Great Events from History

The 19th Century

1801-1900

D1544237

Great Events from History

The 19th Century

1801-1900

Volume 4
1890-1900

Editor

John Powell

Oklahoma Baptist University

SALEM PRESS

Pasadena, California   Hackensack, New Jersey

Editor in Chief: Dawn P. Dawson

Editorial Director: Christina J. Moose
Managing Editor: R. Kent Rasmussen
Manuscript Editors: Desiree Dreeuws, Andy Perry
Production Editor: Joyce I. Buchea
Research Supervisor: Jeffry Jensen
Research Assistant Editor: Rebecca Kuzins

Indexing: R. Kent Rasmussen
Graphics and Design: James Hutson
Layout: William Zimmerman
Photo Editor: Cynthia Breslin Beres
Acquisitions Editor: Mark Rehn
Editorial Assistant: Dana Garey

Cover photos (pictured clockwise, from top left): Rodin's *The Thinker* (The Granger Collection, New York); Immigrants on ship, 1887 (The Granger Collection, New York); Shaka Zulu (The Granger Collection, New York); Hokusai print (The Granger Collection, New York); Eiffel Tower (PhotoDisc); Mexican flag (The Granger Collection, New York)

Copyright © 2007, by SALEM PRESS, INC.

All rights in this book are reserved. No part of this work may be used or reproduced in any manner whatsoever or transmitted in any form or by any means, electronic or mechanical, including photocopy, recording, or any information storage and retrieval system, without written permission from the copyright owner except in the case of brief quotations embodied in critical articles and reviews. For information address the publisher, Salem Press, Inc., P.O. Box 50062, Pasadena, California 91115.

∞ The paper used in these volumes conforms to the American National Standard for Permanence of Paper for Printed Library Materials, Z39.48-1992 (R1997).

Some of the essays in this work originally appeared in the following Salem Press sets: *Chronology of European History: 15,000 B.C. to 1997* (1997, edited by John Powell; associate editors, E. G. Weltin, José M. Sánchez, Thomas P. Neill, and Edward P. Keleher); *Great Events from History: North American Series, Revised Edition* (1997, edited by Frank N. Magill); *Great Events from History II: Science and Technology* (1991, edited by Frank N. Magill); *Great Events from History II: Human Rights* (1992, edited by Frank N. Magill); *Great Events from History II: Arts and Culture* (1993, edited by Frank N. Magill); and *Great Events from History II: Business and Commerce* (1994, edited by Frank N. Magill). New material has been added.

Library of Congress Cataloging-in-Publication Data

Great events from history. The 19th century, 1801-1900 / editor, John Powell.

    p. cm.

Some of the essays in this work appeared in various other Salem Press sets.

Includes bibliographical references and index.

ISBN-13: 978-1-58765-297-4 (set : alk. paper)

ISBN-10: 1-58765-297-8 (set : alk. paper)

ISBN-13: 978-1-58765-301-8 (v. 4 : alk. paper)

ISBN-10: 1-58765-301-X (v. 4 : alk. paper)

[etc.]

1. Nineteenth century. I. Powell, John, 1954- II. Title: 19th century, 1801-1900. III. Title: Nineteenth century, 1801-1900.

D358.G74 2006

909.81—dc22

2006019789

First Printing

PRINTED IN THE UNITED STATES OF AMERICA

CONTENTS

1890's *(continued)*

1900

Appendixes

Indexes

KEYWORD LIST OF CONTENTS

LIST OF MAPS, TABLES, AND SIDEBARS

THE WORLD IN 1801

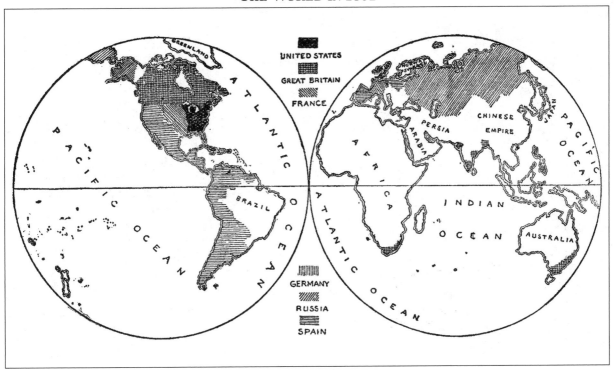

THE WORLD IN 1900

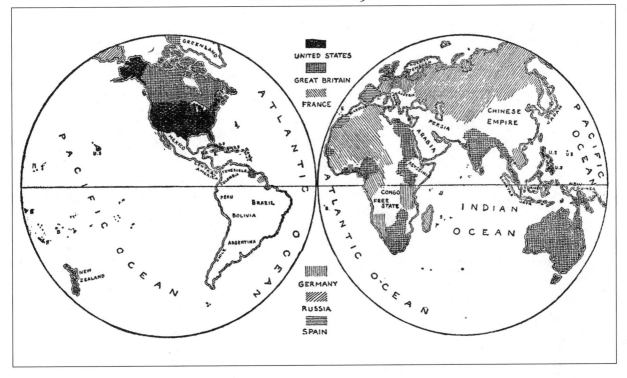

AFRICA AT THE END OF THE NINETEENTH CENTURY

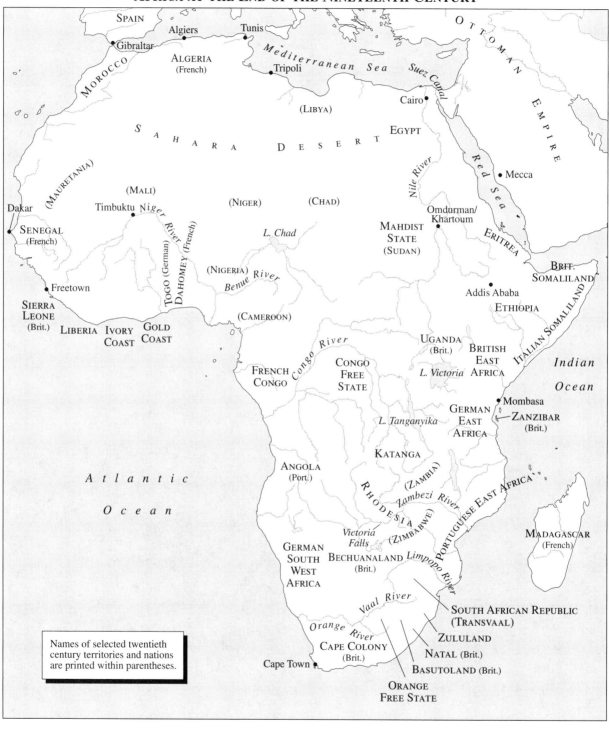

SPAIN

Gibraltar

Algiers

Tunis

MOROCCO

ALGERIA
(French)

Mediterranean Sea

Tripoli

Suez Canal

(LIBYA)

Cairo

EGYPT

OTTOMAN EMPIRE

S A H A R A   D E S E R T

Nile River

Red Sea

Mecca

Dakar

(MAURETANIA)

(MALI)

Timbuktu

Niger River

(NIGER)

(CHAD)

Omdurman/
Khartoum

MAHDIST
STATE
(SUDAN)

SENEGAL
(French)

L. Chad

TOGO (German)
DAHOMEY (French)

(NIGERIA) *Benue River*

ERITREA

BRIT.
SOMALILAND

Freetown

Addis Ababa

ETHIOPIA

SIERRA
LEONE
(Brit.)

LIBERIA

IVORY
COAST

GOLD
COAST

(CAMEROON)

Congo River

FRENCH
CONGO

CONGO
FREE
STATE

UGANDA
(Brit.)

BRITISH
EAST
AFRICA

ITALIAN SOMALILAND

*Indian
Ocean*

L. Victoria

*Atlantic

Ocean*

L. Tanganyika

GERMAN
EAST
AFRICA

Mombasa

ZANZIBAR
(Brit.)

KATANGA

ANGOLA
(Port.)

R
H
O
D
E
S
I
A

(ZAMBIA)

Zambezi River

(ZIMBABWE)

PORTUGUESE EAST AFRICA

MADAGASCAR
(French)

GERMAN
SOUTH
WEST
AFRICA

*Victoria
Falls*

BECHUANALAND
(Brit.)

Limpopo River

Vaal River

SOUTH AFRICAN REPUBLIC
(TRANSVAAL)

ZULULAND

Orange River

CAPE COLONY
(Brit.)

NATAL (Brit.)

BASUTOLAND (Brit.)

Cape Town

ORANGE
FREE STATE

Names of selected twentieth
century territories and nations
are printed within parentheses.

Asia and Australasia at the End of the Nineteenth Century

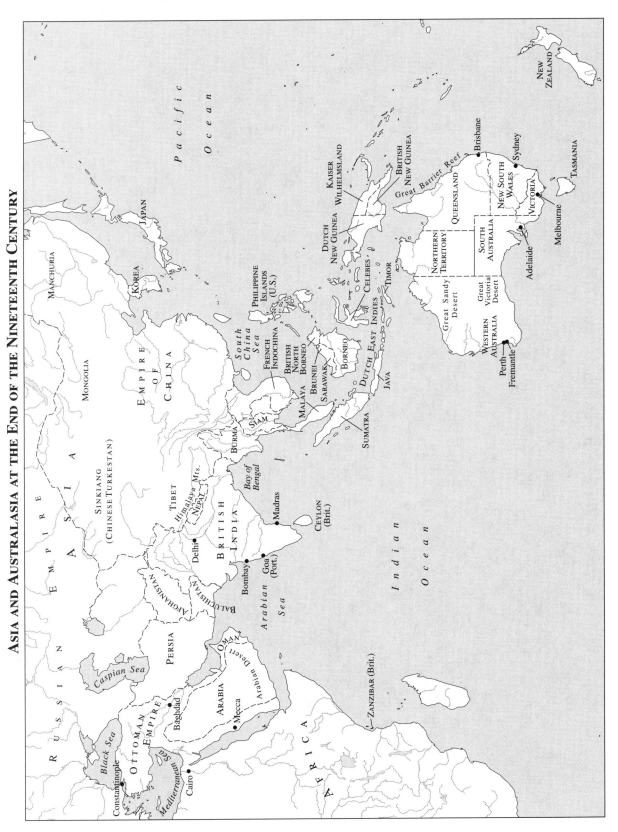

EUROPE AT THE END OF THE NINETEENTH CENTURY

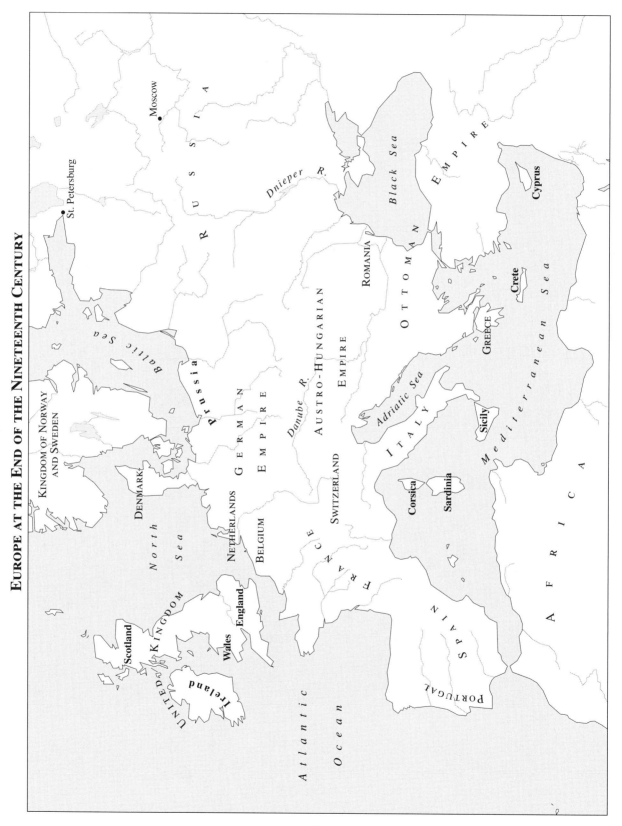

NORTH AMERICA AT THE END OF THE NINETEENTH CENTURY

SOUTH AMERICA AT THE END OF THE NINETEENTH CENTURY

1890
U.S. CENSUS BUREAU ANNOUNCES CLOSING OF THE FRONTIER

*According to a report of the U.S. Census Bureau, the
year 1890 marking the closing of the American
frontier—an event that coincided with the last of the
Indian wars. The report moved a young historian to
develop a thesis on the role of the frontier in U.S.
history that has been debated ever since.*

LOCALE: American Great Plains and Far West
CATEGORY: Expansion and land acquisition

KEY FIGURES

Thomas Jefferson (1743-1826), president of the United
    States, 1801-1809
Frederick Jackson Turner (1861-1932), leading
    American historian of the frontier

SUMMARY OF EVENT

Following the French and Indian War (1756-1763), the
victorious British government issued the Proclamation
of 1763 and created a frontier line between the Allegheny
Mountains and the Mississippi River. This reserved the
land to the west "for the moment" to the American Indians, closing it to settlers and land speculators until King
George III decided what to do with the newly acquired
North American territories that had previously been
dominated by the French. American frontiersmen, such
as Daniel Boone, ignored the British proclamation and
pushed west of the Alleghenies, precipitating pitched
battles with various American Indian tribes, loosely led
by the Shawnee chief Pontiac.

Skirmishes between Native Americans and frontiersmen led Thomas Jefferson to write in the Declaration of
Independence that King George had "endeavored to
bring on the inhabitants of our frontiers, the merciless Indian Savages, whose known rule of warfare is an undis-
tinguished destruction of all ages, sexes, and conditions." Using these words, Jefferson indelibly linked all
American Indian nations to the colonists' definition of
frontier.

In 1890, when the U.S. Census Bureau declared the
frontier to be closed, it used a definition of "frontier" as
an area containing not fewer than two nor more than six
persons per square mile and described as "a line between
Indians and homesteaders." In his report, the director of
the Census Bureau stated that "there can hardly be said to
be a frontier line."

After the Census Bureau report was released, Frederick Jackson Turner, a young history teacher at the Uni-

versity of Wisconsin, was intrigued by its assertion and
concluded that the closing of the frontier symbolized the
end of a great historic movement. He published his thesis
in "The Significance of the Frontier in American History," a paper that he delivered to the American Historical Association in Chicago in 1893. Turner's paper
described the line between American Indians and homesteaders as "a meeting point between savagery and civilization," thereby placing his own signature to Jefferson's
words.

Historians of that time took little exception to the
word "savages" and dwelt instead upon the appealing
thesis of Turner's paper, for it held that U.S. society and
institutions were unique, resulting from the existence of
"an area of free land, its continuous recession, and the advance of American settlement westward." According to
Turner, Europeans had come to America with their cultural baggage, but in the process of adjusting to and ultimately overcoming the primitive environment in which
they found themselves, they were transformed into
something new—Americans living in an American social setting with distinctly American institutions. This
change did not occur all at once as a result of a single
meeting by one group of immigrants with a wilderness
environment. It was, rather, the result of the repetition of
this process on a succession of frontiers over many decades.

Turner noted that there were important differences, as
well as similarities, between frontiers. For example, the
farming frontier of the Midwest was different from the
mining frontier of the Rocky Mountains, and the wood-
land frontier of the seventeenth and eighteenth centuries
was different from the Great Plains frontier of the nineteenth century. At the same time, on virtually all frontiers, the first European immigrants were fur trappers and
traders, who they were followed by cattle raisers, pioneer
farmers, and government-sponsored explorers. To some
areas came miners and ranchers. The process ended with
the establishment of villages and towns.

In Turner's thesis, as an Americanizing influence, the
frontier had several discernible aspects. It transformed
European immigrants of diverse cultural backgrounds
into a composite nationality. It promoted a feeling of
nationalism among the people and produced such nation-
building events as the Louisiana Purchase. It also promoted democracy not only by encouraging individualism and antipathy toward control but also because of the

relative economic equality that existed there. According to Turner, the frontier exerted an important influence on the people living along it. It produced in its inhabitants a combination of coarseness and strength, acuteness and inquisitiveness, practicality and ingenuity, together with restlessness and optimism. While encouraging individualism, the frontier sometimes also encouraged cooperation, especially in defense against the native peoples and in seeking help from government in the form of military assistance and favorable economic legislation.

Less laudable, in Turner's view, was the influence of the frontier in promoting laxity in governmental affairs and business dealings, in its general disrespect for law and order accompanied by an impatience with legal processes, and by its attitude of anti-intellectualism. Turner also implied that the frontier alleviated many social and economic problems inherent in an industrial society and was a safety valve for the discontented.

After a generation of almost universal acceptance, the Turner thesis began to be vigorously attacked during the 1920's, both for what he had said and for what he had failed to say. Historians of a generation that had been reshaped by World War I no longer ignored the exploitation, land thefts, industrialization, lawlessness, and imperialism that had characterized European cultures and that also shaped the United States. Other critics said that Turner had paid no attention to artistic, educational, social, and literary developments; that his terms were ambiguous; that he had failed to test his hypothesis against other frontier experiences; and that his ideas were provincial and some of his statements contradictory. Turner was also criticized for failing to pay attention to the rise of country towns. The rise of towns in the Great Plains between the 1860's and 1890's was a direct result of the expansion of railroading in the United States.

Following the Civil War (1861-1865), rights-of-way were granted to the railroads, virtually wherever they wanted them. Even American Indian reservations were crisscrossed with railroad tracks. Each railroad right-of-way included miles on either side of the tracks, which the

U.S. Lands Settled by 1890

railroads sold to homesteaders to raise money to lay more track. Railroad stops became towns. Grain, meat, and hides exported to the East perpetuated the process. By 1890, there were 197,000 miles of railroad tracks in the United States and almost the same number of miles of telegraph lines.

In 1860, as many as thirty million buffalo may have roamed the Great Plains. In 1885, only five hundred buffalo remained on a reserve in Montana. Killing buffalo made room for cattle and also helped to kill Native Americans. During the 1880's, more than one million Europeans immigrated to the United States. In 1890, in a population of sixty-two million, eight million were engaged in agriculture. The railroads moved ranch and farming products to market.

Turner also failed to take into account other kinds of relevant information in his thesis. For example, in 1890, six corporations controlled 99 percent of private-sector money in the United States. By 1887, the government had substituted agreements for treaties with American Indians. One such agreement granted 160 acres of personal property to American Indian family living on a reservation. The General Allotment (Dawes) Act of 1887 dispersed 32,800 allotments of land to American Indians, covering three million acres, and thus allowed the cession or sale of twenty-eight million acres of allegedly surplus land to white settlers.

Turner defended his thesis by reminding his detractors that he had never claimed the frontier to be the sole force shaping the United States as a nation. He noted that industrialization, social reform, and imperialism were equally important, but that no reasonable person could deny that three centuries of moving west, during which the U.S. people had conquered three thousand miles of wilderness, had left an imprint on U.S. history and the U.S. character.

Turner clearly shaped his thesis on the closing of the frontier to his preconceived notions and had ignored the initial conditions by which the frontier was defined by the king and colonists. He was driven by his zeal to describe a U.S. history and culture characterized by faith in democratic

institutions, an insistence that class lines should never hinder social mobility, an eagerness to experiment, and a preference for the new over the old.

TURNER'S FRONTIER THESIS

The U.S. Census announcement in 1890 of the closing of the American frontier is remembered mostly because of the infamous frontier thesis argued by historian Frederick Jackson Turner. The following is an excerpt from his 1893 paper.

From the conditions of frontier life came intellectual traits of profound importance. The works of travelers along each frontier from colonial days onward describe certain common traits, and these traits have, while softening down, still persisted as survivals in the place of their origin, even when a higher social organization succeeded. The result is that to the frontier the American intellect owes its striking characteristics. That coarseness and strength combined with acuteness and inquisitiveness; that practical, inventive turn of mind, quick to find expedients; that masterful grasp of material things, lacking in the artistic but powerful to effect great ends; that restless, nervous energy; that dominant individualism, working for good and for evil, and withal that buoyancy and exuberance which comes with freedom—these are traits of the frontier, or traits called out elsewhere because of the existence of the frontier. Since the days when the fleet of Columbus sailed into the waters of the New World, America has been another name for opportunity, and the people of the United States have taken their tone from the incessant expansion which has not only been open but has even been forced upon them. He would be a rash prophet who should assert that the expansive character of American life has now entirely ceased. Movement has been its dominant fact, and, unless this training has no effect upon a people, the American energy will continually demand a wider field for its exercise. But never again will such gifts of free land offer themselves. For a moment, at the frontier, the bonds of custom are broken and unrestraint is triumphant. There is not *tabula rasa*. The stubborn American environment is there with its imperious summons to accept its conditions; the inherited ways of doing things are also there; and yet, in spite of environment, and in spite of custom, each frontier did indeed furnish a new field of opportunity, a gate of escape from the bondage of the past; and freshness, and confidence, and scorn of older society, impatience of its restraints and its ideas, and indifference to its lessons, have accompanied the frontier. What the Mediterranean Sea was to the Greeks, breaking the bond of custom, offering new experiences, calling out new institutions and activities, that, and more, the ever retreating frontier has been to the United States directly, and to the nations of Europe more remotely. And now, four centuries from the discovery of America, at the end of a hundred years of life under the Constitution, the frontier has gone, and with its going has closed the first period of American history.

Source: "The Significance of the Frontier in American History" (1893). American Studies at the University of Virginia. Hypertexts collection.

1890's

SIGNIFICANCE

Whatever the strengths and weaknesses of Frederick Jackson Turner's frontier thesis, it is clear that the American frontier was, in fact, closed by 1890. In August, 1886, the Apache leader Geronimo surrendered to U.S. authorities in Arizona. In December, 1890, the great Sioux chief Sitting Bull was murdered by Indian policemen in South Dakota. During that same year, the last battle between regular army and American Indians was fought at Wounded Knee, South Dakota. That battle effectively ended thousands of years of Native American domination over North America. It was no coincidence that the year of Wounded Knee was the same year that the U.S. Census Bureau declared the frontier closed.

—W. Turrentine Jackson,
updated by Glenn Schiffman

FURTHER READING

Axelrod, Alan. *Chronicle of the Indian Wars*. New York: Prentice Hall, 1993. Reference work that surveys the many conflicts between American Indians and U.S. government military and other officials that led to the end of the Indians' way of life and their assimilation and restriction to reservations.

Billington, Ray Allen. *America's Frontier Heritage*. New York: Holt, Rinehart and Winston, 1966. Billington turns away from Turner's hypothesis and focuses instead on the questions about the nature of the frontier experience and the effect that it has it had on the American character.

Bogue, Allan G. *Frederick Jackson Turner: Strange Roads Going Down*. Norman: University of Oklahoma Press, 1998. Scholarly biography of Turner that attempts to show why he should be regarded as one of the most influential historians in American scholarship.

Lewis, Archibald R., and Thomas F. McGann, eds. *The New World Looks at Its History*. Austin: University of Texas Press, 1963. Proceedings of the Second International Congress of Historians of the United States and Mexico, emphasizing the theme of the frontier in history.

Parish, John Carl. *The Persistence of the Westward Movement, and Other Essays*. Berkeley: University of California Press, 1943. Nine essays suggesting that the American westward movement was not one but many movements of population. Parish examines the forces that brought people to the West, their attempts to reproduce the culture of the East and its necessary modifications, and finally the persistence of the westward movement as a state of mind.

Paxson, Frederic Logan. *When the West Is Gone*. New York: Henry Holt, 1930. Consisting of three lectures delivered at Brown University only a few decades after the closing of the frontier, this brief work analyzes U.S. history from the perspective of the shifting frontier.

Turner, Frederick Jackson. *The Frontier in American History*. 1920. Reprint. New York: Dover, 1996.

Cover of an 1889 issue of Harper's Weekly *with an engraving from Frederic Remington's painting titled "The Frontier Trooper's Thanatopsis." The trooper's meditation on death in this picture might be seen as symbolic of the closing the frontier.* (Library of Congress)

Turner's classic exposition of the frontier as a shaper of American history, which he first broached in 1893. Provocative both in its own time and today, this book is available in many editions.

Utley, Robert M. *The Indian Frontier of the American West, 1846-1890.* Albuquerque: University of New Mexico Press, 1984. General history of U.S.-Native American relations that includes a chapter with a useful discussion of the events leading to the Long Walk.

Wyman, Walker D., and Clifton B. Kroeber, eds. *The Frontier in Perspective.* Madison: University of Wisconsin Press, 1957. Thirteen lectures delivered at the University of Wisconsin by eminent historians from Canada, Mexico, and the United States on important aspects of the world frontier and the American frontier.

SEE ALSO: c. 1815-1830: Westward American Migration Begins; Apr. 30, 1860-1865: Apache and Navajo War; Feb. 6, 1861-Sept. 4, 1886: Apache Wars; Dec. 4, 1867: National Grange Is Formed; May 10, 1869: First Transcontinental Railroad Is Completed; c. 1871-1883: Great American Buffalo Slaughter; 1876-1877: Sioux War; Dec. 29, 1890: Wounded Knee Massacre; Jan. 1, 1892: Ellis Island Immigration Depot Opens; May 1-Oct. 30, 1893: Chicago World's Fair; Sept. 6, 1899-July 3, 1900: Hay Articulates "Open Door" Policy Toward China.

RELATED ARTICLES in *Great Lives from History: The Nineteenth Century, 1801-1900:* James Fenimore Cooper; Geronimo; Frederic Remington; Sitting Bull.

February 17-18, 1890
WOMEN'S RIGHTS ASSOCIATIONS UNITE

The merger of the two major national woman suffrage organizations ended the divisiveness that had long hampered the woman suffrage movement and created a body that would play a major role in the eventual ratification of the Nineteenth Amendment.

LOCALE: Washington, D.C.

CATEGORIES: Women's issues; organizations and institutions

KEY FIGURES

Susan B. Anthony (1820-1906) and
Elizabeth Cady Stanton (1815-1902), leaders of the New York-based National Woman Suffrage Association
Lucy Stone (1818-1893), leader of the Boston-based American Woman Suffrage Association
Victoria Woodhull (1838-1927), radical associate of Stanton

SUMMARY OF EVENT

Many of the men and women who campaigned for women's rights during the nineteenth century were also involved in other reformist causes. For example, Elizabeth Cady Stanton and Lucretia Mott attended the first World Anti-Slavery Convention in London in 1840, where women were denied the right to participate. Susan B. Anthony was first involved in the temperance movement, and at an 1852 Sons of Temperance meeting in Al-

bany, New York, she was denied the right to speak. By then, Stanton, Mott, and three others had organized what came to be known as the 1848 Seneca Falls Convention.

During the decade leading up to the Civil War (1861-1865), feminists made modest gains. Limited protection of a married woman's personal property was legislated in Ohio and New York, and increasing numbers of middle-class women were entering the professions. Oberlin College admitted women. Many traditions came under attack. Stanton briefly joined Amelia Bloomer's campaign for women's dress reform and spoke at the 1860 Woman's Rights Convention on the need to reformulate marriage as a civil, not a sacred, contract.

As the Civil War approached, the antislavery movement came to dominate reform causes. Basing their argument on Thomas Jefferson and the Declaration of Independence, feminist leaders asserted that both women and African Americans had natural rights. In general, they were in accord with Frederick Douglass, former slave and abolitionist leader, who argued that, if the U.S. Constitution were interpreted literally, it was an antislavery document, and with Victoria Woodhull, radical speaker and editor, who insisted that women already had the legal right to vote.

With the end of the Civil War in 1865 and proposals to add the Fourteenth Amendment to the Constitution, feminists suffered a setback. While the Constitution previously had not defined citizens as male, the wording of

1890's

this amendment did so. Thus, for the first time, women were explicitly denied rights that were guaranteed to men. Previously, they were denied voting rights by state laws alone. With the passage of the Fourteenth Amendment, only another amendment could enfranchise them. Like many other abolitionist leaders, Wendell Phillips, elected president of the American Anti-Slavery Society in 1865, argued that women should postpone their own campaign for the vote until rights for African Americans had been constitutionally ensured. Some moderate feminists, such as Lucy Stone, agreed.

In May, 1869, that strategy led to a split among suffragists. The New York group, which became the National Woman Suffrage Association (NWSA), was led by Anthony and Stanton. Stanton was the first NWSA president and remained president for twenty-one years. To establish a short-lived newspaper, *The Revolution*, An-

thony and Stanton accepted funds from George Francis Train, a radical Irish American; Train may have been a racist, but his support of organized labor alone would have made him unacceptable to most middle-class reformers. The newspaper's association with Train offended many NWSA members.

When the Fifteenth Amendment was proposed, stating that the vote could not be denied on the basis of color, race, or previous servitude, the NWSA urged inclusion of the word "sex." NWSA leaders took a stand on other issues then considered radical, favoring equal pay for equal work and reform of marriage laws, and attempting to draw public attention to the legal and economic plights of housewives, factory workers, prostitutes, and prisoners. Membership in the NWSA was open to all, but no man could hold office in the organization. The NWSA tended to attract younger women and women from the western frontier, rather than the more sheltered women of eastern cities.

Meanwhile, a Boston-based group, led by Lucy Stone and Henry Blackwell, concentrated on the vote. Founded by Stone, Julia Ward Howe, and Isabella Beecher Hooker, the American Woman Suffrage Association (AWSA) allowed men full participation. The popular Protestant preacher Henry Ward Beecher, Isabella Hooker's brother, became the first AWSA president. When a choice had to be made between the causes of woman suffrage and African American suffrage in order to get legislation passed, the Boston group agreed that woman suffrage must wait. In comparison with NWSA's newspaper, the AWSA newspaper was conservative. Mary Livermore, the editor of *Woman's Journal*, had left the NWSA because of its radical stance on marriage and dress.

The division between the two organizations was hardened by the NWSA's brief acceptance of radical orator Victoria Woodhull. Once a spiritualist healer, Woodhull and her sister, Tennessee Claflin, had become the first female Wall Street brokers. They operated as Woodhull, Claflin & Company and were backed by Cornelius Vanderbilt's money. So long as Vanderbilt money was behind her, Woodhull was treated with respect by the press, but that changed as Vanderbilt's interest waned. In 1870, Woodhull began *Woodhull and Claflin's Weekly*, a

Federal law never restricted the franchise to men, as it was up to the individual states to determine franchise rights. Long before passage of the Nineteenth Amendment, some states did, in fact, permit women to vote. Here women are voting in a Boston election in 1888. (Library of Congress)

newspaper that touched on women's issues ranging from hair-dye poisoning to prostitution. In it, she supported her own candidacy for U.S. president, to run in the 1872 elections as a third-party candidate.

A charismatic orator, Woodhull was initially accepted by Stanton and some others in the NWSA. She spoke to large gatherings on such matters as political and civil service corruption, the unequal division of wealth, and the need to unite labor reformers and suffragists. Her most outspoken opponents were from the Boston faction and included two sisters of Henry Ward Beecher—Catharine Beecher and Harriet Beecher Stowe, the author of *Uncle Tom's Cabin* (1852). As newspapers focused on details of Woodhull's unconventional personal life, she chose to expose the hypocrisy of her critics by publicly revealing the long-standing affair between Henry Ward Beecher and a married woman member of his congregation. The various scandals alienated many of the New York group from Woodhull; the Boston group was enraged.

Through almost two decades, the division between the two associations remained. Both claimed memberships of about ten thousand during this period, while millions of women were drawn into other reformist or self-help movements, including cultural and garden clubs, the Women's National Committee for Law Enforcement, and the Southern Women's Educational Alliance. The largest group was the Women's Christian Temperance Union (WCTU), which claimed a membership of 150,000 in 1892. With its auxiliaries, its membership was more than 200,000. Frances Willard, WCTU leader, worked with both suffrage associations, seeing woman suffrage as the one route to legislation against alcohol.

Alice Stone Blackwell, Lucy Stone's daughter, was among those who saw the need to unite the two suffrage factions into a single, more effective body. She and Rachel Foster Avery, who represented the NWSA, were negotiators. The merger took place at a February 17-18, 1890, meeting in Washington, D.C. Stanton, who was then seventy-five years old, became the first president of the new National American Woman Suffrage Association (NAWSA). Anthony and Stone, who were both in their early seventies, served as vice president and executive committee chair.

SIGNIFICANCE

Stanton resigned as president of the NAWSA in 1892. She was skeptical of the temperance affiliation and the piety and conservatism of the new group. After she left, she continued her radical attack on organized religion. Publication of her 1895 *Woman's Bible* caused such out-

rage that the NAWSA censured Stanton's work at its 1896 meeting. Stanton was followed as president by Anthony and then by Carrie Chapman Catt, an Iowa superintendent of schools, who served from 1900 to 1904. A new vigor was given the suffrage movement, however, only by younger women. Harriot Stanton Blatch, Stanton's daughter, returned to the United States in 1907, after having observed radical British suffrage techniques. She organized the first suffrage parades in New York. Catt returned to power in 1915, and, with the younger generation of radicals, led the way to the Nineteenth Amendment in 1920.

—Betty Richardson

FURTHER READING

Baker, Jean H, ed. *Votes for Women: The Struggle for Suffrage Revisited*. Oxford, England: Oxford University Press, 2002. Solid history of the woman suffrage movement.

Barry, Kathleen. *Susan B. Anthony: A Biography of a Singular Feminist*. New York: New York University Press, 1988. Readable scholarly biography that emphasizes Anthony's public life and covers the many issues and divisions of the suffrage movement.

Blackwell, Alice Stone. *Lucy Stone: Pioneer of Woman's Rights*. 2d ed. Norwood, Mass.: Alice Stone Blackwell Committee, 1930. Reprint. Charlottesville: University Press of Virginia, 2001. Biography of Lucy Stone by her daughter, who presents an insightful and personal view of Stone's personal and public life.

Bordin, Ruth. *Woman and Temperance: The Quest for Power and Liberty, 1873-1900*. Philadelphia: Temple University Press, 1981. Traces the complex relationship between suffrage and the then-more-numerous and powerful forces for temperance, a relationship that led the alcohol industry and drinkers to oppose suffrage.

Flexner, Eleanor. *Century of Struggle: The Woman's Rights Movement in the United States*. Rev. ed. Cambridge, Mass.: Belknap Press of Harvard University Press, 1975. First published in 1959 and extensively revised in 1975, this remains the best basic survey of women's rights issues from colonial times until ratification of the Nineteenth Amendment in 1920.

Griffith, Elisabeth. *In Her Own Right: The Life of Elizabeth Cady Stanton*. New York: Oxford University Press, 1984. The first fully scholarly study of Stanton and her leadership in the women's rights movement.

Gurko, Miriam. *The Ladies of Seneca Falls: The Birth of the Women's Rights Movement*. New York: Macmil-

1890's

lan, 1974. Traces major figures of the women's movement from 1848 through the formation of the NAWSA in 1890.

Kern, Kathi. *Mrs. Stanton's Bible*. Ithaca, N.Y.: Cornell University Press, 2001. Examination of Stanton's nonsexist *Women's Bible*, published in 1895. Kern argues that Stanton's biblical commentary alienated her from less radical members of the women's movement and may have delayed the achievement of woman suffrage.

McFadden, Margaret, ed. *Women's Issues*. 3 vols. Pasadena, Calif.: Salem Press, 1997. Comprehensive reference work with numerous articles on woman suffrage, women's rights organizations, individual leaders, and many related issues.

Sherr, Lynn. *Failure Is Impossible: Susan B. Anthony in Her Own Words*. New York: Times Books, 1995. Collection of excerpts from Anthony's speeches and letters, with commentaries on Anthony's life and career.

Underhill, Lois Beachy. *The Woman Who Ran for President: The Many Lives of Victoria Woodhull*. Bridgehampton, N.Y.: Bridge Works, 1995. Balanced and

scholarly study of the charismatic feminist leader whose scandalous life has caused her to be omitted from or patronized in most early histories.

SEE ALSO: 1820's-1850's: Social Reform Movement; July 19-20, 1848: Seneca Falls Convention; May 28-29, 1851: Akron Woman's Rights Convention; May 10, 1866: Suffragists Protest the Fourteenth Amendment; July 9, 1868: Fourteenth Amendment Is Ratified; May, 1869: Woman Suffrage Associations Begin Forming; Dec., 1869: Wyoming Gives Women the Vote; June 17-18, 1873: Anthony Is Tried for Voting; Mar. 9, 1875: *Minor v. Happersett*; July 4, 1876: Declaration of the Rights of Women; Sept. 19, 1893: New Zealand Women Win Voting Rights; Oct. 27, 1893: National Council of Women of Canada Is Founded.

RELATED ARTICLES in *Great Lives from History: The Nineteenth Century, 1801-1900:* Susan B. Anthony; Henry Ward Beecher; Amelia Bloomer; Matilda Joslyn Gage; Julia Ward Howe; Lucretia Mott; Elizabeth Cady Stanton; Lucy Stone; Victoria Woodhull.

July 20, 1890
HARRISON SIGNS THE SHERMAN ANTITRUST ACT

The Sherman Antitrust Act was the first federal legislation in the United States to outlaw monopolies and restraint of trade. It still forms the centerpiece of U.S. antitrust law.

ALSO KNOWN AS: Sherman Act
LOCALE: Washington, D.C.
CATEGORIES: Laws, acts, and legal history; government and politics; trade and commerce

KEY FIGURES
John Sherman (1823-1900), U.S. senator from Ohio
George Franklin Edmunds (1828-1919), U.S. senator from Vermont, 1866-1891, and chairman of the Senate Judiciary Committee, 1872-1879, 1881-1891
George Frisbie Hoar (1826-1904), U.S. senator from Massachusetts
Benjamin Harrison (1833-1901), president of the United States, 1889-1893
Richard Olney (1835-1917), attorney general, 1893-1895, and secretary of state, 1895-1897
John D. Rockefeller (1839-1937), founder and chief executive of the Standard Oil Company

SUMMARY OF EVENT
The period following the U.S. Civil War was one of rapid economic growth and change in the United States. Creation of a nationwide network of railroads gave individual firms a way to serve a nationwide market, enabling them to grow to a large size to improve their efficiency or simply to gain strategic advantages. A conspicuous firm was the Standard Oil Company, led by John D. Rockefeller. The firm was efficient and progressive in developing petroleum refining, but it was heavily criticized for such actions as pressuring railroads for preferential rebates and discriminatory price-cutting to intimidate competitors.

Standard Oil effectively controlled the petroleum-refining industry by 1879. In addition to lubricants, its principal product was kerosene, aggressively marketed worldwide as the first cheap and convenient source of artificial light. In 1882, the firm was reorganized in the form of a trust, facilitating the acquisition of competing firms. Although the trust form went out of use soon after, the term "trust" became a common name for aggressive big-business monopolies. Other large combinations were soon formed, so that by 1890, large companies controlled the production of such items as whiskey, sugar, and lead, and dominated the nation's railroads.

Opposition to big-business abuses spread among farmers and in small-business sectors such as the grocery business. Popular concern was fueled by writings such as Edward Bellamy's utopian novel *Looking Backward: 2000-1887* (1888), which had sold one million copies within fifteen years after its publication. Individual states adopted antimonopoly legislation or brought court actions against alleged monopolists. By 1891, eighteen states had adopted some sort of antitrust legislation.

Both major political parties had adopted vague antimonopoly statements in their platforms for the 1888 election, but neither rushed to submit appropriate legislation at the next congressional session. President Benjamin Harrison was moved to ask for such a statute in his annual message of December, 1889. A bill introduced by Senator John Sherman of Ohio was extensively revised by the Senate Judiciary Committee, under the able guidance of George Frisbie Hoar and Chairman George Franklin Edmunds. The resulting bill was passed by Congress with virtually no debate and only one opposing vote. President Harrison signed it into law July 20, 1890.

The Sherman Antitrust Act contained three important types of provisions. First, the law outlawed "every contract, combination in the form of trust or otherwise, or conspiracy, in restraint of trade or commerce among the several states or with foreign nations. . . ." This came to be viewed as dealing with "loose combinations" of several firms undertaking joint action. Second, the law made it illegal for any person to monopolize or attempt to monopolize any part of that trade or commerce. This was viewed as dealing with activities of individual large firms. The key terms were not defined, and it remained for lawyers and judges to try to find satisfactory and consistent meanings for them. Third, the law provided for a

---

THE SHERMAN ANTITRUST ACT

The Sherman Antitrust Act comprises sections 1-7 of Title 15 of the U.S. Code. The core sections, 1, 2, and 4, outlaw monopolies and establish the jurisdiction of the courts to enforce that prohibition.

§1 Every contract, combination in the form of trust or otherwise, or conspiracy, in restraint of trade or commerce among the several States, or with foreign nations, is declared to be illegal. Every person who shall make any contract or engage in any combination or conspiracy hereby declared to be illegal shall be deemed guilty of a felony, and, on conviction thereof, shall be punished by fine not exceeding $10,000,000 if a corporation, or, if any other person, $350,000, or by imprisonment not exceeding three years, or by both said punishments, in the discretion of the court.

§2 Every person who shall monopolize, or attempt to monopolize, or combine or conspire with any other person or persons, to monopolize any part of the trade or commerce among the several States, or with foreign nations, shall be deemed guilty of a felony, and, on conviction thereof, shall be punished by fine not exceeding $10,000,000 if a corporation, or, if any other person, $350,000, or by imprisonment not exceeding three years, or by both said punishments, in the discretion of the court.

§4 The several district courts of the United States are invested with jurisdiction to prevent and restrain violations of sections 1 to 7 of this title; and it shall be the duty of the several United States attorneys, in their respective districts, under the direction of the Attorney General, to institute proceedings in equity to prevent and restrain such violations. Such proceedings may be by way of petition setting forth the case and praying that such violation shall be enjoined or otherwise prohibited. When the parties complained of shall have been duly notified of such petition the court shall proceed, as soon as may be, to the hearing and determination of the case; and pending such petition and before final decree, the court may at any time make such temporary restraining order or prohibition as shall be deemed just in the premises.

1890's

variety of means of enforcement. The attorney general was empowered to bring criminal or civil court actions against violators. Civil remedies often proved attractive, because the burden of proof was not so difficult to achieve, and the remedies could involve changing industry structure and behavior, not merely applying punishments. In addition, private individuals could sue offending firms for triple the value of their losses.

Between 1890 and 1904, only eighteen suits were filed under the act. Several of these aimed at collusive rate-fixing by railroads, despite their regulated status under the Interstate Commerce Commission. At the time of the Pullman Strike (1894), the courts held that the Sherman Act could be applied to the activities of labor unions. Unions were repeatedly subjected to injunctions and triple-damage suits for strikes, picketing, and boycotts, even after Congress attempted, in the Clayton Antitrust Act of 1914, to exempt most union activities from antitrust laws.

The Sherman Act's effectiveness was limited severely by the Supreme Court in an 1895 case against the sugar trust, *United States v. E. C. Knight Company*. The ruling in that case defined commerce so narrowly that it excluded almost all forms of interstate enterprise except transportation. The Court was led to make a ruling of this type by the way in which the Justice Department, under Attorney General Richard Olney, framed the case. Collusive behavior among a number of separate firms, however, was not granted such a loophole. In 1899, activities by six producers of cast-iron pipe to agree on contract bids were held illegal in *Addyston Pipe and Steel Co. v. United States*. These two cases indicated that activities involving several firms were much more likely to be found illegal than the operations of a single-firm monopolist. Perhaps in response, the decade of the 1890's witnessed an unprecedented boom in the formation of giant corporations through mergers and consolidations. The process culminated in the creation of United States Steel Corporation in 1901, capitalized at more than one billion dollars.

Again, public outcry arose. Congress appointed an industrial commission in 1899 to consider the trust problem. A preliminary report in 1900 observed that "industrial combinations have become fixtures in our business life. Their power for evil should be destroyed and their means for good preserved." The commission's 1902 report recommended stronger actions against price discrimination. Some large firms were prosecuted successfully. A giant railroad merger was blocked in the *Northern Securities* case of 1904, helping to gain for President Theodore Roosevelt a reputation as a vigorous trust-buster. In 1911, two notorious trusts, Standard Oil and American Tobacco, were convicted of Sherman Act violations. In each case, the convicted firm was ordered to be broken into several separate firms. The Standard Oil settlement made it much easier for new firms to enter petroleum refining, making possible the emergence of such new competitors as Texaco and Gulf Oil. However, prosecution of the ultimate corporate giant, U.S. Steel, was dismissed in 1920.

SIGNIFICANCE

In 1914, Congress adopted the Clayton Act, which amended the Sherman Act to specify business actions to be prohibited. This act outlawed price discrimination, tying and exclusive-dealing contracts, mergers and acquisitions, and interlocking directorships, where these tended to decrease competition or to create a monopoly.

The Federal Trade Commission was also established in 1914, charged with preventing unfair methods of competition and helping to enforce the Clayton Act.

Until 1950, Sherman Act prosecutions tended to be relatively effective against collusive actions by separate firms in interstate commerce, situations involving, for example, price fixing and agreements to share markets, to boycott suppliers, or to assign market territories. On the other hand, individual firms were left relatively free, even if large and dominant. Treatment of individual large firms shifted somewhat after the government successfully prosecuted the Aluminum Company of America (ALCOA) in 1945. The court agreed with the prosecution that the firm's market share was large enough to constitute a monopoly, and that ALCOA had deliberately undertaken to achieve this monopoly. This case provided a basis for successful antitrust actions against United Shoe Machinery Company in 1954 and against American Telephone and Telegraph (AT&T) in 1982. In the AT&T case, the telephone industry was drastically reorganized. The various regional operating companies became independent, and entry into long-distance phone services was opened up for new competitors. The government's ability to block the formation of giant-firm monopoly was strengthened in 1950, when Congress passed the Celler-Kefauver Antimerger Act, which gave the government stronger authority to block mergers that seemed to threaten to produce monopoly.

—*Paul B. Trescott*

FURTHER READING

Blair, Roger D., and David L. Kaserman. *Antitrust Economics*. Homewood, Ill.: Irwin, 1985. This university textbook puts the Sherman Act into a broad economic context.

Hylton, Keith N. *Antitrust Law: Economic Theory and Common Law Evolution*. New York: Cambridge University Press, 2003. Compares the Sherman Antitrust Act and other statutes with antitrust common law.

Kovaleff, Theodore P., ed. *The Antitrust Impulse: An Economic, Historical, and Legal Analysis*. 2 vols. Armonk, N.Y.: M. E. Sharpe, 1994. Diverse essays reexamine the history and impact of the law.

Letwin, William L. *Law and Economic Policy in America: The Evolution of the Sherman Act*. New York: Random House, 1956. Surveys the background and early application of the law, finding it an unsuccessful experiment.

Thorelli, Hans. *The Federal Antitrust Policy: Origination of an American Tradition*. Baltimore: Johns Hopkins University Press, 1955. This encyclopedic study focuses on the political and legal background of the Sherman Act, its legislative history, and its early application.

Whitney, Simon N. *Antitrust Policies: American Experience in Twenty Industries.* 2 vols. New York: Twentieth Century Fund, 1958. Excellent case studies give deeper meaning to the law's application.

SEE ALSO: Apr. 12, 1861-Apr. 9, 1865: U.S. Civil War; Feb. 25, 1863-June 3, 1864: Congress Passes the National Bank Acts; Jan. 10, 1870: Standard Oil Company Is Incorporated; Jan. 2, 1882: Standard Oil Trust Is Organized; Jan. 16, 1883: Pendleton Act Reforms the Federal Civil Service; Feb. 4, 1887: Interstate Commerce Act; July 4-5, 1892: Birth of the People's Party; May 11-July 11, 1894: Pullman Strike; July 24, 1897: Congress Passes Dingley Tariff Act.

RELATED ARTICLES in *Great Lives from History: The Nineteenth Century, 1801-1900:* Benjamin Harrison; John D. Rockefeller.

December 11, 1890

BEHRING DISCOVERS THE DIPHTHERIA ANTITOXIN

Emil von Behring discovered that a toxin produced by the causative agent of diphtheria could be destroyed by blood serum derived from immunized animals. His discovery resulted in the development of a vaccine.

LOCALE: Berlin, Prussia, German Empire (now in Germany)

CATEGORY: Health and medicine

KEY FIGURES

Emil von Behring (1854-1917), German bacteriologist

Shibasaburo Kitasato (1852-1931), Japanese bacteriologist and Behring's collaborator

Paul Ehrlich (1854-1915), German bacteriologist and Behring's collaborator

Edward Jenner (1749-1823), English physician who developed the smallpox vaccine

Edwin Klebs (1834-1913), German bacteriologist who isolated the diphtheria bacillus in 1883

Friedrich August Johannes Löffler (1852-1915), German bacteriologist

Pierre-Paul-Émile Roux (1853-1933), French bacteriologist

Alexandre Yersin (1863-1943), Swiss bacteriologist and Roux's collaborator

Henry Sewall (1855-1936), American physiologist

SUMMARY OF EVENT

During the nineteenth century, there was an enormous growth of knowledge in the field of bacteriology. Much of the expansion resulted from discoveries by German bacteriologist Robert Koch and French chemist Louis Pasteur. The two scientists are considered the founders of modern medical bacteriology and were instrumental in demonstrating the relationship between exposure to bacteria and specific human and animal diseases. These diseases involved causative agents, or pathogens, such as bacteria, which would interact with human and animal hosts and induce illness caused by infection or toxicity. The illnesses were collectively classified as "communicable diseases" since they could be transmitted from one host to another.

Several scientists and physicians focused on prevention and eradication of communicable diseases. Diphtheria was a major communicable disease studied during this period since it was responsible for many deaths, especially among young children. It is transmissible mainly via direct contact with an infected host and ingestion of contaminated raw milk, and possibly via contact with contaminated articles. The disease is caused by a bacterium called *Corynebacterium diphtheriae.* Certain strains of these bacteria are susceptible to genetic alteration by a virus that causes the organisms to produce a toxin which is responsible for the onset of diphtheria and the related symptoms. Infection of humans with these bacteria and absorption of their toxin can result in the formation of lesions in the nasal, pharyngeal, and laryngeal regions of the upper respiratory system. The toxin can also negatively impact other organs and systems, such as the nerves, heart, and kidneys. If the disease is extensive, diphtheria is fatal; the probability of contracting the disease is increased under crowded conditions.

The prevalence of the disease increased concomitantly as population densities increased in cities around the world. The causative agent of the disease was not discovered until 1883, when a German bacteriologist, Edwin Klebs, isolated the bacteria from people with diph-

1890's

Emil von Behring. (Nobel Foundation)

theria. The discovery was not confirmed, however, until 1884, when a German bacteriologist, Friedrich August Johannes Löffler, demonstrated that pure cultures of these organisms would induce diphtheria in experimental animals. Indeed, the original name of the causative agent of diphtheria was Klebs-Löffler bacillus, later renamed to *Corynebacterium diphtheriae*.

Five years later, two other scientists, French bacteriologist Pierre-Paul-Émile Roux and Swiss bacteriologist Alexandre Yersin, were able to separate a chemical toxin from *C. diphtheriae* and demonstrate that the chemical was the actual factor that caused diphtheria. Thus, the foundation was established for development of a means for rendering the toxin innocuous in order to prevent the onset or eradicate the symptoms of the disease in people who were exposed to the toxin-producing bacteria.

The German bacteriologist Emil von Behring and his assistant, a Japanese bacteriologist, Shibasaburo Kitasato, focused on immunization of animals via vaccination. The scope of their research was influenced by concepts established by several other scientists, including an English physician named Edward Jenner, Pasteur, and

the American physiologist Henry Sewall. Jenner developed the concept of vaccination during the late 1790's. Jenner knew that people who had acquired cowpox and survived were immune against future outbreaks and a very fatal disease, called smallpox. Based on this premise, Jenner demonstrated that smallpox could be prevented in humans if they were injected with a small dose of fluid from an active cowpox lesion. He named this process "vaccination" from the Latin *vaccinia*, which means cowpox.

Pasteur applied Jenner's concept to other diseases and developed vaccinations consisting of attenuated bacteria for the prevention of anthrax and rabies during the 1880's. In turn, based on Pasteur's success, Sewall applied the concept to develop a vaccine that would induce immunity against toxic snake venoms. In 1887, he was successful in demonstrating that an animal could be protected from the toxic venom if previously vaccinated with sublethal doses of the toxin.

Behring and Kitasato attempted to extend the already proven concept of immunization via vaccination and apply the technique for control of diphtheria. Thus, combined with data generated by Klebs, Löffler, Roux, and Yersin regarding the toxin-producing *C. diphtheriae*, Behring and Kitasato initiated a series of their own experiments. In 1889, Kitasato had discovered the causative agent of tetanus, which was also found to be a toxin-producing bacterium.

Behring's experimental design involved preparing a pure culture of a live, toxin-producing strain of *C. diphtheriae* in a nutrient broth, separating the toxin generated by the bacteria in the broth from the organisms via filtration, and injecting graduated sublethal doses of the toxin under the skin of healthy rabbits and mice. Several days later, he injected the inoculated animals with live, active *C. diphtheriae* bacteria. Behring's experiment was a success.

On December 11, 1890, Behring reported in a journal article that the animals vaccinated with *C. diphtheriae* toxin prior to injection with active *C. diphtheriae* bacteria did not develop diphtheria. Control animals which were not vaccinated, however, developed the disease subsequent to injection with active organisms. Thus, Behring demonstrated that the experimental animals were able to develop an induced immunity to the *C. diphtheriae* toxin via vaccination because of the formation of a protective toxin-destroying agent produced within their blood serum. (One week earlier, Behring and Kitasato had coauthored a journal article which reported similar findings for experiments using toxin produced by tetanus bacilli.) The two scientists referred to the protective toxin-destroying agent within the blood sera of immunized animals as an "antitoxin."

SIGNIFICANCE

As a result of Behring's discovery of diphtheria antitoxin, the foundation was established to develop an efficient vaccine and to determine an optimal dose for human use. Progress was demonstrated within a year, because of experiments conducted by German bacteriologist Paul Ehrlich, whose work involved determining if serum derived from animals and humans known to contain the antitoxin could be injected in others to induce immunization. This concept became the foundation of what is called "serotherapy" to induce "passive immunity." A person is considered to have been passively immunized when they become immune to toxin because of injection with serum containing antitoxin from another immunized person or animal. In other words, passive immunity implies the transfer of immunity from one host to another via vaccination with antitoxin instead of active toxin.

Ehrlich's assistance to Behring was also instrumental in establishing some insight into the administration of safe and effective doses of vaccine for clinical use. Within a year of Behring's discovery of the diphtheria antitoxin, clinical trials were established with humans to determine if diphtheria could be prevented and possibly cured. The clinical trials were successful; thus, the era of vaccinating humans, especially children, with diphtheria antitoxin had begun. The process, however, was not totally efficient, and scientific research continued. Nevertheless, immunization to prevent and cure diphtheria via vaccination was gaining widespread use, and a significant decline in the disease was apparent by the beginning of the twentieth century.

Behring's discovery of the diphtheria antitoxin influenced several major advances in the area of medical science. The concept of serotherapy as a form of vaccination was developed to induce passive immunity against the *C. diphtheriae* toxin. The process was later applied by other scientists to control the impact of other bacterial and viral agents found to be pathogenic to humans and animals. Concomitantly, a greater understanding of the human immune system was gained, especially relative to the concept of antibody (for example, antitoxic protein in blood serum) response to antigen (for example, *C. diphtheriae* toxin). Finally, as a result of the vaccine, countless lives of people who were afflicted with the dreaded disease of diphtheria were saved, while even more peo-

ple were spared the experience of contracting the illness. In acknowledgment of Behring's discovery and its positive impact realized at that time and perceived for the future, he was awarded the first Nobel Prize in Physiology or Medicine in 1901.

—Michael S. Bisesi

FURTHER READING

Asimov, Isaac. *Asimov's Biographical Encyclopedia of Science and Technology*. New rev. ed. Garden City, N.Y.: Doubleday, 1972. This reference provides biographical summaries of 1,195 great scientists, including those who established the foundation and influenced the discovery of the diphtheria antitoxin.

Chase, Allan. *Magic Shots*. New York: William Morrow, 1982. This book provides a historical perspective regarding discoveries of various vaccines that had a positive influence in medicine. The book refers the reader to several of the original journal articles that reported the discoveries.

Lagerkvist, Ulf. *Pioneers of Microbiology and the Nobel Prize*. River Edge, N.J.: World Scientific, 2003. Behring is one of the scientists prominently featured in this book about Nobel Prize-winning microbiologists. The book contains a section about Behring's life and his scientific discoveries. One of the few books about Behring written in English.

Walker, M. E. M. *Pioneers of Public Health*. New York: Macmillan, 1930. This book contains a chapter about Hermann Biggs, an American physician instrumental in encouraging the use of the diphtheria antitoxin to prevent diphtheria. The chapter provides a historical account of the discovery of the antitoxin and development of vaccine.

Waller, John. *The Discovery of the Germ: Twenty Years That Transformed the Way We Think About Disease*. New York: Columbia University Press, 2002. Waller examines the breakthroughs in microbiology that occurred between 1879 and 1900, including the discoveries of Koch and Pasteur. Places Behring's work in a larger medical and historical context.

Walsh, James Joseph. *Makers of Modern Medicine*. Reprint. Freeport, N.Y.: Books for Libraries Press, 1970. The book contains a chapter about Joseph O'Dwyer, an American physician who relentlessly studied the efficacy of using diphtheria antitoxin and eventually succeeded in demonstrating its true value.

Wood, William Barry. *From Miasmas to Molecules*. New York: Columbia University Press, 1961. The book provides a historical perspective as well as ex-

1890's

panded scientific explanations of the diphtheria bacilli: antitoxin and immunity.

SEE ALSO: Oct. 16, 1846: Safe Surgical Anesthesia Is Demonstrated; May, 1847: Semmelweis Develops Antiseptic Procedures; 1857,: Pasteur Begins Developing Germ Theory and Microbiology; 1880's: Roux Develops the Theory of Mitosis; 1882-1901: Metchnikoff Advances the Cellular Theory of Immu-

nity; Mar. 24, 1882: Koch Announces His Discovery of the Tuberculosis Bacillus; Jan. 23, 1897: "Aspirin" Is Registered as a Trade Name; Aug. 20, 1897: Ross Establishes Malaria's Transmission Vector; 1898: Beijerinck Discovers Viruses; June, 1900-1904: Suppression of Yellow Fever.

RELATED ARTICLES in *Great Lives from History: The Nineteenth Century, 1801-1900:* Emil von Behring; Robert Koch.

December 29, 1890
WOUNDED KNEE MASSACRE

This last major confrontation between American Indians and U.S. government troops represented the end of violent resistance by Native Americans to the loss of their independence and signaled the closing of the American frontier.

ALSO KNOWN AS: Battle of Wounded Knee
LOCALE: Wounded Knee Creek, near Pine Ridge, South Dakota
CATEGORIES: Atrocities and war crimes; indigenous people's rights; wars, uprisings, and civil unrest

KEY FIGURES
Sitting Bull (1831-1890), last great Sioux warrior chief
Big Foot (c. 1825-1890), chief of the Minneconjou Sioux
Wovoka (Jack Wilson; c. 1858-1932), Paiute messiah of the Ghost Dance religion
William Cody (Buffalo Bill; 1846-1917), frontier scout and showman
James W. Forsyth (1835-1906), Seventh Cavalry officer in charge at Wounded Knee
James McLaughlin (1842-1923), agent in charge at the Standing Rock reservation
Nelson A. Miles (1839-1925), commander of the Division of the Missouri

SUMMARY OF EVENT
On December 15, 1890, two weeks before the Battle of Wounded Knee was fought, Sitting Bull, the last great Sioux warrior chief, was killed in an effort to suppress the Ghost Dance religion, which had been begun by Wovoka. Wovoka's admixture of American Indian and Christian beliefs inspired hope in an eventual triumph of the American Indians over the white settlers, who, Wovoka envisioned, would fall through the earth and disap-

pear forever. Although Wovoka preached passivity and patience, some of his zealous disciples carried a more aggressive message. Among them were a Minneconjou Sioux named Kicking Bear and his brother-in-law Short Bull. They and other followers of Wovoka introduced the Ghost Dance to the Dakota reservations, including Standing Rock and Pine Ridge.

In an effort to suppress Ghost Dancing, James McLaughlin, the government agent in charge of the Standing Rock reservation, first arrested Kicking Bear, then moved against Sitting Bull, an old adversary and, in McLaughlin's mind, the symbolic center of tribal unrest. McLaughlin was convinced that Ghost Dancing could be suppressed only if Sitting Bull were in prison. He called Sitting Bull a fomenter of disturbances, prompting General Nelson A. Miles, U.S. Army Commander of the Missouri Division, to send William Cody to Standing Rock to persuade the chief to negotiate with Miles. However, McLaughlin complained to Washington and had Cody's mission aborted.

What followed was a fiasco. Forty-three American Indian police, commanded by Lieutenant Bull Head, surrounded Sitting Bull's cabin and ordered him to come outside. Sitting Bull obeyed, but one of the assembled Ghost Dancers, angered at the arrest, shot Bull Head with a rifle. While attempting to fire back at his assailant, Bull Head accidentally shot Sitting Bull at the same moment that another American Indian policeman fired a lethal shot through the old chief's head.

When news of Sitting Bull's death reached Big Foot, the chief of the Minneconjou at Cherry Creek, he decamped his followers and started a journey toward Pine Ridge, hoping to find protection under Chief Red Cloud. His band consisted of 120 men and 230 women and children. Big Foot himself was ill with pneumonia and had to make the journey in a wagon. On December 28, near Porcupine Creek, the Indians encountered troops of the Seventh U.S. Cavalry under the command of Major Samuel Whitside. Although near death, Big Foot arranged a meeting with Whitside, who informed the chief that his orders were to escort the Indians to Wounded Knee Creek. Big Foot agreed to comply with Whitside's directions, because Wounded Knee was on the way to Pine Ridge. Whitside then had his men move Big Foot to an army ambulance to make his trip more comfortable.

The combined Indian trains reached Wounded Knee Creek before nightfall. Whitside oversaw their encampment south of his military bivouac and provided them with rations, tents, and a surgeon to tend Big Foot. He also took measures to ensure that none of the Indians could escape by posting sentinels and setting up rapid-fire Hotchkiss guns in key positions.

During the night, the remaining Seventh Cavalry troops arrived, and command of the operation passed from Major Whitside to Colonel James W. Forsyth. The colonel told the junior officer that he had received orders to accompany Big Foot's bands to the Union Pacific Railroad for transport to a military prison in Omaha. The next morning, on December 29, after issuing hardtack rations to the Indians, Colonel Forsyth ordered them to surrender their weapons, and his soldiers stacked up the Indians' arms and ammunition. Not satisfied that all weapons had been turned in, Forsyth sent details to search the Indians' tipis. The searchers then ordered the Indians to remove their blankets, which, the soldiers assumed, masked hidden weapons.

The situation grew tense. The Indians were both humiliated and angry, but they were badly outnumbered and almost all of them had been disarmed. Only the Minneconjou medicine man Yellow Bird openly protested. He began performing Ghost Dance steps and chanted lines from the holy songs that assured the Indians that their Ghost Shirts would not let the soldiers' bullets strike them.

The soldiers found only two rifles during the last search, but one of them belonged to a deaf Sioux brave named Black Coyote, who resisted them. Soldiers grabbed him and spun him around, attempting to disarm him, and at that point Black Coyote fired his rifle, possibly by accident. The debacle followed has been called a battle, but it was little more than a massacre. The soldiers

Cavalry troops fighting the Sioux at Wounded Knee Creek. (Francis R. Niglutsch)

1890's

opened fire on the unarmed Minneconjou at once, slaughtering many of them with repeated volleys from their carbines. Most of the Indians tried to flee, but the Hotchkiss guns opened up on them from their hillside positions. Firing at a rate of almost one round per second, the soldiers' shots tore into the camp, indiscriminately killing braves, women, and children. The Hotchkiss guns turned the rout into a massacre.

When it was over, Big Foot and more than half his followers were dead or seriously wounded. One hundred fifty-three lay dead on the ground, but many of the fatally wounded had crawled off to die elsewhere. One estimate claimed that there were barely more than fifty Indian survivors, only those transported after the massacre. Twenty-five soldiers were killed; most had been shot accidentally by their own comrades, not by Indians.

After the wounded troopers were decamped and sent to Pine Ridge, a detail of soldiers rounded up the surviving Indians: four men and forty-seven women and children. Placed in wagons, they also set out for Pine Ridge, leaving their dead to a blizzard that prevented their immediate burial and froze them into grotesque, hoary reminders of the debacle.

SIGNIFICANCE

An inquiry followed the events at Wounded Knee, prompted by General Miles, who brought charges against Forsyth, but the colonel was exonerated and nothing else came of the investigation. The affair traditionally has been viewed as the last armed resistance of American Indians to reservation resettlement. It and the death of Sitting Bull, both in 1890, although not singled out, were certainly factors in the conclusions of Frederick Jackson Turner, who claimed in his renowned 1893 thesis that the U.S. frontier closed during the year of the massacre.

For American Indians, however, the infamous day did not die with the victims. On February 27, 1973, more than two hundred members of the American Indian Movement (AIM) took the reservation site at Wounded Knee by force, proclaiming it the Independent Oglala Sioux Nation and demanding that the federal government make amends for past injustices by reviewing all American Indian treaties and policies. Federal marshals immediately surrounded the group. After a two-month standoff, the marshals persuaded the Indians to surrender with promises of a public airing of grievances. For American Indians, Wounded Knee has remained an important symbol of the Euro-American injustice and suppression of their people.

—John W. Fiero

FURTHER READING

Allen, Charles Wesley. *Autobiography of Red Cloud: War Leader of the Oglalas.* Edited by R. Eli Paul. Helena: Montana Historical Society Press, 1997. First publication of a memoir that the Sioux chief Red Cloud dictated three years after the massacre at Wounded Knee.

Anderson, Gary Clayton. *Sitting Bull and the Paradox of Lakota Nationhood.* New York: Longman, Addison-Wesley, 1996. Biography of the last great Sioux chief that focuses on the challenges Sitting Bull faced in leading his people.

Brown, Dee. *Bury My Heart at Wounded Knee: An Indian History of the American West.* New York: Holt, Rinehart and Winston, 1970. Readable, popular account of the displacement and oppression of American Indian nations by European settlers, from the beginnings of European settlement in North America to the massacre of 1890. Includes a helpful but now dated bibliography.

Jensen, Richard E., R. Eli Paul, and John E. Carter. *Eyewitness at Wounded Knee.* Lincoln: University of Nebraska Press, 1992. Fine collection of photographs from the Wounded Knee battlefield and related sites, with essays on the American Indian perspective, the U.S. Army's role, and the distorted media coverage.

Klein, Christina. "'Everything of Interest in the Late Pine Ridge War Are Held by Us for Sale': Popular Culture and Wounded Knee." *Western Historical Quarterly* 25 (Spring, 1994): 45-68. Argues that commercial exploitation of Wounded Knee in Buffalo Bill Cody's Wild West show, photographs, and the dime novel played as significant a role as the military in defeating the Ghost Dancers' dreams of American Indian autonomy. Includes photographs.

Neihardt, John G. *Black Elk Speaks: Being the Life Story of a Holy Man of the Oglala Sioux.* 1932. Reprint. Lincoln: University of Nebraska Press, 1979. This classic work chronicles the spiritual odyssey of Black Elk, a holy man of the Oglala Sioux. Provides important insight into American Indian beliefs and an account of the Wounded Knee Massacre.

Utley, Robert M. *The Lance and the Shield: The Life and Times of Sitting Bull.* New York: Ballantine Books, 1994. Nearly definitive biography of Sitting Bull that portrays the Sioux chief as a complex leader.

_____. *Last Days of the Sioux Nation.* New Haven, Conn.: Yale University Press, 1963. Highly regarded, sensitive, and evenhanded study that documents the events leading up to Wounded Knee. Contains a chapter on sources, making it invaluable for further study.

Voices from Wounded Knee, 1973. Rooseveltown, N.Y.: Akwesasne Notes, 1974. With edited transcripts of interviews, documents the efforts of the Oglala Sioux to gain national sympathy for the plight of the American Indian by their stand at Wounded Knee Creek in 1973. Includes a chronicle of events from 1868 to 1973 and an account of the 1890 massacre.

SEE ALSO: Aug. 17, 1862-Dec. 28, 1863: Great Sioux War; June 13, 1866-Nov. 6, 1868: Red Cloud's War; Dec. 21, 1866: Fetterman Massacre; Oct. 21, 1867: Medicine Lodge Creek Treaty; June 27, 1874-June 2, 1875: Red River War; 1876-1877: Sioux War; June 25, 1876: Battle of the Little Bighorn; 1890: U.S. Census Bureau Announces Closing of the Frontier.

RELATED ARTICLES in *Great Lives from History: The Nineteenth Century, 1801-1900:* William Cody; Red Cloud; Sitting Bull.

1891
NAISMITH INVENTS BASKETBALL

Basketball, invented by James Naismith, is a traditionally American game first played as an indoor sport in YMCA gymnasiums during winter months. The game was quickly embraced, and it spread rapidly throughout the world to become not only a playground and school sport but also an Olympic and professional sport.

LOCALE: Springfield, Massachusetts

CATEGORIES: Sports; organizations and institutions

KEY FIGURES

James Naismith (1861-1939), Canadian-born American physical education instructor

Luther Halsey Gulick (1865-1918), Naismith's supervisor

Amos Alonzo Stagg (1862-1965), football and basketball coach

Frank Mahan (1867-1905), early basketball player, coined the term "basketball"

SUMMARY OF EVENT

Basketball, a traditionally American game that has achieved international popularity, was invented in 1891 by James Naismith while he was a student at a training school (now Springfield College) for leaders of the Young Men's Christian Association (YMCA). Luther Gulick, the school's dean,

asked Naismith and fellow student Amos Alonzo Stagg to form a football team. Stagg became the captain and Naismith played center.

Football and baseball were popular with the students, who were also YMCA directors, but they were unhappy with the indoor gymnastics classes that they taught during the winter months. The marching drills, Indian-club and medicine-ball routines, and calisthenics did not ap-

Dr. James Naismith (in suit) with his first basketball team in Springfield, Massachusetts. (Hulton Archive/Getty Images)

1890's

BASKETBALL'S ORIGINAL RULES

1. The ball may be thrown in any direction with one or both hands.

2. The ball may be batted in any direction with one or both hands.

3. A player cannot run with the ball. The player must throw it from the spot on which he catches it, allowances to be made for a man who catches the ball when running if he tries to stop.

4. The ball must be held by the hands. The arms or body must not be used for holding it.

5. No shouldering, holding, pushing, tripping or striking in any way the person of an opponent shall be allowed; the first infringement of this rule by any player shall come as a foul, the second shall disqualify him until the next goal is made, or, if there was evident intent to injure the person, for the whole of the game, no substitute allowed.

6. A foul is striking the ball with the fist, violation of Rules 3, 4, and such as described in Rule 5.

7. If either side makes three consecutive fouls it shall count as a goal for the opponents (consecutive means without the opponents in the meantime making a foul).

8. A goal shall be made when the ball is thrown or batted from the grounds into the basket and stays there, providing those defending the goal do no touch or disturb the goal. If the ball rests on the edges, and the opponent moves the basket, it shall count as a goal.

9. When the ball goes out of bounds, it shall be thrown into the field of play by the person touching it. He has a right to hold it unmolested for five seconds. In case of a dispute the umpire shall throw it straight into the field. The thrower-in is allowed five seconds; if he holds it longer it shall go to the opponent. If any side persists in delaying the game the umpire shall call a foul on that side.

10. The umpire shall be the judge of the men and shall note the fouls and notify the referee when three consecutive fouls have been made. He shall have power to disqualify men according to Rule 5.

11. The referee shall be judge of the ball and shall decide when the ball is in play, in bounds, to which side it belongs, and shall keep the time. He shall decide when a goal has been made and keep account of the goals, with any other duties that are usually performed by a referee.

12. The time shall be two fifteen-minute halves, with five minutes rest between.

13. The side making the most goals in that time shall be declared the winner. In the case of a draw the game may, by agreement of the captains, be continued until another goal is made.

Source: "Dr. Naismith's Original 13 Rules." Basketball Hall of Fame.

ever, was found to be no more helpful than the German and French systems. Naismith suggested inventing a new sport.

Naismith tried to adapt soccer, lacrosse, and rugby to indoor play, but he had no luck. He imagined using a large ball that would be advanced not by running, which would involve tackling, but by passing. He solved the problem of scoring when he created a goal by adapting a childhood game called Duck on the Rock, which involved lobbing small stones onto a large rock and knocking off the rocks of the opposition. He then assumed that if he placed the goal on the floor, players would be able to surround it and thus prevent scoring entirely. Placing the goal over the players' heads solved the problem. He secured peach baskets (fifteen inches in diameter) that he got from the school's janitor and raised them ten feet above the floor; he used a soccer ball as the first basketball. He also substituted the center jump for the rugby scrimmage to put the ball in play.

Naismith's thirteen original rules, which included fouls, goals, and out-of-bounds penalties, were posted on the bulletin board at the Armory Street YMCA gymnasium. He later tried the game with his class, dividing the eighteen players into two teams, one captained by Eugene Libby of Redlands, California, the other by Duncan Patton of Canada, two men who had been playing Naismith's other games for two weeks. Each team had a goalkeeper, two guards, three center men, two wings, and a home man or goal thrower (three centers, three forwards, and three guards).

Acting as the sole official in the game, Naismith threw the ball up between a center from each team, and play began. As Naismith later acknowledged, there were many fouls at first, probably because the players were accustomed to the roughness of football. Initially, all the players tried to score, but eventually there was some semblance of teamwork as players learned that those closest to the basket had a better chance of scoring. In that first classroom game, played on a very small court (approximately thirty by fifty feet) and with only imaginary boundary lines, only one goal was scored, a shot by Wil-

peal to them. Gulick called upon Naismith to find an alternative training system and sent him to Martha's Vineyard, Massachusetts, to study Baron Nils Posse's Swedish gymnastics system. The Swedish system, how-

liam R. Chase of New Bedford, Massachusetts, from midcourt. Afterward, a player had to climb a ladder to retrieve the ball from the peach basket, prompting Naismith to think of a better way for the ball's return to the court.

Naismith's students went home for Christmas break and took the game with them; it became popular immediately. When Frank Mahan returned to Springfield, he met with Naismith to discuss what to call the game. Mahan first suggested "Naismith ball," but Naismith objected; then he suggested "basketball," and Naismith agreed. The thirteen rules and Naismith's instructions were printed January 15, 1892, in the *Triangle*, the school newspaper, which had national distribution. Naismith's nine-man team, called the Flying Circus and captained by Mahan, became the first basketball team in history.

By April, *The New York Times* was covering the sport, which was played primarily at YMCAs. On February 12 and March 15, the Central and Armory branches of the New York YMCA played each other, but the most important public game was played March 11, 1892, at the International YMCA Training School in Springfield. Naismith, Gulick, Stagg, and four others played against seven students. (Naismith had said that the game could be played by any number of players.) Naismith's team lost, 5-1. The only faculty member to score was Stagg, whose aggressive play earned him a black eye. In 1896, Stagg also appeared in a game between a YMCA team made up of University of Iowa students and another of University of Chicago students. That same year Yale University organized the first regular college games, playing Trinity, Wesleyan, and the University of Pennsylvania.

Because the YMCA was an international movement, the game spread to more than one dozen countries by 1900. Naismith went to the University of Kansas to coach basketball, and Gulick helped modify the rules and publicize basketball internationally. By 1900, American soldiers had played basketball in the Philippines and in China.

SIGNIFICANCE

Basketball became to the winter season what baseball and football were to the rest of the year. Whereas ice hockey was established in some parts of the north, there was no national winter sport in the United States until the creation of basketball. Naismith invented the game, and Gulick popularized it through his involvement with the YMCA. Within just a few short years, however, the game was too big for one individual to administer.

In 1896, control of the game passed to the Amateur Athletic Union of America, and in 1908 the National Collegiate Athletic Association (NCAA) determined college rules for the sport. During the twentieth century basketball became an Olympic sport (baseball gained Olympic status late in the twentieth century, and American football has remained an American sport), and it is played professionally around the globe. U.S. Olympic basketball teams traditionally were made up of college players who brought home many gold medals, until other countries became competitive in the sport. When Olympic teams were allowed to use professional players during the early 1990's, the U.S. squad was nicknamed the Dream Team and won international fame. Over the next decade, basketball won greater popularity around the world, and during the early twenty-first century, other nations began to challenge American dominance in the sport.

—*Thomas L. Erskine*

FURTHER READING

Bjarkman, Peter C. *The Biographical History of Basketball*. Chicago: Masters Press, 2000. Acknowledges Naismith as the founder of basketball but points out that Naismith saw basketball as essentially a way to provide off-season exercise for his football players. Notes that only about six of Naismith's original thirteen rules are still in effect.

Cosentino, Frank. *Almonte's Brothers of the Wind: R. Tait McKenzie and James Naismith*. Burnstown, Canada: General Store Publishing House, 1996. Ties the careers of the two men together in terms of physical education and health.

Fox, Larry. *Illustrated History of Basketball*. New York: Grosset & Dunlap, 1974. Fox's first three chapters cover Naismith's invention of basketball and the game's rapid increase in popularity.

Naismith, James. *Basketball: Its Origin and Development*. New York: Association Press, 1941. The game's inventor discusses how the game changed since its inception.

Peterson, Robert W. *Cages to Jump Shots: Pro Basketball's Early Years*. Lincoln: University of Nebraska Press, 2002. Peterson explores the earliest years of basketball, from its inception in 1891 to 1954. Also looks at how the sport and the makeup of teams have been affected by social trends.

Webb, Bernice Larson. *The Basketball Man: James Naismith*. Lawrence: University Press of Kansas, 1973. Biography of Naismith that explores the game's origins.

1890's

SEE ALSO: c. 1845: Modern Baseball Begins; 1869: Baseball's First Professional Club Forms; Apr. 6, 1896: Modern Olympic Games Are Inaugurated.

RELATED ARTICLE in *Great Lives from History: The Nineteenth Century, 1801-1900:* William Gilbert Grace.

March 11, 1891

STROWGER PATENTS AUTOMATIC DIAL TELEPHONE SYSTEM

Almon Brown Strowger's automatic dialing system provided one-wire signaling that ultimately proved to be a practical way to provide automatic switching on the Bell telephone network.

LOCALE: Kansas City, Missouri

CATEGORIES: Inventions; communications; manufacturing

KEY FIGURES

Almon Brown Strowger (1839-1902), Missouri undertaker who invented automatic telephone dialing

A. E. Keith (fl. late nineteenth century), Strowger's associate who helped refine Strowger's invention

John Erickson (fl. late nineteenth century) and *Charles J. Erickson* (fl. late nineteenth century), engineers who developed Strowger's invention commercially

SUMMARY OF EVENT

After Alexander Graham Bell invented the telephone, much of the research and development in the growing telephony industry was directed to the need for switching equipment that would provide reliable and convenient access for increasing numbers of users linked to growing telephone networks. During the decade and a half that followed Bell's first dramatic demonstration of the telephone in 1876, all telephone calls between two points had to be manually connected by operators—a bottleneck that often resulted in delays and other problems during times of peak telephone use.

Telephone subscribers also realized that, during periods of high demand, operators were in a position to control which users would get priority access. Users were also concerned about privacy and fairness. Operators could listen in on conversations and were in a position to control whether calls even went through. Some subscribers expressed concern that operators might be tempted to become involved in schemes concocted by third parties to interfere with, or even sabotage, competition among commercial establishments. That concern was expressed

by Almon Brown Strowger, a Kansas City, Missouri, undertaker who, despite a lack of technical training and expertise, set out to invent a way for telephone users to bypass operators automatically to ensure that calls would go through and that they would be private.

Strowger had become convinced that his own funeral business was being victimized by unscrupulous telephone operators who were deliberately giving incorrect phone numbers to callers attempting to reach him, or, when correct numbers were requested, engaging busy signals rather than putting the calls through. Recognizing that the only recourse was to find a way to bypass human operators, Strowger determined to invent an automatic switching system capable of doing just that.

All previous attempts to develop automatic switching systems had failed. In 1879, for example, the Connolly-McTighe patent, issued on December 9 to M. D. Connolly, T. A. Connolly, and T. McTighe, had provided specifications for the first automatic telephone switch, but it ultimately proved a failure. In 1884, Ezra Gilliland developed a primitive system that proved reliable but inefficient. It worked but was capable of serving only fifteen telephones. Strowger learned from those ideas when he proposed and patented a system that could handle up to ninety-nine telephones on March 11, 1891.

Each Strowger telephone had two buttons that could be pressed up to nine times each to achieve the required digits for any two-digit number from zero to ninety-nine. In the telephone central office, each electric pulse created when the buttons were pushed moved a mechanical arm so that the contact points were placed directly in line with those of the exact numbers requested. This innovation was quickly accepted as the key to automatic switching, and in 1891 Strowger set up the Strowger Automatic Telephone Exchange to exploit his patent by manufacturing the switches designed according to the specifications set forth in his patent. That company would be absorbed into the Automatic Electric Company in 1908.

Strowger's automatic switch was not a complete success initially, although the underlying principle upon which it was based was sound. Shortly after acquiring the patent, Strowger became associated with A. E. Keith, John Erickson, and Charles J. Erickson. All were talented engineers who helped develop his automatic switch concept into a workable and dependable system. In November, 1892, the first Strowger system was installed in LaPorte, Indiana, making it the first automatic central switching facility in the world. Over the next fifteen years, the system was repeatedly tested, modified, and remodified.

Around the turn of the twentieth century, the American Telephone and Telegraph Company was examining and testing automatic switching systems that were being proposed by other companies. Meanwhile, the Automatic Electric Company pressed on with development and deployment of its Strowger system. It installed systems capable of handling up to six thousand lines each in several cities including Grand Rapids, Michigan, and Dayton, Ohio.

Despite the growing track record of the Strowger system, the future of automatic switching was seen as uncertain by the Bell company, which had set up its own automatic systems in many small towns and rural areas. These systems had proved less reliable and more costly than manual switching because they required constant technical maintenance and support, and they did not eliminate completely the need for manual operators. To early telephone designers, this meant that automatic switching was not a true substitute for manual switching. Instead, it was perceived to be simply a costly enhancement of the existing system that, over the years, had become increasingly efficient and less costly per subscriber as the numbers of telephone subscribers increased.

Bell company officials were also concerned that automatic switching put responsibility for making telephone connections on the shoulders of the customers, instead of the operators. They reasoned that that might result in the public perception that the quality of service had been lowered. From the beginning, American Telephone and Telegraph officials had insisted that automatic switching must be both cost effective and reliable and represent a tangible improvement in overall quality of telephone service for the customers.

Despite the concerns about privacy and access, manual switching centers had been evolving also. They were streamlined gradually for efficiency and cost effectiveness, often handling ten thousand lines or more. Telephone company officials remained unconvinced about the practicality of automatic switches until 1914. By that time, the Automatic Electric Company had refined and enhanced the Strowger switch to the point where it per-

formed most of the functions of manual operators. The breakthrough came in 1905, when a new electronic pulsing scheme was incorporated that required only one wire. Until that time, two wires were required to send electronic signal pulses back and forth between stations and central switches. A timing scheme was introduced that eliminated the need for the second line, and a major advance in technical efficiency was suddenly at hand.

Strowger died several years before his automatic switching concept achieved its full potential as the primary automatic switching technology employed by the Bell system. In May, 1916, the Automatic Electric Company and Western Electric, the telephone equipment manufacturing branch of American Telephone and Telegraph, signed an agreement that gave Western Electric the right to manufacture Strowger automatic dialing equipment, although Automatic Electric would continue to supply equipment to the parent company for many years. In 1917, the Strowger switch was ordered for a new Bell central office in Norfolk, Virginia, and from that point on was the accepted switching technology in all Bell system installations. Automatic Electric continued to supply equipment to Bell until 1936.

SIGNIFICANCE

The Strowger automatic dialing system represented a change from the way telephone service had been provided during the early years. Bell officials had assumed that manual operators would always be involved in connecting calls because the system was too technically complicated for most subscribers to master. During those years, subscribers simply picked up their telephone receivers and gave quick pulls on hand cranks to signal operators to come on the line. Callers then gave the operators the numbers—or sometimes only the names—of the parties they wished to reach, and the operators placed their calls.

Station dialing required callers to do everything. They had to punch in the numbers of the desired parties accurately and then wait for the connections to go through. This process was complicated when long-distance toll calls were placed, and company officials worried that the public would perceive automatic dialing to be a degradation in the quality of the service to which they had become accustomed.

By 1914, Bell operators were discovering that a significant portion of the public had already been exposed to automatic dialing with few complaints about the added effort of station dialing. For almost fifteen years, the Automatic Electric Company had been selling ever-

1890's

improving Strowger equipment to independent telephone companies around the country that could not afford to employ full-time operators. That equipment had gained a good reputation among the independent companies for reliability and economy, and was particularly valuable in systems where peak demand could not be handled efficiently by manual operators. During the same period, Bell was buying up many of these independents, in the process acquiring the installed equipment. Telephone subscribership was continuing to skyrocket, and, in desperate need of a way to accommodate that growth, the company began to run its own tests and use the Bell Research Laboratory to refine the Strowger concept for use on the nationwide system. That the concept ultimately became the basis for the design of the automatic rotary dial telephone bears witness to the significance of the unique and innovative ideas proposed by Strowger.

—Michael S. Ameigh

FURTHER READING

Brooks, John. *Telephone: The First Hundred Years*. New York: Harper & Row, 1976. Excellent corporate history of the Bell telephone system that includes many anecdotes and colorful stories about the early years of telephony, giving life and context to otherwise highly technical descriptions.

Casson, Herbert. *The History of the Telephone*. Chicago: A. C. McClurg, 1910. Rare glimpse into the early days of telephony as described by many of the innovators who participated in the development of the nationwide telephone network.

Danielian, Noorbar R. *AT&T: The Story of Industrial Conquest*. New York: Vanguard Press, 1939. Good look at some of the personalities involved in the development of the world's largest telephone network.

Fagen, M. D., ed. *A History of Engineering and Science in the Bell System: The Early Years, 1875-1925*. New York: Bell Telephone Laboratories, 1975. Large work prepared by the Bell technical staff as part of a multivolume set tracing the corporate and technical history of the company. Contains detailed and well-illustrated descriptions of the Strowger dialing apparatus from the very first prototype through its evolution to the rotary dialing mechanisms still in use.

Hill, R. B. "Early Work on Dial Telephone Systems." *Bell Laboratories Record* 31 (March, 1953). A good overview of the technical developments in dial switching during the earliest years.

_____. "The Early Years of the Strowger System." *Bell Laboratories Record* 31 (March, 1953). Good overview of the technical developments in dial switching during the earliest years.

Rhodes, Frederick Leland. *Beginnings of Telephony*. New York: Harper & Bros., 1929. Another early look at behind-the-scenes research and development that shaped telephone technology during its first quarter century.

SEE ALSO: May 24, 1844: Morse Sends First Telegraph Message; June 25, 1876: Bell Demonstrates the Telephone; Dec. 24, 1877: Edison Patents the Cylinder Phonograph; June, 1896: Marconi Patents the Wireless Telegraph; Dec. 15, 1900: General Electric Opens Research Laboratory.

RELATED ARTICLES in *Great Lives from History: The Nineteenth Century, 1801-1900:* Alexander Graham Bell; Thomas Alva Edison.

May 15, 1891
PAPAL ENCYCLICAL ON LABOR

As the world confronted the new challenges of industrialization, the resulting social dislocations, and answers offered by anarchism and socialism, Pope Leo XIII presented a Roman Catholic perspective founded on traditional theology and the realities of the changing social, political, and economic environment. Although not all embraced it, his encyclical Rerum novarum *served as a seminal statement on labor that shaped papal attitudes for seven decades.*

LOCALE: Rome, Italy
CATEGORIES: Religion and theology; business and labor

KEY FIGURES

Leo XIII (Vincenzo Gioacchino Pecci; 1810-1903), Roman Catholic pope, 1878-1903
Matteo Liberatore (1810-1892), Italian theologian, philosopher, and writer
Camillo Mazzella (1833-1900), Roman Catholic cardinal, 1886-1900
Tommaso Maria Zigliara (1833-1893), Roman Catholic cardinal, 1879-1893

SUMMARY OF EVENT

The second half of the nineteenth century witnessed the increasingly frenetic industrialization of Europe and North America. On both continents, this process produced societies that faced new and revolutionary changes that severely challenged the traditional relationships between employers and employees, as well as between states and their citizens. Burgeoning populations ensured ample labor forces but also seemed to recommend a cold and often cruel treatment of this "factor of production" to owners and managers. European nation-states, many of which had only recently come into existence as modern nation-states, struggled to find a role in this rapidly changing landscape and wavered between paternalistic interference and negligent laissez-faire policies.

Early trade unionism promised some relief and power for the working classes, but this movement met strong opposition from capitalist owners and the liberal governments that tended to reflect their values. In the United States, the picture was much the same, as "robber barons" and ambitious industrialists took advantage of every opportunity to reduce costs and maximize profits, while the federal government remained ambivalent. Al-though Christianity had a long tradition of moral teaching on many social issues, this new and evolving situation—which pitted capitalism, private property rights, and ownership privileges against the social, economic, and even physical welfare of the laboring classes—demanded to be addressed by the most powerful of Christian voices, that of the Roman Catholic pope.

The very forces that had unleashed industrialization, modern nationalism, and increasing secularization in society had weakened papal authority and muffled its voice. Indeed, the papacy was noted for its championing of the interests of the wealthy European classes, the traditional allies of the clerical class. Nonetheless, in the person of Pope Leo XIII, the Roman Catholic Church had a leader who was unusually engaged in contemporary social matters and who was willing to use his pulpit for the common good.

Vincenzo Gioacchino Pecci, who took the name Leo XIII upon being elected pope in 1878, was a diplomatic and well-traveled cleric who understood the political and economic forces at work in industrializing Europe better than did most leaders in Rome. Pope Pius IX, Leo's predecessor, had ruled the Catholic world for three decades as an antiliberal autocrat and a self-styled martyr to Italy's 1870 unification. Leo's instincts and experience led him to take a different road as supreme pontiff.

As papal political power had disintegrated, Pius had created a powerful diplomatic infrastructure in Catholic Europe and beyond, one that held sway even in such antagonistic states as imperial Germany. Inheriting this tool, Leo went to work establishing a staunch moral voice, disembodied from any political base and beholden to no particular interests. In dealing with states, he deftly balanced traditional Catholic or papal positions with a willingness to compromise on minor matters. He could, at the same time, adopt the works of the thirteenth century theologian Thomas Aquinas as the Church's official doctrine and applaud achievements of the modern world that did not unduly threaten Church teaching.

During the very first year of his reign, 1878, Leo promulgated *Quod apostolici*, which spoke out against the class struggle noted and encouraged by Marxists and socialists. In *Arcanum*, two years later, Leo reaffirmed the human family as the basis of society, refuting those who would radically alter fundamental social relationships. As bishop of Perugia, Pecci had befriended many Catholic socialists—while dismissing socialism itself—and

1890's

had founded the Gardens of Saint Philip Neri, a local Catholic organization that promoted social justice along lines set down by French Catholic workers associations. Even so, when the Catholic Union of Freiburg, which had been established by a Catholic bishop, asked Leo in 1887 to convene an international convention to discuss the major social issues of the day, Leo refused, citing his unwillingness to confront the Italian government. That government, still relatively new, remained steadfastly opposed to any potentially provocative gathering.

Leo sought a way openly to embrace the growing movement known as Social Catholicism and just as openly to strike a blow against socialism and communism. In the 1880's, he began collecting information and opinions on the condition of modern labor both from the-

orists and from those engaged directly with Social Catholicism. With Leo's encouragement, the Jesuit editors of *Cività Cattolica*, a journal that incorporated and espoused the ideas of Thomas Aquinas, published a series of articles on social issues and the moral theology that should be brought to bear in understanding and confronting them. Leo then harnessed one of these editors, Matteo Liberatore, to draft a papal encyclical formally addressing the condition of the working class from these Catholic perspectives. Cardinals Tommaso Maria Zigliara and Camillo Mazzella and several papal secretaries helped shape the work, and Leo polished the final document. It is generally known, as most encyclicals are, by its opening words, *Rerum novarum*, "of new matters."

Rerum novarum was issued on May 15, 1891, and is divided into five unequal parts. In the first, Leo utilizes four classic Catholic arguments based on theology and reason that uphold the validity of private property and freedom of its use. With this argument, he sought to buttress the foundations of liberal capitalism and undermine its socialist and communist critics. In the second section, the pope laid out both the theoretical underpinnings of the Church's role in shaping society and a blueprint for the exercise of that role. Recognizing that the Church had long since lost any ability to enforce its will, Leo outlined the ways in which teaching and preaching could constitute a powerful—and necessary—moral voice to guide all the world's people.

Leo expanded on the theme of teaching and preaching in the third part of the encyclical, including positive activity by the Church and lay Catholics alike. Provision of social welfare for the needy, promotion of social justice, and organization to oppose arbitrary and oppressive treatment by the powerful classes lay at the heart of Leo's conception of Catholic-led social action. The fourth part of the encyclical laid out a positive role for the state in providing an environment that was conducive to an equitable and just relationship between capital and labor.

As he rejected socialism, so Leo rejected the laissez-faire state. Instead, he promoted a polity that protected both property rights and the God-given rights of working people to

Coronation of Pope Leo XIII. (Francis R. Niglutsch)

safe and fair workplace conditions, a living wage, and justice in disputes. In the final section of the document, Leo extolled the benefits of voluntary trade unionism and envisioned Catholics creating parallel organizations that would provide voices for the working class and leverage against intransigent capitalists. Leo would have the state embrace such organizations rather than oppose them: He hoped that capitalist states would see their value as bulwarks against socialist or communist alternatives.

Rather than merely condemning exploitation or defending property rights, Leo presented a nuanced and interconnected analysis of contemporary issues and called upon the Church, modern nation-states, workers, and employers to engage symbiotically for the benefit of all. *Rerum novarum* thus put forward a clearly articulated rationale for social and political action designed to help workers gain social justice without impairing the ability of capitalists to increase profits. It recognized the complexity of the contemporary landscape, while nevertheless envisioning traditional teaching as still not only relevant but crucial to that landscape. The forcefulness of Leo XIII's vision for the betterment of society made his encyclical a landmark statement in the social history of modernization.

SIGNIFICANCE

Rerum novarum was the first comprehensive statement of papal attitude toward the problems of labor during the Industrial Revolution. It consistently shaped statements of papal social teaching over the succeeding seven decades, a period sometimes characterized by its "Leonine" policy. Nonetheless, its acceptance was anything but uniform. Leo's endorsement of the interventionist state fell flat among free market liberals, while his support for private property displeased the more radical among the working classes. Others condemned the papacy for daring to intervene in arguably nonreligious matters. Catholicism, though, could now be accepted as a constructive presence in the industrializing world, and those who operated between the radicals and the hardcore capitalists could view the papacy as a force for moderation rather than a source of traditionalist inertia.

Leo's vision of a Catholicism that was continually strengthened and made ever more relevant by its engagement in the modern economic and social worlds was left unachieved. He wanted to see the papacy rise from its near-death to a new pinnacle of influence, as

Catholic moral law became the foundation of a new, industrialized Western society. Despite its seminal role in articulating Catholic social teaching, however, *Rerum novarum* neither directed the development of liberal economic development nor halted the progress of leftist political action.

—Joseph P. Byrne

FURTHER READING

Coleman, John, and Gregory Baum, eds. *Rerum Novarum: A Hundred Years of Catholic Social Teaching.* New York: Trinity Press International, 1991. A centenary compilation of short articles dealing with the impact of *Rerum novarum* on subsequent developments in Catholic social theory and practice.

Holland, Joe. *Modern Catholic Social Teaching: The Popes Confront the Industrial Age, 1740-1958.* New York: Paulist Press, 2003. Focuses on the background to, content of, and ripple effects of *Rerum novarum* in subsequent papal documents, with substantial coverage of the encyclical itself.

John Paul II. *On the Hundredth Anniversary of Rerum Novarum: Centissimus Annus.* Washington, D.C.: United States Catholic Conference, 1991. Contains text of John Paul II's letter, published on the centenary of *Rerum novarum*, which reflects on the encyclical's relevance over the century and for Christians in the contemporary world.

Leo XIII. *The Great Encyclical Letters of Pope Leo XIII, 1878-1903: Or, A Light in the Heavens.* Rockford, Ill.: Tan Books, 1995. A ready source for the full texts of *Rerum novarum* and other encyclicals of Pope Leo XIII.

1890's

1892
AMERICA'S "NEW" IMMIGRATION ERA BEGINS

Economic and political changes in both Europe and the United States, as well as new developments in transportation, launched a fundamentally new era that brought large numbers of immigrants to the United States from eastern and southern Europe for the first time.

LOCALE: Ellis Island, New York
CATEGORIES: Immigration; sociology; economics

KEY FIGURE
Josiah Strong (1847-1916), prominent Protestant
　clergyman who opposed unrestricted immigration

SUMMARY OF EVENT
In 1808, the U.S. government purchased Ellis Island from the state of New York for ten thousand dollars. This new federal property, located in New York Harbor about one mile south of Manhattan Island, served first as a fort and later as an arsenal. Until 1882, the state of New York had guided the influx of immigration from the old Castle Garden station at the tip of Manhattan. The opening of Ellis Island on January 1, 1892, as the first federal immi-

gration station symbolized a new era for the United States as well as the beginning of the end of free immigration to the New World.

The U.S. Congress had begun the selective process of excluding undesirable elements among those immigrating to the United States with the passage of the federal Immigration Act of 1882. That measure was designed to prevent the immigration of persons who had criminal records and those who were mentally incompetent or indigent. During that same year, Congress also passed the Chinese Exclusion Act (later extended to all Asians) barring an entire nationality from entry as racially undesirable for a period of ten years. In 1904, that law's provisions were extended indefinitely, to be repealed only in 1943.

Most immigrants who came to the United States before the 1890's had come from northern and western Europe. During the 1880's a fundamental change occurred. In addition to the traditional immigrants, who shared common language patterns with persons already in the United States, people from Mediterranean and Slavic countries began to arrive in increasing numbers. The extent of the change can be measured by comparing two of the peak years in U.S. immigration. In 1882, 87 percent of the 788,000 immigrants came from northern and western Europe. In 1907, only 19.3 percent were from those regions, while 80.7 percent came from southern and eastern Europe.

A great impetus to immigration was the transportation revolution made possible by steamships. In 1856, more than 96 percent of U.S. immigrants crossed oceans on sailing ships, on voyages that took between one and three months. By 1873, the same percentage of immigrants traveled by steamships, which took only ten days. The new steamships were specifically designed for passengers, and while still subject to overcrowding and epidemics, they were a major improvement over the sailing ships because their passengers had to endure overcrowding for much briefer periods. Steamship companies competed for immi-

Eastern European immigrants crossing the Atlantic to North America in 1899. (Library of Congress)

EUROPEAN EMIGRATION TO THE UNITED STATES IN 1900

Numbers indicate
emigrants in thousands

SCANDINAVIA
31

IRELAND
36

GREAT
BRITAIN
13

GERMANY
19

Atlantic

Ocean

RUSSIA AND THE
BALTIC STATES
91

FRANCE
3

CENTRAL
EUROPE
115

ITALY
100

ROMANIA, BULGARIA,
AND TURKEY
7

SPAIN AND
PORTUGAL
2

M e d i t e r r a n e a n   *S e a*

1890's

grant business and maintained offices in Europe. The Hamburg-Amerika line, for example, had 3,200 U.S. agencies throughout Europe. More than half of the immigrants in 1901 came with prepaid tickets supplied by relatives in the United States.

As the older agricultural economies of Europe were replaced by industrial economies, many Europeans moved from farms to cities in search of employment. When they were unsuccessful in that search, they were easily persuaded to try the New World, where jobs were said to be plentiful. The same railroad-building process that opened the American West to the immigrant made it easier and cheaper for the Europeans to reach their coastal areas and embark for the United States.

Most of the emigration from southern Europe was occasioned by economic distress. Southern Italy's agricul-

ture was severely affected by competition from Florida in oranges and lemons, as well as by a French tariff against Italian wines. The Italian emigration began with 12,000 in 1880 and reached a peak of nearly 300,000 in 1914. After new U.S. laws restricting immigration took full effect, Italian immigration fell to 6,203 in 1925.

From Russia and other Slavic areas, emigration was also caused by political and religious problems. Russian Jews fled in reaction to the riots set off by the assassination of Czar Alexander II in 1882, the pogroms of 1881-1882 and 1891, and the 1905-1906 massacres of thousands of Jews. Major Jewish immigration to the United States began with 5,000 people in 1880 and reached a peak of 258,000 in 1907. Some two million Roman Catholic Poles also arrived between 1890 and 1914. In 1925, however, the Immigration Service recorded only 5,341

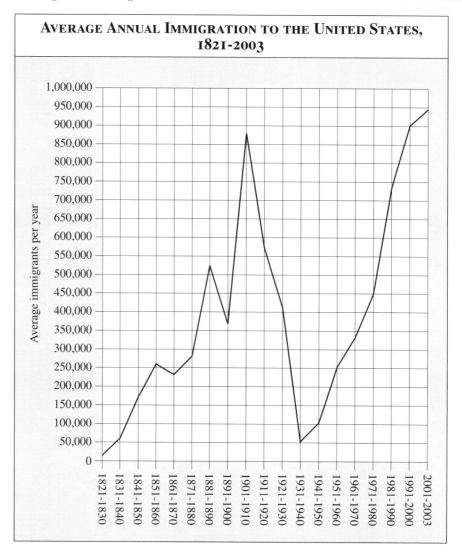

AVERAGE ANNUAL IMMIGRATION TO THE UNITED STATES, 1821-2003

entrants from Poland and 3,121 from Russia and the Baltic States.

Two issues caused the greatest concern to American nativists during the 1890's: the tendency of the new immigrants to congregate in the cities, and the fact that they spoke seemingly unassimilable languages, such as Yiddish, Polish, and Russian. One of the first articulate spokesmen against unrestricted immigration, the Reverend Dr. Josiah Strong, was alarmed by the concentration of foreign peoples in cities. Strong's famous book, *Our Country*, published in 1885, clearly stated what many other U.S. citizens feared: that the new influx of immigrants would create permanent slums and perpetuate poverty in the United States.

The urban nature of the settlement was unavoidable.

U.S. agriculture was suffering from the same shocks that had disrupted European agriculture, and the Populist movement in the country made clear that the myth of utopia in the western United States was no longer believable. Most new immigrants were attracted by the pull of U.S. industry and opportunity, and they came to the United States with the express purpose of settling in cities. In addition, new industrial technology had reduced the demand for skilled labor, while the need for unskilled and cheap factory help increased. To add to the social clash between the new and old immigrants, the arrival of a new labor force in great numbers probably allowed some older laborers to move up to more important supervisory and executive positions.

Many new immigrants did not share the optimism and

enthusiasm of established Americans. Some tended to be pessimistic and resigned, distrustful of change, and unfamiliar with democratic government after having lived in autocratic societies. Near the beginning of the era of new immigration, the Panic of 1893 developed and was followed by a depression that lasted until 1897. This economic downturn seemed to confirm the fears of people already settled in the United States that the country and its system of government were failing. The new immigration, however, was but one of the major social, cultural, and economic changes taking place in the turbulent United States of the 1890's.

In 1907, Congress created the Dillingham Commission to investigate the problems of immigration. Many of the commission's findings reflected the fears of citizens concerning the new immigration and led to the passage of restrictive legislation during the 1920's. Unrestricted immigration ended with the passage of the National Origins Act of 1924, which limited the number of new immigrants to 154,277 per year. Each country's quota could be no more than 2 percent of the number of people born in the country who were counted in the 1890 U.S. census, a year in which few born in southern and eastern Europe were part of the U.S. population.

After World War II, when the Atlantic Ocean reopened to civilian passenger travel, planes began replacing ships as vehicles of immigration, and there was no need for Ellis Island. By the time Ellis Island finally closed as a reception center in 1954, few European immigrants still came to the United States by ship, and the Immigration Service could handle all the new arrivals at Manhattan's docks. By then, much of the fear of the "new" immigration had evaporated. Italians, Slavs, and Jews had not, after all, remained in permanent slums, mired in perpetual poverty, as Strong had feared. Moreover, they and their descendants had fought side by side with U.S. soldiers of British and German ancestry in World War I and World War II.

SIGNIFICANCE

During the 1940's, there was much criticism of the rigidity of the immigration restriction legislation that hampered attempts to deal with the problems of war refugees. Not until 1965, however, would the rigid quota system established in 1924 be replaced with a more flexible system. When that reform opened the door to increased entry by Asians and Latin Americans, complaints about the new "new immigrants" began to echo nineteenth century uneasiness about the former "new immigrants."

—*Richard H. Collin, updated by Milton Berman*

FURTHER READING

Brownstone, David M., Irene M. Franck, and Douglas L. Brownstone, eds. *Island of Hope, Island of Tears.* New York: Penguin Books, 1986. Interviews with elderly people who went through Ellis Island during the early years of the twentieth century provide highly personal accounts of members of the generation of "new" immigrants. Many photographs.

Daniels, Roger. *Coming to America: A History of Immigration and Ethnicity in American Life.* New York: HarperCollins, 1990. Well-written, scholarly account of U.S. immigration from the colonial period through the 1980's.

Gabaccia, Donna R. *Immigration and American Diversity: A Social and Cultural History.* Malden, Mass.: Blackwell, 2002. Survey of American immigration history, from the mid-eighteenth century to the early twenty-first century, with an emphasis on cultural and social trends, with attention to ethnic conflicts, nativism, and racialist theories.

Greene, Victor R. *A Singing Ambivalence: American Immigrants Between Old World and New, 1830-1930.* Kent, Ohio: Kent State University Press, 2004. Comparative study of the different challenges faced by members of eight major immigrant groups: the Irish, Germans, Scandinavians and Finns, eastern European Jews, Italians, Poles and Hungarians, Chinese, and Mexicans.

Handlin, Oscar. *The Uprooted.* 2d ed. Boston: Little, Brown, 1973. Dramatic narrative focusing on the life experiences of immigrants to the United States.

Higham, John. *Strangers in the Land: Patterns of American Nativism, 1860-1925.* New Brunswick, N.J.: Rutgers University Press, 1955. Analysis of the nativist movements whose pressure led to the passage of immigration restriction.

Meltzer, Milton. *Bound for America: The Story of the European Immigrants.* New York: Benchmark Books, 2001. Broad history of European immigration to the United States written for young readers.

Reimers, David M. *Still the Golden Door: The Third World Comes to America.* New York: Columbia University Press, 1985. Study of twentieth century immigration to the United States, primarily after World War II.

Wepman, Dennis. *Immigration: From the Founding of Virginia to the Closing of Ellis Island.* New York: Facts On File, 2002. History of immigration to the United States from the earliest European settlements of the colonial era through the mid-1950's, with liberal extracts from contemporary documents.

1890's

SEE ALSO: 1840's-1850's: American Era of "Old" Immigration; 1849: Chinese Begin Immigrating to California; Jan. 31, 1858: Brunel Launches the SS *Great Eastern*; Mar. 3, 1875: Congress Enacts the Page Law; May 9, 1882: Arthur Signs the Chinese Exclusion Act; Nov. 12, 1882: San Francisco's Chinese Six Companies Association Forms; Mar. 13, 1887: American Protective Association Is Formed; Sept. 18, 1889: Addams Opens Chicago's Hull-House; Jan. 1, 1892: Ellis Island Immigration Depot Opens; May 4, 1892: Anti-Japanese Yellow Peril Campaign Begins; May 10, 1895: Chinese Californians Form Native Sons of the Golden State.

RELATED ARTICLE in *Great Lives from History: The Nineteenth Century, 1801-1900:* Samuel Gompers.

1892-1895
TOULOUSE-LAUTREC PAINTS *AT THE MOULIN ROUGE*

Henri de Toulouse-Lautrec's At the Moulin Rouge *illustrated the practices of bohemian Paris at the turn of the century, in particular the nightlife crowd of dancers and drinkers at the dance hall Moulin Rouge. The image retained the Impressionist interest in capturing a single fleeting moment, but it employed the artist's idiosyncratic style and thematic concerns to do so, creating an art that was uniquely Toulouse-Lautrec's.*

LOCALE: Montmartre, Paris, France
CATEGORY: Art

KEY FIGURES
Henri de Toulouse-Lautrec (1864-1901), French artist
Edgar Degas (1834-1917), French painter and sculptor
La Goulue (Louise Weber; 1866-1929), French cabaret dancer
Jane Avril (1868-1943), French cabaret dancer

SUMMARY OF EVENT

The French post-Impressionist painter, illustrator, and lithographer Henri de Toulouse-Lautrec captured the effervescent fervor of bohemian Paris in his many paintings and posters. He represented and glamorized the less civilized individuals of society, particularly the patrons and entertainers of the pleasure district of Montmartre. Between 1892 and 1895, Toulouse-Lautrec painted *At the Moulin Rouge*, which embodied the nineteenth century voyeuristic taste in nighttime entertainment, portraying patrons of a nightclub as simultaneously observing and observed.

In the swell of the Industrial Revolution, the last decade of the nineteenth century in France (the fin de siècle) was fraught with uncertainty over the stability and the social path of the Third Republic (1870-1940). After the common working man had been replaced by machines and after personal vices became regulated by the new regime, mass socialism and burgeoning feminism began to propose radical solutions to the ills of a new industrial age. For some, this transitional period encouraged what was then viewed as irresponsible and depraved behavior and frenetic, even fatalistic, states of mind. The end of the nineteenth century also witnessed the rise and downward spiral of the dance hall and other bohemian entertainments in the hilltop Montmartre district, technically just outside Paris. Montrmartre was crowded with cabarets, café-concerts, bars, brothels, and other salacious venues. The area was a popular locale in which to meet and drink, especially considering that wine was made locally, at a nunnery in the district.

The disreputable atmosphere of Montmartre was associated in the Parisian popular mind with the bohemian artist. The bohemian lifestyle was introduced to the Parisians by Slavic and Hungarian artists who frequented French academic art circles. Many believed the stereotype of the gypsy, the wandering vagrant artist who was the quintessential bohemian individual. This stereotype, while a gross abstraction of reality, was embraced as a model by many artists, writers, dancers, philosophers, and dreamers in late nineteenth century French culture. During this period, sometimes referred to as the belle époque, some French entertainers, artists, and intellectuals began to emulate what they saw as an ideal and carefree lifestyle.

The most famous concert venue and dance hall in Montmartre—and the stage for many French artists' opuses—was the Moulin Rouge, named for its recognizable red windmill. The Moulin Rouge opened on October 5, 1889, to an eager bohemian public that included Henri de Toulouse-Lautrec. The nightly finale at the Moulin Rouge was a new dance phenomenon called the cancan. Known for their physical limberness and their loose morals, the cancan dancers were popular for their wild performances and particularly for raising their brightly colored skirts to kick their long legs up to eye-level. This was the world that Toulouse-Lautrec anxiously joined as a spectator and also came to represent in his art.

Henri de Toulouse-Lautrec was born into aristocracy on November 24, 1864, to the Comte Alphonse-Charles de Toulouse in Albi, France, with a rich aristocratic genealogy one thousand years in the making. As a child, Toulouse-Lautrec was often ill and injured. He broke both of his legs on separate occasions as an adolescent, and a bone disease prevented him from growing to a mature height. It was arguably Toulouse-Lautrec's inability to participate in many aristocratic pastimes and outdoor activities that inspired him to become an artist.

Toulouse-Lautrec began working in the academic style of painting under the tutelage of L. J. F. Bonnat and Fernand Cormon. By the mid-1880's, he was frequent-ing Montmartre, as well as the galleries and exhibitions of the Impressionist painters. In 1885, Toulouse-Lautrec became fascinated with Edgar Degas, whose voyeuristic images of women (often ballet dancers) in private scenes later proved to be incredibly influential on Toulouse-Lautrec. The majority of the Impressionists focused their attention on the effect of light in nature, while Degas, whose oeuvre included natural imagery as well, often chose to depict the play of light on interior space. He represented the interiors of public arenas, such as ballet studios, as well as private settings, such as women's boudoirs.

Toulouse-Lautrec's interest in the Montmartre night-life brought him to nightly cabarets and dance halls, where he would sketch rough drawings on paper that would be continued as drawings or paintings on canvas the next day. He was befriended by social outcasts, particularly by prostitutes. Toulouse-Lautrec favored this vulgar and garish nightlife; he focused on the impover-

Henri de Toulouse-Lautrec's At the Moulin Rouge. (Hulton Archive/Getty Images)

1890's

ished and depraved, because they did not fit into the mold of proper society—just as he did not fit into his birthplace in French aristocracy. Prostitutes allowed Toulouse-Lautrec to draw them in the most intimate of environments and poses; he produced at least fifty images depicting the lifestyle of the French brothels, or *maisons closes*, between 1885 and 1895. His subjects varied from prostitutes to the patrons of the various establishments of Montmartre to cabaret performers. It was his depictions of the nightly performers, which he exhibited in the various cafés of the district, that won him his initial commissions to produce commercial playbills and posters in 1891.

Although Toulouse-Lautrec is widely known for the lithographic posters he produced to advertise the nighttime attractions of Montmartre, perhaps his most recognized image is from an oil painting: *At the Moulin Rouge* depicted an evening scene of patrons at the nightclub. It captured a single, informal moment among the celebrated members of the Montmartre nightlife. In the painting's background, a cabaret dancer adjusted her hair in a mirror. The dancer portrayed was Louise Weber, better known as La Goulue, or "the glutton," as she could drink any man under the table. Toulouse-Lautrec produced numerous images of La Goulue, returning to the Moulin Rouge repeatedly to observe her. She was the subject of his first lithograph, *Moulin Rouge: La Goulue* (1891).

Also depicted in this sensationalized atmosphere were the dancer Yvette Guilbert, music critic Édouard Dujardin, and the back of a fiery redhead believed to be the dancer Jane Avril—another popular subject of Toulouse-Lautrec. The faces of these subjects were shadowed by the dim, artificial light of the nightclub. However, there was one face that stood out from the rest. A cropped visage of actress May Milton loomed on the right side of the canvas with a garish green face. Her face appeared ominous and eerie, even sickly. The green skin tone imparted by Toulouse-Lautrec was meant to capture the reflection of artificial light upon Milton's luminescent face powder.

Artistically, *At the Moulin Rouge* evinced the same post-Impressionist qualities prized in the lithographs of Toulouse-Lautrec. The artist created roughly hewn, two-dimensional, linear forms and engaged in expressionistic uses of color. The human shape was exaggerated almost to abstraction in his work, yet its representation somehow remained brutally honest, much like the environment that produced the work. Toulouse-Lautrec used more rounded, although still rather jagged, lines to trace

the figures of La Goulue and Jane Avril, which contrasted with the harsh diagonals of the room itself. He chose a color palette that was unflattering to his subjects yet visually engaging, with various spots of color designed to lead the eye around the image. For example, the vibrant red of Avril's hair against her trademark black attire complemented the acidic green of Milton's goblin-like face.

The lithographic quality of Toulouse-Lautrec's drawings and paintings stemmed from his interest in Japanese woodblock prints from the Edo period (1615-1868). Images of Japanese *ukiyo-e*, or "images of the floating world," were similar to a genre of images popular with the Impressionists and post-Impressionists, ranging from scenes of nature to theater to prostitution. Many French artists from these stylistic periods credited Japanese woodblock prints with their inspiration, leading them to create asymmetrical compositions and broad areas of color that echoed the two-dimensionality of the woodblock prints.

SIGNIFICANCE

Henri de Toulouse-Lautrec's *At the Moulin Rouge* is remembered for its skilled craftsmanship and the psychological insight it provided into a world that was more foreign than familiar to the majority of Parisians. Toulouse-Lautrec took a region infamous for its vulgarity and debauchery and humanized the ill-fated creatures of the night that inhabited it, making them intriguing. His artistic innovations influenced his fellow post-Impressionist painters Vincent van Gogh and Georges Seurat, as well as the succeeding expressionist painter Georges Rouault. Toulouse-Lautrec's death from alcoholism in 1901 put an end to a brilliant career at the young age of thirty-six. Despite the short life of the belle époque, its history remains vibrant and intriguing to many modern theorists and filmmakers.

—Emilie B. Fitzhugh

FURTHER READING

Cabanne, Pierre. *Henri de Toulouse-Lautrec, the Reporter of Modern Life*. Paris: Editions Pierre Terrail, 2003. Focuses on the development of the entertainment genre of images popular in nineteenth century Paris, crediting some of his contemporary influences.

Hanson, Lawrence and Elisabeth. *The Tragic Life of Toulouse-Lautrec*. New York: Random House, 1956. A thorough biographical narrative.

Heller, Reinhold. *Toulouse-Lautrec: The Soul of Montmarte*. New York: Prestl, 1997. Provides a look at the dichotomy of Toulouse-Lautrec's life from his early development in the aristocracy and his fascination with dance halls and cabarets.

Nord, Philip. *Impressionists and Politics: Art and Democracy in the Nineteenth Century*, London: Routledge, 2000. Offers a balance of facts and the psychology behind the interaction of art and politics as the Impressionists were moving away from government sanctioned schools and sets the stage for the social climate in which Henri de Toulouse-Lautrec emerged.

SEE ALSO: 1824: Paris Salon of 1824; Oct.-Dec., 1830: Delacroix Paints *Liberty Leading the People*; 1855: Courbet Establishes Realist Art Movement; May 15, 1863: Paris's Salon des Refusés Opens; Apr. 15, 1874: First Impressionist Exhibition; Late 1870's: Post-Impressionist Movement Begins.

RELATED ARTICLES in *Great Lives from History: The Nineteenth Century, 1801-1900:* Edgar Degas; Vincent van Gogh; Georges Seurat; Henri de Toulouse-Lautrec.

January 1, 1892
ELLIS ISLAND IMMIGRATION DEPOT OPENS

The Ellis Island immigration center opened as the nation's major point of entry for immigrants coming into the United States from Europe. More than twelve million such immigrants would be processed in the facility before it finally closed sixty-two years later.

LOCALE: Ellis Island, New York
CATEGORIES: Immigration; government and politics

KEY FIGURES
Benjamin Harrison (1833-1901), president of the United States, 1889-1893
John R. McPherson (1833-1897), U.S. senator from New Jersey
Annie Moore (1877-1923), first immigrant processed at Ellis Island
Samuel Ellis (d. 1794), American businessman

SUMMARY OF EVENT
Ellis Island, which now covers a land area of about 27.5 acres, has been known by a variety of names during its history. Early Dutch settlers called it Oyster Island, because they used the site for shucking oysters. When the British took possession of New Amsterdam, changing its name to New York, they called the island Gibbet Island, indicating that it was a place for executing pirates. Purchased by a businessman named Samuel Ellis late in the eighteenth century, the island took the name of its new owner. In 1808, Ellis's heirs sold the island to the federal government for $10,000. For a few years, it again served as a major execution post, but just before the U.S. Civil War it become a military arsenal. After the war, the future use of the island became the subject of heated political debate when New Yorkers learned that it contained

enough munitions, if exploded, to destroy all of Manhattan, Brooklyn, and Jersey City.

By 1880, a gigantic wave of immigrants from a variety of European countries was beginning to enter the United States. In contrast to earlier waves, a large percentage of these immigrants came from southern and eastern Europe, particularly Italy, Poland, Bohemia, and Russia. As a result of this so-called New Immigration, the United States would be increasingly marked by an unprecedented diversity in religion and other cultural traits. Nor surprisingly, Americans accustomed to perceiving their countrymen as being white, Anglo-Saxon Protestants (WASPs) were often concerned about this new diversity. Fears were exacerbated by the tendency of new immigrants to be poor, uneducated, and victims of religious or political oppression. Recurring stories in newspapers and magazines told about alleged incidents of European nations dumping criminals and insane persons into boats headed to America.

At that time, the states were still largely in control of regulating immigration policy. Because so many new immigrants entered the United States at New York, the New York State Immigration Commission was particularly important in shaping this policy. Since 1855, New York City's center for processing immigrants had been located at Castle Garden, on the southern tip of Manhattan. Between 1855 and 1890, almost eight million immigrants, or two out of three persons coming to America, passed through this facility.

During the 1880's, Congress began to pass new federal regulations for potential immigrants. A congressional statute of 1882 prohibited entrance into the country by "any convict, lunatic, idiot, or any person unable to

LATE NINETEENTH CENTURY U.S. IMMIGRATION LAWS

1882	First federal immigration law is enacted, barring lunatics, convicts, and those likely to become public charges.
1882	Chinese Exclusion Act denies entry to Chinese laborers.
1885	Foran Act prohibits importing contract labor but not skilled labor for new industries, artists, actors, lecturers, or domestic servants; it also permits assisting the immigration of friends and relatives.
1891	All national immigration is placed under full federal control.
1891	Legislation adds health requirements to immigration restrictions.
1893	Legislation requires ship owners to prepare manifests providing detailed information on individual immigrant passengers.

take care of himself or herself without becoming a public charge." However, with the sheer number of immigrants growing daily, the overcrowded conditions and resulting confusion at Castle Garden made it almost impossible for New York bureaucrats to investigate aliens sufficiently to enforce this law and prevent undesirables from escaping into the city. In addition, a congressional investigation confirmed long-standing reports that New York's immigration officials were guilty of taking bribes and profiting from the sale of railroad tickets. In 1890, Congress responded by closing Castle Garden and creating the federal Bureau of Immigration as part of the U.S. Treasury Department.

Congressional leaders also concluded that the federal government should construct a new immigration center. A joint committee was appointed to suggest a desirable location. The committee soon decided that the most secure location would be one of the government-owned islands in New York harbor. Their first choice was Bedloe's Island, where the Statue of Liberty had been built four years earlier, but the suggestion aroused a storm of protests. Led by Senator McPherson of New Jersey, the committee then proposed Ellis Island, even though it would have to be greatly enlarged to accommodate the expected number of immigrants. New Yorkers, eager to eliminate the dangerous munitions dump still housed on the island, strongly supported the recommendation.

In May, 1890, Congress voted to accept the joint committee's choice and appropriated funds to establish the nation's first federal immigration center. The next year, work began on a large, three-story reception center 400 feet long and 150 feet wide. The project also included a

hospital, a generating plant, and a boiler house. All of the buildings were made of Georgia pine. The construction of a sea wall and a landfill doubled the size of the island, from 3.5 acres to more than 7 acres. The ambitious project was designed to accept up to ten thousand immigrants per day. Within two years, enough buildings had been set up to begin processing immigrants, but the entire installation would not be completed until June 14, 1897.

Meanwhile, federal investigators discovered that New York officials were misusing the state's immigration commission for political purposes. In 1891, Congress and President Bejmain Harrison responded to the scandal by passing legislation that placed the regulation of immigration exclusively under the authority of the federal government. The 1891 law also expanded the category of prohibited immigrants to include anyone with a contagious disease or a criminal record, and it required steamship companies to return rejected aliens to their homelands free of charge.

On New Year's Day, 1892, the Ellis Island Immigration Station officially opened. At 8:00 that morning, several large ships were already waiting to land. The first person to enter the country through Ellis Island was the fifteen-year-old Annie Moore, described as a "rosy-cheeked Irish girl." Superintendent John C. Weber presented her with a ten-dollar gold piece. She and her two younger brothers passed the inspection and were allowed to take the ferryboat to the barge office. About 700 immigrants were processed at the station on the first day, and a total of 445,987 immigrants, including Israel Baline (Irving Berlin), arrived on Ellis Island during its first year of operation.

All of the immigrants processed at Ellis Island were checked for disabilities, diseases, and legal difficulties. Frequently, one or two members of a family were sent back to their home countries. Immigrants had no right to a legal hearing if authorities ordered them deported. About one thousand persons each month were found "undesirable," as a result of which the receiving station received the nickname Island of Hope, Island of Tears. With immigrants speaking so many different languages, the clerks sometimes wrote approximations of their names or simply used English phonetic spellings.

Within five years, 1.5 million immigrants had landed

on Ellis Island, but on June 15, 1897, the day after the facility was completed, the original wooden buildings on the island burned to the ground. While new buildings were under construction, immigrants had to pass through the temporary depot of the Battery's Barge Office. In December, 1900, although its new brick and limestone buildings were still incomplete, Ellis Island resumed processing immigrants. The main building, called the Great Hall, attracted much attention: It was a huge, fireproofed structure in French Renaissance style with four turrets. The impressive array of buildings, costing more than one million dollars, suggested the importance of immigration to the country at that time. Federal officials made the mistake, however, of designing the new complex for only 500,000 immigrants per year, seriously underestimating the number of persons who would enter the country in subsequent decades.

Until passage of the Immigration Act of 1924, the "golden door" to the United States was open to European immigrants with relatively few restrictions. As the number of immigrants decreased to a trickle after 1924, Ellis Island was used primarily for law-enforcement purposes. On November 12, 1954, what had by then become the Immigration and Naturalization Service moved to Lower Manhattan and officially closed all the buildings on the island. In 1965, however, the site became part of the Statue of Liberty National Monument, and the Ellis Island Immigration Museum was opened to the public in 1990.

SIGNIFICANCE

Between 1892 and 1924, Ellis Island served as the primary receiving station for the largest and most successful wave of mass migration in modern history. Like the Statue of Liberty that stands nearby, the island came to symbolize the promises, hopes, and dreams of opportunity and freedom that lured millions of impoverished and oppressed peoples to immigrate to America. During the early twenty-first century, almost 40 percent of the U.S. population—more than 100 million Americans—were able to trace their ancestry through at least one person who entered the country through Ellis Island.

—Thomas Tandy Lewis

FURTHER READING

Benton, Barbara. *Ellis Island: A Pictorial History*. New York: Facts On File, 1985. Fascinating collection of photographs accompanied by a concise history of the island.

Bolino, August. *The Ellis Island Source Book*. Washington, D.C.: Kensington Press, 1985. Excellent source of information about the history of the island; especially good on legal matters.

Carmack, Sharon D. *Guide to Finding Your Ellis Island Ancestors*. Cincinnati, Ohio: Family Tree Books, 2005. In addition to practical advice about locating and using ancestral records, the book describes immigrants' experiences on the island.

Coan, Peter M. *Ellis Island Interviews: Immigrants Tell Their Stories in Their Own Words*. New York: Barnes & Noble Books, 1997. Following a helpful introduction, this book contains 114 fascinating interviews selected from the Ellis Island Oral History Project.

Foner, Nancy. *From Ellis Island to JFK: New York's Two Great Waves of Immigration*. New Haven, Conn.: Yale University Press, 2000. Scholarly summary of both the 1880-1920 wave and the post-1970 wave of immigration to the United States.

Sandler, Martin. *Island of Hope: The Journey to America and the Ellis Island Experience*. New York: Scholastic, 2004. Illustrated account of the experiences of individual immigrants; primarily for young readers.

Tifft, Wilton. *Ellis Island*. Chicago: Contemporary Books, 1990. Excellent historical text with many revealing photographs of the immigrants.

Wasserman, Fred, ed. *Ellis Island: An Illustrated History of the Immigration Experience*. New York: Macmillan, 1991. Beautiful volume containing many hundreds of photographs of immigrants, buildings, and artifacts.

Young, Robert. *A Personal Tour of Ellis Island*. Minneapolis, Minn.: Lerner, 2001. One of several well-illustrated books written primarily for young readers.

SEE ALSO: c. 1815-1830: Westward American Migration Begins; 1840's-1850's: American Era of "Old" Immigration; 1845-1854: Great Irish Famine; Feb. 4, 1846: Mormons Begin Migration to Utah; June 15, 1846: United States Acquires Oregon Territory; 1849: Chinese Begin Immigrating to California; Mar. 13, 1887: American Protective Association Is Formed; 1890: U.S. Census Bureau Announces Closing of the Frontier; 1892: America's "New" Immigration Era Begins; 1896: Immigrant Farmers Begin Settling Western Canada.

RELATED ARTICLE in *Great Lives from History: The Nineteenth Century, 1801-1900*: Benjamin Harrison.

1890's

February, 1892
DIESEL PATENTS THE DIESEL ENGINE

German thermal engineer Rudolf Diesel developed and patented a prototype of an internal combustion engine that he believed could one day be operated on vegetable oils and other plentiful fuels rather than on petroleum.

LOCALE: Berlin, Prussia, German Empire (now in Germany)

CATEGORIES: Inventions; science and technology; transportation

KEY FIGURES

Rudolf Diesel (1858-1913), German thermal engineer

Sadi Carnot (1796-1832), French physicist

Alphonse Beau de Rochas (1815-1893), French engineer and inventor

Nikolaus August Otto (1832-1891), German engineer and inventor

Eugen Langen (1833-1895), Otto's partner in building internal combustion engines

Étienne Lenoir (1822-1900), French engineer and inventor

Carl von Linde (1842-1934), German refrigeration engineer and industrialist

SUMMARY OF EVENT

Rudolf Diesel spent his early years in Paris, where he lived with his parents, natives of Bavaria holding Bavarian citizenship. When the Franco-Prussian war erupted in 1870, the Diesel family, faced with the prospect of deportation from France, moved to London. Soon, young Rudolf was sent to Augsburg, Germany, his father's home town, to continue his schooling.

When he was old enough to begin his higher education, Diesel entered the Technische Hochscule, a university-level technical institute in Munich, where he showed a particular aptitude for engineering. Carl von Linde, a noted authority on refrigeration engineering who was associated with the Technische Hochschule, recognized Diesel's exceptional aptitudes while the youth was still a student and took a special interest in him. With von Linde's encouragement, Diesel performed experiments that involved using ammonia to fuel an expansion engine. In 1880, von Linde employed Diesel in his corporation, stationing him in Paris. By 1890, Diesel moved to Berlin to take a new job with von Linde's company. It was there that he first conceived of developing an internal combustion engine different from those produced

earlier by Nikolaus August Otto in Germany and Étienne Lenoir in France.

Diesel's ideas were not yet fully formed, so in February, 1892, he applied for a development patent on his engine. The German government issued the development patent, and the following year, Diesel published a more comprehensive explanation of the engine as he conceived it. This description, *Theorie und Konstruktion eines rationellen Wäremotors* (theory and construction of a rational heat motor), enabled Diesel to obtain a patent in 1893 for the compression-ignition engine that is now commonly referred to as the diesel engine.

The concept of compression ignition was articulated as early as 1824 by the French physicist Sadi Carnot, but no practical application of this technology appeared until 1876, when Otto built a working model of an engine in which the mixture of fuel and air was compressed in the cylinder before ignition. Fourteen years earlier, Alphonse Beau de Rochas had conceived theoretically of an engine built according to these principles, but he did not create any working models. Lenoir began building internal combustion engines in 1862 and produced about five hundred of them, all based upon concepts relating to the steam engine. Lenoir's engines used sliding valves to admit and dispel combustion gases.

It took another fourteen years after Otto unveiled his model in 1876 before Diesel conceived of his engine in detail. Otto and Eugen Langen—his partner in their joint venture, the Gasmotorenfabrik—built some five thousand engines before Diesel patented his engine. Their engines were more practical than Lenoir's in that they used flywheels to carry the pistons through their rest phases. Diesel's engine differed from those developed by Otto and Lenoir in that its power was achieved by compressing air in the cylinder. The air was compressed to a pressure of about five hundred pounds per square inch, at a temperature of about one thousand degrees Fahrenheit. Fuel was then ignited by pressure rather than by a spark and burnt before the piston descended. This action occurs so slowly that there is no significant increase in pressure resulting from the ignition. Previous engines had depended upon a spark to ignite the fuel in their cylinders. Diesel's model depended on heated, compressed air to achieve this ignition.

Whereas previous internal combustion engines had been powered by gasoline, Diesel's engine could operate on a variety of fuels. Indeed, his first working model was fueled by powdered coal, which was in plentiful supply but which quickly proved to be a less-than-ideal fuel for the engine. Diesel soon replaced powdered coal with alcohol and other liquid fuels.

As soon as the idea of Diesel's engine was protected by a patent, the inventor set about building working models. He received backing and encouragement from the Maschinenfabrik of Augsburg and the powerful Krupp enterprises. By 1897, he had produced several working models, the most promising of which was a four-stroke engine with a single perpendicular cylinder that served as the compression chamber. This early diesel engine delivered twenty-five horsepower.

Remarkably, Diesel's engine was sufficiently simple in its design that its commercial possibilities became evident quite quickly. The engine was pressed into service in a variety of ways that, by the turn of the century, brought Diesel remarkable wealth through royalties. For all of its promise and actual success, however, the engine was not without serious drawbacks. The early diesel engines were much larger and considerably heavier than the gasoline engines they were designed to replace. They

also produced considerable air pollution, but comparable gasoline engines caused comparable amounts of pollution as well.

Because of their size, the earliest diesel engines were most appropriate for use as stationery sources of power. Eventually, they were used to power large ships and locomotives. During World War I, they provided power for Germany's fleet of submarines. It was not until the second quarter of the twentieth century, however, that diesel engines were commonly used to power trucks, which currently remains one of their major applications. Diesel engines have a much longer life than gasoline-powered engines, and they require considerably less upkeep than their gasoline-powered counterparts. They also can burn less expensive fuel, including easily replenishable vegetable oils.

SIGNIFICANCE

Diesel engines are the engines of choice for most trucks, locomotives, ships, buses, and stationary power plants. They are durable engines that, when Diesel first developed them, were too heavy and cumbersome to be practical for any but the largest vehicles. The power and cost-efficiency of the diesel engine made it possible for such vehicles to be put to work, however, and in some cases made it possible for them to exist at all.

Eventually, the weight of the diesel engine was reduced sufficiently to make practical its use in private passenger vehicles. Diesel-powered passenger automobiles have generally been more popular in Europe than in the United States, probably because the price of gasoline is much higher in Europe than it is in the United States, making diesel automobiles practical choices purely on economic grounds. Diesel envisioned his engine as running on vegetable oils and other renewable resources. The oil industry, however, created a new type of gasoline that could power a diesel engine so that it could still make profits from diesel-powered automobiles. During the early twenty-first century, a new interest in the use of biological fuels in diesel engines, commonly referred to as "biodiesel," began to gain strength, motivated by increasing gasoline prices.

—*R. Baird Shuman*

FURTHER READING

Alternatives to Traditional Transportation Fuels, 1993. Washington, D.C.: Energy Information Administration, 1995. A major section on diesel engines is informative in addressing alternative fuels, such as vegetable oils, that can be used in diesel engines.

Rudolf Diesel. (Library of Congress)

1890's

Hill, Stephen H. *Automotive Diesel Technology Programs*. Washington, D.C.: United States Department of Energy, 1977. Hill discusses in detail the potential of using diesel engines in private passenger automobiles as a means of reducing the consumption of petroleum-based fuels in the United States.

Jefferson, C. M., and R. H. Barnard. *Hybrid Vehicle Propulsion*. Boston: WIT Press, 2002. The authors' three-page discussion of the diesel engine is informative, especially the section on the efficiency of diesel engines. The authors discuss the advantages of diesel engines in hybrid vehicles.

Nitske, Robert, and Charles Morrow Wilson. *Rudolf Diesel: Pioneer of the Age of Power*. Norman: University of Oklahoma Press, 1965. This well-researched book's age does not diminish its importance to those interested in the development of diesel technology and in the life of Rudolf Diesel. Strongly recommended.

Rosbloom, Julius. *Diesel Handbook: A Practical Book of Instruction for Engineers and Students on Modern Diesel Engineering—Land, Marine, Locomotive, and Automotive and Portable Installations*. Jersey City, N.J.: Diesel Engineering Institute, 1935. This early consideration of diesel engineering demonstrates the range of possibilities this technology permits. Despite its age, this is a valuable presentation.

SEE ALSO: Mar. 24, 1802: Trevithick Patents the High-Pressure Steam Engine; September 27, 1825: Stockton and Darlington Railway Opens; July 21, 1836: Champlain and St. Lawrence Railroad Opens; June 15, 1844: Goodyear Patents Vulcanized Rubber; 1850: First U.S. Petroleum Refinery Is Built; 1860: Lenoir Patents the Internal Combustion Engine; Jan. 10, 1870: Standard Oil Company Is Incorporated; May, 1876: Otto Invents a Practical Internal Combustion Engine; Jan. 29, 1886: Benz Patents the First Practical Automobile; Dec. 7, 1888: Dunlop Patents the Pneumatic Tire.

RELATED ARTICLES in *Great Lives from History: The Nineteenth Century, 1801-1900:* Carl Benz; Gottlieb Daimler; Rudolf Diesel; Étienne Lenoir; Nikolaus August Otto.

May 4, 1892
ANTI-JAPANESE YELLOW PERIL CAMPAIGN BEGINS

Anti-Japanese and anti-immigrant fears and hatred led to racist polemics in local newspapers and the formation of anti-Japanese associations, including those of organized labor. They also led to boycotts against Japanese merchants and white merchants who employed Japanese workers and led to legislation that limited the civil rights of Japanese American immigrants.

ALSO KNOWN AS: Yellow Terror

LOCALE: San Francisco, California

CATEGORIES: Civil rights and liberties; immigration; laws, acts, and legal history; diplomacy and international relations

KEY FIGURES

Henry Gage (1852-1924), governor of California, 1899-1903

James Phelan (1861-1930), San Francisco mayor in 1900

Theodore Roosevelt (1858-1919), president of the United States, 1901-1909

Eugene E. Schmitz (1864-1928), San Francisco mayor in 1905

SUMMARY OF EVENT

In 1890, there were only some two thousand Japanese living in America, working mainly as laborers and farmhands in California and the Pacific Northwest. Nevertheless, the use of Japanese to break a labor strike in the coal mines in British Columbia began what was to become a widespread anti-Japanese campaign.

Typical of the political rhetoric that was to become prevalent was a slogan used during a political campaign in 1887, when a "Dr. O'Donnell" of San Francisco included the slogan "Japs must go" in his campaign. Although the slogan had little effect on his failed political campaign, it was nevertheless a sign of things to come.

In 1889, the editor of the *San Francisco Bulletin* began a series of editorials attacking Japanese immigrants and making a case that they were dangerous to white American workers and to American culture. On May 4, 1892, he wrote, "It is now some three years ago that the *Bulletin* first called attention to the influx of Japanese into this state, and stated that in time their immigration threatened to rival that of the Chinese, with dire disaster to laboring interests in California." The *San Francisco*

Bulletin's "Yellow Peril" campaign (named "yellow" for the skin-color designation of peoples of Asia) helped strengthen the growing anti-Japanese fervor in California. The campaign was not only against Japanese laborers, who were thought to be threatening the livelihoods of "real" American workers, but also against their perceived threat to American culture. Met with hostility, prejudice, and discrimination, Japanese in many urban areas settled into ethnic enclaves known as Japantowns, where they could secure employment and feel safe and comfortable among fellow compatriots.

On June 14, 1893, the San Francisco board of education passed a resolution requiring that all Japanese persons must attend the already segregated Chinese school instead of the regular public schools. Because of Japanese protests, the resolution was rescinded; however, it marked the beginning of legal discrimination against the Japanese in California. In 1894, a treaty between the United States and Japan allowed citizens open immigration, but both governments were given powers to limit excessive immigration. In 1900, because of American protests, Japan began a voluntary program to limit Japanese emigration to the United States.

This turn-of-the-century toy gun bears the message "Chinese must go." When its trigger is pulled, the figure in the hat kicks the Chinese figure. (Asian American Studies Library, University of California at Berkeley)

The Alaskan gold rush of 1896-1899 attracted a great number of white laborers, and when the Northern Pacific and Great Northern Railroads worked to build a connecting line from Tacoma and Seattle to the east, extra laborers were needed. The companies turned to Japanese immigrants as workers. Some of these laborers came from Japan and Hawaii. The rapid influx of Japanese laborers created further anti-Asian sentiments and hostility.

With the 1882 Chinese Exclusion Act up for renewal in 1902, the anti-Japanese sentiment occurred in the overall context of a growing anti-Asian movement, especially among labor unions and various political groups. In April of 1900, the San Francisco Building Trades Council passed a resolution to support the renewal of the Chinese Exclusion Act and to add the Japanese to this act to "secure this Coast against any further Japanese immigration, and thus forever settle the mooted Mongolian labor problem." The county Republican Party lobbied extensively to get the national Republican Party to adopt a Japanese exclusion plank in their national platform. San Francisco mayor James Phelan and California governor

Henry Gage joined the calls for Japanese to be included in the renewal of the Exclusion Act. However, when the exclusion law was extended in 1902, Japanese people were not included.

After the defeat of Russia by Japan in the Russo-Japanese War, a growing fear of Japanese power led to further agitation and political tactics to limit Japanese immigration and influence in America. Whereas Chinese were hated and despised by various politicians, labor leaders, and some regular citizens, Japanese were feared.

SIGNIFICANCE

The Yellow Peril campaign of the nineteenth century did not stop with the beginning of the twentieth century. In 1905, the *San Francisco Chronicle* launched another anti-Japanese campaign, emphasizing the dangers of future immigration. Later, the San Francisco Labor Council, at the urging of a local doctor and with the support of San Francisco mayor Eugene E. Schmitz, launched boycotts against Japanese merchants and white merchants who employed Japanese workers. Later that year, sixty-seven labor organizations formed the Asiatic Exclusion League (sometimes called the Japanese and Korean Exclusion League), and the American Federation of Labor passed a resolution that the provisions of the Chinese Exclusion Act be extended to include Japanese and Koreans.

In 1906, anti-Asian sentiments continued to grow. San Francisco was struck by a devastating earthquake in April, and civil unrest increased. Japanese persons and businesses were attacked and looted. On October 11, 1906, the San Francisco School Board ordered that all Japanese, Korean, and Chinese students attend a segregated "Oriental school." (This regulation was later changed to include only older students and those with limited English proficiency.) Japan protested that the school board's action violated the U.S.-Japan treaty of 1894, bringing the San Francisco situation into international focus. To assuage Japan, President Theodore Roosevelt arranged with the school board to rescind its order in exchange for federal action to limit immigration from Japan.

In the ensuing U.S.-Japan "Gentlemen's Agreement," Japan promised not to issue passports to laborers planning to settle in the United States and recognized U.S. rights to refuse Japanese immigrants entry into the United States. In an executive order issued on March 14, 1907, Roosevelt implemented an amendment to the Immigration Act of 1907, which allowed the United States to bar entry of any immigrant whose passport was not issued for direct entry into the United States and whose immigration was judged to threaten domestic labor conditions.

Although anti-Japanese sentiments lessened during World War I after Japan joined the Allies in the war against Germany, almost immediately following the war these sentiments resurfaced. The 1917 and 1924 Immigration Acts barred Asian laborers from the United States. In California, a campaign to pass the 1920 Alien Land Act attracted the support of the American Legion and the Native Sons and Daughters of the Golden West.

—*Gregory A. Levitt*

FURTHER READING

Ichihashi, Yamato. *The American Immigration Collection: Japanese in the United States*. 1932. Reprint. New York: Arno Press, 1969. A thorough description of Japanese immigration into the United States with an excellent chapter on anti-Japanese agitation.

McWilliams, Carey. *Prejudice: Japanese-Americans, Symbol of Racial Intolerance*. 1944. Reprint. Hamden, Conn.: Archon Books, 1971. A dated but excellent account of anti-Japanese American prejudice and discrimination up to World War II. New foreword by McWilliams.

Takaki, Ronald. *Strangers from a Different Shore: A History of Asian Americans*. 1989. Rev. ed. Boston: Little, Brown, 1998. An excellent overview of the broader picture of Asian immigration and settlement in the United States.

Wilson, Robert A., and Bill Hosokawa. *East to America: A History of the Japanese in the United States*. New York: William Morrow, 1980. An excellent account of Japanese immigration and settlement in the United States.

SEE ALSO: 1840's-1850's: American Era of "Old" Immigration; Jan. 24, 1848: California Gold Rush Begins; 1849: Chinese Begin Immigrating to California; July 28, 1868: Burlingame Treaty; May 10, 1869: First Transcontinental Railroad Is Completed; Mar. 3, 1875: Congress Enacts the Page Law; May 9, 1882: Arthur Signs the Chinese Exclusion Act; Nov. 12, 1882: San Francisco's Chinese Six Companies Association Forms; Mar. 13, 1887: American Protective Association Is Formed; 1892: America's "New" Immigration Era Begins; May 10, 1895: Chinese Californians Form Native Sons of the Golden State.

RELATED ARTICLE in *Great Lives from History: The Nineteenth Century, 1801-1900:* Stephen J. Field.

July 4-5, 1892
BIRTH OF THE PEOPLE'S PARTY

Agrarian unrest increased in the decades following the Civil War in the United States. It finally gave rise to a grassroots populist movement that created the People's Party. The party's presidential candidates could not raise the funds necessary to mount a serious challenge to more conservative politicians, however.

ALSO KNOWN AS: Populist Party
LOCALE: Omaha, Nebraska
CATEGORIES: Government and politics; organizations and institutions

KEY FIGURES

Ignatius Donnelly (1831-1901), leader of the Minnesota Alliance and writer
James G. Field (1826-1901), Populist vice-presidential candidate in 1892
Leonidas LaFayette Polk (1837-1892), president of the Southern Alliance and editor of the *Progressive Farmer*
Thomas Edward Watson (1856-1922), Populist vice presidential candidate in 1896
James Baird Weaver (1833-1912), Populist presidential candidate in 1892

SUMMARY OF EVENT

Political activists completed the organization of the People's Party of the United States of America, also known as the Populist Party, at the nominating convention held in Omaha, Nebraska, July 4-5, 1892. The formation of a new political party had been discussed for several years in a series of farmer-oriented conventions. Representatives of the powerful Northern and Southern Farmers' Alliances, together with certain labor groups, such as the Knights of Labor, and some smaller organizations of farmers, met at St. Louis in December, 1889, to consider merging and cooperating in political action. At that time they were unable to effect a union of their organizations, but they did discover that many of their political demands were identical. Farmers and workers both agreed that fundamental changes needed to be made in American banking practices, as well as in regulating railroads and in providing for the arbitration of labor disputes.

These political demands were enunciated further at another convention held at Ocala, Florida, in December, 1890. Then, at the National Union Conference held in Cincinnati in May, 1891, Ignatius Donnelly—leader of the Minnesota Alliance and a noted author—demanded the immediate formation of a third party, but Leonidas LaFayette Polk—president of the Southern Alliance and editor of the influential *Progressive Farmer*—wrote a letter advising delay. Polk was backed by James B. Weaver from Iowa. A compromise was reached whereby an executive committee was to begin preparations for establishing a new party, but formal organization would be delayed until after a reform convention met in St. Louis in February, 1892. The vast majority of delegates to this convention were representatives of the Farmers' Alliances, but a substantial number of seats were reserved for representatives from certain labor unions.

The convention met, heard speeches, adopted a platform, and adjourned. By arrangement, the delegates remained in their seats and reorganized as a political action group. They accepted a motion to appoint a committee to confer with the executive committee that had been appointed at Cincinnati regarding the calling of a national nominating convention. The combined executive committee, in the patriotic mode of the time, adopted plans to authorize 1,776 delegates to meet in a nominating convention on July 4, 1892, in Omaha.

The strength of the People's Party centered in areas where commercial farming of staple crops, such as cotton and wheat, was dominant. These farmers believed that they were at the mercy of monopolies and speculators, and they demanded government legislation regarding the control of money, transportation, and land. The years following the end of the U.S. Civil War (1861-1865) had proved financially devastating for the nation's farmers as the money supply of the country contracted. The war had contributed to widespread inflation and the depreciation of the value of the dollar. Bankers had pushed for the return to a hard money standard and for holding the supply of money in circulation constant to prevent further inflation. Although the complexities of monetary theory were difficult for people to understand, the result was easily seen: With the supply of money held constant, the more farmers, as a whole, produced, the less each individual farmer would be paid.

By 1892, several previous attempts at forming a third political party had been made. The National Labor Union of 1871, the Greenback Party, and the Union Labor Party had all been inspired by difficulties caused by monetary policies. Each of these parties had appealed to slightly different segments of the population. The People's Party would come the closest to uniting rural farmers with ur-

1890's

ban labor interests. Still, sectional differences delayed the formation of the party for several years. The Southern Alliance believed that it could capture the Democratic organization, while many Northern Alliance groups wanted to form new parties.

The memory of the Civil War remained strong, and Democratic politics had different connotations in different regions. Still, both groups experienced considerable success with their respective strategies in the off-year election of 1890. In the South, four governors and forty-four congressmen who were committed to Alliance principles were elected as Democrats; in the states of the Great Plains, the Populists as an independent party gained

the election of two U.S. senators. By 1892, many southern farmers were disillusioned with the concessions made by the national Democratic Party and were more willing to join a third party movement. The Southern Alliance members were, however, never united on the new strategy. For example, African American farmers who were active in the Southern Alliance had always strenuously opposed cooperating with the Democrats, while white farmers generally supported cooperation.

The 1892 Omaha nominating convention of the People's Party accepted the report of its platform committee. Donnelly's ringing denunciation of the corruption of the two major parties, Congress, the state legislatures, and the bench was adopted as the preamble to the platform. The body of the platform called for an inflated currency (specifically, "free silver," or the unlimited coinage of silver and gold and a "circulating medium" of not less than fifty dollars per capita), a graduated income tax, the establishment of postal savings banks, the nationalization of the railroads, and the prohibition of alien ownership of land. Finally, the committee presented several resolutions that it did not consider as an integral part of the platform. These resolutions included demands for the secret ballot, the initiative and referendum, direct election of senators, and one-term limitations on the presidency. Expression of sympathy for labor and a demand for the restriction of "undesirable immigration" were also included in the attached resolutions.

The majority of the thirteen hundred delegates who attended the Omaha convention probably favored Judge Walter Q. Gresham as their presidential candidate. Gresham would have given a degree of respectability to the new party, and he was believed to be sympathetic to most Populist views. The judge refused to allow his name to be put in nomination, however, and James B. Weaver, an Iowa Alliance leader who had been the Greenbacker presidential candidate in 1880, was nominated on the first ballot. A southerner was needed to give the ticket balance, and James G. Field, a former Confederate officer from Georgia,

---

PLATFORM OF THE PEOPLE'S PARTY

After assembling a party platform at its nominating convention on July 4, 1892, the People's Party published that platform, excerpted below, in the Omaha Morning World-Herald *on July 5.*

Wealth belongs to him who creates it, and every dollar taken from industry without an equivalent is robbery. "If any will not work, neither shall he eat." The interests of rural and civil labor are the same; their enemies are identical. . . .

FINANCE.—We demand a national currency, safe, sound, and flexible issued by the general government only, a full legal tender for all debts, public and private, and that without the use of banking corporations; a just, equitable, and efficient means of distribution direct to the people, at a tax not to exceed 2 per cent, per annum, to be provided as set forth in the subtreasury plan of the Farmers' Alliance, or a better system; also by payments in discharge of its obligations for public improvements. . . .

We demand a graduated income tax.

We believe that the money of the country should be kept as much as possible in the hands of the people, and hence we demand that all State and national revenues shall be limited to the necessary expenses of the government, economically and honestly administered. We demand that postal savings banks be established by the government for the safe deposit of the earnings of the people and to facilitate exchange.

TRANSPORTATION.—Transportation being a means of exchange and a public necessity, the government should own and operate the railroads in the interest of the people. The telegraph and telephone, like the post-office system, being a necessity for the transmission of news, should be owned and operated by the government in the interest of the people.

LAND.—The land, including all the natural sources of wealth, is the heritage of the people, and should not be monopolized for speculative purposes, and alien ownership of land should be prohibited. All land now held by railroads and other corporations in excess of their actual needs, and all lands now owned by aliens should be reclaimed by the government and held for actual settlers only.

William Jennings Bryan. (Library of Congress)

was nominated. The first Populist presidential ticket had been formed.

SIGNIFICANCE

In the presidential election of 1892, Grover Cleveland collected 277 electoral votes to 145 for the Republican candidate, Benjamin Harrison; the People's Party garnered only 22, all in the western states. The Populists polled 1,041,028 popular votes compared to Cleveland's winning total of 5,556,543. In 1894, the Populists increased their combined popular vote to 1,471,600.

The presidential election year of 1896 saw the People's Party fuse with the Democratic Party, which had nominated William Jennings Bryan. Bryan, who shared many Populist views, especially in regard to the importance of "free silver," was also nominated by the Populists, although they chose a different vice presidential candidate, Thomas E. Watson, in an attempt to maintain their separate party identity. William McKinley, the Republican candidate, easily defeated the Democratic-Populist ticket. Backed by business interests with deep pockets, the Republicans were able to outspend both the Democrats and the Populists. Standard Oil alone contrib-

uted $250,000 to the campaign, an immense sum for that time. Bryan was forced to campaign by commercial carrier, subject to the tight structure of standard railroad timetables, while McKinley enjoyed a private train. It is thus not surprising that the Populists failed to win as a third party and that they failed when they supported Bryan. Their appeal to the American populace was never sufficient to build a strong base for a major party.

—Mark A. Plummer,
updated by Nancy Farm Mannikko

FURTHER READING

Argersinger, Peter H. *The Limits of Agrarian Radicalism: Western Populism and American Politics.* Lawrence: University Press of Kansas, 1995. Intriguing analysis of why rural concerns failed to galvanize the American populace as a whole.

Crossen, Cynthia. "The Man Who Made Political Campaigns All About the Money." *Wall Street Journal* (Eastern edition), March 24, 2004, p. B1. Describes the introduction of new methods of fund-raising in American campaigns. Focuses on Marcus A. Hanna's fund-raising and promotional efforts on behalf of William McKinley during the presidential campaign of 1896, in which he defeated the Democratic-Populist ticket.

Goodwyn, Lawrence. *The Populist Moment: A Short History of the Agrarian Revolt in America.* New York: Oxford University Press, 1978. A condensed version of Goodwyn's larger work, *Democratic Promise*, intended for a general audience. *Democratic Promise*, a massive scholarly work, is considered the definitive history of the Populist movement.

Griffiths, David B. *Populism in the Western United States.* Lewiston, Idaho: Edwin Mellen Press, 1992. Good discussion of the Populist movement in the western states.

McMath, Robert C. *American Populism: A Social History, 1877-1898.* New York: Hill and Wang, 1993. An accessible overview of Populism and the People's Party.

Ostler, Jeffrey. *Prairie Populism: The Fate of Agrarian Radicalism in Kansas, Nebraska, and Iowa, 1880-1892.* Lawrence: University Press of Kansas, 1993. Detailed history of Populism in the prairie states.

SEE ALSO: Feb. 12, 1873: "Crime of 1873"; Jan., 1884: Fabian Society Is Founded; Nov. 4, 1884: U.S. Election of 1884; Feb. 4, 1887: Interstate Commerce Act; July 20, 1890: Harrison Signs the Sherman Antitrust

1890's

Act; May 11-July 11, 1894: Pullman Strike; Nov. 3, 1896: McKinley Is Elected President; Mar., 1898: Russian Social-Democratic Labor Party Is Formed; Feb. 27, 1900: British Labour Party Is Formed.

RELATED ARTICLES in *Great Lives from History: The Nineteenth Century, 1801-1900:* Grover Cleveland; Marcus A. Hanna; Benjamin Harrison; William McKinley.

August 3, 1892
HARDIE BECOMES PARLIAMENT'S FIRST LABOUR MEMBER

Keir Hardie recognized that neither William Ewart Gladstone's Liberal Party nor Lord Salisbury's Conservative Party was willing to address the needs and conditions of the British working class. Attracted to socialist theory, Hardie succeeded in gaining election to the House of Commons as a Labour member of Parliament in 1892 and formed the Independent Labour Party in 1894.

LOCALE: London, England

CATEGORIES: Government and politics; social issues and reform; business and labor

KEY FIGURES

Keir Hardie (1856-1915), Scottish member of Parliament, 1892-1895, 1900-1915

William Ewart Gladstone (1809-1898), prime minister of Great Britain, 1868-1874, 1880-1885, 1886, 1892-1894

Henry Broadhurst (1840-1911), British trade unionist and politician

Robert Bontine Cunninghame Graham (1852-1936), British writer and politician

Third Marquis of Salisbury (Robert Cecil; 1830-1903), prime minister of Great Britain, 1885-1886, 1886-1892, 1895-1902

Ramsay MacDonald (1866-1937), prime minister of Great Britain, 1924, 1929-1931, 1931-1935

SUMMARY OF EVENT

The last three decades of the nineteenth century witnessed a substantive shift in British politics that was caused by the expansion of the franchise (more people gained the right to vote), the continuing expansion of industrialization, and the ascendancy of new political leaders such as the Liberal William Ewart Gladstone and the Conservatives Benjamin Disraeli, Randolph Churchill, and the third marquis of Salisbury. While both Liberal and Conservative governments responded to the extension of democracy and industrialization by being more aggressive in domestic legislation, neither party was willing to address the mounting economic and social distress that afflicted the working class. Hours of work, safety, wages and benefits, pensions, education, and health care problems were all major issues that dominated the lives of the working class and yet had no champion in Parliament. Critics of the major parties emerged, including some who were influenced by the writings of Karl Marx. The Fabian Society was formed in 1884 and served as an important instrument of this criticism; while it achieved some limited successes, however, it was not competitive with the major political parties.

The founder of the British Labour Party, Keir Hardie, came from humble, working-class Scottish origins. Ori-

Keir Hardie. (Library of Congress)

ginally named James Kerr, Hardie was the son of Mary Kerr and a miner; when he was three years old, his mother married David Hardie and his name was changed to James Keir Hardie. His mother imposed her atheist views on her son; later, he would become a devout Christian. Hardie had little formal education and started working in coal mines at the age of eleven. The work was difficult and dangerous. Hardie later reported that he had witnessed the tragedy of the Blantyre coal mine in 1877: More than two hundred miners were killed in the accident. Shortly thereafter, Hardie left the coal mines and fields and became involved in the trade union movement.

At first, Hardie utilized his skills as a writer and journalist to advance his ideas to improve the lives of labor, especially those who worked in the mines. During the early 1880's, Hardie considered himself to be a Gladstone Liberal. He achieved some recognition of his Liberal affiliation through his writings and his presentations to local groups. However, Hardie came to recognize that he was not comfortable within the Liberal Party. His attacks in 1887 and 1889 on Henry Broadhurst, a Liberal member of Parliament who served also as the secretary of the Trades Union Congress, were indicative of his mounting disenchantment with the Liberal Party. Hardie condemned Broadhurst for owning stock in companies and for not using his position in the House of Commons to improve working conditions.

During the same period, Hardie came under the influence of Robert Bontine Cunninghame Graham, a socialist and a Liberal member of Parliament. Although not a member of the proletariat, Cunninghame Graham established the Scottish Labour Party in 1888 and had Hardie elected secretary. Cunninghame Graham did not fit the image of a socialist; he possessed resources and had a reputation as a writer and international traveler. Nonetheless, he was a fervent socialist and led the Scottish Labour Party during its brief history. Hardie assisted in the development of the new party's agenda, which included nationalization of major industries, universal health care, and improved working conditions. During the late 1880's, Hardie abandoned all hope that the Liberal Party could implement the level of economic change that was needed to correct the multitude of abuses and hardships that confronted the working class.

In 1888, Hardie ran for a seat in the House of Commons as an Independent Labour candidate. He refused any support from the Liberals and would not identify himself as affiliated with the Liberal Party; he was defeated by a wide margin. However, Hardie did campaign as a Liberal candidate in the West Ham South district of London in 1891 and won election to the House of Commons. The following year, he dropped his association with the Liberals and stood for reelection. Hardie was elected as an Independent Labour candidate on August 3, 1892. His election resulted from the support of a few socialists and many Liberals.

Between 1892 and 1895, Hardie made his mark on British political history; he began publishing a weekly newspaper, the *Labour Leader*, to advance socialist principles, and he created and organized the Independent Labour Party (1893-1894). Throughout his public career as a socialist leader, Hardie never called for the overthrow of the government, but he did call for the abandonment of capitalism and the triumph of socialism. In 1895, he was defeated in the general election.

During the following years, Hardie traveled extensively throughout the world and worked to establish a worldwide socialist network. In 1900, Hardie became the chair of the Labour Representation Committee, an alliance among the trade unions and the Independent Labour Party. In the same year, he again won election to the House of Commons as the representative from Merthyr Tudful. During the first decade of the twentieth century, Hardie became increasingly committed to feminism as well as socialism; at the same time, a new generation of Labour leaders was emerging. Ramsay MacDonald, later to become the first Labour prime minister, became powerful through political dealings with the Liberal Party. The Liberals recognized the growing support for Labour and, after negotiations with MacDonald, agreed not to contest fifty seats in the general election of 1906, hoping to forge an alliance with Labour against the Tories. Labour won twenty-nine seats in the Commons and became a major force in British political life.

During the last decade of his life, Hardie wrote and traveled extensively, supported feminism, and opposed police brutality. After the British declaration of war on Germany on August 4, 1914, Hardie organized antiwar activities but gained little support. Both the Left and the Right condemned his antiwar positions, and some labeled Hardie as a traitor. By the summer of 1915, Hardie was a broken man; he died on September 26, 1915, in Glasgow, Scotland.

SIGNIFICANCE

As Keir Hardie struggled during the 1880's and 1890's to identify a political path to achieve his social and economic agenda, he discovered that neither of the major political parties—the Conservatives and the Liberals— recognized or accepted any responsibility for the untena-

1890's

ble living and working conditions that prevailed among the British working class. Hardie sought to eliminate abuses and hardships that affected the general population and to improve their quality of life in housing, old-age pensions, education, and transportation. Hardie's success in becoming the first Labour member of Parliament in 1892 was followed by the formal establishment of the Labour Party in 1894.

During the Labour Party's early years, Hardie's leadership was challenged by more doctrinaire and left-wing factions; the pragmatic and democratic Hardie was not a Marxist but shared many goals in common with that more radical approach to the problems and issues of the period. By the late 1920's, the Labour Party had eclipsed the Liberal Party and had become the principal rival of the Conservatives. Labour's success was based on its clear identity with the working class; as the franchise expanded and women became increasingly politically active, support for the Labour Party expanded as well. While differing in many ways, the Labour Party of Tony Blair is directly linked to the values first advanced within Parliament by Keir Hardie.

—William T. Walker

FURTHER READING

Benn, Caroline. *Keir Hardie*. London: Richard Cohen Books, 1997. A solid political biography of Hardie that focuses on the evolution of his political thought and values.

Davies, Andrew. *To Build a New Jerusalem: The British Labour Party from Keir Hardie to Tony Blair*. London: Abacus, 1996. Contains a valuable chapter on Hardie's contribution as the founder of the Labour Party.

Howell, David. *British Workers and the Independent Labour Party, 1888-1906*. London: Palgrave Macmillan, 1983. A scholarly and sympathetic assessment of Hardie's understanding and appreciation of the conditions and needs of the British working class and his views as a socialist.

Jeffreys, Kevin, ed. *Leading Labour: From Keir Hardie to Tony Blair*. London: I. B. Tauris, 1999. Useful study of all of the leaders of the Labour Party; provides a sympathetic account of Hardie's difficulties in establishing the Independent Labour Party as a force in British politics.

McLean, Iain. *Keir Hardie*. London: Allen Lane, 1975. A brief but reliable account of Hardie's life and his sympathy for the plight of British workers.

Morgan, Kenneth O. *Keir Hardie: Radical and Socialist*. London: Phoenix Giant, 1997. A reliable biography of Hardie that is based on both primary and secondary sources.

Reid, Fred. *Keir Hardie: The Making of a Socialist*. London: Croom Helm, 1978. Sympathetic account that focuses on Hardie's transformation from Liberal and journalist to socialist and politician.

Stewart, William. *J. Keir Hardie: A Biography*. Westport, Conn.: Greenwood Press, 1970. A comprehensive and solid biography that is centered on Hardie's continuing identity with the British working class.

SEE ALSO: 1824: British Parliament Repeals the Combination Acts; May 9, 1828-Apr. 13, 1829: Roman Catholic Emancipation; June 4, 1832: British Parliament Passes the Reform Act of 1832; 1833: British Parliament Passes the Factory Act; Aug. 14, 1834: British Parliament Passes New Poor Law; July 26, 1858: Rothschild Is First Jewish Member of British Parliament; Aug., 1867: British Parliament Passes the Reform Act of 1867; June 2, 1868: Great Britain's First Trades Union Congress Forms; Jan., 1884: Fabian Society Is Founded; Dec. 6, 1884: British Parliament Passes the Franchise Act of 1884; Feb. 27, 1900: British Labour Party Is Formed.

RELATED ARTICLES in *Great Lives from History: The Nineteenth Century, 1801-1900:* Benjamin Disraeli; William Ewart Gladstone; Keir Hardie; Third Marquis of Salisbury.

1893
MUNCH PAINTS *THE SCREAM*

Edvard Munch, a Norwegian painter and printmaker who was one of the most influential expressionists of the late nineteenth and early twentieth centuries, created his masterpiece, The Scream, *considered the artistic epitome of existential angst. The painting, which also depicts Munch's own feelings of social anguish and alienation, is one of the most recognizable works of modern art.*

LOCALE: Oslo, Norway
CATEGORY: Art

KEY FIGURES

Edvard Munch (1863-1944), Norwegian artist
Hans Jaeger (1854-1910), Norwegian novelist
Christian Krohg (1852-1925), Norwegian genre and
     portrait painter and author
Søren Kierkegaard (1813-1855), Danish theologian
     and philosopher
Stanisław Przybyszewski (1868-1927), Polish novelist,
     essayist, and dramatist
Henrik Ibsen (1828-1906), Norwegian playwright and
     poet
August Strindberg (1849-1912), Swedish dramatist and
     novelist

SUMMARY OF EVENT

Norwegian artist Edvard Munch had introduced feeling into painting with his masterpiece *The Scream* (1893). Other artists, such as Paul Gauguin, also professed a desire to incorporate feeling into their paintings, but Munch was interested in feelings induced by situations of anxiety, strain, or distress. He dealt with the individual confronted with dilemmas, the individual involved in situations over which he or she had no control, the individual who felt or sensed that the world was a strange and alien place.

Munch had parallel interests with many of his friends, who also were leading writers and intellectuals of the day. Hans Jaeger, Stanisław Przybyszewski, August Strindberg, and Henrik Ibsen shared with Munch certain life attitudes, social concerns, and psychological insights. Munch had produced paintings that rivaled the theater and the novel, and his works were comparable to some of the strongest literary productions at the end of the nineteenth century.

As a young artist from a conservative, middle-class family headed by a strict and deeply religious father,

Munch came into contact with members of a Bohemian and radical avant-garde circle in Kristiania (Oslo). The circle members' way of life and vehement criticism of the prevailing social order were in acute contrast with anything Munch had ever known. Two significant influences on Munch at that time were well-known painter Christian Krohg, who became his teacher and mentor, and Hans Jaeger, an anarchist writer whose advocacy in his novels of free love led to his banishment from Norway. For Munch, life in bohemian Kristiania included his own unhappy affairs with several women and many encounters with death in his immediate family.

In 1885, Munch had spent several weeks in Paris, where he was influenced by both Impressionism and post-Impressionism. A state grant had enabled him to return to Paris in 1889, but by then he had been drawn to the strongly Symbolist cultural atmosphere of Parisian theater and literature and the works of Stéphane Mallarmé, Paul Verlaine, and Joris-Karl Huysmans, among others. He also renewed his friendship with Jaeger, now living in Paris. It was at that time, also, that Munch had declared in a journal entry that he would no longer paint interiors with people reading or knitting but would instead create "living" people who breathe and feel and suffer and love.

With this declaration, he had conceived the idea for his "Frieze of Life," a series of paintings and prints that dealt with ordinary people and the crises they continually confront, especially those of sickness, anxiety, love, and death. The series had been patterned after the great painting cycles of the past that recorded the life of Jesus Christ, the Virgin, or the saints. Much like Vincent van Gogh, Munch, too, endured great personal suffering and sought to transform himself through art; the anguish of others became a metaphor of his own anguish.

The best known of all Munch's work in the Frieze of Life is *The Scream*, which he began in late 1893. Munch had described this scene in a journal entry of January, 1892, relating that, as he walked along a road with two friends, he felt a tinge of melancholy as the sun was setting. Then, suddenly, the sky had become a bloody red. Feeling tired, he stopped and leaned against a railing, looking at the flaming clouds hanging like blood and a sword over the blue-black fjord and the city. His friends had walked on but he stood still, trembling with fright; he then felt a loud, unending scream piercing nature.

In *The Scream*, one sees a figure (likely the artist) transposed by his feelings by screaming, in such a way

Edvard Munch's masterpiece, The Scream. (AP/Wide World Photos)

Several scholars have pointed out that until Émile Durkheim's *Le Suicide: Étude de sociologie* (1897; *Suicide: A Study in Sociology*, 1951) proved otherwise, the sunset hour was believed to be the most common time for suicides. Because Munch, in some of his journal entries, described his own suicidal ideation, it would seem that the painting indeed reflects Munch's own personal angst at that moment. Moreover, Munch stated that, at the time he heard the scream in nature, he suffered from a fear of open places or spaces and a fear of heights.

Søren Kierkegaard, in his *Begrebet Angest* (1844; *The Concept of Dread*, 1944) had described the fear of heights as evidence of anxiety that, when combined with fear of open places or spaces, becomes symptomatic of a greater anxiety—the fear of death. A story in Norwegian literature relates the tale of travelers who hear a cry in a desolate landscape. Later in the story, the travelers are told that once a year in this part of the world a cry is heard: the cry of the world.

Munch could link what was "inside" the figure with what was "outside" the figure through his choice of color and through a confluence of certain painted rhythms and movements. Like Van Gogh, he preserved the expressive possibility of space, so that the painting shows an interesting synthesis of a pronounced "surfaceness," which is the result of drawing and the application of flat color, and the calculated use of fleeting orthogonals, which increase the velocity of seeing into the painting. Impressionism had eliminated deep space in painting.

The coincidence of subject and nature in Munch's work also differs from the Impressionist approach. When an Impressionist confronts nature, he or she will develop a mood conditioned by pleasurable experiences. There are no Impressionist paintings that are the result of distressing moods. The Impressionist is congenial to those conditions in nature that produce reverie, or joyful, thoughtful, pleasurable moods. Essentially, however, the Impressionist is responding to conditions outside of himself or herself. Contrarily, Munch saw nature through the eyes of a mood, always selecting moments in nature that are coincident with moods of depression, anxiety, or death.

SIGNIFICANCE

Edvard Munch's *The Scream* remains the ultimate crystallization of humanity's existential angst, a pioneering depiction of Munch's own torment that laid the founda-

that even the gender of the figure is indeterminate. With the figure, the artist projects a particular body image. He sets up certain rhythms of consciousness that are carried over into the environment, swirling along the fjord, as if nature and the figure had impregnated each other, leading to a resonance shared by both nature and the figure.

One of the most dramatic aspects of the painting is the sky, with the blood-red clouds that, like tongues of fire, bite into the yellow background. This depiction of clouds had its source in a meteorological phenomenon that occurs in late autumn on the shores of Oslo Fjord. During early evenings after a rainstorm, the setting sun creates a stunning visual effect, such as had been depicted by Munch in his painting. Still, Munch's profound experience of the moment has not been refuted. (Some scholars have suggested the unique atmospheric effects of the 1883 eruption of the Indonesian volcano Krakatoa might have influenced Munch's heightened experience of the weather in Norway at that time.)

tion for the expressionist movement in Europe. Other artists of the period had been trying to evoke personal anguish through their own work, but none, perhaps, could do so with the precision and simplicity, yet directness, of Munch. *The Scream*'s colors and "moving" brush strokes show nothing less than the screaming figure's inner turmoil, and Munch's painting leaves one with a gut feeling that the artist indeed had something to relate.

In 1892, Munch had received an invitation for a one-person show from the Association of Berlin Artists, introducing a new, significant phase of his life. Although this exhibition in Berlin caused a scandal among traditionalists, and was, therefore, closed after a week, he nevertheless found support from younger artists in Berlin and was soon recognized in Germany and central Europe as one of the creators of a new style.

German expressionism would come into being in Germany and Austria around 1900 and persist until the beginning of the Weimar Republic (c. 1920-1921). Responding to Munch's influence, German expressionists looked upon the work of art as the bearer or carrier of very intense feelings that the artist and his or her viewers had about the world. Expressionists believed that expressionism should be a kind of inner process, based upon intuition and on the ecstatic.

Like all movements, however, expressionism had its contradictions, its seeming inconsistencies, and its plurality of sources. Within German expressionism, there were two distinct groups: Die Brücke (The Bridge) and Der Blaue Reiter (The Blue Rider). Of the two groups, The Bridge was most greatly influenced by Munch's work. The Bridge artists preserved the motif; they were not interested in abstraction or in formal theorizing about art. The motif was essential to them as a metaphor that could express their emotional and spiritual experiences as well as their worldview, which looked upon the world as potentially a hostile and dangerous place. Like

Munch, they focused upon basically unpleasant subjects and those difficult moments in human existence.

—LouAnn Faris Culley

FURTHER READING

Heller, Reinhold. *Edvard Munch: The Scream.* New York: Viking Press, 1973. The most complete analysis of this work, both in terms of meaning and technique.

Hodin, Paul. *Edvard Munch.* London: Thames and Hudson, 1985. A scholarly analysis covering all of Munch's work, with 160 plates discussed in depth.

Munch, Edvard. *The Private Journals of Edvard Munch: We Are Flames Which Pour Out of the Earth.* Madison: University of Wisconsin Press, 2005. English translation of Munch's private diaries. Spans the period from the 1880's to the 1930's.

Prideaux, Sue. *Edvard Munch: Behind "The Scream."* New Haven, Conn.: Yale University Press, 2005. A comprehensive biography of Munch, with chapters exploring his life and world before, during, and after his painting *The Scream.* Includes maps and illustrations, some in color.

Schroeder, Klaus, ed. *Edvard Munch: Theme and Variation.* Ostfildern, Germany: Hatje Cantz, 2003. Essays by well-known scholars provide an expansive analysis of the development of theme and variation in Munch's work.

SEE ALSO: Oct.-Dec., 1830: Delacroix Paints *Liberty Leading the People*; Apr. 15, 1874: First Impressionist Exhibition; Late 1870's: Post-Impressionist Movement Begins; 1886: Rise of the Symbolist Movement.

RELATED ARTICLES in *Great Lives from History: The Nineteenth Century, 1801-1900:* Paul Gauguin; Vincent van Gogh; Henrik Ibsen; Søren Kierkegaard.

1890's

1893-1896
NANSEN ATTEMPTS TO REACH THE NORTH POLE

Fridtjof Nansen was renowned for his east-to-west crossing of Greenland. During his quest to reach the North Pole, he and a companion traveled to the farthest point north ever accomplished. Launched with his crew from his ship the Fram, *both expeditions contributed greatly to the scientific understanding of the Arctic region.*

LOCALE: Norway; Greenland; Arctic Ocean
CATEGORIES: Exploration and discovery; environment and ecology

KEY FIGURES
Fridtjof Nansen (1861-1930), Norwegian polar explorer
Colin Archer (1832-1921), Scottish ship designer
Otto Sverdrup (1854-1930), Norwegian polar explorer
Fredrik Hjalmar Johansen (1867-1913), Norwegian polar explorer
Frederick George Jackson (1860-1938), British polar explorer

SUMMARY OF EVENT
Fridtjof Nansen, one of the fathers of nineteenth century Polar exploration, was one of the most capable and confident explorers of his day and was able to combine his intellectual ideas with their practical application. He kept valuable diaries and scientific notes and published books of his Arctic experiences and observations. His interest in the Arctic began in 1882, when he took passage on the Norwegian sealing vessel *Viking*, which sailed to the Arctic Ocean.

During the Arctic journey on the *Viking*, Nansen made valuable scientific notes and sketches, recording his observations of winds, currents, ice movements, and fauna. He also began formulating his plans for crossing Greenland and the theories that would influence his later Arctic explorations. After the *Viking* voyage, he served as curator of the natural history collection at the Bergen Museum and gained his doctorate from the University of Christiania in 1887.

In 1887, at the age of twenty-seven, Nansen began meticulous preparations for his expedition to cross the Greenland icecap. His planned route involved landing on the largely uninhabited east coast and going west, the route opposite that cho-

sen by earlier explorers. An east-to-west route would allow Nansen to go straight home after the expedition, rather than having to retrace his steps to gain ship's passage. The route also forced the expedition to move forward regardless of the circumstances, because there were no settlements to which he could return. The University of Christiania recommended the project, but Norway's national assembly, the Stortinget, or Storting, was hesitant to fund such a potentially hazardous expedition. Nansen instead relied on the donation of a wealthy Copenhagen merchant for the needed funds.

Six men set forth on Nansen's expedition in June of 1888 and spent the next month trying to reach the shore of Greenland to begin their trek across the continent's icy interior. Nansen's expedition finally reached the eastern shore and set off, reaching the west coast in September. The men endured the common Arctic hardships of near disasters on the ice, insufficient food, and temperatures well below freezing. Along the way, expedition members kept records of meteorological conditions and other

Fridtjof Nansen. (R. S. Peale/J. A. Hill)

NANSEN'S POLAR EXPEDITION

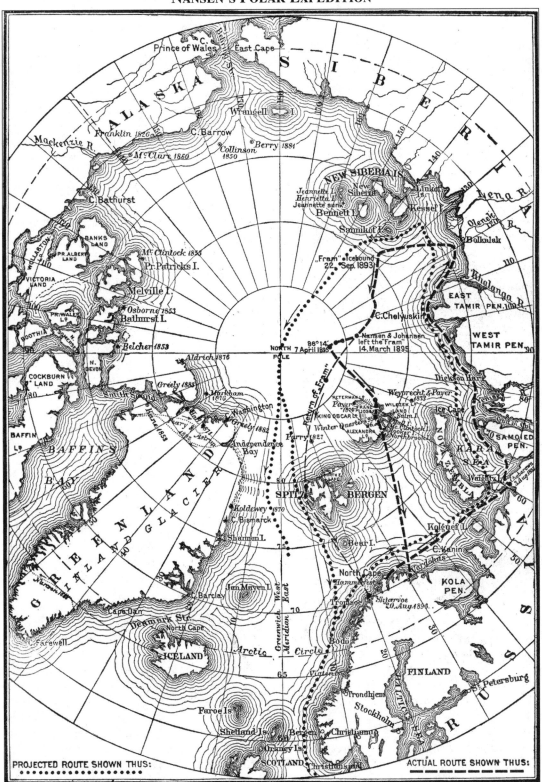

PROJECTED ROUTE SHOWN THUS:
•••••••••••••••••••••

ACTUAL ROUTE SHOWN THUS:

phenomena. The expedition wintered at the west coast settlement of Godthaab, where Nansen studied the Inuit. Nansen had learned to speak the Inuit language prior to leaving Norway and would later publish a book entitled *Eskimo Life* (1958). The men returned to Norway the following spring and were greeted as national heroes. Nansen had achieved renown as a premier Arctic explorer and scientist.

Nansen's Arctic experiences and his study of earlier, ill-fated expeditions, such as the expedition (1879-1881) launched by the United States aboard the *Jeannette*, helped him formulate theories about Arctic Ocean currents. These speculations would drive his famous attempt to reach the North Pole. The Arctic Ocean had remained largely an enigma. By studying driftwood that had traveled from Siberia to Greenland, including remnants of the *Jeannette*, Nansen became convinced that an Arctic current flowed from Siberia "up" to the North Pole and back "down" to Greenland.

Nansen devised a plan to build a sturdy ship that could withstand the pressure of the ocean's pack ice and then drift, frozen into the ice, to the North Pole. Scholars from the Royal Geographical Society of London were skeptical of Nansen's proposed plan. Some doubted a ship could survive in the ice and others doubted his polar-drift theory. Nansen received more support from his home country: The Sorting, the Norwegian king, and private individuals all helped to fund his venture.

Nansen spent three years preparing for the expedition to the North Pole and working with renowned Scottish shipbuilder Colin Archer to design what became known as the *Fram* ("forward"). The *Fram* was a uniquely designed ship with a three-layered hull that was more than two feet thick, braced with heavy beams, and rounded, which enabled it to rise up out of the ice rather than be crushed within it, as had been the fate of many other ships. The *Fram*, with an ironclad front and back, weighed four hundred tons and had the equipment necessary to make needed tools and supplies. A windmill and dynamo provided sporadic electric light and the "Nansen cooker" allowed the preparation of hot foods. Nansen even kept games and books on board to prevent boredom during the long voyage and dark Arctic winters.

Twelve men accompanied Nansen on his expedition, which left Norway in June of 1893, carrying provisions for six years and fuel oil for eight years. Otto Sverdrup, chosen to be the *Fram*'s captain, had already accompanied Nansen across Greenland. The thirty-five-year-old Nansen left behind a wife named Eva and a six-month-old daughter named Liv.

The *Fram*, disproving the skeptics at home, froze into the pack ice in September of 1893, successfully remaining watertight and secure. The ship's unique design proved successful, and it survived being frozen within the heavy pack ice. During the three years in which the expedition was frozen in the ice, Nansen and his crew made more scientific notes, including descriptions of the wonders of the aurora borealis (northern lights) and the Arctic flora and fauna.

By March of 1895, it had become clear to Nansen that the ship would not drift over the North Pole as he had hoped. With Hjalmar Johansen, Nansen would make an attempt to reach the North Pole using skis and dog sleds. Sverdrup would remain in charge of the frozen-in *Fram* and its crew. Nansen and Johansen took dogs, kayaks, and sleds and set out for the North Pole on March 14, but they were forced to turn for Franz Josef Land after reaching 86 degrees 12 minutes north latitude on April 8, only 224 nautical miles from the pole. The three-hundred-mile journey took five months and marked the farthest anyone had reached north during the nineteenth century.

Nansen and Johansen wintered in a stone hut on an island Nansen later would name Jackson Island. The following May, they encountered British explorer Frederick Jackson, part of the Jackson-Harmsworth Arctic expedition of 1894-1897. The three returned to Jackson's headquarters and later sailed to a port in northern Norway. Also in 1896, shortly after Nansen arrived in Norway, the *Fram* finally broke free of the pack ice and made its way home, having drifted west with the currents as Nansen had predicted. Nansen and his partner rejoined the *Fram* as it made its way down the Norwegian coast to Christiania (now Oslo), reaching the city on September 9, 1896, after a voyage of more than thirty-five months. Once again, Nansen had added to his renown as an Arctic scientist and explorer, and once again he received a hero's welcome.

SIGNIFICANCE

Fridtjof Nansen's expedition was the first voyage to reach the heart of the Arctic, and it compiled critical information on ocean currents, winds, and temperatures. The expedition proved that the Arctic Ocean was a deep, ice-covered ocean and that a current of warm water flowed below the polar ice. Nansen's theory of the drift of the polar currents was also proved correct. The crew's observations greatly benefited the new science of oceanography, which would become the focus of Nansen's future work.

In the years following his return, Nansen planned a

major expedition to the South Pole, but his trip was forever derailed by his academic studies and statesmanship. Fellow Norwegian explorer Roald Amundsen would be the one to take the reins of the *Fram* on future explorations. Finally, Nansen won the 1922 Nobel Peace Prize for his efforts on behalf of World War I prisoners of war and refugees and his work with famine victims in various parts of the world.

—*Marcella Bush Trevino*

FURTHER READING

Huntford, Roland. *Nansen: The Explorer as Hero*. New York: Barnes & Noble Books, 1998. A 610-page work that focuses on the *Fram* expedition and Nansen's attempt to reach the North Pole, with frequent quotations from Nansen's own diaries, letters, and writings.

Markham, Clements R. *The Lands of Silence: A History of Arctic and Antarctic Exploration*. Mansfield Centre, Conn.: Martino, 2005. Good overview of exploration in the Arctic and Antarctic regions. Originally published 1921.

Mills, William J., ed. *Exploring Polar Frontiers: A Historical Encyclopedia*. Santa Barbara, Calif.: ABC-Clio, 2003. Useful overview of key figures and polar expeditions.

Nansen, Fridtjof. *The Farthest North*. Northampton, Mass.: Interlink Books, 2003. Nansen's 832-page account of his journey on the *Fram* and his attempt to reach the North Pole. Originally published in 1898.

SEE ALSO: 1818-1854: Search for the Northwest Passage; 1820-early 1840's: Europeans Explore the Antarctic.

RELATED ARTICLES in *Great Lives from History: The Nineteenth Century, 1801-1900:* Sir John Franklin; Sir James Clark Ross; David Thompson.

May 1-October 30, 1893
CHICAGO WORLD'S FAIR

The World's Columbian Exposition in Chicago displayed many of the most impressive technological advances of the nineteenth century, offered visitors intriguing speculations about technological advances, and marked a cultural watershed in American history.

ALSO KNOWN AS: World's Columbian Exposition; Great White City

LOCALE: Chicago, Illinois

CATEGORIES: Architecture; cultural and intellectual history; science and technology

KEY FIGURES

Daniel Hudson Burnham (1846-1912), young Chicago architect who was chief executive of the fair

Richard Morris Hunt (1827-1895),

Charles Follen McKim (1847-1909) and

Henry Van Brunt (1832-1903), architects who planned the fair on classical lines

Frederick Law Olmsted (1822-1903), leading landscape painter who chose Jackson Park as the site for the fair

John Wellborn Root (1850-1891), consulting architect for the fair

SUMMARY OF EVENT

Also known as the World's Columbian Exposition, the Chicago World's Fair opened its five-month run on

May 1, 1893. The movement to celebrate the four-hundredth anniversary of Christopher Columbus's discovery of America with a world's fair had begun in 1889, when four cities, Chicago, New York, Washington, and St. Louis, petitioned Congress for the right to stage a fair. Competition was keen. Most of the established cities regarded Chicago as a brash upstart and argued that they had the advantages of denser populations and longer traditions. Chicago, however, pledged to invest ten million dollars in its fair, and Congress, convinced of the midwestern city's resolve, voted in 1890 to award to Chicago the World's Columbian Exposition.

Banker Lyman Gage was chosen president of the planning committee, and plans for what was to be the famous "Great White City" were begun. A committee of six thousand, the largest such body ever assembled, planned all aspects of the fair. The site for the fair was chosen on February 11, 1891, when Frederick Law Olmsted, the great U.S. landscape artist and city planner, selected Jackson Park, an undeveloped stretch of swamp and scrub bounded by Lake Michigan but accessible to the center of Chicago.

The architectural planning of the fair has engendered historical controversy. The distinctive part of the design, the unified architectural planning that made the Great White City a realization of classical architectural forms

1890's

The Electricity Building at the Chicago World's Fair. (Planet Publishing Company)

rather than a celebration of the new Chicago architecture, came about when five Chicago architectural firms asked five outside architects, mainly from New York, to help in designing the fair. John Wellborn Root was the chief architect, but when he suddenly died before the designs were completed, executive authority passed to Daniel Hudson Burnham, one of the younger Chicago architects. Burnham offered no resistance to the New Yorkers, who were at the head of the architectural profession. Richard Morris Hunt, Charles Follen McKim, and Henry Van Brunt were New York architects who took charge of the preparations. They determined that the Middle West should have a display of the best architecture, which in the New Yorkers' eyes did not include the brash new designs of the Western, or Chicago, school.

While celebrating the anniversary of Columbus's opening of the New World, the fair was also to be both a tribute to the dynamic growth of Chicago as a new me-

tropolis and a symbol to the rest of the world that the United States had come of age. The physical scale of the fair was vast, covering more than six hundred acres—nearly one square mile. The magnificent Roman classical architecture, which seemed even more miraculous in its juxtaposition with the brash and rough metropolis of Chicago, dominated the entire scene.

The Manufacturers Building was 1,687 feet (514 meters) long and 787 feet (240 meters) wide; a complete ten-story building could have been laid inside it. The Palace of Fine Arts was of equally enormous proportions, covering more than 600,000 square feet (55,740 square meters). It was the one building that would remain in place after the fair was over. Marshall Field, founder of the wholesale and retail firm that bears his name, was asked for one million dollars in order to establish an exhibit of exposition displays in the building. Preservation was not possible, however, as the original materials were meant to be temporary. Field hired Burnham to plan the new building.

A material called "staff," invented in France about 1876, was used heavily in the buildings of both the earlier Paris Exposition and at the Columbian Exposition. Staff was composed of powdered gypsum, with alumina, glycerine, and dextrine. It could be molded into almost any shape, was waterproof, and cost less than one-tenth as much as marble or granite. Sixty-five foreign countries built pavilions. The sixteen leading European and Asian nations constructed lavish buildings, within which they displayed their finest wares. The fair also had the first Ferris wheel ever erected in America. Invented by George Washington Gale Ferris, it was a revolving structure that was 250 feet (76.2 meters) high, had thirty-six cars, cost fifty cents for a ride of two revolutions, and was filled day and night with riders.

Electric lighting was still new in 1893, and the fair used an electrical power station that generated three times more power than was being used for the rest of Chicago. The fair used eight thousand arc lamps and glow-worm-sized incandescent lights, the first electric intramural train with a third rail electrically stimulated, and displays of boats of warlike usage. Companies that provided dynamos and other electrical equipment were Edison, Western Electric, and Westinghouse. The Siemens-Halske Company (now Siemens) of Berlin sent a special 1,500-horsepower plant for incandescent lighting. The Palace of Fine Arts still survives in Chicago as the Museum of Science and Industry; the contemporary artist-sculptor Augustus Saint-Gaudens mirrored most public opinion when he asserted that it was the greatest building since Greece's Parthenon.

The World's Columbian Exposition was at the center of the great Chicago cultural outburst and renaissance. The Chicago Symphony, the Public Library, the Art Institute, the Newberry Library, and the University of Chicago all began their development or rebirth in a new form during the same decade. As a national achievement, the fair was even more significant. Its Women's Building was designed by a Bostonian, Sophia B. Hayden. A Board of Woman Managers and female commissioners worked in the administration of affairs with each state and in every foreign country. The official guide mentions that women exhibitors could compete with men in any department on a common level with men, with "sex not to be recognized or considered." Specific mention is made in the guide that a "young lady of California is exhibiting specimens of wrought-iron work of her own design."

The artificiality of the fair notwithstanding, many Americans became aware for the first time that there was such a thing as art in architecture; the large amount of building that followed in the growing American cities was done more carefully and produced better-designed buildings, regardless of style, than would have been built had the fair not taken place.

A new wealthy class had developed in the United States as a result of the profits from U.S. industrialism, and the newly rich wished to memorialize themselves by association with what they regarded as the eternal glory of art. The fair was one aspect of this desire; the beginnings of great American art collections was another and more lasting effect. The spirit of upper-class responsibility for American cultural leadership was symbolized and encouraged by the fair. Saint-Gaudens had exclaimed at a meeting of the planners, "This is the greatest meeting of artists since the fifteenth century," and the same feeling was communicated to the American people, who could take pride in an indigenous culture for the first time.

For city planning, the fair was vital. When urban planners saw what planning could do for a section of Chicago swampland, there resulted, among other plans, the imaginative Burnham Chicago Plan of 1909, and the revival of Pierre Charles L'Enfant's plan for Washington, D.C. What followed was an important time for city planning in an increasingly urban United States. The main controversy of the fair revolved around the reactionary classical architecture, but that controversy was relatively unimportant. Tourists and critics visiting Chicago saw the work of the Chicago school of architecture and were impressed by it.

The great triumph of the fair was the cultural pride that it instilled in the United States—a pride that was sorely needed in the wake of the Panic of 1893 and the ensuing economic depression. The fair set a high standard to emulate, and it pointed the way for future cultural and urban aspirations. By associating themselves with ancient civilizations, Chicago and the United States were suggesting that America was the home of a new, more glorious Renaissance. The fair was as important to rising U.S. nationalism as Frederick Jackson Turner's frontier thesis of U.S. history, which, like the fair, was presented in 1893 in Chicago.

SIGNIFICANCE

By the time the Columbian Exposition closed on October 30, more than 27 million people had visited the exhibits that had been mounted by representatives from seventy-seven different nations. The exposition was one of the

1890's

few world's fairs to make a profit, returning 14 percent to its astonished stockholders, who had not expected to break even. The effect of the fair upon art, architecture, and urban development in the United States was profound, and its effect upon Europe's recognition of the new United States is difficult to overestimate.

—*Richard H. Collin, updated by Norma Crews*

FURTHER READING

Columbian Guide Company. *Official Guide to the World's Columbian Exposition.* Chicago: Author, 1893. Official guide to the fair, with prices for everything from baths to boat rides.

Dybwad, G. L., and Joy V. Bliss. *Annotated Bibliography, World's Columbian Exposition, Chicago 1893.* Albuquerque, N.Mex.: Book Stops Here, 1992. Comprehensive bibliography of materials published on the Columbian Exposition.

Findling, John E., ed. *Historical Dictionary of World's Fairs and Expositions, 1851-1988.* Westport, Conn.: Greenwood Press, 1990. Handy reference work with concise synopses of all the world's fairs between 1851 and 1988, including the Chicago fair.

Larson, Erik. *The Devil in the White City: Murder, Magic, and Madness at the Fair That Changed America.* New York: Crown, 2003. Best-selling history of the Chicago World's Fair that centers on the fascinating lives of Daniel Hudson Burnham, who planned the fair, and Henry H. Holmes, a serial killer who built a hotel near the fair so he could attract his victims.

Muccigrosso, Robert. *Celebrating the New World: Chicago's Columbian Exposition of 1893.* Chicago: Ivan R. Dee, 1993. Presents a layout of the fair, gives detailed information about its buildings and their contents, and highlights important inventions that were displayed at the exposition.

Rydell, Robert W. *All the World's a Fair: Visions of Empire at American International Expositions, 1876-1916.* Chicago: University of Chicago Press, 1984. Scholarly analyses of American fairs and expositions around the turn of the twentieth century that focuses on connections between them and American imperialism.

Rydell, Robert W., John E. Findling, and Kimberly D. Pelle. *Fair America: World's Fairs in the United States.* Washington, D.C.: Smithsonian Institution Press, 2000. Less dense than Rydell's 1984 book, this little volume offers brief accounts of all world's fairs held in the United States.

Weimann, Jeanne Madeline. *The Fair Women.* Chicago: Academy Chicago, 1981. Interesting account of the Women's Building at the World Columbian Exposition.

SEE ALSO: 1850's-1880's: Rise of Burlesque and Vaudeville; May 1, 1851-Oct. 15, 1851: London Hosts the First World's Fair; Apr., 1869: Westinghouse Patents His Air Brake; May 10-Nov. 10, 1876: Philadelphia Hosts the Centennial Exposition; 1878: Muybridge Photographs a Galloping Horse; Oct. 21, 1879: Edison Demonstrates the Incandescent Lamp; 1883-1885: World's First Skyscraper Is Built; May 8, 1886: Pemberton Introduces Coca-Cola; 1890: U.S. Census Bureau Announces Closing of the Frontier; Nov. 16, 1896: First U.S. Hydroelectric Plant Opens at Niagara Falls.

RELATED ARTICLES in *Great Lives from History: The Nineteenth Century, 1801-1900:* Daniel Hudson Burnham; William Cody; Marshall Field; Frederick Law Olmsted; Augustus Saint-Gaudens; Lucy Stone; Louis Sullivan.

September 19, 1893
NEW ZEALAND WOMEN WIN VOTING RIGHTS

Women in New Zealand, including Maori women, gained voting rights following a strong suffrage movement, an absence of entrenched conservative forces, growth in female education, women's entry into paid employment, and a favorable political climate after a long depression. New Zealand women became the first women of any nation to gain suffrage rights and to vote in national elections.

ALSO KNOWN AS: Electoral Act of 1893
LOCALE: New Zealand
CATEGORIES: Government and politics; women's issues; laws, acts, and legal history; organizations and institutions; social issues and reform

KEY FIGURES

Kate Sheppard (1848-1934), New Zealand suffrage movement leader
Mary Leavitt (1830-1912), American organizer of the Women's Christian Temperance Union
Meri Te Tai Mangakahia (1868-1920), Maori suffragist
Mary Ann Müller (1820-1901), British-born feminist
Mary Wollstonecraft (1759-1797), British feminist and author
Harriet Taylor Mill (1807-1858), British social-political writer
Richard John Seddon (1845-1906), prime minister of New Zealand, 1893-1906

SUMMARY OF EVENT

In 1879, the government of New Zealand granted suffrage to all men; however, most women were not allowed to vote, even at the local level. From 1867 to 1875, only women ratepayers (taxpayers) could vote in municipal elections. In 1877, that right was somewhat extended when women householders were given the right to vote and to stand for school committees and educational boards.

As a former British colony, New Zealand derived its political system from British law. Similarly, women ratepayers in Great Britain could stand for and vote only in elections for local school boards since 1870, while suffrage was granted to male adults aged twenty-one and older. Women did not fare any better in Australia, another former British colony, even though the state of South Australia became the first in the world to adopt adult male suffrage in 1856. (Three more Australian states followed suit in 1860.) Starting their suffrage movement during the late 1880's, New Zealand women achieved their goal with the last petition in 1893.

The first New Zealand advocate of women's rights and suffrage was British-born feminist writer Mary Ann Müller. Because her husband disapproved of her feminist views, she wrote under the nom de plume Femina. Her pamphlet, *An Appeal to the Men of New Zealand* (1869), attacked old customs and prejudices and advocated voting rights for women. The article was praised by British philosopher and economist John Stuart Mill, whose *The Subjection of Women* (1861) supported woman suffrage. Other British political radicals who inspired New Zealand suffragists included Harriet Taylor Mill and Mary Wollstonecraft. Harriet Taylor Mill, married to John Stuart Mill, wrote "Enfranchisement of Women," which had been published in 1851 in the *Westminster Review*. Wollstonecraft made the case for woman suffrage with her *A Vindication of the Rights of Woman* in 1792.

A number of New Zealand politicians were sympathetic with women's demand for the national-election vote. Before 1885, voting advocates had introduced electoral bills that included clauses to enfranchise women ratepayers and, eventually, all women. However, these attempts at legislation failed to pass either the New Zealand house of representatives or the conservative upper house, the legislative council.

Women in New Zealand did not have an organized voice for voting rights until the founding of the New Zealand Women's Christian Temperance Union (WCTU) in 1885. Mary Leavitt, an American WCTU member, introduced the temperance movement to New Zealand and then to Australia one year later. Temperance societies were formed, both in New Zealand and the Old World, to fight social problems. The 1880's saw New Zealand enter a period of economic depression and poverty, sexual license, and general disorder. Alcoholism negatively affected women and the financial security of their families. Some groups in the WCTU devoted themselves to charitable activities such as running soup kitchens and night shelters and helping people in hospitals and prisons. Other political groups campaigned for equal divorce laws, the raising of the age of consent (twelve at that time), preschool education, and women's suffrage. Kate Sheppard proved to be another critical leader in the suffrage movement. She strongly believed that New Zea-

1890's

land women should get the vote first before they could obtain protective legislation for women and children.

After 1890, the WCTU had broadened the base of its movement and presented petitions to Parliament, including the 1891 petition, which had been signed by nine thousand women. The electoral bill for women's suffrage passed the lower house but was defeated by the upper house. Another petition with twenty thousand signatures was presented to Parliament in 1892. The liquor industry, which opposed women's suffrage because once granted, women would use the vote to prohibit alcohol, began circulating its own antisuffrage petitions in public houses. The Roman Catholic Church also objected to more rights for women, and other conservative institutions and groups considered woman suffrage a threat to traditional life and values. Even Prime Minister Richard John Seddon, who was on the liquor-trade side, opposed woman suffrage.

In 1893 the WCTU gathered nearly thirty-two thousand signatures—almost one quarter of the adult women in New Zealand—to accompany what had been the largest petition of its kind in New Zealand and other Western countries up to that time. The petition was sent to Parliament, and it passed the lower house. Once again the liquor industry petitioned the upper house to reject it. Because the legislative council was almost evenly divided on the bill, Prime Minister Seddon realized he would need one more opposition vote to defeat it. He tried to persuade one councilor to change his supporting vote. Two opposition councilors, however, reacted to Seddon's tactics by changing sides and voting in favor. The bill passed 20-18 on September 8 and was sent to the governor, Lord Glasgow, for his consent.

Antisuffrage petitions again were circulated, and some opposition councilors urged the governor not to sign the bill into law. Lord Glasgow, however, signed the bill on September 19, and the bill became the Electoral Act of 1893. New Zealand women won voting rights just ten weeks before the next national election. The suffrage act included the voting rights of Maori women as well. Led by suffragist Meri Te Tai Mangakahia, Maori women demanded inclusion in the act, and they won the same rights as non-Maori women.

The woman suffrage movement achieved its goal in about eight years. Kate Sheppard's leadership undoubtedly helped bring about its success. (Her political advocacy on behalf of women's rights has been acknowledged with her image on New Zealand's ten-dollar note.) The movement succeeded also because of the growth of female education and because of women's entry into paid employment. Women's advances into many traditionally male occupations made women's political exclusion even more unjust and illogical. Furthermore, an absence of entrenched conservative forces in pioneering New Zealand, as well as the liberal political climate after the economic depression, in which the country was ready to accept new ideas and radical reform, also helped the cause.

SIGNIFICANCE

Woman suffrage was a major advance toward equality in citizenship for women in New Zealand. The movement and the electoral act served as shining examples to women around the world who had been struggling for emancipation from their legal and social subjection. Australia was the next country to follow New Zealand in granting voting rights for women. The state of South Australia enfranchised women in 1894, and the state of Western Australia did so in 1899. Australian women won the national vote in 1902.

Britain did not grant women the right to vote in local elections until it enacted the Local Government Act of 1894, which gave voting rights to married women. British and American women's active participation in World War I also helped change public attitudes toward women's political enfranchisement. The Twentieth Amendment to the U.S. Constitution, ratified in 1920, secured women's suffrage in the United States. British women age thirty and older won the vote in 1918, and, by 1928, all women of voting age could vote. Two other countries, Finland in 1906 and Norway in 1913, granted women suffrage prior to World War I.

In 1919, the Women's Parliamentary Rights Act was passed by the New Zealand parliament. This monumental law made all New Zealand women eligible for election to the national parliament.

—Anh Tran

FURTHER READING

Arneil, Barbara. *Politics and Feminism*. Malden, Mass.: Blackwell, 1999. A comprehensive review of the major currents in Western feminism. Recommended as a companion text for courses in feminism, feminist theory, or Western political thought.

Baker, Jean H., ed. *Votes for Women: The Struggle for Suffrage Revisited*. New York: Oxford University Press, 2002. A collection examining the struggle of American women for suffrage rights. Essential reading for studies in American politics and in women's political participation specifically.

Dubois, Ellen C. *Women Suffrage and Women's Rights*. New York: New York University Press, 1998. A collection that provides an excellent review of the woman suffrage movement, including international and American suffrage in the context of women's broader concerns for social and political justice.

Grimshaw, Patricia. *Women's Suffrage in New Zealand*. 2d ed. Auckland, New Zealand: Auckland University Press, 1987. Comprehensive account that describes the contributions of Maori women to achieve voting rights for both Maoris and all women in New Zealand.

Marshall, Susan E. *Splintered Sisterhood: Gender and Class in the Campaign Against Women Suffrage*. Madison: University of Wisconsin Press, 1997. Analyzes the often violent style of antisuffrage protest.

Rei, Tania. *Maori Women and the Vote*. Wellington, New Zealand: Huia, 1993. Excellent overview of Maori women's political activity, published for the suffrage centennial. Features a portrait of Mangakahia on the cover.

Walter, Lynn, ed. *Women's Rights: A Global View*. Westport, Conn.: Greenwood Press, 2001. Case studies exploring the problems surrounding the fight for women's rights in different countries. A cross-cultural study in attitudes toward women and efforts to provide women the same rights as men.

SEE ALSO: July 19-20, 1848: Seneca Falls Convention; Aug. 28, 1857: British Parliament Passes the Matrimonial Causes Act; May, 1869: Woman Suffrage Associations Begin Forming; Dec., 1869: Wyoming Gives Women the Vote; July 4, 1876: Declaration of the Rights of Women; Feb. 17-18, 1890: Women's Rights Associations Unite; Oct. 27, 1893: National Council of Women of Canada Is Founded.

RELATED ARTICLES in *Great Lives from History: The Nineteenth Century, 1801-1900:* Meri Te Tai Mangakahia; Richard John Seddon; Sir Julius Vogel; Frances Willard.

October, 1893-October, 1897
BRITISH SUBDUE AFRICAN RESISTANCE IN RHODESIA

In contrast to the many sub-Saharan African countries colonized by European imperial powers, Zimbabwe was colonized by a private British company. British occupation began peacefully but soon faced violent resistance on such a large scale that imperial troops had to be brought in to impose order. The Ndebele and Shona revolts were among the largest, bloodiest, and most sustained attempts by Africans to resist colonization.

ALSO KNOWN AS: Ndebele War; Anglo-Ndebele War; Chimurenga
LOCALE: Zimbabwe
CATEGORIES: Wars, uprisings, and civil unrest; expansion and land acquisition; colonization

KEY FIGURES
Lobengula (c. 1836-1894), ruler of the Ndebele Kingdom
Mtshani Khumalo (c. 1830's-1907), cousin of Lobengula who commanded the Imbizo regiment
Cecil Rhodes (1853-1902), English financier and politician in South Africa
Charles Dunell Rudd (1844-1916), British businessman who acted as Rhodes's agent in Zimbabwe

Leander Starr Jameson (1853-1917), Scottish physician and associate of Rhodes
Patrick William Forbes (1861-1923), British army officer who served in the British South Africa Police
Allan Wilson (1856-1893), Scottish commander of the ill-fated Shangani Patrol during the Ndebele War
Herbert Charles Onslow Plumer (1857-1932), commander of the first British imperial unit to fight in the 1896 revolt
Edwin Alfred Harvey Alderson (1859-1927), British army officer who commanded the Mashonaland Field Force

SUMMARY OF EVENT
Creation of the modern nation of Zimbabwe began during the 1890's, when the region was occupied by agents of the British South Africa Company and transformed into the colony of Rhodesia (later Southern Rhodesia). Before that time, the region was made up of scores of independent African states. Most were Shona-speaking societies, but the single largest African state was the Ndebele, or Matabele, Kingdom, in the southwestern region that Europeans called Matabeleland.

1890's

JAMESON'S CAMPAIGNS IN SOUTHERN AFRICA

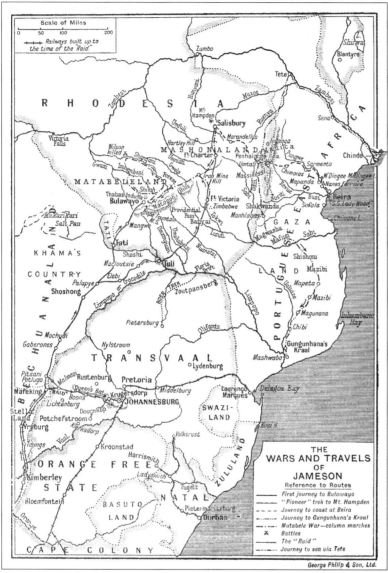

Source: Ian Colvin, *The Life of Jameson* (London, 1923)

premacy of the Ndebele and set a pattern of applying to the Ndebele rulers for permission to work in the region. By the late 1880's, Mzilikazi's son and successor, Lobengula, was generally recognized as the principal power in the region.

In 1888, South African industrialist Cecil Rhodes sent Charles Dunnel Rudd into Zimbabwe as the head of a negotiating team to seek an exclusive mining concession from Lobengula for his syndicate. On October 30, 1888, Lobengula signed what became known as the Rudd Concession. One of the most controversial documents in Southern African history, the written English version of the concession differed from the version presented to the Ndebele in their own language and later became a subject of misunderstanding and Ndebele resentment that contributed to the outbreak of war. The Ndebele saw the concession as a grant of severely limited prospecting rights, but in the view of Rhodes's group, the concession granted it exclusive control over all mineral resources between the Limpopo and Zambezi Rivers. Rhodes used the concession to obtain from the British government a royal charter authorizing him to form a private commercial company to occupy, administer, and develop the region north of the Limpopo.

When Lobengula learned of Rhodes's interpretation of the concession, he publicly repudiated it. Meanwhile, Rhodes used his royal charter to form the British South Africa Company, a London-based organization that would eventually administer the territories that later formed modern Zimbabwe and Zambia. Rhodes's immediate goal, however, was to establish a company presence in Mashonaland from which it could expand its authority. To that end, he sent his associate Leander Starr Jameson to Matabeleland to persuade Lobengula to retract his repudiation of the Rudd Concession. Meanwhile, Lobengula sent envoys to England to

Offshoots of South Africa's Zulu who had adopted Zulu military techniques and organization, the Ndebele had settled in Zimbabwe under their founder-king Mzilikazi in 1839. By far the most powerful state in the region, the Ndebele Kingdom maintained tributary relationships with many Shona states and often raided other communities in the region to the northeast and east that Europeans dubbed Mashonaland. When European hunters, traders, prospectors, and missionaries began entering the region during the 1850's and 1860's, they recognized the su-

solicit advice from the British crown on how to deal with the growing number of Europeans pressuring him for concessions.

In early 1890, the BSAC organized an expedition to occupy Mashonaland. Known as the Pioneer Column, that body comprised about seven hundred heavily armed European men and two hundred Ngwato auxiliaries from Botswana. In June, the column entered Zimbabwe from Botswana, moving along the southern and eastern fringes of the Ndebele sphere of influence. On September 30, after erecting forts in several locations, the column halted in northern Mashonaland, where it established Fort Salisbury on the site that later became Zimbabwe's capital, Harare. Operating under the pretense that it was acting with Lobengula's permission, the occupation was conducted without reference to the rights of the Shona peoples.

After establishing its presence in Mashonaland, the chartered company began building European settlements and distributing mining rights. In May, 1891, the British government declared a protectorate over both Mashonaland and Matabeleland and recognized the BSAC as the protectorate's government. These developments naturally alarmed the Ndebele, but Lobengula merely continued to seek advice from the British high commissioner in South Africa. Meanwhile, the company worked to portray the Ndebele as dangerous predators by publicizing incidents involving Ndebele-Shona hostilities.

On July 18, 1893, the Ndebele mounted a punitive raid on the tributary Shona chiefdom near Fort Victoria. Jameson, the company's chief administrator in Mashonaland, ordered Patrick William Forbes, the commander of the company's British South Africa Police, to prepare for war. In early October, as Lobengula continued his efforts to negotiate peace, three separate British columns began marching on Matabeleland. On October 15, the columns starting from Fort Salisbury and Fort Victoria converged at Iron Mine Hill and continued moving southwest, toward Lobengula's capital at Bulawayo. The third column, made up of members of the Bechuanaland Border Police, advanced on Bulawayo from the southwest.

The battles that ensued were comparatively brief conflicts with only a few significant military engagements. The first battle occurred on October 25 near the headwaters of the Shangani River, where Forbes's main column fought a much larger Ndebele force commanded by Mtshani Khumalo, the chief of the Imbizo regiment. The Ndebele surrounded the British column and recaptured cattle that the British had collected but were repelled by machine guns, which gave the British overwhelming superiority in firepower. Two days later, Forbes's column repelled a second major Ndebele attack at the Bembezi River in a similar fashion. These battles were the largest actions in the war, but only a few hundred Ndebele were killed in them.

As Forbes's column advanced on Bulawayo, Lobengula had his capital torched and retreated north, all the while continuing his futile attempts to negotiate with the invaders. On November 4, Forbes occupied Bulawayo, where the Bechuanaland Border Police column arrived one week later, after skirmishing with an Ndebele force commanded by Gampu at the Mangwe Pass. The British then turned their attention to capturing Lobengula. As the column's progress was slowed by heavy rains and swollen rivers, Forbes sent three dozen men north under the command of Major Allan Wilson to continue the pursuit along the Shangani River. Wilson's patrol was annihilated in early December.

Forbes's main column then encountered heavy Ndebele resistance as it retreated to Bulawayo. After reports of Lobengula's death—to un-

Contemporary drawing of an Ndebele regiment advancing on the British column at the Shangani River on October 25, 1893. (Arkent Archive)

1890's

1765

known causes—were received, the British declared the end of the war and the abolishment of the Ndebele Kingdom. Under Jameson's direction, the British then began building settlements and setting up an administration in and around Bulawayo.

Despite the British occupation of Matabeleland, the war had not really ended. The conflict's last major engagement had been a disastrous British defeat, large parts of Matabeleland remained unpacified, the Ndebele military system remained largely intact, and the Ndebele retained most of their firearms. The 1893 war was merely a prelude to the much larger conflict that began in 1896.

Between the spring of 1896 and the fall of 1897, a large part of Zimbabwe's peoples rose in violent rebellion against the BSAC and European settlers. The Ndebele and Shona shared many of the same grievances: British seizures of cattle, forced labor, land encroachments, and abusive company administrators. Moreover, they recognized that the British had failed to legitimize their claims to sovereignty. The Ndebele also had the additional grievance of British refusal to let them restore their kingship.

The revolts were, in part, triggered by a series of natural disasters in early 1896 that many Africans blamed on the European occupiers. Within a short period, most of the country was beset by drought, locusts, and a cattle plague known as rinderpest, which had swept down through eastern Africa after first appearing in Somalia in 1889. Ndebele leaders appear to have begun planning their revolt in February, 1896, a few months after most of the BSAC's police troops had evacuated the country to participate in the Jameson Raid in the Transvaal. The depletion of British troop strength left Zimbabwe vulnerable to disturbances.

On March 20, Ndebele men began killing African police officers and European settlers around Filabusi. By April, virtually all districts in the former kingdom and its tributaries were in revolt. The company responded by organizing the Bulawayo Field Force, which put both European and African volunteers under arms.

Most of the Ndebele joined the revolt, but they lacked a unified command structure. The rebels fought in three main groups. One centered on the Khumalo royal family in the north; another was based by the Insiza River in southeastern Matabeleland; and a third, less tightly organized, group fought in the rugged Matopo Hills. Some former military commanders, such as Mtshani, remained neutral, while others, including Gampu, supported the British, especially in the southwest, where they helped keep open the supply routes to South Africa.

In the initial fighting, the Ndebele drove European settlers from the outlying regions of Matabeleland and turned their offensive against fortified centers in Bulawayo and other major settlements. Unable to cope with the rebellion on its own, the company called in imperial help. In mid-May, the first imperial unit, the Matabeleland Relief Force, arrived under the command of British colonel H. C. O. Plumer. From that point, the Ndebele revolt became an increasingly defensive guerrilla war against imperial troops. In early June, General Frederick Carrington arrived to take command of all imperial troops. With him was Colonel Robert Stephenson Smyth Baden-Powell, who would later achieve renown in the South African War and found the Boy Scouts movement.

In late June, the Ndebele situation improved when the Shona began to revolt and when Lobengula's son Nyamanda was proclaimed king by one faction of the rebels. However, by then many Ndebele were already surrendering because of supply and ammunition shortages. The conflict then became mainly a protracted guerrilla war in the Matopo Hills, in which difficult terrain greatly favored the Ndebele. In late August, Cecil Rhodes himself came to the Matopos and personally participated in peace negotiations that led to a settlement with the southern rebels. By December, almost all rebels had surrendered.

Meanwhile, a second revolt began in late June in central Mashonaland, where the Shona caught Europeans by surprise. Because the Shona had lived under scores of autonomous polities throughout the nineteenth century, both the causes and the course of their revolt were more complex than those of the Ndebele. Only about one-third of the Shona joined the revolt. Most Shona lived in areas in which British settlement had been most disrupted. Many rebel leaders had earlier traded with Portuguese coming up from Mozambique for firearms to use against Ndebele raids. Many Shona who collaborated with the British were from communities that had been preyed upon by the Ndebele but who had not traded with the Portuguese. Most Shona in the far northern, far eastern, and southeastern parts of Mashonaland remained neutral.

To an extent greater than in the Ndebele revolt, indigenous religious leaders played a prominent role in the Shona revolt. The most notable of these were the spirit mediums known as Kaguvi, or Kagubi, by the Upper Umfuli River, and Nehanda in the Mazoe Valley. Both mediums sent out messengers to exhort Shona chiefs to support the rebellion. The Kaguvi medium was supported by the Ndebele Mwari cult leader Mkwati, who went to Mashonaland to help encourage rebellion there.

The Shona revolt shocked Europeans, who had believed that the Shona had docilely acquiesced to European occupation. However, the ferocity and persistence with which the Shona fought rapidly changed European views. At first the Shona revolt was aided by the removal of all European troops to Matabeleland. In August, however, Lieutenant Colonel Edwin Alfred Harvey Alderson arrived in Mashonaland at the head of fresh imperial troops in the Mashonaland Field Force. Alderson began launching assaults on Shona strongholds in Mashonaland's rocky terrain, which gave the Shona more fortified positions than the Ndebele had outside the Matopos.

In October, after the Ndebele revolt was effectively suppressed, Carrington shifted his troops into Mashonaland. Despite the concentration of imperial forces, the British made little progress during the next two months. In December, the BSAC asked the imperial troops to withdraw from the country to save money, and the company's own police took over. Fighting abated during the ensuing rainy season, and attempts at peace negotiations in January, 1897, were unsuccessful. As heavy fighting resumed in March, the company forces scarcely knew where to strike because the Shona had no centralized command structure. Eventually, however, the British wore down the Shona by ruthlessly blasting rebels from caves with dynamite. By October, all the major rebel leaders were killed or captured, and the revolts were over.

SIGNIFICANCE

Although the brief Ndebele War of 1893 led to the occupation of central Matabeleland by the BSAC, it was actually an inconclusive affair that might be seen as a prelude to the Ndebele and Shona uprisings of 1896-1897. The 1893 conflict taught the Ndebele the futility of using traditional fighting techniques against British machine guns. When they fought the British in 1896, they avoided open battles and concentrated on hit-and-run guerrilla techniques. The Shona fought the same way and managed to prolong their own rebellion by taking advantage of the many naturally fortified positions in their region.

The revolts involved the majority of Zimbabwe's African communities and killed about one in every ten Europeans in the country. All European development of the country was halted for more than one year, and the BSAC's inability to subdue the uprisings on its own nearly forced its collapse. However, with the help of British imperial troops, the risings were suppressed, and the conquest of Zimbabwe was effectively completed.

After the revolts ended, the British disarmed the rebels, executed many of their leaders, and replaced many traditional Ndebele and Shona leaders with government-appointed chiefs. The independence of the Ndebele and Shona was decisively ended and the BSAC was left firmly in control. From that time until the modern nationalist movement of the 1970's, the country's white administration experienced no significant violent resistance from the black African majority.

—R. Kent Rasmussen

FURTHER READING

Baden-Powell, R. S. S. *The Matabele Campaign, 1896.* 1897. Reprint. New York: Negro Universities Press, 1970. One of many memoirs of the 1898-1897 rebellions written by a British army officer.

British South Africa Company. *The '96 Rebellions.* Bulawayo: Books of Rhodesia, 1975. Facsimile reprint of the chartered company's own publication, *Reports on the Native Disturbances in Rhodesia, 1896-7* (London, 1898), containing its official account of the revolts.

Cobbing, Julian. "The Absent Priesthood: Another Look at the Rhodesian Risings of 1896-1897." *Journal of African History* 18, no. 1 (1977): 61-84. Revisionist study of the Shona and Ndebele revolts that rebuts T. O. Ranger's argument that religious leaders played a major leadership role. Includes a map.

Dodds, Glen Lyndon. *The Zulus and Matabele: Warrior Nations.* Harrisburg, Pa.: Arms and Armour Press, 1998. Popular survey of the military aspects of Ndebele and Zulu history by a writer who grew up in Zimbabwe's Matabeleland. Includes chapters on the Matabele War and the 1896 rebellion.

Glass, Stafford, *The Matabele War.* London: Longmans, 1968. Still the only full-length scholarly study of the Ndebele War.

Ranger, T. O. *Revolt in Southern Rhodesia, 1896-7: A Study in African Resistance.* Evanston, Ill.: Northwestern University Press, 1967. Innovative and influential study of the revolts that was the first serious attempt to discern patterns of organization and planning in the African revolts. Illustrations, maps, index.

Rubert, Steven C., and R. Kent Rasmussen. *Historical Dictionary of Zimbabwe.* 3d ed. Lanham, Md.: Scarecrow Press, 2001. General reference work on Zimbabwe that contains extensive entries on all aspects of British colonization and African resistance. All the entries on precolonial history are written by an authority on Ndebele history.

Selous, F. C. *Sunshine and Storm in Rhodesia.* 1896. Re-

1890's

print. Bulawayo: Books of Rhodesia, 1968. Facsimile reprint of a firsthand account of the Ndebele side of the 1896 revolts by a hunter intimately familiar with Matabeleland who fought against the Ndebele. Contains many contemporary photographs and drawings, a map of Matabeleland, and an index.

Wills, W. A., and L. T. Collingridge. *The Downfall of Lobengula*. 1894. Reprint. Bulawayo: Books of Rhodesia, 1971. Facsimile reprint of the British South Africa Company's official history of the Ndebele War. Contains chapters by participants and eye witnesses. Most of the descriptions of military actions were written by Major P. W. Forbes, a British army officer who was the principal commander of the company forces

during the 1893 war. Includes many illustrations, several detailed folding maps, and an index.

SEE ALSO: c. 1817-1828: Zulu Expansion; Jan. 22-23, 1879: Battles of Isandlwana and Rorke's Drift; Jan. 22-Aug., 1879: Zulu War; 1884: Maxim Patents His Machine Gun; Mar. 13, 1888: Rhodes Amalgamates Kimberley Diamondfields; Dec. 29, 1895-Jan. 2, 1896: Jameson Raid; Oct. 11, 1899-May 31, 1902: South African War.

RELATED ARTICLES in *Great Lives from History: The Nineteenth Century, 1801-1900:* Sir Robert Stephenson Smyth Baden-Powell; Cetshwayo; Lobengula; Cecil Rhodes.

October 27, 1893
NATIONAL COUNCIL OF WOMEN OF CANADA IS FOUNDED

The National Council of Women of Canada gathered numerous organizations of differing viewpoints under its aegis, helping to empower women through education, debate, and participation in public-policy making. By the end of the 1890's, the group had achieved a number of objectives on behalf of women in the areas of labor, justice, education, and nursing.

LOCALE: Canada

CATEGORIES: Women's issues; organizations and institutions; government and politics; social issues and reform

KEY FIGURES

Lady Aberdeen (1857-1939), first president of the National Council of Women of Canada, 1893-1898

Adelaide Hunter Hoodless (1857-1910), first NCWC treasurer and founder of the Women's Institute in 1897

Henrietta Edwards (1849-1931), women's rights activist, founder of the Working Girls' Association, and founding NCWC member

SUMMARY OF EVENT

Twenty-two Canadian delegates attended the meeting of the International Council of Women (ICW) that was held in conjunction with the World Congress of Women and the World Exposition in Chicago in May, 1893. Adelaide Hunter Hoodless, one of the Canadian delegates, remarked that Canada was the only country at the conference with no official organization. Hoodless and other

delegates would soon meet and discuss the question of founding such an organization for Canada.

About fifteen hundred women, representatives of most women's organizations in Canada, met in Toronto five months after the meeting in Chicago, forming the National Council of Women of Canada (NCWC) on October 27, 1893. Lady Aberdeen, the ICW president, was elected president of the newly formed NCWC. Another founder was Henrietta Edwards, an early women's right activist and also the founder of the Working Girls' Association in 1875. The NCWC joined the ICW officially in 1897.

As outlined in its constitution, which was drafted by the clerk of the House of Commons, the NCWC was structured to be similar to the ICW in administration and organization, and in spirit: The ICW was made up of women's organizations from around the world; the NCWC came to be an association of already established groups. The ICW provided a means of communication among women's organizations around the world; the NCWC was to establish a communication network among associations for the exchange of goals and the means to achieve them. Finally, the ICW had no power over its members; similarly, any association that joined the NCWC would not lose its independence.

The NCWC's strength came from the councils and their membership. By the end of 1890's, the NCWC had more than two hundred local councils and six affiliated national organizations, among them the Young Women's Christian Association (YWCA) and the Dominion

Order of the King's Daughters. Local membership consisted of philanthropic organizations, educational institutions, church aid and missionary aid societies, and religious associations.

There also were eight national-level standing committees made up of local-council representatives. NCWC yearbooks contained reports from these committees. NCWC funding came from three sources: membership fees, donations, and fund drives. Local meetings were concerned with social issues and the running of cities, but they also were interested in the shaping of the country. Their discussion resulted in petitions to local and provincial governments and in memoranda to the NCWC. The press and personal relationships were also used as tools of persuasion.

The NCWC had a number of characteristics, which also were used as the basis for criticism. First, it was predominantly Anglophone and Protestant. As a result, the English language, values, institutions, and projects were supported and promoted. Except in Montreal, the group was not able to recruit French-speaking women in Quebec. Also in Montreal, the active orders of Catholic women seldom joined NCWC activities. Second, its members were from the middle or upper classes, and they focused their work mostly in towns and cities, not in rural areas. Racial minority groups were usually recipients of NCWC work. Leaders of other organizations were usually from the middle and upper classes, but their members were from different social strata. For example, many factory workers, shop girls, and servants joined the YWCA.

Finally, NCWC philosophy was neither particularly innovative nor radical. Its agenda emphasized the betterment of existing social conditions rather than the initiation of challenges to the established norms or to demands for a new social order. It would not get involved with such issues as women's rights and the sweating system, which exploited women garment workers. The preservation of the family and the state were major objectives in the preamble to the NCWC constitution. Devoted members such as Hoodless believed women's destiny was in the home, and she never supported women's suffrage. On the contrary, the Women's Christian Temperance Union (WCTU) and the YWCA were involved in lobbying for major legislative reform programs. The "radical" associations joined the NCWC because they hoped to convert the organization's conservative majority to support their agenda.

The NCWC achieved a number of objectives at both the local and national levels. Besides its response to disaster relief, it worked effectively for the just treatment of women by the justice system and in the workplace, worked toward increased educational training and other related opportunities, and worked for increased and sufficient medical care.

First, women inspectors were hired at factories and workshops in Ontario and later in Quebec. Provisions of the Factory Act of Ontario, extended to include shop girls, provided for better working conditions. There were changes in arrangements for women prisoners in various places where female police matrons were appointed, while young girls were sent to a separate facility.

Second, in 1898, women were appointed to boards of school trustees in New Brunswick, Nova Scotia, and British Columbia. Other educational appointments included those to school commissions, advisory boards, and boards of education. Hoodless, who had campaigned for the importance of training in domestic science (home economics), saw her proposal implemented in Ontario in 1898 and in the organization of cooking classes and schools.

Finally, educating mothers about infant care started in 1896 as health cards were distributed door to door and at meetings in poor districts. The NCWC's most important achievement was providing care to poor people—immigrants in remote areas, Western farmers, and urban industrial workers. The goal was accomplished with the founding of the Victorian Order of Nurses in 1898. The following year saw nurses sent to fifteen branches and cottage hospitals established for children in Halifax, Regina, and Victoria.

SIGNIFICANCE

A number of volunteer-service organizations run by and for women had already existed by the time the National Council of Women of Canada was founded in 1893. As a group consisting of specific organizations, however, the NCWC had proved to be an effective voice for women in voluntary work and various initiatives and lobbying efforts.

Also, while many organizations were founded to achieve a specific goal (for example, women's suffrage) and then fade away after that goal was achieved, the NCWC was meant to survive and expand. Its staying power could be explained by its vision of consensus, in which women could cooperate to find solutions to agreed-upon issues. In addition to being the voice of female opinion and the lobbyist of policies for women and children, the NCWC provided women a place for political and social education. Also, with the inclusion of different religious organizations against the background of bitter

1890's

religious conflicts during the 1890's, the organization had raised consciousness of religious tolerance.

Before the women's vote was granted, the NCWC had succeeded in drawing together both conservative and radical elements under its aegis. The NCWC was able to fulfill its vision by providing a locus for disparate groups of Canadian women.

—*Anh Tran*

FURTHER READING

Bumsted, J. M. *The Peoples of Canada: A Post-Confederation History*. New York: Oxford University Press, 2004. A survey of Canada's history from the late 1880's to the early twenty-first century. Discusses Canada's social, cultural, political, and economic conditions and provides documentation and analysis of social reform.

Bystydzienski, Jill M., and Joti Sekhon, eds. *Democratization and Women's Grassroots Movements*. Bloomington: Indiana University Press, 1999. Sixteen case studies in Canada and across the world on how community-based actions, programs, and organizations contribute to the creation of a civil society and thus enhance democracy.

Naples, Nancy A. *Grassroots Warriors: Activist Mothering, Community Works, and the War on Poverty*. New York: Routledge, 1998. Voices of women who fought for social and economic justice in New York City and Philadelphia. Influence of gender, ethnicity, and class on political consciousness and practice.

Strong-Boag, Veronica, and Anita Clair Fellman, eds. *Rethinking Canada: The Promise of Women's History*. New York: Oxford University Press, 1997. A blend of classic essays and contemporary writings, featuring key developments in Canadian history and highlighting women's distinct experiences, identities, and aspirations.

Trimble, Linda, and Jane Arscott. *Still Counting: Women in Politics Across Canada*. Peterborough, Ont.: Broadview Press, 2003. Examination of women's involvement in Canadian politics and the need to rethink masculinist political culture.

SEE ALSO: July 19-20, 1848: Seneca Falls Convention; Aug. 28, 1857: British Parliament Passes the Matrimonial Causes Act; May, 1869: Woman Suffrage Associations Begin Forming; Dec., 1869: Wyoming Gives Women the Vote; June 17-18, 1873: Anthony Is Tried for Voting; July 4, 1876: Declaration of the Rights of Women; Feb. 17-18, 1890: Women's Rights Associations Unite; Sept. 19, 1893: New Zealand Women Win Voting Rights.

RELATED ARTICLES in *Great Lives from History: The Nineteenth Century, 1801-1900:* Susan B. Anthony; Hubertine Auclert; Mary Ann Shadd Cary; Dame Millicent Garrett Fawcett; Helene Lange; Lucretia Mott; Anna Howard Shaw; Elizabeth Cady Stanton; Lucy Stone; Victoria Woodhull.

1894-1895
KELLOGG'S CORN FLAKES LAUNCH THE DRY CEREAL INDUSTRY

An accidental discovery by the Kellogg brothers led to the making of corn flakes, the first mass-produced, ready-to-eat breakfast cereal. The popularity of Kellogg's Corn Flakes spawned countless imitators as the cereal industry experienced massive growth.

LOCALE: Battle Creek, Michigan
CATEGORIES: Business and labor; health and medicine; agriculture

KEY FIGURES
John Harvey Kellogg (1852-1943), doctor, medical superintendent of the Battle Creek Sanitarium, inventor
W. K. Kellogg (1860-1951), inventor who founded the Battle Creek Toasted Corn Flake Company

Ella Eaton Kellogg (1853-1920), dietician who managed the Battle Creek Sanitarium kitchen
Ellen G. White (1827-1915), Seventh-day Adventist leader who founded the Health Reform Institute
James Caleb Jackson (1811-1895), doctor who founded the first edible cereal product in 1863
C. W. Post (1854-1914), founder of Post Cereals

SUMMARY OF EVENT
Until the late nineteenth century, most Americans ate the same types of breakfast that their European ancestors had eaten. Diets had been rich in meat, which could be preserved easily in the days before refrigeration. Before being edible, grains had to be cooked and made into bread or gruel. Canned foods were yet to be introduced, and

fruit and vegetables were scarce when out of season. Nutritional science was in its infancy, and consumers had no way of knowing if they were getting a healthy diet.

One of the first groups to promote diet as a means of improving health was the Seventh-day Adventists. In addition to their religious beliefs, they also advocated moderate eating habits, temperance, and vegetarianism. In 1866, Seventh-day Adventist leaders Ellen G. White and James White had established the Health Reform Institute in Battle Creek, Michigan. The institute, which featured water treatments known as hydrotherapy, was successful, but it lacked the expertise of a medical doctor. To that end, the Whites partially financed the medical education of one of their parishioners, a teenager named John Harvey Kellogg. Kellogg would complete his medical training and then return to the institute, which he did in 1875. One year later, he became its medical director.

Kellogg immediately began instituting changes in the facility, including changing its name to Battle Creek Medical and Surgical Sanitarium. "The San," as it was soon called, was to become a place where people not only came to get well but also learned to stay well. Kellogg shifted the sanitarium's focus from theology to medical and dietary treatment. His "Battle Creek Idea" revolved around preventive and curative treatments such as a healthy diet, plenty of exercise, and a variety of hydrotherapies. Kellogg encouraged his patients to avoid all meat products and base their diet on vegetables, fruits, nuts, and grains.

Kellogg's mission tapped into what had been a growing health craze in the latter part of the nineteenth century. People believed they could gain control of their bodies through diet, exercise, and other modern curatives. Vegetarianism and temperance were among the popular fads, and the Battle Creek Idea fit right into that scheme. In 1877, one year after Kellogg took over, the San treated three hundred patients. By 1886, less than ten years later, that number had quadrupled, and the San had become the largest institution of its kind in the world.

Kellogg hired his business-minded younger brother, W. K. Kellogg, to handle the bookkeeping and marketing, and he placed his wife, Ella Eaton, in charge of the San's kitchen. A trained dietician, Eaton oversaw the creation of more than eighty new grain- and nut-based dishes designed to replace meat in the diets of wealthy clients.

This first print advertisement for Kellogg's Corn Flakes was published in 1906. (Hulton Archive/Getty Images)

1890's

The breakfast product that would be the precursor to Kellogg's Corn Flakes was developed in 1894 as an alternative to the hard-to-chew zwieback toast. To create a product that would be easier to chew and digest, the Kelloggs experimented with a variety of grain combinations. The successful corn flakes recipe was developed by accident when a batch of cooked wheat was left to sit out all night. The next morning, the cooked wheat was processed through heavy rollers and emerged in flake form. The end product, then called Granose, was served, with salt, to sanitarium patients. Kellogg applied for his "Flaked Cereals and the Process of Preparing Same" patent on May 31, 1895. The patent application covered the original wheat flakes, as well as barley, oats, corn, and other grains.

Technically, Granose was not the first breakfast cereal, but it was the first to be available in a ready-to-eat form. Another early health pioneer, James Caleb Jackson, invented a cereal product called Granula in 1863, but the bran-based nuggets were so dense that they had to be soaked overnight before they could be eaten.

Patients wanted to purchase the Granose cereal and other sanitarium foods, leading the Kellogg brothers to found the Sanitas Nut Food Company to market their food products. Kellogg had little interest in the business end of cereal manufacturing; his priority was the health and well-being of his patients. W. K. Kellogg, frustrated by his brother's lack of interest, decided to form his own cereal company to take advantage of the new fad.

A devastating fire at the sanitarium in 1902 put those plans on hold, and not until 1906 did the new company, the Battle Creek Toasted Corn Flake Company, go into business. This small company, which had started out in a one-story wooden factory, would grow to become the Kellogg Company, the world's largest cereal manufacturer.

By his own choice, Dr. Kellogg did not profit from his discovery, instead supporting his large family (which included forty foster and adopted children) with the proceeds of his writing. He remained the director of the sanitarium until his death in 1943.

The Kellogg brothers were not the only people to succeed in the early days of the cereal industry. Inspired by their success, a former sanitarium patient named C. W. Post began manufacturing cereal and grain-based products in 1895. His first offering was Postum, a grain-based coffee substitute, but he quickly followed with Grape Nuts cereal in 1898 and his own version of the flaked cereal in 1904, first called Elijah's Manna and then renamed Post Toasties in 1904.

SIGNIFICANCE

The early days of the cereal boom have been compared to the California gold rush or a boomtown in an oil-producing region. Would-be cereal barons took advantage of the Battle Creek Medical and Surgical Sanitarium's reputation by prominently advertising that their products, too, were "Made in Battle Creek." With no regulations in place to prevent fraud, some cereal companies extolled the exaggerated health benefits of their products. At its peak, the cereal boom spawned forty-four

companies hoping to create the next profitable product in the ready-to-eat breakfast cereal market. Few of the early cereal companies survived the boom, but Kellogg's and Post continued their success; another contemporary, the Battle Creek Cereal Food Company, became part of the Ralston Purina Company in 1927.

The breakfast cereal industry continued to grow throughout the twentieth century, aided by the burgeoning advertising industry. These multibillion dollar industries have changed the way many Americans start their days. In an ironic twist, the same product that started out as "health food" during the late nineteenth century would come under fire in the late twentieth century. Nutritional experts decried the amounts of sugar, processed flour, and artificial colors and flavors in a product that has been marketed primarily to children.

—*P. S. Ramsey*

FURTHER READING

Bruce, Scott, and Bill Crawford. *Cerealizing America: The Unsweetened Story of American Breakfast Cereal*. Boston: Faber & Faber, 1995. Overview of the American cereal industry, from its roots in Seventh-day Adventism and the health and diet movement to corporate mainstay.

Money, John. *The Destroying Angel: Sex, Fitness, and Food in the Legacy of Degeneracy Theory, Graham Crackers, Corn Flakes, and American Health History*. Amherst, N.Y.: Prometheus Books, 1985. Focuses on the more puritanical United States at the end of the nineteenth and beginning of the twentieth centuries and the products and practices designed to help fight patients' baser urges.

Schwarz, Richard W. *John Harvey Kellogg, M.D.* Nashville, Tenn.: Southern, 1970. A biography of John Harvey Kellogg, co-inventor of corn flakes, the first ready-to-eat breakfast cereal.

SEE ALSO: Summer, 1831: McCormick Invents the Reaper; 1840: Liebig Advocates Artificial Fertilizers; 1870-1871: Watch Tower Bible and Tract Society Is Founded; May 8, 1886: Pemberton Introduces Coca-Cola.

1894-1896
OTTOMANS ATTEMPT TO EXTERMINATE ARMENIANS

Troubled and angered by the extent of Armenian nationalism and opposition to Ottoman rule, Sultan Abdülhamid II is said to have killed more than 100,000 Armenians in acts of genocide that created an enormous outcry around the world. Great-power politics precluded any direct intervention, however, by the Western world.

ALSO KNOWN AS: Hamidian Massacres

LOCALE: Armenian Anatolia; Kurdistan; Turkish Armenia; Constantinople, Ottoman Empire (now Istanbul, Turkey)

CATEGORIES: Atrocities and war crimes; wars, uprisings, and civil unrest; diplomacy and international relations; human rights

KEY FIGURES

Abdülhamid II (1842-1918), Ottoman sultan, r. 1876-1909

Mihran Damadian (1863-1945), Armenian Hunchak revolutionary

Hamparsum Boyadjian (1867-1915), Armenian Hunchak revolutionary

SUMMARY OF EVENT

The Armenian people historically are residents of the region corresponding to the ancient kingdom of Van, located near the Caucasus on the plateau between the Black and Caspian Seas. After centuries of occupation by warring empires, the Armenians had to contend with further oppression by the Ottoman sultans in the 1860's, motivating the afflicted to offer resistance in the form of a nationalist movement. After protests by the Armenian mountaineer population for having to pay taxes to the central government and Kurdish chieftains, Ottoman troops were sent to subdue the population, resulting in widespread massacres.

A second wave of massacres came in 1875 in Zeytoun, but this wave had been merely a harbinger of things to come. With the loss of Ottoman control of the Balkans and the dwindling income of the empire, the Armenians continued to be targets of insidious political and military terror. In 1894-1896, there was another series of massacres in Sassoun, which then spread to other parts of Turkish Armenia. When Mihran Damadian and Hamparsum Boyadjian, two leaders of the Hunchakists (a Marxist Armenian revolutionary party), tried to organize an armed insurrection (tacitly encouraged by Russia), the sultan characterized the protest and isolated acts of brigandage as an open revolt and ordered a ruthless massacre.

The massacre lasted twenty-four days between August 18 and September 10 and was horrifying in its scale. Young men were bound hand and foot, laid out in a row, and burned alive. Many men were bayoneted, women raped, children cudgeled to death, and unborn babies torn from their mothers' wombs. Churches were attacked and set on fire. Great Britain and the other great powers refrained from action. Armenians were of marginal significance to the Western leaders who had imperial, colonial, and mercantile aspirations in the Ottoman Empire. Instead of intervening directly, the Powers crafted the May reform project that the sultan would stall and finally reject. No reparation or remedy was ever afforded the Armenians.

Ottoman sultan Abdülhamid II. (R. S. Peale/J. A. Hill)

ARMENIAN MASSACRES, 1894-1896

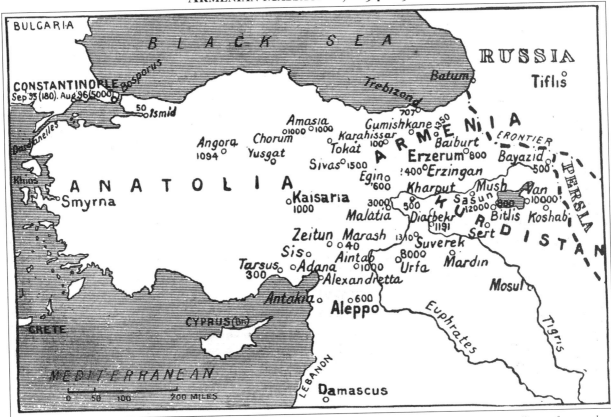

Contemporary map of the Armenian massacres, with estimated numbers of people killed at each site. The spellings of many place names differ from modern spellings but should be recognizable.

In September of 1895, members of the Hunchak committee of Constantinople organized a demonstration that was to move from the cathedral of Kumkapi to the Sublime Porte (High Gate of the palace and chief office of justice), where a memorandum was to be placed that denounced the massacre of Armenians, the mistreatment of prisoners, corrupt tax collectors, the migration of nomadic Kurds to Armenian *vilayets* (main administrative districts), and the lack of equality before the law. The document also demanded reforms of police and gendarmerie, economic changes, and a general amnesty of Armenians in detention or exile. The demonstrators (roughly four thousand persons) were split into groups, one of which became involved in a bloody incident.

Major Servet Bey, the aide-de-camp of the minister of police, insulted a student who had challenged his authority, only to have the Armenian shoot him dead with a revolver, propelling a Turkish retaliation that was immediate and brutal. Soldiers and police rushed upon the

demonstrators, killing forty and wounding hundreds. In another section of town, Kurds hunted down Armenians (even infants and the elderly) and clubbed them to death as Turkish police and soldiers often watched silently or joined in the murders. As the massacres continued for the next week, those who suffered the most were the poor working classes, but no Armenian of any social class was safe. Turks surrounded and burned churches, where thousands of Armenians had sought refuge.

The sacrilegious acts accentuated the deep religious animosity of Muslim Turks against Christian Armenians, an animosity that was stoked to fever-heat by the sultan and his Ottoman henchmen, who exploited the theocratic principle of *ummet* (a grouping of peoples sharing the same religion) to deepen the cleavage between Turks and Armenians. Historians tend to see the massacre at Sassoun as having facilitated the Constantinople carnage and for paving the way for the outbreak of empirewide massacres.

On October 2, 1895, after two unknown assailants shot and wounded Bahri Paşa, the notorious former governor of Van, and the local commandant in Trebizond—where seven thousand Armenians lived—armed Turks attacked the Armenian quarter under the pretext of searching for the attackers. As the governor sent telegraph reports to Sultan Abdülhamid II on the progress of the massacre, soldiers and brigands devastated the Armenian community. Unsuspecting pedestrians and innocent shopkeepers were shot in the street; stores and homes were ransacked with the intention of impoverishing and blotting out all Armenians. By the end of the slaughter (which started and ended with a bugle signal), 920 Armenians lay dead and the rest faced starvation. What became known as the autumn killings continued in various Armenian districts.

The historical record is appallingly gruesome: unprovoked attacks on Armenians at Akhisar; major massacres at Bitlis and Gumush-khana (October 25), where survivors were forced to convert to Islam; eight hours of pillaging and killing in Baiburt on October 27; a two-day massacre at Urfa (October 27-28) precipitated by a quarrel between a Turk and an Armenian, leading to their deaths and a full-scale attack by the whole Turkish-Kurdish population; and agony in Erzerum (October 30), where all night and day Armenians were slaughtered and hung from butchers' hooks before their bodies, soaked in oil, were thrown onto fires. The fundamental patterns in all the attacks remained the same: the deliberate provocation of the Armenians to instigate a protest or quarrel or bloody incident, followed by massive retaliation by the provokers.

In mountainous Zeytoun, Armenians felt threatened by the influx of new Turkish military units, the erection of new barracks and munitions depots, and social and economic injustices. Turks would "buy" goods without paying for them, sexually molest children, verbally abuse priests and mountaineers, and resort to tax-related acts of confiscation. After Zeytounis retaliated for the burning down of select villages, the Turks engaged them in ferocious battles. However, the fifteen hundred insurgents, equipped with only flintlock and old rifles, could not be broken. Beyond the massive battlefield casualties in the course of the uprising (October 24, 1895-February 2, 1896), thousands of Turkish soldiers froze to death in subzero winter temperatures, and thousands of others died from their wounds.

The six Western powers—Great Britain, Austria, Italy, Germany, Russia, and France—offered to mediate the matter, and an accord was put into effect on February 12, 1896. The sultan agreed to tax relief for the Zeytounis and to specific reforms in law and government. In return, the Armenians surrendered their weapons, and their four top leaders were expelled from the Ottoman Empire. In this way, Zeytoun escaped the massacres, while the sultan was saved from an alarming situation.

Although organized for defense, Van was the target of a massacre that lasted nine days (June 15-23, 1896). Leaders of the three Armenian parties established a Joint Directorate of Defense, with 200 armed and 700 unarmed men in the Armenakan group, 125 in the socialist Dashnak contingent, and only 25 in the well-disciplined Hunchak. In the intense, last-ditch battle, only 35 Armenians survived and the cream of their youth and intellectuals perished. Farther from Van, in the outlying villages, Armenian losses were even greater, though only rough estimates exist on the number of casualties.

Following the examples of the Armenakans and Hunchaks in the organization of the Sassoun outbreak and Grand Porte protest, a small band of Dashnaks in August 14-26, 1896, raided and captured the Ottoman Bank (which contained flourishing British, French, and other European investments). Running low in ammunition and fearing Turkish vengeance and European rejection, the rebels agreed to mediation, which led to the rebel's surrender and exile in France. Government reprisals against the Armenian population resulted in nearly six thousand fatalities in three days, fatalities suffered within sight of the European embassies.

SIGNIFICANCE

The Hamidian Massacres, as they are also called, showed the ability of the Turks to implement a systematic policy of murder and plunder against a minority population and to grant immunity to criminal parties in the face of international protest. When it was found that police repression alone could not prevent the renaissance of a major communal group, a policy was devised by which to reduce that group, seriously harm its economic base, humiliate its leadership, and reassert the strength of the Turkish government.

In addition to showing that collective punishment could take the form of mass murder, the massacres taught several lessons. One lesson was that a communal group could be seen as a threat to the establishment by virtue of its ideology and ability to influence its social and political context. A second lesson was that the group could seem a threat if it appeared to be linked to external powers dangerous to the ruling class or state. A third lesson was that the faster and higher a group rose, the more in-

1890's

tense would become the government's opposition to that group, leading to violence and massacres. The massacres of 1894 to 1896 set a precedent for the twentieth century Armenian genocide and, indeed, for the subsequent genocide of European Jews by the Nazis.

—*Keith Garebian*

FURTHER READING

Dadrian, Vahakn N. *The History of the Armenian Genocide: Ethnic Conflict from the Balkans to Anatolia to the Caucasus.* New York: Berghahn Books, 2003. An Armenian historian's account of the breakdown of Armenian-Turkish relations during and after Abdülhamid II's reign.

_____. *Warrant for Genocide: Key Elements of the Turko-Armenian Conflict.* New Brunswick, N.J.: Transaction, 1999. Excellent on the advent of Armenian revolutionaries and the Ottoman Turkish backlash. Extensive end notes.

Kirakossian, Arman J. *The Armenian Massacres, 1894-1896: U.S. Media Testimony.* Detroit, Mich.: Wayne State University Press, 2004. Reprints of a number of articles and essays from the period of the massacres.

Ternon, Yves. *The Armenians: History of a Genocide.* Translated by Rouben C. Cholakian. Delmar, N.Y.: Caravan Books, 1981. A good overview of the revolutionary movement, the massacres, and the twentieth century genocide. Includes notes, a bibliography, and a geographical index.

SEE ALSO: Mar. 1, 1811: Muḥammad ʿAlī Has the Mamlūks Massacred; May, 1876: Bulgarian Revolt Against the Ottoman Empire; Apr. 24, 1877-Jan. 31, 1878: Third Russo-Turkish War.

RELATED ARTICLES in *Great Lives from History: The Nineteenth Century, 1801-1900:* Abdülhamid II; Clara Barton.

January 4, 1894
FRANCO-RUSSIAN ALLIANCE

The Franco-Russian alliance was formed to offset the power of the Triple Alliance between Italy and the Austro-Hungarian and German Empires. The combination of the two alliances divided Europe into two increasingly hostile diplomatic and military camps, setting the stage for World War I.

ALSO KNOWN AS: Dual Entente
LOCALE: Paris, France; St. Petersburg, Russia
CATEGORY: Diplomacy and international relations

KEY FIGURES

Alexander III (1845-1894), czar of Russia, r. 1881-1894

Nikolay Karlovich Giers (1820-1895), Russian minister of foreign affairs, 1882-1895

Gustave Louis Lannes (Marquis de Montebello; 1838-1907), French ambassador to Russia

Raoul Le Mouton de Boisdeffre (1838-1919), chief of the French general staff

Nikolay Obruchev (fl. late nineteenth century), chief of the Russian general staff

William II (1859-1941), emperor of Germany, r. 1888-1918

Otto von Bismarck (1815-1898), chancellor of the German Empire, 1871-1890

SUMMARY OF EVENT

The Franco-Russian alliance, concluded in 1894, represented the climax of the growing rapprochement between the two nations and also demonstrated the declining relationships each had experienced with Germany and Great Britain since 1885. Both France and Russia feared the preeminence of Germany in Europe, based on the Triple Alliance among Germany, the Austro-Hungarian Empire, and Italy. France could neither forgive nor forget the stinging defeat of 1871 and the loss of Alsace-Lorraine to the newly united German Empire. Tension between France and Germany was exacerbated by the Boulanger crisis of 1886-1889 and the increase in the size of the German army provided by the bills of 1887 and 1890. Russia for its part had pledged benevolent neutrality with Germany in the Reinsurance Treaty of 1887 if either should be attacked by a third great power, but Russia too was suspicious of Germany.

German chancellor Otto von Bismarck compromised any chance of friendship with Russia by persuading the Reichstag to put through a sharp increase of the German tariff on agricultural imports, an increase which proved to be injurious to Russian landowners. These landowners began to pay more heed to the anti-German propaganda put forth by the Pan-Slavs. Moreover, Bismarck forbade the Reichsbank to accept Russian securities as collateral for Russian industrialization loans. In 1890, William II dismissed Bismarck and decided to forego renewal of the Reinsurance Treaty. Four days before the old agreement expired, he signed the Heligoland Treaty with Great Britain, gaining the strategic North Sea island by granting the British some territorial concessions in Africa. Both Russia and France regarded the Heligoland Treaty as the basis of the Quadruple Alliance.

While Germany was Russia's chief rival on the Continent, Great Britain had thwarted the imperialistic hopes of Russia in the Middle East and in Asia. At the same time, Britain was France's rival in Africa and southeast Asia. Russia and France began to look toward each other for mutual trust and protection, although the wide divergence between the autocracy of the one and the republicanism of the other meant that their friendship grew slowly. A French loan of five hundred thousand francs to Russia in December of 1888 helped to nullify Bismarck's financial sanction, and larger loans were given by France to Russia in the following year. In return, Russia agreed to purchase five hundred thousand rifles from France.

In July of 1891, Czar Alexander III and Nikolay Karlovich Giers, the Russian minister for foreign affairs, played host to a French naval squadron at Kronstadt. The spectacle of the autocratic czar of all the Russias standing bareheaded at attention for the playing of the national anthem of republican France created a sensation throughout Europe. It was becoming clear that neither the Russian nor the French government would allow ideological differences to stand in the way of cooperation against the Triple Alliance. The enthusiasm generated by this visit paved the way in August for an exchange of notes between the two governments. In these notes, they agreed to mutual consultations if either were threatened by attack.

Czar Alexander and Giers remained cautious. It was not until August 17, 1892, that they were persuaded by the French to consider the draft of a military convention. General Raoul Le Mouton de Boisdeffre agreed on behalf of the French general staff to come to the aid of Russia if Russia were attacked by Germany or Austria supported by Germany. General Nikolay Obruchev agreed on behalf of the Russian general staff to aid France if France were attacked by Germany or Italy supported by Germany. Both France and Russia agreed not to conclude a separate peace. It was not, however, a binding agreement, because the czar and Giers refused to ratify the agreement until 1893.

Editorial cartoon by John Tenniel (1820-1914) depicting the German emperor William II as a ship's captain dismissing his pilot, Otto von Bismarck. The caption reads, "Dropping the pilot. The Prussian Bully has no further use for Prince Bismarck."

Giers was particularly concerned about the terms of the military convention, which had been worked out by Boisdeffre and Obruchev without the participation of any representative of the Foreign Ministry. The two military men were naturally concerned with strictly military issues rather than the general political context. They focused their attention on how wars could be won rather than on how they might be averted or limited. Giers was reluctant to assume military obligations toward France that might seriously restrict Russia's room to maneuver in a diplomatic crisis. Nevertheless, a series of events undercut his resistance to the military convention.

In 1893, Great Britain appeared to move closer to the Triple Alliance, Germany increased its army even further, and the visit of the French fleet to Kronstadt was returned by an equally cordial visit of the Russian fleet to Toulon in October. Czar Alexander became convinced that Russia should ratify the military convention with France despite Giers's reservations. Finally, on December 27, Giers notified the French ambassador to St. Petersburg, Gustave Louis Lannes, the marquis de Montebello, that Russia formally approved the draft of the military convention that had been drawn up by the chiefs of the French and Russian general staffs in August of 1892. Lannes, who had worked hard to secure agreement, was able to announce the approval of the French government on January 4, 1894.

SIGNIFICANCE

The Franco-Russian alliance, or the Dual Entente as it came to be called, divided Europe into two armed camps in the decade before 1914. For ten years before 1914, it tended to stabilize rather than endanger the tranquillity of the Continent. France felt secure against Germany, and Russia believed that it had obtained greater assurance than before. Both countries saw the alliance as a means of countering the challenge given by British imperial policy outside Europe, and there were actually occasions in 1894 and 1895 when the Franco-Russian alliance made common cause with Germany against Great Britain.

The balance of power shifted between the Dual Entente and the Triple Alliance, as Italy virtually deserted the latter in 1902 and then Britain began to make overtures to the former. Faced with a serious German challenge to Britain's naval supremacy, the British government decided in 1904 to settle its colonial rivalries with France in Africa and southeast Asia. Britain and Russia reached a similar agreement in 1907 concerning long-standing differences in the Middle East and Asia. Clashes for supremacy in Morocco and in the Balkans continued to be heated. After 1904, however, international crises of these types began to be seen against the background of two gigantic armed camps created by competitive alliances, and events in 1914 brought about international conflict in World War I.

—*Edward P. Keleher, updated by Richard D. King*

FURTHER READING

Berghann, V. R. *Imperial Germany, 1871-1918: Economy, Society, Culture, and Politics*. Rev. and expanded ed. New York: Berghahn Books, 2005. Comprehensive and accessible survey of Germany history, organized thematically. Includes a chapter on foreign policy before and after World War I.

Bridge, F. R., and Roger Bullen. *The Great Powers and the European States System, 1815-1914*. New York: Longman, 1980. A concise introduction to European international relations from the defeat of Napoleon to the outbreak of World War I.

Kennan, George F. *The Fateful Alliance: France, Russia, and the Coming of the First World War*. New York: Pantheon Books, 1984. Diplomat and historian George Kennan produced this informative study of the negotiations that resulted in the Franco-Russian alliance in 1894.

Kennedy, Paul. *The Rise and Fall of the Great Powers: Economic Change and Military Conflict from 1500 to 2000*. New York: Random House, 1987. A sweeping history that examines the impact of economic change on international politics since the Renaissance.

Kissinger, Henry. *Diplomacy*. New York: Simon & Schuster, 1994. A historical account of statesmanship and the balance of power since the seventeenth century.

Langer, William L. *The Franco-Russian Alliance, 1890-1894*. Cambridge, Mass.: Harvard University Press, 1929. Reprint. New York: Octagon Books, 1977. More than a history of Franco-Russian relations, this book studies European diplomacy from the fall of Bismarck to the signing of the alliance.

MacKenzie, David. *Imperial Dreams, Harsh Realities: Tsarist Russian Foreign Policy, 1815-1917*. Fort Worth, Tex.: Harcourt Brace College, 1994. An introduction to the history of Russian foreign policy during the last century of the czarist regime.

Taylor, A. J. P. *The Struggle for Mastery in Europe, 1848-1918*. Oxford, England: Clarendon Press, 1954. A classic history that studies in detail the operation of the balance of power in Europe.

SEE ALSO: Jan. 18, 1871: German States Unite Within German Empire; May 6-Oct. 22, 1873: Three Emperors' League Is Formed; June 13-July 13, 1878: Congress of Berlin; May 20, 1882: Triple Alliance Is Formed; Jan., 1886-1889: French Right Wing Revives During Boulanger Crisis; 1889: Great Britain Strengthens Its Royal Navy; May 18-July, 1899: First Hague Peace Conference.

RELATED ARTICLE in *Great Lives from History: The Nineteenth Century, 1801-1900:* Otto von Bismarck.

May 11-July 11, 1894
PULLMAN STRIKE

In the Pullman Strike, a major struggle between railroad management and labor resulted in federal intervention. The government successfully employed the Sherman Antitrust Act to prosecute the striking workers, setting a precedent that stood as an impediment to collective bargaining until the passage of the Clayton Antitrust Act in 1914.

LOCALE: Pullman, Illinois

CATEGORIES: Business and labor; government and politics; laws, acts, and legal history; social issues and reform

KEY FIGURES

Eugene V. Debs (1855-1926), president of the American Railway Union

George Mortimer Pullman (1831-1897), president of the Pullman Palace Car Company

Thomas W. Heathcoate (fl. late nineteenth century), chairman of the Pullman strike committee

Clarence Darrow (1857-1938), special counsel to the American Railway Union

Edwin Walker (fl. late nineteenth century), special counsel to the General Managers Association and special federal attorney during the strike

John Peter Altgeld (1847-1902), governor of Illinois

Grover Cleveland (1837-1908), president of the United States, 1885-1889, 1893-1897

Richard Olney (1835-1917), U.S. attorney general

John P. Hopkins (1858-1918), mayor of Chicago, 1893-1895

SUMMARY OF EVENT

The Pullman Strike of 1894 was one of the farthest reaching labor-management disputes in United States history. Conducted in the midst of the most catastrophic depression to date, it was the most dramatic of a large number of strikes affecting the nation. The labor upheaval started in Pullman, Illinois, nine miles south of Chicago. What began as a dispute between the Pullman Palace Car Company (PPCC) and three thousand employees developed into a bitter struggle between twenty-four railroads serving Chicago and the American Railway Union (ARU), whose members voted to support their striking brethren in Pullman by boycotting Pullman cars. Before the strike ended, railroad traffic was stopped from Ohio to California, and the federal government had intervened in support of the PPCC and the railroads.

The town of Pullman was already famous. Built in 1880 by George Mortimer Pullman, the town was widely, although not universally, acclaimed as a unique experiment. It housed all the essentials of life, from food stores to educational and entertainment centers to a multidenominational church. Despite the intentions of its founder, however, it was not a happy place. The preponderance of men among its 8,603 inhabitants indicated a social instability caused partly by George Pullman's refusal to sell homes to his workers. The rents, fixed by Pullman to provide a return of 6 percent, were higher than in nearby towns. There was little democracy in the town government, and the company interfered with elections.

As landlord, George Pullman imposed middle-class values that restricted his workers' personal freedom. Among other things, they resented the strict prohibition of alcoholic beverages. Sufficiently concerned with his workers' souls to erect a community church, Pullman rented the structure at fees too high for most religious denominations to pay. Additional grumbling occurred over company charges for utilities. Residents claimed that company spies watched them, and in the plant workers suffered from blacklisting and a policy of granting nearly absolute power to shop foremen.

In the depression of the 1890's, while continuing to pay the usual dividends of 8 percent, the company drastically cut wages. Wage cuts of 30 to 50 percent, without corresponding cuts in already high rents, made it difficult for workers to provide adequate care for their families. In response, the workers formed a grievance committee to discuss their situation with the company. The vice president met with the committee, promising that no reprisals would be taken against workers for voicing their concerns. However, he then proceeded to fire three committee leaders, convincing many workers that a strike remained as the only practical option.

By the spring of 1894, desperate workers began flocking to the ARU, which, under the leadership of Eugene V. Debs, had recently won an astounding victory over the Great Northern Railroad. Led by Thomas W. Heathcoate, the chairman of the Pullman Strike committee, the emboldened workers decided to strike the PPCC on May 11. A month later, despite Debs's opposition, an ARU convention voted to stop handling Pullman cars after the company ignored efforts to settle the dispute. The union, by detaching Pullman cars from the trains, sought to deplete the revenues of the PPCC and force negotiations. Anticipating trouble with the railroads, Debs tried unsuccessfully to get support from the railroad brotherhoods, which opposed his industrial unionism, and from Samuel Gompers of the American Federation of Labor, who charged Debs with dual unionism. African American railroad workers were less than cooperative. In spite of Debs's urging, African Americans had been barred from ARU membership in a narrowly passed provision to the ARU constitution.

Although Pullman workers received support from the ARU, the PPCC found stronger allies in the railroads, already organized into the General Managers Association (GMA), an organization of twenty-four railroad companies operating in or through Chicago. The railroads were determined to honor their contracts with the PPCC, insisting that trains run with Pullman cars attached. Alarmed at the rapid growth of the ARU, they were eager for a chance to crush it. The strike began on June 26, with workers either walking off the job or detaching Pullman cars. Railroad workers in twenty-three states honored

the strike, producing a rapid halt in most freight traffic. The GMA retaliated by recruiting strike breakers. Fearing federal intervention, Debs ordered that violence be avoided and offered to operate passenger and mail trains without Pullman cars attached. The railroads refused. By the end of June, fifty thousand workers were idle across two-thirds of the country, and a stalemate had been reached.

From Washington, D.C., the administration of President Grover Cleveland followed the strike with growing alarm, while in Illinois, Chicago Mayor John P. Hopkins and Governor John Peter Altgeld, both sympathetic toward the union, kept police and National Guardsmen alerted for possible trouble. With local police ready to preserve law and order but unwilling to break the strike, the GMA worked through subterfuge to involve the federal government. Hoping to create public discontent, the GMA permitted transportation inconveniences, rejected freight shipments, and curtailed passenger service. Meanwhile, Attorney General Richard Olney, a former railroad lawyer, instructed federal district attorneys to

U.S. troops protecting a train during the railroad workers strike. (Library of Congress)

punish those stopping the mail. On June 30, Olney hired additional federal marshals, although mail trains continued to run on schedule. Next, he named Edwin Walker, a counsel to the railroads, as special federal attorney. Walker, in effect, assumed command of Justice Department affairs in Chicago.

On July 1, rioting broke out in a Chicago suburb which, together with exaggerated and alarmist newspaper reports of violence, gave Olney an excuse to intervene. On July 2, the federal government secured an injunction against the ARU under the Sherman Antitrust Act, and the next day President Cleveland, ignoring Governor Altgeld, sent in federal troops to protect the United States mails. At the time, local officials had the situation in hand and Altgeld stood ready to use National Guardsmen if needed. The use of the Sherman Antitrust Act against a union, which Congress never intended, was only slightly less startling than the terms of the injunction issued by two federal judges with railroad sympathies. In a sweeping denial of basic rights, the court enjoined union leaders from communicating with their own membership. Had this order been obeyed, it would have destroyed the ARU. On advice of special counsel Clarence Darrow, Debs ignored the injunction, an action for which he later went to jail.

Far from restoring order, the arrival of federal troops led to increased violence on July 5 and 6, when mobs destroyed more than $340,000 worth of railroad property. Unqualified and hastily deputized federal marshals contributed to the violence. With the arrest of ARU leaders on conspiracy charges, however, the strike weakened. By July 11, trains were operating in most of the nation, although the strike continued officially for three more weeks.

SIGNIFICANCE

Apart from property damage, forfeited earnings and wages, and business losses, the Pullman Strike destroyed the ARU as an effective organization. It introduced new and threatening antilabor weapons, and it led to the eventual dissolution of the model town of Pullman after repeated court suits. Finally, although a presidential commission subsequently absolved the strikers of all responsibility, Debs lost faith in the capitalist system and became a devout convert to socialism during his six months of incarceration. The strikers were also casualties. Many workers returning to their jobs found out that they had been permanently replaced and blacklisted from future railroad work. The failure of the strike was a major defeat for labor unions in the United States. The

ARU had fought an unenviable two-front war against organized management and concerted efforts by the federal government to stop the strike. Few would venture such a battle again.

—Merl E. Reed, updated by Irwin Halfond

FURTHER READING

Brommel, Bernard J. *Eugene V. Debs, Spokesman for Labor and Socialism*. Chicago: Kerr, 1978. Based on manuscript sources, this biography provides an excellent overview of Debs's life and his role in the Pullman Strike.

Ginger, Ray. *The Bending Cross: A Biography of Eugene V. Debs*. New Brunswick, N.J.: Rutgers University Press, 1949. Reprint. Kirksville, Mo.: Thomas Jefferson University Press, 1992. Still the most readable and reliable biography of the great labor leader to date. The 1992 reprint offers a new bibliography and pictures.

Lindsey, Almont. *The Pullman Strike*. Chicago: University of Chicago Press, 1942. Although dated and written in dramatic form, this is a good starting point for the background and major events of the Pullman Strike.

Potter, David M. *The Chicago Strike of 1894: Industrial Labor in the Nineteenth Century*. New York: Holt, Rinehart and Winston, 1963. The best overview for the general reader of the forces leading up to and the events of the Pullman Strike.

Smith, Carl S. *Urban Disorder and the Shape of Belief: The Great Chicago Fire, the Haymarket Bomb, and the Model Town of Pullman*. Chicago: University of Chicago Press, 1995. Provides an interesting sociological account of the conditions among the railroad workers that made the Pullman Strike possible, if not inevitable.

Warne, Colston E., ed. *The Pullman Boycott of 1894: The Problem of Federal Intervention*. Boston: D. C. Heath, 1955. Presents views by the major participants and investigative materials by U.S. government agencies.

SEE ALSO: Sept.-Nov., 1880: Irish Tenant Farmers Stage First "Boycott"; Dec. 8, 1886: American Federation of Labor Is Founded; Feb. 4, 1887: Interstate Commerce Act; July 20, 1890: Harrison Signs the Sherman Antitrust Act; July 4-5, 1892: Birth of the People's Party.

RELATED ARTICLES in *Great Lives from History: The Nineteenth Century, 1801-1900:* John Peter Altgeld; Grover Cleveland.

1890's

July 8, 1894-January 1, 1896
KABO REFORMS BEGIN MODERNIZATION OF KOREAN GOVERNMENT

Japan forced Korea to introduce the far-ranging Kabo reforms, intended to modernize the country along the Japanese model and to safeguard Japanese interests in Korea. The popularity and effects of the reforms were seriously undermined by the Japanese murder of Korean queen Min in 1895, and Korea aligned itself with Russia after 1896 and retreated from the reforms.

LOCALE: Korea

CATEGORIES: Government and politics; laws, acts, and legal history; diplomacy and international relations; social issues and reform

KEY FIGURES

Kojong (Yi Myong-bok; 1852-1919), king of Korea, r. 1864-1897, and emperor of Korea as Kwangmu, r. 1897-1907

Min (Myongsong Hwanghu; 1851-1895), queen of Korea, r. 1866-1895

Ōtori Keisuke (1832-1911), Japanese minister to Korea

Kim Hong-chip (1842-1896), Korean prime minister

Miura Gorō (1846-1926), Japanese minister to Korea

Taewon-gun (Yi Ha-ung; 1821-1898), Korean grand prince

Pak Yong-hyo (1861-1939), Korean cabinet minister and former rebel

Jung Bong-jun (d. 1895), Tonghak leader

SUMMARY OF EVENT

By the early 1890's, Japan had strong commercial and political interests in Korea. These were suddenly threatened by the Korean Tonghak Rebellion, which demanded not only better government but also expulsion of the Japanese from Korea. The quasi-religious Tonghak ("Eastern learning") movement (known as Ch'ŏndogyo, or "religion of the heavenly way," after 1905) arose in Korea during the mid-nineteenth century. Its founder, Cho'oe Che-u, was executed in 1864. By 1893, the movement petitioned the Korean king Kojong to exonerate its dead leader. Kojong refused in spite of mass appeal, and the Tonghak rose in rebellion.

In spring, 1894, the Tonghak brought much of southwestern Korea under their control. On May 31, their new leader, Jung Bong-jun, captured the town of Chŏnju, south of Seoul. Alarmed, the Korean government secretly requested Chinese help on June 3. Japan decided also to send troops to Korea. Between June 8 and 10, Chinese warships brought twenty-five hundred soldiers to the Korean town of Asan, south of Seoul. On June 9, the Japanese minister to Korea, Ōtori Keisuke, arrived at Inch'ŏn and marched into Seoul with three hundred marines. On June 10, while Japanese warships landed more soldiers, Korean officials made peace with the Tonghak. They agreed to the Tonghak's reformist demands, aimed at ending misrule and despotism and bestowing more rights to common people. Jung Bong-jun, satisfied, put down his arms and left Chŏnju.

With both Japanese and Chinese troops in Korea, Japanese prime minister Itō Hirobumi proposed that Korea be forced to modernize. China refused and argued for mutual troop withdrawal, which would return the Korean status quo. On June 26, Ōtori met King Kojong and demanded reforms. Two days later, he inquired if Korea still considered itself a vassal of China, as it had most recently expressed in October, 1882. On June 30, Korea declared its independence from China to Ōtori.

On July 3, Ōtori met Kojong and demanded sweeping administrative, economic, social, military, and educational reforms, modeled on Japan's modernization under the Meiji Emperor. Intimidated by the Japanese military, on July 8 Kojong set up a committee for reform that was to consult with Japanese advisors. This was the beginning of the Kabo reforms, named after the Korean name for the year 1894. The Korean committee considered the reforms, some of which were similar to those demanded by the Tonghak, as well as those demanded by the progressive party behind the failed Kapsin coup of December, 1884.

While it was still considering the reforms, Ōtori demanded that Korea break off relations with China. Faced with refusal, on July 23 Japanese troops arrested King Kojong and Queen Min and empowered the king's father, Yi Ha-ung, as the Taewon-gun or grand prince of Korea. On July 25, the Taewon-gun canceled Korea's treaty with China. On the same day, the Japanese defeated China in a naval battle off Korea. On July 29, the conflict between the Japanese and Chinese spread to the land of Korea, and on August 1, Japan declared war on China.

The Taewon-gun appointed Prime Minister Kim Hong-chip to supervise the Kabo reforms. The reforms effected a separation of the national and the royal household, established a ministry of finance also responsible for tax collection, and created an independent judiciary and police system. The reforms gave nobles and commoners equal legal status, ending the social status system that had separated them. They also abolished slavery and human trafficking. Certain professions, such as butchery, acting, and innkeeping, were freed from their previous social ostracism. Widows were allowed to remarry, and child marriage was abolished. There was an emphasis on good government and creating new educational opportunities, as the traditional Korean examination system was abolished. Korean currency was based on the silver standard, but Japanese currency was also allowed to circulate, benefiting Japan.

With the king and queen released, the pro-Japanese reformer Pak Yong-hyo was pardoned for his participation in the Kapsin coup. He returned to Korea from Japan and became a cabinet member on October 20. Considering the reformers to be Japanese puppets, in November, the Tonghak rebelled again. They were defeated by December, however; Jung Bong-jun was captured on December 30 and beheaded in April, 1895. On April 17, China signed the Treaty of Shimonoseki, formally conceding defeat and ending the Sino-Japanese War. Japan further encouraged Korean reforms. On June 23, 1895, the last of the 421 Kabo reform articles was promulgated.

Many Koreans associated the Kabo reforms with Japanese imperialism. Queen Min leaned toward Russia. Fearing for his life, reformer Pak fled for Japan on July 6, 1895. Japan grew exasperated at Korea's unwillingness to enforce the Kabo reforms. Queen Min was identified as the leading antagonist. The new Japanese minister to Korea, Miura Gorō, arrived in Seoul on September 3 with secret instructions to kill Queen Min. Miura gathered Japanese journalists and gangsters known as *sōshi*, as well as Japanese police and military men in Korea. Learning that Queen Min planned to disband a unit of Japanese-trained Korean soldiers, he acted. On October 5, he persuaded the Taewon-gun to support the conspiracy. At three in the morning on October 8, as ordered by Miura, a gang of Japanese woke the Taewon-gun and transported him to the royal palace, forcing their way inside.

As light broke, the Japanese seized Kojong and his son and demanded the king identify his queen. When he refused, the gangsters seized court ladies. Finally breaking into the queen's chambers, they saw a woman of royal stature and composure and mortally stabbed her. The Japanese stripped naked the dying woman, who was indeed Queen Min, and ogled her nude body before covering her in a bed sheet. They dragged the dying queen outside, killed three of her court ladies, and burned their bodies.

Miura pronounced the incident a coup of the Taewon-gun. The assassination was observed, however, by an American and a Russian living in the palace, so the world was alerted to the truth. Coming on the heels of Western accounts of the Japanese massacre of the Chinese population of Lüshun (Port Arthur) in November, 1894, the murder of Queen Min significantly harmed Japan's international reputation. Miura was recalled on October 19. The same month, Japan's Prime Minister Itō ended pressure on the Korean government to reform. One final reform installed the Western calendar in Korea on January 1, 1896. Forcing male Koreans to cut their topknotted hair met with such resistance that it was soon abandoned.

On February 11, 1896, Kojong escaped with his new consort, Lady Om, to the Russian legation in Seoul. From safety, he deposed Prime Minister Kim Hong-chip and other Kabo reformers, who were killed by a mob in the streets of Seoul. Japanese influence and the Kabo reforms were further challenged by another Korean uprising that was finally defeated by spring, 1896.

SIGNIFICANCE

Japan forced the Kabo reforms on the Korean government in order to safeguard its own economic and political interests. Even though the reforms were of a progressive nature, often along the lines previously demanded by Korean intellectuals, popular leaders, and rebels also seeking reform, they were forever associated with the Japanese invaders. The murder of the conservative Queen Min turned her into a Korean martyr. This further blemished the Kabo reforms.

Progressive Koreans tried to reap the benefits of the Kabo reforms by instituting the Independence Club (Tongnip Hyophoe) in Seoul in 1896. Kojong vacillated between promoting reform and insisting on royal prerogatives. In a desperate attempt to upgrade Korea's international standing, he pronounced himself emperor Kwangmu and turned the kingdom into the Taehan (Great Han) Empire on October 12, 1897. With members of the Independence Club pushing for democratic reforms, the emperor at first sought to accommodate them, but in December, 1898, he turned against the club and imprisoned many of its leaders.

The Kabo reforms failed to modernize Korea. During the early twentieth century, after defeating Russia in 1905, Japan finally annexed Korea in 1910. Any possible alliance of reformist Koreans and Japan failed in the face of naked Japanese imperialism.

—*R. C. Lutz*

1890's

FURTHER READING

Hatada, Takahashi. *A History of Korea*. Translated by Warren Smith and Benjamin Hazard. Santa Barbara, Calif.: ABC-Clio, 1969. Chapter 6 treats the Kabo reforms in the light of Korea's lost autonomy. Appendix, index, maps, and tables.

Joe, Wanne. *A Cultural History of Modern Korea*. Elizabeth, N.J.: Hollym Press, 2000. Includes a passionately pro-Korean, very detailed rendition of the reforms. Focuses on Korean nationalism. Illustrations, maps, notes, bibliography, index.

Keene, Donald. *Emperor of Japan*. New York: Columbia University Press, 2002. Biography of the Meiji emperor of Japan. Chapters 44, 45, and 47 give a detailed account of the Kabo reforms from a Japanese point of view. Notes, index, bibliography, illustrations.

Oliver, Robert. *A History of the Korean People in Modern Times*. Newark: University of Delaware Press, 1993. Chapters 3 and 4 treat the reforms and give biographies of Korean progressives. Notes, references, indexes.

Shin, Yong-ha. *Modern Korean History and Nationalism*. Translated by N. N. Pankaj. Seoul, Republic of Korea: Jimoondang, 2000. Chapter 3 deals with the Kabo reforms in light of the failed Tonghak Rebellion and focuses on Korean nationalism. Bibliography, glossary, index.

Tennant, Roger. *A History of Korea*. London: Kegan Paul International, 1996. Chapters 30 and 31 deal with the Kabo reforms. Notes, bibliography, index.

SEE ALSO: Jan. 3, 1868: Japan's Meiji Restoration; 1870's: Japan Expands into Korea; July 23, 1882-Jan. 9, 1885: Korean Military Mutinies Against Japanese Rule; Feb. 11, 1889: Japan Adopts a New Constitution; Aug. 1, 1894-Apr. 17, 1895: Sino-Japanese War.

RELATED ARTICLE in *Great Lives from History: The Nineteenth Century, 1801-1900:* Mutsuhito.

August 1, 1894-April 17, 1895
SINO-JAPANESE WAR

The Sino-Japanese War was the first stroke in the development of modern Japanese imperialism. Followed by the Russo-Japanese War a decade later, it propelled Japan to world power status and established a Japanese hegemony in East Asia.

LOCALE: Japan; China; Korea
CATEGORY: Wars, uprisings, and civil unrest

KEY FIGURES

Heihachirō Tōgō (1848-1934), Japanese naval commander
Oyama Iwao (1842-1916), Japanese military commander
Tokutomi Sohō (1863-1957), Japanese political theorist and military strategist
Yoshida Shōin (1830-1859), Japanese political theorist
Friedrich Ratzel (1844-1904), German political theorist

SUMMARY OF EVENT

The Sino-Japanese War of 1894-1895 was the result of geopolitical tensions whose foundations lay in a newly established Japanese strategic culture that sought to project the nation's power and protect its security. This aggressive worldview was based upon an energetic military-industrial complex that had been created in the years directly following the Meiji Restoration and was driven by Japan's decision to adopt Western science and technology. By the latter part of the nineteenth century, Japan had developed an international philosophy based upon the application of European geopolitical thought to the empire's situation in East Asia. Japanese theorists such as Tokutomi Sohō began to create a grand strategy that reflected the geopolitical model found in the organic state theory of Friedrich Ratzel. Based upon social Darwinist principles, this system was predicated on the beliefs that, like an organism, the nation-state had to grow or die and that only the strongest nations had the right to survive and prosper.

Sohō also incorporated into his geopolitical philosophy the theories of Yoshida Shōin, who earlier had written that Japan's long-term security depended on an aggressive, expansionist policy. Shōin was the first intellectual to forecast the potential dangers posed by Russia and China to Japan's security, and he identified the geopolitical importance of Manchuria and Korea to the future of the Japanese nation. Sohō synthesized the ideas of Ratzel and Shōin to develop the first Japanese imperialist theory. He advocated the establishment of an East Asian Japanese sphere of influence created by military

CHINA AND JAPAN

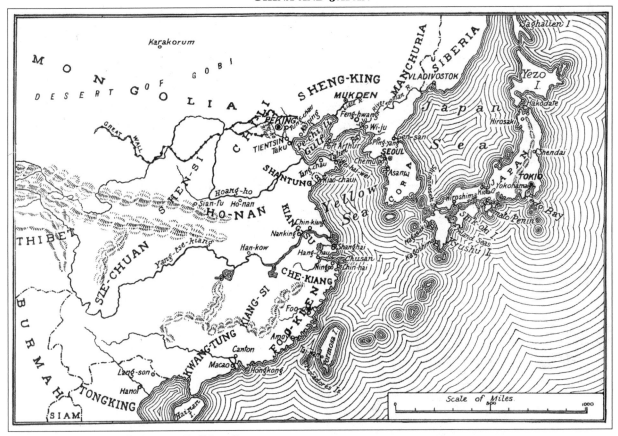

Note: Place names use nineteenth century English spellings.

conquest. Sohō believed such a sphere would establish Japan as a major force in world politics and enable it to expand Asia's "greatest civilization" into the rest of the region.

This theory gave rise to a grand strategy predicated upon economic and military strength. Japanese industrial success would provide both the wealth and the technology needed to develop a military capable of defending the nation against Western imperialism. The Meiji government began to create a new army based upon the German model. Every Japanese man would serve a period of active duty in which he would acquire the skills of the modern soldier. He would then be placed in the ready reserve, available for duty at any time over the next decade. The army again used the German model when it created a general staff to oversee its long-term planning, intelligence gathering, and logistical needs. This German connection also reinforced contemporary European geopolitical theories that called for imperial expansion

and warned against the acquisition of territory by foreign rivals within Japan's geographic realm of security.

The Japanese perception of encroachment by potential rivals began as early as the late 1850's, when France established control over parts of Southeast Asia that would become known as French Indochina. The French expansion coincided with the British acquisition of Burma and its competition with Russia over control of Central Asia. This so-called Great Game between Great Britain and Russia over the gateway to East Asia was viewed by Japan as a potential threat to its long-term security.

The Meiji government viewed the Great Game as all the more problematic because China was being ravaged by colonial partition and could not be counted on as an adequate buffer against European expansionism. Japan would eventually regard Russia as the greatest threat, when the Russians established a strong presence in northeast Asia and began to plan the construction of the Trans-Siberian Railroad. Japanese strategists viewed this great "heartland" power's ability to project its military might deep into Japan's strategic realm as a danger to the nation's security.

Japan's response to these geopolitical challenges was to attempt to establish control over the centuries-old East Asian "land bridge," Korea. This strategy would bring Japan into direct conflict with China. The Chinese for centuries had dominated Korea and believed they had the right to control the peninsula. When the Meiji government was first established, it had attempted to break China's centuries-long diplomatic dominance, but both Korea and China rejected Japan's advances, leading to increased tension among the three nations. These tensions increased until they caused a diplomatic crisis in 1875, when Chinese ships fired on Japanese naval vessels off the coast of Korea. The crisis was resolved with an agreement that granted Japan both economic and military privileges on the Korean peninsula.

Early in 1894, the corruption and inefficacy of the Ko-

Chinese herald reading the government's declaration of war against Japan. (Francis R. Niglutsch)

rean government led to the outbreak of the Tonghak Rebellion. Korea, unable to defeat the rebels, called upon its traditional protector, China, for assistance. Japan responded to the rebellion by sending in its own troops, bringing China and the Meiji government face to face on the peninsula. Japan, not content with the concessions it had gained in 1875, had been seeking an opportunity to bring Korea under its direct control since the early 1880's. Japanese strategists considered Korea to be the lynchpin in the nation's plans to keep the Europeans, especially the Russians, out of its sphere of influence. As the July Crisis of 1894 developed, both the Chinese and the Japanese military positioned themselves for action.

The first engagement took place in July, before war had been formally declared. Japanese ships, under the command of Captain Heihachirō Tōgō, engaged Chinese ships off the coast of Inchon Harbor, sinking a vessel that was attempting to transport a large contingent of Chinese troops to reinforce this strategic area. Instead, the Japanese landed a unit of marines and brought the harbor under the control of Japan's military. War was subsequently declared on August 1, 1894, and by September the Japanese had captured the strategic city of Pyongyang. This victory allowed the Japanese to drive deeply into Chinese territory, opening the northern half of the Korean peninsula to Japan's forces.

The Japanese navy then delivered a fatal blow to the Chinese fleet in the Battle of the Yellow Sea. Twelve Japanese men of war attacked the Chinese contingent, destroying most of its battleships and bringing the vital waterway under the control of Japan. The eastern coast of China was left undefended. When this development was coupled with another victory at the Yalu River, the Japanese were provided with a clear avenue of attack at the most strategic fortification in the Chinese defensive line, the city of Lüshun (Port Arthur).

Constructed during the late nineteenth century, Lüshun was an Asian Maginot Line consisting of twenty-two fortified positions and protected by seventy large and extremely accurate artillery emplacements. These fortifications protected the Liaodong Peninsula, which was the terminal of the South Manchurian Railway. This important transportation system connected the area to all the major railroad lines in northern China. It was also to provide the linkage to the eastern section of the Trans-Siberian Railroad, whose construction was being organized by the Russian government. The

Japanese forces entering China after crossing the Yalu River. (Francis R. Niglutsch)

geopolitical significance of this peninsula made it a primary objective of the Japanese military.

The Chinese army believed that the fortifications at Lüshun were impenetrable, and this false sense of security emboldened them to launch a series of hostile actions that backfired, filling the Japanese forces with a terrible resolve. The Chinese military placed advertisements all over the city, offering money to anyone who produced the body of a Japanese soldier. The decapitated and mutilated remains of these soldiers were then placed hanging upside down around the Lüshun fortifications. The heads of the soldiers were placed on spikes in full view of the Japanese army.

Japan attacked Lüshun. General Oyama Iwao executed a brilliant attack, penetrating the fortifications; in short order, the invincible fortress fell to the Japanese forces. With both the Yellow Sea and Lüshun under Japanese control, Iwao launched another successful attack on Shantung Province. This victory left the Chinese capital of Beijing open to attack, and the Manchu forces sued for peace, signing the Treaty of Shimonoseki on April 17, 1895.

SIGNIFICANCE

The Sino-Japanese War of 1894-1895 altered the strategic situation in East Asia. China was forced to turn over the island of Taiwan, and this placed the Japanese navy within striking distance of the Chinese mainland. Japan also gained control over both Lüshun and the Liaodong Peninsula. This gave Japan a direct avenue of attack against Russian territory in northeast Asia. The Russian government concluded that force had to be used to remove the Japanese threat.

Shortly after the turn of the twentieth century, the two competitors clashed in the Russo-Japanese War of 1904-1905. Japan was once again successful, defeating both Russian naval and land forces. This victory catapulted Japan into a position of prominence in East Asia until 1945. Russia's disastrous defeat undermined czarist authority and initiated the Revolution of 1905.

—Richard D. Fitzgerald

FURTHER READING

Beasley, W. G. *Japanese Imperialism, 1894-1945*. Oxford, England: Clarendon Press, 1987. Provides an excellent overview of the history of modern Japanese imperialism. Maps, index.

Edgerton, Robert B. *Warriors of the Rising Sun: A History of the Japanese Military*. Boulder, Colo.: Westview Press, 1997. Gives a detailed account of the rise and evolution of the Japanese military from the late nineteenth century to the end of World War II. Maps, index.

Hoyt, Edwin P. *Japan's War: The Great Pacific Conflict*. New York: Da Capo Press, 1989. One of the most respected accounts of the causes and effects of Japanese militarism in East Asia. Maps, index.

SEE ALSO: Mar. 31, 1854: Perry Opens Japan to Western Trade; 1860's: China's Self-Strengthening Movement Arises; Jan. 3, 1868: Japan's Meiji Restoration; Apr. 6, 1868: Promulgation of Japan's Charter Oath; 1870's: Japan Expands into Korea; July 8, 1894-Jan. 1, 1896: Kabo Reforms Begin Modernization of Korean Government; Nov. 14, 1897: Scramble for Chinese Concessions Begins; May, 1900-Sept. 7, 1901: Boxer Rebellion.

RELATED ARTICLES in *Great Lives from History: The Nineteenth Century, 1801-1900:* Mutsuhito; Saigō Takamori.

October, 1894-July, 1906
DREYFUS AFFAIR

In the so-called Dreyfus affair, a Jewish French officer was wrongfully convicted of treason by the army, which then refused to exonerate him. The controversy over the affair undermined the conservative leadership of the French army, triggered a democratic reform of the officer corps, and led to laws mandating the separation of church and state in France.

LOCALE: Paris and Rennes, France; Devil's Island, French Guiana

CATEGORIES: Laws, acts, and legal history; military history; government and politics; religion and theology

KEY FIGURES

Alfred Dreyfus (1859-1935), French army officer convicted of treason

Émile Zola (1840-1902), prominent French novelist

Édouard Drumont (1844-1917), anti-Semitic editor of *La Libre Parole*

Ferdinand Walsin Esterhazy (1847-1923), French army officer who committed the crimes of which Dreyfus was convicted

Auguste Mercier (fl. late nineteenth century), French minister of war in 1894

Hubert Henry (1846-1898), French army officer involved in the affair

Georges Picquart (1854-1914), French army officer involved in the affair

SUMMARY OF EVENT

In October of 1894, Captain Alfred Dreyfus, an artillery officer serving on the general staff of the French army, was arrested and charged with selling French military secrets to the Germans. The charge by the Statistical Section, the counterespionage agency of the French army, was based entirely on circumstantial evidence. A letter enumerating a list, or *bordereau*, of certain military memoranda which the writer later hoped to send to the German military attaché, Colonel von Schwarzkoppen, was purloined from the latter's mail by a French spy and submitted to the French counterespionage unit. It exaggerated the significance of the document and wrongly inferred its author to be an artilleryman. The *bordereau* was handwritten, but Major Hubert Henry, the chief of intelligence, and his associate, Colonel Mercier du Paty de Clam, ignored the caution of professional graphologists and concluded that Dreyfus had written the list.

Aware of the possible diplomatic consequences of a public trial, the French government urged the minister of war, General Auguste Mercier, to move slowly and secretly. News leaked out, however, to the right-wing, anti-Semitic press, which clamored for vigorous prosecution of Dreyfus's treason. Succumbing to this pressure, Mercier ordered a court-martial. In a secret trial, Dreyfus was pronounced guilty on December 22, but only after seriously irregular procedures, such as keeping knowledge of crucial evidence from the defense. In addition, Major Henry was so certain of Dreyfus's guilt, despite flimsy evidence, that he lied before the court. Nevertheless, Dreyfus was sentenced to public degradation and to life imprisonment on Devil's Island in French Guiana.

The majority of French citizens who followed the trial were satisfied. Because Dreyfus was a Jew, the outcome was welcomed by anti-Semites such as Édouard Drumont, editor of *La Libre Parole*. However, the number of those who did not accept the verdict increased as the years passed. In addition to Dreyfus's family, these included Joseph Reinach, a Jewish politician and member of the Chamber of Deputies; Auguste Schuerer-Kestner, vice president of the Senate; and Major Georges Picquart, who had succeeded Henry as chief of the counterespionage Statistical Section.

In March of 1896, Picquart discovered fragments of an express letter that Schwarzkoppen had torn up unsent but which had been found by a French agent. This letter, known as the *petit bleu* (little blue), was addressed to Major Ferdinand Walsin Esterhazy, a scoundrel badly in need of money who was known to visit the German embassy. The letter proved that Esterhazy was in Schwarzkoppen's pay. Picquart became convinced that the original *bordereau* had been in the handwriting of Esterhazy, not Dreyfus. He laid the information before the French general staff, but to avoid reopening the Dreyfus case the War Office hushed up the matter and had Picquart transferred to another post. After Picquart had left the Statistical Section, Major Henry, to protect himself, his superiors, and the honor of the French army, forged and falsified evidence in order to strengthen the case against Dreyfus.

Angry at the treatment he had received, Picquart disobeyed orders and related the evidence he had gathered to a lawyer, who in turn contacted others known to be sympathetic to Dreyfus. Growing doubt that Dreyfus had been given a fair trial led to his case's being taken up by Georges Clemenceau, the Radical Republican and newspaper editor, and eventually to the publication of Émile Zola's famous article, "J'Accuse," January 13, 1898, in the newspaper *L'Aurore*. The famous novelist denounced the War Office for protecting Esterhazy while condemning an innocent man. Zola was brought to trial and convicted of libel for writing the article, but the sensationalism surrounding his trial renewed general interest in the Dreyfus case. Picquart was also arrested on trumped-up charges of divulging secret military documents.

The case was gradually transformed into the Dreyfus affair, the greatest public controversy to rock the Third Republic. The investigation was reopened, and Henry committed suicide when his forgeries were brought to light. The matter of Dreyfus's fate was almost lost in a nationwide furor that came close to resembling a civil

Alfred Dreyfus on trial. (The Co-Operative Publishing Company)

war. On one side were Drumont and other anti-Semites, ultranationalists, certain Roman Catholic organizations, such as the Assumptionist religious order, and the newspaper *La Croix*, gathered under the anti-Dreyfusard banner to defend an authoritarian, integrally Catholic vision of France, symbolized by the honor of the army, against its secularistic, Jewish, and socialist enemies.

On the opposing side were Clemenceau and the Dreyfusards, dedicated to the ideals of a secular, democratic republic, threatened at its foundations by the injustice done to Dreyfus and by the army's criminal attempts at a cover-up. At the peak of this conflict the government agreed to Lucie Dreyfus's request for a new trial for her husband. The case was handled eventually by a united Appeals Court. Its judges saw clearly that, on the basis of the evidence presented, Dreyfus had been wrongfully convicted. While this court could have simply reversed the original verdict, it ordered a second court-martial, to permit Dreyfus to be cleared by his peers.

The judges at the Rennes court-martial in September, 1899, were faced with a dilemma: If Dreyfus were found innocent, they would destroy the prestige of the former war minister, Mercier, who continued to believe that Dreyfus had been guilty. Such a decision would also endanger their own chances for promotion and their social standing. For these reasons, and because the defense handled the case poorly, the verdict once again went against Dreyfus, but this time his sentence was reduced. Ten days following the court-martial, President Émile Loubet, at the request of Prime Minister Pierre Marie René Waldeck-Rousseau, pardoned Dreyfus. The government and the army hoped that the Dreyfus affair had come to an end.

The controversy, however, was not over. Alfred Dreyfus and his family pressed for full restoration of his rank and honor. Radicals, socialist-radicals, and socialists continued to use the Dreyfus affair to attack the Assumptionists and other anti-Dreyfusard organizations, claiming that by lining up with those who opposed justice for Dreyfus, these institutions exposed their basic antirepublican nature. It took almost seven more years of legal work for justice to be served to its chief victims. On July 12, 1906, the Court of Appeals finally reversed his conviction. The legislature immediately restored Dreyfus and Picquart to the ranks they would have earned—major for the former and brigadier-general for the latter. On July 22, Dreyfus was awarded the Legion of Honor.

SIGNIFICANCE

The Dreyfus affair contributed to bitter criticism of and demoralization within the French army, to the dissolution of the religious congregations, and finally to the passage of a bill separating church and state in France in 1905. The Dreyfus affair had caused a serious breach in French society, which continued at least until the outbreak of World War I, and it helped to impel the French

---

"J'ACCUSE. . . !"

French novelist Émile Zola's open letter, "I Accuse . . . ! Letter to the President of the Republic," was published in L'Aurore *(the dawn) on January 13, 1898. An extremely long missive defending Alfred Dreyfus and attacking the French establishment, the letter takes its famous title from its conclusion, in which Zola leveled specific charges at those he considers responsible for the Dreyfus affair.*

I accuse Lt. Col. du Paty de Clam of being the diabolical creator of this miscarriage of justice—unwittingly, I would like to believe—and of defending this sorry deed, over the last three years, by all manner of ludicrous and evil machinations.

I accuse General Mercier of complicity, at least by mental weakness, in one of the greatest inequities of the century.

I accuse General Billot of having held in his hands absolute proof of Dreyfus's innocence and covering it up, and making himself guilty of this crime against mankind and justice, as a political expedient and a way for the compromised General Staff to save face.

I accuse Gen. de Boisdeffre and Gen. Gonse of complicity in the same crime, the former, no doubt, out of religious prejudice, the latter perhaps out of that esprit de corps that has transformed the War Office into an unassailable holy ark.

I accuse Gen. de Pellieux and Major Ravary of conducting a villainous enquiry, by which I mean a monstrously biased one, as attested by the latter in a report that is an imperishable monument to naïve impudence.

I accuse the three handwriting experts, Messrs. Belhomme, Varinard and Couard, of submitting reports that were deceitful and fraudulent, unless a medical examination finds them to be suffering from a condition that impairs their eyesight and judgement.

I accuse the War Office of using the press, particularly *L'Éclair* and *L'Écho de Paris*, to conduct an abominable campaign to mislead the general public and cover up their own wrongdoing.

Finally, I accuse the first court martial of violating the law by convicting the accused on the basis of a document that was kept secret, and I accuse the second court martial of covering up this illegality, on orders, thus committing the judicial crime of knowingly acquitting a guilty man.

---

insistence upon a state-church separation that remains among the most stringent in the world.

—*Harold A. Schofield, updated by Charles H. O'Brien*

FURTHER READING

Bredin, Jean-Denis. *The Affair: The Case of Alfred Dreyfus*. Translated by Jeffrey Mehlman. New York: George Braziller, 1986. A thorough, well-balanced work, especially useful for the legal process. The author also evokes the national passions that swirled around Dreyfus.

Brown, Frederick. *Zola: A Life*. New York: Farrar, Straus and Giroux, 1995. Massive, meticulously researched account of Zola's life, with analyses of all of his novels, set within the context of Second Empire and Third Republic France.

Chapman, Guy. *The Dreyfus Case: A Reassessment.* New York: Reynal and Hitchcock, 1955. A serious attempt to correct misconceptions fostered by partisans of Dreyfus. Chapman argues Dreyfus was the victim, not of anti-Semitism but of misplaced loyalties among the military.

Forth, Christoper E. *The Dreyfus Affair and the Crisis of French Manhood.* Baltimore: Johns Hopkins University Press, 2004. A gendered study of the Dreyfus Affair, relating contemporary French ideologies of masculinity to Dreyfus's Jewishness.

Halasz, Nicholas. *Captain Dreyfus: The Story of a Mass Hysteria.* New York: Simon & Schuster, 1955. A traditional interpretation, this work highlights the heroic aspects of the case: justice versus reason of state.

Hoffman, Robert Louis. *More than a Trial: The Struggle over Captain Dreyfus.* New York: Free Press, 1980. Focused on the controversy surrounding Dreyfus, a virtual civil war. Draws mainly on polemical tracts and other common artifacts of the struggle.

Kleeblatt, Norman L., ed. *The Dreyfus Affair: Art, Truth, and Justice.* Berkeley: University of California Press, 1987. This exhibition catalog includes eight diverse articles and several hundred photographs, caricatures, and other visual items.

Lindemann, Albert S. *The Jew Accused: Three Anti-Semitic Affairs (Dreyfus, Beilis, Frank), 1894-1915.* New York: Cambridge University Press, 1991. Places the anti-Semitism of the Dreyfus affair in comparative perspective and historical context.

Wilson, Stephen. *Ideology and Experience: Antisemitism in France at the Time of the Dreyfus Affair.* Rutherford, N.J.: Fairleigh Dickinson University Press, 1982. A well-documented study, explaining the social function of anti-Semitism in France at the time of the Dreyfus affair with special attention to Édouard Drumont.

SEE ALSO: July 26, 1858: Rothschild Is First Jewish Member of British Parliament; c. 1865: Naturalist Movement Begins; Jan., 1886-1889: French Right Wing Revives During Boulanger Crisis; Feb., 1896-Aug., 1897: Herzl Founds the Zionist Movement.

RELATED ARTICLE in *Great Lives from History: The Nineteenth Century, 1801-1900:* Émile Zola.

December 22, 1894
DEBUSSY'S *PRELUDE TO THE AFTERNOON OF A FAUN* PREMIERES

Often identified as marking the birth of modern music, Claude Debussy's nine-minute orchestral composition radically subverted traditional ideas of musical structure and tonality. It also deployed striking timbres and complex, fluctuating rhythms to create a dreamlike mood. Debussy's innovations made him one of the most influential composers in twentieth century music.

ALSO KNOWN AS: *Prélude à l'après-midi d'un faune*
LOCALE: Paris, France
CATEGORY: Music

KEY FIGURES

Claude Debussy (1862-1918), French composer
Stéphane Mallarmé (1842-1898), French poet
Richard Wagner (1813-1883), German operatic
  composer
Nikolay Rimsky-Korsakov (1844-1908), Russian
  composer
Arnold Schoenberg (1874-1951), Austrian composer

SUMMARY OF EVENT

Claude Debussy premiered his watershed composition, *Prélude à l'après-midi d'un faune* (*Prelude to the Afternoon of a Faun*) on December 22, 1894. His unprecedented use of sustained atonal passages dislocated the diatonic scale (a division of the octave into five whole-tone and two half-tone intervals), which had organized Western music since the beginning of classicism. His chromaticism—moving melodies and chords through a series of half-tone steps—drew upon the compositions of such precursors as Hector Berlioz, Frédéric Chopin, Robert Schumann, and Richard Wagner. However, his whole-tone progressions, the opposite musical extreme, represented the most decisive innovation in Western music until Arnold Schoenberg's perfection of the twelve-tone scales fifteen years later.

In 1889, when Debussy returned to Paris after a two-year fellowship in Rome, he had already gone twice to the annual festival of Richard Wagner's operas in Beyreuth. Debussy became one of the French popularizers and performers (in piano reductions of the orchestral operatic scores) of Wagner's music, whose harmonies and parallel chords appeared in Debussy's later orchestral works. He acquired several other influences as well: The Russian composer Nikolay Rimsky-Korsakov inspired Debussy's use of the flute in *Prelude to the Afternoon of a Faun*. The complex rhythms and the non-Western scales and timbres of Javanese gamelan music, which Debussy heard shortly after his return, also influenced him.

Debussy's original inspiration for his landmark piece was a long poem, *L'Après-midi d'un faune* (1876; *The Afternoon of a Faun*, 1956), by the master of French Symbolism, Stéphane Mallarmé. Mallarmé hosted a famous writers' and artists' salon on Tuesday afternoons. Debussy attended regularly and became friends with the older man. The two had even planned to collaborate in a stage production of *The Afternoon of a Faun*. In it, apparently, Mallarmé would have read sections of the poem aloud, interspersed with the performance of sections of Debussy's composition. Mallarmé postponed the event indefinitely, however, perhaps out of anxiety over the public reception.

In both the poem and the musical work, a faun—a mythic creature from ancient Greece, half-man and half-goat—awakens on a hot, drowsy summer afternoon from a dream in which he was about to ravish two nymphs he had surprised and seized while they were sleeping. They elude him and slip away, diving beneath the water of a pond. He tries to recapture them, first by retelling the adventure as a story, then by playing a melody on his panpipes that would recall the experience. When these two attempts fail, the faun fantasizes briefly about raping the queen of the gods, but, fearing punishment, he withdraws by falling asleep again, to seek the nymphs in his dreams.

Debussy's whole-tone and chromatic motifs thoroughly undermine a listener's sense of a dominant tonality. His orchestral composition opens with a dreamy, unaccompanied flute line starting on G-sharp, which proves to be the relative minor tone of the E-major scale. The flute plays the E, resolving the scale, only after thirty measures, during which it has drifted chromatically and played two "tritones," series of three successive whole-note intervals (an augmented fourth, or exactly one-half octave). Commonly known as the *diabolus in musica* (the devil in music), this traditionally forbidden sequence dislocates a melodic line from any clear sense of a dominant tonality.

The flute in the opening evokes the panpipes, conven-

tionally associated with Pan, the ancient Greek nature god, who once pursued and tried to rape the nymph Syrinx. Her sisters saved her by transforming her into a stand of reeds beside a pond. To commemorate his desire for her, Pan cut some of the reeds and made them into a musical instrument on which he often played. Fragments of Debussy's opening flute motif recur throughout the composition, but Debussy relies more heavily on distinctive musical timbres than on musical themes and their development. His violins suggest the rich emotional textures of the human voice and human sensibility; his harp arpeggios imply the sudden appearance and disappearance of the naiads, the water-dwelling nymphs. Skillfully harmonized, the prominent woodwinds create a lush, languorous, sensuous atmosphere. The piece's coda recapitulates its initial theme in a simplified form.

Debussy's piece seems to follow the poem closely at each stage. The music even has the same number of measures (110) as the poem has verses (classical twelve-syllable alexandrines). However, twentieth century composer Leonard Bernstein, arguing an opposing position with equal plausibility, claimed that *Prelude to the After-*

Claude Debussy. (Library of Congress)

noon of a Faun was actually an essay on the key of E major, flirting with the breakdown of conventional tonality only in order to retreat repeatedly from the brink. By contrast, Arnold Schoenberg's *Five Pieces* of 1909, by inventing and systematically applying the twelve-tone system, actually marks the origin of a new music, which then coexists with the old without ever replacing it.

SIGNIFICANCE

Few people attended the first performance of *Prelude to the Afternoon of a Faun*, but its impact has grown ever since. The Russian Vaslav Nijinski (1890-1950), among the greatest ballet dancers of all time, created a ballet with revolutionary choreography based on Debussy's composition. Debussy refused to adopt any familiar, consecrated musical form for the orchestra, such as the symphony or sonata. His whole-tone and chromatic motifs thoroughly undermined listeners' sense of a dominant tonality. His series of parallel chords (a device forbidden in conventional composition theory, although found in Wagner) overwhelmed habitual ideas of harmony and musical structure, as did his incomplete chord progressions, his parenthetical episodes (unrelated musical materials separating statements of the leading themes), and his contrapuntal juxtaposition and compression of two or more musical motifs at once. He developed these devices throughout his later orchestral works.

Debussy is widely known as the major "Impressionist" composer, by analogy with the Impressionist movement in painting. The title of several of Debussy's major orchestral compositions—*La Mer* (the sea), *Nuages* (clouds), *Fêtes* (parties), and *Jeux* (games)—seem to justify the label, because in them he seems to be "painting after nature." However, the composer himself strongly objected to being called "Impressionist," because, like his master Mallarmé, he was seeking to suggest moods and ideas, not to depict scenes.

Compared to Schoenberg's influence on modern music, the influence of Debussy has been the more profound and lasting. His example strongly affected Igor Stravinsky, Béla Bartók, George Gershwin, and Pierre Boulez, among many others. For this reason, he may be the most significant composer of the twentieth century.

—*Laurence M. Porter*

FURTHER READING

Bernstein, Leonard. *The Unanswered Question: Six Talks at Harvard.* Cambridge, Mass.: Harvard University Press, 1976. A definitive analysis of *Prelude to the Afternoon of a Faun* by a great conductor and teacher. Strongly rebuts the conventional opinion that Debussy was a striking innovator, convincingly explaining the piece as a conservative delaying action, as was Mallarmé's poem.

Brown, Matthew. "Tonality and Form in Debussy's *Prélude à l'après-midi d'un faune.*" *Music Theory Spectrum* 15, no. 2 (Fall, 1993): 127-143. Agreeing with Bernstein, Brown asserts that conventional tonal analysis can effectively explain the composition of the prelude, but that Debussy innovated by eliminating conventional harmonic cadences (resolutions), inserting parenthetical thematic episodes, compressing several themes into one polyphonic statement, and favoring recognizable tonal patterns over conventional melodies.

Code, David J. "Hearing Debussy Reading Mallarmé: Music Après Wagner in the *Prélude à l'après-midi d'un faune.*" *Journal of the American Musicological Society* 54, no. 3 (2001): 493-554. Cole carefully compares Debussy's score with Mallarmé's text, claiming that the composer was a careful, sophisticated reader who followed the poem much more closely than is commonly believed.

Debussy, Claude. *Prelude to the Afternoon of a Faun: An Authoritative Score; Mallarmé's Poem; Backgrounds and Sources; Criticism and Analysis.* Edited by William W. Austin. New York: W. W. Norton, 1970. Still the fundamental, essential reference text for students of music.

Griffiths, Paul. *A Concise History of Avant-Garde Music from Debussy to Boulez.* New York: Oxford University Press, 1978. Includes a dense, provocative discussion of Debussy's decisive, influential innovations in musical style.

Lesure, François, and Roy Howat. "Debussy (Achille-) Claude." In *The New Grove Dictionary of Music and Musicians*, edited by Stanley Sadie. 2d ed. London: Macmillan, 2001. An authoritative overview of the composer's life and works.

Lockspeiser, Edward. *Debussy: His Life and Mind.* 2 vols. Reprint. New York: Cambridge University Press, 1983. Chapter 14, "Mallarmé," traces the poet's influence on and friendship with the composer.

Parks, Richard S. *The Music of Debussy.* New Haven, Conn.: Yale University Press, 1989. A technical analysis of pitch, timbre, and structure in Debussy's music.

Staines, Joe, ed. *The Rough Guide to Classical Music.* London: Penguin Books, 2001. This user-friendly, non-technical guide contains intelligent, knowledge-

1890's

able comments on many major composers and compositions, and evaluates current recordings well. It lucidly contrasts Debussy with Schoenberg.

Wenk, Arthur. *Claude Debussy and Twentieth-Century Music.* Boston: Twayne, 1983. Explains the influences on Debussy of Javanese gamelan music, Symbolist poetry, and contemporary Russian composers. Discusses Debussy's circular rather than linear structure and his tonal organization.

SEE ALSO: Apr. 7, 1805: Beethoven's *Eroica* Symphony Introduces the Romantic Age; May 7, 1824: First Performance of Beethoven's Ninth Symphony; Jan. 2, 1843: Wagner's *Flying Dutchman* Debuts; Aug. 13-17, 1876: First Performance of Wagner's Ring Cycle.

RELATED ARTICLES in *Great Lives from History: The Nineteenth Century, 1801-1900:* Hector Berlioz; Nikolay Rimsky-Korsakov; Robert Schumann; Richard Wagner.

1895-1898
HEARST-PULITZER CIRCULATION WAR

The rival newspapers of Hearst and Pulitzer competed for readership by printing sensational news stories pitched at the lowest common denominator, thus inaugurating the modern conception of journalism for a mass audience.

LOCALE: New York, New York

CATEGORIES: Journalism; business and labor; crime and scandals

KEY FIGURES

William Randolph Hearst (1863-1951), owner of the *New York Journal*

Joseph Pulitzer (1847-1911), owner of the *New York World*

Morrill Goddard (fl. late nineteenth century), chief of Hearst's Sunday edition

Frederic Remington (1861-1909), Hearst's illustrator in Cuba

Richard Harding Davis (1864-1916) and

Karl Decker (fl. late nineteenth century), Hearst reporters in Cuba

Valeriano Weyler y Nicolau (1838-1930), commander of Spanish forces in Cuba

Enrique Dupuy de Lôme (1851-1904), Spanish minister to the United States

William McKinley (1843-1901), president of the United States, 1897-1901

SUMMARY OF EVENT

The pattern of modern journalism was established by Joseph Pulitzer. Born in Hungary in 1847, Pulitzer arrived in the United States in 1864 to fight with the Union Army. After the Civil War (1861-1865), the penniless young immigrant settled in St. Louis, Missouri, where, by virtue of his intelligence and hard work, he soon be-

came not only a successful reporter but also a lawyer and crusading politician. Pulitzer served in the Missouri legislature and worked as a reporter on the *St. Louis Post* and the *Westliche Post*, a leading midwestern German newspaper. In 1876, he purchased the *Post* and the *St. Louis Dispatch*, consolidating them into the *Post-Dispatch*. This venture was such a success that the young publisher turned his attention to the world of New York journalism. In 1883, he purchased the *New York World* from the financier Jay Gould, and in 1887 Pulitzer established the *Evening World*.

It was with the *World* that Pulitzer set the pattern for the so-called new journalism. Interesting news stories written in a simple, easily comprehended style were presented in a sensational manner to appeal to the widest possible reading audience. The *World* led crusades, such as collecting funds to build the pedestal for the Statue of Liberty, as well as exposés of the white slave traffic, the Louisiana lottery, the ill treatment of immigrants at Ellis Island, and the questionable activities of many large industrial concerns. Stunts also were part of the new journalism. The *World*, for example, sponsored a trip around the world by journalist Nellie Bly, who outdid Jules Verne's fictitious Phileas Fogg of *Le Tour du monde en quatre-vingts jours* (1873; *Around the World in Eighty Days*, 1873) by arriving back in New York after slightly more than seventy-two days. Newspaper illustrations appeared in the *World*, as did high-quality editorials. Pulitzer also conducted imaginative promotional campaigns to increase circulation.

In 1887, the twenty-four-year-old William Randolph Hearst assumed control of the *San Francisco Examiner*, succeeding his wealthy father. Copying Pulitzer's methods, Hearst soon transformed the newspaper into a model of journalistic sensationalism. Like Pulitzer, Hearst was confident that he could become successful in New York City. In 1895, after receiving $7.5 million from the sale of his father's mining stock, Hearst bought the *New York Morning Journal*. The Hearst-Pulitzer circulation war had begun.

Hiring brilliant journalists at any cost, Hearst soon staffed the *Journal* with the nation's brightest talent. The *Journal* carried so many illustrations and so emphasized scandal, crimes, and disaster that its circulation rose dramatically, causing Pulitzer to reduce the price of his morning paper to one cent. In the midst of the 1896 presidential election, Hearst established the *Evening Journal* to compete with Pulitzer's *Evening World*; by the end of 1897, the *Journal*, by continuing to stress sex-and-crime sensationalism, surpassed the *World* in circulation. Competition between Hearst and Pulitzer eventually focused on their Sunday editions, with Hearst finally buying away from the *World* all of its Sunday staff. The chief of

Hearst's Sunday edition, Morrill Goddard, pioneered in Sunday sensationalism by developing a panoply of crime, sports, pseudo-scientific articles, "lonely hearts" columns, and above all, a colored supplement of comics known as the *American Humorist*. It was the most popular of these comic characters, the "Yellow Kid," that led to the name "yellow press" to identify the Hearst-Pulitzer brand of sensational journalism.

Some historians have claimed that, had it not been for the Hearst-Pulitzer circulation war, there would have been no Spanish-American War. Although this is a questionable assertion, it is undeniably true that between 1895 and 1898 the *Journal* and the *World* conducted the most emotional campaign of jingoism in the history of U.S. journalism—a campaign that undoubtedly stimulated the fervor of countless people in the United States for war with Spain. Pictures, headlines, and news stories in these newspapers indicted the Spanish for perpetrating atrocities in Cuba. Concentration camps, the mutilation of women and children, and the gruesome activities of the Spanish commander, General Valeriano Weyler y Nicolau (nicknamed "the Butcher" by the papers), were daily fare in the *Journal* and the *World*.

Initially, the *World*'s correspondents were superior in uncovering or fabricating atrocity stories, but as the competition increased, Hearst dispatched more talent to Cuba. Perhaps the best known of his correspondents were writer Richard Harding Davis and illustrator Frederic Remington, whom Hearst sent to Cuba on his yacht *Vamoose*. Remington is reported to have sent Hearst a telegram that read, "Everything is quiet. There is no trouble here. There will be no war. Wish to return. Remington." To this, Hearst sent the prompt reply, "Please remain. You furnish the pictures and I'll furnish the war. Hearst."

Another of Hearst's reporters, Karl Decker, rescued Evangelica Cisneros, niece of Salvador Cisneros, the president of the rebel government, from a prison, smuggled her out of Cuba, and took her to New York and Washington, D.C., where she received a tumultuous welcome, including a meeting with President William McKinley. The *Journal* also printed the

Front page of the New York World *two days after the USS* Maine *exploded in Havana Harbor.* (Library of Congress)

"de Lôme letter," in which Enrique Dupuy de Lôme, the Spanish minister to the United States, called President McKinley a "would-be politician." Perhaps the height of the circulation war occurred after the U.S. battleship *Maine* exploded and sank in Havana harbor on February 15, 1898. No guilty party was ever discovered. However, the *Journal* immediately blamed the Spanish, proclaiming in banner headlines: "Destruction of the Warship *Maine* Was the Work of an Enemy." The *World* also exploited the sinking to inflame the nation's passion for war, and other newspapers joined in the outcry.

SIGNIFICANCE

As the circulations of both the *World* and the *Journal* passed one million, it was evident that other newspapers, such as the *Chicago Tribune*, *Chicago Times-Herald*, *Boston Herald*, and *San Francisco Chronicle*, also had begun to appreciate the benefits of the new journalism. More to the point, they had no choice but to emulate the tactics of Pulitzer and Hearst unless they wished to be driven out of business by competitors with fewer scruples. The tactics and methods of the Hearst-Pulitzer circulation war spread throughout the country, and they have continued to be staples of U.S. journalism ever since.

—*William M. Tuttle, updated by Michael Witkoski*

FURTHER READING

Brian, Denis. *Pulitzer: A Life*. New York: John Wiley & Sons, 2001. The only comprehensive biography since Swanberg. Relies heavily upon information contained in earlier works.

Littlefield, Roy. *William Randolph Hearst: His Role in American Progressivism*. Lanham, Md.: University Press of America, 1980. One of the Hearst newspapers' greatest claims was that they served as a spokesperson for the common American. The extent to which this was true, and Hearst's use and misuse of that role, is the crux of Littlefield's study.

Mott, Frank Luther. *American Journalism: A History, 1690-1960*. Boston: Houghton Mifflin, 1962. The single most valuable survey to date of U.S. newspapers throughout most of the nation's history. Especially pertinent when it comes to the Hearst-Pulitzer struggle for readership. Contains excellent reproductions of actual pages, which give a true feel for what journalism looked like during the period of the circulation wars.

Robinson, Judith. *The Hearsts: An American Dynasty*. Newark: University of Delaware Press, 1991. Although unique in many ways, William Randolph Hearst had a background and left a legacy. This volume places the Hearst family in the context of American life.

Swanberg, W. A. *Citizen Hearst: A Biography of William Randolph Hearst*. New York: Charles Scribner's Sons, 1961. Although it has been updated by specialized studies in some areas, this work remains the place to start for an understanding of Hearst and his career.

_____. *Pulitzer*. New York: Charles Scribner's Sons, 1967. Presents the basic, indispensable information about Hearst's great rival and one of the major figures in U.S. journalism. Shows the personal nature of the circulation struggle during the period of yellow journalism.

Turner, Hy B. *When Giants Ruled: The Story of Park Row, New York's Great Newspaper Street*. New York: Fordham University Press, 1999. This history of the New York City newspaper business during the mid-nineteenth and early twentieth centuries includes information about Pulitzer and the other publishers of the era. Chronicles the newspaper circulation wars and the contributions of reporters, illustrators, and cartoonists.

SEE ALSO: Sept. 3, 1833: Birth of the Penny Press; Sept. 18, 1851: Modern *New York Times* Is Founded; 1880's-1890's: Rise of Yellow Journalism; Apr. 24-Dec. 10, 1898: Spanish-American War.

RELATED ARTICLES in *Great Lives from History: The Nineteenth Century, 1801-1900*: Joseph Pulitzer; William McKinley; Frederic Remington.

January 24, 1895
HAWAII'S LAST MONARCH ABDICATES

Queen Liliuokalani of the kingdom of Hawaii surrendered power to a provisional government established by a coup. The queen's forced abdication led to Hawaii's annexation by the United States, which culminated in statehood in 1959.

LOCALE: Honolulu, Kingdom of Hawaii (now in Hawaii)

CATEGORIES: Government and politics; wars, uprisings, and civil unrest; indigenous people's rights

KEY FIGURES

Liliuokalani (Lydia Kamakaeha; 1838-1917), queen of Kingdom of Hawaii, r. 1891-1893

Sanford Ballard Dole (1844-1926), American planter who became the first and only president of the Republic of Hawaii

John L. Stevens (1820-1895), American minister to the Kingdom of Hawaii

Grover Cleveland (1837-1908), president of the United States, 1885-1889, 1893-1897

William McKinley (1843-1901), president of the United States, 1897-1901

SUMMARY OF EVENT

Soon after her coronation on January 17, 1891, Queen Liliuokalani came into conflict with the members of her government's cabinet, which consisted mostly of non-Hawaiians (*haole* in the Hawaiian language). These men represented the moneyed aristocracy of Hawaii, who controlled the kingdom's imports and exports. By 1891, exports alone, nearly all to the United States, were worth nearly $275 million.

It was this same group of cabinet members who had forced the queen's predecessor and brother, King David Kalakaua, to sign the so-called Bayonet Constitution of 1887, which severely curtailed the power of the monarchy and the rights of the indigenous peoples of Hawaii. Liliuokalani wished to abolish this constitution and return some measure of power to native-born Hawaiians. Liliuokalani had begun to lobby for a new constitution, or, at minimum, a return to the older constitution of 1864, the last truly Hawaiian constitution. As a native Hawaiian, Liliuokalani was vitally interested in preserving the rights of native Hawaiians, who were losing in the political arena to the American *haole*. Soon after she announced her intentions, elements of the government,

with the support of the planter aristocracy, began planning the coup that would end her reign.

On January 17, 1893, the Committee of Safety, and its militia of local, supportive citizens, began carrying out the coup by taking over government buildings and disarming the royal guard. The committee, made up of non-Polynesians, many of whom were members of the Annexation Club, a group actively seeking annexation of Hawaii by the United States, included some of the most prominent names in Hawaiian politics. The committee instituted its provisional government and chose Sanford Ballard Dole, who was a known moderate, as the new president. The committee hoped his moderate politics would provide wider support for the revolution.

One day before the coup, John L. Stevens, the U.S. minister to Hawaii and an ardent supporter of Hawaiian annexation, ordered U.S. Marines from the cruiser USS *Boston* ashore to "protect American interests." The Marines took up station guarding Iolani Palace, the official

Queen Lilioukalani around 1893. (Hawaii State Archives)

LILIUOKALANI IN HER OWN WORDS

Hawaii's last monarch was forced to abdicate as queen by a provisional government with plans to annex Hawaii to the United States. In her memoir Hawaii's Story by Hawaii's Queen, *published a few years after she was dethroned, Liliuokalani, in the excerpt here, tells how she had no choice but to sign her "act of abdication." Doing so would protect those who had been loyal to her and her government and also prevent her own execution for "treason."*

For the first few days nothing occurred to disturb the quiet of my apartments save the tread of the sentry. On the fourth day I received a visit from Mr. Paul Neumann [her commissioner], who asked me if, in the event that it should be decided that all the principal parties to the revolt must pay for it with their lives, I was prepared to die? I replied to this in the affirmative, telling him I had no anxiety for myself, and felt no dread of death. He then told me that six others besides myself had been selected to be shot for treason, but that he would call again, and let me know further about our fate. I was in a state of nervous prostration, as I have said, at the time of the outbreak, and naturally the strain upon my mind had much aggravated my physical troubles; yet it was with much difficulty that I obtained permission to have visits from my own medical attendant.

About the 22d of January a paper was handed to me by Mr. Wilson [her marshal], which, on examination, proved to be a purported act of abdication for me to sign. It had been drawn out for the men in power [the provisional government] by their own lawyer, Mr. A. S. Hartwell, whom I had not seen until he came with others to see me sign it. The idea of abdicating never originated with me. I knew nothing at all about such a transaction until they sent to me, by the hands of Mr. Wilson, the insulting proposition written in abject terms. For myself, I would have chosen death rather than to have signed it; but it was represented to me that by my signing this paper all the persons who had been arrested, all my people now in trouble by reason of their love and loyalty towards me, would be immediately released. Think of my position—sick, a lone woman in prison, scarcely knowing who was my friend, or who listened to my words only to betray me, without legal advice or friendly counsel, and the stream of blood ready to flow unless it was stayed by my pen.

Source: Liliuokalani, *Hawaii's Story by Hawaii's Queen* (1898), chapter 44.

has caused United States Troops to be landed in Honolulu and declared that he would support the said Provisional Government."

President Grover Cleveland, unhappy with events in Honolulu, dispatched James H. Blount as his agent to investigate the coup. It was Blount's opinion that the actions of Minister Stevens were a prime factor in the success of the revolution and that those actions had violated Hawaiian sovereignty. President Cleveland subsequently sent a letter to Congress in which he admitted that the deposing of the queen was a direct result of the interference in Hawaiian affairs by the United States. The president ended any debate on annexation pending further study by the White House.

With the failure of immediate annexation, the Committee of Safety held a constitutional convention and proclaimed the founding of the Republic of Hawaii on May 30, 1894. This action was taken after the report of Minister Blount prompted President Cleveland to begin debate concerning American restoration of Liliuokalani to the throne. The committee believed it needed a more permanent government if it were to thwart any attempt to restore the monarchy. The committee elected Dole as the republic's first and only president.

Following a rebellion in 1895, led by the Hawaiian-born man Robert William Wilcox, the government tried Liliuokalani for misprision, the crime of having knowledge of a rebellion and not reporting it. Convicted, her initial sentence was five years at hard labor, but Dole commuted her sentence to imprisonment. She was confined in a small room at the Iolani Palace, the building that had been hers as queen. She remained in prison until released on parole on February 6, 1896. She later left Hawaii to undertake a world tour. She joined the Mormon Church in 1916 and died the following year at her Washington House home in Honolulu. She is best remembered for writing "Aloha Oe," the song most associated with Hawaii.

President William McKinley's administration, on July 7, 1898, annexed Hawaii to the United States. This decision was indicative of the expansionist atmosphere of the McKinley administration and the needs of the Spanish American War for a refueling station for the American Pacific fleet to reach its territories in the Phil-

residence of the ruler of Hawaii, as well as other strategic buildings in Honolulu in support of the revolutionaries.

Queen Liliuokalani's resignation statement accused the United States of collusion in the revolution. The queen's letter, which survived only because Hawaii's provisional government failed to read the letter, having simply acknowledged its receipt, contains a concise accusation. In the letter, the queen wrote, "I Yield to the superior force of the United States of America, whose minister plenipotentiary, His Excellency John L. Stevens,

ippines. The official annexation of Hawaii signified the end of the short-lived Republic of Hawaii and a much fuller participation by the United States in Hawaiian affairs. Hawaii would remain an American territory, would become famous in part because of the Japanese attack on Pearl Harbor on December 7, 1941, and eventually would achieve statehood on August 21, 1959.

SIGNIFICANCE

The dethroning of Queen Liliuokalani led to the final annexation of Hawaii to the United States. With American expansion into the Pacific Ocean, the strategic location of Hawaii as a refueling and resupply point for vessels bound for central and western Pacific locations made its control important to the U.S. government. Denying control of the Hawaiian Islands to other, potentially hostile countries such as Great Britain, France, and Japan was equally important to the U.S. government. Although thwarted by the Cleveland administration's unwillingness to expand into Hawaii at the expense of the Hawaiian people and of Hawaiian sovereignty, the dethroning of Liliuokalani paved the way for the government of the Republic of Hawaii to continue lobbying for such annexation until a president who would agree with their ideas came into office.

With Hawaii a part of the United States, tariff issues ceased to be problems for Hawaiian planters, and the sugar and pineapple trade to the continental United States began to flourish. Japanese expansion, already prevalent at the beginning of the twentieth century, was firmly stopped at the 154th parallel, and U.S. imperialism acquired a stepping stone allowing greater influence into the Pacific Ocean basin in the twentieth century. Although U.S. hegemony would be challenged in 1941, an Allied victory in World War II ensured that the Pacific would remain a U.S. zone of control. Hawaii remained the key to that control.

On November 23, 1993, the U.S. Congress passed and President Bill Clinton signed into law a joint resolution that apologized to the people of Hawaii for the actions of agents of the United States who aided and abetted the revolutionaries in overthrowing the Kingdom of Hawaii in January of 1893. The law specifically acknowledged that by its actions, the United States had deprived the rights of indigenous Hawaiians to self-determination.

—*Bruce S. Stewart*

FURTHER READING

Allen, Helena G. *The Betrayal of Liliuokalani, Last Queen of Hawaii: 1838-1917*. Glendale, Calif.: Ar-
thur H. Clark, 1982. A detailed assessment of the later years of the Hawaiian monarchy and the events of Liliuokalani's life as told from her writings and the memoirs of her heirs.

Conroy, Francis Hilary. *The Japanese Expansion into Hawaii, 1868-1898*. Saratoga, Calif.: R. & E. Research Associates, 1973. An assessment of the growing immigration of Japanese into Hawaii and Japanese influences on the islands.

Guzzetti, Paula. *Last Hawaiian Queen, Liliuokalani*. London: Marshall Cavendish, 1997. An updated biography of the last queen of Hawaii.

Kuykendall, Ralph S. *The Hawaiian Kingdom, 1854-1874: Twenty Critical Years*. Honolulu: University of Hawaii Press, 1953. A discussion of the early influences of Americans in the Hawaiian Islands.

Liliuokalani. *Hawaii's Story by Hawaii's Queen*. Honolulu: Mutual, 1990. In this biographical work, originally published in 1898, Liliuokalani tells the story of the last days of the Kingdom of Hawaii and the circumstances surrounding her forced abdication. Includes chapters on subsequent U.S. government investigations into the coup of 1893 and events leading up to the takeover of the monarchy. Introduction by Glen Grant.

Morris, Aldyth. *Liliuokalani*. Honolulu: University of Hawaii Press, 1995. The story of the overthrow of the Hawaiian monarchy, the provisional government, and annexation.

"Native Hawaiians Seek Redress for U.S. Role in Ousting Queen." *The New York Times*, December 11, 1999, p. A20. A report about Hawaiians seeking redress for the U.S. involvement in Liliuokalani's overthrow. Discusses then-president Bill Clinton's apology for the incident.

Osborne, Thomas J. *Empire Can Wait: American Opposition to Hawaiian Annexation, 1893-1898*. Kent, Ohio: Kent State University Press, 1981. An analysis of American opposition to the annexation of Hawaii.

Stevens, Sylvester K. *American Expansion in Hawaii: 1842-1898*. 1945. Reprint. New York: Russell & Russell, 1968. Examines American commercial and political expansion into Hawaii.

SEE ALSO: Dec. 31, 1853: Gadsden Purchase Completes the U.S.-Mexican Border; Feb. 4, 1899-July 4, 1902: Philippine Insurrection.

RELATED ARTICLES in *Great Lives from History: The Nineteenth Century, 1801-1900:* Grover Cleveland; Kamehameha I; Liliuokalani; William McKinley.

1890's

January 27, 1895
TCHAIKOVSKY'S *SWAN LAKE* IS STAGED IN ST. PETERSBURG

Choreographed by Marius Petipa and Lev Ivanov, the performance of Tchaikovsky's Swan Lake *at St. Petersburg brought music, drama, and dance together in an intense and lyrical unity which revolutionized Russian ballet and set the standard for classical ballet. The St. Petersburg staging of the ballet remains the one most often followed today.*

LOCALE: St. Petersburg, Russia
CATEGORIES: Dance; theater; music

KEY FIGURES
Peter Ilich Tchaikovsky (1840-1893), Russian
    composer
Marius Petipa (1818-1910), French ballet dancer,
    ballet master, and choreographer
Lev Ivanov (1834-1901), Russian dancer, teacher,
    choreographer, and ballet master
Pierina Legnani (1863-1923), Italian prima ballerina

SUMMARY OF EVENT
Peter Ilich Tchaikovsky's *Lebedinoe ozero* (1877; *Swan Lake*) has become one of the best-known and most appreciated of all classical ballets. The dual role of its heroine Odette/Odile is the trial by which every classical ballerina assures her claim to greatness. However, although it was the first ballet that Tchaikovsky wrote, it was also the last of his ballets to enjoy success. Tchaikovsky first tried his hand at writing a "ballet" in the summer of 1871, while he was staying with his sister Alexandra Davydova at her estate in the Ukraine. He was very devoted to her children and created a ballet for them based on fairy tales of swan queens. Once back in Moscow, he apparently talked about his "ballet" at a social gathering at the home of Vladimir Petrovich Begichev, the intendant of the Russian Imperial Theatres of Moscow. The possibility of a full-scale ballet was subsequently discussed by the artists, writers, and composers present. Thus, in May of 1875, Begichev commissioned Tchaikovsky to write a score for a ballet derived from his improvised children's entertainment to be called *Swan Lake*.

Although Begichev and a dancer in the Moscow Bolshoi Ballet Company, Vasily Fedorovich, are credited with writing the first libretto for the ballet, Tchaikovsky is believed to have had considerable influence on the dramatic narrative. The legend of the Swan Maiden was centuries old, and tales of women turned into swans abounded in the folklore of both Eastern and Western culture, but the precise story told in the ballet is not to be found elsewhere. Thus, *Swan Lake* has many cultural ancestors but the story of Swan Lake can be considered as Tchaikovsky's own tale.

The fact that Tchaikovsky had so much influence upon the story is somewhat unusual, since he was also responsible for the musical score. Ballets at that time were created in a fashion which may seem peculiar to a modern afficionado. The librettist of a ballet would simply choose a story or legend and create a ballet of five or six acts. The librettist wrote the entire story of his ballet; it was then put into the hands of a choreographer who created the dance movements, from whom it traveled to a composer who wrote the music and then into the hands of various designers of costumes and sets. In other words, there was very little collaboration among the various artists who created and performed a ballet.

Rehearsals for *Swan Lake* began in March of 1876 and went on for eleven months. Julius Wentzel Reisinger, an Austrian who was the Moscow ballet master at the time, was put in charge of the choreography. It seems that he found it impossible to create dances to Tchaikovsky's music, however: He eliminated parts of the score or replaced them with other music, and at times he left the choreography of their roles to the individual dancers. The premiere performance of the ballet was given by the Moscow Bolshoi Company on March 4, 1877.

The ballet was poorly received and severely criticized for its weak choreography and a general lack of talent among its dancers, costumers, set designers, and orchestra. Tchaikovsky's music was rejected as too dramatic and emotional. It seemed to be in the dark, brooding style of Richard Wagner, while the audience was accustomed to light, airy scores. Although *Swan Lake* was viewed as a failure, it was performed forty-one times, and it remained part of the Moscow Bolshoi repertoire until 1883. All of the seats were sold out for thirty-three of these performances. Still, the ballet was looked upon as a failure.

During the late 1880's, Marius Petipa, the ballet master and choreographer for the St. Petersburg Ballet Company, asked Tchaikovsky to compose a musical score for the ballet *Spyashchaya krasavitsa* (1889, *Sleeping Beauty*). The ballet was a great success, bringing renown to both Petipa and Tchaikovsky. In 1892, Petipa once again called upon Tchaikovsky for a musical score. This time, it was for a Christmas ballet, *Shchelkunchik* (1892;

The Nutcracker). Petipa fell ill and had to assign the choreography of *The Nutcracker* to his assistant, Lev Ivanov. The first performance was somewhat poorly received, but the ballet was soon successful.

As a consequence of the success of *Sleeping Beauty* and *The Nutcracker*, the possibility of a St. Petersburg production of *Swan Lake* soon materialized. Tchaikovsky did not live to see his ballet performed in St Petersburg; he died of cholera in 1893. The following year, a memorial concert was presented for him. For this performance, Lev Ivanov choreographed act 2 of *Swan Lake*. Ivanov's choreography of the lakeside scene was especially successful, as he used the corps de ballet as an integral part of the ballet's drama. Pierina Legnani, the Italian ballerina who reigned as prima ballerina of the St. Petersburg Company, performed the role of the Swan Queen.

The performance was well received, and Ivan Vsevolozhsky, director of the Imperial Theatre, asked Petipa to choreograph a complete production of the ballet. Petipa made several changes in the music and the libretto of the ballet. In collaboration with Ricardo Drigo, the chief orchestra conductor of the company, he asked Tchaikovsky's brother Modeste to alter the score to include more character dances. In the libretto, he changed Odette's persecutor. Originally, her wicked stepmother had changed her into a swan. Von Rothbart had merely been her stepmother's accomplice. Petipa eliminated the stepmother and made von Rothbart a wicked magician totally responsible for Odette's plight. He also changed the ending. Tchaikovsky's ending had been tragic, with Prince Siegfried and Odette being swept under the water of the lake and dying, united forever in death. Petipa, who liked happy endings, concluded the ballet with the lovers united to live happily ever after. His version of *Swan Lake* remained an intensely dramatic ballet, however.

Petipa divided the choreography of the ballet with Ivanov. Petipa choreographed act 1 and most of act 3, and Ivanov choreographed acts 2 and 4, plus two dances in the ballroom scene of act 3, the Venetian Dance and the Czardas. Ivanov once again used the corps de ballet as an integral part of the drama of the ballet and created lyrical dances emphasizing the beauty and flowing movements of swans. His pas de quatre, the Dance of the Little Swans, was particularly lyrical, with a soft ethereal quality. Petipa's choreography of the court scenes

had an energy and quickness of movement that created a definite contrast to the pas de quatre.

The Black Swan pas de deux of act 3 was perhaps the most striking dance in the ballet. Legnani performed the role of Odette/Odile. Aware of the effect of her performance of thirty-two fouettés in his *Cinderella* (1893), Petipa included them as Odile's means of seducing Siegfried. Composed of many different kinds of dancing, including classical, character, folk, and a considerable amount of mime, *Swan Lake* was truly representative of the genius of Petipa. Ivanov's contributions were also significant, as he was able to bring together music and dance in a perfect combination. On January 27, 1895 (January 15 by the Eastern Orthodox calendar then in use in Russia), Swan Lake premiered at the Marinsky Theatre in St. Petersburg with Pierina Legnani in the role of Odette/Odile and Pavel Gerdt in that of Siegfried.

Scene from a 1943 Australian production of Swan Lake, *in which Robert Helpmann and British ballerina Margot Fonteyn danced the lead roles.* (Hulton Archive/Getty Images)

1890's

SIGNIFICANCE

In bringing together the talents of Tchaikovsky, Petipa, Ivanov, and Legnani, the St. Petersburg performance of *Swan Lake* epitomized the beauty and richness of ballet and assured the existence of the art in its highest form. *Swan Lake* became the embodiment of Russian classical ballet's ideals. It was both technically and emotionally demanding. It required dancers who were accomplished both as actors and as dancers. The full range of emotion portrayed in the ballet coupled with the technical difficulty of the dance movements combined to create a standard for ballet choreography and performance which persists to this day.

—*Shawncey Webb*

FURTHER READING

Anderson, Jack. *Dance*. New York: Newsweek Books, 1974. Although this book is rather old, it has an excellent discussion of the creation and performance of *Swan Lake* and is very well illustrated.

Scholl, Tim. *From Petipa to Balanchine: Classical Revival and the Modernization of Ballet*. Reprint. New York: Routledge, 2001. Original and somewhat controversial argument that Balanchine's choreography was a direct twentieth century response to Petipa's work. Rejects a line of modernization through Fokine and Diaghilev.

Souritz, Elisabeth. *The Great History of the Russian Ballet: Its Art and Choreography*. Richford, Vt.: Park-stone Press, 1999. Detailed, in-depth treatment of ballet technique and performance in accord with Russian standards.

Wiley, Roland John. *The Life and Ballets of Lev Ivanov: Choreographer of the Nutcracker and Swan Lake*. Oxford, England: Oxford University Press, 1997. Richly documented presentation of the career of Ivanov; includes discussions of the state of dance in Russia in Ivanov's time and of his influence on later choreographers, especially Mikhail Fokine. Contains a chapter on *Swan Lake* and a chapter on libretti for ballets.

_____. *Tchaikovsky: Ballets—Swan Lake, Sleeping Beauty, Nutcracker*. Oxford, England: Oxford University Press, 1991. Includes discussion of the negotiations between Tchaikovsky and the Imperial Theater, a chapter on the production of Swan Lake in Moscow, and a chapter on the production in St. Petersburg. Useful appendixes, including the scenarios of Tchaikovsky's ballets (both Moscow and St. Petersburg performances).

SEE ALSO: Mar. 12, 1832: *La Sylphide* Inaugurates Romantic Ballet's Golden Age; Jan. 2, 1843: Wagner's *Flying Dutchman* Debuts; c. 1869: Golden Age of Flamenco Begins; Aug. 13-17, 1876: First Performance of Wagner's Ring Cycle.

RELATED ARTICLES in *Great Lives from History: The Nineteenth Century, 1801-1900:* Peter Ilich Tchaikovsky; Richard Wagner.

February 24, 1895-1898
CUBAN WAR OF INDEPENDENCE

After it became clear that Cuba's Ten Years' War against Spain had failed to achieve lasting reforms, new hostilities broke out and achieved great success in Cuba's Oriente province. The savage fighting of the new revolt would combine with Spain's repressive reaction to bring the United States into the conflict and lead to the Spanish-American War.

LOCALE: Cuba
CATEGORIES: Wars, uprisings, and civil unrest; government and politics

KEY FIGURES

José Martí (1853-1895), Cuban rebel leader, poet, and secretary-general of the Cuban provisional government

Calixto García Íñiguez (1839-1898), Cuban rebel leader in the Oriente province

Antonio Maceo (1845-1896), Cuban rebel field commander

Máximo Gómez y Báez (1836-1905), military commander of Cuban rebel forces

Tomás Estrada Palma (1835-1908), president of the exiled Cuban revolutionary government

Valeriano Weyler y Nicolau (1838-1930), Spanish commander in Cuba, 1896-1897

Arsenio Martínez de Campos (1831-1900), Spanish captain-general and military commander in Cuba, 1895-1896

Antonio Cánovas del Castillo (1828-1897), Spanish prime minister, 1875-1881, 1883-1885, 1890-1892, and 1895-1897

Lithograph sold in the United States in support of the Cuban nationalist movement. (Library of Congress)

Práxedes Mateo Sagasta (1825-1903) Spanish prime minister, 1871-1872, 1874, 1881-1883, 1885-1890, 1892-1895, 1897-1899, 1901-1902

SUMMARY OF EVENT

The Treaty of Zanjón ended the Cuban insurrection known as the Ten Years' War (1868-1878). It provided for a cease-fire between Cuban rebels and the Spanish colonial administration in Havana. Both sides agreed on the implementation of significant reforms. The Spanish regimes that followed in the wake of the Zanjón agreement, however, dragged their feet; only the abolition of slavery was carried out, and only then at a comparatively late date (1886). Furthermore, Spanish colonial policies enacted during the late 1880's and early 1890's were damaging the Cuban economy: Heavier taxation of Cuban exports and the abrogation of trade terms with the United States resulted in a 40 percent decline in trade revenue.

Cuban exiles in the United States established a rebel government in New York City to organize and coordinate efforts aimed at securing independence. It was led by journalist and poet José Martí and former insurgent general Tomás Estrada Palma. Both would assume prominent positions in the provisional government that was to be proclaimed: Estrada Palma as president, and Martí as secretary-general. They were assisted by, among others, certain veteran generals of the Ten Years' War: Máximo Gómez y Báez, Antonio Maceo, and Calixto García Íñiguez.

On February 24, 1895, revolts broke out in the countryside of at least three provinces. The first clash occurred between Cuban and Spanish forces at Los Negros on March 10. The Spanish defeat there resulted in the dispatching of some thirty thousand reinforcements from Spain and Puerto Rico. On March 31, Maceo, who had sailed from Central America, made a landing at Baracoa and proclaimed the provisional government, while Martí and Gómez, using Haiti as their base, landed on April 13. Battles at Sabana de Jaibo, Jobito, Arroyo Hondo, Ramon de las Juagas, and Cristo resulted in further Spanish setbacks.

Martí, who in many ways was the voice and inspiration of the revolution, was surprised and killed at Dos Rios on May 19, and his men were slaughtered. As more recruits joined the rebellion and volunteers kept trickling into Cuba, Spanish captain-general Arsenio Martínez de Campos launched a determined but failed attack on Maceo at Peralejo on July 13, 1895. He nearly lost his life and was forced to retreat. Thereafter, lapsing into depression and becoming increasingly ineffectual, Martínez de Campos was replaced by General Valeriano Weyler y Nicolau on February 10, 1896.

Weyler y Nicolau set about with the ruthless resolve that earned him the sobriquet of "butcher" in the American press. Maceo and Gómez had been freely ranging across the island—sometimes independently, and sometimes in concert—raiding and destroying government facilities and supplies and breaching the *trochas* (entrenchment ditches across the width of Cuba) that had been in place since the Ten Years' War. Maceo and Gómez were joined by General Calixto García Íñiguez, who disembarked in Cuba on March 25, 1896.

After proclaiming martial law and bolstering the number of troops patroling the *trochas*, Weyler y Nicolau sought to destroy the rebel power base by ordering the entire populations of certain target regions into concentration camps. This *reconcentrado* policy was initially successful in hampering rebel operations, though Maceo's forces remained very active. In the long term the brutality of Weyler y Nicolau's policy drew sharp attack from William Randolph Hearst's *New York Morning Journal* and *New York Evening Journal*, Joseph Pulitzer's *New York World*, and other publications. Reports of atrocities of greater and lesser veracity poured out of Cuba and began inflaming American public opinion against Spain. Disease, starvation, and executions resulting from the *reconcentrados* killed a conservatively estimated 480,000 people. On December 7, 1896, Maceo

was ambushed and killed at Punta Brava while riding to Gómez's assistance.

Weyler y Nicolau's heavy-handed methods slowly ground down or impeded rebel resistance in the western and central regions, and a relentless campaign of maneuver, terror, and retaliation raged in the rebellion's Oriente province stronghold between Weyler y Nicolau and García Íñiguez. Known now as "the fox," García Íñiguez proved an elusive and resourceful opponent, slipping away from royalist forces to capture Jiguani (March 13, 1897) and Victoria de las Tunas (August 30).

The inauguration of William McKinley as president of the United States on March 4, 1897, brought into power an administration that was much more favorable toward the Cuban rebel cause than was that of the outgoing Grover Cleveland administration. Estrada Palma skillfully exploited American sympathy to successfully lobby Washington for interventionist legislation. On August 8, 1897, Spanish prime minister Antonio Cánovas del Castillo, leader of the Conservative Party and a supporter of Weyler y Nicolau's policy, was assassinated

Cuban president Tomás Estrada Palma with his cabinet in 1902. (Library of Congress)

and his successor, Liberal Party leader Práxedes Mateo Sagasta, dismissed Weyler y Nicolau (October 31). By the end of the year, the Sagasta regime had drawn up a plan for partial Cuban autonomy. It was too late, and too little.

García Íñiguez's army resumed its aggressive campaigning. On November 28, 1897, the rebels had forced the surrender of the Spanish garrison at Guisa, and 1898 saw the capitulation of the fortresses at Bayamo, Holguin (García Íñiguez's birthplace), and Gibara. García Íñiguez's troops had triumphed in a pitched battle at Rejondon de Baguanos (February 1, 1898) as well. The Cuban War of Independence was then absorbed in (some might even assert, overshadowed by) the U.S. declaration of war against Spain on April 22, 1898, and the swift, decisive conflict known as the Spanish-American War.

SIGNIFICANCE

Although the United States made short work of the underequipped and demoralized Spanish forces, the Cuban War of Independence, in which the guerrillas had more than held their own against vastly superior numbers, had given the Cubans such a sense of pride and independence that any prior inclinations favoring annexation by the United States had been cast aside.

Recognizing the reality posed by Cuban nationalist sentiment, the Congress of the United States had passed the Teller Amendment (1898) disclaiming any intentions by the United States to make Cuba a colonial possession. After an interim period of U.S. military governance, Cuba became an independent republic in 1902, with Tomás Estrada Palma as its first president.

—*Raymond Pierre Hylton*

FURTHER READING

Belnap, Jeffrey, and Raul Fernandez. *Jose Marti's "Our America": From National to Hemispheric Cultural Studies*. Durham, N.C.: Duke University Press, 1998. A collection of essays that attempt to shed light on the mercurial and dynamic genius who was the visionary behind the Cuban rebellion.

Ferrer, Ada. *Insurgent Cuba: Race, Nation, and Revolution, 1868-1898*. Chapel Hill: University of North Carolina Press, 1999. Focuses on the multicultural factors involved in the Cuban revolt, which is depicted as running against the conventional late nineteenth century attitudes on race.

Foner, Philip S. *Antonio Maceo: The Bronze Titan of Cuba's Struggle for Independence*. New York: Monthly Review Press, 1977. An engrossing biography of one of the pivotal guerrilla chieftains, arguably the most formidable rebel leader, during the early phases of the Cuban War for Independence.

Rubens, Horatio S. *Liberty: The Story of Cuba*. 1932. Reprint. New York: Arno Press, 1970. Extols the virtues and strengths of the Cuban guerrilla fighters to legendary proportions. However, the work is still useful.

Schmidt-Nowara, Christopher. *Empire and Antislavery: Spain, Cuba, and Puerto Rico, 1833-1874*. Pittsburgh: University of Pittsburgh Press, 1999. Traces the development of revolutionary ideology in nineteenth century Cuba within the broader context of Spanish (and Puerto Rican) abolitionism and politics.

Thomas, Hugh. *Cuba: The Pursuit of Freedom*. New York: Harper & Row, 1971. As in all works by the prolific historian Thomas, this work is meticulously written, and presents facts with great detail. A definitive chronicle of the Cuban ordeal.

U.S. RESOLUTION RECOGNIZING CUBAN INDEPENDENCE

The U.S. government officially supported the Cuban movement for independence from Spain and condemned Spain for its poor treatment of the Cuban people. The April 20, 1898, congressional resolution, excerpted here, also stated that, if necessary, the U.S. would use military force against Spain to ensure Cuba's sovereignty.

Whereas, the abhorrent conditions which have existed for more than three years in the Island of Cuba, so near our own borders, have shocked the moral sense of the people of the United States, have been a disgrace to Christian civilization, culminating, as they have, in the destruction of a United States battle-ship, with two hundred and sixty-six of its officers and crew, while on a friendly visit in the harbor of Havana, and can not longer be endured, as has been set forth by the President of the United States in his message to Congress of April eleventh, eighteen hundred and ninety-eight. . . .

Resolved . . . First. That the people of the Island of Cuba are, and of right ought to be, free and independent.

Second. That it is the duty of the United States to demand, and the Government of the United States does hereby demand, that the Government of Spain at once relinquish its authority and government in the Island of Cuba, and withdraw its land and naval forces from Cuba and Cuban waters. . . .

Turton, Peter. *Jose Marti: Architect of Cuba's Freedom.* London: Zed Books, 1986. A definitive and complimentary portrayal of Martí as a near-mystical figure.

SEE ALSO: Oct. 10, 1868-Feb. 10, 1878: Cuba's Ten Years' War; 1880's-1890's: Rise of Yellow Journal-ism; Apr. 24-Dec. 10, 1898: Spanish-American War; Feb. 4, 1899-July 4, 1902: Philippine Insurrection.

RELATED ARTICLES in *Great Lives from History: The Nineteenth Century, 1801-1900:* Miguel Hidalgo y Costilla; Isabella II; William McKinley; José Martí; Joseph Pulitzer.

May 10, 1895

CHINESE CALIFORNIANS FORM NATIVE SONS OF THE GOLDEN STATE

Second-generation Chinese Americans, hoping to change the traditional thinking of their elders and the racist bias of whites regarding assimilation with American mainstream culture, formed an alliance to address the concerns of Chinese immigrants and their American-born families. Their organization became a major social and political force for the Chinese American community of San Francisco and other U.S. cities.

ALSO KNOWN AS: Chinese American Citizens Alliance
LOCALE: San Francisco, California
CATEGORIES: Immigration; civil rights and liberties; social issues and reform; organizations and institutions

KEY FIGURE

Chun Dick (fl. late nineteenth century), San Francisco resident who incorporated the association

SUMMARY OF EVENT

Chinese immigration to the United States began during the mid-nineteenth century. The migration pattern of the Chinese was the same wherever they went: Peasants from rural areas in China migrated to cities looking for work, without securing a sustainable income, and men (mostly young men) left China while their families remained. Their purpose in leaving was twofold: to earn money to send home to their families and to return to China once they secured sufficient money (around five hundred dollars) to support their families comfortably.

Travel to the United States was beyond the financial capability of most Chinese, so to secure passage to America most indentured themselves (contracted their labor in advance) to a merchant or a labor agent, a system called the credit-ticket arrangement whereby merchants advanced Chinese money for passage to the United States and kept collecting it for years.

The California gold rush of 1848-1849 had drawn many with its promises of gold-filled streets; in fact, the Chinese name for San Francisco is "Old Gold Mountain." Not all Chinese immigrants, however, willingly left China. Many emigrated because of famine and political and social unrest in southern China. Others were victims of the so-called Pig Trade, which replaced slavery after it was outlawed following the U.S. Civil War (1861-1865). They chose the United States because of exaggerated tales of wealth and opportunity spread by traders and missionaries.

After the Chinese landed in the United States, labor agents, under the credit-ticket arrangement, gained almost complete domination of their indentured workers and kept them in isolated communities which the agents controlled. These areas became known as Chinatowns. Moreover, many Chinese, not wanting to remain permanently in the United States, had little incentive to assimilate. Their unwillingness or inability to become acculturated into the American "melting pot" became an indictment against all Chinese. Although most Chinese wanted to return to China, many could not secure sufficient money for return passage and never returned to their homeland.

Life in California during the late nineteenth century was difficult at best for most Chinese. The Chinese communities organized *Hui-Guan* (merchant guilds) that served as welcoming committees, resettlement assistance services, and mutual help societies for newly arrived immigrants. Chinese immigrants were also organized by the Chinese Consolidated Benevolent Association (also known as the Chinese Six Companies), originally agents of Chinese firms in Hong Kong who had established the "coolie trade" to San Francisco. ("Coolie" is a derogatory term used to name unskilled laborers.) The Six Companies kept traditional Chinese rules, customs, and values as the basis for appropriate behavior, helping protect Chinese from an increasingly anti-Chinese atmosphere.

Anti-Chinese sentiments and violence against Chinese began almost as soon as they arrived in North America. These attitudes existed at the top levels of government and labor unions as well as with local citizens. During the mid- to late nineteenth century, various political parties, including the Know-Nothing Party, the Democratic Party, and the Republican Party, promoted anti-Chinese platforms. During this time, workers' unions organized anti-Chinese activities, and anti-Asian sentiments were propagated by newspapers in western states.

In 1871, about twenty Chinese in Los Angeles were killed and their homes and businesses looted and burned. In 1877, a similar incident occurred in San Francisco. In Chico, California, five farmers were murdered. Anti-Chinese riots broke out in Denver, Colorado, and in Rock Springs, Wyoming. In 1885, Chinese workers, employed as strikebreakers, were killed at a Wyoming coal mine. Chinese residents in Seattle and Tacoma, Washington, were driven out of town and thirty-one Chinese were robbed and murdered in Snake River, Oregon. In 1905, sixty-seven labor organizations, in order to prevent employers from hiring Asians, formed the Asiatic Exclusion League.

During the early 1890's, the Chinese Six Companies lost face when they influenced Chinese not to sign documents required by the Geary Act (1892), an extension of the Chinese Exclusion Act of 1882, which required all Chinese residing in the United States to obtain a certificate of eligibility with a photograph within a year. When the Geary Act was ruled legal, thousands of Chinese Americans became illegal immigrants in the United States.

Following the ruling on the act, the Tongs, secret societies of criminals that originated in China, used this opportunity to take control of the Chinatowns. The result was a vicious and bloody civil war among Chinese Americans—in which local police, for the most part, played a very limited role. Among first-generation Chinese, few actively opposed the rule of the Tongs. Perhaps accustomed to bandits, clan warfare, and warlords in southern China and imbued with the Daoist spirit of letting things alone, most Chinese did their best to survive without resisting Tong leaders.

Many young American-born Chinese opposed these "old ways" of doing things. They accepted the notion that they were never going to return to China and they wanted to adopt American ways and fit into American culture. They soon formed the group Native Sons of the Golden State in an effort to assimilate into American mainstream culture. Chun Dick incorporated the group on May 10, 1895. He was followed by Walter U. Lum, Joseph K. Lum, and Ng Gunn, who reorganized Native Sons several years later. The Native Sons' headquarters was located on the second floor of a building at 753 Clay Street in San Francisco. The first officers were The Chen, Kun Wu, and Tai-yung Li.

The Native Sons of the Golden State emphasized the importance of naturalization and voters' registration. All members were urged to become American citizens and to vote. The organization also encouraged active participation in the civic affairs of mainstream American life. The leaders thought that some of the anti-Chinese sentiments and discriminatory actions were, in part, due to the traditional attitudes and behaviors of the Chinese immigrants themselves: remaining isolated, not learning English, and not taking part in politics.

SIGNIFICANCE

As the organization grew, it established chapters in Oakland, Los Angeles, San Diego, Chicago, Portland, Detroit, Pittsburgh, and Boston, eventually changing its name to the Chinese American Citizens Alliance (CACA) in 1915 to recognize the chapters outside California. Women were accepted into the fraternal order in 1977.

In 1913, CACA defeated a California law designed to prevent Chinese from voting. The group fought against the National Origins Act, or Immigration Act of 1924, and sought the right for Chinese men to bring their wives to the United States.

CACA helped defeat the Cinch bill of 1925, which attempted to regulate the manufacture and sale of Chinese medicinal products such as herbs and roots. By promoting numerous social functions—dances, sporting events, dinner parties, and the like—CACA also helped keep Chinese American communities together and moved them toward assimilation. CACA fought against the stereotyped portrayals of Chinese in films, newspapers, and magazines as heathens, drug addicts, or instigators of torture.

—*Gregory A. Levitt*

FURTHER READING

Daniels, Roger. *Asian America: Chinese and Japanese in the United States Since 1850.* Seattle: University of Washington Press, 1988. An excellent overall account of Asian America that includes a brief description of the Chinese American Citizens Alliance.

Dillon, Richard H. *The Hatchet Men: The Story of the*

1890's

Tong Wars in San Francisco Chinatown. New York: Coward-McCann, 1962. A dated but interesting account of the violence in San Francisco's early Chinatown under the "rule" of the Tongs.

Ng, Franklin, ed. *Asian American Family Life and Community.* New York: Garland, 1998. Examines the social, economic, and family histories of Asians in America. Includes the chapter "The Chinese American Citizens Alliance: An Effort in Assimilation, 1895-1965."

Takaki, Ronald. *Strangers from a Different Shore: A History of Asian Americans.* 1989. Rev. ed. Boston: Little, Brown, 1998. An account of Asians coming to live in America, which provides some discussion of the Chinese American Citizens Alliance in the 1940's and the late 1980's.

Tsai, Shih-Shan Henry. *The Chinese Experience in America.* Bloomington: Indiana University Press, 1986. Places the alliance in historical context.

SEE ALSO: 1840's-1850's: American Era of "Old" Immigration; Jan. 24, 1848: California Gold Rush Begins; 1849: Chinese Begin Immigrating to California; July 28, 1868: Burlingame Treaty; Mar. 3, 1875: Congress Enacts the Page Law; May 9, 1882: Arthur Signs the Chinese Exclusion Act; Nov. 12, 1882: San Francisco's Chinese Six Companies Association Forms; 1892: America's "New" Immigration Era Begins; May 4, 1892: Anti-Japanese Yellow Peril Campaign Begins; Mar. 28, 1898: *United States v. Wong Kim Ark.*

June 20, 1895
GERMANY'S KIEL CANAL OPENS

After eight years of construction, the Kiel Canal was opened to oceangoing vessels sailing between the Baltic and North Seas. The canal's construction demonstrated the ability of the new German Empire to carry out a large-scale project, and with the buildup of the German navy in the two decades following the canal's opening, the massive engineering project was a sign of Germany's arrival on the world stage.

LOCALE: Duchy of Schleswig-Holstein, Germany
CATEGORIES: Transportation; engineering; economics; trade and commerce

KEY FIGURES
Otto von Bismarck (1815-1898), German chancellor, 1871-1890
William I (1797-1888), king of Prussia and German emperor, r. 1871-1888
William II (1859-1941), king of Prussia and German emperor, r. 1888-1918
Helmuth von Moltke (1800-1891), chief of the Prussian general staff

SUMMARY OF EVENT
The irregular geographic configuration of northern Europe, with the Baltic Sea virtually cut off from the North Sea and the Atlantic Ocean, made inevitable the linking of the two seas with a canal. Until that time, seagoing vessels had to navigate around the Danish peninsula and through the difficult passage of the sound between Denmark and Sweden, a distance of about five hundred miles. The vast growth of oceangoing shipping after 1500 made the elimination of that trip one that engaged many minds.

The eighteenth century was the great age of canal building, so it is hardly surprising that a plan emerged at that time to link the Baltic with the North Sea across the southern reaches of the Danish peninsula. The land through which such a canal would have to pass, the duchies of Schleswig and Holstein, were governed by members of the Danish royal family. In 1784 a canal was built between Kiel on the Baltic and the town of Tönning on the shores of the Elbe River north of Hamburg, the great North Sea port. Known as the Eider Canal, it utilized the Eider River, which flowed across much of Schleswig-Holstein. In 1785 it was opened to international traffic, but it was quite shallow, required three to four days to pass through, and comparatively little use was made of it.

The picture changed during the 1860's, and for several reasons. First, as a result of several wars fought in that decade, Schleswig-Holstein was added to the kingdom of Prussia. In 1871, Prussia became the core of the new German Empire, which was rapidly industrializing and eager to become a major European power. Second,

Fireworks illuminate the sky during celebrations at the opening of the Kiel Canal. (Francis R. Niglutsch)

oceangoing shipping was expanding quite rapidly in the latter part of the nineteenth century, and the new German Empire aspired to play an important role in the world economy. Third, nations with large private freight and passenger traffic believed they needed to protect those national assets by the building of a navy. All these factors came together to renew interest in a new, and bigger, canal through Schleswig-Holstein, connecting the two northern European seas.

Local support for a new canal was strong. In 1868 a Kiel Canal construction committee submitted a proposal for a canal to the legislature of the North German Union, a predecessor organization of the German Empire proclaimed in 1871. This petition was passed on to Bismarck in his capacity as chancellor, a role he was also to occupy in the empire. In the 1870's commercial interests in Hamburg took up the cause, particularly the ship-owning interests.

Shipping companies made contact with Bismarck, who favored the canal. Opposing the canal were the mili-

tary authorities, notably General Helmuth von Moltke, the architect of Prussia's victory over France in 1870. Moltke argued that the costs of building such a canal would be too great and would detract from military expenditures. Bismarck, however, who saw the canal as a way of winning the support of conservative agricultural interests and the growing class of large industrialists, defied Moltke's opposition. Bismarck's great coup was winning the support of the emperor, the elderly William I, who argued that completion of the canal was an urgent military need. The imperial support enabled Bismarck to win the approval of the Reichstag for the construction of the canal in 1886.

The canal, which actually begins at the Kiel harbor at Holtenau, runs for 98.7 kilometers (61.3 miles) to Brunsbüttel on the banks of the Elbe River, northwest of the port of Hamburg. Besides two double locks, which were completed in 1892 and sit at each end of the canal, there are no breaks in the passageway from the Baltic to the North Sea. The original plan called for a minimum depth for the canal of 8.5 meters, a minimum width at the bottom of 22 meters, and a breadth on the surface of 58 meters. The radius of turns could not be less than 250 meters, but at the request of the German navy during construction this figure was increased to 1,000 meters, and the length of various bends in the route was increased from 250 to 450 meters. At midstream the depth was increased to 9 meters, and the breadth on the surface was expanded from 58 to 67 meters. These changes reflect the growing interest, which had been fueled by the new emperor William II, in the construction of a powerful navy to challenge the British navy.

The construction of the canal was entrusted to a special commission created by the Reichstag in 1886. The route was divided up into four (later five) administrative sections. The first of these was responsible for the construction of the double locks at the Elbe end of the canal, and the remainder were assigned appropriate segments to direct construction work. Large excavators dug the canal, and more than seven thousand workers were hired, including masons, machinists, and blacksmiths. The canal cut across four rail lines, four major roads, and numerous smaller ones. The rail lines entailed the construction of bridges, both fixed spans and those with turning segments, as did the major roadways. Pilots would be required on vessels traversing the canal, but the commission ordered lights on the banks to guide the pilots. Steam engines were placed at each end of the canal to power dynamos that would light up the lights.

Construction was completed in 1895 at a total cost of 156 million marks, some 900,000 marks below the amount budgeted, but the Reichstag added another 1.7 million marks to pay for the elaborate dedicatory ceremonies on June 20, 1895. Emperor William II, grandson of the emperor who had lent his support to the creation of the canal, presided over the ceremonies, and he immediately christened the canal the Kaiser Wilhelm Kanal, in honor of his grandfather. The dedication began in Hamburg and wound up with a parade of vessels passing through the canal for more than eight hours. The following day, in Kiel, a cornerstone was laid that was patterned after the cornerstone laid by Emperor William I at the opening eight years earlier.

SIGNIFICANCE

The Kiel Canal was touted as a major construction achievement, comparable to the Suez Canal. Later commentators also likened it to the Panama Canal. The canal was, however, not without its negative aspects.

Despite the canal's broad dimensions, many ships still ran aground on the banks or collided with concrete embankment structures. In an effort to avoid changing elevations, the canal had been planned, and built, to run largely along the route of the eighteenth century Eider Canal, whose route in turn had been dictated by the need to use natural waterways wherever possible. These circumstance contributed to many of the accidents that plagued the early years of the canal's operations.

Although the canal saved vessels traveling between the North Sea and the Baltic Sea some five hundred miles, the saving of time was much less, because ships had to move at very slow speeds through the canal. Because oceangoing ships continued to grow in size throughout the twentieth century, the canal has since required two expansions. By the late twentieth century, however, many vessels were much too large to fit through the canal, so its usefulness has diminished.

The construction of the canal served as concrete evidence of the growing industrial, commercial, and naval power of the German Empire. It was justified in part by the needs of the new German navy, which in turn contributed to the growing estrangement between Germany and Great Britain in the early years of the twentieth century, an estrangement that led to World War I. As trade became more global, the importance of the traffic on the Baltic Sea and the North Sea lessened, and the canal served relatively fewer users. It demonstrated both the capabilities and the pride, some would say hubris, of the new German Empire, leading shortly to the empire's collapse in World War I.

—Nancy M. Gordon

FURTHER READING

Feuchtwanger, Edgar. *Imperial Germany, 1850-1918.* New York: Routledge, 2001. A well-written and richly detailed account of the German Empire. Has only one specific reference to the canal, but it provides good background.

Henderson, W. O. *The Rise of German Industrial Power, 1834-1914.* Berkeley: University of California Press, 1975. Contains the most extensive information in English about the canal.

Lagoni, Rainer, Hellmuth St. Seidenfus, and Hans-Jürgen Teuteberg, eds. *Nord-Ostsee-Kanal.* Kiel, Germany: Wachholtz Verlag, 1995. Commissioned by the German Transport Ministry, this book, graced with many photographs, contains exhaustive information about the canal. In German.

Pflanze, Otto. *Bismarck and the Development of Germany.* Princeton, N.J.: Princeton University Press,

1990. Vol. 3 includes "The Period of Fortification, 1880-1898," detailing Bismarck's role in creating the canal.

SEE ALSO: May 22-June 20, 1819: *Savannah* Is the First Steamship to Cross the Atlantic; Oct. 26, 1825: Erie Canal Opens; 1847: Hamburg-Amerika Shipping Line Begins; Jan. 31, 1858: Brunel Launches the SS *Great Eastern*; Nov. 17, 1869: Suez Canal Opens.

RELATED ARTICLE in *Great Lives from History: The Nineteenth Century, 1801-1900:* Ferdinand de Lesseps.

September 18, 1895
WASHINGTON'S ATLANTA COMPROMISE SPEECH

One of the most controversial addresses in African American history, Booker T. Washington's speech at the Atlanta Exposition proposed an accommodation between black and white southerners that would be mutually beneficial but which relegated African Americans to an inferior position.

ALSO KNOWN AS: Atlanta Exposition Address
LOCALE: Atlanta, Georgia
CATEGORIES: Education; economics; social issues and reform

KEY FIGURES
Booker T. Washington (1856-1915), prominent African American educator
W. E. B. Du Bois (1868-1963), African American intellectual who opposed Washington's philosophy

SUMMARY OF EVENT
Born a slave on a small Virginia plantation, Booker T. Washington gained his freedom at the end of the Civil War (1861-1865), when he was only nine years old. After emancipation, he worked in a salt furnace and coal mine and learned to read by studying spelling books and occasionally attending a school for African American children. In 1872, he enrolled at Hampton Institute in Virginia, a technical and agricultural school established for emancipated slaves. After graduating, he taught in Malden, West Virginia. He later returned to Hampton Institute to serve as a dormitory moderator to a group of newly admitted Native American students and to administer Hampton's night school.

In May, 1881, Washington received an invitation to join a group of educators from Tuskegee, Alabama, to help establish a technical and agricultural college for African American students. Tuskegee Institute opened on July 4, 1881, with Washington as its principal. Tuskegee's first academic building was a dilapidated church, and its first dormitories were shacks and cabins, but Washington raised funds, acquired land, supervised the construction of buildings, and recruited talented faculty members. Within a decade, the school had gained a national reputation for providing outstanding technical and occupational training to black students.

Booker T. Washington. (Library of Congress)

1890's

Washington toured the country, soliciting donors, recruiting students, and making speeches that extolled the value of the occupational training being delivered at Tuskegee Institute.

In the spring of 1895, Washington was invited to join a planning committee for the forthcoming Atlanta Cotton States and International Exposition, which was to be held in September. The exposition was designed to highlight the South's most recent developments in agricultural technology. Washington was asked to deliver one of the key addresses during the exposition's opening ceremonies. His speech was to focus on the role of African Americans in the South's agricultural economy. Washington saw the address as an opportunity to discuss the achievements that African Americans had made in the South since emancipation and to stress the need for further advancements.

On September 18, 1895, Washington delivered his speech before an audience of several thousand listeners. He opened by thanking the directors of the Atlanta Exposition for including African Americans in the event and expressed his hope that the exposition would do more to "cement the friendship of the two races than any occurrence since the dawn of our freedom." He went on to predict that the exposition would awaken among both white and black southerners "a new era of industrial progress." He illustrated his point by telling a parable of a ship lost at sea whose crew members were desperate for fresh water. The captain of another ship, hearing the pleas for water from the distressed vessel, urged the lost sailors, "Cast down your bucket where you are." When the captain of the lost ship followed that advice, his crew members brought aboard sparkling fresh water flooding into the Atlantic Ocean from the Amazon River.

Washington then urged his African American listeners to cast down their buckets "in agriculture, mechanics,

---

"CAST DOWN YOUR BUCKETS"

Booker T. Washington built his 1895 Atlanta speech around the metaphor of an oceangoing ship desperate for fresh water whose crew had to be reminded that they need not seek elsewhere, as they were in the midst of the fresh effluent water of the Amazon River.

A ship lost at sea for many days suddenly sighted a friendly vessel. From the mast of the unfortunate vessel was seen a signal, "Water, water; we die of thirst!" The answer from the friendly vessel at once came back, "Cast down your bucket where you are." A second time the signal, "Water, water; send us water!" ran up from the distressed vessel, and was answered, "Cast down your bucket where you are." And a third and fourth signal for water was answered, "Cast down your bucket where you are." The captain of the distressed vessel, at last heeding the injunction, cast down his bucket, and it came up full of fresh, sparkling water from the mouth of the Amazon River.

To those of my race who depend on bettering their condition in a foreign land or who underestimate the importance of cultivating friendly relations with the Southern white man, who is their next-door neighbor, I would say: "Cast down your bucket where you are" — cast it down in making friends in every manly way of the people of all races by whom we are surrounded.

Cast it down in agriculture, mechanics, in commerce, in domestic service, and in the professions. And in this connection it is well to bear in mind that whatever other sins the South may be called to bear, when it comes to business, pure and simple, it is in the South that the Negro is given a man's chance in the commercial world, and in nothing is this Exposition more eloquent than in emphasizing this chance. Our greatest danger is that in the great leap from slavery to freedom we may overlook the fact that the masses of us are to live by the productions of our hands, and fail to keep in mind that we shall prosper in proportion as we learn to dignify and glorify common labor . . .

To those of the white race who look to the incoming of those of foreign birth and strange tongue and habits for the prosperity of the South, were I permitted I would repeat what I say to my own race, "Cast down your bucket where you are." Cast it down among the eight millions of Negroes whose habits you know, whose fidelity and love you have tested in days when to have proved treacherous meant the ruin of your firesides. Cast down your bucket among these people who have, without strikes and labor wars, tilled your fields, cleared your forests, builded your railroads and cities, and brought forth treasures from the bowels of the earth, and helped make possible this magnificent representation of the progress of the South. . . .

---

in commerce, in domestic service, and in the professions." He said that black people would prosper "in proportion as we learn to dignify and glorify common labour and put brains and skill into the common occupations of life. . . ." He added that "no race can prosper till it learns that there is as much dignity in tilling a field as in writing a poem."

Washington also told his white listeners to cast down their own buckets among the South's African Americans, who have, without strikes and labour wars, tilled your fields, cleared your forests, builded your railroads and cities, and brought forth treasures from the bowels of the earth, and helped make possible this magnificent representation of the progress of the South.

He encouraged white southerners to educate African Americans in "head, heart, and hand" so that they would remain "the most patient, faithful, law-abiding, and unresentful people that the world has seen." He asserted that in "all things purely social we can be as separate as the fingers, yet one as the hand in all things essential to mutual progress."

Washington concluded his speech by expressing his belief that the

wisest among my race understand that the agitation of questions of social equality is the extremest folly, and that progress in the enjoyment of all the privileges that will come to use must be the result of severe and constant struggle rather than of artificial forcing.

He emphasized that African Americans must achieve economic self-reliance before they received "all the privileges of the law," that the "opportunity to earn a dollar in a factory just now is worth infinitely more than the opportunity to spend a dollar in an opera-house." Before surrendering the podium, Washington pledged to his audience his untiring effort to solve the racial animosities in the South and thereby bring to the region "a new heaven and a new earth."

Washington's address was enthusiastically received. Afterward, former Georgia governor Rufus Bullock grasped Washington's hand and offered his congratulations. Others rushed to shake Washington's hand. Over the next few days, newspapers in the North and South praised the speech in editorials. President Grover Cleveland wrote a congratulatory note. Washington received dozens of invitations to speak around the country and deliver his pragmatic message of black economic self-reliance and political accommodationism.

Critics of Washington's accommodationist philosophy soon surfaced as well. They accused Washington of making an unsatisfactory compromise by accepting an inferior social and political position for African Americans in exchange for economic opportunities. These critics argued that the tools for economic independence alone would not lead African Americans toward full citizenship and that the widespread segregation of and discrimination against African Americans in the United States, especially in the South, was proof of the flaws of Washington's reasoning.

Perhaps the most eloquent critic of Washington's message was W. E. B. Du Bois. In *The Souls of Black Folk* (1903), Du Bois, who would later found the National Association for the Advancement of Colored People (NAACP), asserted that Washington "represents in Negro thought the old attitude of adjustment and submission," that the ideas expressed in what he called Washington's "Atlanta Compromise" were merely "a gospel of Work and Money" that prompted African Americans to surrender political power, civil rights, and opportunities for higher education. In contrast to Washington, Du Bois advocated that African Americans receive the right to vote; civic equality; and opportunities for higher academic education, as opposed to the kind of occupational training offered at Tuskegee Institute.

SIGNIFICANCE

Despite criticisms, Washington remained an important African American spokesman. In 1901, he published *Up from Slavery*, an autobiography that chronicled his rise from slavery to national prominence. This rags-to-riches story was translated into several languages, giving Washington an international reputation. During that same year, he founded the National Negro Business League. He wrote several other books on the African American experience, including *Frederick Douglass* (1907) and *The Story of the Negro* (1909). He died at Tuskegee Institute in 1915.

The issues that Washington articulated in his Atlanta Exposition Address continued to influence African American dialogue throughout the twentieth century. Although Du Bois was proven correct in his belief that economic advancements for African Americans would not be forthcoming until they achieved political rights and social equality, Washington's message—that African Americans must be allowed to enjoy the fruits of America's economic prosperity—was repeated by African American civil rights leaders throughout the twentieth century.

—*James Tackach*

FURTHER READING

Baker, Houston A., Jr. *Turning South Again: Re-thinking Modernism/Re-reading Booker T. Washington*. Durham, N.C.: Duke University Press, 2001. Strongly critical analysis of Washington's ideas that attacks Washington for his fear of offending whites, for

1890's

founding Tuskegee Institute on the site of an abandoned plantation, and for training black people to work in servile occupations.

Bontemps, Arna. *Young Booker: Booker T. Washington's Early Days*. New York: Dodd, Mead, 1972. Bontemps, an African American poet and critic, traces Washington's life from its beginnings through the Atlanta address.

Brundage, Fitzhugh, ed. *Booker T. Washington and Black Progress: "Up from Slavery" One Hundred Years Later*. Gainesville: University Press of Florida, 2003. Collection of essays examining Washington's autobiography from various perspectives. Several place Washington's thought in a broad economic context.

Du Bois, W. E. B. *The Souls of Black Folk*. 1903. Reprint. New York: Penguin Books, 1989. In chapter 3 of his study of African American life, Du Bois critiques the ideas expressed in Washington's Atlanta Exposition Address.

Franklin, John Hope, and Alfred A. Moss, Jr. *From Slavery to Freedom: A History of African Americans*. 8th ed. Boston: McGraw-Hill, 2000. Chapter 14 of this extensive history of African Americans discusses Washington's philosophy and its critics.

Harlan, Louis R. *Booker T. Washington: The Making of a Black Leader, 1856-1901*. New York: Oxford University Press, 1972. This first volume in a two-volume biography of Washington contains a detailed discussion of the Atlanta address.

Smock, Raymond W., ed. *Booker T. Washington in Perspective: Essays of Louis R. Harlan*. Jackson: University Press of Mississippi, 1988. Collection of twelve essays on Washington by his leading biographer, Louis R. Harlan.

Verney, Kevern. *The Art of the Possible: Booker T. Washington and Black Leadership in the United States, 1881-1925*. New York: Routledge, 2001. Study of Washington's ideas and achievements, explaining his responses to segregation and his opposition to black urban migration. Compares Washington to Frederick Douglass, W. E. B. Du Bois, and Marcus Garvey.

Washington, Booker T. *Up from Slavery*. 1901. Reprint. New York: Bantam Books, 1970. In chapters 13 and 14, Washington describes the events leading to the Atlanta Exposition Address, records the entire address, and discusses reactions to it.

SEE ALSO: July 6, 1853: National Council of Colored People Is Founded; Jan. 1, 1857: First African American University Opens; Mar. 3, 1865: Congress Creates the Freedmen's Bureau; May 18, 1896: *Plessy v. Ferguson*.

RELATED ARTICLES in *Great Lives from History: The Nineteenth Century, 1801-1900:* Grover Cleveland; Booker T. Washington.

November 9, 1895
RÖNTGEN DISCOVERS X RAYS

Wilhelm Conrad Röntgen's discovery of X rays had both practical and philosophical consequences. The penetrating power of this wavelength of electromagnetic radiation led to its wide use in medical and industrial applications. Meanwhile, the vision of the world revealed by X-radiography seemed to confirm the late nineteenth century worry that the world was less solid and less stable than it seemed.

LOCALE: Würzburg, Bavaria, German Empire (now in Germany)

CATEGORIES: Physics; science and technology; inventions; photography

KEY FIGURES

Wilhelm Conrad Röntgen (1845-1923), German experimental physicist

Sir William Crookes (1832-1919), British inventor

Heinrich Hertz (1857-1894), German physicist

Philipp Lenard (1862-1947), German experimental physicist

Ludwig Zehnder (1854-1935), Röntgen's laboratory assistant and colleague

SUMMARY OF EVENT

X rays were discovered in 1895 by Wilhelm Conrad Röntgen, a professor of physics at the University of Würzburg. He was investigating the radiation produced in a partially evacuated glass bulb when a high voltage was applied. Sir William Crookes in 1869 had published a research report in which he described the bright glow that occurred inside such a bulb. Another physicist, Philipp Lenard, had then shown that the electrical discharge inside the glass bulb could penetrate a thin aluminum window, producing an external beam that traveled through several centimeters of open air. This beam was called a "cathode ray," because it originated at the negative voltage terminal, or cathode. Lenard was able to trace the path of cathode rays by coating a small screen with fluorescent paint that glowed in the dark when radiation struck it. He showed that cathode rays could be deflected by a magnet.

Röntgen was an experienced experimentalist with twenty-five years of laboratory research and more than forty technical publications. Using the same type of apparatus as Crookes and Lenard had used, he first confirmed their observations for himself. In order to see the external beam more clearly, he surrounded the glass bulb with opaque, black paper, so the light produced inside the bulb would be blocked out and the external beam would show up more clearly. On November 9, 1895, according to his laboratory notebook, he noticed something quite unusual. A piece of cardboard coated with fluorescent paint, lying on the table more than a meter away, started to glow whenever the electric discharge was turned on. This was a startling observation, because cathode rays could not travel that far. Was there another, unknown type of radiation coming through the black paper?

Working by himself, Röntgen began a systematic investigation of the mysterious radiation. He observed fluorescence at a distance of as much as two meters from the discharge tube. Since the radiation had penetrated opaque, black paper, he decided to test various other materials for their transparency. Even behind a book of one thousand pages, he found that the fluorescent screen lit up brightly. Blocks of wood and sheets of aluminum transmitted the radiation fairly well, but two millimeters of lead was enough to block it. When holding his hand between the discharge apparatus and the fluorescent screen, Röntgen was able to see the shadow of the bones inside the faint outline of his fingers.

Further experiments showed that photographic plates were sensitive to the radiation. This enabled Röntgen to make a permanent record of his observations. He had to be careful not to store unused photographic plates near the apparatus, however, or they would become fogged by stray radiation. In his publications, Röntgen referred to the new type of radiation as "X rays," because they were a mystery. He used a glass prism to see if X rays could be refracted like ordinary light, but the result was negative. He also found that X rays were not reflected by a mirror and could not be focused by a lens. Diffraction gratings, which had been used to measure the wavelengths of visi-

Wilhelm Conrad Röntgen. (Library of Congress)

ble light with high precision, had no effect on X rays, and a magnet caused no deflection in their path.

On December 22, 1895, Röntgen asked his wife to help him in the laboratory. He placed an X-ray tube just underneath a table, while she held her hand on the table surface with a photographic plate above her hand. The exposure time was about five minutes. When Röntgen developed the photograph, it showed the bones in her hand with her wedding ring on one finger. A photography assistant made multiple prints from this and several other negatives. On January 1, 1896, Röntgen sent a ten-page article with photographs to the Physical-Medical Society of Würzburg, as well as to colleagues at other universities. The pictures created a sensation. Nothing like them had ever been seen before.

Within a few days, newspapers all over Europe had published stories and photographs about this new scientific development. A flood of messages came to Röntgen with invitations to give lectures and demonstrations. He turned them all down, except one that he could not refuse from the emperor of Germany, William I. On January 13,

X RAYS AND CONRAD'S *HEART OF DARKNESS*

The discovery of X rays by Wilhelm Conrad Röntgen had theoretical and philosophical consequences at least as significant as its practical effects. By allowing people to see through solid matter, X rays rendered more plausible the contemporary theory of the ether, which asserted that all matter was not "really" solid, but was composed of etherial waves or vibrations. Novelist Joseph Conrad first encountered both X rays and ether theory at a dinner party in September of 1898, as he recounts in the letter excerpted below. Some critics believe that the vision of an insubstantial universe Conrad experienced through the X-ray machine was a direct inspiration for his novella Heart of Darkness, *which he published the following year.*

The secret of the universe is in the existence of horizontal waves whose varied vibrations are at the bottom of all states of consciousness. If the waves were vertical the universe would be different. . . . Therefore it follows that two universes may exist in the same place and in the same time—and not only two universes but an infinity of different universes—if by universe we mean a set of states of consciousness; and not, *all* (the universes) composed of the same matter, *all matter* being only that thing of inconceivable tenuity through which the various vibrations of waves (electricity, heat, sound, light, etc.) are propagated, thus giving birth to our sensations—then emotions—then thought. Is that so?

These things I said to the [Doctor] while Neil Munro stood in front of a Röntgen machine and on the screen we contemplated his backbone and his ribs. The rest of that promising youth was too diaphanous to be visible. It was so—said the Doctor—and there is no space, time, matter, mind as vulgarly understood, there is only the eternal something that waves and an eternal force that causes the waves—it's not much—and by virtue of these two eternities exists that Corot and that Whistler in the dining room upstairs (we were in a kind of cellar) and Munro's here writings and your Nigger and Graham's politics and Paderewski's playing (in the phonograph) and what more do you want?

What we wanted (apparently) was more whisky.

Source: Joseph Conrad, Letter to Edward Garnett (September 29, 1898). In *The Collected Letters of Joseph Conrad* (New York: Cambridge University Press, 1986), vol. 2, pp. 94-95.

from many scientists who were experimenting with X rays. One person sent a photograph of a fish showing its detailed bone structure. His friend Ludwig Zehnder, whom he had known since graduate school in Zürich, took several photographs of the human body, which he pasted together to obtain a complete skeleton from head to foot. There were some crackpot letters, such as the one asking for a sum of money to solve the secrets of weather forecasting with X rays. The greatest honor for Röntgen was to be awarded the Nobel Prize in 1901, the first year in which the award was given.

SIGNIFICANCE

Röntgen felt that the benefits of X rays should be available to humankind without restrictions. He therefore did not take out a patent on his discovery, although doing so could have made him wealthy. His apparatus was not expensive or difficult to duplicate. The most difficult aspect of its construction was the need for a professional glass blower to make a specialized glass bulb with two metal electrodes inside that were connected by wires going through the glass to two terminals on the outside. Many hospitals and research laboratories were able to set up their own X-ray machines. Within one year of Röntgen's initial publication, nearly one thousand articles on X rays had appeared in various technical journals.

The medical profession enthusiastically welcomed X rays as a new diagnostic tool. Doctors were able to determine the severity of broken bones and to locate swallowed objects or bullets embedded in the body. Annual chest X rays for school children became a routine procedure to diagnose early signs of tuberculosis. Irradiation of cancerous tumors was found to be a beneficial therapy, as long as the dose was carefully regulated. In the 1970's, a major improvement in X-ray technology, called the CT scan, was developed. A narrow beam of X rays was swept across a portion of the body from many different angles, and the information was then correlated by a computer to produce a picture on a screen.

Röntgen traveled to Berlin with his X-ray apparatus and showed to the assembled court how metal objects inside a closed box could be photographed. On January 23, he gave a lecture to the faculty and students at his own university. He told the audience about his experiments, giving credit for earlier contributions to Heinrich Hertz, who had discovered radio waves in 1888, and to Lenard. Toward the close of the lecture, Röntgen made an X-ray photograph of a faculty colleague's hand, which was quickly developed and passed around the room. Prolonged applause came as the lecture ended.

Over the next several weeks, Röntgen received letters

Among its industrial applications, the X-ray apparatus came into common use at airports to inspect baggage before boarding. X rays have been used to search for hidden microphones in the wall of a room before a diplomatic conference. In the pipeline industry, after individual sections of pipe had been welded together, portable X-ray machines have been used to detect possible hairline cracks at the welds that might later allow fluid to leak out. X-ray analysis has been widely used by chemists to determine the structure of complex molecules, such as the deoxyribonucleic acid (DNA) helix. Röntgen's discovery of X rays stands as a good example of pure research that led to a multitude of practical applications that could not have been anticipated.

—Hans G. Graetzer

FURTHER READING

Farmelo, Graham. "The Discovery of X-rays." *Scientific American*, November, 1995, 86-91. Describes Röntgen's experimental setup and contains reprints of the earliest X-ray photographs, including the one of his wife's hand.

Hart, Michael H. *The One Hundred: A Ranking of the Most Influential Persons in History*. New York: Galahad Books, 1982. A fascinating collection of short biographies about the most famous artists, political leaders, theologians, and scientists, including Röntgen.

Kevles, Bettyann. *Naked to the Bones: Medical Imaging in the Twentieth Century*. Reading, Mass.: Addison-Wesley, 1998. Discusses Röntgen's discovery and its medical applications, with modern improvements in imaging technology using computers; intended for the general reader.

Nitske, W. Robert. *The Life of Wilhelm Conrad Röntgen: Discoverer of the X Ray*. Tucson: University of Arizona Press, 1971. The best biography of Röntgen available in English, containing fascinating anecdotes about his personal life and scientific career. Photographs, a bibliography, and translations of his three X-ray publications.

Turner, G. L. "Röntgen, Wilhelm Conrad." *Dictionary of Scientific Biography*. Vol. 11. New York: Charles Scribner's Sons, 1981. An authoritative, short biography of Röntgen's life and professional career.

Walker, James S. *Physics*. 2d ed. Upper Saddle River, N.J.: Pearson/Prentice Hall, 2004. College-level textbook describing the operation of an X-ray tube, including Röntgen's contribution.

SEE ALSO: 1803-1808: Dalton Formulates the Atomic Theory of Matter; 1816: Laënnec Invents the Stethoscope; Nov. 6, 1820: Ampère Reveals Magnetism's Relationship to Electricity; Oct., 1831: Faraday Converts Magnetic Force into Electricity; Dec. 14, 1900: Articulation of Quantum Theory.

RELATED ARTICLE in *Great Lives from History: The Nineteenth Century, 1801-1900:* Wilhelm Conrad Röntgen.

1890's

November 27, 1895
NOBEL BEQUEATHS FUNDS FOR THE NOBEL PRIZES

After making a vast fortune from his invention of dynamite, land mines, and other explosives, Alfred Nobel sought to bestow a positive legacy upon society by leaving most of his wealth to establish the renowned Nobel Prizes.

LOCALE: Sweden
CATEGORY: Cultural and intellectual history

KEY FIGURE

Alfred Nobel (1833-1896), Swedish inventor and philanthropist

SUMMARY OF EVENT

Alfred Nobel was one of the most successful entrepreneurs and industrialists in Europe by the time he died on December 10, 1896. He had led an exciting life but one that was somewhat lacking in fulfillment. In the years immediately before his death, he pondered many philosophical questions, including the matter of how his life would be viewed after his death. He had never married, had no offspring, and despite his enormous wealth, he was troubled at the thought that he would likely be remembered, if at all, as the inventor of dynamite, which, despite its commercial usefulness, is also dangerous.

Alfred's father, Immanuel Nobel, was in the construction business in Sweden, but his business failed in the 1830's, plunging the elder Nobel into bankruptcy when Alfred was a child. Immanuel staged a substantial comeback by setting up a plant in St. Petersburg, Russia, to manufacture land mines and other munitions, for which

Russia had a great demand during its battles in the Crimean War (1853-1856). In time, Immanuel was sufficiently successful to bring his wife, Andrietta, and his sons to St. Petersburg, where Alfred received an excellent education from carefully selected tutors. Adept at languages, Alfred was soon fluent not only in his native Swedish but also in Russian, German, English, and French. In his later life, he conducted business in all of these languages.

Nobel also was intrigued by chemistry and could divert himself for hours doing chemical experiments under the direction of one of his Russian tutors, Nikolai Zinin, who had studied in Paris with a noted French chemist, Théophile-Jules Pelouze. Eventually, Nobel spent a year in Paris studying with Pelouze and becoming a highly proficient chemist.

Nobel was extremely interested in explosives and had a familiarity with them through his exposure to his father's munitions factory. When the Crimean War ended, the Russians no longer needed the materials that his father produced. During the next several years, Nobel doggedly continued his experiments until he discovered a type of porous sand, *Kieselguhr*, that, mixed with nitro-

Alfred Nobel. (Library of Congress)

glycerin, forms a paste that is much easier and safer to work with than liquid nitroglycerin. He called this new product dynamite, a word derived from the Greek word *dynamos*, meaning "power." The demand for such a material was enormous as both Europe and the United States embarked on extensive construction projects to expand their infrastructures, building roads, bridges, tunnels, and various structures that required precision blasting.

By the time he was forty, Alfred Nobel was one of the richest people in the world. His wealth increased exponentially in the years that followed, as demand for his products grew and as oil properties he owned in Russia rewarded him handsomely. The question of what his lasting legacy would be concerned him greatly. Nobel was cosmopolitan, a scientist, widely read in philosophy, and a chemist who also loved literature. He wrote considerable poetry and one play, *Nemesis*. He had strong moral underpinnings that made it incumbent on him to contribute permanently to society.

Perhaps sparking his interest in establishing permanent prizes to recognize exceptional contributions to humankind was his receiving, along with his father, the Letterstedt Prize by the Royal Swedish Academy in 1868. Nobel was deeply moved at being chosen to receive such an award, whose stated purpose was to recognize "important discoveries of practical value to humanity." These words, used to describe the Letterstedt Prize, are remarkably similar to some of the language Nobel used in drafting his last will and testament, in which he established the Nobel Prizes.

Nobel executed his will at Paris's Swedish-Norwegian Club on November 27, 1895, one year before his death. The will provided for a small number of relatives and friends, distributing about 6 percent of his total assets among them. The remaining 94 percent was, according to his instructions, to be invested by his executors in safe securities, the income from which was to be distributed annually in equal portions to those chosen as recipients by the Nobel Foundation in specified categories. Nobel's will was challenged by some of his relatives, so the foundation was not established until 1900, after legal problems had been resolved. Nobel specifically directed that nationality should not be considered in selecting recipients of the prizes.

Prizes, in accordance with Nobel's wishes, fell into five categories, going to those who in the preceding year are deemed by the Nobel Prize Committee to have made the most significant contributions to society in chemistry, physics, physiology or medicine, literature, and peace. The prizes have been awarded annually since

1901. In 1969, one additional category, economic sciences, was added to the five existing categories.

The list of Nobel laureates contains scientists of the stature of Albert Einstein, Marie Curie, and Linus Pauling; writers such as William Faulkner, T. S. Eliot, and Toni Morrison; physicians and physiologists such as Ivan Petrovich Pavlov and Sir Alexander Fleming; and advocates of peace such as Woodrow Wilson, Albert Schweitzer, and Wangari Muta Maathai.

SIGNIFICANCE

During the early twenty-first century, the Nobel Prizes remained the most prestigious of all recognitions of excellence among thousands of awards given in various fields worldwide each year. The Nobel awards each carry a cash prize in excess of $1 million. Awards are sometimes made to more than one person in a given field, especially in the sciences, where collaborative work is frequent and recognized as a single contribution.

Nobel was initially criticized for not earmarking the awards for Swedes, or, more broadly, to Scandinavians, but such a restriction would have violated Nobel's cosmopolitanism. Awards have gone to individuals from many countries and from six of the seven continents, exactly what Alfred Nobel had hoped for. His influence through the prizes he established has grown steadily through the years.

—*R. Baird Shuman*

FURTHER READING

Abrams, Irwin, ed. *The Words of Peace: The Nobel Peace Prize Laureates of the Twentieth Century*. New York: Newmarket Press, 2000. Selections from the acceptance speeches of Nobel Peace Prize recipients, with a foreword by former U.S. president and Nobel laureate Jimmy Carter.

Calvin, Melvin. *Following the Trail of Light: A Scientific Odyssey*. Washington, D.C.: American Chemical Society, 1992. Calvin, although focusing on the Nobel Prizes in chemistry, provides useful information about the establishment of the prizes in general.

Evanloff, Michael, and Marjorie Fluor. *Alfred Nobel: The Loneliest Millionaire*. Los Angeles: W. Ritchie Press, 1969. This sympathetic presentation of Nobel as a human suffering from concerns about producing destructive weapons is insightful and penetrating.

Fant, Kenne. *Alfred Nobel: A Biography*. Translated by Marianne Ruuth. New York: Arcade, 1993. Fant demonstrates his understanding of Nobel's life and of his motivations for establishing the Nobel Prizes.

Halasz, Nicholas. *Nobel: A Biography of Alfred Nobel*. New York: Orion Press, 1959. Although superseded by Fant's later biography, this biography is easily accessible to those wishing to understand Nobel's contributions to society.

Leroy, Francis, ed. *A Century of Nobel Prizes Recipients: Chemistry, Physics, and Medicine*. New York: Marcel Dekker, 2003. An encyclopedic collection of prize winners in three of the six categories. Includes illustrations, a bibliography, and an index.

Levinovitz, Agneta Wallin, and Nils Ringertz, eds. *The Nobel Prize: The First One Hundred Years*. London: Imperial College Press, 2001. The first two selections in this collection focus, respectively, on the life and philosophy of Nobel and on the establishment of the Nobel Prizes. A comprehensive, accurate overview.

Magill, Frank N., ed. *The Nobel Prize Winners: Literature*. 3 vols. Pasadena, Calif.: Salem Press, 1987. An excellent source listing the recipients of the Nobel Prize in Literature, through the year 1987. Includes a bibliography and an index.

_____. *The Nobel Prize Winners: Physiology or Medicine*. 3 vols. Pasadena, Calif.: Salem Press, 1991. An excellent source listing the recipients of the Nobel Prize in Physiology or Medicine, through the year 1991. Includes a bibliography and an index.

Thee, Marek, ed. *Peace! By the Nobel Peace Prize Laureates: An Anthology*. Paris: UNESCO, 1995. A 570-page anthology of works by peace prize recipients. From UNESCO's Cultures of Peace series.

SEE ALSO: Aug. 22, 1864: International Red Cross Is Launched; Oct., 1867: Nobel Patents Dynamite; 1882-1901: Metchnikoff Advances the Cellular Theory of Immunity; 1888-1906: Ramón y Cajal Shows How Neurons Work in the Nervous System; June, 1896: Marconi Patents the Wireless Telegraph; Dec. 14, 1900: Articulation of Quantum Theory.

RELATED ARTICLES in *Great Lives from History: The Nineteenth Century, 1801-1900:* Alfred Nobel; Bertha von Suttner.

1890's

December 28, 1895
FIRST COMMERCIAL PROJECTION OF MOTION PICTURES

Moving pictures were developed during the early 1890's by several different inventors, including Thomas Alva Edison, whose kinetoscope was a peep-show device accommodating one viewer at a time. The Lumière brothers' cinematograph, by contrast, projected a moving image onto a screen so that many spectators could view it at once. When the device was first used to entertain a paying audience in a Paris café, the cinema was born.

LOCALE: Paris, France

CATEGORIES: Motion pictures; inventions; science and technology; photography

KEY FIGURES

August Lumière (1862-1954), French filmmaker and inventor

Louis Lumière (1864-1948), French filmmaker, inventor, and brother of August

William Dickson (1860-1935), American photographer and inventor

Thomas Alva Edison (1847-1931), American inventor and entrepreneur

Edwin S. Porter (1870?-1941), American director

Georges Méliès (1861-1938), French filmmaker

Eadweard Muybridge (1830-1904), British photographer and inventor

Étienne-Jules Marey (1830-1904), French photographer and inventor

SUMMARY OF EVENT

When Eadweard Muybridge visited Thomas Alva Edison on February 25, 1888, in Orange, New Jersey, he showed the famous inventor his zoöpraxiscope, a machine that projected images onto a screen in such a way as to create the illusion that they were moving, and the two men discussed combining that machine with Edison's phonograph. Edison planned to call the new invention a kinetoscope, meaning "moving view," but the combination did not succeed. The following year, Edison gave William Dickson, a photographer who worked with Edison on his experiments, the task of creating a device that would combine moving images with recorded sound. Dickson was to make a device involving moving photographic images, however, unlike the hand-painted images of the zoöpraxiscope. While traveling in Europe, Edison also met Étienne-Jules Marey, who had photo-graphed a continuous series of images on a film strip that passed before a single camera lens.

Marey's ideas were used by Dickson and his assistant, William Heise. The two created a camera that used a .75-inch strip of film that was exposed by means of a horizontal-feed system, utilizing a row of perforations on the bottom edge of the band. On May 20, 1891, Edison demonstrated a peep-hole viewing machine that featured Dickson on camera bowing, smiling, and taking off his hat. In three months, Edison submitted patents for "his" kinetograph (the camera) and kinetoscope (the peep-hole viewing device). The following year, Edison and Dickson made a vertical-feed motion picture camera that used 1.5-inch film strips. They employed this device to make more experimental films, one of which featured Dickson and Heise congratulating each other on their invention.

Edison in 1892 constructed the first dedicated motion picture studio, the Black Maria (named for its resemblance to contemporary black police wagons), and he shifted to commercial filmmaking. *Blacksmith Scene*, one of his early films, was demonstrated at the Brooklyn Institute on May 9, 1893. Edison marketed his kinetoscope machines and the films to be shown in them to penny arcades and other such venues in large cities, where they became extremely popular despite the brevity of the films, which lasted less than twenty seconds each. As the novelty of an image in motion wore off, however, the popularity of the new devices began to wane. Meanwhile, the cinematograph of August and Louis Lumière, a device which projected moving images onto a screen, was becoming popular in France.

Edison initially resisted screen projection for simple economic reasons. Since each of his peep-show devices only occupied a single viewer at a time, he could easily sell a half-dozen or more kinetoscopes to each venue. A venue using motion picture projectors would need at most two such devices, so Edison believed that his machine sales would plummet if he switched to projection. He failed, at first, to take into account the extent to which the content of the films themselves could drive a motion picture industry. Films of the 1890's were often demonstrations of technology rather than aesthetic objects— and this was far more true of Edison's films than of the Lumières' films.

Just as Edison, despite the pioneering work of other people, received most of the credit for the development of the motion picture in America, August and Louis

Lumière have been regarded as the inventors of French film, although they, too, had been preceded by other inventors. Among the most significant of the earlier French inventors was Lèon Bouly, who in 1893 secured a patent for his cinematograph but could not pay the yearly patent fee. The enterprising Antoine Lumière—father of Louis and August who had had one of his employees take apart the Edison kinetoscope—picked up Bouly's patent and the term "cinematograph" and took out a patent for his sons. The brothers should be credited, however, for developing the motion picture business in France. Above all, they should be credited for the quality of the films they produced.

The cinematograph, an incredibly efficient, boxlike device, was actually three devices in one. It was a camera, a film processor, and a projector, and it was still compact enough to be easily portable. The Lumières began making films with the device at the end of 1894, and they gave technical demonstrations of motion picture projection beginning in March, 1895. Their most famous exhibition, however, was the evening of short films they presented on December 28, 1895, at the Grand Café, in the Boulevard des Capucines, Paris. This presentation is generally credited as being the first projection of motion pictures onto a screen for a paying audience and therefore as the beginning of the motion picture industry. There is evidence, however, that an exhibition given by German motion picture inventors Max and Emil Skladanowsky may deserve that title, as it may have occurred more than a month earlier.

The Lumières' films were short, like Edison's, and like his, they were concerned with everyday life. The earliest films of both producers fall into the category of "actualities," a now-forgotten genre of nonfictional films resembling extremely short documentaries in which the point is merely to show a brief scene from life. As Edison had filmed workers (in *Blacksmith Scene*, for example), the Lumières' first film, *La Sortie des usines Lumière* (1895; workers leaving the Lumière factory), was typical of their films. Among the most striking of those early films was *L'Arrivée d'un train en gare de la Ciotat* (1895; the arrival of a train at Ciotat station). Some spectators reportedly reacted to the latter film as though the train were coming directly at them. While the earliest Lumière films were set in France, the brothers began to venture to other parts of the world to make their films, bringing actualities of exotic locales back to France.

Edison eventually recognized the need to compete with the projectors invented by others, including those of the Lumière brothers and the Skladanowsky brothers. Edison's employees found an answer to this competition in the phantoscope, a machine that had an intermittent action that stopped each frame in front of the light source, making modern film projection possible. The machine's inventors, Francis Jenkins and Thomas Armat, quarreled, and Armat took the machine to Edison, who renamed it the "vitascope," emphasizing its ability to capture life. Edison's reputation as the Wizard of Menlo Park, as well as the new name he gave the device, provided the vitascope with commercial viability.

The vitascope was introduced on April 23, 1896, at Koster and Bial's Music Hall, where six films were shown, all of them quite short, ten or fifteen seconds being the maximum length. Production shifted from the

1890's

"BIOGRAPH: THE MARVEL OF SCIENCE"

One of the earliest motion picture projectors in America was the Biograph, created by the American Mutoscope and Biograph Company, which would go on to produce D. W. Griffith's first films. Excerpted below is a description of the first Biograph exhibition in Cincinnati, published in the Cincinnati Enquirer *in late 1896.*

To see Niagara taken with all its water drops in paroxysm, lost to their level, threatened with death by vapor, the rapids full of delugers out deluged, drowners drowning, furies flying, is to arrest the heart and make science-devout the audience which came only to leer at lewdness. Gods they never feared. But knowledge in its apparitions makes them worshipers. Upon a sheet shaken by the stage drafts the enormous cataract records its living countenance. Its least rills of water spill spill like its rivers. The leaves, the jar or the wind shook on the trees at the cataract's border were not overlooked by the camera. Forever they will shake, having been caught in the act like the minutest things.

See, also, the greater dragon than that red one in Revelations, the Empire State express, at 60 miles an hour, repeating its convulsive chariot race against Apollo's steeds! You see it coming, head on, almost a mile away. Track-menders look at it, hasten their work, and finally clear the track. It expands as it draws nearer, puffs every puff of smoke, flashes its driving rod, rises on the sheet to near the top of the stage, veers off as if to run out at the wings, and leaves the oldest among us appalled.

Source: "Biograph: The Marvel of Science." *Cincinnati Enquirer* (November 2, 1896).

Black Maria, where the popular *May Irwin Kiss* (1896) was filmed, to the outdoors when the Edison Company created a new, portable camera. *Herald Square*, *Central Park*, and *Elevated Railway, 23rd Street New York* were all actualities, similar to the Lumière films popular in Europe (and soon, six weeks later, to make their debut in America).

Both Edison's vitascope and the Lumières' cinematograph were shown internationally before 1900. In 1896, for example, Lumière films shown in Bombay were the first films to be exhibited in India. The Lumières also influenced Edison's filmmakers. *Employers Leaving Factory* (1896) was an American remake of the earlier Lumière film, and indeed, such "remakes" of the films of others were quite common in the early years of cinema. Film historian Charles Musser believes that the device of mounting a camera on a train in Edison's *Niagara Falls, Gorge* (1896) was inspired by the Lumières' *Grand Canal, Venice* (1896). The Lumière comedy *L'Arroseur arrosée* (1896; the waterer watered) was particularly influential. Now commonly thought of as the first fiction film, the first narrative film, and the first comedy, it was twice adapted and modified by Edison's company. Lumière military scenes and illustrations of news stories were also quickly adapted by Edison filmmakers.

In fact, the Lumière cinematograph, which showed films at Keith's Union Square Theater in New York, was strong competition for Edison, whose equipment was simply not its equal. The highest-quality American films were made by the American Mutoscope and Biograph Company (commonly known as Biograph). Edison's films were shown at his Eden Musée, also located in New York. Film in 1896-1897 was still a novelty and often competed with or supplemented vaudeville. Edison had a great deal of American competition, especially with Biograph, which had been associated with Dickson, who had created the mutoscope (another peep-show device). Edison resorted to patents, despite the fact that his inven-

Early advertisement for Vitascope projectors. (Hulton Archive/Getty Images)

tions were hardly original, and then to lit-igation, as he attempted to take control of the film business.

By 1900, filmmaking had not changed a great deal; editing and various cine-matic effects such as the iris did not be-come common until after 1900, when Edwin S. Porter, who had worked on Edi-son's machines, became involved in pro-duction and directing. Porter, who would become the director of Edison's most fa-mous and popular films, had seen Geor-ges Méliès's fantasy narrative film *La Voyage dans la lune* (1902; the trip to the moon). He understood the importance of a story line, and in 1902-1903, he pro-duced four story films, including the highly regarded *Great Train Robbery* (1903) and *Life of an American Fireman* (1902-1903), the latter of which was mod-eled after a magic lantern show of the same name.

Porter also understood the reluctance of film exhibi-tors to accept premade story films: They did not want to cede creative control to film producers, at a time when each exhibitor was accustomed to assembling his or her own unique show, rather than offering a standardized product. Some of the earliest narrative films, for exam-ple, were sold shot by shot. Exhibitors could buy as many or as few shots as they liked and assemble them to create films of varying lengths. Porter helped standardize the earliest conventions of film editing and narrative by per-suading some film exhibitors to purchase and project multishot films that had been assembled by the film-maker in advance. Once that step had been accom-plished, it was possible for a conventional cinematic lan-guage to be invented, and the art of cinema had truly begun.

SIGNIFICANCE

The evolution of film editing and narrative conven-tions—so central to the history of cinema as an art form—was slow at first, but between roughly 1907 and 1917, what is now known as classical cinema developed. By that time, the actualities so popular between 1895 and around 1904 had largely been replaced by narrative films. It is easy, then, to discount the earliest films of 1895-1896 as merely proofs of concept for the technol-ogy rather than artistic works in themselves. The films of August and Louis Lumière, however, clearly fall in the

---

MÉLIÈS'S CAREER IN CINEMA BEGINS

Georges Méliès, one of the most famous film makers of the preclassical period, was a stage magician when moving pictures were first invented. He was one of the first to recognize the potential of the new technology to create illusion, in addition to capturing reality. Reproduced below is his own account of his first encounter with the Lumière cinematograph, after which he immediately decided to make moving pictures of his own.

. . . a *still* photograph showing the place Bellecour in Lyon was pro-jected. A little surprised, I just had time to say to my neighbor:

"They got us all stirred up for projections like this? I've been doing them for over ten years."

I had hardly finished speaking when a horse pulling a wagon began to walk towards us, followed by other vehicles and then pedestrians, in short all the animation of the street. Before this spectacle we sat with gaping mouths, struck with amazement, astonished beyond all expression.

Source: Georges Sadoul, *Histoire générale du cinéma* (Paris: Denoël, 1946-1954), quoted and translated in Tom Gunning, "An Aesthetic of Astonishment: Early Cinema and the (in)Credulous Spectator," *Art and Text* 34 (1989), p. 35.

---

latter category. The care with which they were composed and the sheer beauty they retain more than one hundred years later speak to the depth of the Lumières' accom-plishment and mark them as the first true filmmakers.

—*Thomas L. Erskine*

FURTHER READING

Abel, Richard. *The Ciné Goes to Town: French Cinema, 1896-1914*. Berkeley: University of California Press, 1994. Exhaustive study of French cinema from its in-ception until World War I.

Burch, Noël. *Life to Those Shadows*. Translated and edited by Ben Brewster. Berkeley: University of Cali-fornia Press, 1990. An extremely important examina-tion of emergent cinema on its own terms, under-standing it as an art in its own right, distinct from the classical cinema that followed rather than merely a primitive attempt at such an art.

Elsaesser, Thomas, with Adam Barker, eds. *Early Cin-ema: Space, Frame, Narrative*. London: BFI, 1990. An anthology of short essays by all of the most impor-tant and influential theorists of early cinema, includ-ing Tom Gunning, Miriam Hansen, Charles Musser, Noël Burch, André Gaudreault, and others.

Hendricks, Gordon. *Origins of the American Film*. New York: Arno Press, 1972. Attempts to give due credit to William Dickson, whom Hendricks believes to be responsible for Edison's motion picture camera.

Musser, Charles, "At the Beginning: Motion Picture, Production, Representation, and Ideology at the Edison and Lumière Studios." In *The Silent Cinema Reader*, edited by Lee Grieveson and Peter Krämer. New York: Routledge, 2004. Some material is similar to Musser's work in his own book, but this essay includes much new material on the Lumières.

_____. *Before the Nickelodeon: Edwin S. Porter and the Edison Manufacturing Company.* Berkeley: University of California Press, 1991. Focuses on Porter's role in the development of cinema; Musser devotes the third chapter of his book to Edison from 1888 to 1895.

Phillips, Ray. *Edison's Kinetoscope and Its Films: A History to 1896.* Westport, Conn.: Greenwood Press, 1997. Thorough treatment of the films (all of which are listed, with many described) made by Edison's film company.

Whissel, Kristen. "The Gender of Empire: American Modernity, Masculinity, and Edison's War Actualities." In *A Feminist Reader in Early Cinema*, edited by Jennifer M. Bean and Diane Negra. Durham, N.C.: Duke University Press, 2002. Places Edison's early war actualities in the context of modernity, American imperialism, and gender.

SEE ALSO: 1839: Daguerre and Niépce Invent Daguerreotype Photography; 1850's-1880's: Rise of Burlesque and Vaudeville; Dec. 24, 1877: Edison Patents the Cylinder Phonograph; 1878: Muybridge Photographs a Galloping Horse; Oct. 21, 1879: Edison Demonstrates the Incandescent Lamp; May, 1887: Goodwin Develops Celluloid Film; June, 1896: Marconi Patents the Wireless Telegraph.

RELATED ARTICLE in *Great Lives from History: The Nineteenth Century, 1801-1900:* Thomas Alva Edison.

December 29, 1895-January 2, 1896
JAMESON RAID

An abortive attempt to overthrow the Afrikaner government of the Transvaal in South Africa, the Jameson Raid increased tensions between the British government and the region's two Afrikaner republics and contributed significantly to the outbreak of the South African War nearly four years later.

LOCALE: South Africa
CATEGORIES: Diplomacy and international relations; wars, uprisings, and civil unrest; crime and scandals

KEY FIGURES
Cecil Rhodes (1853-1902), mining magnate and prime minister of the Cape Colony, 1890-1896
Leander Starr Jameson (1853-1917), British South Africa Company's administrator of Rhodesia
Paul Kruger (1825-1904), president of the Transvaal's South African Republic, 1883-1902
Sir Hercules Robinson (1824-1897), governor of the Cape Colony and British high commissioner of South Africa, 1881-1889, 1895-1897
Joseph Chamberlain (1836-1914), British colonial secretary, 1895-1903
Third Marquis of Salisbury (Robert Cecil; 1830-1903), British prime minister and foreign secretary, 1895-1902

SUMMARY OF EVENT
Throughout the nineteenth century, South Africa's Afrikaner people continually resisted British interference and domination, as evidenced by the fact that thousands of them left the Cape Colony during the 1830's and set up their own republics inland. During the 1890's, they and the British continued to be at odds over which groups would control the destiny of South Africa. After the discovery of gold in the Afrikaner-ruled Transvaal, British interest in creating a consolidated South Africa under their authority increased significantly. British capital flowed into the Transvaal mining industry, providing the British government with a vested interest in controlling that industry's progress and profits. However, the Transvaal's Afrikaners intended to use their republic's mineral wealth to ensure their independence from British authority. Into this situation stepped the millionaire English businessman, imperialist, and prime minister of Britain's Cape Colony, Cecil Rhodes.

By 1893, Rhodes was leading a chartered company that controlled what is now Zimbabwe, immediately north of the Transvaal. He had also formulated a plan to overthrow the Afrikaner government in the Transvaal and open the region to British development and control. Rhodes believed the Transvaal's South African Republic to be weak and unable to respond to a major internal challenge. Under his plan, a column of British troops entering the Transvaal from the north would incite a rebellion among the mainly British Uitlanders, or outsiders, living and working in the Transvaal.

The Transvaal's Uitlanders had long caused difficulties for the Afrikaners, and they formed an organization called the Transvaal National Union in 1892. They opposed the severe voting restrictions imposed on newcomers by the Afrikaner government, the governments' forced conscription for its wars of expansion, and Afrikaner monopolies in politics and business. To Rhodes, the Uitlanders appeared to be the perfect on-the-spot constituency to rise up against the Afrikaners and support a British takeover. When the conservative government of Lord Salisbury came to power in London in 1895, Rhodes found many politicians in the British government interested in his plan. Among them was Joseph Chamberlain, the new secretary of state for the colonies and an avid imperialist. With his support, Rhodes moved ahead with his arrangements.

Rhodes developed a strategy with his allies in South Africa and laid his plans. Under the command of his close associate Dr. Leander Starr Jameson, his troops would be stationed at the border between British Bechuanaland and the Transvaal under the guise of protecting a railway from aggressive Tswana groups. When the Transvaal's Uitlanders—who would be supplied with smuggled weapons—rose in revolt, Rhodes would then leak a fake letter to Cape Colony newspapers pleading for British intervention to stop the chaos. In response, Jameson would then lead his massed troops into the Transvaal to put down the insurgency. Meanwhile, Sir Hercules Robinson, the governor of Cape Colony and British high commissioner for South Africa, would wait for the right time to respond to the requests for mediation, effectively

THE JAMESON RAID

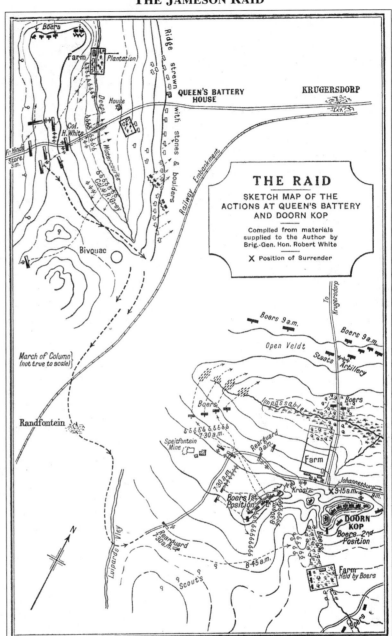

Source: Ian Colvin, *The Life of Jameson* (London, 1923)

ensuring imperial control over the Transvaal government.

As the moment approached for Rhodes's coup, all the pieces seemed to be in place. However, there was one fatal flaw: The Uitlanders, whom Rhodes expected to instigate the uprising, were not as motivated to take action as

1890's

he had believed. Although many of them had initially been interested in his plan as a way to promote a change in Transvaal government policies, many of them wanted to postpone action. Despite their lackluster support, Jameson decided to go ahead with the plan under the belief that once his force entered the Transvaal, the Uitlanders would be roused to action. To prevent Rhodes from ordering him to halt, he cut all his lines of communication with the south and then proceeded across the border.

Jameson's invasion of the Transvaal did move the Uitlanders to take action to encourage the president of the South African Republic, Paul Kruger, for reforms, but not to take up arms or in any other way justify Jameson's rash undertaking. Jameson never got close to the major mining center, Johannesburg, as government troops met his detachment and forced him ignominiously to surrender. The entire invasion lasted only five days.

Jameson's raid had failed miserably and left the British government in an embarrassing diplomatic position. High Commissioner Robinson did travel to the Transvaal as planned, but not to oversee the establishment of British authority. Instead, he went there to plead for clemency on behalf of Jameson and his imprisoned followers. Rhodes, who had not tried to stop Jameson, even after the Uitlanders wavered in support, was forced to resign as prime minister of the Cape Colony. Chamberlain's government distanced itself as much as possible from the fiasco, denying any involvement.

President Kruger responded remarkably moderately. He released Jameson and his troops to the British to be tried, and the Uitlanders who had joined in the plot served prison time in the Transvaal. Rhodes's reputation suffered severely at first. However, when Germany's Emperor William II sent a congratulatory message to Kruger, the British saw his action as a clear sign of German involvement in Transvaal affairs. In the public eye,

Cartoon by Francis Carruthers Gould (1844-1925) lampooning the disastrous Jameson Raid. The cartoon's panels mimic the panels of the famous medieval Bayeaux Tapestry, which chronicles William the Conqueror's invasion of England in 1066.

Rhodes was redeemed and his conniving was forgiven. He once again became the hero of imperialism, and the British government rebounded from the scandal.

SIGNIFICANCE

Although Kruger reacted mildly in response to what could certainly be considered a hostile invasion, the Jameson Raid served to sour the already shaky relations between the Afrikaners and British. From the Afrikaner point of view, it became obvious that the British were intent to undermine the sovereignty of the South African

Republic. Kruger became a national hero in the Transvaal, strengthening resolve not to consider any British participation in his government. The Jameson Raid made it all the more clear to Afrikaners that British Uitlanders posed a threat to their security, justifying their excluding Uitlanders from participation in their government and economy. Continued Afrikaner conflict with the British appeared almost inevitable.

From the British perspective, the Jameson Raid was a humiliation. Despite that fact, Chamberlain and Rhodes were both convinced consolidating South Africa under British rule was the only way to bring peace, security and prosperity to the entire region. The looming German threat and apparently close German relations with the Transvaal only served to increase anxiety in Great Britain that the gold mines and South Africa itself were in danger. For the British, the only solution was incorporating the Transvaal into the British Empire. In a sense, therefore, the Jameson Raid was a trial run for future imperialist efforts to control South Africa, and the British intended to continue until their imperial objectives were appeased. The eventual result was the outbreak of the South African War in 1899.

—Branden C. McCullough

FURTHER READING

Butler, Jeffrey. *The Liberal Party and the Jameson Raid.* London: Oxford University Press, 1968. Discusses the response of the Liberal Party in Great Britain to the Jameson Raid and the subsequent political fallout in Parliament.

Davidson, Apollan B. *Cecil Rhodes and His Time.* Translated by Christopher English. 2d ed. Pretoria, South Africa: Protea Book House, 2003. Up-to-date biography of Cecil Rhodes that discusses his role in South African politics.

Makhura, Tlou John. "Another Road to the Raid: The Neglected Role of the Boer-Bagananwa War as a Factor in the Coming of the Jameson Raid, 1894-1895." *Journal of South African Studies* 21, no. 2 (June, 1995): 257-267. Brief study that makes a compelling case for attributing the support for the raid of British living in the Transvaal to their resentment of the Afrikaner war with the Baganawa people.

Pakenham, Elizabeth. *Jameson's Raid.* London: Weidenfeld & Nicolson, 1960. Attempt to unravel the complicity of all the various parties involved in planning and carrying out the Jameson Raid.

Phimister, Ian. "Unscrambling the Scramble for Southern Africa: The Jameson Raid and South African War Revisited." *South African Historical Journal* 28 (1993): 214-220. New look at the role of the Jameson Raid in the objectives of the British imperial machine.

Rhoodie, Denys. *Conspirators in Conflict: A Study of the Johannesburg Reform Committee and Its Role in the Conspiracy Against the South African Republic.* Cape Town, South Africa: Tafelberg-Uitgewers, 1967. Brief analysis of the Uitlanders, their connections with Cecil Rhodes, and their part in the Jameson Raid.

Van der Poel, Jean. *The Jameson Raid.* London: Oxford University Press, 1951. Classic account of the raid, placing it in the context of British imperialism.

SEE ALSO: 1835: South Africa's Great Trek Begins; Jan. 22-Aug., 1879: Zulu War; Dec. 16, 1880-Mar. 6, 1881: First Boer War; June 21, 1884: Gold Is Discovered in the Transvaal; Mar. 13, 1888: Rhodes Amalgamates Kimberley Diamondfields; Oct., 1893-Oct., 1897: British Subdue African Resistance in Rhodesia; Oct. 11, 1899-May 31, 1902: South African War; Oct. 13, 1899-May 17, 1900: Siege of Mafeking.

RELATED ARTICLES in *Great Lives from History: The Nineteenth Century, 1801-1900:* Joseph Chamberlain; Paul Kruger; Cecil Rhodes; Third Marquis of Salisbury.

1890's

1896
BROOKS BROTHERS INTRODUCES BUTTON-DOWN SHIRTS

Brooks Brothers, a clothing design and manufacturing company, introduced the innovative button-down collar shirt, changing the style of men's shirts in the United States and creating a classic item of fashion. The collar design was inspired by the buttoned-collar shirts of English polo players.

LOCALE: New York, New York
CATEGORIES: Fashion and design; trade and commerce; manufacturing; business and labor

KEY FIGURES

John E. Brooks (fl. late nineteenth century), designer of the button-down shirt
Henry Sands Brooks (1770-1833), founder of Brooks Brothers

SUMMARY OF EVENT

The style of men's clothing in the United States during the latter years of the Gilded Age, which began during the late nineteenth century, was similar in design to items of apparel worn by Europeans. On both sides of the Atlantic, the men's fashion industry was influenced by English designers and clothing manufacturers. Cross-Atlantic exchange did little to enhance innovativeness in the cut, color, and fabric of clothing designed, manufactured, or sold in the United States.

Even though items of men's apparel extended beyond the basic utilitarian purpose of covering for a naked body into the social realm of status, they were not designed or produced for comfort, practicality, or elegance. Stiff, drab, staid, and durable constituted the standards for the tailoring or mass production of men's garments and accessories at the end of the nineteenth century.

Change in the men's clothing industry, unlike that in the world of women's fashion, rarely occurred and was slow to win acceptance. In 1896, however, Brooks Brothers, a manufacturer and retailer of men's clothing, quietly but dramatically introduced changes that set aside the physically and emotionally restrictive clothing norms of the past and established a new set of standards based on comfort, quality, and style. The fashion items that Brooks Brothers used to create a new fashion statement were the button-down shirt, or button-down polo shirt; the three-button, soft-shoulder sack suit; and the Scottish Harris tweed sport coat.

The instigator of fashion innovativeness, Brooks

Brothers was by 1900 one of America's premier manufacturers and retailers of men's clothing. For more than eight decades, the company, not especially known for its design creativity, worked to establish its high rank among men's clothiers on the bases of quality and service. With the simultaneous marketing of three newly designed items of apparel, Brooks Brothers secured a favored position within the retail trade that it would retain for most of the twentieth century. Although the sack suit and the Harris tweed coat became accepted items of men's wear, it was the button-down shirt or button-down polo shirt that proved to be one of America's most significant design and retail successes. Of the three apparel items, it was the button-down shirt that gained over time the label of classic. First worn by political and business leaders, it filtered down into the common culture of American life.

The button-down shirt was the design creation of the grandson of the founder of the Brooks Brothers company, John E. Brooks. Like his grandfather, he had a keen eye for designs that were stylish as well as potentially profitable. While traveling in England in 1900, he attended a polo match and soon became more interested in the garb worn by the players than in the activity on the playing field. Of particular interest to him were the shirts worn by the polo players. He observed that the English polo players used buttons to secure the points of their collars, keeping them from flapping in the wind.

Reasoning that such accoutrements could be adapted to shirts worn by American men, he returned home and submitted a design for a shirt made of cotton, in a number of colors and colored stripes, with an attached, narrow rolled collar that included a button to hold the top of the shirt together and two buttons, one on each side of the shirt, to hold down the flaps of the collar. Company directors approved the idea. They believed that the button-down shirt was marketable, for it filled the need of the American male for garments that were stylish yet functional. They accepted the design for manufacturing and marketing because they considered it a visual representation of the Brooks Brothers philosophy of selling, at a reasonable price, quality merchandise to male customers who valued refined items of apparel.

The button-down-collar shirt was first sold at the Brooks Brothers flagship store in New York City in the fall of 1900. The comfort and tasteful yet subtle styling of the shirt quickly captured the attention of many customers. The button-down shirt quickly was deemed practical by the men who first wore it.

The button-down-collar shirt was, in its initial stage of introduction in 1900 and 1901, a success. It was more comfortable, less restricting, and less troublesome than its predecessors, with its attached, unstarched collar, and it fitted with ease under a suit coat. Furthermore, it held a necktie more securely in place and thus proved to be highly practical, especially for office-type work.

Although the button-down collar was received favorably by many American men, during the first two decades of the new century it was not the sole or the dominant style. The body of most shirts sold in Europe and the United States had been altered during the 1880's. The shoulder yoke was introduced, along with proportioned sleeves with cuffs that either were curved or were in the French style. Shirt bodies were either white, plain colored, or striped, with collars and cuffs either the same color as the body or white. Most collars were starched and detachable. It was not until about 1930 that the detachable shirt collar was abandoned by the fashion industry.

The body of the button-down shirt was similar to that of most tailored or manufactured shirts sold in 1900 and did not change greatly thereafter. With the introduction of the button-down collar, the body of the shirt was only slightly altered. The original button-down shirt was constructed with a shoulder yoke that was shallower, sleeves that were straighter, and a buttoned front that was plainer. The cuffs of the button-down shirt were left round. The collar and cuffs of the shirt were the same color as the body, and the colors used were the same as for past Brooks Brothers shirts, no different from those used by other clothiers. The innovation came in the collar, which was attached to the shirt body, was narrower, and had its characteristic buttonholes to allow it to be fastened to the shirt body.

The buttons for the button-down shirt were selected carefully by Brooks Brothers. Most were made of seashells, usually with two holes bored for attachment by thread to the shirt. In the United States, by the end of the 1890's, John F. Boepple had been manufacturing buttons made of freshwater mussel shells harvested from the Mississippi River or its tributaries. Less costly than buttons made from ocean shells, mussel-shell buttons were used particularly in mass-produced, ready-made men's, women's, and children's clothing. Brooks Brothers continued to use the more expensive and more iridescent buttons made from ocean shells. Shirts could be purchased ready-made by the Brooks Brothers factory or could be made by hand.

The introduction of the button-down collar gave rise to a wider acceptance of the four-in-hand tie made in small-patterned or striped silk, which had been introduced in 1890. The bow tie, the ascot, and a large and rather thick four-in-hand knot were all used with high collars; a smaller and less thick tie was needed to accommodate the button-down collar. Consequently, Brooks Brothers scaled the size and thickness of the four-in-hand downward so that it could be used with the button-down collar. In doing so, the company created an elegant neckwear accessory.

SIGNIFICANCE

After its introduction to the public in 1900, the button-down shirt remained the biggest seller of all items manufactured and sold by Brooks Brothers. In the modern age of mass production and marketing, other clothiers soon adopted the style.

The shirt's value soon was recognized by President Theodore Roosevelt, President Woodrow Wilson, investment banker J. P. Morgan, and members of the Vanderbilt and Astor families. Both Roosevelt's and Wilson's inaugural clothing, including suits, shirts, and ties, was furnished by Brooks Brothers. Later, other presidents from Herbert Hoover to John F. Kennedy were Brooks Brothers customers. The cap that President Franklin D. Roosevelt wore was a Brooks Brothers creation.

After World War II, the button-down shirt was the most popular shirt style in America. It became a major component, along with the sack suit, of the Ivy League look of the late 1940's and 1950's. Brooks Brothers became a public corporation, passing out of family ownership and operation. It was purchased by Garfinckel's in 1946; by Allied Corporation in November, 1981; by Campeau Corporation in November, 1986; and by Marks & Spencer in April, 1988. It retained its reputation as a clothier of distinction, however, in part because of its continual sale and marketing of button-down shirts.

—*The Editors*

FURTHER READING

Ash, Juliet, and Lee Wright, eds. *Components of Dress: Design, Manufacturing, and Image-Making in the Fashion Industry*. New York: Routledge, 1988. A small, very readable volume. Short chapters on a number of topics, from World War I fashion to influences on dress styles by minorities, are interesting and

1890's

informative. Includes a picture of workers in a Brooks Brothers factory.

Bigelow, Marybelle S. *Fashion in History: Apparel in the Western World*. Minneapolis, Minn.: Burgess, 1970. Covers fashion history from antiquity to the modern era. Illustrated with reproductions of clothing. The various sections on men's clothing provide information on the evolution as well as the innovativeness of style.

Boucher, François. *Twenty Thousand Years of Fashion: The History of Costume and Personal Adornment*. Rev. ed. New York: Harry N. Abrams, 1987. Color plates illustrate fashion from ancient times to the modern era. Reproductions of Impressionist paintings are true to colors of the originals. Includes a helpful, lengthy glossary of fashion terms and items.

Colle, Doriece. *Collars, Stocks, Cravats: A History and Costume Dating Guide to Civilian Men's Neckpieces, 1655-1900*. Emmaus, Pa.: Rodale Press, 1972. Limited in readable material, but many drawings by the author provide precise data on collars, stocks, and cravats that can be used to date costumes and portraits. A general reference work, with illustrations, on styles of neckwear of various eras. Appendix B contains an account of neckpieces in art.

Laver, James. *Costume and Fashion: A Concise History*. 4th ed. New York: Thames and Hudson, 2002. Discusses men's and women's fashions from early antiquity into the twentieth century. Includes lovely black-and-white drawings.

Schoeffler, O. E., and William Gale. *Esquire's Encyclopedia of Twentieth Century Men's Fashions*. New York: McGraw-Hill, 1973. Informative coverage of men's fashion up to the early 1970's. Informative biographical sketches of leading designers. Reproductions of ads, sketches, and drawings, along with inclusion of quotations from primary sources, add effective dimensions to this study. Glossary.

Tortora, Phyllis G., and Keith Eubank. *A Survey of Historic Costume: A History of Western Dress*. 4th ed. New York: Fairchild, 2005. Very readable. Begins with the ancient world and covers fashion through the twentieth century. Illustrated, with a thorough bibliography.

Waugh, Norah. *The Cut of Men's Clothes, 1600-1900*. New York: Theatre Arts Books, 1964. Informative section on nineteenth century tailoring. Valuable information on the use of pattern blocks and measurement in producing mass-produced clothes. Patterns with measurements of different styles are included. The quotations from primary sources are insightful.

Yarwood, Doreen. *Costume of the Western World: Pictorial Guide and Glossary*. New York: St. Martin's Press, 1980. Illustrations and black-and-white drawings by the author. Concise but valuable glossary of fashion items and terms.

SEE ALSO: Apr. 6, 1808: American Fur Company Is Chartered; 1869: First Modern Department Store Opens in Paris; Aug., 1872: Ward Launches a Mail-Order Business; May 8, 1886: Pemberton Introduces Coca-Cola.

RELATED ARTICLES in *Great Lives from History: The Nineteenth Century, 1801-1900:* Marshall Field; Montgomery Ward.

1896
IMMIGRANT FARMERS BEGIN SETTLING WESTERN CANADA

To develop Canada's national economy and foster political unification, the government began a campaign to encourage immigrant farmers to settle in western Canada. The campaign led to the first mass migration of Europeans to Canada and the expansion of agriculture and other industries benefiting both the prairie region and the nation as a whole.

LOCALE: Western Canada

CATEGORIES: Immigration; agriculture; business and labor; expansion and land acquisition; government and politics

KEY FIGURES

Clifford Sifton (1861-1929), Canadian minister of the interior, 1896-1905

Sir Wilfrid Laurier (1841-1919), Canadian prime minister, 1896-1911

Frank Pedley (1858-after 1913), Canadian superintendent of immigration

William Forsythe McCreary (1856-unknown), Canadian commissioner of immigration

SUMMARY OF EVENT

Toward the end of the nineteenth century, Canada encountered a demographic crisis, as emigration began surpassing immigration. Canadian leaders had sought immigrants to populate the country's vast western territory but were initially unsuccessful. Canada's western prairies challenged farmers, who often abandoned these lands because of their severe climates and harsh living conditions. During the 1880's, approximately one million people moved from Canada to the United States, where they received free land offered by the Homestead Act of 1862.

Sir Wilfrid Laurier, a liberal politician who won the 1896 election for Canadian prime minister, named Clifford Sifton, a farmer's son, minister of the interior with the assignment to direct western settlement. Sifton, a former Manitoba legislator, capably formulated plans to achieve settlement goals, emphasizing agriculture as essential for Canadian prosperity and focusing on inviting skilled farmers to immigrate. Sifton rejected urban immigrants, however, whom he feared would abandon farmland for cities. Because administrative requirements had impeded some settlers, Sifton closed the Dominion Lands Board, which he blamed for complicating procedures. He clarified the immigration branch's mission to recruit and assist immigrants, and he selected Frank Pedley as his superintendent of immigration in Ottawa and William Forsythe McCreary as commissioner of immigration in Winnipeg.

Sifton believed competent farmers could create an economically appealing situation that would attract businesses and industries to western Canada. He sought to achieve the immigration of many people quickly, and he offered commissions to immigration agents and employees as an incentive for immigration staff to secure as many acceptable immigrants as possible.

During the mid-1890's, Canada had became attractive to immigrants for several reasons. While available farmland in the United States decreased because of settlement and land-law changes, Canada offered ample agricultural resources, especially for growing wheat. International markets demanded Canadian agricultural products because many industrialized nations had limited foodstuff on hand. Crops sold at high prices, assuring farmers some financial security after economic crises had depressed global markets in previous years. People considered immigrating to Canada because European populations significantly increased, overcrowding communities. Canada offered freedom from the oppressive political systems and religious controls of some countries.

Sifton identified incentives to lure agricultural immigrants to Canada. He streamlined the Dominion Lands Act of 1872 to provide adults twenty-one years or older with 160 acres of land if those settlers would reside on that land three years, erect a homestead shelter, grow crops on thirty acres, and give the government ten Canadian dollars to register a claim. To ensure there were enough lands to distribute, Sifton persuaded the Canadian Pacific Railway and other railroads to release lands the government had given them to back railroad bonds and pay for constructing and maintaining lines. Sifton ceased all federal land grants for railroads. He promised immigrants reduced or sponsored transatlantic passage from their homelands and affordable transportation costs, particularly low rail rates to ship goods, within Canada. He encouraged the idea that free land in the United States was scarce and that Canada was the only place to find such opportunities.

Applying business methods to immigration recruitment, Sifton organized an effective campaign. Promotional materials distributed in Europe and Great Britain

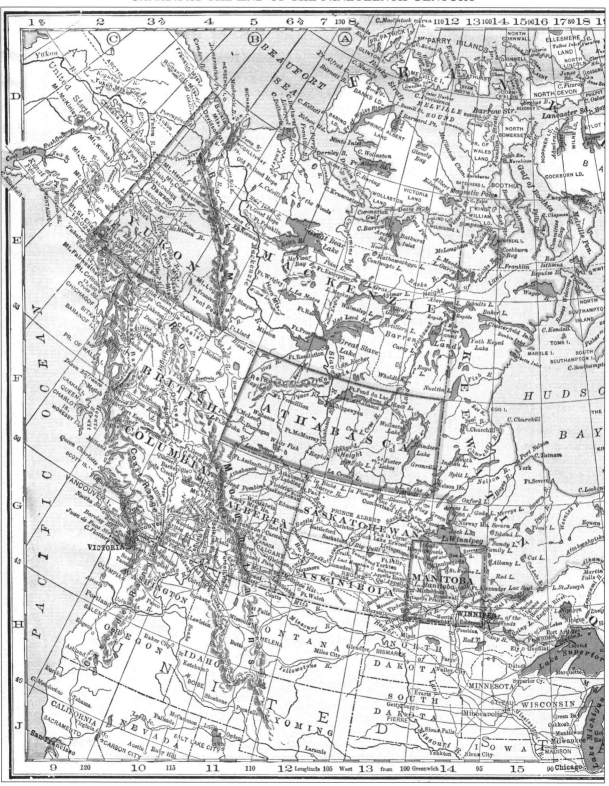

1832

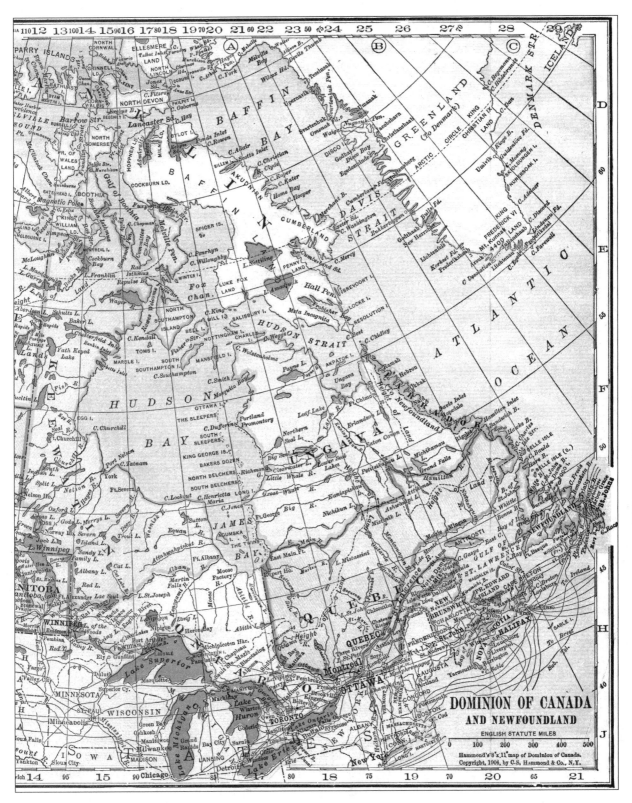

DOMINION OF CANADA
AND NEWFOUNDLAND

ENGLISH STATUTE MILES

0   100   200   300   400   500

Hammond's 8"x 11" map of Dominion of Canada.
Copyright, 1904, by C.S. Hammond & Co., N.Y.

1890's

1833

focused on free farms for immigrants. Sifton established immigration offices in other countries and arranged for translators to prepare brochures that portrayed western Canada as a paradise. Forbidding references to cold temperatures, snow, and isolation, Sifton insisted agents show appealing images, which were contrary to common perceptions of the Canadian prairie.

Sifton hired writers to prepare praiseworthy letters and essays in European newspapers and placed advertisements. He invited to Canada reporters representing United States and European periodicals. The reporters in turn would view the western Canadian sites and then recommended them to readers. Sifton's representatives touted immigration at public events, especially agricultural fairs and meetings. By 1903, promoters showed audiences a film featuring western Canada. Successful immigrants urged their families and friends to join them.

In addition to recruiting northern Europeans, Sifton considered settlers from the United States, an option previous officials had dismissed. U.S. farmers were familiar with prairie climate and soils, and would have an easier time adjusting to the Canadian climate. Also, Sifton believed that U.S. agriculturists possessed funds, equipment, and skills they could invest in Canadian farming. He directed agents to discuss immigration with white U.S. farmers and to urge the farmers to move their operations and livestock to the Canadian prairie by stressing its similarities with lands they cultivated in the Midwest and western United States. Immigration officials excluded minority farmers, especially African Americans, often rejecting their petitions for homestead lands. Sifton also discouraged immigration by Italians, Jews, and Asians because he believed they would not pursue work in agriculture. Recruitment materials omitted references to people of color and other ethnic minorities.

Sifton believed that central, southern, and eastern Europeans, particularly Ukrainians, Germans, Galicians, Russian Doukhobors, Austro-Hungarians, Poles, and Slavs, would be valuable immigrants. He noted that the attributes of peasants included a strong work ethic and an affinity for agriculture, envisioning that such immigrants could perform seasonal work as needed, migrating across the land to harvest crops. Sifton wanted farmers who would persevere no matter how harsh their environment. Many immigrants were overwhelmed by the large acreage given to them. Some immigrants were uninterested in acquiring homesteads and instead worked for the railroad or other industries.

Sifton circumvented some European laws and poli-

cies overseeing emigration. France, for example, discouraged emigration in order to maintain a sufficient military force. Establishing a contract with the North Atlantic Trading Company, an Antwerp group of steamship agents, Sifton secretly offered financial rewards per immigrant to middlemen who persuaded and transported people to Canada. Sifton paid priests to encourage French Canadians living in the United States to return to Canada. Critics accused Sifton of profiting from his immigration duties, but proof of this was lacking.

Sifton urged immigrants to settle lands adjacent to people from their native country so they could form communities. Such ties strengthened settlements and often led to more immigration. Immigrants would arrive already knowing some settlers. Canadian settlement requirements for immigrants split some ethnic groups. Most Russian Doukhobors, for example, resisted swearing oaths of allegiance, and were thus prevented from participating in any government activities, including education and registering vital records.

Many Canadians resisted Sifton's plans to recruit immigrants but were unable to prevent his efforts. Public reaction targeted some immigrant groups as inferior. Canadians protested that their country risked losing its British culture because immigrants insisted on using their native languages and were uninterested in assimilating. Violent anti-immigration groups often destroyed immigrants' property, and xenophobic attitudes and taxes hindered some immigration. The "alien" labor act (1897) provided measures to restrict foreigners, and by 1898, Sifton was demanding the deportation of Italians who were not settling farmland.

SIGNIFICANCE

Clifford Sifton's immigration policies transformed Canada's western lands into a productive agricultural region. Two million immigrants, mostly skilled farmers, from the United States, European continent, and Great Britain emigrated to Canada between 1896, when Sifton initiated his campaign, and 1911. Immigrants diversified Canada demographically. They applied their expertise to cultivating the Canadian prairies, yielding income from previously fallow land. While Clifton and politicians promoted immigration, scientists and engineers improved agriculture. Farmers benefited from growing wheat and grains suitable for prairie conditions, and they adopted better agricultural tools and methods. Canadian leaders improved transportation systems, mainly railroads, to ease the shipping of goods to numerous markets and make shipping more affordable.

Sifton's settlement plan succeeded so well that available lands soon dwindled. Ambitious agriculturists requested lands the government had protected for First Nations peoples, arguing they had more land than their population needed. Sifton agreed. Government leaders seized some indigenous peoples' lands for settlers.

By 1905, the year Sifton resigned his post as minister of the interior, western expansion resulted in officials designating Alberta and Saskatchewan as provinces. Sifton's successor, Frank Oliver, pursued more restrictive immigration policies, seeking only U.S., British, and Canadian settlers for prairie lands. The Immigration Acts of 1906 and 1910 reinforced entry restrictions. Sifton's immigration program had initiated changes that molded western Canada into a thriving agricultural and industrial region for white settlers compatible with eastern provinces and integral in international trade.

—*Elizabeth D. Schafer*

FURTHER READING

Bumsted, J. M. *Canada's Diverse Peoples: A Reference Sourcebook*. Santa Barbara, Calif.: ABC-Clio, 2003. Includes a chapter discussing immigration from 1867 to 1914, supplemented with a time line and a bibliography. A volume in the Ethnic Diversity Within Nations series.

Draper, Paula, Franca Iacovetta, and Robert Ventresca, eds. *A Nation of Immigrants: Women, Workers, and Communities in Canadian History, 1840's-1960's*. Toronto: University of Toronto Press, 1998. Analyzes female immigrants in western Canada and their experiences as domestics and laborers and efforts to retain ethnic and cultural customs while assimilating into communities.

Hall, David J. *Clifford Sifton*. 2 vols. Vancouver: University of British Columbia Press, 1981, 1985. A comprehensive biography that devotes one chapter to Sifton's immigration policies and discusses them in relation to his other political interests. Illustrations, bibliography, index.

Kaye, Vladimir J. *Early Ukrainian Settlement in Canada, 1895-1900: Dr. Josef Oleskow's Role in the Settlement of the Canadian Northwest*. Toronto: University of Toronto Press, 1964. This volume in the Canadian Centennial series explores the experiences of an immigration agent and of European immigrants during the first years of Sifton's efforts to populate western Canada. Foreword by George W. Simpson.

Troper, Harold M. *Only Farmers Need Apply: Official Canadian Government Encouragement of Immigration from the United States, 1896-1911*. Toronto: Griffin House, 1972. Expanded version of a thesis written at the University of Toronto, examining the agriculturists Sifton identified as suitable for immigration and how agents recruited those farmers.

SEE ALSO: 1829-1836: Irish Immigration to Canada; 1845-1854: Great Irish Famine; May 20, 1862: Lincoln Signs the Homestead Act; 1872: Dominion Lands Act Fosters Canadian Settlement; 1873: Ukrainian Mennonites Begin Settling in Canada; Jan. 1, 1892: Ellis Island Immigration Depot Opens; July 11, 1896: Laurier Becomes the First French Canadian Prime Minister.

RELATED ARTICLES in *Great Lives from History: The Nineteenth Century, 1801-1900:* Mary Ann Shadd Cary; Sir John Alexander Macdonald; Susanna Moodie; Thomas Talbot; Catharine Parr Traill.

1890's

February, 1896-August, 1897
HERZL FOUNDS THE ZIONIST MOVEMENT

Austrian journalist Theodore Herzl wrote A Jewish State *in 1896, in response to growing European anti-Semitism. Abandoning his former assimilationist ideas, Herzl helped create the World Zionist Organization, which paved the way for the creation of a Jewish state.*

LOCALE: Vienna, Austria

CATEGORIES: Social issues and reform; religion and theology; immigration

KEY FIGURES

Theodor Herzl (1860-1904), Austrian journalist and first president of the World Zionist Organization

Max Nordau (1849-1923), Austrian writer

Aḥad Ha'am (Asher Ginzberg; 1856-1927), Russian agnostic rabbi

Chaim Weizmann (1874-1952), Russian Jewish chemist

SUMMARY OF EVENT

During the nineteenth century, European Jews fell into three main groups based upon their attitude toward their homeland: traditional Orthodox, Reform, and Zionist. Orthodox Jews adhered to traditional beliefs and, at least in Russia, were restricted by law in their daily life. Symbolically, Jerusalem remained the center of Orthodox religious life, with the phrase "Next year in Jerusalem" being repeated at each Passover Seder. Even the worst conditions seemed endurable by focusing on the promise of a Messiah who would someday lead his people back to Israel, reversing the centuries of exile begun when the Romans burned the temple and expelled the Jews in 70 C.E.

Other Jews, influenced by Enlightenment thinkers like Moses Mendelssohn, embraced Reform Judaism. For them, assimilation into European culture was the answer. The ancient longing for the Messiah and a return to Israel was abandoned. The Reform Jews' only link to their ancestral home was through charity, as they assisted the handful of poor religious Jews then living in Jerusalem, praying and studying the Talmud.

A major turning point in Jewish history came with the French Revolution of 1789. The new French constitution granted Jews freedom, repealing their 1306 expulsion. Similar freedoms were soon granted throughout other western European nations. These developments were a boon to assimilationist Jews, who emerged into leadership positions in government, medicine, law, and finance.

During the nineteenth century, however, nationalism was on the rise as an ideology throughout Europe. The various Italian and German states, for example, united into two nations based upon the ethnic and linguistic ties of their people. This new nationalist ideology countered Reform Jews' assimilationist ideas, resurrecting hopes of a Jewish homeland. Thus, a third Jewish movement arose that sought a return to Jerusalem by political means. Rather than assimilate or wait for the Messiah to lead them, this third group of Jews decided to bring about their own return home. Their movement became known as Zionism, named for an ancient Jerusalem hill.

The Austrian journalist Theodor Herzl—a Jew who had thrived by assimilation—is often called the founder of Zionism. The critical dates in the foundation of the movement were February, 1896, when Herzl published *Der Judenstaat* (*A Jewish State: An Attempt at a Modern Solution of the Jewish Question*, 1896), and August, 1897, when the first Zionist Congress was held in Basle, Switzerland. While it is true that the term "Zionism" was popularized only under Herzl, however, the idea had been present throughout the nineteenth century. This was

Theodor Herzl. (Library of Congress)

a time of renewed interest in the Middle East in general, with the building of the Suez Canal and with a new age of explorers and archaeologists who reported stories of their travels. By mid-century, every European nation and the United States had consulates in Jerusalem.

A succession of Jewish thinkers continued to visit the topic of Jewish nationalism. Among them were the Sarajevo-born Rabbi Yehuda Alkalai, the Polish Talmudic scholar Rabbi Zvi Hirsch Kalischer, the German socialist Moses Hess, the Odessa physician Leo Pinsker, and the Russian agnostic Ahad Ha'am. The reason for a resurgence of nationalistic Jewish ideas was quite simple: The plague of anti-Semitism had not died, in spite of the Enlightenment and the rise of democratic ideas.

Alkalai, Kalischer, and Hess were affected deeply by news of the ritual murder of Jews in Damascus in 1840. It was in Germany in the 1870's, however, that the situation turned drastic following a major financial crisis. The historian Heinrich Treitschke referred to the Jews as "our misfortune," and Wilhelm Marr coined the term "anti-Semitism." The hatred of Jews now moved from religious bigotry to racism, as the idea of the Aryan superrace emerged. In 1881, the Russian czar, Alexander II, was assassinated. The event opened the door for the worst pogroms yet seen, which lasted through the turn of the century.

In 1881 in various Russian cities, Jews began organizing as "Lovers of Zion" to mobilize for emigration. At a time when one million Russian Jews emigrated to North America, twenty thousand made the first *aliya* (voyage of return to Israel), traveling to what was then Palestine. Some of them established agricultural settlements there with the financial support of wealthy European Jews such as Moses Montefiore and Baron Edmond Rothschild.

Thus, the ideas of Zionism were well under way when Herzl appeared on the scene. As had been true of the other Zionist intellectuals, the catalyst for Herzl's conversion to Zionism was a confrontation with anti-Semitism. An assimilated Jew, he had prospered in western Europe. However, while in Paris as a correspondent for the *Neue Freie Presse* (new free press), he was personally affected by the so-called Dreyfus affair, the 1894 trial of Alfred Dreyfus. A Jewish captain in the French army, Dreyfus was convicted of spying for Germany and imprisoned. Even when evidence surfaced that he was innocent, the government refused for years to exonerate him. Herzl became convinced that European Jews would never be completely free.

At first, Herzl sought financial assistance for Jewish emigration to places such as Argentina. In a period of five days during the summer of 1895, he sketched out his ideas in a sixty-five-page pamphlet that he originally intended as an address to the Rothschild family. In February, 1896, he published it as *A Jewish State*. Later, Herzl acknowledged that he wrote independently, unaware of the writings of Pinkser, Hess, and the other early Zionists.

Herzl then called for like-minded Jews to organize at a series of congresses. The First Zionist Congress was held in Basle, Switzerland, in August, 1897. While Herzl addressed the two hundred delegates with his rallying call, it was Max Nordau, another Austrian writer, who served as Herzl's right-hand man, articulating the precarious status of European Jewry. Herzl was elected as president of the World Zionist Organization, whose single goal was the creation of a home for Jews in Palestine. By 1899, the World Zionist Organization had created its own bank. By 1901, it had created the Jewish National Fund for the purpose of purchasing land.

Herzl worked tirelessly to complete the work of six congresses before his death at the age of forty-four on July 3, 1904. He was not without opposition within the Jewish ranks. Ahad Ha'am spoke against him and quit the movement after the first congress. Ahad Ha'am's disciple, Chaim Weizmann, and Martin Buber formed their own "democratic" faction within the organization.

Herzl's method was diplomacy, and he was not afraid to compromise. Since Palestine was under the control of the Ottoman Empire, he met with the sultan, offering him financial assistance to help pay off the debts of the already crumbling empire. The sultan welcomed Jews to settle within the empire—but not in Palestine, not in massive settlements, and not organized as a Jewish state. Herzl turned to the British for an alternative location for a Jewish homeland. Already, Argentina and several North American sites had been suggested. The British discussed the possibility of Cyprus or Sinai. Finally, they offered the Jews a section of Uganda and Kenya in East Africa. At the sixth Zionist Congress in 1903, Herzl's proposal to accept Uganda was accepted by a vote of 295 to 178. Herzl had not abandoned the idea of a state in Palestine, however. Eventually, he thought, the Ottoman Empire would collapse or at least agree to accept a Jewish state within it. In the meantime, the Jews of Europe could not wait. Uganda would serve as a temporary refuge.

SIGNIFICANCE

On May 14, 1948, when David Ben Gurion read the proclamation establishing the State of Israel, Herzl's photo

1890's

1837

was prominently displayed above his head. Herzl, more than any other individual, had created the irreversible momentum that had brought about the Jewish state. However, things did not develop as Herzl might have expected. By the time of his death in 1904, he had failed in his effort to unite European Jews. Assimilated Jews of western Europe were afraid that the Zionist movement would jeopardize their standing in society. Many of the eager Russian Jews had already rejected Herzl's long-term approach. The mantle of leadership fell upon the Russian chemist Chaim Weizmann, who reversed the vote on Uganda. Other Russian Jews, such as David Ben Gurion, ignored Herzl's cautious approach and took part in the second *aliya* in the early decades of the twentieth century.

It was Herzl's lobbying efforts among the British, however, that helped pave the way for success, especially when Weizmann moved to London and contributed significantly to the British war effort. In the Balfour Declaration of 1917, Great Britain was the first government to express support for the establishment of a Jewish state. When the Ottoman Empire was dismantled after World War I, the British Mandate was established for control of Palestine from 1920 to 1948, leading to increased Jewish immigration, as European anti-Semitism too continued to grow. Although Herzl was intent on direct negotiation with Ottoman leaders, he seemed less aware of the role of the one-half million Arab inhabitants of Palestine and their growing anxiety over Zionism. This anxiety would lead to a century of conflict between Jews and Arabs in Palestine.

— *Fred Strickert*

FURTHER READING

Avineri, Shlomo. *The Making of Modern Zionism: Intellectual Origins of the Jewish State*. 1970. Reprint. New York: Basic Books, 1990. An analysis of the role of seventeen contributors to Zionism, emphasizing the philosophical underpinnings of the movement.

Dowty, Alan. *The Jewish State: A Century Later*. Berkeley: University of California Press, 2001. An analysis of contemporary Israel in view of its roots in the Zionist movement.

Hertzberg, Arthur. *The Zionist Idea: A Historical Analysis and Reader*. Reprint. New York: Jewish Publication Society, 1997. A collection of selections from thirty-seven writers who influenced the development of Zionism.

Herzl, Theodor. *The Jew's State*. Translated by Henk Overberg. Northvale, N.J.: Jason Aronson, 1997. Herzl's landmark statement of Zionist philosophy; one of the founding texts of the movement.

Laqueur, Walter. *A History of Zionism*. Reprint. New York: Schocken Books, 2003. The classic scholarly study of Zionism, first published in 1972.

Lownthal, Marvin, ed. and trans. *Diaries of Theodor Herzl*. Gloucester, Mass.: Peter Smith, 1990. Herzl's own reflections upon his life and work are recorded in these personal diaries.

Pawel, Ernest. *The Labyrinth of Exile: A Life of Theodor Herzl*. New York: Farrar, Straus and Giroux, 1992. Places Herzl in his historical and cultural setting.

SEE ALSO: 19th cent.: Arabic Literary Renaissance; 1814-1879: Exploration of Arabia; 1839-1847: Layard Explores and Excavates Assyrian Ruins; Sept. 12, 1853: Burton Enters Mecca in Disguise; July 26, 1858: Rothschild Is First Jewish Member of British Parliament; Oct., 1894-July, 1906: Dreyfus Affair.

RELATED ARTICLES in *Great Lives from History: The Nineteenth Century, 1801-1900:* Alexander II; Theodor Herzl.

March, 1896-November, 1899
SUDANESE WAR

During the Sudanese War, British and Egyptian forces crushed Sudanese rebels to reestablish imperial control and to forestall rival European imperial powers from planting their flags at the headwaters of the Nile.

LOCALE: Sudan

CATEGORIES: Wars, uprisings, and civil unrest; expansion and land acquisition

KEY FIGURES

Horatio Herbert Kitchener (1850-1916), British commander-in-chief of Anglo-Egyptian invasion force

The Mahdi (Muḥammad Aḥmad ibn as-Sayyid ʿAbd-Allāh; 1844-1885), Sudanese Islamic revolutionary leader

ʿAbd Allāh (1846-1899), khalifa and ruler of Sudan, r. 1885-1899

SUMMARY OF EVENT

From the 1820's through the 1890's, khedival Egypt dominated the Sudan. Although it provided few services in return, the Egyptian regime squeezed local peoples for taxes and manpower. To the Sudanese, this was to be expected from "Turks"—their generic name for all Muslim outsiders from the north. To the Sudanese, Turks had no redeeming values, aside from the fact that they were powerful and well armed. Under Egyptian rule, rebellion became a regular feature of life in the Sudan. However, rebellion did not become a major problem until 1881. During that year, as government officials focused on Cairo, where Colonel Ahmad Urabi was organizing a military coup, a local insurrection broke out on the Nile River's Aba Island in the Sudan. Under the battle cry of "Believe in the power of God, not of the Turks!" the Islamic fundamentalist Muḥammad Aḥmad ibn as-Sayyid Abd-ʿAllāh enjoined his followers to throw out the Su-

Mahdist army advancing on Omdurman. (Francis R. Niglutsch)

THE MAHDIST STATE AND THE ETHIOPIAN EMPIRE

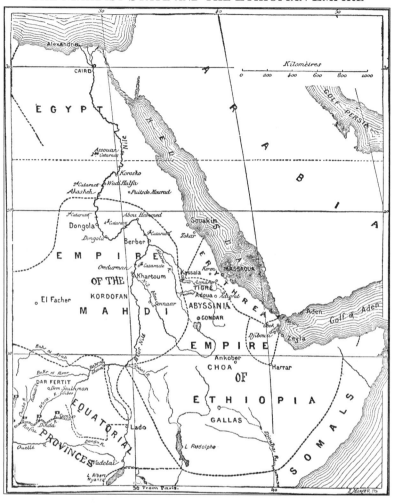

dilemma, as one of the fundamental reasons for crushing Urabi was to ensure that Egypt paid off its massive debts to European investors. This was important, as German and French bankers could easily turn to their home governments if Egypt failed to make interest payments on its loans. This in turn could jeopardize Great Britain's veiled protectorate and threaten its control of the now vital Suez Canal. Thus. it was a primary concern for every British proconsul to make sure his Egyptian puppets maximized revenues and minimized expenses.

One way to accomplish this goal was to cut back on the government payroll, especially by reducing expenses in the recently defeated Egyptian army. Thus, as the Mahdi expanded his forces between 1882 and 1884, Egypt sent little military assistance to relieve its beleaguered garrisons. Finally, the Egyptian government decided to evacuate the Sudan. This was a major undertaking, and involved the hiring of the British officer Charles George Gordon, a former governor-general of the Sudan who had become an iconic hero to the Victorian public. Sent to organize an evacuation of the Sudanese capital, Khartoum, Gordon instead

dan's despised Egyptian regime. The Sudanese people declared him to be the Mahdi, the Deliverer whom Islam promised would unite and purify Muslims immediately before the end of the world. Increasing his following through skillful use of religious appeals, diplomacy, and politics, the Mahdi established an Islamic theocracy on the Nile, but only after a violent campaign that drew world attention.

The Mahdi's campaign coincided with Colonel Urabi's failed effort to establish an Egyptian nationalist regime in Cairo. Instead of freeing Egypt from Ottoman control, the coup led to British occupation in 1882 and the establishment of the so-called "veiled protectorate" that would govern Egypt until 1914. From that time, Great Britain maintained a powerful interest in all affairs relating to Egypt. At first, this new situation presented a

attempted to defend the city. An epic siege resulted, ending in 1885 with Gordon's death and a general massacre by the Mahdi's forces. Gordon's death was an international news event that evoked a strong reaction in Great Britain. British troops had made a half-hearted effort to relieve Khartoum in 1884-1885 but failed to arrive in time. In effect, the Sudan was abandoned to the Mahdists. This did not sit well with the British public, who demanded that the death of a British hero be avenged. Vengeance was not the sole reason for a campaign of reconquest. The British public also recoiled from tales of savage injustice in the Sudan and the Mahdist endorsement of slavery.

The actions of the Mahdi and his successor, Khalifa ʿAbd Allāh, appeared to reinforce such tales as the Mahdists launched poorly planned invasions of Egypt. Mahdist armies demanded submission to their leaders and promised fire and sword to all who refused to submit. The Mahdist invasions were repulsed, but British officials feared the possibility that infiltrating Mahdists might stir up trouble among Egyptian Muslims. Meanwhile, the politics of imperialism eventually forced Great Britain to reconsider its interests in the Sudan. By 1890, three other imperialist powers were probing the Sudan's poorly defined frontiers. To the east of the Sudan, where Italy had gained control over the former Egyptian possession of Eritrea, Italian forces were fighting Mahdist armies and moving inland. In the south, the Congo Free State, really the private possession of King Leopold II of Belgium, was sending African soldiers into regions that had been part of the Egyptian Sudan. Finally, and from the British perspective the most serious threat to the Sudan, a column of French troops under Captain Jean-Baptiste Marchand had begun an epic march that would end up in the tiny Nile village of Fashoda.

British officials had every reason to fear the consequences of any military success by Italian, Congo Free State, or French forces in the Sudan. Explorers, such as Samuel Baker, had firmly established that the southern Sudan, with its many lakes and gigantic swamps, was a major source of the Nile. As virtually all of Africa was considered to be fair game during the age of imperialism, there appeared to be no force in place to stop another power from colonizing the southern Sudan and taking control of the Nile's headwaters. Such control might even allow for a diversion of these waters that could have serious consequences for Egypt that would in turn threaten Britain's control of the Suez Canal. It is thus not difficult to understand the March 12, 1896, decision of the cabinet of British prime minister Salisbury to approve an Anglo-Egyptian force to retake the Sudan.

Commanded by General Herbert Kitchener, a veteran of the 1884-1885 campaign, this force was a state-of-the-art army. Combining well-trained Egyptians, Sudanese loyalists, and regular British and Scottish troops, it numbered 25,800 men. It was the largest British army sent to fight in Africa until the South African War of 1899-1902. Its troops employed modern breach-loading and magazine-fed rifles. Their artillery included Maxim machine guns and the new quick-fire field artillery that were coming into use during the mid-1890's. Armored gunboats ensured that there would be no naval opposition for control of the vital Nile River, while telegraphs and railroads increased the data- and supply-gathering capabilities of Kitchener's troops. All these advantages, combined with effective training and leadership, created a sense of superiority.

Kitchener developed a careful strategy that provided for a slow but steady advance with secure lines of supply. Skirmishes and even a major battle at Atbara on April 8, 1898, could not halt his advance. By late July, Kitchener's army was advancing on Khartoum. It deployed near Omdurman, a suburb of Khartoum on the west side of the Nile, on September 1. The next day, a massive battle erupted as more than thirty thousand Mahdists charged the Anglo-Egyptian lines. This was folly in the extreme, as the most poorly equipped allied forces possessed firepower superior to the best of what the Mahdists had. Attacking Kitchener's position actually strengthened his already significant advantage, allowing his men to employ cover and fight close to their reserves and supplies. The Mahdist strategy all but ensured an Anglo-Egyptian victory.

The Twenty-first Lancer Regiment, which included future British prime minister Winston S. Churchill among its officers, provides a case study for the tremendous advantages held by Anglo-Egyptian soldiers at Omdurman. Charging into a mass of Mahdists, the cavalrymen suffered heavy casualties in hand-to-hand combat. After breaking away, they dismounted, employed their rifles, and broke every attack launched by the more numerous enemy. After the Mahdists failed to destroy this small unit cut off from support, they appeared to have no chance of defeating Kitchener's main force. By noon, 11,000 Mahdists were dead, and another 16,000 had been captured. Anglo-Egyptian losses were 48 dead and 434 wounded.

The khalifa escaped Omdurman and the fall of Khartoum, leaving only minutes before British forces entered the city. Retreating westward into remote Kordofan, he rebuilt some of his army. However, he was defeated and killed at Umm Diwaykarat on November 24, 1899. His death marks the end of the significant fighting, but the Mahdist general Osman Digna remained at large until January of 1900.

SIGNIFICANCE

Destroying the Mahdist state secured Egypt from invasion, established the Anglo-Egyptian Sudan, and eliminated the possibility of a French, Italian, or Congo Free State takeover of the headwaters of the Nile. It also made Kitchener a household name in Great Britain, and ensured his future advancement to the highest ranks of the Royal Army.

—*John P. Dunn*

1890's

FURTHER READING

Churchill, Winston S. *The River War*. London: Longmans, Green, 1899. A later winner of the Nobel Prize in Literature, Winston Churchill had an excellent writing style that enhances his firsthand account of the Omdurman campaign.

Harrington, Peter, and Sharp, Frederic, eds. *Omdurman 1898: The Eye-Witnesses Speak*. London: Greenhill Books, 1998. Compilation of firsthand British accounts of the Sudanese War.

Holt, P. M. *The Mahdist State in the Sudan, 1881-1898*. New York: Oxford University Press, 1970. Excellent scholarly work based on Sudanese primary sources. Remains the best work on the Sudanese War in the English language.

Magnus, Sir Philip. *Kitchener, Portrait of an Imperialist*. London: John Murray, 1958. Standard biography of the British military commander in the Sudanese War.

Neillands, Robin. *The Dervish Wars: Gordon and Kitchener in the Sudan, 1880-1898*. London: John Murray, 1996. Study of British imperial interests in the Sudan that both students and scholars of the subject will find useful.

Zulfo, Ismat Hasan. *Karar: The Sudanese Account of the Battle of Omdurman*. London: Frederick Warne, 1980. Important book based on Arabic sources and oral tradition. Especially good on the makeup, training, and weapons of the Sudanese.

SEE ALSO: Sept. 13, 1882: Battle of Tel el Kebir; Mar. 13, 1884-Jan. 26, 1885: Siege of Khartoum; Nov. 15, 1884-Feb. 26, 1885: Berlin Conference Lays Groundwork for the Partition of Africa; Mar. 1, 1896: Ethiopia Repels Italian Invasion; July 10-Nov. 3, 1898: Fashoda Incident Pits France vs. Britain.

RELATED ARTICLES in *Great Lives from History: The Nineteenth Century, 1801-1900:* Charles George Gordon; The Mahdi; Third Marquis of Salisbury.

March 1, 1896
ETHIOPIA REPELS ITALIAN INVASION

A latecomer to the European scramble for African territories, Italy focused its colonizing efforts on Eritrea and Ethiopia in Northeast Africa. After years of treaty disputes and diplomatic intrigue, Ethiopia's Emperor Menelik II ended Italian aspirations with a resounding victory at the Battle of Adwa. The defeat of Italy affirmed Ethiopian independence and challenged the prevalent racial attitudes of nineteenth century Europe.

LOCALE: Ethiopia and Eritrea

CATEGORIES: Colonization; wars, uprisings, and civil unrest

KEY FIGURES

Yohannes IV (1831-1889), emperor of Ethiopia, r. 1872-1889

Menelik II (1844-1913), emperor of Ethiopia, r. 1889-1913

Oreste Baratieri (1841-1901), Italian general

Ingida Alula (1847-1897), Ethiopian general

Francesco Crispi (1819-1901), prime minister of Italy, 1887-1891, 1893-1896

SUMMARY OF EVENT

The Italo-Ethiopian wars were the product of Italy's efforts to subjugate Northeast Africa's fiercely independent Ethiopian Empire. The roots of the conflict go back to 1884, when Great Britain facilitated an agreement between Egypt and Ethiopia called the Hewett Treaty. One of the stipulations of this pact was that the Egyptian Red Sea port of Massawa, which served as Ethiopia's primary connection with the world outside its isolated highlands, remained free for Ethiopian transit. However, Great Britain refused to enforce this accord and invited its ally Italy to assume control of Massawa from Egypt in 1885. Italy claimed willingness to accede to the demands of the Hewett Treaty, but instead blocked Ethiopian access through the port and used it as a base for its ambitions to colonize Ethiopia.

The Italian motives became immediately clear to Ethiopian emperor Yohannes IV. Italy had engaged in discussion with Menelik, who was then king of the semi-independent state of Shoa to the south. Even though Menelik had sworn fealty to Yohannes, the emperor knew Menelik desired his title and feared the Italians wished to use him for their own ends. Indeed, Italy had been sending Menelik arms and asking to make treaties independent of Yohannes.

While negotiating with Menelik, the Italians slowly extended their influence inland from Massawa, occupying the important trade route town of Sahati, in blatant

Ethiopian emperor Menelik II (under umbrella) negotiating peace terms with Italian commissioners. (Francis R. Niglutsch)

disregard for the Hewett Treaty, which designated Sahati as exclusively Ethiopian. Ras Ingida Alula, the emperor's general based in the northern province of Tigre, immediately threatened to march on Sahati. The Italians reiterated their peaceful intentions, but Ras Alula would hear none of it. He ordered the Italians to evacuate Sahati. The Italians refused, so Ras Alula attacked the Italian garrison at Sahati, but was repulsed. Italian troops were sent to relieve Sahati, and en route Ras Alula attacked them at Dogali and destroyed the force. In Italy, the Dogali Massacre, as it was so named, elicited outrage and cries for retribution. Italy demanded territorial concessions and compensation for what it considered to be unwarranted aggression on the part of Ras Alula. Yohannes refused such extravagant terms, providing Italy with the excuse to attack and occupy Ethiopia.

Hoping that Menelik would attack Yohannes, the Italians prepared for war to take advantage of the situation when it occurred. Yohannes realized his difficult position, for it appeared Menelik was conspiring against him, and his army was weak and needed provisions. Yohannes marched on Shoa to gain supplies from that rich

region and to force Menelik to acquiesce; however, he was unsuccessful. Shortly afterward, Sudanese Mahdists attacked Yohannes's western borders, seeing the unbalanced situation in Ethiopia as a perfect time to strike. Yohannes was killed in battle with the Mahdists at Metemma in February, 1889.

Once news of the emperor's death reached Shoa, Menelik immediately claimed the title for himself, as there was little competition to his ascendancy outside of Tigre, where Ras Alula supported the previous emperor's son as the heir. On May 2, 1889, before his crowning ceremony, however, he signed the Treaty of Wichale with Italy. Italy's prime minister Francesco Crispi immediately proclaimed Ethiopia a protectorate of Italy on the basis of Article 17 of the treaty. The Italian version of the treaty stated that Menelik gave consent for Italy to conduct all foreign policy matters on his behalf. The Amharic-language version that Menelik had was quite different; it said that Menelik could choose to use Italian offices if he wished. Menelik thus felt no obligation to forsake his rights of sovereignty. At first he thought the discrepancy a mistake and hoped for alteration. Only later did he perceive the treachery involved. He wasted no time in abrogating the article, but to no avail.

With the acquiescence of other European powers, Italy recommenced its expansion inland in Northeast Africa by occupying Asmara. While still pressing for Ethiopian acceptance of the Treaty of Wichale, General Oreste Baratieri took command of the new Italian colony of Eritrea on the Red Sea. Wanting access to the healthier highlands, he began to move on Tigre. Reading the signs of Italian invasion, Menelik prepared for war as well as he could. He began importing arms through Djibouti, a French colony on the coast. Internally, Ethiopia united against the potential Italian invasion, with even Ras Alula submitting to the emperor. By late 1895, Ethiopia had mobilized for war.

General Baratieri had ordered the occupation of Adigerat as a fortified base from which to push into the highlands in 1895. Later that year, Baratieri won his last victory at Debra Aila, annexing the province of Tigre to the Eritrean colony. The supremely confident Italian military leaders expressed little concern when they learned that Ethiopian troops were moving into the vicinity of Atzala. However, when the Italians marched out to meet the Ethiopian army, they received an unexpected surprise. The mass of Ethiopian troops attacked their position. Horribly outnumbered, the Italians suffered their first real defeat at the Battle of Amba Alagi. Humbled but vengeful, the troops retreated to Adigerat and the fortress of Mequelle.

The Italian general had little notion of the extent of the Ethiopian army, which numbered at least 100,000 men. Menelik sent part of his army to lay siege to the Italian position at Mequelle, which was in dire need of supplies and water. Having little choice in the matter, General Baratieri arranged a cease-fire agreement. Menelik II accepted it and agreed to escort the survivors of Mequelle to Adigerat. He was now in a strategically powerful position.

General Baratieri had just under 45,000 troops available to him, and he, like Menelik, lacked provisions. Blind to the reality of his army's situation in Ethiopia, Prime Minister Crispi pressed General Baratieri into action to salvage Italian pride. Arrogant and lacking good intelligence about Menelik's troop movements, Baratieri decided to leave the confines of his fortress. After a winter of fighting and waiting, Menelik learned of the Italian advance on March 2, 1896.

Menelik positioned his force just outside Adwa. A lack of communication and errors in movement due to inaccurate knowledge of the terrain assisted in the wholesale slaughter of the Italian army. Outflanked and outnumbered, Baratieri's army was virtually destroyed, with over 7,000 men dead and 10,000 wounded. Another 2,000 or so were taken prisoner. Although the Ethiopian army also sustained heavy losses, it remained intact and in control.

SIGNIFICANCE

As a direct consequence of the Battle of Adwa, Crispi's government in Italy fell and Menelik II was able to dictate his own peace terms. His foremost demand was the delineation of boundaries between Ethiopia and Eritrea and annulment of the Treaty of Wichale. The victory at Adwa ensured that one subtantial part of sub-Saharan Africa would not fall under European colonial rule. Moreover, the Ethiopian victory represented not only a defeat over imperialism but also a symbol for Africans across the continent with which to identify. Ethiopia had asserted its right to independence and its ability to defend that right, a powerful sentiment for other Africans under the yoke of imperialism during the decades that followed.

European states, which had long ignored Ethiopia as a secondary power, or no power at all, now had little choice but to negotiate with Ethiopia on equal terms. In Europe, the ideological effect was most important. An African power had defeated a European power, and handily. To many Europeans, the Ethiopian victory at Adwa symbolized the waning of European power in the world. Moreover, Menelik and his army powerfully contradicted European attitudes of race. This war shook the foundations of European social Darwinism and scientific racism to its core and forced a painful reevaluation among many Europeans as to the moral justification of imperialism. Italy's humiliation at Adwa would also provide Benito Mussolini's Fascist government a powerful motivation for returning to Ethiopia in 1935.

—*Branden C. McCullough*

FURTHER READING

Berkeley, G. F. H. *The Campaign of Adowa and the Rise of Menelik*. 1902. Reprint. New York: Negro Universities Press, 1969. Contemporary account that provides a detailed account of troop movements and the command decisions for the military engagements.

Caulk, Richard A. *"Between the Jaws of Hyenas": A Diplomatic History of Ethiopia, 1876-1896*. Edited by Bahru Zewde. Wiesbaden, Germany: Harrassowitz Verlag, 2002. This massive work treats the entire war in detail, including the intrigues of Menelik's relationship with Italy before his ascendancy to emperor and the Treaty of Wichale.

Lāpiso Dé Delébo. *The Italo-Ethiopian War of 1887-1896: From Dogali to Adwa*. Addis Ababa: Artistic Print Enterprise, 1996. Survey that expands the scope of the war, discussing the evolution of hostilities and the buildup to Adwa.

Marcus, Harold. *The Life and Times of Menelik II: Ethiopia, 1844-1913*. Lawrenceville, N.J.: Red Sea Press, 1995. Biography of Menelik by a leading scholar of Ethiopian history. Particularly important for portraying the Ethiopian view of the war.

Work, Ernest. *Ethiopia: A Pawn in European Diplomacy*. New York: MacMillan, 1936. This classic work is essential for understanding the maneuvering of Italian foreign policy toward Ethiopia.

SEE ALSO: Apr., 1868: British Expedition to Ethiopia; Sept. 13, 1882: Battle of Tel el Kebir; Mar. 13, 1884-Jan. 26, 1885: Siege of Khartoum; Mar., 1896-Nov., 1899: Sudanese War; July 10-Nov. 3, 1898: Fashoda Incident Pits France vs. Britain.

RELATED ARTICLE in *Great Lives from History: The Nineteenth Century, 1801-1900:* Menelik II.

April 6, 1896
MODERN OLYMPIC GAMES ARE INAUGURATED

The Olympic festival in Athens, Greece, successfully combined ancient and modern traditions and practices to establish what remains the most prestigious international sports spectacle.

ALSO KNOWN AS: Games of the I Olympiad
LOCALE: Athens, Greece
CATEGORIES: Sports; organizations and institutions

KEY FIGURES

Pierre de Coubertin (1863-1937), French aristocrat, founder of the modern international Olympic festival

Panayótis Soútsos (1806-1868), Greek poet, first to propose the revival of the ancient Olympics

Evangelis Zappas (1800-1865), Greek businessman, sponsor of the first revived Olympic games

William Penny Brookes (1809-1895), English doctor

Demetrios Vikelas (1835-1908), Greek merchant, first president of the International Olympic Committee

Constantine (1868-1923), prince of Greece, later King Constantine I, r. 1913-1917, 1920-1922

John Connolly (1868-1957), American athlete, journalist, and novelist

Spiridon "Spiros" Louis (1873-1940), Greek shepherd and water carrier

SUMMARY OF EVENT

Many people played a part in the modern revival of the Olympic Games. Panayótis Soútsos published his poem in the Nauplion, Greece, newspaper in 1833, providing the first call for a revival of the ancient festival. Soútsos later presented a detailed plan for the games to the Greek government. Some of his ideas were implemented through the generosity of Evangelis Zappas, who funded successful Olympic competitions for Greek athletes at Athens in 1859 and (after his death) in 1870 and 1875. Meanwhile, William Penny Brookes celebrated annual "Olympian" festivals at his village of Much Wenlock in Shropshire, England, beginning in 1850. These festivals grew into regional and then national competitions at London in 1866 and Birmingham in 1867, and Brookes later proposed international games as well.

The person who would finally achieve the goal of an international competition was a French nobleman and education reformer, Baron Pierre de Coubertin, who would found the modern Olympic Games. Troubled by his own country's military weakness and impressed by the focus on physical fitness at English schools such as Rugby, Coubertin campaigned for the introduction of organized athletics into French education. He also felt French interests would be served by friendly competitions with the international elite. The June, 1894, conference he organized in Paris led directly to the establishment of the International Olympic Committee (IOC) and the 1896 Olympic Games in Athens, Greece. Thanks in good measure to the enthusiastic support of Demetrios Vikelas, the first president of the IOC; Crown Prince Constantine, the president of the organizing committee; and of many other Greeks, the festival began in the ancient Panathinaiko Stadium (restored in 1895 by George

Averoff, a Greek businessman and philanthropist) on April 6, 1896. The day was March 25 by the Greek calendar—Greek Independence Day, the opening date that had been suggested by Soútsos.

Between forty and seventy thousand spectators filled the stadium for the opening ceremonies at 3:30 P.M., and as many as thirty thousand more watched from the hills around the stadium. After the Olympic hymn played, athletes ran the heats of the 100-meter dash. The first final, the triple jump, followed the 100-meter dash and was won by John Connolly, an American, who became the first Olympic champion in some fifteen hundred years. (Connolly would later write a historical novel about the games.) A Frenchman finished the triple jump in second place.

Connolly's victory ceremony featured the raising of the U.S. flag, and the prizes were awarded at the end of the festival on April 15. Victors won an olive branch and a silver medal, which bore an image of the Greek god Zeus on one face and the Athenian Acropolis on the other face. Runners-up took home a bronze medal and a laurel branch. A herald announced each medalist's name, country, and event, and King George I of Greece presented the prizes, congratulating each athlete in his own native tongue.

The ten days of this first modern Olympiad included forty-three events in athletics, cycling, fencing, gymnastics, shooting, swimming, tennis, weightlifting, and wrestling; bad weather forced the cancellation of scheduled competitions in rowing and sailing. Two hundred forty-one athletes from fourteen countries participated, with the Greeks making up the largest team and earning the most medals. The Americans, with eleven first-place finishes, won the most events. The Germans, the largest foreign contingent, also did well.

Among individual performances, two American brothers, John and Sumner Paine, both became Olympic champions in shooting. Paul Masson of France won three cycling events and Alfred Hajos (Guttmann) of Hungary won both the 100-meter and the 1,200-meter swimming race. An English student, John Boland, came to Athens as a tourist and ended up winning the tennis competition,

The dramatic high point of the first modern Olympiad was the marathon, which was won by a Greek shepherd, Spiridon Louis. King George I of Greece became so excited that he ran with Louis after he entered the stadium. (Francis R. Niglutsch)

despite playing in leather-soled shoes with heels. Robert Garrett, Jr., an American college student, triumphed in both the shot put and the discus throw. Ironically, his unfamiliarity with discus throwing proved to be an advantage because his Greek rivals mimicked what they thought to be the classical technique and threw stiffly with their arms alone. Garrett used the leverage of his legs to earn a narrow victory. Carl Schumann of Germany won in gymnastics and Greco-Roman wrestling and also competed in athletics and weightlifting.

The most dramatic and popular achievement, however, was that of Greek shepherd and water carrier Spiridon "Spiros" Louis, who became the winner of the first marathon ever run despite stopping at a tavern for a glass of wine along the distance of about twenty-five miles. (The modern distance for marathon races was not set until 1908.) Louis's victory in this race, based on ancient legends about the Athenian defeat of Persian invaders at Marathon in 490 B.C.E., established the event as a staple in athletic competitions. The marathon also guaranteed the success of the 1896 Olympiad.

Subsequent festivals at Paris (1900) and St. Louis (1904) were not as well attended or received, partly because of their uneasy link with world fairs. However, another Athens Olympiad, the 1906 Games, again organized by Prince Constantine, reawakened interest in the Olympic movement and put it on the course that led to the contemporary festival and its global reach.

SIGNIFICANCE

The 1896 Olympic Games was a creative mix of the ancient and the modern. The herald's proclamation echoed the practices of antiquity, and the flag-raising inaugurated a new tradition. Victors' prizes included the olive branch of the original games—cut from the same sacred grove at Olympia—and the silver medals of Zappas's revivals. Only men took part, as in the ancient games, but men from all over the world, not Greeks alone. Most entered on their own, as in antiquity, but the Greeks and Hungarians were official representatives of their countries.

Events ranged from the ancient discus throw to the shooting of up-to-date pistols and rifles. No combination of old and new had a greater or more harmful effect than the exclusion of all but amateurs from the 1896 games. This was justified by the symbolic nature of prizes at an-

cient Olympia, but it misrepresented the realities of Greek competition.

The original Olympic victors earned rich rewards from their native cities and often won money and other prizes of value at festivals before and after competing at Olympia. Amateurism, an invention of the 1860's, effectively reserved the modern Olympics for those wealthy enough to train, travel, and compete with no thought of expense or material rewards; amateurism as Olympic policy continued for some one hundred years. It was only at the end of the twentieth century that the more open, modern international Olympics had returned to the true spirit of the ancient games. Unfortunately, the international cooperation and harmony that Coubertin hoped the games would foster have not yet been achieved.

—*Mark Golden*

FURTHER READING

De Coubertin, Pierre. *Olympic Memoirs*. Lausanne, Switzerland: International Olympic Committee, 1979. First published in French in 1931, a firsthand account by a major figure in the Olympic revival, as essential as it is misleading.

Llewellyn Smith, M. *Olympics in Athens, 1896: The Invention of the Modern Olympic Games*. London: Profile Books, 2004. A lively and updated treatment by a former British ambassador to Greece.

Mandell, Richard D. *The First Modern Olympics*. Berkeley: University of California Press, 1976. A standard account of the 1896 Olympic Games.

Young, David C. *A Brief History of the Olympic Games*. Malden, Mass.: Blackwell, 2004. A good overview by an authority on both the ancient and the modern Olympics.

_____. *The Modern Olympics: A Struggle for Revival*. Baltimore: Johns Hopkins University Press, 1996. A path-breaking investigation that corrects many misconceptions about the origins of the modern festival.

SEE ALSO: c. 1845: Modern Baseball Begins; Aug. 22, 1851: *America* Wins the First America's Cup Race; 1869: Baseball's First Professional Club Forms; 1891: Naismith Invents Basketball.

RELATED ARTICLE in *Great Lives from History: The Nineteenth Century, 1801-1900:* William Gilbert Grace.

1890's

May 18, 1896
PLESSY V. FERGUSON

One of the most notorious decisions in the history of the U.S. Supreme Court, Plessy v. Ferguson *not only upheld racial segregation in the United States, it also lent the sanction of the Supreme Court and created the contentious doctrine of separate but equal that a later Court would eventually overturn as a self-contradiction.*

LOCALE: Washington, D.C.
CATEGORIES: Laws, acts, and legal history; government and politics; social issues and reform; civil rights and liberties

KEY FIGURES
Homer Adolph Plessy (1862-1925), New Orleans resident of one-eighth African ancestry
Albion Winegar Tourgée (1838-1905), Plessy's chief attorney
Henry B. Brown (1836-1913), associate Supreme Court justice, 1890-1906
John Marshall Harlan (1833-1911), associate Supreme Court justice, 1877-1911
Louis A. Martinet (d. 1917), New Orleans man who led a challenge to the separate but equal doctrine
John H. Ferguson (fl. late nineteenth century), judge of the Criminal District Court for Orleans Parish
Charles E. Fenner (1834-1911), associate Louisiana Supreme Court justice

SUMMARY OF EVENT
On July 10, 1890, the Louisiana General Assembly, over the objection of its eighteen African American members, enacted a law that read, in part:

> . . . all railway companies carrying passengers in their coaches in this state shall provide equal but separate accommodations for the white and colored races, by providing two or more passenger coaches for each passenger train, or by dividing the passenger coaches by a partition so as to secure separate accommodations.

The Louisiana law empowered train officials to assign passengers to cars; passengers insisting on going into a car set aside for the other race were liable to a twenty-five-dollar fine and twenty days' imprisonment. In addition, the company could refuse to carry an obstreperous passenger and, if it were sued for doing so, was immune from damages in state courts. A third section outlined the

penalties for noncomplying railroads and provided that "nothing in this act shall be construed as applying to nurses attending children of the other race."

At first the Separate Car Bill was stymied by the black legislators and by railroad officials who were as anxious to avoid the economic burden of providing separate facilities as they were to avoid a boycott of irate black passengers. After the black legislators had helped to override the veto of a major lottery bill, however, the legislature revived the Separate Car Bill and enacted it by a safe margin.

After its enactment, some of the railroad companies were inclined to disregard the law, and they apparently collaborated with black people to test its validity. In 1890, the railroads had unsuccessfully challenged a Mississippi separate but equal law; the Supreme Court of the United States had held in *Louisville, New Orleans, and Texas Railway Co. v. Mississippi* that such a law, when applied solely to travel within the state, did not encroach upon interstate commerce.

The prominent black community of New Orleans organized to mount a legal attack upon the new law. A group calling itself the Citizens' Committee to Test the Constitutionality of the Separate Car Law, led by Louis A. Martinet and Alexander A. Mary, organized to handle the litigation and enlisted the services of Albion Winegar Tourgée. Tourgée was to serve as chief counsel and devote his considerable talents to rallying public opposition to the Jim Crow system typified by the Louisiana law. The new counsel had served as a classical carpetbagger in North Carolina during Reconstruction and, among other accomplishments, had published a number of novels about the Reconstruction era, among them *A Fools Errand* (1879), *An Appeal to Caesar* (1884), and *Bricks Without Straw* (1880).

Martinet engaged James Walker to assist in handling the Louisiana phase of the controversy. Before the first test of the Louisiana law (also featuring an African American who could "pass for white") could be settled, the Louisiana Supreme Court decided in *State ex rel. Abbot v. Hicks* (1892) that the 1890 law could not be applied to interstate travelers since it was an unconstitutional regulation of interstate commerce. The *Plessy* case, then, relitigated the question raised in the 1890 Mississippi railroad case, but as a problem in the constitutional law of civil liberties rather than one of interstate commerce.

The person recruited to test the segregation law was Homer Adolph Plessy, a person of seven-eighths Caucasian and one-eighth African ancestry, in whom "the mixture of colored blood was not discernible." On June 7, 1892, holding a first-class ticket entitling him to travel on the East Louisiana Railway from New Orleans to Covington, Louisiana, Plessy took a seat in the car reserved for whites. The conductor, assisted by a policeman, forcibly removed Plessy and, charging him with violating the segregation law, placed him in the parish jail. The state prosecuted Plessy in the Orleans Parish criminal district court before Judge John H. Ferguson. Plessy's plea that the law was unconstitutional was overruled by Ferguson, who directed the defense to address itself to the questions of fact. Having no defense in the facts, Tourgée and Walker appealed Ferguson's ruling on the law's constitutionality to the Louisiana Supreme Court by asking that court to issue a writ of prohibition which in effect would have directed Ferguson to reverse his ruling on the constitutional question.

On December 19, 1892, Associate Judge Charles E. Fenner of the Louisiana Supreme Court ruled the law constitutional in an opinion that served as a model for that written later by Justice Henry B. Brown of the U.S. Supreme Court. After a delay of almost four years—a delay that Tourgée encouraged on the grounds that it gave the opponents of segregation needed time—the U.S. Supreme Court heard the arguments in Plessy's case on April 13, 1896. On May 18, 1896, Justice Brown handed down the majority opinion, supported by six other justices (Justice David Brewer did not participate, and Justice John Marshall Harlan dissented).

Justice Brown first disposed of Tourgée's argument that the segregation law was a "badge of servitude," a vestige of slavery prohibited by the Thirteenth Amendment (1865). Decisions in the 1872 Slaughterhouse cases and the 1883 Civil Rights Cases, wrote Brown, indicated that it was because the Thirteenth Amendment barred only outright slavery and not laws merely imposing "onerous disabilities and burdens" that the movement for the Fourteenth Amendment had been successful. Later in his opinion Brown blended the "badge of servitude" argument of the Thirteenth Amendment with his treatment of the equal protection question:

We consider the underlying fallacy of the plaintiff's argument to consist in the assumption that the enforced separation of the two races stamps the colored race with a badge of inferiority. If this be so, it is not by reason of anything found in the act, but solely because the colored race chooses to put that construction upon it.

If Plessy was to gain any relief, it had to be from the Fourteenth Amendment, but that amendment, according to Brown

merely . . . enforced the absolute equality of the two races before the law, but in the nature of things it could not have been intended to abolish distinctions based upon color, or to enforce social, as distinguished from political, equality, or a commingling of the two races upon terms unsatisfactory to either.

To support his point, Brown cited state school segregation and antimiscegenation laws and federal laws prescribing segregated schools for the District of Columbia. Special stress was placed on the 1849 decision of *Roberts v. Boston*, in which Chief Justice Lemuel Shaw of the Massachusetts Supreme Judicial Court had upheld the

---

PLESSY V. FERGUSON

The majority opinion in Plessy v. Ferguson *was rendered by Justice Henry B. Brown. Brown endorsed the argument of Lousiana that it was constitutionally permissible to mandate "equal but separate accomodations" for black and white train passengers. (The more famous phrase, "separate but equal," appears only in Justice Harlan's dissent.)*

We consider the underlying fallacy of the plaintiff's argument to consist in the assumption that the enforced separation of the two races stamps the colored race with a badge of inferiority. If this be so, it is not by reason of anything found in the act, but solely because the colored race chooses to put that construction upon it. The argument necessarily assumes that if, as has been more than once the case, and is not unlikely to be so again, the colored race should become the dominant power in the state legislature, and should enact a law in precisely similar terms, it would thereby relegate the white race to an inferior position. We imagine that the white race, at least, would not acquiesce in this assumption. . . . Legislation is powerless to eradicate racial instincts, or to abolish distinctions based upon physical differences, and the attempt to do so can only result in accentuating the difficulties of the present situation. If the civil and political rights of both races be equal, one cannot be inferior to the other civilly or politically. If one race be inferior to the other socially, the constitution of the United States cannot put them upon the same plane.

constitutionality of separate but equal schools for Boston. Brown did not mention that the Massachusetts legislature had repudiated Shaw's doctrine in 1855.

To the plaintiff's argument that the principle of segregation could be used by the state to enforce extreme and arbitrary forms of racial discrimination, Brown responded that every exercise of state power must be "reasonable, and extend only to such laws as are enacted in good faith for the promotion of the public good, and not for the annoyance or oppression of a particular class." There was nothing unreasonable about the Louisiana law according to the Court; in determining what is reasonable, state legislators could "act with reference to the established usages, customs, and traditions of the people, with a view to the promotion of their comfort, and the preservation of the public peace and good order." Finally, Brown in his opinion delivered a famous statement on the relationship between law, prejudice, and equality:

> The [plaintiff's] argument also assumes that social prejudice may be overcome by legislation, and that equal rights cannot be secured to the negro except by an enforced commingling of the two races. We cannot accept this proposition. If the two races are to meet on terms of social equality, it must be the result of natural affinities, a mutual appreciation of each other's merits and a voluntary consent of individuals.

The law in question interfered with the "voluntary consent of individuals."

Tourgée's fears were realized: The Court had sanctioned Jim Crowism. What comfort African Americans derived from the case had to be found in the strong dissenting opinion of Justice Harlan, who once again proved himself to be a staunch champion of a broad interpretation of the Reconstruction amendments. Harlan construed the ban on slavery to cover segregation laws; he insisted on Tourgée's thesis that a railroad was a public highway and that under the Fourteenth Amendment government could make no racial distinctions whether one considered the case under the privileges and immunities, due process, or equal protection clauses of that amendment.

Harlan attacked the Court's reliance on pre-Fourteenth Amendment precedents; his most memorable language appeared in connection with his charge that the majority usurped constitutional power by assuming authority to decide on the "reasonableness" of state social legislation:

> The white race deems itself to be the dominant race in this country. And so it is, in prestige, in achievements, in education, in wealth, and in power. So, I doubt not that it will continue to be for all time, if it remains true to its great heritage and holds fast to the principles of constitutional liberty. But in view of the Constitution, in the eye of the law, there is in this country no superior, dominant, ruling class of citizens. There is no caste here. Our Constitution is color-blind, and neither knows nor tolerates classes among citizens. In respect of civil rights, all citizens are equal before the law.

Harlan turned out to be a competent soothsayer:

> The destinies of the two races in this country are indissolubly linked together, and the interests of both require that the common government of all shall not permit the seeds of race hate to be planted under the sanction of law.

JUSTICE HARLAN'S DISSENT

Justice John Marshall Harlan was the sole dissenter in Plessy v. Ferguson. *He argued that the segregation law in Louisiana violated the "true intent and meaning" of the Thirteenth and Fourteenth Amendments.*

The white race deems itself to be the dominant race in this country. And so it is, in prestige, in achievements, in education, in wealth, and in power. So, I doubt not, it will continue to be for all time, if it remains true to its great heritage, and holds fast to the principles of constitutional liberty. But in view of the constitution, in the eye of the law, there is in this country no superior, dominant, ruling class of citizens. There is no caste here. Our constitution is color-blind, and neither knows nor tolerates classes among citizens. In respect of civil rights, all citizens are equal before the law. The humblest is the peer of the most powerful. The law regards man as man, and takes no account of his surroundings or of his color when his civil rights as guarantied by the supreme law of the land are involved. It is therefore to be regretted that this high tribunal, the final expositor of the fundamental law of the land, has reached the conclusion that it is competent for a state to regulate the enjoyment by citizens of their civil rights solely upon the basis of race.

In my opinion, the judgment this day rendered will, in time, prove to be quite as pernicious as the decision made by this tribunal in the Dred Scott Case.

SIGNIFICANCE

Despite Harlan's impassioned words, it would take the general public and the justices of the Supreme Court decades to adopt his views and interpretation of the Constitution. *Plessy v. Ferguson*'s strong sanction of segregation lasted formally in transportation until the Court's decision in *Henderson v. United States* (1950) and in education until *Brown v. Board of Education of Topeka, Kansas* (1954). Antimiscegenation laws were not outlawed until 1967 in *Loving v. Virginia*.

—*James J. Bolner, updated by Brian L. Fife*

FURTHER READING

Fireside, Harvey. *Separate and Unequal: Homer Plessy and the Supreme Court Decision that Legalized Racism.* New York: Carroll & Graf, 2004. A detailed look at the legacy of the Court's decision in *Plessy v. Ferguson.*

Kauper, Paul G. "Segregation in Public Education: The Decline of *Plessy v. Ferguson.*" *Michigan Law Review* 52 (1954): 1137-1158. Kauper contends that the Court did not deal definitively with the validity of segregation legislation, relying instead on its view of "reasonableness."

Lofgren, Charles A. *The Plessy Case: A Legal-Historical Interpretation.* New York: Oxford University Press, 1987. In tracing the history of transportation law, Lofgren concludes that *Plessy* did not cause Jim Crow but instead confirmed the American racism of its era.

Mueller, Jean West, and Wynell Burroughs Schamel. "*Plessy v. Ferguson* Mandate." *Social Education* 53 (1989): 120-122. Traces the historical events leading to the Court's ruling, as well as teaching strategies for instructors.

Roche, John P. "*Plessy v. Ferguson:* Requiescat in Pace?" *University of Pennsylvania Law Review* 103 (1954): 44-58. Roche believes that the *Plessy* decision reflected the political climate of its time and was a judicial attempt to deal with a social and political problem.

Woodward, C. Vann. *American Counterpoint: Slavery and Racism in the North-South Dialogue.* Boston: Little, Brown, 1971. Woodward discusses the irony of Justice Brown's and Harlan's positions, in the light of the origins of the two men.

SEE ALSO: Nov. 24, 1865: Mississippi Enacts First Post-Civil War Black Code; Dec. 6, 1865: Thirteenth Amendment Is Ratified; Apr. 9, 1866: Civil Rights Act of 1866; July 9, 1868: Fourteenth Amendment Is Ratified; Oct. 15, 1883: Civil Rights Cases; 1890: Mississippi Constitution Disfranchises Black Voters; Sept. 18, 1895: Washington's Atlanta Compromise Speech.

RELATED ARTICLES in *Great Lives from History: The Nineteenth Century, 1801-1900:* Stephen J. Field; Roger Brooke Taney; Booker T. Washington.

June, 1896
MARCONI PATENTS THE WIRELESS TELEGRAPH

Capable of sending Morse code signals through airwaves, Guglielmo Marconi's wireless telegraph ushered in a revolutionary period in communications that would later include radio broadcasting, television, radio astronomy, and radar.

LOCALE: London, England
CATEGORIES: Communications; science and technology; radio and television

KEY FIGURES

Guglielmo Marconi (1874-1937), Italian inventor of the radio
Samuel F. B. Morse (1791-1872), American inventor of the telegraph
Karl Ferdinand Braun (1850-1918), German physicist who shared a Nobel Prize with Marconi
James Clerk Maxwell (1831-1879), Scottish physicist who first postulated electromagnetic theory
Heinrich Hertz (1857-1894), German physicist who first experimentally proved electromagnetic theory

SUMMARY OF EVENT

Communication during the late nineteenth century was firmly based on the electric telegraph, invented by Samuel F. B. Morse in 1838. In both the United States and Europe, telegraph lines strung along poles connected even the most remote settlements. Transatlantic communication had even been possible since 1866, when a cable had been successfully placed across the ocean. Telegraphs

Guglielmo Marconi (right) and the American chemist Irving Langmuir (1881-1957) in the General Electric Research Laboratory in 1922. (Library of Congress)

Six years later, a young Italian by the name of Guglielmo Marconi came across a report on Hertz's experiments and decided that here was a method that could be used to communicate Morse code without wires. Using equipment invented by a number of other scientists, he attempted to lengthen the distance the electromagnetic waves could be transmitted. When the distance grew to more than a mile, he tried to attain a patent in his native Italy in 1895. With telegraphy firmly in place on land, the only function the patent officials saw for the device was to allow ships to communicate with each other and the shore. Marconi headed to England, thinking his chances for approval might be better in a country with the largest fleet in the world. While in Great Britain, he received a patent for the wireless telegraph in June, 1896.

Marconi was not satisfied with a device that could only transmit within a one-mile radius, so he continued to improve the wireless telegraph. Over the next few years, the distance increased to four, then seven, and then twelve miles. In 1899, Marconi succeeded in transmitting from England to France across the English Channel, a distance of thirty miles. Marconi focused on maritime events, such as yacht racing, and worked to provide ways for ships to signal distress at sea. He also sought to provide a wireless telegraph in those areas inaccessible to or awkward for telegraph poles, such as on the coast, where winds off the ocean regularly destroyed telegraph lines connected to lighthouses, or across wide rivers, where telegraph lines could not be strung with ease.

Also in 1899, Marconi moved to the United States and set up the Marconi Wireless Telegraph Company of America. He began marketing his device and became quite successful. Competitors quickly arose, however, and one of the early problems of radio communications was interference among competing stations. The different stations needed a way to transmit at different frequencies so that receivers could distinguish the desired signal. Marconi again experimented with devices developed by other inventors until he had a tuner that would radiate

could only use the Morse code, a system of dots and dashes devised by Morse, instead of either the alphabet or voice to communicate messages. Nevertheless, skilled operators familiar with the code made the system workable.

The beginnings of a new system that would eventually lead to both voice and music being broadcast throughout the world without the use of wires were not obvious at first. For decades, physicists had known that electromagnetic waves act at a distance without a physical medium. In 1873, James Clerk Maxwell provided the equations that explained the theory behind such an effect, but it was not until 1888 that Heinrich Hertz studied electromagnetic radiation in the laboratory. A current discharging in one part of the laboratory sent electromagnetic waves over to a detector in another part of the laboratory. The detector would spark in response. Hertz published his findings, but he never considered the possibility that electromagnetic waves could be used to communicate information.

strongly with little interference. He received a patent for the mechanism in 1900.

The next step for Marconi was to attempt to broadcast radio waves across even greater distances than before. He was convinced that transatlantic signaling could be accomplished. Prevalent theories deemed this impossible. Radio waves travel at the speed of light in straight lines. After radio waves passed the horizon, they would merely radiate out into space, not follow the curvature of the earth to reach far distant places. Since Marconi was already obtaining distances twice as long as that required to reach the visible horizon, he saw no reason why the distance could not be increased even further.

In order to achieve radio signals across the Atlantic, Marconi built huge power stations with tall antennas, one at Poldhu in Cornwall, England, and one at St. John's in Newfoundland, Canada. By special arrangement, the station at Poldhu would broadcast the letter "s" in Morse code on certain days at certain times. Marconi would be listening at those times for the signal. On December 12, 1901, he heard the signal from a distance of two thousand miles. He had no disinterested witnesses at the event, however, nor did the telegraphy monopoly on Newfoundland allow him to continue his experiments at St. John's. Marconi repeated the event on board a ship with several witnesses, again asking that the same signal be sent from Poldhu. Again, he received signals at a distance of two thousand miles, establishing the ability of radio waves to travel at distances conducive to transatlantic communication.

Theories abounded concerning radio's newfound ability to transmit over such long distances. The one most accepted was that a region of the atmosphere must reflect the radio waves, allowing them to extend farther than expected. It was not until the 1920's that researchers experimented with sending radio waves up into the atmosphere to discover various regions that reflected radio waves in various ways. This layer of the atmosphere is called the ionosphere. During the day, sunlight ionizes molecules within this region and hinders radio transmissions; at night, the effect is lessened.

Marconi might have impressed the world with the first transatlantic radio transmission, but in the meantime he had his hands full trying to keep his company competitive. The radio wave detector of the time was a coherer, a tube of glass full of metallic particles that would cohere when radio waves passed through them. At a tap, they would fall apart again. Marconi designed a magnetic detector in 1902 that could work continuously. His new detector was also faster and longer lasting than a coherer.

SIGNIFICANCE

Marconi's invention replaced the telegraph as the sole means of communicating news across long distances and became the most versatile means of communication of the twentieth century, with applications in entertainment, news broadcasts, military detection systems, and astronomy. In 1909, Guglielmo Marconi was recognized for his work on the wireless telegraph with the Nobel Prize in Physics, shared with German physicist Karl Ferdinand Braun, who had also done research on wireless telegraphy. Braun is known for improving radio antennas so that their range became greatly increased and for inventing the crystal radio receiver and the cathode-ray tube.

Radio as Marconi envisioned it used long waves at high energies to travel. He was certain that long waves were necessary for long distances, and large power stations were set up to propagate these waves. Radio amateurs, limited to small power supplies, were forced to use shortwave radio and achieved good results. Shortwave radio was able to maintain contact more regularly than long wave, and it traveled longer distances, too. In the 1920's, Marconi reversed his position and began researching shortwave radio. His efforts provided a reliable means for long-distance communication.

—*Rose Secrest*

FURTHER READING

Coe, Lewis. "Without Wires." In *The Telegraph: A History of Morse's Invention and Its Predecessors in the United States*. Jefferson, N.C.: McFarland, 1993. Traces Marconi's earliest breakthroughs and the transformation of nineteenth century communications systems from telegraph to early radio.

Leinwoll, Stanley. *From Spark to Satellite: A History of Radio Communication*. New York: Charles Scribner's Sons, 1979. Carefully reports the history, the people, the scientific theory, and the technology of radio from Marconi to radio astronomy.

Pierce, John R., and A. Michael Noll. "Electric and Electronic Devices: The Physics of Communication Systems." In *The Science of Telecommunications*. New York: Scientific American Library, 1990. A clear, detailed description of the device Marconi invented, with color photographs, electrical diagrams, and a brief biography.

Rhoads, B. Eric. "Who Really Invented Radio?" *Audio* 79 (December, 1995): 26-31. A brief yet thorough summary of the technology and inventors of early radio. Clearly explains radio's mechanisms and early patents, with many pertinent photographs.

1890's

Strebeigh, Fred. "Messages by Wireless." In *Inventors and Discoverers: Changing Our World*, edited by Elizabeth L. Newhouse. Washington, D.C.: National Geographic Society, 1988. Traces the history of wireless communication from the first laboratory transmissions to television, with numerous color photographs coupled with informative captions.

Weightman, Gavin. *Signor Marconi's Magic Box: The Remarkable Invention of the Nineteenth Century and the Amateur Inventor Whose Genius Sparked a Revolution*. Cambridge, Mass: Da Capo Press, 2003. Biography of Marconi tracing his invention and its effects upon twentieth century culture.

SEE ALSO: Nov. 6, 1820: Ampère Reveals Magnetism's Relationship to Electricity; 1839: Daguerre and Niépce Invent Daguerreotype Photography; Jan. 10, 1840: Great Britain Establishes Penny Postage; May 24, 1844: Morse Sends First Telegraph Message; Apr. 3, 1860-Oct. 26, 1861: Pony Express Expedites Transcontinental Mail; Oct. 24, 1861: Transcontinental Telegraph Is Completed; July 27, 1866: First Transatlantic Cable Is Completed; June 23, 1868: Sholes Patents a Practical Typewriter; June 25, 1876: Bell Demonstrates the Telephone; Dec. 24, 1877: Edison Patents the Cylinder Phonograph; Mar. 11, 1891: Strowger Patents Automatic Dial Telephone System; Dec. 28, 1895: First Commercial Projection of Motion Pictures.

RELATED ARTICLES in *Great Lives from History: The Nineteenth Century, 1801-1900:* James Clerk Maxwell; Samuel F. B. Morse; Aleksandr Stepanovich Popov.

July 11, 1896
LAURIER BECOMES THE FIRST FRENCH CANADIAN PRIME MINISTER

Wilfrid Laurier's oratory made him a hero in Quebec and earned him a national reputation among Liberal Party members. In 1887 he was chosen opposition leader in Parliament, and, nine years later, he defeated Sir Francis Tupper to become Canada's first French Canadian prime minister.

LOCALE: Canada
CATEGORY: Government and politics

KEY FIGURES
Sir Wilfrid Laurier (1841-1919), opposition leader, 1887-1896, and Liberal prime minister, 1896-1911
Edward Blake (1833-1912), leader of parliamentary Liberals, 1880-1887
Sir Mackenzie Bowell (1823-1917), Conservative prime minister, 1894-1896
Sir John Alexander Macdonald (1815-1891), Conservative prime minister, 1867-1873, 1878-1891
Louis Riel (1844-1885), French Canadian rebel leader
Sir Charles Tupper (1821-1915), Conservative prime minister, 1896

SUMMARY OF EVENT
Wilfrid Laurier's rise to political prominence during the 1880's and 1890's benefited from growing French Canadian discontent with their position in the Dominion of Canada. In 1864, Quebec proponents of confederation claimed the confederation agreement provided for provincial autonomy in cultural and religious matters while protecting the rights of minorities. Quebec would maintain its established French language and the Roman Catholic religion while respecting the practices of its Protestant and English-speaking minorities. Protestant English-speaking provinces would extend similar protection to their French-speaking and Catholic minorities. In the eyes of many Quebecers, the execution of Louis Riel in 1885 and passage of the Manitoba Schools Act in 1890 violated that agreement, demonstrating that neither the federal government nor English-speaking provinces considered French and Catholic minorities equals within the nation.

In 1885, Riel had led an armed rebellion to support land claims by his French-speaking followers. He was captured, tried for treason, convicted, and hung on November 16, 1885, despite serious questions whether he was sufficiently sane to be responsible for his acts. Quebecers, who doubted that an English-Canadian would have been treated as Riel had been treated, celebrated him as a martyr who died defending French minority rights. In a March, 1886, debate concerning Riel's execution, Laurier achieved national renown in the Liberal Party through a speech in which he mounted a powerful attack on the conservative government, accusing it of bringing on rebellion by ignoring the legitimate griev-ances of Riel's followers.

Edward Blake, the leader of the parliamentary Lib-erals, had used Laurier as a major party spokesman in his unsuccessful 1887 election campaign against John Alex-ander Macdonald. After his defeat Blake had resigned and persuaded the Liberals to choose Laurier as his suc-cessor, claiming that a French Canadian as head of the party could unite Canadians. Laurier's highly visible position on the national scene helped Liberals become dominant in Quebec, despite opposition from Catholic bishops who viewed liberalism as a heretical and revolu-tionary doctrine.

When the Liberal government of Manitoba abolished French as an official language in the province, ended funding of church-run schools, and established in its place a state-financed nondenominational school sys-tem, Laurier faced an almost impossible dilemma. The 1870 act organizing the province had guaranteed equal rights to English-language Protestant schools and French-language Catholic schools. Quebecers believed manda-tory nondenominational English-language schools were, in effect, Protestant schools designed to destroy French Canadian culture and Catholicism. They demanded that the federal government intervene to restore the 1870 act's provisions.

Laurier sympathized with his fellow Catholics but could not offer open support without splitting his party. Not only was Manitoba governed by Liberals, but also many Ontario Liberals, whose support was vital to Laur-ier's continuance as leader, sympathized with Manitoba. Laurier temporized and refused to take a stand, claiming that responding was the responsibility of the Conserva-tive government. Macdonald was as cautious as Laurier and referred the entire matter to the court system.

Manitoba's actions intensified the increasingly con-tentious ethnic and religious tensions in late nineteenth century Canada. Growing immigration steadily reduced the French presence in the country, arousing French Ca-nadians' fears that they were an increasingly embattled minority. Few immigrants to Canada came from France or Belgium, the flow of English-speaking newcomers in-creased, and those from other European countries pre-ferred to learn English rather than French.

As the century progressed, racist ideas encouraged by social Darwinist philosophies assured Anglo-Saxons they were the top of the evolutionary ladder, while all other linguistic and ethnic groups were inferior. The preference for learning English by immigrants from the Ukraine and Hungary appeared to validate this view,

Sir Wilfrid Laurier. (Library of Congress)

1890's

raising questions over the propriety of using public funds to teach what was believed an inferior language: French. Extremists asserted that, as part of the British Empire, Canadians should use only English. Proponents of this view formed a so-called equal rights association, whose definition of "equal rights" required ending all legal or constitutional provisions granting French equal rights with English, or Catholicism equal rights with Protes-tantism. Young Quebecers reacted by joining nationalist groups and demanding that the federal government pro-tect French rights in Manitoba.

Conservatives were no more eager than was Laurier to address an issue that threatened to split their party be-tween British Empire loyalists, who called for complete cultural uniformity in Canada, and French and Catholic party members. The Manitoba schools question re-mained in limbo while it shuttled back and forth between the Canadian courts and the British Law Lords, then the final court of appeal on Canadian legal matters. When the Law Lords in January, 1895, finally ruled that Ottawa had the power to reverse the Manitoba act, the issue could no longer be avoided.

Mackenzie Bowell, a weak prime minister, dithered

and lost support of his cabinet; Sir Charles Tupper took over the Conservative leadership. On January 21, 1896, arguing that Parliament had an obligation to fulfill promises made to French Catholics, Tupper presented a remedial bill that would force Manitoba to honor the 1870 act. Although the Quebec hierarchy called on Laurier to support the bill, he refused to do so, asserting that as a member of Parliament he had to consider the national interest, not just those of Catholics, and claimed that compromise was still possible, despite six years of stalemate. Acting as a partisan opposition leader determined to thwart Conservative initiatives, Laurier used every possible obstructive tactic to keep Tupper from bringing his bill to a vote before the current parliament's scheduled end on April 26. Tupper was forced to withdraw his bill and call an election for June 23, 1896.

Tupper was confident of victory. Quebec's bishops instructed the faithful to vote only for supporters of the remedial bill. Tupper expected Quebec voters would follow their bishop's directive and vote Conservative, and he also believed Protestant voters would reject a Catholic candidate for prime minister. He proved mistaken in both suppositions. Laurier asked Quebec voters whether they trusted a fellow French Canadian or an English Protestant to protect their interests, and they responded by ignoring the bishops and voting 3 to 1 for Laurier. Except for a few Protestant clergymen who predicted eternal damnation for anyone helping elect a Catholic prime minister, most provinces divided their votes. The Quebec landslide thus gave Liberals a secure majority in the new Parliament, making Laurier the first French Canadian prime minister. He took office on July 11.

SIGNIFICANCE

Sir Wilfred Laurier moved to ease ethnic and religious hostility by accepting an agreement that ratified most acts of the Manitoba government. The school system would remain nondenominational, and teaching would be conducted in English. Catholics were permitted to have religious instruction for thirty minutes at the end of each school day and, if parents of ten students whose native tongue was not English requested it, there could be classes in a language other than English. This latter provision, however, was dropped in 1916 when the possibility of German classes infuriated wartime chauvinists. French Canadian nationalists were deeply disappointed

and Quebec's bishops angrily protested Laurier's compromise, arguing that it abandoned Catholic rights. The country, however, mostly accepted his resolution of the controversy.

With the Manitoba school question out of the way, Laurier concentrated on national problems involving trade, tariffs, and railroads. He would prove to the country over the next fifteen years that a French Canadian prime minister could provide effective leadership for Canada.

—Milton Berman

FURTHER READING

Mann, Susan. *The Dream of a Nation: A Social and Intellectual History of Quebec*. 2d ed. Montreal: McGill-Queen's University Press, 2002. Describes rising Quebec nationalism in the 1890's.

Morton, Desmond. *A Short History of Canada*. 3d rev. ed. Toronto: McClelland & Stewart, 1997. A concise narrative puts the 1896 election in critical perspective.

Neatby, H. Blair. *Laurier and a Liberal Quebec: A Study in Political Management*. Toronto: McClelland and Stewart, 1973. Analyzes Laurier's political activities in Quebec.

Schull, Joseph. *Laurier: The First Canadian*. Toronto: Macmillan of Canada, 1965. A detailed biography, very favorable to Laurier.

Silver, A. I. *The French-Canadian Idea of Confederation, 1864-1900*. 2d ed. Toronto: University of Toronto Press, 1997. Describes increasing French Canadian disillusionment with the idea of confederation.

Spigelman, Martin. *Wilfrid Laurier*. Rev. ed. Markham, Ont.: Fitzhenry & Whiteside, 2000. Brief, mostly laudatory biography of Laurier.

SEE ALSO: July 1, 1867: British North America Act; Oct. 11, 1869-July 15, 1870: First Riel Rebellion; Nov. 5, 1873-Oct. 9, 1878: Canada's Mackenzie Era; Sept., 1878: Macdonald Returns as Canada's Prime Minister; Mar. 19, 1885: Second Riel Rebellion Begins; 1896: Immigrant Farmers Begin Settling Western Canada.

RELATED ARTICLES in *Great Lives from History: The Nineteenth Century, 1801-1900:* Sir John Alexander Macdonald; Louis Riel; Sir Charles Tupper.

August 17, 1896
KLONDIKE GOLD RUSH BEGINS

When gold was found in Canada's Klondike Valley, the discovery sparked a frenzied gold rush, bringing in a wave of more than 100,000 prospectors to face the grueling conditions and extreme weather of the northern territory, while causing a financial ripple effect through the global economy.

LOCALE: Klondike, Yukon, Canada
CATEGORIES: Earth science; exploration and discovery; economics

KEY FIGURES

George Washington Carmack (c. 1850-1922), prospector whose claim on Bonanza Creek began the Klondike gold rush
Kate Carmack (Shaaw Tláa; b. c. 1862), possibly the first prospector to find gold in Bonanza Creek
Robert Henderson (1857-1933), prospector who may have been the first to strike gold in the Klondike
Jack London (1876-1916), prospector and author
Skookum Jim (c. 1855-1916), Tagish Indian and brother-in-law and mining partner of George Washington Carmack

SUMMARY OF EVENT

In August of 1896, a whoop and holler shattered the silence of the Klondike Valley, when George Washington Carmack, his wife, Kate Mason Carmack, and his two Indian companions, Tagish Charlie and Skookum Jim, greeted Carmack's discovery of gold. Their exclamations echoed through the Yukon into Alaska and rippled eventually into the lower forty-eight states by way of Seattle, where a ship delivered the largest shipment of gold dust ever handled at that port. Soon, the whole world was listening, captivated by the promise of riches and adventure found in Bonanza Creek.

Three weeks before Carmack and his partners were

Klondike mining camp.

ROUTES TO THE KLONDIKE

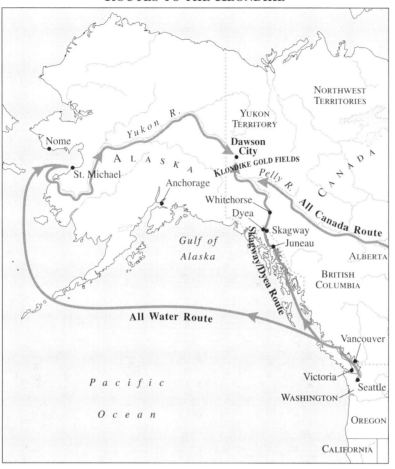

nanza, where nuggets lay in the ground for the picking. It was not until two years later, when it was too late to stake a claim, that Henderson discovered that the two creeks were one and the same.

On August 17, 1896, after Carmack had panned out enough gold dust for a "grub stake," he made his way to Forty Mile, where he announced his discovery. The stampede did not begin immediately. Miners at Forty Mile were skeptical. Carmack was married to an Indian, Kate Carmack, and consequently did not enjoy a good reputation. Carmack had never been a zealous prospector; the Indian life of fishing and hunting had appealed to him more than the grind of gold mining. Still, miners could not ignore such an electrifying report, especially after Carmack had shown them a shotgun shell filled with coarse gold. Soon, men traveled upriver from Forty Mile to have a look, and by the time winter came, the reports of other miners confirmed the strike.

By early winter, most of the men of Forty Mile had rushed to the new ground and staked claims. It was said that butchers dropped their aprons on the spot, druggists ground up their last prescriptions, and clerks tallied up their final bill of sale, all with the urge to head north to the Klondike. The Klondike was a magnet that drew miners, and others, from everywhere.

Victims of the Klondike fever numbered in the tens of thousands—casual laborers, farmers, students, bankers, and miners. Some, such as George Pilcher and Wyatt Earp, preferred to go on their own. Others, such as Will Ballou and John Hewitt, formed joint companies with like-minded neighbors who were willing to pool their resources. Many were backed by investors who wanted a share in the northern enterprise. Guidebooks advised readers on transportation routes, including an all-water route to the goldfields from the West Coast, a steerage passage from Seattle to Skagway in Alaska, and a trail one could hike and climb into the interior over the Chilkoot Pass and White Pass.

Most of the 1897-1898 argonauts (adventurers on a

able to get downstream to the mining settlement of Forty Mile to register their claim, they held a meeting on the hill overlooking Rabbit Creek. During this meeting, they decided to change the name of the creek. The miners in the north were mostly veterans of former gold rushes. They had a habit of changing the names of gold-bearing creeks to traditional mining names such as "Bonanza," thus removing the strangeness from a strange country. Rabbit Creek became a name on old maps, and Bonanza became the name that lured thousands north for the world's last great gold rush.

There was a time when the creek was not so well known. Over the hill from Bonanza Creek, a prospector named Robert Henderson was seeking that elusive strike. It was Henderson who suggested that Carmack try his luck on Rabbit Creek, and it was Henderson who continued to prospect just a stone's toss away from the wealth of Rabbit Creek, while hearing of a creek called Boquest) chose Seattle as their port of embarkation to the north. Among the sixty thousand stampeders was Jack London. He and his partners were among the thirty to forty thousand argonauts to choose one of the passes from the head of Lynn Canal as their route to the Klondike. From the coast to Dawson City was six hundred miles, but it was the first eighteen miles, from Dyea to the summit, that caused the most anxiety to travelers.

The trails, especially the Chilkoot Trail, had always been difficult to travel. At the base of the mountains, eight miles from the coast, the slope ascended sharply for ten miles to the summit, an elevation of thirty-five hundred feet. Crossing the pass under ideal weather conditions on the hard-packed snow of early spring was difficult, but undertaking it during a winter blizzard through deep, soft snow was extremely treacherous. What made the Chilkoot Trail a cruel punishment for most stampeders was tackling it time after time, weighed down by heavy backpacks. Most brought one thousand to two thousand pounds of supplies, which meant that twenty or more crossings had to be made after one's base depot was made at camp. Pack animals could not make it over the Chilkoot; the White Pass Trail proved a death trap for horses and mules. Hundreds fell from the twisting, narrow trail into the valley below; others foundered in deep snow or mud, or broke their legs fording the rocky streams, leaving a trail lined with rotting carcasses.

Two thundering avalanches of snow and ice killed many prospectors. In September, 1897, fierce winds loosened the glacier's edge, releasing a lake that heavy rains had built up on the glacier. More than a score of men were struck with typhoid fever in 1898. Drowning on the upper Yukon accounted for many other deaths. Still other menaces were spinal meningitis, starvation, frostbite, claim jumping, and robbery. The next stage of the journey called for boat building. Men sweated through the arduous winter work of building boats without benefit of sawmills. This work strained many men beyond endurance; it ended partnerships and dissolved families.

All was not grimness on the Klondike Trail. Gamblers ran their games wherever a number of people gathered. All the entrepreneurs along the trail contributed to a carnival mood. Many argonauts seemed more interested in fun than in gold.

SIGNIFICANCE

Within two years, thirty to forty thousand persons were added to Alaska's population, with a corresponding increase in its commerce and material prosperity. In 1897

alone, $22 million was taken from the Klondike field. The discovery of gold prompted people to start spending money around the globe, ending the economic depression that had made life difficult in the latter part of the nineteenth century. The irresistible pull of the Klondike gold exerted its influence on men and women of all ranks and stations of life throughout North America and beyond.

—*Susan M. Taylor*

FURTHER READING

Adney, Tappan. *The Klondike Stampede*. Vancouver: University of British Columbia Press, 1994. A factual story of the adventurous people who brought the Alaskan Yukon to the nation's attention.

Berton, Pierre. *The Promised Land: Settling the West, 1896-1914*. Toronto: McClelland & Stewart, 1984. The final volume in the author's tetralogy of the national dream, the Klondike gold rush.

Dobrowolsky, Helene. *Law of the Yukon: A Pictorial History of the Mounted Police in the Yukon*. Whitehorse, Y.T.: Lost Moose, 1995. Examines the law enforcement role of the Northwest Mounted Police during the Klondike gold rush.

Hitchcock, Mary E. *Two Women in the Klondike*. Fairbanks: University of Alaska Press, 2005. A contemporary account of the Klondike experience, with descriptions of life on the frontier. An abridged edition of Hitchcock's work first published in 1899.

Hunt, William R. *North of 53°: The Wild Days of the Alaskan-Yukon Mining Frontier, 1870-1914*. New York: Macmillan, 1974. A rigorous social document supported by the records and diaries of the people who built Alaska.

Matthews, Richard. *The Yukon*. New York: Holt, Rinehart and Winston, 1968. An intriguing history of the Yukon as a study of contrasts in peoples, wealth, and cultures.

Mayer, Melanie J. *Klondike Women: True Tales of the 1897-98 Gold Rush*. Athens: Swallow Press/Ohio University Press, 1989. Firsthand accounts of the adventures, challenges, and disappointments of women on the trails to the Klondike.

Morse, Kathryn Taylor. *The Nature of Gold: An Environmental History of the Klondike Gold Rush*. Seattle: University of Washington Press, 2003. Explores the environmental impact of the gold rush. Includes a foreword by environmental writer and scholar William Cronon.

Schell, Karen. *Westward Expansion II*. 9 vols. Farm-

1890's

ingdale, N.Y.: Cobblestone, 1993. Gives a rich, complex image of the people, time, and places of the Klondike gold rush.

Wilson, Graham, ed. *The Last Great Gold Rush: A Klondike Reader*. Whitehorse, Y.T.: Wolf Creek Books, 2002. An anthology of writings on the Klondike gold rush. Chapters include "The Outfit of an Argonaut," "A Woman Pioneer in the Klondike and Alaska," "The Saloon in Skagway," "The Spell of the Yukon," "Sheep Camp Washed Away," "The Chilkoot Pass," and "The Grand Cañon of the Yukon."

SEE ALSO: Jan. 24, 1848: California Gold Rush Begins; 1849: Chinese Begin Immigrating to California; 1851: Gold Is Discovered in New South Wales; Mar. 23, 1858: Fraser River Gold Rush Begins; Mar. 30, 1867: Russia Sells Alaska to the United States; May 23, 1873: Canada Forms the North-West Mounted Police; June 21, 1884: Gold Is Discovered in the Transvaal.

RELATED ARTICLES in *Great Lives from History: The Nineteenth Century, 1801-1900:* Wyatt Earp; Stephen J. Field.

November 3, 1896
MCKINLEY IS ELECTED PRESIDENT

In a presidential election that was dominated by debate over the silver and gold standards, William McKinley recaptured the presidency for the Republican Party and oversaw the beginning of the Republicans' thirty-six-year domination of Congress.

ALSO KNOWN AS: Election of 1896
LOCALE: United States
CATEGORY: Government and politics

KEY FIGURES
William McKinley (1843-1901), Republican who was elected president, 1897-1901
William Jennings Bryan (1860-1925), Democratic presidential candidate
Grover Cleveland (1837-1908), president of the United States, 1885-1889, 1893-1897
Marcus A. Hanna (1837-1904), Republican campaign manager
Garret Augustus Hobart (1844-1899), Republican vice presidential candidate
Arthur Sewall (1835-1900), Democratic vice presidential candidate
Thomas Edward Watson (1856-1922), Populist vice presidential candidate

SUMMARY OF EVENT
The Republicans approached the November 3, 1896, U.S. elections confident that they would regain the presidency that they had relinquished only twice since the Civil War (1861-1865), both times to Grover Cleveland, in 1884 and 1892. The failure of the Cleveland administration to deal effectively with the severe economic depression that followed the Panic of 1893 had led to significant losses for the Democrats in the 1894 elections. Republicans gained more than one hundred seats in the House of Representatives, the largest transfer of congressional strength in U.S. history up to that time. Moreover, the Democratic Party was dangerously split over the issue of silver, and President Cleveland had been repudiated by many in his own party. The Republicans, controlling the House of Representatives and seeing the continuing difficulties of the opposing parties, were certain that they could defeat the Democrats and the Populists in the presidential race.

The leading candidate for the Republicans was William McKinley, a former governor of Ohio, who had the nomination assured by the time that the Republican National Convention assembled in St. Louis on June 16, 1896. As the most popular leader in his party, McKinley defeated his disorganized rivals and won the nomination easily on the first ballot. He selected Garret Augustus Hobart of New Jersey as his running mate. Their platform promised to preserve the existing gold standard but to seek a wider use of silver through international agreements. The East liked the platform's pledge for gold; the West admired its bow toward silver. McKinley expected to base his campaign on the gold standard and the protective tariff. The Republicans did not anticipate a serious challenge from the eventual Democratic nominee.

The Democrats were hopelessly divided about silver and its inflationary implications. Cleveland and his allies favored the gold standard. Party members in the South and West wanted free silver—the rapid expansion of the money supply—to raise agricultural prices and make debts easier to pay. The prosilver forces controlled the platform at the national convention that met in Chicago in July. No clear front-runner for the nomination had emerged, but a young Nebraskan named William Jennings Bryan hoped to sway the delegates when he spoke for silver during the debate on the platform.

Bryan's "Cross of Gold" speech became an eloquent statement of the free-silver cause, and his oratory captivated the audience. The next day, the thirty-six-year-old Bryan was nominated on the fifth ballot. To balance the ticket, the convention chose Arthur Sewall, a Maine banker who favored free silver, as Bryan's running mate. Some Democrats who advocated remaining on the gold standard bolted the party and formed the Gold Democrats.

The nomination of Bryan and the adoption of a free-silver plank in the Democratic platform placed the Populists, whose national convention gathered on July 22 in St. Louis, in a dilemma. If they nominated Bryan and thereby fused with the Democrats, they would advance the cause of free silver but render their own party irrelevant. However, if they were to nominate a separate ticket, that might guarantee a victory for McKinley and the Republicans. The delegates decided to endorse Bryan for president and select their own vice presidential candidate. They chose Thomas Edward Watson of Georgia, a longtime Populist leader. As a result, there were two Bryan tickets in the field, with different vice presidential candidates. Bryan never accepted Watson as an official candidate, but the result was a good deal of confusion on many state ballots.

Free silver became the dominant issue of the election. Debtors and those who mined silver believed that silver should be minted in unlimited quantities at the fixed silver-to-gold ratio of sixteen to one. They argued that increasing the money supply would raise prices for agricultural products and make debts easier to pay. Supporters of the gold standard countered that inflation would penalize those with savings and those on fixed incomes. Silver supporters within the Republican ranks held a national convention and supported Bryan and Sewall. The Gold Democrats nominated John M. Palmer of Illinois as their presidential candidate. Prohibitionist and Socialist-Labor Party candidates were also on the ballot in many states.

Bryan waged a vigorous personal campaign. He traveled eighteen thousand miles, made more than six hundred speeches, and was heard by an estimated 500,000 people. Crowds cheered the Boy Orator of the Platte, as Bryan was known. The Democrats' main asset was Bryan himself. Otherwise, the party had little money or effective campaign resources. In the East, conservative Democrats supported McKinley or the Gold Democrats. The major battleground of the election became the Midwest.

Knowing that he could not match Bryan's skills as a speaker, McKinley conducted a "front-porch" campaign from his home in Canton, Ohio. Republican groups came to meet with him and hear short, effective speeches that McKinley gave about the dangers of free silver and

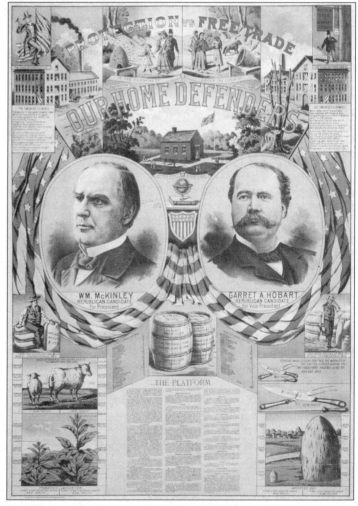

Republican campaign poster for William McKinley and his running mate, Garret A. Hobart. (Library of Congress)

1890's

ELECTORAL VOTES IN THE 1896 PRESIDENTIAL ELECTION

the virtues of the protective tariff. McKinley warned workers that inflation would erode the value of their paychecks. Under the leadership of campaign manager Marcus A. Hanna, the Republicans raised four million dollars from large contributors and corporations. Hanna used the money on a campaign of education that saw 250 million pamphlets of Republican literature distributed to the voters. Speakers for McKinley crisscrossed the North in a well-organized drive to arouse Republican voters.

At the outset of the campaign, a wave of enthusiasm swept the country for Bryan. Some conservatives warned that the nation stood on the brink of social revolution. It proved difficult, however, for Bryan to sustain his one-issue campaign throughout the entire presidential contest. By the middle of the fall, the luster of the silver issue was becoming tarnished, and the Republicans surged ahead in the key states. McKinley's pluralistic and inclusive style attracted voters, particularly in the industrial states, to his message. Meanwhile, the divided and underfinanced Democrats could not overcome the obstacles that the Cleveland administration had imposed upon them.

The excitement and controversy of the 1896 cam-

paign produced a large voter turnout in percentage terms. Women and members of minorities were still barred from voting in many states, but more than 75 percent of the eligible male electorate went to the polls in the North. Two million more people voted than in the previous presidential contest. McKinley captured 271 electoral votes, and Bryan had 176 (including 27 Bryan-Watson electors). Bryan's strength lay in the plains and southern states; McKinley ran well in the industrial Midwest. The popular vote totals were 7,104,779 for McKinley to Bryan's 6,502,925.

SIGNIFICANCE

After the election, Bryan and the Democrats alleged that corporations supporting McKinley and Hanna had coerced workers into voting Republican, but Bryan's inflationary ideas were a better explanation of why so many industrial employees voted Republican. The outcome of the election completed the electoral upheaval of the 1890's and made the Republicans the majority party for a generation. McKinley was reelected in 1900 but was assassinated the following year and succeeded by his vice president, Theodore Roosevelt.

McKinley interpreted his electoral victory in 1896 as a victory for the gold standard and the concomitant interests of big-business industrialism over agrarian Populism. Passage of the Dingley Tariff Act in 1897 and the Gold Standard Act in 1900 attest that victory.

—Lewis L. Gould,
based on the original entry by Mark A. Plummer

FURTHER READING

Gould, Lewis L. *The Presidency of William McKinley.* Lawrence: University Press of Kansas, 1980. The first chapter looks at the 1896 election and McKinley's rise to national prominence. The book stresses McKinley's skill as a politician.

Gould, Lewis L., and Craig H. Roell, eds. *William McKinley: A Bibliography.* Westport, Conn.: Meckler, 1988. Exhaustive listing of articles and books on Mckinley and the 1896 election that were published before 1988.

Jones, Stanley L. *The Presidential Election of 1896.* Madison: University of Wisconsin Press, 1964. Balanced and fair treatment of the election that contains a wealth of information about the activities of all the major participants in the 1896 contest.

McGerr, Michael. *The Decline of Popular Politics: The American North, 1865-1928.* New York: Oxford University Press, 1986. Review of campaign styles, useful for placing the partisan techniques in 1896 within a historical context.

Morgan, H. Wayne. *From Hayes to McKinley: National Party Politics, 1877-1896.* Syracuse, N.Y.: Syracuse University Press, 1969. Well-written narrative history of U.S. politics during the late nineteenth century. Argues that the outcome of the 1896 election was the culmination of Republican policies of nationalism and economic development.

Phillips, Kevin. *William McKinley.* New York: Times Books/Henry Holt, 2003. This analysis of McKinley's presidency argues that McKinley was a "near great" president, whose place in history has been diminished because he was unable to complete his second term.

Williams, R. Hal. *Years of Decision: American Politics in the 1890's.* Prospect Heights, Ill.: Waveland Books, 1993. Excellent narrative. Includes information on the election of 1896 and its significance. Good discussion on the emotions the election aroused.

SEE ALSO: Mar. 5, 1877: Hayes Becomes President; Nov. 4, 1884: U.S. Election of 1884; July 4-5, 1892: Birth of the People's Party; July 24, 1897: Congress Passes Dingley Tariff Act; Apr. 24-Dec. 10, 1898: Spanish-American War.

RELATED ARTICLES in *Great Lives from History: The Nineteenth Century, 1801-1900:* Grover Cleveland; Marcus A. Hanna; William McKinley.

November 16, 1896
FIRST U.S. HYDROELECTRIC PLANT OPENS AT NIAGARA FALLS

The electric power plant at Niagara Falls in upstate New York was a milestone in the development of the electric power industry. The first hydroelectric plant in the United States, it not only powered industry but also lit up and electrified urban areas and, later, small towns and rural areas. It eventually inspired the worldwide adoption of alternating current.

LOCALE: Niagara Falls, New York
CATEGORIES: Engineering; science and technology

KEY FIGURES
Thomas Alva Edison (1847-1931), inventor and founder of the Edison General Electric Corporation
George Westinghouse (1846-1914), inventor and industrialist whose company built the power plant at Niagara

Nikola Tesla (1856-1943), Croatian-born inventor who worked with Westinghouse to develop alternating current technology

SUMMARY OF EVENT
In the 1880's, Thomas Alva Edison was the undisputed master of electrical inventions. Called the Wizard of Menlo Park after the location of his New Jersey research and development laboratory, his inventions included motors, generators, and a lighting system designed to run on direct current (DC). He had made major improvements in Samuel F. B. Morse's telegraph and in Alexander Graham Bell's telephone. Edison's most famous innovations were the phonograph and the incandescent light bulb, and he eventually obtained more than one thousand patents.

In 1888, a competing electrical system using alternating current (AC) was introduced by the Westinghouse Electric Corporation. George Westinghouse had purchased the patents for AC motors and generators from a young Serbian immigrant, Nikola Tesla, who had arrived in the United States in 1884. Tesla was a high school student when he had seen his teacher demonstrate a DC electric motor. A large amount of sparking showed where the current entered the central coil of the motor as it made intermittent contact during each rotation. Following that demonstration, Tesla conceived the idea that alternating current, whose direction of flow would change in synchronism with the rotation of the armature, could eliminate the sparking. It remained an idea in his head until several years later when he built a working model and eventually obtained a U.S. patent.

Westinghouse was interested in Tesla's AC motor because he was already in the business of manufacturing transformers. The transformer is a rather simple device with two coils of wire of different sizes wound around an iron core. It is used to increase or decrease an AC voltage. Westinghouse visualized an electric power distribution system in which transmission lines would carry electricity efficiently at a high voltage that could be stepped down by transformers to a safe level for users. He was enthusiastic about the advantages of AC, whereas Edison was committed to DC. Newspapers during the early 1890's wrote about the "battle of the currents," as the two industrialists competed for contracts.

In the 1880's, the mining industry in Colorado was using steam engines for tunneling and rock crushing. If a mine was located above timberline, however, fuel for the engine had to be laboriously carried up by donkeys. Westinghouse made a proposal to mine owners for a cheaper system that would use electric motors. The electricity would be generated by a hydroelectric plant at a low elevation and brought up to the mine by high-voltage transmission lines. Transformers would convert the AC voltage down to a safe level for electric motors to drive the mining equipment. Westinghouse obtained a contract at Telluride, Colorado, where such an electrical system was installed in 1891. Technical problems had to be solved to erect wooden power poles in rocky ground and then to fasten bare copper cables to them with insulators that had to withstand 5,000 volts. Westinghouse lost money on this enterprise, but he demonstrated that an AC system could operate with reliability.

Edison scored a triumph for DC in 1892 when his company built the Pearl Street power plant in New York City. The plant used a steam engine to turn an electric generator from which insulated copper wires, buried underground, carried the current to subscribers in the nearby financial district. It worked well but had one major limitation: The area that could be electrified was restricted to less than one mile from the central station. Beyond that distance, there was too much loss of power from the large currents in the copper wires.

In 1892, Chicago was preparing to be the host city for

Niagara Falls in 1913, viewed from the Canadian side of the border. (Library of Congress)

the Columbian Exposition, set to celebrate the four hundredth anniversary of Christopher Columbus's voyages to the Americas. To bring in visitors, the exposition was to be lit up after dark by thousands of electric lights. Both Edison and Westinghouse bid on the contract to install and maintain the lighting system. Westinghouse submitted the low bid for a generator and distribution system to light up more than 100,000 bulbs. The exposition and its display of electric lights were a great success, attracting more than fourteen million visitors.

During the late 1880's, several New York businessmen had expressed interest in a project to harness the tremendous energy of Niagara Falls. The original plan was to divert some of the water above the falls into a canal, along whose banks more than two hundred water wheels would be installed for sawmills and other industrial applications. The diverted water would be returned to the river through a tunnel below the town of Niagara.

Excavation for the intake canal and the return flow tunnel began in 1890, but a major change of plans soon followed. Engineers in Switzerland had just completed a hydroelectric plant whose output was transmitted at high voltage over several miles of copper wire with little loss of power. After inspecting this plant, the American engineers made the momentous decision to change from water wheels to electricity. The Westinghouse Corporation won the construction contract based on its expertise at the Telluride mine, the Chicago Exposition, and other lighting installations, and construction began on the Niagara power plant late in 1893.

The plant's design consisted of ten turbines located 140 feet below the level of the falls, fed by a downward stream of water going through long chutes from the intake canal. Each turbine was connected to an AC generator, producing a total output that would be greater than all the electric power systems then operating in the United States. It was an ambitious plan requiring turbines and generators larger than had ever been built before. The output of the Tesla generators at the falls was connected

---

TESLA ON THE FIRST ELECTRIC POWER PLANT IN NORTH AMERICA

Inventor Nikola Tesla, with inventor George Westinghouse and helped by the earlier work on electricity by Thomas Alva Edison, utilized the awesome power of Niagara Falls to build the first hydroelectric power plant in North America. In January of 1897, just months after the first electricity raced from the plant to the city of Buffalo in New York, Tesla spoke before a group of local residents, in a speech excerpted here, discussing the significance of the Niagara plant.

[T]hat monument at Niagara . . . is a monument worthy of our scientific age, a true monument of enlightenment and of peace. It signifies the subjugation of natural forces to the service of man, the discontinuance of barbarous methods, the relieving of millions from want and suffering. No matter what we attempt to do, no matter to what fields we turn our efforts, we are dependent on power. Our economists may propose more economical systems of administration and utilization of resources, our legislators may make wiser laws and treaties, it matters little; that kind of help can be only temporary. If we want to reduce poverty and misery, if we want to give to every deserving individual what is needed for a safe existence of an intelligent being, we want to provide more machinery, more power. Power is our mainstay, the primary source of our many-sided energies. With sufficient power at our disposal we can satisfy most of our wants and offer a guaranty for safe and comfortable existence to all, except perhaps to those who are the greatest criminals of all—the voluntarily idle. In the great enterprise at Niagara we see not only a bold engineering and commercial feat, but far more, a giant stride in the right direction as indicated both by exact science and philanthropy. Its success is a signal for the utilization of water powers all over the world, and its influence upon industrial development is incalculable. We must all rejoice in the great achievement and congratulate the intrepid pioneers who have joined their efforts and means to bring it about.

---

to transformers that converted the generators to a high voltage with low current for efficient cross-country transmission to the city of Buffalo, twenty-five miles away. In Buffalo, transformers reconverted the power back to a safe low voltage with high current to operate lighting for streets, homes, businesses, and industrial motors. The Niagara power plant was constructed in stages as the demand for electricity developed.

Tesla's AC electric motor and generator, which he had envisioned as a student and later patented, was completed by Westinghouse, and the first electricity reached Buffalo at midnight on November 16, 1896. A dedicatory dinner was held in Buffalo on January 12, 1897. Tesla, during his dinner address, described his vision of electricity's future and its potential benefits.

SIGNIFICANCE

After the success of the Niagara Falls power plant, the use of electricity increased rapidly. To be profitable, commercial power plants first catered to large industrial users and municipalities rather than to residential customers. For example, because aluminum metal can be extracted from its ore only by electrolysis, and not by smelting, a refinery was built by the Aluminum Company of America at Niagara, marking the start of large-scale electrochemical industry. At the municipal level, cities could now power their trolleys, or streetcars, by overhead electric lines, replacing the outmoded trolleys pulled by horses.

During the early twentieth century, thousands of smaller communities built their own power plants. A typical installation consisted of a coal-fired boiler that produced high-pressure steam to turn the blades of a turbine connected to the shaft of a generator. The plant's output was distributed within the town limits for businesses, homes, and streetlights. Home appliances such as washing machines and vacuum cleaners became popular to reduce the drudgery of housework. There were no power lines to serve farmers, however, and no interconnections between neighboring towns.

By 1934, about one-third of American homes were connected to electricity, but it was unequally distributed. In Chicago, almost everyone had electricity, but in rural areas less than 10 percent had access. Under President Franklin D. Roosevelt, the Rural Electrification Administration (REA) was formed to bring the benefits of electricity to people in the countryside. Also, individual power plants gradually were connected into larger grids to improve reliability in case of a local power failure. The steam engine initiated the first industrial revolution, but electrification brought about a second industrial revolution whose impact on modern society continues.

—Hans G. Graetzer

FURTHER READING

Baldwin, Neil. *Edison: Inventing the Century.* New York: Hyperion, 1995. Reprint. Chicago: University of Chicago Press, 2001. Critically acclaimed comprehensive biography, providing information on Edison's personal life and career. Baldwin argues that Edison embodied the American potential for techno-

logical change; his book describes the cultural context of Edison's inventions.

Coltman, John W. "The Transformer." *Scientific American* (January, 1988): 86-95. A well-written article on transformers and their importance for AC electric power distribution systems, with helpful diagrams.

Hughes, Thomas P. *Networks of Power: Electrification in Western Society, 1880-1930.* Baltimore: Johns Hopkins University Press, 1983. Discusses the role of Westinghouse in developing AC for use in electrical utilities.

Hunt, Inez, and Wanetta Draper. *Lightning in His Hand: The Life Story of Nikola Tesla.* Denver, Colo.: Sage Books, 1964. A biography of Tesla's life and scientific accomplishments, with many fascinating anecdotes and sixteen pages of photographs.

Jonnes, Jill. *Empires of Light: Edison, Tesla, Westinghouse, and the Race to Electrify the World.* New York: Random House, 2003. The best book available on the AC versus DC controversy, describing confrontations between Westinghouse and Edison to establish the superiority of their respective systems.

Moran, Richard. *Executioner's Current: Thomas Edison, George Westinghouse, and the Invention of the Electric Chair.* New York: Alfred A. Knopf, 2002. Tells the story of Edison's campaign to discredit alternating current technology by frightening the public with the potential hazards of electrocution.

SEE ALSO: c. 1801-1810: Davy Develops the Arc Lamp; Nov. 6, 1820: Ampère Reveals Magnetism's Relationship to Electricity; Oct., 1831: Faraday Converts Magnetic Force into Electricity; Apr., 1869: Westinghouse Patents His Air Brake; Oct. 21, 1879: Edison Demonstrates the Incandescent Lamp; May 1-Oct. 30, 1893: Chicago World's Fair; Dec. 15, 1900: General Electric Opens Research Laboratory.

RELATED ARTICLES in *Great Lives from History: The Nineteenth Century, 1801-1900:* Alexander Graham Bell; Thomas Alva Edison; Michael Faraday; Sir William Robert Grove; James Clerk Maxwell; Charles Proteus Steinmetz; Joseph Wilson Swan; Nikola Tesla; George Westinghouse.

1897

ELLIS PUBLISHES *SEXUAL INVERSION*

With the publication of Sexual Inversion, *the first volume of his seven-volume* Studies in the Psychology of Sex, *Havelock Ellis initiated his challenge against the repressive sexual attitudes of the Victorian era.*

ALSO KNOWN AS: *Studies in the Psychology of Sex*
LOCALE: England
CATEGORIES: Health and medicine; psychology and psychiatry; social issues and reform

KEY FIGURES
Havelock Ellis (1859-1939), English physician and sexologist
John Addington Symonds (1840-1893), English poet and critic
Sigmund Freud (1856-1939), Austrian psychoanalyst

SUMMARY OF EVENT

Havelock Ellis was born in Croydon, Surrey, England, in 1859 in the twenty-second year of Queen Victoria's long reign, which was marked by a sexual orthodoxy that eschewed open references to sex and sexuality. It was commonly assumed that women were not supposed to enjoy sex, that sexual activity was to occur within marriage, and that sex involved dutiful heterosexual intercourse aimed at procreation rather than pleasure.

Victorian attitudes toward sex did little to dispel sexual desire. Beneath the smooth surface of proper Victorianism were significant ripples that took the form of premarital sex, extramarital sex, homosexuality, masturbation, and countless behaviors considered deviant. Occasionally some of these cross-currents surfaced, as when Irish playwright Oscar Wilde was brought to trial in 1895, convicted of engaging in homosexual conduct, and imprisoned for two years.

Ellis was raised in a permissive atmosphere. He was schooled at home by his mother, Susannah, and in private schools until he was sixteen years old. At sixteen, Ellis, unsure what he wanted to do with his life, sailed to Australia on one of the ships owned by his father. In Australia, Ellis obtained a teaching job that he held for four years before deciding that he wanted to become a physician. He returned to England in 1879 and, in 1881, began medical studies at St. Thomas's Hospital in London. He passed his medical examinations with modest grades by the mid-1880's.

In 1880, Ellis began serving as editor of the *Westminster Review*. This position gave him access to many of the

more interesting and iconoclastic social circles flourishing in and around London at that time. He established friendships with such luminaries as George Bernard Shaw and Bertrand Russell, both of whom became active supporters of Ellis when his writings on sex were attacked. By the time he completed his medical training, Ellis knew that his greatest interest was in the psychology of sex, which he now set about exploring as objectively as he could, employing scientific research methodologies.

During this period, Sigmund Freud's psychoanalytical writings about human sexuality were topics of considerable discussion in many of the circles in which Ellis traveled. A growing sexual freedom became evident on the Continent, although England still clung to its Victorian traditions. Merely to study sexual topics and present one's findings was considered quite revolutionary and, by some Victorians, dangerously subversive.

Among those persons with whom Ellis came into contact at that time was John Addington Symonds, regarded as a pioneer in the field of homosexual rights and gay memoir. Symonds, also gay, already had gained a considerable reputation as a scholar with the publication of his monumental and authoritative seven-volume work *The Renaissance in Italy* (1875-1886). It was Symonds who, based on primary sources, first claimed that Michelangelo had been gay. Symonds had been open about his own sexual orientation.

In 1890, Ellis published *The New Spirit*, in which he decried the sexual repression evident in Victorian society and in which he championed the rights of women. He followed this book in 1894 with *Man and Woman: A Study of Secondary and Tertiary Sexual Characteristics* (rev. 1929), in which he emphasized the naturalness of human sexual desire, a concept the Victorians had yet to accept.

Early in the 1890's, Ellis began a collaboration with Symonds that continued until Symond's death in 1893. The book that grew out of this collaboration was the first volume of what became a seven-volume work, *Studies in the Psychology of Sex* (1897-1910, 1928). The first volume, *Sexual Inversion* (1897), was considered quite sensational. It was the first book to study homosexuality as something other than a pathological condition and to study it through the calculated use of scientific research methodologies. Later volumes of *Studies in the Psychology of Sex* also investigated another taboo that was sel-

ON SEXUAL INVERSION IN WOMEN AND MEN

*Havelock Ellis's revolutionary views on homosexuality were presented in the first volume–*Sexual Inversion–*of his* Studies in the Psychology of Sex. *The following excerpts are taken from a later edition (1927).*

The terms usually adopted in the present volume are "sexual inversion" and "homosexuality." The first is used more especially to indicate that the sexual impulse is organically and innately turned toward individuals of the same sex. The second is used more comprehensively of the general phenomena of sexual attraction between persons of the same sex, even if only of a slight and temporary character. It may be admitted that there is no precise warrant for any distinction of this kind between the two terms. The distinction in the phenomena is, however, still generally recognized; thus Iwan Bloch applies the term "homosexuality" to the congenital form, and "pseudo-homosexuality" to its spurious or simulated forms. Those persons who are attracted to both sexes are now usually termed "bisexual," a more convenient term than "psycho-sexual hermaphrodite," which was formerly used. There remains the normal person, who is "heterosexual."

Homosexuality is not less common in women than in men. In the serio-comic theory of sex set forth by Aristophanes in Plato's *Symposium*, males and females are placed on a footing of complete equality, and, however fantastic, the theory suffices to indicate that to the Greek mind, so familiar with homosexuality, its manifestations seemed just as likely to occur in women as in men. That is undoubtedly the case.

There are a multitude of social questions which we cannot face squarely and honestly unless we possess such precise knowledge as has been here brought together concerning the part played by the homosexual tendency in human life. Moreover, the study of this perverted tendency stretches beyond itself;

> O'er that art
> Which you say adds to Nature, is an art
> That Nature makes.

Pathology is but physiology working under new conditions. The stream of nature still flows into the bent channel of sexual inversion, and still runs according to law. We have not wasted our time in this toilsome excursion. With the knowledge here gained we are the better equipped to enter upon the study of the wider questions of sex.

Source: Havelock Ellis, *Sexual Inversion* (1927).

many case studies provided by Symonds were the most enticing parts of the study. Despite the study's scientific approach, Victorian readers found it prurient and sought to limit its distribution. In 1898, less than one year after *Sexual Inversion* was published, a British book merchant was arrested and tried for selling the book. During the trial, the presiding judge rejected Ellis's claim that the book was a work of science, calling the claim a pretense the author had adopted in order to justify selling "a filthy publication." Noted playwright Shaw and philosopher-mathematician Bertrand Russell came to Ellis's defense in England, as did Henry L. Mencken in the United States, but to no avail.

Sexual Inversion was banned from being sold to the general public, and as the six final volumes of *Studies in the Psychology of Sex* were readied for publication, they could not be published in England but were printed in the United States by a publisher of medical texts. Not until 1935 were these banned volumes legally sold to anyone other than physicians, social workers, criminologists, and approved professionals.

Some critics of Ellis's work consider it too didactic, noting that it focuses too much on morality and contending that this focus compromises the objectivity of Ellis's conclusions. Certainly, Ellis frequently departs from the dispassionate point of view that scientific investigation demands. His view of sex is that it must be accompanied by love to be satisfactory. However admirable a notion, it is one that is difficult if not impossible to quantify, and it weakens the scientific objectivity of Ellis's studies. Still, his studies remain exceedingly important and notable in the history of modern sexology.

SIGNIFICANCE

The publication of *Sexual Inversion* and subsequent volumes of *Studies in the Psychology of Sex* in both the United States and Germany established Havelock Ellis as a pioneer in the study of sexual behavior. His name,

dom discussed in Victorian society: masturbation. The work exploded popular myths warning that masturbation leads to blindness, and it argued that the practice is universal, natural, and harmless.

In *Sexual Inversion*, Ellis differentiates between homosexuality and "inversion," considering the former an expression of sexual desire. He considered "inversion" a congenital condition. Many readers believed that the

along with that of Sigmund Freud, will forever be associated with the scientific study of sex. The anecdotal nature of many of Ellis's investigations make them suspect as studies that have unquestionable scientific legitimacy, even though his analyses of these case studies are generally penetrating and insightful.

The suppression of Ellis's work failed to keep that work from reaching a public that had long desired a public discussion of sexual matters. Had the public distribution of Ellis's work never been questioned or censored, it is possible the work would have received quite a different response, especially from the general public and other nonmedical professionals.

—*R. Baird Shuman*

FURTHER READING

Bland, Lucy, and Laura Doan. *Sexology in Culture: Labeling Bodies and Desires*. Chicago: University of Chicago Press, 1998. Chapter 10 provides an overview of the professional relationship between Havelock Ellis and Sigmund Freud.

Collis, John Stewart. *Havelock Ellis, Artist of Life: A Study of His Work and Life*. New York: W. Sloane, 1959. A fair assessment of Ellis's consideration of the relationship between romantic love and sex.

Ellis, Havelock. *Havelock Ellis on Life and Sex: Essays of Love and Virtue*. Garden City, N.Y.: Garden City, 1937. Ellis's most cogent essays on the relationship between love and sex.

Grosskurth, Phyllis. *Havelock Ellis: A Biography*. New York: Alfred A. Knopf, 1980. Among the most dependable assessments of Ellis as a writer on sexual matters and as someone confronting his own demons.

Powell, Anthony. *Under Review: Further Writing on Writers, 1946-1990*. Chicago: University of Chicago Press, 1994. Provides an overview of Ellis and his work in a three-page essay on the noted sexologist.

Robinson, Paul. *The Modernization of Sex: Havelock Ellis, Alfred Kinsey, William Masters, and Virginia Johnson*. New York: Harper & Row, 1976. Robinson devotes a forty-one-page chapter to discussing Ellis as a modernist.

SEE ALSO: 1882: First Birth Control Clinic Opens in Amsterdam; 1900: Freud Publishes *The Interpretation of Dreams*.

RELATED ARTICLE in *Great Lives from History: The Nineteenth Century, 1801-1900:* Oscar Wilde.

1897-1901
ABEL AND TAKAMINE ISOLATE ADRENALINE

At almost exactly the same time, the American researcher John Jacob Abel and the Japanese researcher Jokichi Takamine independently isolated adrenaline, or epinephrine, the main hormone of the adrenal medulla, which controls blood pressure and the "fight or flee" mechanism in higher organisms.

LOCALE: Baltimore, Maryland; New York
CATEGORIES: Biology; genetics; chemistry; health and medicine; science and technology

KEY FIGURES

John Jacob Abel (1857-1938), American physician, biochemist, and pharmacologist
Jokichi Takamine (1854-1922), Japanese-born American chemist
Carl F. W. Ludwig (1816-1895), German physiologist and physician with whom Abel trained

SUMMARY OF EVENT

Adrenaline, or epinephrine, is a member of the very important group of biological messengers called hormones. These messengers control many biochemical processes necessary for the life and well-being of the whole body. They are produced in tiny amounts by organs called endocrine glands. Endocrinology, the study of the hormones, is named after these glands, which secrete hormones into the blood. The blood then takes hormones to other "target" organs, where their effects occur. The messages embodied in hormones integrate body functions, allowing them to occur with great flexibility.

Some hormones cause their effects by a mechanism that involves direct stimulation of the expression of genes in target organs. Adrenaline exemplifies another group of hormones that cause their effects by a process called a second messenger mechanism. Here, a hormone causes the production of a second chemical, the second messenger, that actually produces the effect.

Adrenaline is made by the central portion (medulla) of the adrenal glands, twin endocrine glands located atop the kidneys. It is produced from the amino acids phenylalanine and tyrosine. Adrenaline secretion triggers a series of body processes often called the "fight or flee" responses. These responses include accelerated heart rate and output, accompanied by increased energy and strength. They may explain, for example, the unexpected strength that sometimes enables a 150-pound person to lift a telephone pole off a loved one in an emergency situation.

A prominent biochemical event related to fight or flee responses is the greatly increased breakdown of the main energy reserve, glycogen (a complex carbohydrate), in muscle and liver. This prepares the body to use the energy reserve and leads to the physical responses required to fight or flee. The understanding of this process was elucidated in the 1970's. Yet, it might not have occurred if John Jacob Abel and Jokichi Takamine had not isolated adrenaline between 1897 and 1901.

Abel's contribution is a consequence of his lifelong effort to carry the use of the precepts and methodology of chemistry to the practice of medicine and biology. This commitment developed after he received his doctoral degree from the University of Michigan in 1883. At that time, Abel engaged in six years of postgraduate work in Germany, where he worked with famous biologists, including Carl F. W. Ludwig, at Leipzig. For the next two years, Abel engaged in additional training in biochemistry and pharmacology, fine-tuning his interests in those fields. He returned to the United States and accepted a position at the University of Michigan, where Abel offered courses on various aspects of biochemistry and pharmacology, including "the influence of drugs in metabolism of tissues." By 1893, Abel had become the first professor of pharmacology at Baltimore's Johns Hopkins University, a position he occupied until retirement.

Abel steadfastly worked on many aspects of drug and hormone research throughout his life and trained numerous biomedical scientists in the intelligent use of chemistry in their endeavors. He warned developing researchers constantly that sensible investigators must work in areas where "molecules and atoms rather than multicellular tissues or unicellular organisms are the units of study."

The work with epinephrine that Abel carried out, from 1895 to 1905, was only one of his major efforts. It is one for which he became well known. In 1897, Abel published on the isolation of this substance from adrenal glands. Then, in 1899, he named it epinephrine (the pre-

ferred name for the hormone today). The chemical Abel actually isolated was not the free hormone, but rather a modified substance, called monobenzyl adrenaline. It was not until 1901 that Takamine isolated the pure, "free" hormone from the adrenal glands of beef cattle. The chemical structure of the hormone was not proven, however, until it was chemically synthesized by a third researcher in 1904.

Takamine received undergraduate and graduate degrees at the Universities of Tokyo and Glasgow. In 1894, he moved to the United States and founded a private research laboratory, where he isolated bovine adrenaline. In 1901, Takamine described his endeavor at a medical convention at Johns Hopkins University and patented his method for production of the hormone.

Takamine and Abel each recognized the other's contribution to the discovery and isolation of adrenaline, which was the first hormone ever isolated in a pure and stable form. Both became prominent for their efforts, and the most immediate benefit of their dual discovery was the fact that medical practitioners found out quickly that adrenaline could be utilized to stop bleeding during surgery.

SIGNIFICANCE

The pioneering efforts of Abel and Takamine to isolate adrenaline are viewed as being among the most important fundamental discoveries in life science; they produced pure samples of the first hormone ever isolated. Study of the pure adrenaline—in their laboratories and by numerous other researchers—laid many ground rules for the methodology utilized in study of other types of hormones. Furthermore, it led to many important discoveries, including the identification of several hormones related structurally to epinephrine (the catecholamines); explanation of the endocrine actions of the catecholamines; and development of modern explanations for aspects of nervous transmission in mental health and disease.

The widespread impact of the discovery of adrenaline on medical science arose from understandings of its actions in preparing living organisms to flee from danger or to fight—the so-called fight or flee responses. This was caused by the biological effects of the hormone, including increased alertness, elevated heart rate and blood pressure, and increased blood levels of glucose (the source of most of the body's energy). For example, it was examination of the basis for adrenaline effects on glucose levels that led Eugene Sutherland to identify the second messenger mechanism for adrenaline action. Once the second messenger process in adrenaline action was understood, other researchers showed that the mechanism could be applied to explanation of the action of many other hormones.

The observation that adrenaline caused increased mental alertness led to the development of many stimulants, once its chemical structure had been identified as 3,4-dihydroxyphenyl-2-methyl-aminoethanol. The first such chemicals were the structurally related drugs known as the amphetamines (for example, Benzedrine and methedrine). The earliest amphetamines were made by German organic chemists of the 1930's to mimic adrenaline action in a manner that would enable soldiers to fight better in situations where they needed to stay awake for long periods of time.

Eventually, abuse of catecholamine-related drugs (such as the amphetamines) was useful also; understanding of such abuse helped other scientists identify the catecholamine involvement in nervous transmission. In fact, the current explanations of mania, depression, and their effective treatment began with the catecholamine hypothesis of affective disorders, which was proposed in 1965. This hypothesis supposed that depression arises from suboptimum catecholamine production or utilization, while mania is caused by its excess. Spinoffs of successful application of the hypothesis include the choice of new drugs for therapeutic use on the basis of their effect on catecholamine levels and the implication of other "biogenic amines" (for example, serotonin), related structurally to catecholamines, in nerve transmission and its diseases.

—Sanford S. Singer

FURTHER READING

Geiling, E. M. "John Jacob Abel." In *Dictionary of Scientific Biography*, edited by Charles Coulston Gillispie. Vol. 1. New York: Charles Scribner's Sons, 1971. This brief biographical sketch provides insight into Abel's personality and wide impact on biochemistry and pharmacology.

Harrow, Benjamin. *Textbook of Biochemistry*. 10th ed. Philadelphia: W. B. Saunders, 1971. This textbook, first published in 1938, describes briefly the original methodology for isolation and for chemical synthesis of adrenaline. Also provides several important early references on the hormone.

Lamson, Paul D. "John Jacob Abel—A Portrait." *Bulletin of The Johns Hopkins Hospital* 68 (1941): 119-157. This very pleasant and entertaining article is a detailed personal account of Abel's life and career. It provides very interesting and engaging reading and describes Abel both as an individual and as a scientist.

Lehninger, Albert L., David L. Nelson, and Michael M. Cox. *Principles of Biochemistry*. 4th ed. New York: Freeman, 2005. Chapter 25 of this excellent college textbook concisely describes the chemistry, biochemistry, and mechanism of epinephrine. It is especially valuable as a relatively simple, technical explanation of the hormone and its actions and the second messenger mechanisms of hormone action with adrenaline and other hormones.

Murnaghan, Jane H., and Paul Talalay. "John Jacob Abel and the Crystallization of Insulin." *Perspectives in Biology and Medicine* 10 (1967): 334-380. This review of Abel's work on insulin emphasizes its importance and describes the skepticism with which his contemporaries met the concept of a protein hormone. It also places the impact of Abel's research in the broad context of biochemistry of the first half of the twentieth century and cites references on Abel's life and endeavors.

Sutherland, E. W. "Studies on the Mechanism of Hormone Action." *Science* 177 (1972): 401-408. This article explains the important aspects of the Sutherland group's developing understanding of cyclic AMP function in epinephrine action. The evolution of the second messenger concept is well developed by its originator.

Voegtlin, Carl. "John Jacob Abel, 1857-1938." *Journal of Pharmacology and Experimental Therapeutics* 67 (1939): 373-406. This article describes Abel's scientific work, providing details about the discovery and study of adrenaline. Makes clear Abel's excellent scientific ability and aspects of his personality.

White, James T. "Jokichi Takamine." In *The National Cyclopedia of American Biography*. Vol. 40. New York: James T. White, 1955. This brief biographical sketch is one of the only readily available references on Takamine's life and work. It discusses some aspects of his early life as well as his education, career, and accomplishments. Takamine is portrayed as a very solid scientist and a successful entrepreneur.

SEE ALSO: 1816: Laënnec Invents the Stethoscope; 1838-1839: Schwann and Virchow Develop Cell Theory; 1857: Pasteur Begins Developing Germ Theory and Microbiology; 1888-1906: Ramón y Cajal Shows How Neurons Work in the Nervous System.

RELATED ARTICLE in *Great Lives from History: The Nineteenth Century, 1801-1900:* Louis Pasteur.

1890's

January 21-May 20, 1897
GRECO-TURKISH WAR

Greek Christians living under Ottoman rule in Crete were denied both the practice of their religious faith and a say in their governance. Joined by the Greek army, the Cretan Christians rebelled and fought against the Ottomans. Although they ultimately lost their battles, their island was eventually freed from the Ottomans with the help of European powers and was united with Greece in 1912.

LOCALE: Crete, Thessaly, Epirus, and Macedonia
CATEGORIES: Wars, uprisings, and civil unrest; expansion and land acquisition

KEY FIGURES
George I (1845-1913), king of Greece, r. 1863-1913, second son of King Christian IX of Denmark
Constantine I (1868-1923), son of King George I, led the Greeks against the Turks in the 1897 war, king of Greece, r. 1913-1917, 1920-1922
George (1869-1957), second son of King George I, governor of Crete, 1898-1906
Third Marquis of Salisbury (Robert Cecil; 1830-1903), prime minister of Great Britain, 1885-1886, 1886-1892, 1895-1902, and foreign secretary in 1887

SUMMARY OF EVENT
The island of Crete and its Greek population came under Ottoman rule in 1669. Crete's population, which by 1760 was approximately 20 percent Christian and 80 percent Muslim, dynamically changed, and by 1895 was 80 percent Christian and 20 percent Muslim. As the Cretan Christian population rose to a majority, their lack of representation and power in the government caused conflict between them and their Muslim landlords. The Organic Statute in 1868 gave concessions to the Christians from the ruling Porte (government of the Ottoman Empire). The Christians were officially given the right to have a Christian governor in Crete, representation on the council, and to have the Greek language recognized as an official language.

The Pact of Halepa, granted in 1878, gave the Christians of Crete further rights, including a majority representation on the general assembly of Crete. Both the Organic and Halepa Pacts turned out to be more about promises than about practices from the Porte, causing discontent and conflict between the Cretan Christians and their rulers.

In December of 1895, the Porte appointed a Muslim governor to Crete. By February of 1896, the island had seen frequent racial-religious murders. In May, a violent uprising in Canea caused the deaths of many Cretan Christians. The great powers—Great Britian, Russia, France, and Italy—sent warships to Crete to try to keep the peace. Crete appealed to Greece for help and protection. The powers, who were still distraught from dealing with the Armenian massacres, urged the Greek government to not get involved in the rebellion in Crete.

The powers approached the Porte about the need for the Christians in Crete to have representation in the government in order to maintain the peace. The Porte refused to grant any privileges to the Christians until they stopped rebelling. Cretan rebellions continued. The European powers and rebel leaders met at Constantinople and decided to reinstate a Christian governor in Crete and to force the Porte to uphold the reforms given to the Christians in the Halepa Pact. In June of 1896, Russia acted on behalf of the ambassadors to present these demands to the Porte. The Porte conceded to the terms, but by that time the reforms were not acceptable to the Christian leaders in Crete. Not believing that the reforms would be enforced, the Cretan Christians insisted that they be annexed to Greece.

The European powers did not feel that annexation to Greece was a practical alternative. They were afraid that it would lead to further conflict in Europe and uprisings in Macedonia and elsewhere, dividing the Ottoman Empire into warring factions. The powers decided to ask Greece to stop shipments of supplies to Crete and to encourage the Christians in Crete to agree to the concessions the Turks were offering. Greece would not cooperate with the powers because it believed the powers did make the Porte live up to its promises to Greece in the Greeks' successful fight against Ottoman rule.

In response, the powers decided to form their own blockade of supplies going to Crete by blocking both Cretan and Greek ports. England's third marquis of Salisbury, under the pressure of public opinion in Great Britain, suggested that a blockade by only one of the powers would be effective enough to bring Greece into compliance. The powers failed to work in concert because of public opinion and because of political ties through marriages (King George I's relation to Denmark).

In August of 1896 the Porte made an offer to appoint a Christian governor in Crete and to allow the Christian

Cretans power in their own governance. Cretan Christians finally accepted the terms, but when they saw no real changes in their involvement in the government and that the Christian governor was merely a figurehead without any real power, they decided to rebel.

During the last part of the nineteenth century, Greek foreign policy was geared toward expansion. Control over Macedonia was a prime concern in the eastern Mediterranean. When it became clear that Bulgaria had been making plans to annex Macedonia rather than work with the Greeks and Serbs to make Macedonia an autonomous state with equal treatment for all nationalities, the Serbs and Greeks founded secret organizations to promote their causes. The Greeks formed the Greek National Society to support schools and to promote Hellenistic (Greek) propaganda and to defend the rights of Hellenism abroad. The National Society quickly evolved into a force to promote expansion and to resist the oppression of Greek Christians in areas under Ottoman control. Between two-thirds to three-fourths of the Greek army's officers belonged to the National Society.

The Greek National Society initially was reluctant to put its effort into annexing Crete, preferring to further Greek interests and control in Thessaly, Epirus, and then Macedonia. In 1986, however, when it appeared that the promises made to the Cretan Christians by the Porte were once again empty, some of the members of the society went to Crete to help organize a revolt. In February of 1897 fighting broke out around Canea; within two days the town was on fire. Messages were sent to the Greek consul in Athens that Turkish soldiers were shooting the Cretan Christians. Greece responded by sending warships and transports to protect Greek nationals. In March, Greek forces claimed Crete in the name of King George I. This show of force on Greece's part worried the powers, including Germany and Austria, who sent three thousand marines to the region in an attempt to quell the rebellion.

Greece sent forty-five thousand troops to Thessaly and approximately twenty-five thousand to Epirus to confront the Turkish troops. The National Society attacked Turkish posts in Macedonia. The Ottoman gov-

Turkish troops crossing the frontier into Greece. (Francis R. Niglutsch)

1890's

ernment broke off all negotiations and declared war. The Greeks were the underdogs in a war that would last thirty days. The Turks, who had more than one million soldiers in the field, had been expertly trained by the Germans and were adequately armed with state-of-the-art weapons. The Greeks had less than 100,000 men, led by officers who were political appointees more than trained soldiers.

With these weaknesses, Prince Constantine led approximately forty-five thousand troops to Thessaly. He was met by six divisions of Turkish soldiers and was easily turned back. The Turks defeated the Greeks at Meluna Pass and Larissa. The Greek troops rallied in Velestino but were attacked and driven out when they moved to Pharsala. In Epirus, fifteen thousand Greek troops tried to hold a line from Arta to Peta but were defeated by a larger and better-trained army of Turks.

On May 21, the fighting was ended, and an armistice was signed on December 4. Crete was given autonomy and protection under the European powers, and the Turkish troops were forced to leave Crete. Greece was required to pay a large indemnity to Turkey, and at the request of Germany was put under international control of its finances. Prince George of Greece was appointed governor of Crete from 1898 until his resignation in 1906. Not until 1912 would Crete finally achieve its goal of being united with Greece.

SIGNIFICANCE

The Greco-Turkish War exemplified the Cretans' desire to unite with Greece. It also gave a clear message to Europe, the Middle East, and the various nationalities under the control of the Ottoman Empire that the Ottoman army was extremely strong, well trained, and well equipped. For those in doubt of the future of the Turkish Empire, the war proved that the empire remained powerful. Interestingly, Crete and Greece, as the "losers" of the war, nevertheless were victorious when Turkish troops left Crete and Crete become autonomous and protected by the European powers.

—Toby Stewart and Dion C. Stewart

FURTHER READING

Campbell, John. *Modern Greece*. New York: Praeger, 1968. Detailed history of Greece between the seventeenth and twentieth centuries, including the political climate behind the history.

Desch, Michael. "Democracy and Victory." *International Security* 28, no. 1 (2003): 352-361. Discusses the pros and cons of political regimes winning wars and how the Greco-Turkish War defies the hypothesis.

Holland, Robert. "Nationalism, Ethnicity, and the Concert of Europe." *Journal of Modern Greek Studies* 17, no. 2 (1999): 253-276. A detailed history of Crete's fight for union with Greece.

Langer, William. *The Diplomacy of Imperialism*. New York: Alfred A. Knopf, 1950. A detailed study of the Greco-Turkish War and the role of the great powers.

Stallman, R. W., ed. *The War Dispatches of Stephen Crane*. New York: New York University Press, 1964. Crane's actual observations of the Greco-Turkish War, which he covered as a journalist. A fun read as well as a good, but at times biased, history.

SEE ALSO: Mar. 7, 1821-Sept. 29, 1829: Greeks Fight for Independence from the Ottoman Empire; Sept. 24, 1829: Treaty of Adrianople; 1863-1913: Greece Unifies Under the Glücksburg Dynasty.

RELATED ARTICLES in *Great Lives from History: The Nineteenth Century, 1801-1900:* Third Marquis of Salisbury; Alexander and Demetrios Ypsilantis.

January 23, 1897

"Aspirin" Is Registered as a Trade Name

While researching therapeutics for relieving arthritis pain, Felix Hoffman reformulated earlier work with acetylsalicylic acid and developed a method to efficiently synthesize a less irritating, more stable form of the drug, which was named aspirin. Aspirin soon became the first drug to be artificially synthesized in large quantities.

Locale: Elberfeld, Germany

Categories: Inventions; chemistry; health and medicine

Key Figures

Charles Gerhardt (1816-1856), French chemist

Felix Hoffman (1868-1946), German chemist

Edward Stone (1702-1768), British clergyman and amateur naturalist

Hermann Kolbe (1818-1884), German chemist

Summary of Event

The earliest medical text known to exist dates from the Sumerian city-states period around 3000 B.C.E. Among the extant "prescriptions" discovered from this period is a transcribed stone, known as the Ur III tablet, which lists plants such as myrtle or willow for the treatment of illness. The Ebers Papyrus (c. 1550 B.C.E.), discovered in the 1860's by German Egyptologist George Ebers, has a reference to the use of willow in the treatment of ear infections and its use in a salve that helps make muscles more supple. While the precise meaning of the writings on the tablet and papyrus is unclear, the general interpretation is that each describes the use of willow for treating pain.

Because willow is among the plants that contain salicylates, the active ingredient of aspirin, the assumption is that these prescriptions represent the earliest descriptions of the chemical for treating inflammation. Hippocrates (c. 450 B.C.E.), in his cornucopia of medical treatments, also included willow tree bark to relieve headaches and the pain of childbirth. Willow bark was used also by the Romans during the period around the turn of the common era (100 B.C.E.-100 C.E.) for treating various types of pain, including muscle and joint aches and ear infections. Most of these remedies included diverse mixtures of various agents, but there existed a strong and persistent belief in the analgesic properties of plant extracts.

Much of the knowledge associated with plant or herbal medicine remained anecdotal until the mid-seventeenth and eighteenth centuries. In 1633, a Spanish monk in Central America described a "fever tree," a cinchona, the bark of which, when made into a powder, would relieve the symptoms of malaria. The extract, named *quina* or quinine after the Peruvian name *kina*, represented the first remedy that could be studied.

In the 1750's, Edward Stone, a British clergyman as well as an amateur naturalist, observed that the bitter taste of the willow bark was similar to that of the cinchona. Furthermore, he noticed that by chewing ground powder from the willow, the pain associated with ague, a fever (as in malaria) often marked by headache, muscle pain, and sweating, could be relieved. Stone reported his findings to the British Royal Society. His work was acknowledged, but the true significance of his discovery was overlooked.

The active ingredient from willow, salicylic acid, was not isolated until the 1820's. In 1826, Italian scientist Luigi Brugnatelli partially purified what he called "salicin," a highly impure form of salicylic acid. A few years later, French pharmacist Henri Leroux prepared several grams of a crystalline form of the chemical. In 1838, Italian chemist Raffaele Piria named the crystal salicylic acid (SA) The purified form was found to have pain-relieving benefits, and it joined the list of treatments available in some European apothecary shops.

Because it is an acid, SA has a number of unpleasant side effects, mainly stomach irritation. Aware that SA was both a possible therapeutic agent and an organic one, French chemist Charles Gerhardt began to study its molecular structure. Techniques in chemistry during the mid-nineteenth century were crude, and Gerhardt's initial interest was first to classify the molecule. He observed that the basis for SA's irritating properties was in the hydroxyl (-OH) group. He modified the structure by replacing the hydrogen with an acetyl group, thereby creating acetylsalicylic acid (ASA), tantalizingly close to the structure found in today's aspirin. Gerhardt's primary challenge was to accomplish the process in a timely manner and to make it a relatively simple procedure, something he never was able to carry out. After several unsuccessful attempts, he moved on to other endeavors.

Others attempted to continue Gerhardt's work in developing more efficient means of synthesizing modified

1890's

forms of SA. In part, the impetus for the work was the belief that the compound could serve as a food preservative, despite its taste. Among the more successful chemists was Hermann Kolbe. Best known for his research on structural theory related to inorganic and organic molecules, Kolbe found he could efficiently synthesize various forms of SA from relatively simple molecules. The ability to synthesize large quantities of ASA was applied by one of Kolbe's students, Friedrich von Heyden, whose chemical factory, Heyden Chemical, was founded in 1874, mostly to produce the molecule. SA became the first artificially produced pharmaceutical substance; ironically, its application was in part based upon assumed antiseptic properties, properties it did not possess.

In 1894, Felix Hoffman was hired by Friedrich Bayer and Company. Hoffman showed an early interest in science and was trained as a pharmaceutical chemist. Anecdotal evidence suggests he began looking into the development of pain relievers as a means to relieve the arthritis suffered by his father. While his father in all likelihood did suffer from arthritis, the reality of Hoffman's work suggests other reasons for his research. By the 1890's, it was clear that SA provided benefits as an analgesic. What was needed was a more efficient method of production as well as a means to chemically modify the structure to increase its stability and eliminate side effects, all in keeping with the role of Bayer as a pharmaceutical company; Hoffman was assigned the task. While researching the background of the chemical, Hoffman found Gerhardt's original paper.

By treating SA with various chemicals, Hoffman found a method to neutralize its acidic properties without inhibiting its analgesic properties. Ironically, using the same modification procedure on a different chemical, Hoffman also discovered morphine.

Hoffman's reformulated ASA quickly underwent simple field trials. The analgesic was given to dentists, who found that it relieved toothaches. On January 23, 1899, ASA was given the trade name aspirin because it could also be obtained from the meadowsweet plant, genus *Spiraea* (aspirin = "a" for acetylation; "spir" from the plant name; "in," commonly used at the time as a drug name ending). First sold as a powder, Bayer aspirin was marketed in tablet form in 1915, the first such drug to be sold in such a manner.

SIGNIFICANCE

Aspirin can be considered one of the earliest wonder drugs. Initially manufactured by Bayer as an analgesic, or pain reliever, acetylsalicylic acid is more commonly known by its registered trade name, Bayer aspirin. It has been utilized as an anti-inflammatory, as a means to treat and even prevent heart attacks or certain forms of stroke because of its anticlotting ability, and as a possible preventive for certain forms of colon cancer.

A variety of companies market generic forms of the drug under several trade names, but Bayer AG remains the most prominent drug manufacturer of aspirin. It produces approximately 50,000 tons of ASA each year. Estimates are that 137 million tablets are consumed each day worldwide.

The pharmacological basis for the function of ASA was determined only during the 1970's. Pharmacologist John R. Vane at the University of London observed that the active ingredients in aspirin could prevent the action of prostaglandins, molecules released in the body during inflammatory activity. With the determination of the role played by prostaglandins in inflammation and blood clotting, for example, it finally became possible to understand how aspirin plays an inhibitory role in a variety of functions in the human body.

—*Richard Adler*

FURTHER READING

Banks, Grace. "John R. Vane." In *The Nobel Prize Winners: Physiology or Medicine*. Vol. 3. Pasadena, Calif.: Salem Press, 1991. Examines how Vane determined how aspirin treats inflammation and headaches.

Feldman, David. *How Does Aspirin Find a Headache?* New York: HarperCollins, 2005. This book's title refers to one of the numerous questions addressed that are both trivial and more scholarly in nature, making an enjoyable read.

Jeffreys, Diarmuid. *Aspirin: The Remarkable Story of a Wonder Drug*. London: Bloomsbury, 2004. Historical account of the history and discovery of aspirin as well as the fortuitous events that led to its widespread application.

Mann, Charles, and Mark Plummer. *The Aspirin Wars: Money, Medicine, and One Hundred Years of Rampant Competition*. New York: Alfred A. Knopf, 1991. The history of the marketing competition behind one of the most successful pharmaceuticals in modern medical history.

Van Dulken, Stephen. *Inventing the Nineteenth Century: One Hundred Inventions That Shaped the Victorian Age*. New York: New York University Press, 2001. Among the inventions examined is the development of aspirin.

SEE ALSO: Oct. 5, 1823: Wakley Introduces *The Lancet*; Oct. 16, 1846: Safe Surgical Anesthesia Is Demonstrated; Dec. 11, 1890: Behring Discovers the Diphtheria Antitoxin; Aug. 20, 1897: Ross Establishes Malaria's Transmission Vector; 1898: Beijerinck Discovers Viruses; June, 1900-1904: Suppression of Yellow Fever.
RELATED ARTICLE in *Great Lives from History: The Nineteenth Century, 1801-1900:* William Thomas Green Morton.

July, 1897-July, 1904
BJERKNES FOUNDS SCIENTIFIC WEATHER FORECASTING

Vilhelm Bjerknes developed and tested the first hydrothermodynamic mathematical model capable of making weather predictions, thereby transforming weather forecasting from an arcane art into the modern science of meteorology.

ALSO KNOWN AS: Computational hydrodynamics
LOCALE: Stockholm, Sweden
CATEGORIES: Earth science; physics; science and technology; mathematics

KEY FIGURES
Vilhelm Bjerknes (1862-1951), Norwegian theoretical physicist and quantitative meteorologist
Nils Ekholm (1848-1923), Swedish aeronomist and experimental meteorologist
J. W. Sandstrøm (1874-1947), Swedish postdoctoral student in fluid dynamics and atmospheric geophysics

SUMMARY OF EVENT
The gradual development of modern predictive meteorology—which employs only empirical observation and mathematical analysis—was the result of a complex interaction of technological, scientific, and military-economic factors. During the nineteenth century, earlier efforts at studying weather processes predominantly used historical data statistics (the rudiments of so-called synoptic meteorology) and personal experience. The would-be forecaster learned to infer roughly how a weather system—then defined by crudely mapping field measurements of barometric pressure near the earth's surface—would move or change character. Such inferences were generally inaccurate.

Following the near destruction of both the French and British fleets in the Black Sea during the Crimean War (1853-1856), telegraphy became more widely used to disseminate the relatively sparse atmospheric information then available. However, even after the International Meteorological Committee began making efforts in 1873 to standardize, synchronize, and increase observational stations to facilitate international meteorological data exchange, predictions remained neither detailed nor specific as to time and location. Indeed, they typically amounted only to very general forecasts (for example, dry, changeable, or wet), and coastal gale warnings for broad areas were made at most only eighteen hours in advance.

After three decades of empirically studying the formation and progression of large-scale weather systems, by the end of the nineteenth century, meteorologists had reaped only a meager harvest in terms of organized theory and improved predictive capability. Although several separate hydro- and thermodynamic theories for idealized atmospheric conditions had been advanced, these theoretical efforts were divorced almost entirely both from practical forecasting requirements and from detailed physical understanding of the complex processes actually responsible for the change and motion of weather phenomena. Some meteorologists went so far as to abandon completely the possibility of improving rational weather prediction.

Several technological advances and political events, however, brought a new impetus to a new generation of physical meteorologists and oceanographers. These advances included a more widespread network of greater economic and military requirements, as well as opportunities for meteorological observations and predictions of greater geographic extent and accuracy. Other motivations for developing meteorology included the associated aerodynamic stimuli to enhance theories of aerodynamic fluid flow for improved aircraft construction and, independently, attempts at theoretical mechanization of electromagnetic wave fields via quantitative analogues with hydrodynamics. The latter were developed by the physicists Heinrich Hertz, Philipp Lenard, Carl Anton Bjerknes, and his son, Vilhelm.

Despite general neglect by the physics community at large, the Bjerknes concentrated on the problem of for-

1890's

mulating a complete and common set of equations for electromagnetic and hydrodynamic force and flux fields. One of the chief analogues was the mathematical similarity between fluid and electromagnetic "solenoids of circulation." When, in July, 1897, Vilhelm Bjerknes first presented his two extensions of Lord Kelvin's circulation theorems in a lecture to the Stockholm Physics Society, he mentioned no applications whatsoever. Soon after, Bjerknes was approached by his colleagues Nils Ekholm and Svante August Arrhenius, experts in aeronomy and meteorology, respectively, concerning the potential applications of Bjerknes's fluid mechanical analogues to the quantitative study of meso-scale atmospheric motions. As evidenced by Bjerknes's subsequent 1898 lecture and paper "On a Hydrodynamic Circulation Theorem and Its Application to the Mechanics of the Atmosphere and Global Oceans," Bjerknes had begun to consider circulation-theorem applications to polar and continental atmospheric and ocean-flow phenomena.

From 1850 to 1905, it was widely believed that so-called extratropical cyclones were initiated solely by local thermal motion and maintained by the liberated thermal heat of convection. In 1891, Ekholm had shown empirically that the atmosphere frequently has characteristics similar to those of the fluid later postulated by Bjerknes for his electrohydrodynamic circulation theorems. Most noticed by Ekholm in 1898 was the incongruity between lines of equal value of pressure and density in the vicinity of cyclonic (low-pressure) systems. In response to these suggestions (and the receipt of unique upper-air data recording the passage of a cyclone and anticyclone over the Blue Hill Observatory near Weston, Massachusetts), Bjerknes, together with his assistant J. W. Sandstrøm, returned to the circulation theorems, now directly analyzing them from a geophysical applications perspective rather than electromagnetic analogy.

During his initial studies, Bjerknes generalized the previous propositions of Kelvin and Hermann von Helmholtz on the velocity of circulation and conservation of vorticity. Bjerknes's generalization was based on introducing a broader interpretation of the definition of fluids. Whereas earlier views assumed a unique (hydrodynamic) relationship between pressure and volume, in his publications "The Dynamic Principles of Circulation and Motion in the Atmosphere" (1900) and "Circulation Relative to the Earth" (1901), Bjerknes expanded his circulation theorem further to its now-classic form by including terms for Coriolis forces arising from the earth's rotation and approximations for viscous-thermal losses caused by friction from the atmospheric fluid. Using

their equations, Bjerknes and Sandstrøm were theoretically able to reconstruct successfully the changes in direction and intensity of the Massachusetts low-pressure system. Although constructed in retrospect, this reconstruction is believed to be the first scientific "prediction" of weather phenomena in history.

Except for acoustic waves, all atmospheric motions may be characterized as flow circulations along closed streamlines. The area distribution of horizontal atmospheric velocity may be represented in terms of two scalar quantities: relative vertical vorticity and horizontal divergence. The former is twice the angular velocity of an air particle around a vertical axis relative to the earth. The latter is the relative expansion rate of an infinitesimal horizontal area moving with the air. The horizontal velocity field can be decomposed mathematically into one horizontal component containing all the vorticity and no divergence and likewise into another all-divergence/no-vorticity component. These two components of total atmospheric air mass motion have different behaviors. For example, whereas small-scale convection and internal-gravity waves are associated with the first component, large-scale atmospheric motions of interest to international forecasting are predominantly controlled by the latter, revealed by isobaric contour maps having predominantly horizontal circulations and, hence, vorticity-component dominance.

In Bjerknes's initial geometrical interpretation of his circulation theorems as a series of solenoids, because of the tendencies toward rotation in the crisscross lattice of intersecting surfaces, occurrence of skewed distributions of pressure and density should result in overall spatial circulation. Bjerknes's circulation theorem also can explain smaller-scale reciprocating air circulations, such as land-sea breezes and mountain-valley winds. In both cases, circulation is maintained to satisfy the basic vorticity continuity and conservation conditions. Because of radiative heating, mountain slope air temperature increases more in the daytime than does air temperature at equal pressure away from the mountain. Consequently, there arises a day wind blowing up the slope and a night wind blowing downward, as first rigorously demonstrated by Julius Wagner von Jauregg in 1932 using Bjerknes's continuity equation.

In *Lehrbuch der rosmischen Physik* (1903; treatise of cosmic physics), Arrhenius was the first to include independently Bjerknes's circulation theorem as the basis for a chapter on the thermomechanics of the atmosphere and oceans. Later in 1903, Bjerknes himself explicitly formulated and published a major proposal for predicting weather rationally. The proposal was more fully explained in his July, 1904, publication *Das Problem der Wettervorhersage, betrachtet vom Standpunkte der Mechanik und der Physik* (the problem of weather prediction considered from the standpoint of mechanics and physics). These latter publications outline two basic conditions for an improved predictive meteorology based on his prognostic circulation equations: sufficient knowledge of the state of the atmosphere at a given place and time based on a sufficient number of accurate measurements, and sufficiently accurate knowledge of the quantitative physical laws by which one atmospheric state at a given place and time evolves into another.

Since manual solution of equations over many separate observation (grid) points and times was practically impossible (until the advent of computers), Bjerknes and Sandstrøm suggested employing a physical-graphical approximation method. To evaluate the resulting circulation integrals, approximate two-dimensional surfaces of equal pressure (isobars) and of equal specific volume (1/density = isosters) were drawn at specified regular intervals. These surfaces subdivide the three-dimensional atmospheric space into tubes of isobaric-isosteric solenoids. It can be shown, through application of Stokes's theorem of integral calculus, that the integration value is equal to the number of solenoids enclosed by the curve around which the circulation integral is taken.

SIGNIFICANCE

Although a number of British and German observational meteorologists before him had varyingly suggested that cyclones could be associated with regional motion of large-scale circulation air bodies, these anticipations were formalized and subsumed in Vilhelm Bjerknes's work. Because they not only included rigorous derivations and predictions but also tied these to the best available observational data, as underscored by Hans Ertel, Bjerknes's publications had a greater impact on reconceiving the atmosphere as multiple dynamically related air masses instead of a unified global static air mass than the earlier (1903) but purely theoretical hydrodynamic studies of French physicist Jacques Hadamard. In addition to becoming the object of further theoretical efforts to reprove and improve its formulation, Bjerknes's circulation theorems not only became the basis of his later Bergen School of dynamic meteorology but also had the greatest impact on German, French, British, and American quantitative meteorology.

In addition to Vilhelm and his son Jacob's publications (1910 and 1918, respectively) on atmospheric flow-

line convergence and divergence in cloud/precipitation formation and cyclonic squall-lines, in 1921, Jacob Bjerknes and Halvor Skappel Solberg extended this work in *Meteorological Conditions for the Formation of Rain*, introducing the concepts of warm and cold fronts into predictive meteorology. A year later, they published *Life Cycle of Cyclones and the Polar Front Theory of Atmospheric Circulation* (1822), in which their prior descriptive model of cyclones was shown to be a special case, or rather a single stage, in the genesis and development of cyclones, from incipient unstable atmospheric waves through occluded/stalled fronts and dying frontal vortices.

Notwithstanding the fact that polar fronts do not account for all low-pressure systems, much of the conceptual and theoretical apparatus as well as nomenclature developed by the Bjerkneses and their colleagues remains intact in contemporary pedagogic and predictive meteorology. Further confirmatory and developmental studies by Tor Harold Percival Bergeron in 1926 and by Carl-Gustaf Arvid Rossby, Erik Herbert Palmén, and others in the 1930's more closely defined additional frontal and cyclonic phenomena and locally predictive models by developing the kinematic principles of airmass analysis.

—Gerardo G. Tango

FURTHER READING

Bates, Charles C., and John F. Fuller. *America's Weather Warriors, 1814-1985*. College Station: Texas A&M Press, 1986. Discusses the development and application of the Bergen School's efforts of fifty years of military weather predictions.

Bjerknes, Vilhelm, and Johann Sandstrøm. *Dynamic Meteorology and Hydrography*. Vol. 1. Washington, D.C.: Carnegie Institution, 1910. Discusses the theoretical derivations, experimental confirmations, and potential applications of the circulation theorems to predicting atmospheric conditions. Illustrated with numerous maps and diagrams. Written at a higher technical level requiring a solid undergraduate background in partial differentiation equations and/or hydrodynamics.

Cox, John D. *Storm Watchers: The Turbulent History of Weather Prediction from Franklin's Kite to El Niño*. Hoboken, N.J.: John Wiley & Sons, 2002. Comprehensive history of weather prediction includes a chapter on Vilhelm Bjerknes, Lewis Fry Richardson, Jacob Bjerknes, Tor Bergeron, Carl-Gustaf Rossby, and Sverre Pettersen.

Friedman, Robert Marc. *Appropriating the Weather: Vilhelm Bjerknes and the Construction of a Modern Meteorology*. Ithaca, N.Y.: Cornell University Press, 1989. Friedman traces in nonmathematical detail the historical-conceptual details of the revolution in meteorology initiated by Bjerknes. Friedman's philosophical thesis is that Bjerknes "appropriated" the tools of hydrodynamics and the problems of synoptic meteorology to construct a new predictive meteorology.

Holmboe, Jorgen, George E. Forsythe, and William Gustin. *Dynamic Meteorology*. New York: John Wiley & Sons, 1945. Basic textbook used to instruct flyers and meteorologists. Develops Bjerknes's basic thermohydrodynamic principles directly from physical concepts.

Kutzbach, Gisela. *The Thermal Theory of Cyclones: A History of Meteorological Thought in the Nineteenth Century*. Boston: American Meteorological Society, 1979. Presents a thematic analysis of the historical evolution of Euro-American meteorology. Discusses Bjerknes's numerical-observational predictive program from 1903 to 1905.

SEE ALSO: July, 1830: Lyell Publishes *Principles of Geology*; Oct. 4, 1853-Mar. 30, 1856: Crimean War; Apr., 1898-1903: Stratosphere and Troposphere Are Discovered; 1899: Hilbert Publishes *The Foundations of Geometry*; 1900: Wiechert Invents the Inverted Pendulum Seismograph.

RELATED ARTICLES in *Great Lives from History: The Nineteenth Century, 1801-1900:* John Dalton; Joseph-Louis Gay-Lussac; Joseph Henry; Alexander von Humboldt; Sir Joseph Norman Lockyer; Mary Somerville.

July 24, 1897
CONGRESS PASSES DINGLEY TARIFF ACT

The Dingley Act instituted protective tariff policies that led to a major rift between the Republican Party, in favor of the tariff, and the Democratic Party, against the high tariff. The act became the focus of intense criticism and debate after 1900, as Democrats argued the high tariff helped large corporations at the expense of consumers and as some Republicans, especially from midwestern states, sought some sort of reform of the tariff law.

ALSO KNOWN AS: Dingley Tariff; Dingley law
LOCALE: Washington, D.C.
CATEGORIES: Laws, acts, and legal history; trade and commerce; economics

KEY FIGURES
Nelson Wilmarth Aldrich (1841-1915), chair of the U.S. Senate Finance Committee
Grover Cleveland (1837-1908), twenty-second (1885-1889) and twenty-fourth (1893-1897) president of the United States
Nelson Dingley (1832-1899), chair of the House Ways and Means Committee
William McKinley (1843-1901), president of the United States, 1897-1901
Thomas Brackett Reed (1839-1902), speaker of the House of Representatives

SUMMARY OF EVENT
One of the most controversial political issues of the late nineteenth century was the protective tariff. Republicans argued that high customs duties on imports to the United States protected U.S. businesses from foreign competition and provided jobs to farmers and workers. Democrats countered that the policy raised prices to consumers and favored some businesses at the expense of others. The tariff became a key issue dividing the two major parties, with the Republicans united behind protection and most Democrats advocating lower tariffs.

In the presidential elections of 1888 and 1892, the two parties had offered very different approaches to trade policy. The Republicans received support for protectionism in 1888; the Democrats elected Grover Cleveland in part on the promise of lower tariffs in 1892. Republicans had enacted the protective McKinley Tariff in 1890 and saw their control of the House of Representatives vanish as voters rejected the higher prices associated with the law.

When the Democrats regained the White House in 1893 under President Cleveland, they had endeavored to pass a law to lower the tariff. Divisions within the party over other issues and the onset of the economic depression of the 1890's made it difficult for the Democrats to agree on a reform law. The result was the Wilson-

Gorman Tariff of 1894, which lowered rates somewhat but also made concessions to protectionist sentiment within the Democratic Party in order to get a bill through Congress. Cleveland let the bill become law without his signature, and the Republicans hammered away at the measure in the congressional elections of 1894. When the Republicans regained the House in that year, they promised that if a Republican president were elected in 1896, the tariff would be revised upward.

The Republican nominee in 1896 was William McKinley, who had long been associated with the protective tariff in the House. By that time, however, McKinley had decided that it would be wise to include a policy of reciprocal trade whereby the United States would moderate its tariff rates in return for concessions from trading partners. The new president was not a free trader. Reciprocity would occur within the protective system, but he envisioned an expansion of trade with this approach.

William McKinley delivering his inaugural address on March 4, 1897, four months before Congress passed the Dingley Tariff Act. (Library of Congress)

After he defeated William Jennings Bryan in 1896, McKinley urged Congress to move ahead quickly on a tariff law. He summoned the lawmakers into session in March, 1897. Planning meant that the House could act quickly on the tariff. The chairman of the House Ways and Means Committee, Nelson Dingley, reported out a new tariff bill, called the Dingley Tariff, on March 18, three days after the session opened. The speaker of the House, Thomas Brackett Reed, used the power of the Republican majority to push the bill through within three weeks of the opening of the session.

The situation was more complex in the Senate, where Republican control was less secure. There the Dingley Tariff became entangled with another issue. To achieve a greater use of silver in international trade, the United States had opened negotiations with France about an agreement on a policy known as international bimetallism. The French indicated interest in helping the United States if they could receive some concessions for their products in the new tariff bill. These elements led Nelson Wilmarth Aldrich, chair of the Senate Finance Committee, to produce an initial tariff measure in the Senate that recognized French desires, including lower rates on French luxury products.

As time passed, however, the various interest groups within the Republican coalition increased the pressure for higher tariff rates. The result was a bill that raised duties on such products as wool and woolen clothing, while hiking rates on French items such as silks, gloves, and olive oil. When the bill became more protectionist, Senate supporters of international bimetallism pushed the idea of tariff reciprocity treaties as a way of promising future concessions to France and other nations. The Senate bill, as passed on July 7, included language that allowed the president to negotiate treaties for a reduction of up to 20 percent on the duties in the Dingley bill.

The conference committee of the House and Senate leaned more toward the protectionist side. The final bill retained the raised duties on wool, silk, and other products of concern to France. There was wording that allowed the president to offer countries reductions on specific items and to negotiate reciprocal trade treaties as well. The bill came out of conference on July 19, and both houses approved it by July 24, 1897. Despite not having a dependable majority in the Senate, the Republicans had passed a tariff bill quickly and with little intraparty friction. The French initiative on international bimetallism collapsed later in the summer, for reasons unrelated to the passage of the Dingley Tariff.

SIGNIFICANCE

Public reaction to the Dingley Act was quiet. The returning prosperity of the summer of 1897 made the action of the Republican Congress seem appropriate. Although

1890's

President McKinley tried to use the reciprocity sections of the law during the remainder of his term and negotiated agreements with France, Jamaica, Argentina, and other nations, the strength of protectionist sentiment on Capitol Hill limited his accomplishments. In his last public speech, on September 5, 1901, in Buffalo, New York, McKinley argued for reciprocity as a policy of the future and sought to guide public opinion to tolerance of freer trade. The next day he was shot and, with his death on September 14, 1901, reciprocity waned. The new president, Theodore Roosevelt, proved willing to let Congress have its way on the tariff.

Until 1900, the Dingley Tariff enjoyed general political acceptance. As the return of prosperity following the Spanish-American War became more apparent, consumer prices rose and inflation became an issue. The rise of large corporations and public fears about anticompetitive cooperation by those corporations also were associated with the protective policy. Democrats charged that the tariff law had stimulated the growth of giant corporations and raised prices that average citizens had to pay. Within the ranks of the Republicans, sentiment to reform the tariff law grew, especially in the plains states of the Midwest. Party regulars remained steadfast in support of the law, and an internal dispute about the tariff marked the history of the Republicans during the first decade of the twentieth century.

In the presidential election of 1908, public pressure and the attacks of the Democrats led the Republicans to promise a revision of the tariff following the outcome of the race for the White House. The winner, William Howard Taft, followed through on this commitment and set in motion events that led to the enactment of the Payne-Aldrich Tariff of 1909. The controversy that stemmed from that event led, in turn, to a split in the Republican Party and the election of Democrat Woodrow Wilson in 1912. After Wilson took office, the Democratic Congress passed the Underwood Tariff in 1913, which lowered rates and finally replaced the Dingley Tariff completely.

The Republicans achieved substantial political benefits from the Dingley Tariff during the McKinley administration. After 1901, it became a source of persistent friction and opposition internally and from the Democrats. In that period, the law gained its enduring historical reputation as the embodiment of the high protective tariff policies associated with the Republican Party during the last twenty-five years of the nineteenth century.

—Lewis L. Gould,
based on the original entry by Anne Trotter

FURTHER READING

Aaronson, Susan Ariel. *Taking Trade to the Streets: The Lost History of Public Efforts to Shape Globalization.* Ann Arbor: University of Michigan Press, 2001. Although this work focuses on global trade and local activism, it does include the chapter "Same Arguments, Different Context: A Brief History of Protectionism from 1789 to the 1960s," encompassing the time period of the Dingley Act and early Republican protectionist trade policy.

Becker, William H. *The Dynamics of Business-Government Relations: Industry and Exports, 1893-1921.* Chicago: University of Chicago Press, 1982. Considers how U.S. business viewed export policy, and contains useful information on the Dingley Tariff from that perspective.

Gould, Lewis L. "Diplomats in the Lobby: Franco-American Relations and the Dingley Tariff of 1897." *Historian* 39 (August, 1977): 659-680. Uses the French diplomatic archives to trace the relationship between tariff-making and bimetallic diplomacy during the summer of 1897.

_____. *The Presidency of William McKinley.* Lawrence: University Press of Kansas, 1980. Considers the enactment of the Dingley Tariff in the context of the first year of the McKinley administration and traces the president's use of reciprocity as a bargaining tool in trade relations between 1897 and 1901. Good starting point for research on the Dingley law.

Irwin, Douglas A. "Changes in U.S. Tariffs: The Role of Import Prices and Commercial Policies." *American Economic Review* 88, no. 4 (September, 1998). Examines the history of tariffs and trade policies in the second half of the nineteenth century through 1967. Focuses especially on the politics that have led to particular tariff rates.

Northrup, Cynthia Clark, and Elaine C. Prange Turney, eds. *Encyclopedia of Tariffs and Trade in U.S. History.* Westport, Conn.: Greenwood Press, 2003. An informative collection of more than four hundred entries on the tariff acts passed by Congress between 1789 and 1930. Includes primary sources and the texts of the tariffs themselves.

Taussig, Frank W. *The Tariff History of the United States.* New York: Augustus M. Kelley, 1967. In this classic, begun in 1892 and updated yearly with each new tariff act, economics professor and occasional chair of the U.S. Tariff Commission Taussig regards the Dingley Tariff as a transitional measure, reflecting the changing nature of American manufacturing as it faced a new threat of foreign tariff retaliation.

Terrill, Tom E. *The Tariff, Politics, and American Foreign Policy*. Westport, Conn.: Greenwood Press, 1973. Examines the Dingley Tariff from the perspective of whether a search for overseas markets drove U.S. foreign policy during the end of the nineteenth century.

Wolman, Paul. *Most Favored Nation: The Republican Revisionists and U.S. Tariff Policy, 1897-1912*. Chapel Hill: University of North Carolina Press, 1992.

The Dingley Tariff forms the starting point for the author's discussion of Republicans who lobbied for downward revision of the tariff after 1897.

SEE ALSO: Feb. 4, 1887: Interstate Commerce Act; Oct., 1889-Apr., 1890: First Pan-American Congress; July 20, 1890: Harrison Signs the Sherman Antitrust Act; Nov. 3, 1896: McKinley Is Elected President.

RELATED ARTICLES in *Great Lives from History: The Nineteenth Century, 1801-1900:* Grover Cleveland; William McKinley.

August 20, 1897
ROSS ESTABLISHES MALARIA'S TRANSMISSION VECTOR

Several days after allowing mosquitoes to feed on a patient with malaria, Ronald Ross observed the malarial parasite in the stomach of the insect. He observed the parasite migrate to the salivary gland of the insect, suggesting a mechanism of transmission from human to human. Ross subsequently demonstrated that the anopheles *species of the mosquito was the specific vector for transmission of the disease.*

LOCALE: Secunderabad, India
CATEGORIES: Health and medicine; science and technology

KEY FIGURES
Ronald Ross (1857-1932), British physician
Louis-Félix-Achille Kelsch (1841-1911), French pathologist
Camillo Golgi (1843-1926), Italian physician
Sir Patrick Manson (1844-1922), British physician
Alphonse Laveran (1845-1922), French military doctor

SUMMARY OF EVENT

Malaria is an ancient disease whose records go back to the time of the ancient Greeks. Moreover, indirect evidence suggests that the disease goes back several thousand years earlier in the eastern Mediterranean region. The earliest known direct description of malaria is in the writings of Hippocrates (c. 460-c. 370 B.C.E.), who described an illness with intermittent fever that appeared every three to four days and was generally found in people living near areas of dampness or swamps. From Greece, the disease spread to Rome, where its name was coined as a result of the belief that *mala aria*, or bad air,

could be the cause. In 1740, Horace Walpole translated the Latin name into the English "malaria."

By the period of the eighteenth century, theories about the source of the infection began to center on contaminated water. The germ theory of disease, primarily the result of research by Robert Koch and Louis Pasteur, resulted in physicians addressing the possibility of malaria being cause by a germ. The involvement of mosquitoes had historically aroused suspicion. Indeed, a description in Sanskrit literature from fifteen hundred years earlier had suggested a connection between mosquitoes and the disease, but until the nineteenth century, it was not believed that insects served as vectors of disease.

The first demonstration of the role played by parasites other than bacteria in disease came in 1878. Sir Patrick Manson, medical adviser to the British colonial office, reported the presence of the filarial worm in the blood of patients with elephantiasis, a condition marked by significant enlargement of the limbs. At the time, Manson failed to observe the maturation and development of the parasites he had observed, nor did he link the worm with its ingestion and passage through mosquitoes. He mistakenly continued to believe it was the ingestion of contaminated water that spread the disease, not the insect. However, as a result of his extensive studies into such diseases, Manson became known as the founder of tropical medicine, and later, more pejoratively, as Mosquito Manson.

Louis-Félix-Achille Kelsch reported the presence of dark staining inclusion bodies in both red and white blood cells of persons with malaria. The significance of his observation was not understood immediately. In 1880, Alphonse Laveran, a French army surgeon stationed in Algeria, observed a spherical parasite contain-

1890's

Ronald Ross. (Library of Congress)

ing hairs, or flagella. This parasite was likely the male gametocyte of the malarial protozoan, now known by the genus name *Plasmodium*. Émile Roux, a pupil of Laveran while in military school, arranged for a demonstration of "Laveran's bodies" to Roux's skeptical associate, Louis Pasteur. The success of this work later resulted in a successful search for other plasmodia in birds. Several years later, Camillo Golgi, more reknowned for his observation of cellular organelles, also confirmed the presence of "Laveran's bodies." In 1885, Golgi identified three distinct species of the parasite, which are now known as *Plasmodium vivax, Plasmodium falciparum,* and *Plasmodium malariae.*

Ronald Ross was the son of Sir Campbell Ross, a British general in the Indian Army. Born in India, the younger Ross was interested in music and the arts but entered the medical profession, following the wishes of his father. After graduation from medical school in 1879, he served as a surgeon on a series of British ships. Ross became interested in malaria following a London demonstration by Manson in the spring of 1894, at which Ross learned that parasites could be observed in the blood of

patients with the disease. (Manson believed incorrectly, however, that the malarial parasite was acquired through drinking contaminated water.) Ross also became aware of Laveran's belief that these parasites were the actual cause of the disease. Ross's interests continued to lie, however, in the arts. During the summer of 1894, he and his wife lived with friends in Switzerland, and Ross spent the time writing two romance novels.

Returning to medicine in 1895, Ross became increasingly associated with Manson and his work in London on parasitic diseases. Manson taught techniques to Ross necessary for the observation of parasites in blood or tissue. Manson had read Laveran's reports as early as 1889, and he became intrigued by the perceived similarities between the filarial structures and the flagella found on plasmodia. Although his ideas with respect to similarities in lifestyle between the two types of parasites were inaccurate, Manson did correctly suggest that blood cells played a role in the metamorphosis, or life-cycle changes, of these agents. Manson suggested to Ross that he continue with this work upon his return to India.

Ross returned to India in 1895. While on board ship, he began to practice dissection of cockroaches, both to develop expertise in dissection of mosquitoes and to investigate the possibility that cockroaches might carry a parasite similar to those in mosquitoes. Much of his methodology was self-taught. Ross had minimal knowledge of bacteriology, and his expertise in microscopy was primarily learned while working with Manson. He had little knowledge of the life cycle and behavior of the mosquito itself. The initial months of 1895 were spent addressing these deficits.

On August 16, 1897, while Ross was working in Secunderabad, he allowed anopheline mosquitoes to feed on a patient with malaria. On August 20, four days later, he dissected the mosquitoes and found cysts in the stomach tissue containing the malarial parasite. Similar experiments were carried out with two other species of mosquito, *culex* and *aedes*, but the results were negative. Furthermore, volunteers who drank contaminated water did not, with one exception, contract malaria.

It remained to be proven only that the infection of a healthy human with the parasite would result in that person contracting malaria. Ironically, in completing the research necessary to confirm the role of the mosquito in malarial transmission, Ross was betrayed by his mentor, Manson. The Italian physician Giovanni Grassi had been carrying out studies similar to those of Ross and represented Ross's primary competition in the field. Grassi collaborated in his final experiments with Manson, even using Manson's son as one of the subjects for the experiment. Using mosquitoes which had recently fed on a human with malaria, Grassi demonstrated that transmission of the parasite using the *anopheles* vector would result in the transmission of malaria as well.

Ross continued with his work, observing the life cycle of the parasite. Following the rupture of the cysts in the mosquito's stomach, organisms migrated from the stomach to the salivary glands of the mosquito. By 1898, Ross had reported the complete life cycle of the *Plasmodium* parasite, as well as demonstrating that only the single species of mosquito, *anopheles*, was involved in its transmission. In 1902, Ross was both knighted and honored with the Nobel Prize for his work. Laveran received a similar honor from the Nobel committee in 1907 for his discovery of the malarial parasite.

SIGNIFICANCE

While mosquitoes had been suspected prior to this period in the transmission of certain tropical diseases, most notably malaria and yellow fever, the work of Ross and others provided scientific evidence to confirm this suspicion. Furthermore, their work provided an explanation for the presence of these diseases primarily in damp, swampy areas, which were breeding grounds for the insects. In the absence of a treatment (other than quinine) or a vaccine preventive, the explanation also provided a means to address the problem: Breeding grounds for mosquitoes would need to be eliminated.

Wherever possible, swamps were drained, and standing water was treated to kill anopheline mosquitoes. The clearest result of these actions could be observed in Central America: Yellow fever and malaria had ravaged U.S. soldiers during the Spanish-American War, as well as French laborers working in Panama to build a canal across the Central American isthmus. Alhough treatment of water primarily addressed yellow fever, the elimination of mosquito breeding grounds helped control malaria as well.

—Richard Adler

FURTHER READING

Costa, Albert. "Ronald Ross." In *The Nobel Prize Winners: Physiology or Medicine*. Vol. 1. Pasadena, Calif.: Salem Press, 1991. Brief biography of the man who determined the role of mosquitoes in the transmission of malaria. Includes a summary of his career and Nobel reception.

Harrison, Gordon. *Mosquitoes, Malaria, and Man: A History of the Hostilities Since 1880*. New York: E. P. Dutton, 1978. Popular description of malaria and the research carried out by Ross and others to explain its transmission. An in-depth history that includes illustrations.

Haynes, Douglas. *Imperial Medicine: Patrick Manson and the Conquest of Tropical Disease*. Philadelphia: University of Pennsylvania Press, 2001. Biography of the man who was the first to demonstrate the role of mosquitoes in the transmission of parasites to humans.

Lambert, Lisa. "Alphonse Laveran." In *The Nobel Prize Winners: Physiology or Medicine*. Vol. 1. Pasadena, Calif.: Salem Press, 1991. Covers the life and scientific career of the man who discovered the malarial parasite.

Nye, E. R., and M. E. Gibson. *Ronald Ross—Malariologist and Polymath: A Biography*. New York: St. Martin's Press, 1997. Biography of Ross that addresses the complexity of the man as well as his scientific achievements.

SEE ALSO: 1838-1839: Schwann and Virchow Develop Cell Theory; May, 1847: Semmelweis Develops Antiseptic Procedures; 1857: Pasteur Begins Developing Germ Theory and Microbiology; 1867: Lister Publishes His Theory on Antiseptic Surgery; 1880's: Roux Develops the Theory of Mitosis; 1882-1901: Metchnikoff Advances the Cellular Theory of Immunity; Mar. 24, 1882: Koch Announces His Discovery of the Tuberculosis Bacillus; Dec. 11, 1890: Behring Discovers the Diphtheria Antitoxin; Jan. 23, 1897: "Aspirin" Is Registered as a Trade Name; 1898: Beijerinck Discovers Viruses; June, 1900-1904: Suppression of Yellow Fever.

RELATED ARTICLES in *Great Lives from History: The Nineteenth Century, 1801-1900:* Robert Koch; Louis Pasteur.

1890's

November 1, 1897
NEW LIBRARY OF CONGRESS BUILDING OPENS

The Library of Congress expanded dramatically after an 1870 copyright law placed copyrights under the library and provided that two copies of all copyrighted books and publications be placed in its collections. A new building was constructed to accommodate the ever-expanding collections.

LOCALE: Washington, D.C.
CATEGORIES: Architecture; organizations and institutions; cultural and intellectual history

KEY FIGURES

Edward Pearce Casey (1864-1940), architect who was in charge of construction after 1892
Thomas Lincoln Casey (1831-1896), Edward Casey's father, the chief of the Army Engineers who directed construction
Bernard R. Green (1843-1914), Casey's assistant
John L. Smithmeyer (1832-1908) and
Paul J. Pelz (1841-1918), architects who submitted the original plans
Ainsworth Rand Spofford (1825-1908), librarian of Congress, 1864-1897

SUMMARY OF EVENT

The origins of the Library of Congress date back to a congressional act passed on April 24, 1800, that appropriated five thousand dollars to purchase books for the use of Congress and for housing them in a Capitol apartment. By the time it was destroyed during the War of 1812, the library possessed more than three thousand volumes. The library was replaced in January, 1815, with the purchase of Thomas Jefferson's library of six thousand books. A fire in 1851 destroyed thirty-five thousand books of the collection, which had grown by then to fifty-five thousand volumes. Congress immediately voted for funds to expand the holdings of the library and appropriated $72,500 to rebuild its quarters in the Capitol.

During the 1860's, the library was increased by numerous donated collections. The Smithsonian Institution's library of scientific journals and transactions of learned societies was deposited in 1866, and in the following year, the Peter Force collection of Americana was purchased. The library held only 165,000 books by 1870, when an important development took place. An amended copyright law gave copyright to the Library of Congress and stipulated that copyrighted books and other publications must be deposited with the library.

Within two years, it became obvious to Ainsworth Rand Spofford, librarian of Congress from 1864 to 1897, and all who used the library that the Capitol quarters were not adequate for its natural growth and development. The library needed its own building.

After years of architectural debate as to the style—with Italian, French, and German Renaissance, and even Gothic, styles discussed—the building plans of the firm of Smithmeyer and Pelz were accepted. On April 15, 1886, a congressional act created a commission to direct construction, which was in the hands of John L. Smithmeyer. As progress was not made and Congress was in doubt as to the exact cost, a second act, on October 2, 1886, repealed the first, and a ceiling of $4 million was placed on construction costs. General Thomas Lincoln Casey, chief of the Army Engineers, was placed in charge, and he modified the original plans. To the opening session of Congress in December, 1888, he demonstrated that the library would cost $6 million and would be completed within eight years. With congressional approval, construction resumed under Bernard R. Green, superintendent and engineer appointed by General Casey, aided by Paul J. Pelz of the original architectural firm.

Work progressed throughout the 1890's, and in the fall of 1893, the octagonal dome, 140 feet in diameter, was completed. In the autumn of 1897, the new Library of Congress, in Italian Renaissance style finished in New Hampshire granite, was completed at a cost of $6.3 million. On Monday, November 1, the library was opened to the public.

The interior decoration was done by leading artists of the day, under the supervision of Edward P. Casey. One newspaper praised the decoration in the following terms: "It is the interior of the building . . . in which it surpasses furthest anything that the United States has done before in the way of public art."

The operation of the library was directed from the rotunda area, which originally handled 260 readers. The stacks that radiated from the rotunda on three sides rose nine stories and could hold 4.5 million volumes. It was thought at the time that the library would be adequate for fifty years.

Over the years, the library has greatly expanded its size and services. In 1925, the main building was enlarged; in 1939, a five-story annex, the Adams Building, was completed and nearly doubled the original space. Through congressional appropriations, benefactions of public-spirited citizens, transfers from other agencies, deposit of books for copyright, and the operation of a vast network of international exchanges, the library came to contain an unrivaled collection of literary, scientific, artistic, and governmental materials.

In addition to its significant size, the Library of Congress is an international repository, having been charged by Congress in the 1960's to gather "all library materials currently published throughout the world which are of value to scholarship." Materials are collected in Asia, Latin America, and Africa, as well as in Europe and North America, and access to these holdings has been automated. Another change in the library is its expansion of mission, from a resource for Congress to a source of information and materials for numerous publics. This increased access is available within the Library of Congress itself, through the Web, and through the outreach programs the library sponsors and manages.

The library's panoply of materials requires special care to maintain and to preserve their availability to its diverse publics. To accomplish this, the library has a comprehensive preservation program; the most challenging preservation issue is the high acid content of paper characteristic since the mid-nineteenth century. The library's de-acidification program treats, thereby preserving, more than half a million volumes annually. Ad-

ditionally, digitization of many formats now offers the most secure and effective means of preservation and distribution of the world's scholarly treasures.

Generous bequests, international exchange programs, diversification of formats, and expansion of services to its multiple and dispersed publics made the need for additional space obvious. Construction of the "third annex" was completed in 1980. Named in honor of the fourth U.S. president, the James Madison Memorial Building is among the largest library buildings in the world. In appearance, it is simple when compared with the artistic grandeur of the original Jefferson building. It is the home of specific programs of the Library of Congress: processing, copyright, and the Congressional Research Service. The research service, always at the core of the mission of the Library of Congress, is a primary research source for members of Congress.

SIGNIFICANCE

The Library of Congress's collection of more than one hundred million items in nearly five hundred languages and its staff numbering in the thousands honor the goal of its original founders, build on the leadership and diverse vision of its librarians, and equip the Library of Congress to serve both the United States and the world.

—*Russell M. Magnaghi, updated by Ann Thompson*

1890's

The Jefferson Building of the Library of Congress under construction in late 1892. (Library of Congress)

FURTHER READING

Goodrum, Charles A. *Treasures of the Library of Congress*. New York: Harry N. Abrams, 1980. Heavily illustrated description of the unique and specialized collection of the Library of Congress.

Goodrum, Charles A., and Helen W. Dalrymple. *Guide to the Library of Congress*. Rev. ed. Washington, D.C.: Library of Congress, 1988. A brief treatment of the history, collections, and services of the Library of Congress.

_____. *The Library of Congress*. Boulder, Colo.: Westview Press, 1982. Comprehensive treatment of the history, organization, and functions of the Library of Congress.

Johnston, William D. *History of the Library of Congress*. Washington, D.C.: Government Printing Office, 1904. The first volume of an unfinished two-volume set that covers the history of the library from 1800 until 1864.

Thorin, Suzanne E., ed. *Automation at the Library of Congress: Inside Views*. Washington, D.C.: Library of Congress Professional Association, 1986. Describes the development of automation within the Library of Congress.

SEE ALSO: Aug. 10, 1846: Smithsonian Institution Is Founded; July 4, 1848: Ground Is Broken for the Washington Monument; Mar. 2, 1867: U.S. Department of Education Is Created; Feb. 20, 1872: Metropolitan Museum of Art Opens; Oct. 4-6, 1876: American Library Association Is Founded; 1883-1885: World's First Skyscraper Is Built.

RELATED ARTICLE in *Great Lives from History: The Nineteenth Century, 1801-1900:* Rutherford B. Hayes.

November 14, 1897

SCRAMBLE FOR CHINESE CONCESSIONS BEGINS

In the aftermath of Germany's seizure of the Chinese port of Kiaochow, Great Britain, France, and Russia claimed additional concessions from China's Qing Dynasty. The weakened Chinese Empire seemed to be on the brink of partition, but the open door policy of the United States helped maintain the nation's territorial integrity—although it could not save the Qing government from overthrow in 1911.

LOCALE: Chinese coast

CATEGORIES: Diplomacy and international relations; expansion and land acquisition; wars, uprisings, and civil unrest

KEY FIGURES

Cixi (1835-1908), dowager empress of China, r. 1861-1908

Guangxu (1871-1908), Chinese emperor, r. 1875-1908

William II (1859-1941), German emperor, r. 1888-1918

SUMMARY OF EVENT

In 1897, two German Roman Catholic missionaries were murdered in Kiaochow (now Jiaoxian), a port in the Jiao Xian region of China's Shandong Province. Eagerly seizing the opportunity provided by the incident, German emperor William II ordered the occupation of the port and then forced China's Qing government to grant Germany a ninety-nine-year lease on it, followed by other commercial and religious privileges in the province. Other European powers immediately made their own demands for concessions from China, and soon much of coastal China was divided up into colonial spheres of influence belonging to Germany, Russia, Great Britain, and France. By the end of the 1890's, both Chinese and foreigners were predicting that Imperial China would be partitioned by several European powers and Japan.

Under the Qing Dynasty, Imperial China had reached the apex of its international influence in the late eighteenth century. What followed was an era of decline, beginning with a conflict with Great Britain known as the First Opium War (1839-1842) and ending in the Revolution of 1911, which brought about the collapse of Imperial China. In the aftermath of the First Opium War, many of the Chinese concessions made to the British, such as extraterritoriality, were claimed by other foreign nations, including France, the United States, and later Germany, Russia, and a rapidly modernizing Japan. Foreign interest and involvement in China were the result of several factors, including trade and commerce, the desire for national prestige, international rivalries, social Darwinian competition, and the desire of missionaries—both Protestant and Catholic—to Christianize the Chinese. During the 1860's, a self-strengthening movement began developing in the upper reaches of the Chinese

FOREIGN CONCESSIONS IN CHINA

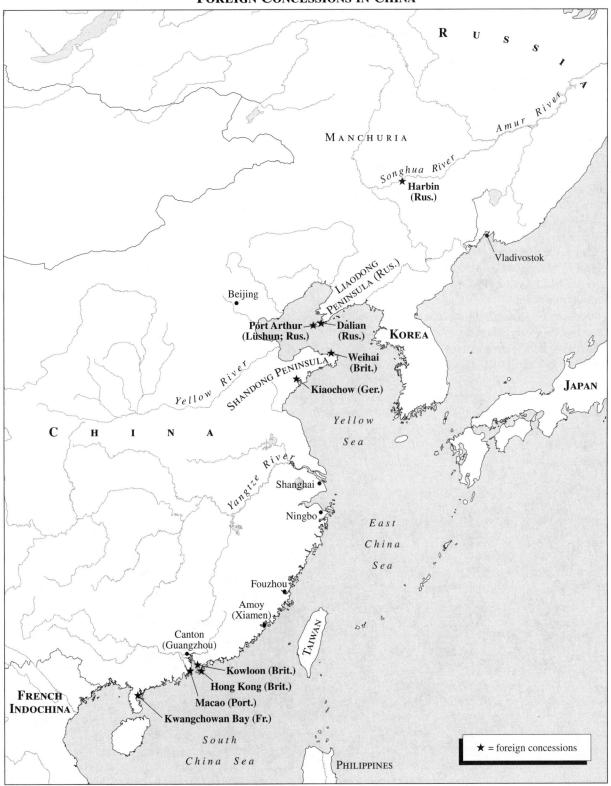

R U S S I A

Amur River

MANCHURIA

Songhua River

★ Harbin
(Rus.)

Vladivostok

LIAODONG
PENINSULA (RUS.)

Beijing

Port Arthur ★ ★ Dalian
(Lüshun; Rus.) (Rus.)

KOREA

★ Weihai
(Brit.)

Yellow River

SHANDONG PENINSULA

★ Kiaochow (Ger.)

C H I N A

Yellow
Sea

JAPAN

1890's

Yangtze River

Shanghai

Ningbo

East
China
Sea

Fouzhou

Amoy
(Xiamen)

TAIWAN

Canton
(Guangzhou)

★ Kowloon (Brit.)

Hong Kong (Brit.)

Macao (Port.)

FRENCH
INDOCHINA

Kwangchowan Bay (Fr.)

South
China Sea

PHILIPPINES

★ = foreign concessions

1889

government and in intellectual circles. The movement represented an attempt to adopt Western technology but retain traditional Chinese Confucian values, but it failed fundamentally to transform China, as the results of the Sino-Japanese War of 1894-1895 revealed.

In the Treaty of Shimonoseki (1895) ending that war, which was easily won by Japan, China was forced to cede Taiwan to Japan. China was also required to abandon its paramount influence in Korea, as well as granting Japan rights in Manchuria's Liaodong Peninsula. Several Chinese officials predicted the partition of China, with Russia and Japan seizing the north, Germany gaining the Shandong Peninsula, Britain dominating the Yangtze region, and France—which had recently staked out an empire in Indochina—occupying China's southern provinces.

However, the foreigners were not united in their imperial ambitions in China. China in the 1895 treaty had given up the Liaodong Peninsula with its port of Dalian and its fortifications at Lüshun (Port Arthur) to Japan, but France, Germany, and Russia, in the so-called Triple Intervention, forced Japan to relinquish that territory. The Triple Intervention resulted in Imperial Japan harboring considerable animosity toward those Western

powers, particularly toward Germany, because the German minister to China appeared to threaten Japan. The primary instigator of the intervention, however, was Imperial Russia, whose trans-Siberian railroad required a direct route across Chinese Manchuria to Vladivostok. Russia hoped to gain concessions in Manchuria from the Qing government as a reward for keeping the Liaodong Peninsula out of Japanese hands, and in September, 1896, a secret agreement was signed between China and Russia, allowing Russia to construct a railroad across Manchuria.

Germany, which was unified only in 1871, was a late arrival in the quest for overseas empire. China was a tempting economic market, but in order to protect Germany's prospective Chinese trade, it was believed necessary to establish a German colony in China that could act as a home base for Germany's East Asian fleet. William II was the major influence on Germany's China policy, but his actions and motives were inconsistent. He believed initially that he was defending Japan against British machinations and hoped that in gratitude Japan would turn over Taiwan to Germany. He then turned against Japan over the issue of the Liaodong Peninsula's dispensation after the Sino-Japanese War. If there was any consis-

Russians forcing Chinese laborers to work in Manchuria. (Francis R. Niglutsch)

tency in William's policy, it was a distrust of Britain's imperial ambitions.

Germany seized its opportunity in 1897. The Russian government had raised no objections to Germany's desire to obtain at least a coaling station in China, and some German missionaries had traveled to the country. Two such Roman Catholic missionaries from the Society of the Divine Word were murdered in Shandong Province on November 1, 1897, by a group of Chinese. William reacted immediately. On November 14, German troops were landed and successfully occupied Kiaochow. The Qing government urged the Germans to withdraw, but on March 6, 1898, the Chinese were forced to grant Germany a ninety-nine-year lease on Kiaochow, which was to be used as a German naval base. A grant followed of railroad and mining privileges in the province. In addition, the Chinese government was required to give further privileges to Christian missionaries, as well as to construct Christian churches.

Other powers immediately made their own demands on China. Russia obtained a twenty-five-year lease on the Liaodong Peninsula and the construction of a branch railroad line from Harbin to Lüshun, which Japan had been forced to relinquish two years earlier. To counterbalance the Russian gains, France gained Kwangchowan Bay (now Zhanjiang Gang), in Guangdong Province, in May, 1898, and Britain demanded the port of Weihai in northeastern Shandong, which became a base for the British Far East Fleet. Britain also obtained Kowloon on a ninety-nine-year lease, adding to the Hong Kong territory it had gained in the Treaty of Nanjing at the end of the First Opium War. Although most of the concessions were formal lease arrangements, usually for ninety-nine years, it was doubtful that any of the foreign powers expected that their nominally leased territories would ever revert to Chinese control.

These developments were met with dismay by Dowager Empress Cixi, who had dominated the Chinese government since 1861. The reigning emperor, Guangxu, was Cixi's nephew, but Cixi allowed him only a modicum of independent authority. Aware of China's weaknesses, as exemplified in the Sino-Japanese War and the subsequent foreign concessions, Guangxu launched a series of reforms in 1898, including modernizing China's administrative, educational, military, economic, and police systems. Cixi, backed by conservatives at court who feared the emperor's modernization and Westernization policies, aborted the so-called Hundred Days of Reform, imprisoning Guangxu and either executing other reformers or driving them into exile.

If the Hundred Days of Reform was one reaction to China's weaknesses, the Boxer Rebellion of 1900 was another. The murder of the Christian missionaries in Kiaochow in 1897 was only one of many antimissionary incidents, which culminated in the appearance of the Yihechuan (Wade-Giles, I-ho ch'üan; the Association of Righteousness and Harmony, most commonly known as the Righteous and Harmonious Fists). This secret society, nicknamed the Boxers by Westerners, practiced a combination of martial arts and spirit possession, in which the initiates believed they were rendered invulnerable to bullets and other weapons. It campaigned under the slogan of "fu-Qing, mie-yang" (support the Qing, exterminate the foreigners). After some vacillation, Cixi gave her support to the Boxers, who in the summer of 1900 seized control of much of Beijing, with the exception of the foreign legation quarter. That quarter was eventually liberated by international army. In the aftermath, China was saddled with an indemnity of $333 million.

SIGNIFICANCE

The scramble for concessions begun by Germany's seizure of Kiaochow in 1897 seemed to many to portend the permanent dismemberment of Imperial China. However, U.S. secretary of state John Hay helped prevent such a dismemberment when he issued two "Open Door Notes." In 1899, he requested that the foreign powers allow equality of commerce in their respective spheres of influence, and in 1900, he stated that the American policy was to preserve China's territorial and administrative integrity, policies also backed by the British. Because of the second note, the consequences of the Boxer Rebellion were relatively limited, whereas it might have been predicted that the West and Japan would have used the rebellion as a justification for making even greater inroads against China's sovereignty.

Cixi and her advisers initiated a program of reform, including abolishing the traditional Confucian educational system and promising constitutional government, but it was too little, too late. Both Cixi and Guangxu died in 1908, and three years later, in the Revolution of 1911, the Qing Dynasty was overthrown, and Imperial China became a republic.

—Eugene Larson

FURTHER READING

Edwards, E. W. *British Diplomacy and Finance in China, 1895-1914.* Oxford, England: Oxford University Press, 1987. An incisive analysis of Britain's relations with China from the Treaty of Shimonoseki to World War I.

Fairbank, John King, and Merle Goldman. *China: A New History*. Enlarged ed. Cambridge, Mass.: Harvard University Press, 1998. One of the best histories of China, including a description of the late nineteenth century concessions.

Lee, Robert. *France and the Exploitation of China, 1895-1901*. Oxford, England: Oxford University Press, 1989. A comprehensive discussion of French involvement in China in the years after the Sino-Japanese War.

Paludan, Ann. *Chronicles of the Chinese Emperors*. New York: Thames and Hudson, 1998. A history of China's emperors, including Cixi and Guangxu, and the era of concessions.

Schrecker, John E. *Imperialism and Chinese National-ism: Germany in Shantung*. Cambridge, Mass.: Harvard University Press, 1971. An excellent analysis of Germany's role in China's Shantung Province.

SEE ALSO: Sept., 1839-Aug. 29, 1842: First Opium War; Jan. 11, 1851-late summer, 1864: China's Taiping Rebellion; 1853-1868: Qing Dynasty Confronts the Nian Rebellion; Winter, 1855-Jan. 2, 1878: Muslim Rebellions in China; Oct. 23, 1856-Nov. 6, 1860: Second Opium War; 1860's: China's Self-Strengthening Movement Arises; Aug. 1, 1894-Apr. 17, 1895: Sino-Japanese War; Sept. 6, 1899-July 3, 1900: Hay Articulates "Open Door" Policy Toward China; May, 1900-Sept. 7, 1901: Boxer Rebellion.

RELATED ARTICLES in *Great Lives from History: The Nineteenth Century, 1801-1900:* Cixi; John Hay.

1898
BEIJERINCK DISCOVERS VIRUSES

The Dutch bacteriologist Martinus W. Beijerinck demonstrated that cell-free extracts prepared from plants with tobacco mosaic disease could transmit the infection to healthy plants. The preparation contained what Beijerinck called contagium vivum fluidum, *infectious material that would replicate only in living tissue, and represented the first evidence for the existence of what became known as viruses.*

LOCALE: Wageningen, the Netherlands

CATEGORIES: Health and medicine; science and technology; agriculture

KEY FIGURES

Martinus W. Beijerinck (1851-1931), Dutch bacteriologist

Adolf Mayer (1843-1942), Dutch agriculturalist

Dmitri Ivanovski (1864-1920), Russian biologist

Friedrich August Johannes Löffler (1852-1915), German professor of hygiene at Greifswald and bacteriologist

Paul Frosch (1860-1928), German bacteriologist

Robert Koch (1843-1910), German bacteriologist

SUMMARY OF EVENT

During the last decades of the nineteenth century, Robert Koch and others discovered that bacteria represented the etiological agents behind many human illnesses. This discovery became the basis for the germ theory of disease, the idea that most illnesses were caused by bacteria. The ability to grow these organisms on laboratory media played a major role in formation of Koch's Postulates, a series of experimental steps linking a disease with a specific organism. The growing list of individual diseases found to be associated with bacterial infections gave rise to a general belief that most diseases were the result of infection by such microscopic agents.

Vaccines had been developed by the 1880's against what we now know to be virally induced diseases, most notably against smallpox and rabies, but there was a significant reluctance to carry out infection in humans of extracts from infected tissues. As a result, the soluble nature of these agents was overlooked, and Koch's Postulates could not be applied. The difficulty in growing many viral agents in the laboratory, as well as lack of animal models, would remain a problem in applying the postulates to viral diseases well into the twentieth century.

The first experimental transmission of a viral disease could arguably be attributed to Adolf Mayer, director of the agricultural station at Wageningen, in the Netherlands. In the 1880's, Mayer studied tobacco mosaic disease (TMD), a name he coined, which was having a significant economic impact on tobacco growers. Mayer demonstrated that one could transmit the disease to healthy plants by spraying them with sap extracted from diseased plants. He attempted to link bacterial agents he isolated from the diseased plants with TMD by applying Koch's Postulates, but his inability to culture any specific organism made this impossible. Despite being unable to isolate the infectious agent, Mayer found that the agent seemed to be removed from tobacco samples by the filtration process he used to look for it. He incorrectly suggested that this was an indication that the agent was a bacterium.

The Russian biologist Dmitri Ivanovski repeated and extended Mayer's work in 1892. Mayer had used a double layer of filter paper to remove any bacteria or other cells from his preparations. Ivanovski, instead of using filter paper, prepared cell-free filtrates from diseased tobacco plants using newly developed porcelain Chamberland filter candles. He was able to transmit TMD to healthy plants even in the absence of bacteria. Ivanovski's conclusion was that a toxin was probably associated with the disease, reflecting the recent discovery by Emil von Behring of the relationship between a toxin and human diphtheria. As late as 1903, however, Ivanovski maintained that the agent behind TMD was probably a bacterium that could not be cultured.

Martinus W. Beijerinck was probably unaware of Ivanovski's earlier work on the nature of the TMD agent. In 1898, he was collaborating with Mayer in the study of the disease and unknowingly repeated the filtration experiments first carried out six years earlier by Ivanovski. Beijerinck's conclusion was that the sap contained a *contagium vivum fluidum*, a contagious living fluid. In a more detailed analysis of the agent, Beijerinck first demonstrated that it would not grow on the culture media generally used to grow or maintain bacteria. Nor would the agent grow in the sap itself. Beijerinck concluded the agent could not be a bacterium. Furthermore, he found that the agent was capable of diffusing through agar, indicating it was a soluble substance, and that it was stable over a period of months even when dried. His work was reported in a publication later that same year.

Beijerinck also carried out studies on the development of TMD itself. He observed that the disease's agent spread through the plant through the phloem and that it had a preference for young growing leaves. By passing the sap from plant to plant, Beijerinck demonstrated that it was capable of reproduction—unlike a toxin, which would have lost viability as it became increasingly diluted. Beijerinck's conclusion that the TMD agent was neither bacterial in nature nor a toxin but that it required living tissue in which to reproduce set his work apart

from that carried out earlier by Ivanovski. Thus, Beijerinck has correctly been given priority in the discovery of viruses.

It was shortly after the work by Beijerinck on TMD was reported that the first demonstration of a disease in animals that could be transmitted by cell-free extracts was carried out. Friedrich August Johannes Löffler, head of a Prussian research commission for the study of foot-and-mouth disease, and his collaborator Paul Frosch, a colleague of Robert Koch at Koch's Institute of Infectious Diseases in Berlin, transmitted the disease using extracts from vesicles isolated from infected cattle. Together, Beijerinck, Löffler, and Frosch demonstrated that some diseases were associated with agents that were too small to be observed with standard microscopes and that required living tissue in which to replicate.

SIGNIFICANCE

Beijerinck was not the first to observe that a filterable agent could serve as an etiological agent for (plant) disease. He demonstrated, however, that such an agent could not be grown in culture media, which likely meant that it was not a bacterium. Furthermore, the fact that the filterable agent could be shown to multiply eliminated the possibility of its being a toxin. Beijerinck's definition of the *contagium vivum fluidum*, however, did not imply a full understanding of the nature and functioning of viruses. The modern concept of a virus required a leap in understanding that was not yet available to the science of the day.

Beijerinck's discoveries were particularly significant in that he demonstrated that the agent required living tissue in which to reproduce. When, shortly afterward, Löffler and Frosch reported that an analogous agent was associated with foot-and-mouth disease in animals, a twenty-five-year debate began over the nature of such "viruses": Were they particles or enzymes? This question was settled only with the independent codiscovery of bacterial viruses by Frederick Twort and Felix d'Herelle, as well as with the development of the electron microscope, which allowed viruses to be visualized.

During these same decades, filterable agents were also demonstrated to be etiological agents of human and other animal diseases, such as yellow fever, polio, rabies, and possibly even cancer. None of these "organisms" could be grown on laboratory media: It was shown that they could replicate only in the animal itself. Scientists gradually came to the conclusion that viruses represented a form of life that could not be considered as either animal or plant.

1890's

Studies of tobacco mosaic virus (TMV) have played a major role in the nascent field of virology. TMV was the first virus to be purified free from host tissue (1935). Unlike most organisms, in which deoxyribonucleic acid (DNA) was determined by the 1940's to be the genetic material, TMV was the first agent found to contain ribonucleic acid (RNA) as a genome.

—*Richard Adler*

FURTHER READING

Dimmock, N. J., A. J. Easton, and K. N. Leppard. *Introduction to Modern Virology*. 5th ed. Malden, Mass.: Blackwell Science, 2001. Abbreviated discussion of the molecular biology of viruses. Introduces the subject with a review of the early history and discovery of viruses.

Fraenkel-Conrat, Heinz. "The History of Tobacco Mosaic Virus and the Evolution of Molecular Biology." In *The Plant Viruses*, edited by M. H. V. van Regenmortel and Heinz Fraenkel-Conrat. New York: Plenum Press, 1986. Discusses the early history of the work carried out by Beijerinck, as well as the role played by TMV in the study of molecular biology of viruses.

Helvoort, Ton van. "When Did Virology Start?" *ASM News* 62 (1996): 142-145. Synopsis of the early years of virology and the changing concept of viral agents.

Knipe, David, Peter Howley, and Diane Griffin, eds. *Fields' Virology*. 2 vols. New York: Lippincott Williams & Wilkins, 2001. Covers most major groups of viruses. The introductory chapter provides extensive coverage of the origin and early history of the subject.

Rott, Rudolf, and Stuart Siddell. "One Hundred Years of Animal Virology." *Journal of General Virology* 79 (1998): 2871-2874. Presentation at the centenary meeting commemorating the discovery of the foot-and-mouth disease virus. Gives the early history of the discovery of filterable agents associated with plant and animal diseases.

Zaitlin, Milton. "The Discovery of the Causal Agent of the Tobacco Mosaic Disease." In *Discoveries in Plant Biology*, edited by S. Kung and S. Yang. Hong Kong: World, 1998. Mayer, Ivanovski, and Beijerinck each played a role in demonstrating the association of a cell-free agent in plant disease. Places their work in the context of contemporary scientific thought.

SEE ALSO: 1816: Laënnec Invents the Stethoscope; 1838-1839: Schwann and Virchow Develop Cell Theory; 1857: Pasteur Begins Developing Germ Theory and Microbiology; 1880's: Roux Develops the Theory of Mitosis; 1882-1901: Metchnikoff Advances the Cellular Theory of Immunity; Mar. 24, 1882: Koch Announces His Discovery of the Tuberculosis Bacillus; Dec. 11, 1890: Behring Discovers the Diphtheria Antitoxin; Jan. 23, 1897: "Aspirin" Is Registered as a Trade Name; Aug. 20, 1897: Ross Establishes Malaria's Transmission Vector; June, 1900-1904: Suppression of Yellow Fever.

RELATED ARTICLES in *Great Lives from History: The Nineteenth Century, 1801-1900:* Emil von Behring; Robert Koch; Louis Pasteur.

March, 1898
RUSSIAN SOCIAL-DEMOCRATIC LABOR PARTY IS FORMED

The Russian Social-Democratic Labor Party was formed by a small group of Russian Marxist revolutionaries. The center of Marxist thought and action in Russia, its radical wing—headed by Vladimir Ilich Lenin—would seize control of the country in the October Revolution less than twenty years later.

ALSO KNOWN AS: Russian Social-Democratic Workers' Party; Russian Social-Democratic Party
LOCALE: Minsk, Russia
CATEGORIES: Organizations and institutions; government and politics; social issues and reform

KEY FIGURES

Vladimir Ilich Lenin (Vladimir Ilich Ulyanov; 1870-1924), leading Russian Marxist
Alexander Kremer (fl. late nineteenth century), leader in the General Jewish Workers' League
Julius Martov (Yuly Osipovich Tsederbaum; 1873-1923), Lenin's assistant until 1903
Georgy Plekhanov (1856-1918), chief exponent of philosophic Marxism in Russia

SUMMARY OF EVENT

The formation of the Russian Social-Democratic Labor Party in 1898 brought at least a semblance of unity to the previously disorganized Marxist movement in Russia. The first Russian Marxist party, the Liberation of Labor, had been founded in Geneva in 1883 by Georgy Plekhanov, who had migrated there from Russia three years earlier. Plekhanov had been a member of the Populist (*Narodnik*) movement of the 1870's but had abandoned Populism in disillusionment over the failure of Russia's peasants to rise up in revolt against the czarist order. Plekhanov now believed that, as industrialization spread in Russia, the industrial working class would fulfill the revolutionary expectations that the Populists had mistakenly assigned to the peasants.

Plekhanov, with the aid of other members of his group, translated the major works of Karl Marx and Friedrich Engels into Russian; the Liberation of Labor then managed to smuggle this material back into Russia. Here it was favorably received by intellectuals and university students who by 1884 had established numerous, though small and ineffective, Marxist groups throughout the country. Generally, until the mid-1890's, these groups were divided by internal polemics rather than united as a militant revolutionary front.

Russian Marxism finally began the process of unification in 1895. Vladimir Ilich Lenin, whose real name was Vladimir Ilich Ulyanov, and his assistant Julius Martov, whose real name was Yuly Osipovich Tsederbaum, organized the scattered groups of the St. Petersburg region into the Fighting Union for the Liberation of the Working Class. Similar unions were established in Moscow and other Russian cities, especially those which were developing into major industrial centers. Social democratic parties were also founded in Poland, Lithuania, and Latvia, which at that time were all part of the Russian Empire.

In 1897, a Jewish social democratic organization, the General Jewish Workers' League, commonly referred to as the *Bund*, came into existence. One of its key members, Alexander Kremer, was instrumental in persuading members of his group to hold a joint meeting with several

Vladimir Ilich Lenin around 1920. (Library of Congress)

other Marxist parties. As a result, in the city of Minsk in March, 1898, there met the First Congress of the Russian Social-Democratic Labor Party. It was hardly a congress, because only nine delegates appeared. Lenin, exiled at that time in Siberia, was not among them. Indeed, it is doubtful whether a unified party emerged from the Minsk congress. The movement had neither a charter nor a program, only a manifesto written by Peter Struve that proved to be unsatisfactory to most party members. No one in attendance at the First Party Congress could imagine that in the coming century a wing of this party would seize power in Russia and subsequently extend its influence throughout the world.

The shallow unity of the Russian Social-Democratic Labor Party lasted only until the meeting of the Second Party Congress in 1903, originally scheduled in Brussels. The intervention of the Belgian police necessitated its transfer to London. Unlike the First Party Congress, the second was dominated by the leading personages of the Russian Social Democratic movement, Lenin, Martov, and Plekhanov. In the course of this congress, a split developed within the party over administrative and ideological questions.

Lenin maintained that membership in the party should be limited to professional revolutionaries who would be bound by iron discipline to obey orders issued by the party's leadership. Opening membership in the party to anyone who wished to join, argued Lenin, would make it too easy for the czarist police to use undercover agents to infiltrate the party's ranks and undermine its effectiveness as an agent of revolution. Lenin's views struck most of the delegates, led by Martov, as inimical to the spirit of democracy. Taking advantage of a walkout staged by the delegates representing the *Bund*, Lenin got himself and Plekhanov elected to key leadership positions by a majority of the remaining delegates. Even though Lenin probably would have lost if the *Bund* delegates had not left, he claimed that his followers were the majority, or Bolshevik, faction, and that Martov's supporters were the minority, or Mensheviks.

Ideologically, Lenin was inclined to believe that the czarist government, following its overthrow, must be succeeded immediately by the dictatorship of the proletariat. The Mensheviks insisted, on the other hand, that the czars must be followed by a bourgeois democratic republic as a necessary prologue to a socialist state. Neither side, it must be stressed, adhered rigidly to its position. Nevertheless, Lenin's insistence on his authoritarian rule over the party and the infallibility of his ideas contributed much to the split that occurred in 1903.

SIGNIFICANCE

For all practical purposes, the split in the party between Bolsheviks and Mensheviks remained permanent. A superficial reconciliation took place at the Fourth Party Congress held in Stockholm, Sweden, in April of 1906. However, in January of 1912, a Bolshevik conference in Prague expelled the Mensheviks from the Russian Social-Democratic Party. By that time, even Plekhanov had broken with Lenin and allied himself with the Mensheviks. In March, 1918, a few months after seizing power in Russia, the Bolsheviks adopted the name Communist Party. Under this name, twentieth century Marxism, despite its great conquests, continued to be threatened by splits between those who considered themselves "orthodox" and those whom they regarded as "revisionist." Thus, like all other great movements of history, communism has been unable to overcome the basic problem of diversity.

—Edward P. Keleher, updated by Richard D. King

FURTHER READING

Baron, Samuel H. *Plekhanov: The Father of Russian Marxism*. Stanford, Calif.: Stanford University Press, 1963. A scholarly study of the life and thought of the first important member of the Russian revolutionary movement to embrace Marxism.

Brovkin, Vladimir N., ed. *The Bolsheviks in Russian Society: The Revolution and the Civil Wars*. New Haven, Conn.: Yale University Press, 1997. Anthology of essays charting the history of Lenin's Bolshevik Party.

Getzler, Israel. *Martov: A Political Biography of a Russian Social Democrat*. Cambridge, England: Cambridge University Press, 1967. Examines the life and thought of a revolutionary Marxist who at one time was Lenin's closest friend but became a leading Menshevik critic of Bolshevik authoritarianism.

Keep, J. L. H. *The Rise of Social Democracy in Russia*. Oxford, England: Clarendon Press, 1963. Analyzes the background to the Bolshevik-Menshevik schism, the critical Second Party Congress, and Bolshevik-Menshevik rivalry during the 1905 revolution.

Pomper, Philip. *The Russian Revolutionary Intelligentsia*. 2d ed. Arlington Heights, Ill.: Harlan Davidson, 1993. This short history of revolutionary movements in nineteenth century Russia is a good introduction to the early development of Russian Marxism.

Service, Robert. *Lenin: A Political Life*. 3 vols. Bloomington: Indiana University Press, 1985-1995. The first volume of this three-part biography focuses on Lenin's early development as a Marxist and his decisive role in fomenting the Bolshevik-Menshevik split.

Tobias, Henry J. *The Jewish Bund in Russia: From Its Origins to 1905.* Stanford, Calif.: Stanford University Press, 1972. A history of the Jewish branch of the Social Democratic movement in Russia and its struggle for the loyalty of Jewish workers.

Wildman, Alan. *The Making of a Workers' Revolution: Russian Social Democracy, 1891-1903.* Chicago: University of Chicago Press, 1967. This scholarly study, which contains a section on the first congress of the Russian Social Democratic Labor Party, focuses primarily on the Mensheviks.

SEE ALSO: Feb., 1848: Marx and Engels Publish *The Communist Manifesto*; Feb. 22-June, 1848: Paris Revolution of 1848; 1867: Marx Publishes *Das Kapital*; 1868: Bakunin Founds the Social Democratic Alliance; Jan., 1884: Fabian Society Is Founded; Feb. 27, 1900: British Labour Party Is Formed.

RELATED ARTICLES in *Great Lives from History: The Nineteenth Century, 1801-1900:* Friedrich Engels; Karl Marx.

March 28, 1898
UNITED STATES V. WONG KIM ARK

The U.S. Supreme Court's Wong Kim Ark *decision held that children born in the United States, even to temporary sojourners, were subject to U.S. jurisdiction regardless of race or nationality. It effectively extended citizenship to any person born on U.S. soil, regardless of parentage.*

LOCALE: Washington, D.C.

CATEGORIES: Laws, acts, and legal history; government and politics; social issues and reform; civil rights and liberties

KEY FIGURES

Melville W. Fuller (1833-1910), chief justice of the United States, 1888-1910

Horace Gray (1828-1902), associate justice of the United States, 1882-1902

John Marshall Harlan (1833-1911), associate justice of the United States, 1877-1911

Wong Kim Ark (b. 1873), man born in San Francisco of Chinese parents

SUMMARY OF EVENT

After the U.S. Civil War (1861-1865), the Constitution of the United States was amended to deal with the end of slavery and the legal status of the freed slaves. Under then-existing law, notably the 1857 decision in *Dred Scott v. Sandford*, even free African Americans could not become citizens. The Thirteenth Amendment ended slavery. The Fourteenth Amendment, which was drafted to confer citizenship on the newly freed slaves and to protect their rights from infringement by state governments, begins: "All persons born or naturalized in the United States and subject to the jurisdiction thereof, are citizens of the United States and of the State wherein they reside."

The Fourteenth Amendment ended neither racial prejudice nor various racially based legal discriminations. In 1882, 1884, and 1894, Congress passed a series of laws known as the Chinese Exclusion Acts. These statutes were designed to keep persons of Chinese ancestry out of the United States. They were particularly aimed at the importation of Chinese laborers and at the "coolie" system—a form of indentured labor. The acceptance of low wages by imported Chinese immigrants angered many Americans.

Wong Kim Ark was born in San Francisco in 1873. His parents were Chinese subjects permanently domiciled in the United States. In modern terminology, they would have been called resident aliens. They had been in business in San Francisco and were neither employees nor diplomatic agents of the government of China. In 1890, they returned to China after many years in the United States. Wong Kim Ark also went to China in 1890, but he returned to the United States the same year and was readmitted to the country on the grounds that he was a U.S. citizen. In 1894, he again went to China for a temporary visit but was denied readmission to the United States on his return in August, 1895.

The federal government's position was that under the Chinese Exclusion Acts, a Chinese person born to alien parents who had not renounced his previous nationality was not "born or naturalized in the United States" within the meaning of the citizenship clause of the Fourteenth Amendment. If the government's position was correct, Wong Kim Ark was not a citizen of the United States and was not entitled to readmission to the country. Wong brought a habeas corpus action against the government in the United States District Court for the Northern District of California. That court's judgment in favor of Wong was appealed to the U.S. Supreme Court by the government.

The case was decided on March 28, 1898. Justice Horace Gray wrote the Supreme Court's opinion for a 6-2 majority. Gray's argument begins with the assumption that the citizenship clause of the Fourteenth Amendment has to be read in the context of preexisting law. The Court's opinion begins with a long review of citizenship practices and legal customs. The U.S. tradition had been to distinguish between "natural-born" and naturalized citizens. This distinction came from English common law.

In England, for hundreds of years prior to the American Revolution (1775-1783), all persons born within the king's realms except the children of diplomats and alien enemies were said to have been born under the king's protection and were natural-born subjects. This rule was applied or extended equally to the children of alien parents. Moreover, the same rule was in force in all the English colonies in North America prior to the revolution, and was continued (except with regard to slaves) under the jurisdiction of the United States when it became independent. The first American law concerning naturalization was passed in the First Congress. It and its successor acts, passed in 1802, assumed the citizenship of all free persons born within the borders of the United States. It was not until the passage of the Chinese Exclusion Acts that any U.S. law had sought to alter the rule regarding natural-born citizens.

On the European continent, however, the law of citizenship was different. Most European countries had adopted the citizenship rules of ancient Roman law. Under the Roman civil law, a child takes the nationality of his or her parents. Indeed, when *United States v. Wong Kim Ark* reached the Supreme Court, the government argued that the European practice had become the true rule of international law as it was recognized by the great majority of the countries of the world.

This was the historical and legal context for the Fourteenth Amendment's language "All persons *born* or naturalized in the United States. . ." (emphasis added). According to Justice Gray, the purpose of the Fourteenth Amendment was to extend the rule providing citizenship for natural-born persons to the freed slaves and their children. The amendment did not establish a congressional power to alter the constitutional grant of citizenship. Gray's opinion reviews many of the Court's prior opinions upholding the principle. The Chinese Exclusion Acts, passed after the passage of the Fourteenth Amendment, could not affect the amendment's meaning, according to the majority, and therefore did not affect the established rule of natural-born citizenship.

The grant of constitutional power to Congress to "establish a uniform rule of naturalization" did not validate the Chinese Exclusion Acts. Wong, as a natural-born citizen, had no need of being naturalized. The Court held that "Every person born in the United States, and subject to the jurisdiction thereof, becomes at once a citizen of the United States, and needs no naturalization." Moreover, the majority held that Congress's power of naturalization is "a power to confer citizenship, not to take it away." In other words,

---

UNITED STATES V. WONG KIM ARK

Justice Horace Gray delivered the opinion of the majority in United States v. Wong Kim Ark. *His decision was based upon the precedents set by international law, as well as statements made by U.S. senators while debating the language and meaning of the Fourteenth Amendment, who had explicitly considered the case of children born to Chinese immigrants.*

The fourteenth amendment affirms the ancient and fundamental rule of citizenship by birth within the territory, in the allegiance and under the protection of the country, including all children here born of resident aliens, with the exceptions or qualifications (as old as the rule itself) of children of foreign sovereigns or their ministers, or born on foreign public ships, or of enemies within and during a hostile occupation of part of our territory, and with the single additional exception of children of members of the Indian tribes owing direct allegiance to their several tribes. The amendment, in clear words and in manifest intent, includes the children born within the territory of the United States of all other persons, of whatever race or color, domiciled within the United States. Every citizen or subject of another country, while domiciled here, is within the allegiance and the protection, and consequently subject to the jurisdiction, of the United States. . . .

To hold that the fourteenth amendment of the constitution excludes from citizenship the children born in the United States of citizens or subjects of other countries, would be to deny citizenship to thousands of persons of English, Scotch, Irish, German, or other European parentage, who have always been considered and treated as citizens of the United States.

CHIEF JUSTICE FULLER'S DISSENT

Chief Justice Melville W. Fuller wrote the dissenting opinion in United States v. Wong Kim Ark, *excerpted below. Justice John Marshall Harlan joined the dissent. Fuller's opinion, excerpted below, was based on the fact that, at the time the case was heard, it was illegal under both U.S. and Chinese law—and according to the terms of treaties between the two powers—for a Chinese citizen to become an American citizen.*

I think it follows that the children of Chinese born in this country do not, ipso facto, become citizens of the United States unless the fourteenth amendment overrides both treaty and statute. Does it bear that construction; or, rather, is it not the proper construction that all persons born in the United States of parents permanently residing here, and susceptible of becoming citizens, and not prevented therefrom by treaty or statute, are citizens, and not otherwise? . . .

It is not to be admitted that the children of persons so situated become citizens by the accident of birth. On the contrary, I am of opinion that the president and senate by treaty, and the congress by legislation, have the power, notwithstanding the fourteenth amendment, to prescribe that all persons of a particular race, or their children, cannot become citizens, and that it results that the consent to allow such persons to come into and reside within our geographical limits does not carry with it the imposition of citizenship upon children born to them while in this country under such consent, in spite of treaty and statute.

In other words, the fourteenth amendment does not exclude from citizenship by birth children born in the United States of parents permanently located therein, and who might themselves become citizens; nor, on the other hand, does it arbitrarily make citizens of children born in the United States of parents who, according to the will of their native government and of this government, are and must remain aliens.

Chief Justice Melville W. Fuller. (Library of Congress)

Congress had the power to establish uniform rules for naturalization but could not alter the plain-language and common-law meaning of the Fourteenth Amendment's citizenship clause.

The dissenting justices saw the case differently. Chief Justice Melville Fuller wrote an extensive dissent in which Justice John Marshall Harlan joined. In their view, the common-law rule sprang from the feudal relationship between the British crown and children born within the realm. American law was not bound to follow the common-law rule, because there were differences between "citizens" and "subjects." In a republic such as the United States, citizenship was a status created by and conferred by the civil law. Because nothing in U.S. law had explicitly endorsed the common-law principle of citizenship, the Fourteenth Amendment did not have to be read so as to include it. Fuller argued that Congress is free to pass statutes that define and interpret the citizenship

clause of the Fourteenth Amendment. In the dissenters' view, then, the Chinese Exclusion Acts could constitutionally limit the reach of the phrase "born or naturalized in the United States and subject to the jurisdiction thereof." Under this interpretation, Wong Kim Ark would not have been a citizen and his exclusion would have been constitutional.

SIGNIFICANCE

The Court's decision in this case was important because it stripped the government of the power to deny the citizenship of persons born in the United States of alien parents. It essentially meant that any person born on U.S. soil, under virtually any circumstances to any parents, would be a citizen of the United States. Beyond establishing a specific limit upon the ability of Congress to pass statutes interpreting or limiting the Fourteenth Amendment, moreover, the decision had a broader implication. It strengthened the principle that Congress lacked the power to pass statutes that modified the meaning of a segment of the Constitution. Congress was bound by the language of the Constitution itself, and changes to the meaning of that language could be achieved only by amending the document.

—*Robert Jacobs*

FURTHER READING

Chan, Sucheng. *Entry Denied: Exclusion and the Chinese Community in America, 1882-1943*. Philadelphia: Temple University Press, 1991. Good discussion of the effects and technical aspects of the Chinese Exclusion Acts.

Corwin, Edward S. *The Constitution of the United States of America: Analysis and Interpretation*. Washington, D.C.: Government Printing Office, 1953. Corwin's monumental compilation of constitutional lore is especially strong on issues such as citizenship, whose fundamental rules date back to the nineteenth century.

Franklin, Frank George. *The Legislative History of Naturalization in the United States: From the Revolutionary War to 1861*. Chicago: University of Chicago Press, 1906. Discussion of naturalization and citizenship precedents of early U.S. history.

Lee, Erika. "Wong Kim Ark: Chinese American Citizens and U.S. Exclusion Laws, 1882-1943." In *The Human Tradition in California*, edited by Clark Davis and David Igler. Wilmington, Del.: Scholarly Resources, 2002. Examines the history of Chinese Americans in California and the effect of the exclusion laws upon them.

McKenzie, Roderick Duncan. *Oriental Exclusion: The Effect of American Immigration Laws, Regulations, and Judicial Decisions upon the Chinese and Japanese on the American Pacific Coast, 1885-1940*. New York: J. S. Ozer, 1971. Discusses the human aspect of the Chinese exclusion laws.

White, Sherwin. *The Roman Citizenship*. London: Oxford University Press, 1973. Complete discussion of the origin of Roman citizenship, the means of acquiring it, and its duties, responsibilities, and privileges.

SEE ALSO: May 9, 1882: Arthur Signs the Chinese Exclusion Act; Nov. 12, 1882: San Francisco's Chinese Six Companies Association Forms; Oct. 15, 1883: Civil Rights Cases; May 10, 1895: Chinese Californians Form Native Sons of the Golden State; May 18, 1896: *Plessy v. Ferguson*.

April, 1898-1903
STRATOSPHERE AND TROPOSPHERE ARE DISCOVERED

Drawing on experimental balloon measurements of atmospheric temperature versus height, Léon Teisserenc de Bort discovered that the stratosphere and troposphere are vertically layered on the basis of thermal inversion.

LOCALE: Trappes (Paris), France
CATEGORIES: Earth science; chemistry; physics; geography

KEY FIGURES
Léon Teisserenc de Bort (1855-1913), French physicist and meteorologist
Richard Assmann (1845-1918), German physicist and meteorologist

SUMMARY OF EVENT
The details of the rate of change of atmospheric temperature versus height have been of basic importance for many years in trying to determine and predict the pro-

cesses governing weather. For example, the variation of wind with height also depends upon vertical temperature variation.

Until the violent eruption of the volcano Krakatoa in the Java Sea in 1883, which produced abnormally high atmospheric concentrations of dust, implying the existence of higher-level global temperature and wind patterns, the body of air above the earth's surface was considered generally a uniform body. William Morris Davis's 1894 text, *Elementary Meteorology*, is representative of knowledge of the upper atmosphere before large-scale kite and balloon soundings. Davis simply divides the earth into geosphere (rock), hydrosphere (water), and atmosphere (air). An empirical formula for atmospheric temperature gradient was developed by Austrian meteorologist Julius Ferdinand von Hann in 1874, based on indirect atmospheric measures such as astronomical observations of the duration of twilight and of meteor burns. Davis proposed that successive isobaric (equipressure) surfaces are separated by greater and greater distances indefinitely out into space. Here, the general distribution of temperature with elevation is simply illustrated as a nearly linear decreasing function.

Balloon ascents to measure upper air temperature were first undertaken by John Jeffries and Jean-Pierre-François Blanchard in 1784 and subsequently by Jean-Baptiste Biot and Joseph-Louis Gay-Lussac in 1804, and continued in England in 1852. Factors influencing balloon performance included the excess of buoyancy forces over balloon gross weight (including human observers) and the maximum size to which the balloon's silk or India rubber envelope would expand in response to decreasing atmospheric pressure. These factors control both maximum ascent ceiling and ascent rate. The need for light gases, such as hydrogen or helium, is to keep the balloon's envelope sufficiently distended. The buoyancy force, which arises from Archimedes' principle, is equal to the air mass displaced by the balloon. As the balloon rises, the air density falls by a factor of about ten for every 6.2 miles (10 kilometers) of ascent, and the balloon's envelope expands in exact proportion to falling density.

Prior to 1890, balloon observations were, for the most part, limited to heights of only a few kilometers by human oxygen consumption, recording mainly local rather than regional or global temperature behaviors. The first attempts at global isothermal charts were published by Hann in Vienna and Alexander Buchan in Edinburgh in 1887 and 1889, respectively. To overcome the human limitation, kites were first employed by Cleveland Abbe in studying winds under a thundercloud at the Blue Hill Observatory in Massachusetts. Nevertheless, for technical reasons, the maximum altitudes attained by kites were only about 5 miles (8 kilometers).

Because of proven dangers to human life in high ascents, small free rubber balloons carrying recently developed self-recording temperature and pressure recorders were first deployed in 1893 by French aeronomist Georges Besançon and were rapidly adopted elsewhere for meteorologic observations. When atmospheric visibility is sufficiently good, larger meteorologic balloons could be followed visually by theodolites to obtain supplementary wind direction data. Theodolites are grid-mounted survey telescopes permitting measurement of height and angular motion. These various observations demonstrated that to at least about 29,500 feet (9,000 meters), temperature decreased in a fairly uniform fashion at a rate of about 1 degree Celsius per every 590-foot (180-meter) rise.

After extensive work in Europe and North Africa with the French government undertaking barometric and other weather observations, in 1897, Léon Teisserenc de Bort founded his own private aeronomic observatory at Trappes near Paris. Earlier, Teisserenc de Bort had pioneered self-recording temperature and barometric pressure sensors; the Austrian physicist Richard Assmann developed the first self-recording hygrometer to measure atmospheric humidity. Using hydrogen-filled balloons specially designed for rapid and near-vertical ascents, Teisserenc de Bort named his surveys "soundings" or "sondings," in analogy to bathymetric depth soundings by sonde-line or acoustic sound at sea. A critical factor was sufficient protection of thermometers from direct solar radiation, as well as recorders that could respond to changing temperature faster than the balloon would rise.

In April, 1898, Teisserenc de Bort used his improved apparatus to begin a long series of regular balloon soundings from Trappes, France. Among other details, he soon discovered unusual temperature records, first believed to be instrument errors, of constant or even increasing temperature conditions from the extreme upper limits of his balloon's ascents. After precluding instrument error and repeating many measurements, in 1899, he published a report indicating that temperatures at heights above which the atmospheric pressure falls below 0.1 (100 millibars) cease to decline with altitude but remain constant over a specific height interval, thereafter slowly increasing.

In his papers of 1904 in the noted French journal *Comptes rendus physique* and his own *Travaux scientifiques de l'Observatoire de météorologie de Trappes* (1909), Teisserenc de Bort gave mean temperatures versus height measured at Trappes between 1899 and 1903. Out of 581 balloon ascents, 141 attained temperature "isothermal" and "inverted" measurements at height records of 8.7 miles (14 kilometers) or more. His data showed that there is a slow temperature decrease up to about 1.2 miles (2 kilometers) above sea level. This is followed by a more rapid decrease up to about 10 kilometers. A very slow or total lack of decrease was measured between 6.8 and 8.7 miles (11-14 kilometers), with an ambient temperature of about −55 degrees Celsius. He called this the "thermal" zone or boundary.

Teisserenc de Bort's observations were almost concurrently confirmed by Assmann's independent series of ascents from Berlin. Assmann and Artur Berson, beginning in 1887, undertook a more extensive series of upper atmospheric soundings, under the aegis of the Prussian Meteorological Office and Aeronautical Section of the

German Army, and later as an independent scientific station at Lindenberg. The details of their seventy ascents between 1887 to 1889 were the first published aeronometric measurements of temperature for several locations, in 1900, and thereafter published regularly in the German journal *Das Wetter*. From a particularly long series of kite soundings from Berlin between October, 1902, and December, 1903, Assmann showed that atmospheric temperature is much more variable at altitudes of 3.5-4 miles (6-7 kilometers) than at ground level.

The effects of diurnal and seasonal changes on upper-level temperatures were also measured. Following the systematic planned simultaneous ascents from many European cities between 1895 and 1899, Assmann assembled a database of more than one thousand of his own observations, with 581 of Teisserenc de Bort, and others from England, Holland, and the Soviet Union, enabling him to compute monthly and annual temperature and wind velocity averages of many altitudes between 0 and 8.7 miles (11 kilometers) over central Europe. Assmann also argued that at about 9 miles (12 kilometers), the upper limit for cirrus clouds, temperature remains constant and later increases slowly. The atmospheric region above these heights of constant temperature was called the stratosphere, the lower region nearest the ground was called the troposphere, and the transition zone was called the tropopause. The mesosphere and thermosphere are above the stratosphere.

SIGNIFICANCE

Meteorologic sounding heights of more than 15 miles (25 kilometers) were achieved in France and Belgium between 1905 and 1907. The Fifth Conference of the International Committee on Scientific Aeronautics at Milan in 1906 saw an increasing number of measurements confirming the temperature results of Teisserenc de Bort and Assmann, notably kite ascents from 1904 to 1905 from the Soviet Union. These data established that above an altitude that geographically varied from about 11 miles (18 kilometers) from the equator to about 6.8 miles (11 kilometers) at 50 degrees north latitude to only about 3.5 miles (6 kilometers) at the poles, atmospheric temperature remained approximately constant over a certain level. (The English meteorologist W. Dines subsequently showed that the stratosphere is high and cold over high pressure and low and warm over low pressure.)

As soon as diverse independent observations had established the troposphere/tropopause/stratosphere, many efforts were made to explain the occurrence of stationary upper-level discontinuities on the basis of the rapidly developing hydrothermodynamics of Vilhelm Bjerknes, Ludwig Prandtl, and others—initially, however, with only very limited success. In 1909, W. Humphreys in the United States and F. Gold in England published what became essentially the generally accepted explanation. In both approaches, it was recognized that it is necessary to consider the thermodynamic balance between absorbed and reemitted solar radiation.

Humphreys' account is less mathematical but equivalent to Gold's account. Briefly, since the average annual temperature in the atmosphere at any location had been shown experimentally not to vary greatly, Humphreys concluded that the absorption of solar radiation is equal basically to the net outgoing reradiation by Earth (discovered previously by S. Langley), using a simple thermodynamic "black body" model. Humphreys concluded that the isothermal/tropopause zone marks the limit of vertical thermal convection and, from this, correctly deduced that the above-lying layers are warmed almost entirely by direct solar radiation (later shown to be dependent upon atmospheric ozone). The increasing temperature trend was shown later to be caused directly by the heat released during the interaction between incoming ultraviolet radiation and atmospheric ozone molecules.

Further direct and indirect studies of the stratosphere and troposphere continued by a variety of means. In studies of ground versus air waves from earthquakes by Emil Wiechert in 1904, and later during World War I, it was noted that loud noises could be heard occasionally at distances ranging from 90 miles (150 kilometers) to more than 240 miles (400 kilometers) from their source, even when observers near the source could barely hear the sounds.

Subsequent studies of the stratosphere by Earth-orbiting satellites include the mapping of the (polar) jet streams and the twenty-six-month quasi-biennial cycle. The original motivation and basis for these and other studies, however, remain the methods and results of Teisserenc de Bort and Assmann.

—Gerardo G. Tango

FURTHER READING

Anthes, Richard A., et al. *The Atmosphere*. 3d ed. Columbus, Ohio: Charles Merrill, 1981. A good general-reader text incorporating almost all meteorologic techniques and findings up to the late 1970's.

Davis, William Morris. *Elementary Meteorology*. Boston: Ginn, 1894. Representative of atmospheric science prior to the experimental results of Teisserenc de

Bort and Assmann and the dynamic meteorologic theory of Bjerknes. Widely available.

Goody, Richard M. *The Physics of the Stratosphere.* Cambridge, England: Cambridge University Press, 1954. A technical account devoted to stratospheric processes. Recommended.

Humphreys, W. J. *The Physics of the Air.* New York: Dover, 1964. Historical-technical account of upper atmospheric science.

_____. "Vertical Temperature Gradient of the Atmosphere, Especially in the Region of the Upper Inversion." *Astrophysical Journal* 29 (1909): 14-26. The first detailed study to incorporate and explain the stratosphere and tropopause in the context of physical theories of atmospheric heating and thermodynamics.

Massey, Harrie Stewart Wilson. *The Middle Atmosphere as Observed by Balloons, Rockets, and Satellites.* London: Royal Society, 1980. General descriptions of many remote sensing methods and typical self-recording instruments.

Pielou, E. C. *The Energy of Nature.* Chicago: University of Chicago Press, 2001. An exploration for all readers into the effects of natural energies upon the earth. Includes the chapters "Solar Energy and the Upper Atmosphere," "Energy in the Lower Atmosphere: The Weather Near the Ground," and "The Warmth of the Earth: Nuclear Reactions Sustain All Life." Includes illustrations.

Seinfeld, John H., and Spyros N. Pandis. *Atmospheric Chemistry and Physics: From Air Pollution to Climate Change.* New York: John Wiley & Sons, 1998. A massive textbook, with more than thirteen hundred pages and hundreds of illustrations, covering the physics and chemistry of Earth's atmosphere. The authors give special attention to, for example, aerosols, the meteorology of air pollution, and the formation and chemistry of clouds. For advanced students.

SEE ALSO: Apr. 5, 1815: Tambora Volcano Begins Violent Eruption; July, 1830: Lyell Publishes *Principles of Geology*; 1850-1865: Clausius Formulates the Second Law of Thermodynamics; Aug. 27, 1883: Krakatoa Volcano Erupts; July, 1897-July, 1904: Bjerknes Founds Scientific Weather Forecasting; 1900: Wiechert Invents the Inverted Pendulum Seismograph.

RELATED ARTICLE in *Great Lives from History: The Nineteenth Century, 1801-1900:* Joseph-Louis Gay-Lussac.

April 24-December 10, 1898

SPANISH-AMERICAN WAR

Drawn into an unwanted war prompted by Spain's inability to find a satisfactory settlement with Cuban rebels, the United States won an easy victory over Spain and found itself with a colonial empire that made it an international power.

LOCALE: Cuba; Philippines

CATEGORIES: Expansion and land acquisition; wars, uprisings, and civil unrest

KEY FIGURES

Pasqual Cervera y Topete (1839-1909), commander of Spain's fleet in the Caribbean

George Dewey (1837-1917), commander of the U.S. Asiatic Squadron

William McKinley (1843-1901), president of the United States, 1897-1901

William Randolph Hearst (1863-1951), New York newspaper publisher

William Thomas Sampson (1840-1902), commander of the U.S. Atlantic Squadron

William Rufus Shafter (1835-1906), commander of the U.S. Expeditionary Force to Cuba

Theodore Roosevelt (1858-1919), assistant secretary of the Navy and later president, 1901-1909

SUMMARY OF EVENT

Cuba became an issue in U.S. foreign policy after its people staged an unsuccessful revolution against Spain in 1895. The Spanish regarded Cuba as an integral part of their nation. To the Spanish, Cuba was "the ever faithful isle," and no Spanish government could long remain in power if it accepted the loss of Cuba without putting up a fight. A bitter war ensued, in which the Spanish controlled major cities such as Havana, while the rebels dominated the countryside. In 1896, the Spanish captain general in Cuba, Valeriano Weyler y Nicolau, announced a tough policy of reconcentration. Cuban civilians in certain parts of the island were to be herded into the Spanish-held towns, where they could no longer assist and supply the rebel armies. Thousands of women

1890's

CARIBBEAN THEATER OF THE SPANISH-AMERICAN WAR

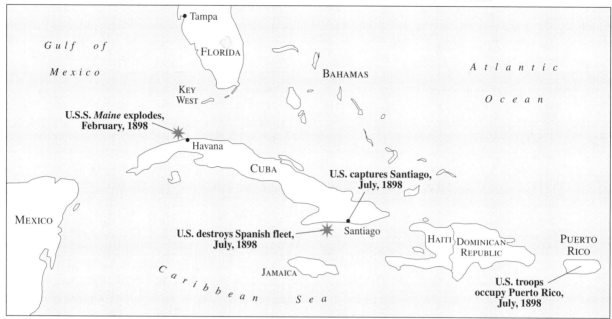

and children died of disease or malnutrition in these overcrowded camps. U.S. opinion, already sympathetic to the Cubans, was outraged. Popular newspapers in the United States published sensational stories about Cuban suffering and Spanish brutalities that fed discontent with the rule of Madrid.

President Grover Cleveland, who occupied the White House during the first two years of the Cuban rebellion, took the position that Spain deserved the chance to defeat the rebellion and resisted pressure from Congress to intervene in the conflict. By the time that Cleveland left office in March, 1897, his policy had failed to persuade the Spanish of the need to negotiate with the rebels, and he had lost the trust of the U.S. people in his foreign policy.

Cleveland's successor, President William McKinley, came into office with two expectations of the Cuban conflict. First, Spain should be allowed to suppress the rebellion, but it had only a limited time to do so. Second, any outcome of the war must

be acceptable to the Cuban rebels. The latter condition virtually ensured a conflict between the United States and Spain, because the rebels would accept nothing less

Theodore Roosevelt (on horse) leading the charge of his Rough Riders up San Juan Hill. From a photograph and painting by Frederick Remington. (P. F. Collier and Son)

than Cuban independence. McKinley played for time, hoping that the Spanish could be persuaded to leave Cuba. Meanwhile, the Spanish stalled, expecting U.S. resolve to falter.

Spanish efforts to conciliate the United States included a modification of their reconcentration policy in November, 1897, and limited autonomy for Cuba. Spain proposed to retain control over Cuba's international relations. However, these steps did not resolve the differences between the United States and Spain. Early in 1898, two events pushed the nations closer to war. In February, the Cubans published a private letter from the Spanish minister in Washington, Enrique Dupuy de Lôme, in which the diplomat made disparaging remarks about President McKinley. The letter also revealed that the Spanish were using delaying tactics. After the letter was publicly revealed, Dupuy de Lôme resigned in disgrace.

One week later, the U.S. battleship *Maine* exploded while docked in Havana harbor, and 260 American sailors were killed. Modern scientific research has concluded that the explosion was an accident caused by an internal problem on the ship. In 1898, however, many Americans believed that Spain had either blown up the ship or failed to prevent its destruction. The episode put the two countries on a collision course toward war. As diplomatic negotiations proceeded, it became apparent that Spain would not grant Cuban independence. The most it would concede was to suspend hostilities, a proposal that neither Washington nor the Cuban rebels would accept.

Meanwhile, the American public was aroused by sensational journalistic coverage of the *Maine* incident. William Randolph Hearst's *New York Journal American* fanned the flames of jingoism by claiming that a secret telegram had been discovered that laid the blame for the *Maine* explosion on Spain. Unfounded reports such as that increased public support for military action and put pressure on McKinley to declare war against Spain.

On April 11, McKinley sent a message to Congress asking for the authority to intervene. and U.S. officials informed Spain that failing to grant independence to Cuba would result in the federal government putting its resolutions into effect. Spain broke relations with the United States, a U.S. blockade of Cuba ensued, and Spain declared war on the United States on April 24. The U.S. president had resisted the popular pressure for war until it became clear that Spain would not yield. The war came about because both nations saw no way out of the diplomatic impasse other than armed conflict. In the United States, this first foreign war in a half century proved popular. Volunteers jammed army and navy recruiting offices.

1890's

1905

The first U.S. victory came on May 1, 1898, when Commodore George Dewey's U.S. Asiatic Squadron captured the entire Spanish fleet at Manila Bay in the Spanish-ruled Philippines. The navy attacked the Philippines as part of a long-standing war plan to induce the Spanish to negotiate an end to the war by threatening their valuable colony in Asia. The victory presented Washington with a new challenge of what to do with this unexpected territorial opportunity. The McKinley administration sent reinforcements to Manila and kept its options open about taking all the islands in a peace settlement.

During June and July, the main focus of military and public attention was on Cuba and the sea and land battles that occurred in the Caribbean. Initial plans for army action in Cuba called for a large-scale landing near Havana during the autumn of 1898. In June, however, the McKinley administration decided to dispatch an expeditionary force of seventeen thousand men to the southeastern Cuban coast. There, in the harbor of the city of Santiago de Cuba, Admiral Pasqual Cervera y Topete's decrepit Spanish fleet had taken refuge. The U.S. Atlantic Squadron, commanded by Admiral William Thomas Sampson, was stationed outside Santiago ready to do battle if Cervera ventured out. The revised U.S. strategy called for the capture of Santiago by land invasion, which would force the Spanish fleet to steam out to virtually certain destruction.

Near Tampa Bay in Florida, the bulk of the regular army, under the command of General William Rufus Shafter, prepared to leave for Cuba. Along with the regulars was the so-called Rough Rider volunteer regiment, of which Lieutenant Colonel Theodore Roosevelt was second in command. Shafter's landing along the coast near Santiago was accomplished late in June. Despite logistical difficulties, the U.S. forces moved forward to engage the Spanish on July 1 near Santiago at the twin battles of El Caney and San Juan Hill. Both battles were U.S. victories. Shafter's troops subsequently occupied the strategic heights above the port city. On July 3, Admiral Cervera, on orders from the government in Madrid, headed out of Santiago harbor and vainly tried to evade the U.S. fleet. By the end of the day, all Spanish ships had been sunk or beached.

Following Cervera's defeat, the end of the war came swiftly. On July 17, after lengthy negotiations, the Spanish soldiers in Santiago surrendered. Puerto Rico was occupied almost without resistance later that month. The Spanish had asked Washington to discuss an end to hostilities during July, and an armistice was declared on August 12. A commission from the United States, led by former secretary of state William R. Day, met with Spanish envoys in Paris in October to arrange peace terms. The Treaty of Paris, signed on December 10, 1898, recognized Cuban independence and ceded Puerto Rico, Guam, and the Philippines to the United States. In partial compensation for the territories, the United States paid Spain twenty million dollars.

SIGNIFICANCE

The war revealed inadequacies in the U.S. Army's ability to mobilize to meet a foreign policy crisis. The resulting outcry over shortages and inefficiencies focused the blame on Secretary of War Russell A. Alger. President McKinley appointed a

The battleship Maine *after it was raised during the early twentieth century.* (Library of Congress)

commission to probe these problems, and out of these deliberations came later military reforms. For the most part, the armed forces performed well under McKinley's leadership. Following the signing of the peace treaty, a bitter struggle over ratification took place in the United States. McKinley effectively mobilized public opinion to secure approval. The outcome of the war left the United States with an overseas empire and new world responsibilities.

The United States entered the Spanish-American War with the ostensible purpose of liberating its Cuban neighbors from European rule. It emerged from the conflict in possession of a distant Philippine empire whose inhabitants then rebelled against U.S. dominance. The war with Spain marked a significant turning point in U.S. history. Acquisition of an overseas empire made the United States a major power on the world stage. Within a few years, however, the people of the United States decided that the expansion achieved during 1898-1899 should not be extended. Disillusionment about the results of imperialism characterized historical memories of the conflict with Spain.

—Lewis L. Gould,
based on the original entry by William I. Hair

FURTHER READING

Campbell, W. Joseph. *Yellow Journalism: Puncturing the Myths, Defining the Legacies.* Praeger, 2003. Overview of the yellow journalism era, which was typified by William Randolph Hearst's sensationalist coverage of the Spanish-American War.

Cosmas, Graham A. *An Army for Empire: The United States Army in the Spanish-American War.* Columbia: University of Missouri Press, 1971. Scholarly but nonetheless highly readable account of U.S. miliary operations in the Spanish-American War.

Gould, Lewis L. *The Spanish-American War and President McKinley.* Lawrence: University Press of Kansas, 1982. Brief survey of the major developments of the war that emphasizes the extent to which McKinley's leadership produced victory for the United States.

Morgan, H. Wayne. *America's Road to Empire: The War with Spain and Overseas Expansion.* New York: John Wiley & Sons, 1965. Offers a vigorous defense of McKinley's policies in 1898; provides a clear, concise statement of the origins and consequences of the war.

Offner, John L. *An Unwanted War: The Diplomacy of the United States and Spain over Cuba, 1895-1898.* Chapel Hill: University of North Carolina Press, 1992. Makes effective use of the archives of the United States, Spain, and other nations to provide a thorough analysis of how the war came about.

Phillips, Kevin. *William McKinley.* New York: Times Books/Henry Holt, 2003. Analysis of McKinley's presidency that shows how McKinley was beginning to transform the United States into a global military power when his life was abruptly ended by an assassin.

Smith, Joseph. *The Spanish-American War: Conflict in the Caribbean and the Pacific, 1895-1902.* New York: Longman, 1994. Surveys the background, causes, and events of the war, with an emphasis on the military history of the conflict. Excellent bibliography.

Trask, David F. *The War with Spain in 1898.* New York: Macmillan, 1981. Perhaps the best one-volume treatment of the war and its military impact.

Traxel, David. *1898: The Birth of the American Century.* New York: A. A. Knopf, 1998. Exploration of the most significant events occurring in 1898. Traxel shows how the Spanish-American War and other events of that year transformed the United States from a rural, isolationist society to a major world power. The book includes an account of the Battle of Manila Bay and Dewey's heroic reception in the United States after his victory.

SEE ALSO: Oct. 10, 1868-Feb. 10, 1878: Cuba's Ten Years' War; 1880's-1890's: Rise of Yellow Journalism; 1895-1898: Hearst-Pulitzer Circulation War; Feb. 24, 1895-1898: Cuban War of Independence; Nov. 3, 1896: McKinley Is Elected President; Feb. 4, 1899-July 4, 1902: Philippine Insurrection; June, 1900-1904: Suppression of Yellow Fever.

RELATED ARTICLES in *Great Lives from History: The Nineteenth Century, 1801-1900:* Stephen Crane; George Dewey; William McKinley.

1890's

July 10-November 3, 1898
FASHODA INCIDENT PITS FRANCE VS. BRITAIN

The culmination of British and French rivalry for control of the Upper Nile, the Fashoda incident took Great Britain and France to the brink of war and changed the course of European domestic diplomacy.

LOCALE: Fashoda, Egyptian Sudan
CATEGORIES: Diplomacy and international relations; expansion and land acquisition

KEY FIGURES
ʿAbd Allāh (1846-1899), khalifa and ruler of Sudan, r. 1885-1899
Third Marquis of Salisbury (Robert Cecil; 1830-1903), British prime minister and foreign secretary, 1895-1902
Théophile Delcassé (1852-1923), French minister of foreign affairs, 1898-1905
Horatio Herbert Kitchener (1850-1916), British general who led the conquest of the Sudan
Jean-Baptiste Marchand (1863-1934), leader of the French expedition to Fashoda

SUMMARY OF EVENT
During the summer of 1897, Great Britain approached its zenith as an imperial power, and the British Empire celebrated the Diamond Jubilee of Queen Victoria's accession to the throne. Nowhere was British imperial power more apparent than in Africa, the arena where the great powers competed for colonies. The most heated imperial rivalry in Africa was between Great Britain and France over Egypt and the large, relatively isolated and desolate area known as the Sudan.

Friction had been increasing in northeastern Africa since the mid-nineteenth century. British and French business interests had combined to construct the Suez Canal and a number of Egyptian railroads, but Ismāʿīl Pasha, the khedive of Egypt, had plunged his country into hopeless debt through reckless spending on private and public projects. To get out of debt, he had sold his Suez Canal company shares to the British government in 1875, thereby focusing British interest on the future of Egypt and the canal.

Resentment in Egypt over foreign control of its affairs led to violence that provoked a British naval bombardment of the port of Alexandria and the appointment of a British consul general to supervise the activities of the new khedive, Muḥammad Tewfik, in order to protect British interests. Egypt had become a British protectorate, and by abstaining from these affairs France had been eased out of the region. The French consoled themselves by searching for other areas in Africa to control.

During the mid-1890's, Great Britain began developing a vision of a continuous strip of British-held territory, "a thin red line" on the map of Africa, stretching from Cairo in the north to the Cape of Good Hope in the south. To make this dream a reality, a gap had to be filled by annexing the area known as the Sudan, between the southern boundary of Egypt and northern Uganda. This area had fallen into the hands of Muḥammad Aḥmad, better known as the Mahdi, and his dervish followers after the defeat and death of the British general Charles George Gordon at Khartoum in 1885. Since that time, Great Britain had not seen fit to challenge the climate, the terrain, and the dervishes who followed the Mahdi's successor, ʿAbd Allāh, known as the khalifa, or caliph. British policy had been to maintain, at least temporarily, the status quo in the Sudan.

Gabriel Hanotaux, France's foreign minister from 1894 to 1898, was a militant expansionist who wanted France to annex as much territory as possible, even if it involved heated diplomacy with other European states. For example, he challenged the British over their long-standing trading rights in Tunisia, which had become a French protectorate in 1881. Hanotaux constantly exerted French claims over Morocco, although the British, Germans, and Spanish also had considerable interests there. His policies were equally aggressive in other parts of Africa and in Asia. Hanotaux's diplomacy was supported by France's equally militant minister of colonies, Théophile Delcassé, and by a host of aggressive French colonialist organizations.

France envisioned a strip of French-held territory stretching across Africa from Senegal on the Atlantic coast in the west to Somaliland on the Red Sea in the east. Still chafing over the British takeover in Egypt, the French planned to control the water supply of Egypt by seizing the headwaters of the Nile River. After a brief period of diplomatic maneuvers and intrigues, which included providing arms to the Ethiopians that enabled them to defeat Italian forces at the Battle of Adowa in 1896, the French launched the operation.

Meanwhile, in the British House of Commons the British minister of war, Sir Edward Grey, announced that any French move toward the Nile River "would be viewed as an unfriendly act," and Great Britain took immediate steps to meet such a threat. Sir Horatio Herbert Kitchener, then the chief commander of the Egyptian army, was provided with a strong Anglo-Egyptian force, and he began the reconquest of the Sudan by moving up the Nile River. At the same time a very small French force of Senegalese soldiers and French officers under Captain Jean-Baptiste Marchand began to move eastward from Brazzaville in the French Congo. Both sides were racing to a derelict fortress at Fashoda, a position of strategic importance for controlling the headwaters of the Nile.

After an epic journey, which included transporting all the parts of a steamboat across the wilderness of central Africa, Marchand arrived at Fashoda on July 10, 1898. Two months later, after defeating the dervishes, Kitchener arrived with five gunboats and a superior force. Marchand expected reinforcements to come from the Red Sea coast, but they did not materialize. The French had won the race to Fashoda, but they were outgunned. Observing correct military etiquette, Marchand and Kitchener drank whiskey and sodas together and decided to fly their nations' flags over different parts of the fortress while awaiting orders from their governments.

The Fashoda confrontation brought Great Britain and France to the brink of war. Public opinion in Europe, inflamed by irresponsible reporting in the press, demanded a decision by force of arms. Théophile Delcassé, who had recently been appointed French minister of foreign affairs, wisely realized that the French position at Fashoda was hopeless. In addition to Kitchener's superiority in troop strength on the spot was Britain's overwhelming naval superiority in the Mediterranean. For France, a military confrontation in that part of Africa was not only undesirable but also potentially catastrophic. Even more significant, the French government was preparing for a dangerous confrontation with Germany. When the time came for a show of force against Germany, France wanted to count on support from Britain. Under unrelenting pressure from the British government led by Lord Salisbury, who was both prime minister and foreign secretary,

the French gave ground and on November 3, 1898, ordered Marchand to withdraw from Fashoda.

Salisbury, who had prepared for the clash at Fashoda since 1897, sincerely believed that any confrontation between France and Britain could only benefit Imperial Germany. Since the 1870's, Salisbury had come to distrust the national and international goals of Germany, fearing that Germany, if not checked, might emerge as the dominant power on the Continent. In the long run, such a development would be a serious blow to British policies. Salisbury also understood that if Britain were to humiliate France, the possibilities of ever achieving a Franco-British rapprochement would be almost nonexistent.

With that in mind, as early as 1897, Salisbury envisioned making France understand that Britain would assist it in obtaining Morocco, if the question of the Nile and Sudan were resolved in Britain's favor. France could receive some minor compensations in the short run, but the Nile question, in the long run, would have to be negotiated with greater colonial questions in mind. French claims were not settled until the following March, when France was obliged to renounce all territory along the Nile River in return for comparatively worthless districts in the Sahara.

Editorial cartoon by Francis Carruthers Gould (1844-1925) commenting on the developing Fashoda crisis. The caption has Captain Jean-Baptiste Marchand saying to the leader of the Anglo-Egyptian expedition, "Do hurry up with those negotiations— it's very uncomfortable up here."

SIGNIFICANCE

Marchand was hailed as a mighty hero upon his return to France, and Kitchener rose to the highest military post in Britain. Beyond mortal glories and reputation, however, was the salient fact that Britain and France would not go to war over Fashoda. What began as a dangerous confrontation on the Nile would end up being an important part of the process bringing Britain and France together, and six years later the two nations would sign the historic Entente Cordiale in London. When France finally went to war against Germany in 1914, it did so as Britain's ally.

—*Jack H. Greising, updated by James J. Cooke*

FURTHER READING

Andrew, Christopher. *Théophile Delcassé and the Making of the Entente Cordiale*. New York: St. Martin's Press, 1968. Best and most detailed work on Delcassé, who was a militant expansionist and who, as foreign minister, had to deal with the Fashoda crisis and its aftermath.

Bates, Darrell. *The Fashoda Incident of 1898: Encounter on the Nile*. New York: Oxford University Press, 1984. Comprehensive scholarly work that covers all aspects of the Fashoda crisis.

Brown, Roger T. *Fashoda Reconsidered*. Baltimore: Johns Hopkins University Press, 1969. Reevaluation of the Fashoda incident that examines its impact on European expansionism and diplomacy.

Lewis, David L. *The Race to Fashoda*. New York: Weidenfeld & Nicolson, 1987. Engaging study of the motivations behind the interest of the great powers in Fashoda and the race to control the Upper Nile.

Neillands, Robin. *The Dervish Wars: Gordon and Kitchener in the Sudan, 1880-1898*. London: John Murray, 1996. Study of British imperial interests in the Sudan that should be of interest to both students and scholars of the subject.

Sanderson, George N. *England, Europe, and the Upper Nile, 1882-1899*. Edinburgh: Edinburgh University Press, 1965. Classic overview of British imperialism in the Upper Nile that places the Fashoda incident in a broad historical context.

Steele, David. *Lord Salisbury: A Political Biography*. London: LCL Press, 1999. Reappraisal of Salisbury's political career that focuses on both his domestic and foreign policies.

SEE ALSO: Nov. 17, 1869: Suez Canal Opens; Mar. 13, 1884-Jan. 26, 1885: Siege of Khartoum; Nov. 15, 1884-Feb. 26, 1885: Berlin Conference Lays Groundwork for the Partition of Africa; Nov., 1889-Jan., 1894: Dahomey-French Wars; Mar., 1896-Nov., 1899: Sudanese War; Mar. 1, 1896: Ethiopia Repels Italian Invasion; May 18-July, 1899: First Hague Peace Conference.

RELATED ARTICLES in *Great Lives from History: The Nineteenth Century, 1801-1900:* Charles George Gordon; The Mahdi; Menelik II; Third Marquis of Salisbury.

October 14, 1898
MOSCOW ART THEATER IS FOUNDED

The founding of the Moscow Art Theater marked a watershed in Russian theater. Rejecting artificiality and stereotype, the founders sought artistic truth in production and repertoire, reaching a new height in naturalism and realism with the plays of Anton Chekhov and the ensemble acting of the company.

ALSO KNOWN AS: Moscow Academic Art Theatre
LOCALE: Moscow, Russia
CATEGORY: Theater

KEY FIGURES

Konstantin Stanislavsky (1863-1938), actor, producer, and founder and director of the Moscow Art Theater
Vladimir Nemirovich-Danchenko (1858-1943), producer, playwright, and founder and director of the theater
Anton Chekhov (1860-1904), Russian playwright
Savva Morozov (1862-1905), merchant, donor, and codirector of the theater

SUMMARY OF EVENT

On June 21, 1897, Konstantin Stanislavsky, a member of an affluent merchant family, and Vladimir Nemirovich-Danchenko, an aristocrat and small landowner, met in the Slaviansky Bazaar restaurant in Moscow. They talked for eighteen hours about the state of Russian theater, adjourning to Stanislavsky's country house in Liubimovka for breakfast. The result of their conversation became the foundation of the Moscow Art Theater.

As a young businessman, Stanislavsky, whose childhood had been filled with performances in his family's house, divided his time between his office and acting in amateur companies. Chairman of the Society of Arts and Letters, he assembled a company of amateurs and professional actors and, between 1888 and 1896, acted in and directed a great range of plays; but he envisioned a more organized theatrical enterprise.

Educated at Moscow University, Nemirovich-Danchenko was a prize-winning dramatist (his play *The Worth of Life* was awarded the Griboyedov prize in 1896), a drama critic, and a teacher of acting at the Philharmonic Dramatic School. Like many of the intelligentsia, he was dissatisfied with Russian theater. No formal theater existed in Russia until 1672, when Czar Alexis commissioned two Germans to produce plays in his palace. During the next two centuries, imperial theaters were established in St. Petersburg and Moscow, subsidized and controlled by the court, a monopoly that existed until 1882.

Private theaters also existed, as landowners and aristocrats conscripted serfs and trained them to be actors. With the emancipation of 1861, many former serfs migrated to the cities to work in factories and industry, where they formed amateur dramatic circles. However, the visit of the German Meiningen Players in 1885 astonished audiences with their realistic attention to the minutiae of life, as well as revealing the shortcomings of Russian enterprises.

Stanislavsky and Nemirovich-Danchenko, each of whom had gained more than decade of theatrical experience, felt that reforms were necessary in the Russian theater. They deplored the lack of artistry and accuracy in scenic design and costume, the lack of discipline in acting companies, and the general behavior of audiences. In their marathon conversation, they had agreed to create a theater that would be an educational institution for both actors and audiences and that certain stage conventions of the eighteenth century, such as stereotyped intonations and gestures, false pathos, and declamation, would be eliminated.

Furthermore, they agreed to assemble a pool of actors, with no stars, who would be guided by a director. Finally, they agreed upon an equal division of responsibility: Nemirovich-Danchenko for the literary content, Stanislavsky for the production form, with each holding veto power. One fundamental disagreement emerged in later years: Nemirovich-Danchenko felt that the production should serve the playwright; Stanislavsky felt that all aspects of the production—text, setting, costumes, props, actors—contributed equally to the totality of the work of art. Financing such an organization would be a problem, but after months of unsuccessful fund-raising, the producers enlisted Savva Morozov, a wealthy Russian industrialist who became a major investor and later a shareholder in the theater.

The company, which included fourteen actors from Stanislavsky's Society of Arts and Letters and twelve from Nemirovich-Danchenko's Philharmonic Drama School, began rehearsals of three plays in June, 1898. Because the Hermitage Theater was unavailable that summer, they secured a barn in Pushkino, outside Moscow, where they lived as a community, bound by an artistic and ideological unity, as only the young, dedicated, and enthusiastic can be. The choice for the opening was a play by Aleksey K. Tolstoi (1817-1875), *Tsar Fyodor Ivanovitch*, a romantic, historical play that idealized sixteenth century Russia and had been banned by censors for thirty years.

The company began with a reading of the play, and followed with long discussions and analyses. All production elements—visual, musical, and verbal—were to merge into an organic whole, surrounded by a wealth of naturalistic detail. Perhaps influenced by the Meiningen Company, members of the Moscow Art Theater journeyed to towns, fairs, and monasteries to seek out authentic objects from the sixteenth century.

On October 14, 1898, *Tsar Fyodor Ivanovitch* opened, and it astounded the audience. The visual aspects—the Archangel's Cathedral, the czar's apartments in the Kremlin, the processions of dignitaries, the costumes of the noblemen—all presented an authentic picture of sixteenth century Russia. Less noticeable to the public but no less innovative was simple and true-to-life acting. This naturalistic approach to production was revolutionary in the Russian theater. Although the reviews were not totally positive, the public embraced the Moscow Art Theater enthusiastically and *Tsar Fyodor Ivanovitch* was a success, both artistically and financially. Not so the other plays of the first season: *The Merchant of Venice, Antigone, La Locandiera, Twelfth Night,* and *The Sunken Bell* were critical and financial failures.

The last play of the season was Anton Chekhov's *The Seagull*. Chekhov, successful as a short-story writer, had mild success with his play *Ivanov*, but the first production of *The Seagull* at the Alexandrinsky Theater in St. Petersburg had been a miserable failure, and he vowed never to write another play. Nemirovich-Danchenko, however, liked *The Seagull*, and although Stanislavsky

1890's

Playwright Anton Chekhov. (Library of Congress)

strongly disagreed, Nemirovich-Danchenko persuaded Chekhov to release the play to the Moscow Art Theater and included it in its 1898-1899 repertoire.

The Moscow Art Theater was in a financial crisis; its continued existence depended upon *The Seagull*'s success. The opening on December 29, 1898, was a tense one for the entire company. The play's emphasis upon trivial but significant details, the importance of subtext, and the lack of both a hero and a linear plot demanded a new theatrical language, but the theater's company, trained in realism, rose to the challenge. Even before the curtain had closed, the audience was in a celebratory frenzy. A new era had begun in the Russian theater.

SIGNIFICANCE

Chekhov's three other plays—*Uncle Vanya, The Three Sisters*, and *The Cherry Orchard*—were produced by the Moscow Art Theater in succeeding seasons. He became identified with the theater, and the theater adopted the seagull for its logo. During the decades that followed its founding, the theater had its successes and failures, while Stanislavsky became increasingly involved with the process of acting. The Stanislavsky method, which contin-

ued to evolve into the 1930's, sought to provide the actor with conscious means to evoke the creative unconscious. Performing a physical action truthfully was a means to plumb the psychological truth of the moment, and terms such as "subtext," "given circumstances," "super-objective," and "the magic if" entered the language of actor training.

The theater altered production values throughout Europe and, after its phenomenal 1920's tour, influenced production values in the United States, particularly with its ensemble acting. The Stanislavsky method, available in his books *An Actor Prepares*, *Building a Character*, and *Creating a Role*, provided the basis for actor training in the Western world. His successors, Richard Boleslavsky, Michael Chekhov, Lee Strasberg, and Paula Strasberg, the actors of the Group Theater of the 1930's, and their descendants in academic institutions continue to train actors using basic principles and exercises.

—*Joyce E. Henry*

FURTHER READING

Benedetti, Jean. "Stanislavsky and the Moscow Art Theatre 1887-1938." In *A History of Russian Theatre*, edited by Robert Leach and Victor Borovsky. New York: Cambridge University Press, 1999. A concise description of the relationship of Nemirovich-Danchenko and Stanislavsky. Includes photographs.

Genard, Gary. "The Moscow Art Theatre's 1923 Season in Boston: A Visit from on High?" *Theatre History Studies* 16 (1996): 15-43. Includes Stanislavsky's impressions of the United States and quotations from American reviews of the Moscow Art Theater's productions.

Nemirovich-Danchenko, Vladimir. *My Life in the Russian Theatre*. Translated by John Cournos. New York: Theatre Arts Books, 1968. An autobiographical, anecdotal account of Nemirovich-Danchenko's relationships with Chekhov, Stanislavsky, Maxim Gorky, Leo Tolstoy, and the Moscow Art Theater.

Slonim, Marc. *Russian Theater from the Empire to the Soviets*. Cleveland: World Publishing, 1961. A thorough account of the beginnings, evolution, and eventual decline of the Moscow Art Theater.

Stanislavski, Konstantin. *An Actor Prepares*. Translated by Elizabeth Reynolds Hapgood. Reprint. New York: Theatre Arts Books, 1989. Written as the diary of an acting student learning the first exercises of the Stanislavsky method.

_____. *Building a Character*. Translated by Elizabeth Reynolds Hapgood. Reprint. New York: Theatre Arts

Books, 1989. Describes external ways to achieve a physical characterization.

_____. *Creating a Role*. Translated by Elizabeth Reynolds Hapbood. Reprint. New York: Theatre Arts Books, 1989. Completes the trilogy and relates the elements of the system to specific plays and roles.

_____. *My Life in Art*. Translated by J. J. Robbins. New York: Theatre Arts Books, 1948. An autobiography describing the beginnings of the Stanislavski system. Lists productions of the Moscow Art Theater from 1898 to 1921.

Swift, E. Anthony. *Popular Theater and Society in Tsarist Russia*. Berkeley: University of California Press, 2002. Locates the Moscow Art Theater within the context of Russian entertainment. Includes photographs.

SEE ALSO: c. 1801-1850: Professional Theaters Spread Throughout America; 1850's-1880's: Rise of Burlesque and Vaudeville; 1878-1899: Irving Manages London's Lyceum Theatre; 1879: *A Doll's House* Introduces Modern Realistic Drama; Oct. 10, 1881: London's Savoy Theatre Opens.

RELATED ARTICLES in *Great Lives from History: The Nineteenth Century, 1801-1900:* Anton Chekhov; Henrik Ibsen; Henry Irving; William Charles Macready.

1899
HILBERT PUBLISHES *THE FOUNDATIONS OF GEOMETRY*

David Hilbert's The Foundations of Geometry *established the basic axiomatic-formalist approach to systematizing mathematics, initiated by compactly deriving a formal axiomatic model for Euclid's geometry.*

LOCALE: Göttingen, Germany
CATEGORY: Mathematics

KEY FIGURES
David Hilbert (1862-1943), German mathematician and logician
Felix Klein (1849-1925), German mathematician and educator
Moritz Pasch (1843-1930), German mathematician
Giuseppe Peano (1858-1932), Italian mathematician and logician

SUMMARY OF EVENT
The modern hypothetico-deductive method in mathematics and the concurrent drive toward abstraction, formalization, and establishing universally applicable foundations may be traced to two principal and near-contemporary sources. One was the development of diverse non-Euclidean geometries and the "Erlanger Programme" efforts at their reconciliation. The other was the group of paradoxes in formal logic and set theory that followed from the invention of quantification theory by Gottlob Frege and the axiomatization of arithmetic by Richard Dedekind and Giuseppe Peano. Carl Friedrich Gauss, Nikolay Ivanovich Lobatchevsky, and János Bolyai in the first three decades of the nineteenth century developed alternate non-Euclidean geometries following the realization that logical negation of Euclid's parallel postulate need not lead to contradiction. Subsequently, they and others found that although the theorems resulting from the new geometric axioms were at odds with observational results of everyday experience, or Immanuel Kant's intuitions, none of the expected logical contradictions appeared in these new geometries.

During the late 1860's, new attention was drawn to non-Euclidean geometry by publications of Hermann von Helmholtz and Ernesto Beltrami. In 1870, Felix Klein discovered a more general model or interpretation of non-Euclidean geometries in the 1859 work of Alexander Cayley, by means of which Klein was able to identify systematically all the primitive objects and relations of the new geometries with corresponding primitives in Euclidean geometry. In 1872, Klein published an important paper, *Vergleichende Betrachtungen über neuere geometrische Forschungen* (equivalency considerations of recent geometric research), which expounded his so-called Erlanger Programme, strongly influencing several generations of mathematicians. This program for the "algorithmic systematization" of geometry and other areas of mathematics expounded the thesis that diverse non-Euclidean geometries could be unified and classifiably related by reconsidering geometry as the more general study of the particular "forms," or formal algebraic properties of spatial configurations of a "manifold" that are left unchanged (invariant) by an underlying group of

HILBERT'S AXIOMS OF GEOMETRY

Geometry, like arithmetic, requires for its logical development only a small number of simple, fundamental principles. These fundamental principles are called the axioms of geometry. The choice of the axioms and the investigation of their relations to one another is a problem which, since the time of Euclid, has been discussed in numerous excellent memoirs to be found in the mathematical literature. This problem is tantamount to the logical analysis of our intuition of space.

The following investigation is a new attempt to choose for geometry a *simple* and *complete* set of *independent* axioms and to deduce from these the most important geometrical theorems in such a manner as to bring out as clearly as possible the significance of the different groups of axioms and the scope of the conclusions to be derived from the individual axioms.

Source: David Hilbert, *The Foundations of Geometry* (1899), Introduction.

transformations (such as rotation, translative motion, and the like).

The new group-theoretical viewpoint of Klein, varyingly adopted by Sophus Lie, Henri Poincaré, Friedrich Schur, Eli Cartan, and others, was subsequently applied to their work on the theory of equations, automorphic functions, and complex function theory, all considered by Klein as "higher geometry." This liberal and novel use of the term "geometry" reflected not only disdain for ancient Euclidean axiomatics employing verbal definitions but also broader visions of the group-theoretic concept as a unifying principle for all mathematics. This view found even greater cultivation in Klein's later work at the University of Göttingen during the 1890's.

Concurrent and partially linked to the Erlanger Programme was reorganization of Euclidean projective geometry by the German mathematician Moritz Pasch in 1882. In the light of the variety of non-Euclidean geometries and the new symbolic logic, concurrent with but independent of Giuseppe Peano, Pasch underscored the distinctions between "explicit" and "implicit" definitions in geometry. An explicit definition expresses a new term by means of terms already accepted in the technical vocabulary at hand. By contrast, implicit definitions broadly define a new term from the total context in which it occurs, recognizing that it is logically impossible to define all terms explicitly without infinite regress or vicious circularity.

Whereas Euclid attempted explicit definitions for all his basic terms such as "point," "line," and "plane," Pasch accepted these terms as primitive or "nuclearly ir-

reducible" implicit definitions. Although the origin of these nuclear propositions in geometry might be based directly on assertions of physical or psychological origins, Pasch emphasized that these propositions, insofar as they are stated and used in mathematics, are stated totally without any regard to extra-geometrical aspects. Following Pasch, Italian mathematician Peano in 1889 gave a new and rigorous reinterpretation of Euclidean geometry using his new symbolic logic. Like Pasch, Peano based his treatment on specific primitive terms and their relations to the intuitive notion of "betweenness." Effectively translating Pasch's treatise into more compact symbolic notation, Peano's geometry remained a purely formal calculus of relations between variables, which remained without any ready applications or continuations by other mathematicians.

As a student at Königsberg between 1884 and 1890, and later as a professor at Halle University in 1891, David Hilbert was exposed to the theory of invariants and notably a wide variety of abstract formalistic approaches to the new axiomatizations of (non-) Euclidean geometry. Some of Hilbert's earliest university lectures, between 1889 and 1891, concerned algebraic and projective geometry. In the fall of 1891, Hilbert attended a lecture by German mathematician Hermann Wiener, where he first learned about the more general validity and scope of the axiomatic method. According to Constance Reid's biography of Hilbert, as early as 1894 in his summer lectures on the foundations of geometry, Hilbert intended to produce the purest possible algebraic system of exact axiomatic non-Euclidean geometry, with Euclid's geometry as a special case.

After extensive studies at the University of Göttingen of number theory and algebra, Hilbert was reinspired to continue his axiomatic foundations of geometry in early 1898, as noted through communications with Schur and Klein. In the summer of 1898, Hilbert gave a lecture series on elements of Euclidean geometry. Hilbert tried not only to synthesize more effectively other efforts to reorganize geometry axiomatically but also to reverse partially the trends toward purely abstract symbolization in geometry, by returning to Euclid's points, lines, and planes and the basic relations of incidence, order, and congruence. Yet, instead of considering only Euclidean geometry, Hilbert began his lectures by explaining that the specific content of Euclid's definitions, interpretation of which had proven so difficult in the case of non-Euclidean geometries, was irrelevant for mathematics and not for the purposes of philosophy, psychology, or physics.

For Hilbert, proper definitional meanings or interpretations of geometrical entities emerge only via their interconnections with whatever basic axioms are selected to define a given system of geometry. As Hilbert and others emphasized, all meanings in geometry are implicit and context-dependent. The "objects" are not to be determined a priori by an individual's psychological or historical perceptions of geometrical shapes in the real world. Hilbert explicitly states that the intuitive basis of fundamental geometrical concepts is mathematically insignificant and that their interconnections come into consideration only through the axioms. In his lectures, Hilbert subsequently proposed to set up on this foundation a simple and (unlike Euclid) complete set of independent axioms, by means of which it would be deductively possible to prove systematically all the long-held theorems of Euclid's geometry, and by implication to do the same for any other non-Euclidean geometry. By employing an algebra utilizing a minimum of new abstract symbols and by keeping his examples in Euclid's axioms, Hilbert was able to formulate and present his (non-Archimidean) conception of the new axiomatic method more clearly and convincingly to a wider audience than did his predecessors.

In-depth analyses of Hilbert's published lecture notes, in *Grundlagen der Geometrie* (1899; *The Foundations of Geometry*, 1902), have been given by many authors. A number of key themes and methodological conclusions common throughout Hilbert's later efforts can be identified readily from Hilbert's work. For the axiomatic reconstruction of any mathematical theory, Hilbert asserted three main requirements to be met by the system of axioms: algebraic independence, set-theoretic completeness, and logical consistency. The requirement of independence asserts that it must be possible to prove any one of the axioms from any others alone or in combination. Hilbert called a geometrical system of axioms complete if it suffices for the verification of all geometric theorems therein. The specific problematics surrounding the completeness requirement are related directly to the subsequent work by Kurt Gödel and Alan Mathison Turing in foundational studies, as well as A. N. Kolmorgorov's axiomatization of Andrey Andreyevich Markov's probability theory.

For Hilbert, the consistency of an axiomatic system

like geometry is directly derivable from that of naïve arithmetic. As well known since René Descartes, analytical geometry simply assigns pairs of real number spatial coordinates to points in plane geometry, with two- and three-variable linear equations defining lines and planes. In 1900, Hilbert stated, as a more general methodological conclusion of his axiomatization of geometry, that it would be possible ultimately to prove the consistency of, for example, Georg Cantor's continuum hypothesis, subsequent arithmetic axioms, and those of mathematical physics, by establishing the correctness of the solutions through a finite number of steps, based on a finite number of hypotheses that must be exactly formulated. A formal axiomatic system is construed not only as a system of specific statements about a given subject matter but also as a system of general conditions for what has been called a general "relational structure," such that the infinite number of formulas in mathematics can be defined completely and consistently by a finite number of formal axioms. Further application of such relational structures to a specific domain of natural science is thus taken to be made by means of a further intuitive or other interpretation of the formal objects and relations of the axioms.

SIGNIFICANCE

Within months of its original German publication, *The Foundations of Geometry* was translated into French, Italian, and English, with a number of important shorter and longer effects on the reformulation and pedagogy of geometry and number theory, which Hilbert next sought to axiomatize. Hilbert and others later showed that other geometries of higher than three dimensions, as well as several other areas of mathematics, were both consistent and complete in Hilbert's sense. Notwithstanding the ingenuity, clarity, and brevity of his system, Hilbert received a number of criticisms, for example, that his axioms were semantically empty denatured symbols dealing with totally abstract things in a rarefied formal system to which no known kind of certain reality or truth could apparently be attached.

A related question was in what sense the logical (nongeometric-specific) meanings of key terms such as "and," "is," "not," and "when" are to be defined. As a response, after a decade of mainly applications-oriented developments in mathematical physics, over the next two decades, Hilbert and his students redoubled further development of his Formalist program by inquiring directly into the logical and philosophical structure of the new foundations. Hilbert subdivided mathematics into three levels: Level 1 is ordinary operational mathematics

1890's

considered as mathematics; level 2 is a system of formal symbols employed by level 1, and defined by level 3, which is an informal meta-mathematical theory about level 2.

An equally serious and longer-lasting criticism of Hilbert's program, by L. E. J. Brouwer and others, was that the question of the absolute consistency of arithmetical axioms employed in Hilbert's relatively consistent foundations of geometry was left unanswered. Under the impact of the antinomies in Cantor's, Bertrand Russell's, and Frege's systems, several critics demonstrated how far, despite all claims, mathematics actually went beyond levels 1 and 2 meaning, expunged formal axioms purportedly divorced from linguistic and psychologistic considerations of evidence or truth. Although the results of Gödel and others suggest that Hilbert's program may never be carried out fully, the practical advantages of Hilbert's abstract approach to mathematics were adopted by numerous physicists as well as mathematicians through his publication *Methoden der mathematischen Physik* (1931-1937; *Methods of Mathematical Physics*, 1953, with Richard Courant).

—*Gerardo G. Tango*

FURTHER READING

Blanché, Robert. *Axiomatics*. Translated by G. B. Kleene. London: Routledge & Kegan Paul, 1962. One of the most cited texts embodying, as well as describing, Hilbert's axiomatic method as comparatively embodied by Euclid, Hilbert, and others.

Hilbert, David, and S. Cohn-Vossen. *Geometry and the Imagination*. Translated by P. Nemenyi. New York: Chelsea House, 1952. Discusses methodological ideas in a popular presentation.

Hilbert, David, and Leo Unger. *The Foundations of Geometry*. 2d ed. La Salle, Ill.: Open Court, 1971. The high technical level and brevity of Hilbert's book makes most of its discussion inaccessible to all but those with graduate-level background in abstract algebra and geometry. Primarily of historical interest.

Mlodinow, Leonard. *Euclid's Window: The Story of Geometry from Parallel Lines to Hyperspace*. New York: Free Press, 2001. Details the development of geometry and Hilbert's contribution.

Poincaré, Henri. *The Foundations of Science*. Translated by George B. Halsted. Lancaster, Pa.: Science Press, 1946. Although written somewhat at odds with Hilbert's *Foundations* (cited above), Poincaré gives an intuition-based introduction to non-Euclidean geometries as well as some of the background to the debates between the formalist (Hilbert), logicist (Russell), and intuitionist (Brouwer) camps.

Reid, Constance. *Hilbert*. New York: Springer-Verlag, 1970. The most informative and readily obtainable English-language account of Hilbert's education, developments, debates, and publications. Discusses Hilbert's controversies with Frege on Hilbert's semantic relativism, as well as an expert summary of Hilbert's main contributions by his onetime student, Hermann Weyl.

Wilder, Raymond L. *The Foundations of Mathematics*. 2d ed. New York: J. Wiley, 1965. An extensive and accessible treatment. Contains a comprehensive bibliography.

SEE ALSO: 1819-1833: Babbage Designs a Mechanical Calculator; 1847: Boole Publishes *The Mathematical Analysis of Logic*; July, 1897-July, 1904: Bjerknes Founds Scientific Weather Forecasting; 1900: Lebesgue Develops New Integration Theory.

RELATED ARTICLES in *Great Lives from History: The Nineteenth Century, 1801-1900:* Gottlob Frege; Carl Friedrich Gauss; Hermann von Helmholtz; Nikolay Ivanovich Lobatchevsky.

1899
JOPLIN POPULARIZES RAGTIME MUSIC AND DANCE

Scott Joplin's ragtime composition "Maple Leaf Rag,"
the first song to sell more than one million copies of
sheet music in the United States, ignited a musical and
dance craze that swept the country. Ragtime, the first
truly American form of music, greatly influenced the
development of jazz.

LOCALE: United States
CATEGORIES: Music; dance

KEY FIGURES
Scott Joplin (1868-1917), influential composer of
    classic piano rags
James Scott (1886-1938), prominent composer of
    technically difficult rags
John Stark (1841-1927), music publisher

SUMMARY OF EVENT
In 1899, the tiny midwestern publishing company John
Stark & Son published a piece of piano music entitled
"Maple Leaf Rag" by a little-known African American
pianist and composer named Scott Joplin. The irresist-
ible instrumental composition quickly became a national
success and ushered in a ragtime craze that swept the
United States in the early years of the twentieth century.
Copies of the sheet music for rags and ragtime songs,
written by scores of composers, both black and white,
were sold by the thousands.

The most immediately distinctive feature of ragtime
music is its bouncy, syncopated rhythm. The pulse and
bounce of ragtime is achieved by a balancing of rhythms
between the pianist's left and right hands. The steady,
even rhythms played by the left hand provide the basis
for the syncopated melodies and counter-rhythms supplied by the right hand. ("Syncopated" refers to rhythms
that accent the offbeats, rather than the regular beats that
are normally accented.)

In ragtime's heyday, the music was played everywhere—from honky-tonks and clubs to middle-class
parlors. In the motion-picture theaters that were spring-
ing up in the early years of the twentieth century, ragtime
piano players provided live accompaniment for many silent films. Ragtime was the first music of African American derivation that crossed over to reach a wide white audience (discounting the clichéd, bastardized music used
in minstrel shows), and it did so at a time of deeply entrenched discrimination and segregation.

Ragtime grew out of African American folk music,

with its emphasis on lively, syncopated rhythms that
urged listeners to dance. Ragtime could have evolved
only in the United States, as in many ways it is actually a
combination of African musical traditions (as passed on
and adapted by generations of African slaves in the
American South) and European musical forms such as
the march. There is a significant difference, however, between rags and earlier African American musical forms:
Rags were written down in standard European-style musical notation.

"Maple Leaf Rag" was not the first rag ever written or
published, and Joplin was not the first ragtime composer.
Different sources date the beginnings of ragtime any-
where from the 1840's to the 1890's. By the 1890's, there
were a number of African American piano players in cities and towns along the Mississippi River who were
playing in a style that was becoming known as "rag" or
"rag time" music. By 1895 or 1896, music had been published that was ragtime in nature, if not in name. "Mississippi Rag," a composition by white Chicago bandleader
William Krell that was published in 1897, is often cited
as the first published rag. "Harlem Rag," by black pianist
Tom Turpin, was published later that year. It was the
success of Joplin's "Maple Leaf Rag," however, that
launched the ragtime craze nationally.

Born in 1868, Joplin moved to St. Louis during the
mid-1880's, before he was twenty years old. He was already an accomplished pianist. He moved to Chicago in
1893 and to Sedalia, Missouri, a few years later. This
move, made because Sedalia's large red-light district
could provide employment for a black pianist, turned out
to be propitious. In Sedalia were both a new college for
African Americans and a white music publisher named
John Stark. The George R. Smith College for Negroes
(which merged with Philander Smith College in Little
Rock, Arkansas, in 1933) gave Joplin the chance to study
music theory and notation. Then, in the summer of 1899,
Stark heard Joplin performing in the Maple Leaf Club,
for which the most famous of all piano rags was named.
Stark was impressed, and he agreed to publish "Maple
Leaf Rag"—two other publishers had turned it down—
and signed Joplin to a five-year contract. The huge success of "Maple Leaf Rag" brought Joplin fame and, if not
riches, at least a measure of financial security.

The song's success shifted the ragtime phenomenon
into high gear. Joplin was one of the most prolific composers of instrumental piano rags, writing about thirty

Sheet music for one of Scott Joplin's popular ragtime songs—the first song to sell more than one million sheets. (Hulton Archive/Getty Images)

himself and another six or seven in collaboration with others. Among the many Joplin rags that appeared in the first years of the twentieth century were "Peacherine Rag" (1901), "The Entertainer" (1902), and "Palm Leaf Rag: A Slow Drag" (1903). Joplin was a particularly influential ragtime figure both because his sheet music sold so many copies and because his work was admired by other ragtime musicians and composers.

Other notable composers of piano rags included James Scott, Joseph Lamb, Tom Turpin, and Scott Hayden (a Joplin protégé). Turpin's "Harlem Rag" and "St. Louis Rag" and Scott's "Frog Legs Rag" and "Hilarity Rag" became standards in the ragtime repertoire. Scott, like Joplin, started young; he had published two rags by the time he was seventeen. Scott's rags are particularly difficult to play, and his music has been called more flamboyant than those of Joplin. Lamb, a white devotee of Joplin's style, is sometimes considered the third great composer of classic rags (alongside Joplin and Scott). There were also a number of women ragtime composers;

May Aufderheide's "Dusty Rag," from 1908, was one of the most popular rags written by a woman.

A distinction should be made among "classic" ragtime (instrumental piano rags), ragtime songs, and the more general use of the term "ragtime" to denote an era and nearly any up-tempo music or dance of the time. A piano rag, strictly speaking, is an instrumental composition. Ragtime songs, less complex than the rags, had both music and words (many of which perpetuated grotesquely stereotyped and racist views of black life). The term "ragtime" is now often used in a general sense to evoke a bygone era existing between the 1890's and the 1920's—a slower, quieter time of pre-World War I innocence and optimism. In this sense, "ragtime" has come to refer to a range of music and dances of the time before the jazz age, including rags, cakewalks, novelty songs, and the popular songs turned out by early Tin Pan Alley composers and musicians.

The defining characteristic of the classic rags was their inventive syncopation, but by 1910 or so, publishers were referring to nearly any up-tempo popular song as "ragtime." The famous song "Alexander's Ragtime Band," for example, written by Irving Berlin in 1911, contains virtually no syncopation. As "Maple Leaf Rag" can in some ways symbolize the beginning of ragtime, so the hugely popular "Alexander's Ragtime Band" symbolizes its coming end. By 1915, ragtime had become watered down by commercial imitation and, as a creative musical form, had run its course.

SIGNIFICANCE

Although the ragtime era lasted for only twenty years at most after publication of the first rag, the effects of the music were felt much longer. Ragtime influenced both the development of jazz and, to a much lesser extent, twentieth century classical music. It would be wrong to claim that ragtime developed into jazz, but jazz would not have developed quite the way it did had it not been for ragtime.

One major contribution that ragtime made to jazz was simply the role of the piano. As the music that was evolving into jazz moved from the parade into the dance hall, honky-tonk, and brothel, the piano began to assume greater importance. The early jazz players' approach to the piano was deeply indebted to ragtime.

There was considerable cultural resistance to the ragtime craze, some of it coming from guardians of morality and some from arbiters of musical taste. Many conservative community leaders considered rags and ragtime dances to be destructive to the morals of youth, much as jazz and rock and roll would be deplored in later generations. There was undeniably a racist element in many of these arguments. Ragtime was also hotly debated in music societies, magazines, and journals, with many classical musicians excoriating it. One conductor declared that ragtime "poisons the taste of the young"; a classical pianist likened it to a "dog with rabies" that had to be exterminated. Nevertheless, ragtime elements began to appear in the work of more open-minded and influential twentieth century composers, both in Europe and in the United States.

Three European composers notable for their inclusion of raglike musical figures were Claude Debussy, Erik Satie, and Igor Stravinsky. American composers drawing upon ragtime have ranged from Henry Gilbert to John Alden Carpenter, but the best known are Charles Ives and George Gershwin. All four were seeking to write classical music with a uniquely American sound; among the sources with which they experimented were spirituals, hymns, folk songs, American Indian music, ragtime, and jazz.

Although ragtime music had faded from mass popularity by World War I, it never quite disappeared. Any piano players who entertained by playing "old-time" or honky-tonk piano had ragtime pieces or ragtime-influenced songs in their repertoire. Moreover, a number of performers and composers (including Eubie Blake, who lived to the age of one hundred) kept the style alive and passed it on to new generations.

During the 1940's, periodic ragtime revivals began occurring, reflecting both the interest and the evolving stylistic interpretations of new devotees. The biggest single ragtime revival occurred in the early and middle 1970's. In the ensuing years, popular interest in ragtime waned once again, but the many recordings and performances of ragtime, as well as the substantial body of scholarship on the music, ensure Joplin and ragtime a secure place in the history of American music.

—*McCrea Adams*

FURTHER READING

Berlin, Edward A. *King of Ragtime: Scott Joplin and His Era*. New York: Oxford University Press, 1994. A comprehensive biography focusing on Joplin's music, with updated information from archives and newspapers. Contains photographs, illustrations, listings of Joplin's works, extensive notes, and a bibliography.

_____. *Ragtime: A Musical and Cultural History*. 1980. Reprint. Berkeley: University of California Press, 2002. A perceptive analysis of the musical and cultural influences on ragtime, with examples.

Blesh, Rudi, and Harriet Janis. *They All Played Ragtime*. New York: Oak, 1971. This pioneering and painstakingly researched study remains an excellent survey of the music, its players, and its composers.

Curtis, Susan. *Dancing to a Black Man's Tune: A Life of Scott Joplin*. Columbia: University of Missouri Press, 1994. Scholarly biography with an interpretation of the communities and societies of Joplin's era. Contains extensive chapter notes and a bibliography.

Gammond, Peter. *Scott Joplin and the Ragtime Era*. New York: St. Martin's Press, 1975. One of a number of short biographies of Joplin written for the newcomer to ragtime. Alternates between chapters on Joplin's life and chapters containing contextual information on ragtime and its era.

Hasse, John Edward, ed. *Ragtime: Its History, Composers, and Music*. New York: Schirmer Books, 1985. An amazingly wide-ranging collection of fine essays on ragtime. Includes essays on Joplin and other major figures, women ragtime composers, musicological examinations, and ragtime's influence on early country music. Also includes Gunther Schuller's "Rags, the Classics, and Jazz."

Jasen, David A., and Gene Jones. *That American Rag: The Story of Ragtime in the United States*. New York: Schirmer Books, 2000. A comprehensive historical overview of ragtime's development in the United States. An excellent reference.

Schafer, William J., and Johannes Riedel. *The Art of Ragtime*. Baton Rouge: Louisiana State University Press, 1973. Aimed at the serious student of ragtime, this work covers a broad area. A scholarly account, rich in detail.

Waldo, Terry. *This Is Ragtime*. New York: Hawthorn Books, 1976. The author, a onetime protégé of ragtime pianist Eubie Blake, surveys ragtime from its beginnings to its resurgence in the 1970's. He devotes separate chapters to ragtime in the 1940's, 1950's, 1960's, and 1970's.

SEE ALSO: Feb. 6, 1843: First Minstrel Shows; 1890's: Rise of Tin Pan Alley Music.

RELATED ARTICLES in *Great Lives from History: The Nineteenth Century, 1801-1900:* Frederick Douglass; Paul Laurence Dunbar; Scott Joplin; Harriet Beecher Stowe.

1890's

1899-1900
REDISCOVERY OF MENDEL'S HEREDITARY THEORY

By 1899, Gregor Mendel had been dead some fifteen years, his notebooks were mostly destroyed, and his work was forgotten. The independent rediscovery of Mendel's work by three scientists and the controversies associated with priority between them led to a reexamination of Mendel's role in science, as well as launching the modern science of genetics.

LOCALE: Central and western Europe
CATEGORIES: Genetics; science and technology

KEY FIGURES

Gregor Mendel (1822-1884), Augustinian monk and geneticist
William Bateson (1861-1926), English zoologist
Erich Tschermak von Seysenegg (1871-1962), Austrian botanist
Carl Erich Correns (1864-1933), German botanist
Hugo de Vries (1848-1935), Dutch botanist
Walter Weldon (1860-1906), British statistician

SUMMARY OF EVENT

The Austrian monk Gregor Mendel is generally considered to be the founder of modern genetics. During the period between 1854 and 1863, he carried out an extensive series of fertilization experiments, utilizing the common garden pea (genus *Pisum*), in which he observed the appearance or disappearance of various traits. Based upon the ratios in which these traits appeared among the plant's offspring, Mendel established what later became known as Mendel's laws of heredity. In 1865, Mendel presented the results of this work before the Brünn (Brno) Natural Science Society. In 1866, his results were published in the relatively obscure scientific journal of the society, *Proceedings of the Brünn Society for the Study of Natural Science*.

Mendel's first law became known in the early twentieth century as the law of segregation, in which genetic factors (*merkmal*) become segregated during the formation of gametes. The second law, the law of independent assortment, reflected his observations that traits often segregated independently of each other. That is, the appearance of a given trait, such as purple flowers, did not affect the probability of the appearance of another trait, such as wrinkled seeds, in the same plant.

The rediscovery of Mendel's work some fifteen years after his death also led to the belief that a combination of factors had resulted in the undeserved if temporary ob-

scurity of that work. These factors included his amateur status in a profession dominated by professional scientists, his presentation and publication in an obscure venue, and even the difficulty of understanding Mendel's use of statistics. Analysis by authors Randy Moore and Robin Henig has suggested it is more likely that his work was simply not considered groundbreaking at the time. As noted by Moore, Mendel's work had appeared in numerous journals and other publications in the years after the initial presentation.

Three individuals are credited with the independent rediscovery of Mendel: Erich Tschermak von Seysenegg, a young Austrian graduate student preparing his thesis; Carl Erich Correns, a German botanist; and Hugo de Vries, a Dutch botanist. Once it became clear that each had independently cited Mendel's work, the question of priority for the rediscovery, particularly between Correns and de Vries, brought those earlier studies to prominence.

Seysenegg published his doctoral thesis in 1900. In-

Gregor Mendel. (Library of Congress)

cluded in his summary was a reference to the earlier work of Mendel, work that he argued was confirmed in his own experiments. Both Moore and Henig point out, however, that Seysenegg never recognized the hereditary principles, Mendel's laws, in the summary of his own work, nor did he understand the significance of the ratios Mendel had reported. It is possible that Seysenegg was aware of Mendel's studies prior to beginning his thesis; his grandfather, Eduard Frenzl, was an Austrian botanist who had feuded with Mendel during the 1850's. Seysenegg's later membership in the Nazi Party and support for eugenics further damaged the credibility of claims to have rediscovered Mendel.

Claims for rediscovery exhibit greater credence in the work by Correns and de Vries. By 1900, De Vries was a highly respected Dutch botanist who had once published his own theory of heredity, emphasizing characters he called "pangenes." In March, 1900, de Vries presented a paper before the Dutch Academy of Science in which he described the appearance of traits in ratios similar to those previously reported by Mendel. Shortly afterward, de Vries published his work and sent a copy of the paper to Correns. While it remains unclear whether de Vries fully understood the significance of the work of Mendel that he had confirmed, his claim to rediscovery stands on firmer ground than does that of Seysenegg.

By the time Correns received a copy of de Vries' paper, he was already familiar with Mendel's work. In fact, he had cited it in an 1899 publication. Correns further noted the importance of the nucleus in the segregation of genetic "factors" (*anlage*). While one could dispute whether the others fully understood the significance of Mendel's ratios, there is no question that Correns did. Correns's use of the term *anlage* in place of Mendel's *merkmal* is evidence of his understanding. Correns argued that a characteristic or trait is determined by its own *anlage*, a principle close to the modern idea of a gene. He also suggested individual *anlage* may be either dominant or recessive.

In his presentation of specific ratios such as the 9:3:3:1 ratio observed in certain dihybrid crosses, Correns reported data that are now often incorrectly attributed to Mendel. Correns provided an explanation for the specific ratios of traits observed in offspring by both Mendel and himself—albeit an abstract explanation in principle. He also explained that *anlage* segregate during meiosis and that cell division results in the formation of gametes. His claim to have rediscovered Mendel's work and understood its signficance is borne out by the fact that he named the abstract cause behind the trait ratios he observed "Mendel's principle."

William Bateson, a zoologist at Cambridge University who learned of Mendel's work by reading the publications of Correns and de Vries, is credited with being among the first to disseminate Mendel's principles. In a lecture before the Royal Horticultural Society at Liverpool in May, 1900, Bateson used Mendel's principles to explain his own investigations. Bateson coined the term "genetics" when applying Mendel's principles to the animal kingdom. He later became the first professor of genetics at Cambridge.

This is not to say that all scientists were in complete agreement with Mendel's observations. Walter Weldon, one of Great Britain's leading statisticians, argued vociferously that other explanations were possible in analyzing Mendel's work. For example, he believed that traits were never lost, but were merely masked (so that it would be possible in principle for any parents to have offspring with any traits). Nevertheless, the ability of others to reproduce Mendel's ratios eventually convinced most skeptics of the "amateur's" accuracy and conclusions.

SIGNIFICANCE

The rediscovery of Mendel's laws brought to the forefront the nascent field of modern genetics. In addition to forming the basis for the terminology that remains instrumental in understanding the field, terminology largely invented by Bateson, the recognition of Mendel's laws of heredity led to the appreciation of the man himself, whose work had been largely forgotten. It is easily overlooked that at the time of the rediscovery, the genetic basis for Mendel's laws was unclear. Chromosomes had been observed by Karl Nageli in the 1840's, but it was only after Walter Sutton—a student at Columbia University in the first years of the twentieth century—observed the pairing and subsequent separation of chromosomes during cell division that the physical explanation for Mendel's laws became apparent.

In retrospect, even if Mendel's work had not reappeared, somebody else would probably have carried out similar work with similar conclusions. Indeed, Correns did exactly that. Mendel was fortunate in choosing plants that would self-pollinate and, more important, tracking traits that we now know to be encoded on different chromosomes. In this respect, the work of a "later Mendel" might not have resulted in reliable interpretations as quickly as Mendel's work did. At any rate, Mendel's work was rediscovered, and its rediscovery formed the foundation upon which the field of genetics advanced during the new century.

—Richard Adler

FURTHER READING

Edelson, Edward. *Gregor Mendel and the Roots of Genetics*. New York: Oxford University Press, 2001. Popular account of Mendel's life and works. Included are controversies dealing with validity of his statistics.

Henig, Robin. *The Monk in the Garden*. New York: Houghton Mifflin, 2000. Well-researched biography of the man considered to be the modern founder of genetics.

Moore, Randy. "The Rediscovery of Mendel's Work." *Bioscene* 27 (2001): 13-24. As noted by the author, Mendel's work was not considered groundbreaking in its time. The controversies associated with priority of rediscovery played a significant role in reinterpreting the significance of Mendel's laws.

Raven, Peter, et al. *Biology*. 7th ed. Boston: McGraw-Hill, 2005. College textbook that provides extensive discussion of Mendel's work and his laws of heredity. Illustrations include summary diagrams, as well as images reproduced from Mendel's notebook.

Stomps, T. "On the Rediscovery of Mendel's Work by Hugo de Vries." *Journal of Heredity* 45 (1954): 293-294. Discusses the controversial role of one of the alleged codiscoverers of Mendel.

Waller, John. *Einstein's Luck: The Truth Behind Some of the Greatest Scientific Discoveries*. New York: Oxford University Press, 2002. Addresses the myths behind scientific achievements. The section about Mendel presents questions about why he was largely ignored by the scientific community during his lifetime.

SEE ALSO: 1809: Lamarck Publishes *Zoological Philosophy*; Nov. 24, 1859: Darwin Publishes *On the Origin of Species*; 1865: Mendel Proposes Laws of Heredity; 1871: Darwin Publishes *The Descent of Man*; 1880's: Roux Develops the Theory of Mitosis; 1883: Galton Defines "Eugenics."

RELATED ARTICLES in *Great Lives from History: The Nineteenth Century, 1801-1900:* Charles Darwin; Gregor Mendel.

February 4, 1899-July 4, 1902
PHILIPPINE INSURRECTION

In a manner similar to U.S. involvement in Iraq more than a century later, the United States entered the Spanish-American War with a plan for helping Filipino rebels defeat their Spanish overlords in the Philippines but with no plan for extricating itself from the conquered colony. As a result, the United States found itself in a costly and unprofitable war with Filipino nationalists.

ALSO KNOWN AS: Filipino War of Independence
LOCALE: Philippine Islands
CATEGORIES: Wars, uprisings, and civil unrest; expansion and land acquisition; colonization

KEY FIGURES
Emilio Aguinaldo (1869-1964), principal leader of the Filipino guerrilla forces
George Dewey (1837-1917), commander of the U.S. Navy's Asiatic Squadron
Frederick Funston (1865-1917), U.S. Army colonel who captured Aguinaldo
Apolinario Mabini (1864-1903), intellectual leader of the Filipino independence movement

William McKinley (1843-1901), president of the United States, 1897-1901
William Howard Taft (1857-1930), first civilian U.S. governor of the Philippines and later president of the United States, 1909-1913

SUMMARY OF EVENT
The Philippine Insurrection, known as the War of Independence by Filipinos, is an early example of a country resisting the rise of the United States as an imperial power. It resulted from misunderstanding and indecision on both sides. U.S. and Filipino forces, which had worked together to end Spanish control of the Philippines in 1898, found themselves fighting as enemies in a long, brutal struggle for domination of the Philippine Islands.

U.S. involvement in the Philippines began during the Spanish-American War of 1898. Before the war even began, U.S. naval strategists had a plan ready for attacking the Spanish fleet at Manila Bay. As relations between the United States and Spain worsened in 1897, Commodore George Dewey, the commander of the U.S. Navy's Asi-

U.S. EXPANSION INTO THE PACIFIC, 1860-1898

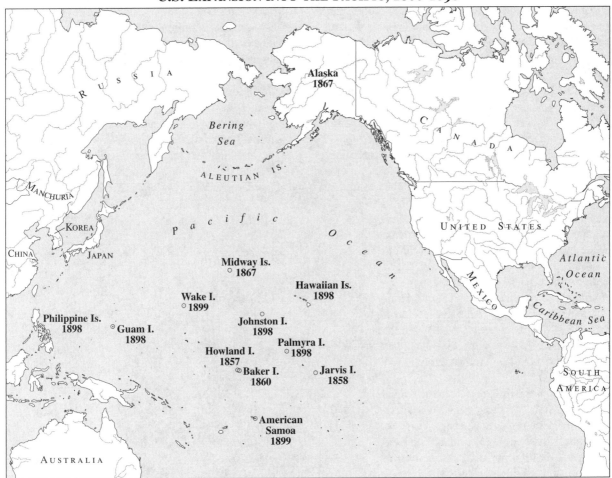

atic Squadron, was ordered to move his fleet to Hong Kong, with instructions to attack Manila Bay if war broke out. War was declared on April 24, 1898. Exactly one week later, Dewey's fleet steamed into Manila Bay. By noon, his ships had sunk or disabled every Spanish ship, without a single loss to the U.S. fleet.

The U.S. government was slow to react to the news of Dewey's overwhelming victory. The almost effortless defeat of the Spanish fleet was unexpected, and President William McKinley had no plan for what to do with the Philippines after the war ended. McKinley considered either taking the entire archipelago, establishing a U.S. naval base in the Philippines, or returning the islands to Spain. Complete independence for the islands was never seriously considered. While McKinley contemplated the fate of the Philippines, relations between the U.S. military occupation force at Manila Bay and the Filipino pop-

ulation deteriorated. At first, the Filipinos welcomed Dewey's forces as liberators. However, the Filipinos soon realized that the Americans intended to control the islands until at least the end of the war and perhaps even longer. In early May, McKinley dispatched an expeditionary force, under the command of General Arthur MacArthur, to Manila Bay. MacArthur arrived in time to accept the Spanish garrison's surrender at the end of the war, an honor that Filipino revolutionary forces had assumed would be theirs.

Filipino insurgents had been fighting the Spanish since early 1896. Spanish efforts to destroy the infant revolution had failed, as rebel leaders fled to the heavily forested hills of the islands to hide and organize bases for guerrilla warfare against the Spanish. In 1897, both sides, weary of the increasingly bloody war, agreed to a cease-fire to discuss peace. The Spanish authorities refused to consider independence, forcing the Filipino insurgents to continue their rebellion. Under the military leadership of Emilio Aguinaldo and the intellectual direction of Apolinario Mabini, rebel leaders established a base of operations at Hong Kong, where they could easily purchase supplies and arms. It was at that time that the Spanish-American War began, bringing an unexpected opportunity for the rebels.

Filipino leaders first believed that the United States would assist them in expelling the Spanish and establishing an independent Philippine state. Aguinaldo accepted anticolonial statements by U.S. consular officers at their face value. The Filipinos soon found, however, that Dewey was more cautious, speaking only of military cooperation to defeat Spain and saying nothing of Filipino independence. Meanwhile, Aguinaldo organized an army of thirty thousand men and won notable victories; nevertheless, the United States held supreme authority, accepting the surrender of Manila Bay and refusing to allow Filipino rebel forces into the city without permission. When the Spanish flag came down, the American Stars and Stripes, not the Filipino revolutionary flag, replaced it.

Faced with the realization that the United States was going to annex the islands, Aguinaldo moved to organize a new government. On June 12, 1898, he proclaimed independence for the Philippines. In September, a constituent assembly was convened, and on November 29, a constitution was adopted. The United States largely ignored this move toward independence. Largely because of racial prejudice against the Philippines' dark-skinned peoples, McKinley's administration assumed that the Filipinos were not ready for self-government. In addition, there was a fear that an independent Philippines might fall easy prey to another ambitious European power, such as Germany or Great Britain. Therefore, the United States proceeded to obtain full control by a provision for annexation of the Philippines in the peace treaty ending the war with Spain.

While the U.S. Senate debated ratification of the peace treaty, a series of clashes between U.S. and Filipino forces that began on February 4, 1899, soon escalated into large-scale fighting. The Philippine Insurrection

against U.S. rule had begun. The United States, because of its decision to assume responsibility for "civilizing" the Filipinos, was forced to wage a bitter war, one that would cost the United States much more money and take many more human lives than the U.S. war with Spain.

The Philippine Insurrection was, in many ways, a prototype of modern guerrilla warfare. Filipino revolutionary leaders quickly lost the support of conservative Filipinos who accepted U.S. rule. As a result, Aguinaldo and his forces retreated to fight the U.S. troops in the jungles, as they had done earlier against Spanish forces. In early 1899, U.S. forces moved into central Luzon, where they captured and burned Malolos, the rebel capital. Rebel

Cover of Judge *magazine with an illustration by Grant E. Hamilton depicting President William McKinley slapping a giant mosquito labeled "Insurgent Aguinaldo." Below "Hit him HARD!," the caption reads, "Mosquitoes seem to be worse here in the Philippines than they were in Cuba."* (Library of Congress)

forces, however, escaped into the hills, where they were supplied by sympathetic villagers until spring rains forced U.S. troops to withdraw.

U.S. commanders finally admitted that Aguinaldo had extensive popular support and that total war was necessary to pacify the islands. The U.S. government responded by sending reinforcements, increasing the number of U.S. troops in the Philippines to seventy-four thousand. As the scale of the fighting rose, vicious tactics and brutality on both sides also increased. Both sides committed atrocities involving soldiers and civilians. U.S. forces systematically burned villages and took hostages in an effort to deny popular assistance to rebel forces. Gradually, the overwhelming strength of the United States prevailed, as U.S. forces took rebel strongholds in the hills and rural regions. By 1901, 639 U.S. garrisons dotted the islands, breaking Filipino resistance.

The insurrection finally collapsed with Aguinaldo's capture in March, 1901. He was treacherously seized by Colonel Frederick Funston and three other U.S. officers pretending to be the prisoners of a group of Filipino defectors, who led the officers directly to Aguinaldo's headquarters in northeastern Luzon. After his capture, Aguinaldo reluctantly took an oath of allegiance to the United States. By July 4, 1901, civil government, under United States auspices, was instituted everywhere in the Philippines, except in southern Mindanao and the Sulu Islands, where Moro tribesmen continued their resistance.

On July 4, 1902, the Philippine Insurrection was formally declared to be over. The United States issued a proclamation of general peace and amnesty. As a result of the struggle, the United States suffered 4,200 dead and 2,800 wounded. While close to 20,000 rebels were killed in the war, another 200,000 Filipinos died from disease, famine, and other war-related causes brought by the U.S. campaign.

William Howard Taft served as the first U.S. governor of the Philippines and later continued to be heavily involved in the administration of the islands as secretary of war and president of the United States. It was Taft who coined the phrase "little brown brothers," which referred to his hope that the United States could somehow "Americanize" the Philippines' native peoples. This phrase remained a strong racial force in U.S. relations with the states in the Pacific and Latin America. The Philippine Islands remained under U.S. jurisdiction until 1934, when Congress passed the Tydings-McDuffie Act, granting independence to the Philippines. However, the developments in the Pacific leading up to World War II

delayed complete independence for the islands until 1946. Modern Filipinos celebrate their independence on the anniversary of June 12, 1898, and regard Emilio Aguinaldo as their national hero.

—*Theodore A. Wilson, updated by William Allison*

FURTHER READING

Brands, H. W. *Bound to Empire: The United States and the Philippines.* New York: Oxford University Press, 1992. Expansive history that emphasizes the interaction of cultural forces in U.S.-Philippine relations and traces the development of the Filipino independence movement.

Dobson, John. *Reticent Expansionism: The Foreign Policy of William McKinley.* Pittsburgh: Duquesne University Press, 1988. One of a few works devoted to McKinley's foreign policy, which Dobson characterizes as ambiguous, indecisive, and reactive.

Karnov, Stanley. *In Our Image: America's Empire in the Philippines.* New York: Random House, 1989. Argues that the United States was inept and ineffective in dealing with the Philippine Insurrection and its aftermath.

Langellier, John P. *Uncle Sam's Little Wars: The Spanish-American War, Philippine Insurrection, and Boxer Rebellion, 1898-1902.* Harrisburg, Pa.: Stackpole Books, 1999. Part of a series of books on the uniforms and equipment of American soldiers in different conflicts, this little book offers vivid illustrations that provide some insights into the nature of the soldiers' experiences in the Philippines.

Miller, Stuart Creighton. *"Benevolent Assimilation": The American Conquest of the Philippines, 1899-1903.* New Haven, Conn.: Yale University Press, 1982. Study of the war in the Philippines and its consequences, including the atrocities committed by the U.S. Army.

Phillips, Kevin. *William McKinley.* New York: Times Books/Henry Holt, 2003. Analysis of McKinley's presidency arguing that McKinley was a "near great" president, whose place in history has been diminished because he was unable to complete his second term. Phillips describes how McKinley began transforming the United States into a global military power, and how many of McKinley's goals were later accomplished by his successor, President Theodore Roosevelt.

Salamanca, Bonifacio S. *The Filipino Reaction to American Rule, 1901-1913.* Quezon City, Philippines: New Day, 1984. A Filipino historian's harsh criticism of

1890's

U.S. policy in the Philippines during the insurrection and the following years of U.S. rule.

SEE ALSO: Oct. 10, 1868-Feb. 10, 1878: Cuba's Ten Years' War; Jan. 24, 1895: Hawaii's Last Monarch

Abdicates; Apr. 24-Dec. 10, 1898: Spanish-American War.

RELATED ARTICLES in *Great Lives from History: The Nineteenth Century, 1801-1900:* George Dewey; William McKinley.

May 18-July, 1899
FIRST HAGUE PEACE CONFERENCE

The First Hague Peace Conference convened at the invitation of Russian czar Nicholas II to discuss nonmilitary means of solving international problems. Twenty-six nations agreed to establish a voluntary permanent court of arbitration, a still-existing international court in the Netherlands.

ALSO KNOWN AS: First International Peace Conference
LOCALE: The Hague, the Netherlands
CATEGORIES: Diplomacy and international relations; laws, acts, and legal history

KEY FIGURES
Nicholas II (1868-1918), czar of Russia, r. 1894-1917
Sir Julian Pauncefote (1828-1902), British ambassador to the United States
Andrew Dickson White (1832-1918), head of the American delegation to the First Hague Peace Conference and U.S. minister to Russia
Alfred Thayer Mahan (1840-1914), American advocate of sea power
William II (1859-1941), emperor of Germany, r. 1888-1918

SUMMARY OF EVENT
As announced by the Russian foreign affairs minister on August 24, 1898, Czar Nicholas II issued an "imperial rescript" inviting the powers with diplomatic representatives at the court of St. Petersburg to participate in an international conference aimed at a "possible reduction of excessive armaments which weigh upon all nations."

The czar's initiative was greeted with different responses. The growing number of pacifists and humanitarians hailed the move as evidence that the czar's promise of peace and progress would be brought to fruition soon after the arrival of the new century. They sincerely believed that a utopian ideal was about to be realized despite the source of the initiative and the signs of war that seemed to lurk everywhere. The antiwar advocates had representatives on the Continent, although they were

particularly strong in Great Britain and the United States. In those two countries, militarism was not deeply rooted, even though 1898 was the year of the Spanish-American War and the confrontation between Great Britain and France at Fashoda.

There was hope that the reduction of armaments would make war less likely and that the products and profits of the rapidly expanding Western industrial complex could be brought to bear on world problems. Arbitration could solve international grievances, as had actually happened in the successful negotiations for damages resulting from the depredations caused by the *Alabama* and other Confederate cruisers during the U.S. Civil War (1861-1865). In 1889, humanitarians were also able to point to the formation of the Interparliamentary Union and the convening of the first Pan-American Congress (1889-1890) as examples of international problems being solved without resorting to war.

On the other side, contemporary political realists of every stripe were suspicious of the czar's motives and were alarmed over possible consequences. It was obvious that the bellicose Emperor William II of Germany, who was already committed to the continuance and expansion of newfound German strength, would not, under any circumstances, agree to disarm an empire created by force of arms. While on friendly terms with Russia, France was shocked at not being consulted by its ally before the proposal was made. The thought of maintaining the status quo as established by the French defeat in the Franco-Prussian War (1870-1871) was totally unacceptable.

Nevertheless, Germany and France, along with twenty-three other nations, accepted the invitation. The reasons for acceptance varied, but generally it was held that the czar should not be offended, and it was unlikely that any enforceable action could come out of such a conference. Furthermore, to decline the invitation would have put a nation in a bad light with liberals, pacifists, humanitarians, socialists, and similar groups.

On close examination, Russian motives do not appear to have been entirely altruistic. The naïve Nicholas II may have been more idealistic than his ministers, but it was clear by 1898 that Russia, already lagging behind the West in economic and industrial development, was unable to compete in the armaments race. The financial burden alone was too great. The Russian finance minister decided that a ten-year international moratorium on armaments could bring the leading military states down to the Russian level.

On May 18, 1899, the First International Peace Conference convened at The Hague in the Netherlands. Among those who attended the conference and who were genuinely interested in the cause of peace were Sir Julian Pauncefote, who represented Great Britain and served as British ambassador to the United States, and Andrew Dickson White, who represented the United States and served as the American minister to Russia.

The voices that were most influential at the conference in the long run belonged to blunt military-naval experts and apostles of military strength such as Captain Alfred Thayer Mahan of the United States, Admiral Sir John Arbuthnot Fisher of Great Britain, and Colonel Gross von Schwarzhoff of Germany. Basing their arguments on individual, sovereign responsibility, their clamor for the necessity of preparedness carried the day. Confronted by the irrefutable military realities of the international situation, the goals of the conference were not realized.

SIGNIFICANCE

The means for preventing armed conflict were approved unanimously by the twenty-six nations present and participating in the conference. International commissions of inquiry were authorized to appease, investigate, and prevent conflict. More important, participants devised a permanent court of arbitration that was authorized to hear and judge disputes that were voluntarily brought to its purview. Although it was not a permanent sitting court, it drew from a pool of jurists who could arbitrate in any given situation. The weakness of this approach was less in its structure than in the reluctance of nations to risk their influence and prestige. Perhaps Nicholas II put it best when he remarked that "Peace is more important than anything, if honor is not affected."

—Jack H. Greising, updated by John Quinn Imholte

1890's

Delegates to the first Hague Peace Conference. (The Co-Operative Publishing Company)

FURTHER READING

Cooper, Sandi E. *Patriotic Pacifism: Waging War on War in Europe, 1815-1914.* New York: Oxford University Press, 1991. This work contains scattered references to both Hague Peace Conferences within a European context.

Davis, Calvin D. *The United States and the First Hague Conference.* Ithaca, N.Y.: Cornell University Press, 1962. Davis explores reasons for the successes of the first conference and what he believes are its more significant failures. Davis also argues that the conference was for the most part unsuccessful in its goals and thus was a failure.

Hull, William I. *The Two Hague Conferences and Their Contributions to International Law.* Boston: Ginn, 1908. Reprint. New York: Garland, 1972. Hull presents a positive assessment of the peace movement's internationalist direction.

Marchand, C. Roland. *The American Peace Movement and Social Reform, 1898-1918.* Princeton, N.J.: Princeton University Press, 1972. Emphasizes in brief references the relationship of the conference and the American peace movement.

Ralston, Jackson H. *International Arbitration from Athens to Locarno.* Stanford, Calif.: Stanford University Press, 1929. Places the origin and outcome of the First Hague Peace Conference in its historical context.

Tuchman, Barbara. "The Steady Drummer: The Hague, 1899 and 1907." In *The Proud Tower: A Portrait of the World Before the War, 1890-1914.* New York: Macmillan, 1966. A popular account of the personalities and highlights of both Hague conferences.

SEE ALSO: Apr. 12, 1861-Apr. 9, 1865: U.S. Civil War; Mar. 13, 1884-Jan. 26, 1885: Siege of Khartoum; Oct., 1889-Apr., 1890: First Pan-American Congress; Jan. 4, 1894: Franco-Russian Alliance; July 10-Nov. 3, 1898: Fashoda Incident Pits France vs. Britain.

RELATED ARTICLE in *Great Lives from History: The Nineteenth Century, 1801-1900:* Bertha von Suttner.

September 6, 1899-July 3, 1900
HAY ARTICULATES "OPEN DOOR" POLICY TOWARD CHINA

U.S. secretary of state John Hay circulated a set of notes articulating an American foreign policy in favor of free trade between China and all nations. The policy, which also officially advocated respect for China's territorial integrity, was never fully put into practice, but it ironically helped the United States to seize a piece of the China trade pie for itself.

LOCALE: Washington, D.C.

CATEGORIES: Diplomacy and international relations; trade and commerce

KEY FIGURES

John Hay (1838-1905), U.S. secretary of state, 1898-1905

William Woodville Rockhill (1854-1914), Hay's adviser on China, who drafted the first of the "Open Door Notes"

William McKinley (1843-1901), president of the United States, 1897-1901

John Bassett Moore (1860-1947), assistant secretary of state

Alfred E. Hippisley (1848-1939), Rockhill's friend, an officer in the Chinese Imperial Maritime Customs Service

Edwin Hurd Conger (1843-1907), U.S. minister to Beijing in 1890

SUMMARY OF EVENT

John Hay's open door policy represented a milestone in the articulation of United States foreign policy in Asia at the turn of the twentieth century. They were circulated to address specific events. However, their cumulative and long-term implications have made them critical to understanding the evolution of the United States as a world power.

By 1890, the U.S. frontier had been declared closed, but Americans were still conditioned to expand. Capital needed sources of investment. Industry required markets. The national ego, convinced that the United States had become a world power, sought an arena in which to assert itself. Mission boards were eager to save new souls. Righteous individuals were eager to shoulder the "white man's burden" and "civilize backward peoples." More reflective persons blamed economic slumps and social ills on overproduction and desired wider markets to solve the problems of overproduction and society at the same time. For these and other reasons, some people in the United States became increasingly interested in

China as a possible target for continued expansion.

At the conclusion of the Spanish-American War (1898), a significant expansionist exercise in itself, the administration of President William McKinley had gained possession of the Pacific islands of Wake, Guam, and the Philippines. The United States began to realize that it not only had a new political interest in Asian developments but it also had the requisite coaling stations to provide itself with a commercial interest in the fabled China market.

For some years, Great Britain had dominated the China market, conducting about 80 percent of China's foreign trade. In part because they could afford to do so, the British had pursued a policy of "open door," or free trade, in China. During the 1880's and 1890's, other European nations began to challenge Great Britain's market hegemony and its open door. Germany, France, Japan, and Russia began carving out individual spheres of influence, in each of which theirs was the only foreign trade permitted. The Chinese people and government remained essentially passive to this exploitation. Britain resented it and officially reasserted the open door. Unofficially, however, the British realized that despite their reassertions, doors were being closed in China.

The British began to seek allies who would be willing to support the open door. In March, 1898, Great Britain's foreign secretary sent a secret message to President McKinley, asking if the United States was interested in concerted action to support free trade in China. At that time, the United States was occupied in the Spanish-American War, and Secretary of State John Sherman's answer was a firm no. The British continued to pay lip service to the open door in 1898 and 1899 but quietly began to create a sphere of influence of their own. Great Britain leased Kowloon, directly opposite Hong Kong, and eyed the Yangtze Valley as a source of exclusive markets.

At the time of the British overture to the United States concerning the open door in China, John Hay was the United States ambassador in London. Hay regretted his

---

HAY'S FIRST "OPEN DOOR" NOTE

On September 6, 1899, John Hay issued the first of his "open door" notes, in response to the German Empire's lease of Kiaochow, China. Hay expressed concern over the potential deleterious effect the lease could have upon the rights and privileges of Americans trading in China.

Earnestly desirous to remove any cause of irritation and to insure at the same time to the commerce of all nations in China the undoubted benefits which should accrue from a formal recognition by the various powers claiming "spheres of interest" that they shall enjoy perfect equality of treatment for their commerce and navigation within such "spheres," the Government of the United States would be pleased to see His German Majesty's Government give formal assurances, and lend its cooperation in securing like assurances from the other interested powers, that each, within its respective sphere of whatever influence—

First. Will in no way interfere with any treaty port or any vested interest within any so-called "sphere of interest" or leased territory it may have in China.

Second. That the Chinese treaty tariff of the time being shall apply to all merchandise landed or shipped to all such ports as are within said "sphere of interest" (unless they be "free ports"), no matter to what nationality it may belong, and that duties so leviable shall be collected by the Chinese Government.

Third. That it will levy no higher harbor dues on vessels of another nationality frequenting any port in such "sphere" than shall be levied on vessels of its own nationality, and no higher railroad charges over lines built, controlled, or operated within its "sphere" on merchandise belonging to citizens or subjects of other nationalities transported through such "sphere" than shall be levied on similar merchandise belonging to its own nationals transported over equal distances.

---

government's refusal to support the British. In 1899, Hay, now secretary of state, determined to render at least tardy support to the open door. Hay brought William Woodville Rockhill, who was familiar with China, to Washington to advise him, and the two awaited an opportunity to make some U.S. commitment in China. In the summer of 1899, Alfred E. Hippisley—a friend of Rockhill and an official of the Chinese Imperial Maritime Customs Service—visited Washington, D.C. Hippisley resented spheres of influence, especially British activities at Kowloon. Hippisley suggested to Rockhill that a U.S. policy statement on an open door might help. Rockhill had little difficulty convincing Hay, and Hay convinced McKinley.

On September 6, 1899, Hay dispatched a series of notes, drafted by Rockhill, to Great Britain, Germany, and Russia, and shortly thereafter to France, Italy, and Japan. These notes, known as the "Open Door Notes," asked the governments of these six nations to agree to three principles: Each nation with a sphere of influence was to respect the rights and privileges of other nations in its sphere; Chinese officials were to continue to collect tariff duties in all spheres; and within its sphere, no nation would discriminate against other nations in levying harbor dues and railroad rates. The responses to Hay's "Open Door Notes" were qualified and evasive. Nevertheless, the secretary of state announced that the China powers had acceded to the U.S. policy.

Hay's high-level commercial diplomacy presupposed that the Chinese would remain passive, but they did not. In the spring of 1900, China exploded in the Boxer Rebellion against the intrusion of Western "barbarians." The United States joined the European powers in dispatching troops to quell the unrest, and on July 3, 1900, Hay sent his second "Open Door Notes." On the advice of Assistant Secretary of State John Bassett Moore, Hay put the United States on record as favoring the maintenance of stability in China, Chinese territorial integrity, and the open door in all parts of China.

The second of the notes, actually a diplomatic circular to U.S. diplomats in major foreign capitals, merely articulated U.S. policy and therefore did not require agreement from the other European nations affected by the action of the Boxers. It was a stronger and more broad-based expression of Hay's position on Chinese territorial integrity and the rule of international law. Hay further confirmed his position during the Boxer attack on foreign legations in Beijing, giving explicit instructions to Edwin Hurd Conger, his minister in Beijing, to support the preservation of China's territorial integrity.

Improving the defenses of the American legation in Beijing during the Boxer Rebellion. (Francis R. Niglutsch)

SIGNIFICANCE

People in the United States, both at the time and after, believed that the open door policy represented a stand by their government against the rapacious European and Japanese powers in China. The reality was not quite so simple and was more practical than high minded. China was not a party to the U.S. action. China never chose the open door. Moreover, indemnities levied by all the powers over the Boxer Rebellion forced China to borrow money from these same powers, further restricting its independence. The Russians used the situation both to withdraw from Beijing and to solidify their control over Manchuria. The third of Hay's notes, his final statement on the open door policy of the United States, was sent during the Russo-Japanese War and was the result of a German request that the warring nations respect China's territorial integrity.

The United States, intentionally or otherwise, took advantage of the modified open door to exploit the China market. Later, the United States used Japan as a nominal ally to pursue power diplomacy in China. In a sense, the United States had taken a stand against European colonialism in order to seize a portion of the European market in China.

—*Emory M. Thomas, updated by Ann Thompson*

FURTHER READING

Clymer, Kenton J. *John Hay: The Gentleman as Diplomat*. Ann Arbor: University of Michigan Press, 1975. Studies Hay's diplomatic thinking. Chapter 4 gives a complete yet succinct description of Hay's views and actions regarding China.

Dennett, Tyler. *John Hay: From Poetry to Politics*. New York: Dodd, Mead, 1934. Awarded the Pulitzer Prize in biography in 1934, this work is still considered the most thorough biography of John Hay. Chapters 24 and 25 discuss the "Open Door Notes."

Dobson, John M. *America's Ascent: The United States Becomes a Great Power, 1880-1914*. De Kalb: Northern Illinois University Press, 1978. Places late nineteenth and early twentieth century Far Eastern policy, including the "Open Door Notes," in context with other diplomatic actions of the United States.

Esherick, Joseph W. *The Origins of the Boxer Uprising*. Berkeley: University of California Press, 1987. Focuses on internal Chinese affairs and the Chinese government before and during the Boxer Rebellion. U.S. policy on the uprising is stated in the second of Hay's notes.

Kennan, George F. *American Diplomacy*. Expanded ed. Chicago: University of Chicago Press, 1984. Contains a section on Alfred E. Hippisley, a major player in the drafting of the first "Open Door Notes."

Kushmer, Howard I., and Anne Hummel Sherrill. *John Milton Hay: Union of Poetry and Politics*. Boston: Twayne, 1977. Chapter 6 provides comprehensive discussion of the "Open Door Notes" in the context of the economic and diplomatic environment within the United States and with other world powers.

Phillips, Kevin. *William McKinley*. New York: Times Books/Henry Holt, 2003. In his analysis of McKinley's presidency, Phillips concludes McKinley was a "near great" president, whose place in history has been diminished because he was unable to complete his second term. Phillips describes how McKinley began transforming the United States into a global military power, and how many of McKinley's goals were later accomplished by President Theodore Roosevelt.

Varg, Paul A. *Open Door Diplomat: The Life of W. W. Rockhill*. 1952. Reprint. Westport, Conn.: Greenwood Press, 1974. Covers the role of William Woodville Rockhill in the preparation of the "Open Door Notes."

Zimmerman, Warren. *First Great Triumph: How Five Americans Made Their Country a World Power*. New York: Farrar, Straus and Giroux, 2002. John Hay's activities as secretary of state to Presidents McKinley and Theodore Roosevelt are examined in this study of five people who helped make America an international power at the start of the twentieth century.

SEE ALSO: Oct. 23, 1856-Nov. 6, 1860: Second Opium War; 1860's: China's Self-Strengthening Movement Arises; Aug. 1, 1894-Apr. 17, 1895: Sino-Japanese War; Nov. 14, 1897: Scramble for Chinese Concessions Begins; May, 1900-Sept. 7, 1901: Boxer Rebellion.

RELATED ARTICLES in *Great Lives from History: The Nineteenth Century, 1801-1900:* John Hay; William McKinley.

1890's

October 11, 1899-May 31, 1902
SOUTH AFRICAN WAR

Great Britain's war with South Africa's two Afrikaner republics ended Afrikaner hopes for maintaining their independence but established the basis for the larger, unified nation that would later fall under Afrikaner domination. The war also introduced deadly forms of modern warfare to Europeans.

ALSO KNOWN AS: Boer War; Second Boer War; Anglo-Boer War
LOCALE: South Africa
CATEGORIES: Wars, uprisings, and civil unrest; expansion and land acquisition; colonization

KEY FIGURES

Louis Botha (1862-1919), Afrikaner commander of the Transvaal's republican army
Joseph Chamberlain (1836-1914), British colonial secretary, 1895-1903
Christiaan Rudolf de Wet (1854-1922), Afrikaner guerrilla commander
Frederick Sleigh Roberts (1832-1914), British commander in chief in South Africa, 1899-1900
Lord Kitchener (Horatio Herbert Kitchener; 1850-1916), chief of staff under Roberts, whom he succeeded as commander in chief, 1900-1902
Paul Kruger (1825-1904), president of the Transvaal's South African Republic, 1883-1902
Sir Alfred Milner (1854-1925), British governor of the Cape of Good Hope and high commissioner for South Africa, 1897-1901
Cecil Rhodes (1853-1902), head of the British South Africa Company and former prime minister of the Cape of Good Hope, 1890-1896
Marthinus Theunis Steyn (1857-1916), president of the Orange Free State, 1896-1902

SUMMARY OF EVENT

The South African War was a large-scale conflict in which the Afrikaner republics of the Transvaal and the Orange Free State faced the full might of Great Britain. Indeed, it pitted the Afrikaners, or Boers, who were mostly farmers of Dutch descent, against the entire British Empire. The number of casualties that the British would eventually suffer in the war would be greater than the entire Afrikaner population of the two republics it conquered.

The area around the Cape of Good Hope had been colonized by the Dutch in 1652. Because of British expan-

sion into the area after 1806, Afrikaner settlers who resented the British advance began migrating into the interior during the Great Trek of 1835-1838. Of the several independent republics they founded in the interior, the two largest and most enduring were the South African Republic, founded in the Transvaal region in 1852, and the Orange Free State, founded in the region between the Orange and Vaal Rivers in 1854.

Discoveries of diamonds at Kimberley in the northern Cape Colony, near the Orange Free State, in 1867, and of gold on the Witwatersrand in the Transvaal in 1886, brought a large influx of foreigners into the area and transformed the economies of these agricultural societies. Under the leadership of Paul Kruger, president of the South African Republic, these outsiders, or Uitlanders, were denied easy access to citizenship and were taxed heavily in an attempt by the Afrikaner government to maintain political control and autonomy. The Afrikaners feared that if the Uitlanders were granted citizenship and representation in their republics, they would eventually seize control of the governments. The British, however, viewed the Afrikaner measures as repressive and protested against them.

The Afrikaners feared that they might lose their independence, and these fears seemed to be confirmed by the Jameson Raid of December, 1895, to January, 1896. The raid was part of a plot designed by Cecil Rhodes to stir up the Uitlanders to rise up against the government of the Transvaal. A major mine owner, Rhodes was also head of the British South Africa Company—which administered the northern colonies that later became Zimbabwe and Zambia—and the prime minister of the Cape Colony. His coconspirator was Dr. Leander Starr Jameson, the administrator of Rhodesia (Zimbabwe). The plot failed, and because Rhodes had pursued his policy against the advice of British colonial secretary Joseph Chamberlain, he resigned as prime minister. Further restrictions on the Uitlanders in the Transvaal also resulted, and the abortive conspiracy led to a military alliance between the Transvaal and the Orange Free State in 1896. Moreover, the Jameson Raid also provoked worldwide sympathy for the Afrikaners and a general denunciation of British policy.

Meanwhile, the British remained concerned about what they considered to be their legitimate commercial interests in the Afrikaner republics. Sir Alfred Milner, the British governor of the Cape Colony, began a long series of negotiations with the Transvaal's President

Kruger in an effort to resolve the grievances of the Uitlanders. In 1898, Milner returned to London to consult with Chamberlain. While he was absent, his subordinate damaged the British position by suggesting that these grievances of the Uitlanders were being exploited from ulterior motives. This indiscreet remark deepened the suspicions of the Afrikaners. In the spring of 1899, Milner warned Chamberlain that the situation in South Africa was becoming worse.

Chamberlain suggested organizing a conference—a proposal that was supported by the Free State's President Marthinus Theunis Steyn, who hosted discussions at Bloemfontein between Milner and Kruger in May, 1899. No agreements were reached. In August, Kruger offered substantial concessions to the Uitlanders, but by then the British had concluded that establishing British hegemony over all of South Africa was the only solution.

As Uitlanders poured out of the Transvaal in September, 1899, the British began a large-scale military buildup in South Africa. This military menace was the subject of an ultimatum from Kruger on October 9, followed by a declaration of war on October 11. The Orange Free State honored the alliance of 1896 by joining its fellow Afrikaner republic in declaring war on the British.

The progress of the South African War can be divided into three well-defined phases. The first, from October, 1899, to February, 1900, was marked by a strong and successful Afrikaner offensive. The Afrikaners invaded Great Britain's Natal colony on the east coast besieged British forces at Ladysmith, Mafeking, and Kimberley. Afrikaner forces also crossed the Orange River that separated the Orange Free State from the Cape Colony. In the second phase, from February to September, 1900, British forces under the command of Field Marshal Frederick Sleigh Roberts occupied all the major towns and annexed the Transvaal. The third and most painful phase, from September, 1900, to May, 1902, was marked by guerrilla warfare by the Afrikaners under the leadership of their generals, notably Louis Botha and Christiaan Rudolf de Wet.

Afrikaner attack on a British convoy during the last months of the South African War, when Afrikaner forces relied heavily on guerrilla tactics. (Francis R. Niglutsch)

After Roberts was made an earl in November, 1900, he handed over command to his chief of staff, General Horatio Herbert Kitchener. Kitchener then began rounding up Afrikaner women and children and placing them in concentration camps. Epidemics soon broke out in the camps, and there was an appalling death rate among prisoners until British officials compelled the military to improve living conditions in the camps. The British also built a system of blockhouses throughout the countryside. They then proceeded to run down the guerrilla bands by combing the country section by section.

SIGNIFICANCE

The signing of the Treaty of Vereeniging on May 31, 1902, ended the most serious challenge to the British Empire since the Napoleonic Wars (1793-1815). The British effort had been marked by the participation of troops from Australia, Canada, and other colonies. The Afrikaners lost their independence and became British subjects. Although the war ultimately established the foundation for the Union of South Africa (later the Republic of South Africa), the bitterness engendered by the war continued to affect the political life of South Africa through the twentieth century.

The cost of the war was high for Britain, with more than 100,000 total casualties. For the Afrikaners, however, the loss of 7,000 lives dead out of a total population of 87,000 was devastating. Meanwhile, as historian Thomas Pakenham observed, the "central tactical lesson of the war eluded the British," who tended to credit Afrikaner marksmanship or the enemy's superior weapons with prolonging the conflict. Instead, the appearance of smokeless guns (witnessed firsthand by American soldiers in Cuba at roughly the same time) and the use of the machine gun, when combined with trenches, had raised the defense to a new preeminence—a status that became even more apparent during World War I.

— *Martin L. Dolan, updated by Larry Schweikart*

FURTHER READING

Bidwell, Shelford, and Dominick Graham. *Fire-Power: British Army Weapons and Theories of War, 1904-1945*. London: Allen & Unwin, 1982. Beginning its narrative shortly after the conclusion of the South African War, this book traces the impact of the British experience in the war on later British military strategy, tactics, and weapons.

Churchill, Winston S. *London to Ladysmith via Pretoria*. Reprint. Rockville, Md.: Wildside Press, 2005. First-person account of Churchill's experiences as a war correspondent in South Africa during the early months of the conflict, when he was captured by Afrikaners.

Farwell, Byron. *The Great Anglo-Boer War*. New York: W. W. Norton, 1990. Solid popular history of the South African War that describes battles and opposing policies, with considerable attention to Kruger's own role.

German General Staff. *The War in South Africa, 1899-1900*. 2 vols. Reprint. Nashville, Tenn.: Battery Press, 1999. Limited edition reprint of the detailed analysis of the South African War compiled by the German general staff for use in officer training. Covers events of the war through September, 1900. Includes illustrations and large, detailed maps.

Holt, Edgar. *The Boer War*. London: G. P. Putnam's Sons, 1958. Before Pakenham's book, this was probably the best single-volume military treatment of the war, although one that ignored the racial elements of the Afrikaner positions.

Pakenham, Thomas. *The Boer War*. New York: Random House, 1979. Thoroughly researched and comprehensive study of the South African War that is unmatched in detail and use of primary sources.

Phimister, Ian. "Unscrambling the Scramble for Southern Africa: The Jameson Raid and South African War Revisited." *South African Historical Journal* 28 (1993): 214-220. Revisionist examination of the Jameson Raid's role in furthering the objectives of the British imperial machine.

SEE ALSO: 1835: South Africa's Great Trek Begins; Jan. 22-Aug., 1879: Zulu War; Dec. 16, 1880-Mar. 6, 1881: First Boer War; June 21, 1884: Gold Is Discovered in the Transvaal; Mar. 13, 1888: Rhodes Amalgamates Kimberley Diamondfields; Oct., 1893-October, 1897: British Subdue African Resistance in Rhodesia; Dec. 29, 1895-Jan. 2, 1896: Jameson Raid; Oct. 13, 1899-May 17, 1900: Siege of Mafeking.

RELATED ARTICLES in *Great Lives from History: The Nineteenth Century, 1801-1900:* Sir Robert Stephenson Smyth Baden-Powell; Joseph Chamberlain; Paul Kruger; Cecil Rhodes.

October 13, 1899-May 17, 1900
SIEGE OF MAFEKING

The masterful British defense of Mafeking under the leadership of Colonel Robert Baden-Powell was the most important psychological turning point in the South African War. The lifting of the siege marked the beginning of the end of Afrikaner resistance and prompted nearly hysterical displays of jingoism in England.

LOCALE: Mafeking, South Africa
CATEGORY: Wars, uprisings, and civil unrest

KEY FIGURES

Robert Stephenson Smyth Baden-Powell (1857-1941), British commander at Mafeking
Lord Edward Herbert Cecil (1867-1918), British major serving under Baden-Powell
Piet Cronje (1840?-1911), Afrikaner commander of the Transvaal troops that besieged Mafeking
Frederick Sleigh Roberts (1832-1914), British commander in chief during the first phase of the South African War
Sir Bryan Mahon (1862-1930), commander of the British relief force

SUMMARY OF EVENT

In August, 1899, Mafeking was an important rail center between Cape Town and Rhodesia. A town with more than nine thousand inhabitants, 80 percent of whom were black, it had simple adobe buildings, arranged in orderly fashion around a small town square. Its unprepossessing appearance belied the strategic importance it would have if a war were to erupt between the British in the Cape Colony and the South African Republic, the Afrikaner republic in the Transvaal that lay only eight miles to the east. If the Transvaal Afrikaners could take Mafeking immediately after the opening of hostilities, perhaps all the Afrikaners would join them in driving the British from South Africa. Colonel Robert Baden-Powell was sent to Mafeking to make sure that this did not happen. Noted for his cunning and ingenuity, he proved the perfect officer for this difficult assignment.

Through August and September, Baden-Powell developed and implemented a plan for the defense of Mafeking that was part bluff and part genius. The town lay in the middle of an arid plain with no natural defensive barriers. To remedy this, Baden-Powell supervised the construction of sixty sandbag forts along a perimeter well beyond the town limits. He expected that the Afri-

kaners would try to take Mafeking using long-range guns purchased from Germany and France. The farther from the center of the town their modern cannons were placed, the less damage the militarily inexperienced Afrikaners would be able inflict. Baden-Powell also wanted to ring Mafeking with land mines but did not have the proper materials to construct them. Working in a makeshift secret laboratory, his men instead created what appeared to be lethal weapons but which in fact were wooden boxes filled only with sand. To convince the spies in Mafeking that the bogus mines were genuine, and to reassure Mafeking's inhabitants that everything was being done to protect them, Baden-Powell periodically secretly detonated a stick of dynamite along the circle of bogus mines to give the appearance of testing them. The controlled explosions convinced both groups.

On October 9, 1899, the South African Republic's president Paul Kruger sent an ultimatum to the British government to remove its troops from South Africa within forty-eight hours or a state of war would exist between his republic and Great Britain. Two days later the first shots of the war were fired, and two days after that, on October 13, the Afrikaner siege of Mafeking began.

General Piet S. Cronje commanded the Afrikaner troops that ringed Mafeking. His demand that the British surrender the town at once was politely refused. Instead of waiting for the enemy to attack, Baden-Powell took the war to the Afrikaners in a series of well-planned forays. These brief sorties convinced him that his adversaries were mostly inexperienced soldiers, and that Cronje believed that heavy casualties would undermine support for the war among Afrikaners. Baden-Powell was determined that the Afrikaners would pay dearly for every foot of ground they might gain.

During the often brutal and seemingly endless Afrikaner shelling that reduced much of Mafeking to rubble, the civilian population behaved with a calm and steady courage. In fact, for the town's young boys, the siege almost became a lark. To curb their energies and prevent a possible tragedy, Baden-Powell charged his subordinate, Major Lord Edward Herbert Cecil, to organize the Mafeking Cadet Corps—the prototype of Baden-Powell's Boy Scouts. The effort was successful, and the boys provided valuable service in a number of roles.

Baden-Powell kept in touch with the outside world by using African runners, who risked their lives every time they slipped through the Afrikaner lines. Through the in-

Revelers in London's Hampstead neighborhood celebrating news of the lifting of the Mafeking siege. So great was British rejoicing that "mafficking" entered the English language as a term for boisterous celebrating, particularly in patriotic causes. "Bravo B.P." is an allusion to Colonel Baden-Powell. (Hulton Archive/Getty Images)

formation the runners brought in, Baden-Powell learned early in the siege that a number of unexpected reverses would prevent General Frederick Sleigh Roberts, the British commander in chief in South Africa, from relieving Mafeking in the foreseeable future. Baden-Powell and his fellow defenders were thus left alone with little hope of reinforcements or supplies. However, Baden-Powell had made his initial plans with that possiblity in mind. Rationing of food, fuel, and other supplies had been routine from the moment that war was declared.

Because the siege had begun in the midst of the Southern Hemisphere's spring, residents of Mafeking had been encouraged to use every available plot of ground to grow fruits and vegetables to supplement the limited supplies of foodstuffs. The result was that everyone received enough rations to maintain an adequate and nourishing—if uninteresting—diet. When the supply of fresh meat from local livestock was exhausted, horses and even stray dogs were consumed. There were certainly complaints about rationing and the often imperious manner in which Baden-Powell managed every aspect of town life during the siege, but most inhabitants of Mafeking did their part to win the struggle against the Afrikaners.

Finally, on May 17, 1900, a relief force under the command of Colonel Bryan Mahon reached Mafeking. After 217 days the siege was lifted, and the Afrikaners retreated. When the news reached London, the city erupted in a celebration of patriotism mingled with relief. The word "mafficking" then entered the language to describe hysterical celebrating, Baden-Powell became a national hero, and the newspapers were filled with details—both genuine and bogus—of his struggle against the Afrikaners. At an age when most army officers were looking forward to winding down their careers, Baden-Powell was about to begin another and more public phase of his life. He was barely forty-three when the Siege of Mafeking was lifted; half of his life—the most public part—lay before him.

SIGNIFICANCE

While Mafeking was certainly valuable militarily, its real importance was psychological. The siege became a test of wills, achieving a significance far beyond its immediate strategic value. The victors at Mafeking would win the war. Because Baden-Powell was able to withstand the repeated Afrikaner attacks until relief arrived,

Kruger did not receive the popular support that was crucial for a Afrikaner victory. Inspired by the resistance of the soldiers and civilians of Mafeking, the British forces achieved the final victory, and all of South Africa was added to the British Empire. However, the most lasting and positive outcome of the siege was the inception of the world scouting movement. Born of necessity in the midst of war, it would, under the leadership of Lord Baden-Powell of Gilwell, transform the lives of millions of young men and women in the twentieth century.

—*Clifton W. Potter, Jr.*

FURTHER READING

Grinnell-Milne, Duncan. *Baden-Powell at Mafeking*. London: Bodley Head, 1957. Although somewhat dated, this is a well-written, concise, and entertaining biography of the hero of Mafeking.

Hillcourt, William, and Olave Lady Baden-Powell. *Baden-Powell, The Two Lives of a Hero*. New York: Gilwellian Press, 1992. This is the best brief, but complete, biography of Baden-Powell, written by two who knew him well.

Hopkins, Pat, and Heather Dugmore. *The Boy: Baden-Powell and the Siege of Mafeking*. Rivonia, South Africa: Zebra Press, 1999. Revisionist study of not only the siege but also Baden-Powell himself and the British presence in South Africa at the end of the nineteenth century.

Jeal, Tim. *Baden-Powell*. New Haven, Conn.: Yale University Press, 2001. Revisionist study that defends Baden-Powell from his late twentieth century critics, particularly those who contend that he used the South African War for his own aggrandizement. It has an extensive bibliography, which will prove useful to scholars.

MacDonald, Robert H. *Sons of the Empire: The Frontier and the Boy Scout Movement, 1890-1918*. Toronto, Ont.: University of Toronto Press, 1993. Interesting study of the genesis of the international scouting movement and Baden-Powell's role in founding it.

Midgley, John F. *Petticoat in Mafeking: The Letters of Ada Cook with Annotations and a Vindication of Baden-Powell*. Kommetjie, South Africa: J. D. Midgley, 1974. Exciting eyewitness account of the siege and liberation of Mafeking.

Plaatje, Sol T. *Mafeking Diary: A Black Man's View of a White Man's War*. Edited by John Comaroff with Brian Willan and Andrew Reed. London: James Currey, 1990. Firsthand account of the siege by a resident African who would later become a prominent journalist and nationalist figure. Plaatje's account provides an interesting alternative to the studies that place an emphasis on the heroic sacrifices made by the British to secure an empire in Africa.

SEE ALSO: 1835: South Africa's Great Trek Begins; Dec. 16, 1880-Mar. 6, 1881: First Boer War; Dec. 29, 1895-Jan. 2, 1896: Jameson Raid; Oct. 11, 1899-May 31, 1902: South African War.

RELATED ARTICLES in *Great Lives from History: The Nineteenth Century, 1801-1900:* Sir Robert Stephenson Smyth Baden-Powell; Paul Kruger.

1890's

1900
FREUD PUBLISHES *THE INTERPRETATION OF DREAMS*

Freud's The Interpretation of Dreams *employed dream analysis to introduce his influential theory that unconscious motives, molded from relationships in childhood, are basic to adult personality.*

ALSO KNOWN AS: *Die Traumdeutung*
LOCALE: Vienna, Austria
CATEGORIES: Psychology and psychiatry; philosophy; literature

KEY FIGURES
Sigmund Freud (1856-1939), Austrian neurologist and founder of psychoanalysis
Josef Breuer (1842-1925), Austrian physician who worked with Freud on hysteria
Erik H. Erikson (1902-1994), German-born American psychoanalyst who modified Freud's ideas

SUMMARY OF EVENT

Die Traumdeutung (1900; *The Interpretation of Dreams,* 1913) is widely considered to be among the greatest works of Sigmund Freud. It is certainly one that Freud himself considered most important, as evidenced by the fact that it is the only one of Freud's early works that he repeatedly revised throughout his career as new information and clinical experience caused him to modify his theories. This work is important because it introduced the core ideas of psychoanalysis, the still influential theory that hidden, unconscious feelings and motives determine both the symptoms of mental patients and the normal thoughts and deeds of everyday life.

Even before he began his study of dreams, Freud, an Austrian neurologist, had already proved himself a capable medical researcher and produced several significant papers on neurological conditions. About 1885, Freud was introduced to the study of hypnotism, and during the 1890's he worked with Josef Breuer to develop a theory of hysteria. Breuer had called to the attention of Freud the case of a young girl who suffered from apparent paralysis and psychic confusion. He noticed that if the girl were allowed to give verbal expression to her fantasies, the symptoms tended to disappear. This would prove to be an important factor in the development of psychoanalysis, which is sometimes referred to as the "talking cure."

Breuer also observed that, whereas the girl could not account for her symptoms in a conscious state, under hypnosis she well understood the connection between her symptoms and past experiences. From this case,

Breuer and Freud developed their theory that hysteria is a condition that imitates a physical or neurological disorder but for which no physical or neurological causes can be discovered. According to the theory, hysteria springs from the repression of desired acts and can be cured only by a kind of catharsis in which unconscious desires are rendered conscious and meaningful.

These studies in hysteria contained one basic idea that Freud was later to develop in his theory of psychoanalysis: that a significant aspect of mental life was "unconscious." Inexpressible in rational language, the unconscious had indirect and sometimes perverse effects upon daily activity. During the 1890's, Freud began to appreciate the general significance of his discovery. He began to analyze his own dreams and unintentional behavior. The unconscious, he realized, could be revealed in many ways other than hypnosis, and its significance was not limited to mental patients. Indeed, Freud came to call

Sigmund Freud. (Library of Congress)

dreams the "royal road" to the unconscious, the privileged arena for finding evidence of unconscious impulses. *The Interpretation of Dreams* was significant, then, in that it introduced psychoanalysis not only as a treatment for hysteria but also as a comprehensive theory of human motivation and development.

The Interpretation of Dreams is distinguished both by the methodology with which it intends to investigate dreams and by the meaning that it assigns to dreams. Freud argues that the meaning of a dream is not to be discovered by some hidden logic, but rather through a process of free association, by getting the dreamer to uncover its meaning. What is the nature of a dream? Basically, Freud sees it as a protector of sleep that simultaneously expresses and censors the unconscious desires that are allowed free play once conscious mental activity is suspended. Thus, the manifest dream (the dream that is remembered in a conscious state) is not the same as the latent dream thought or desire, because this desire is often of such a nature (usually sexual) that it conflicts with the requirements of society and the moral code that the individual imposes upon him- or herself. The manifest dream partly censors this unconscious desire and at the same time expresses it in symbolic form. The decoding of such symbolism is the entrance into the complexes that, if not understood and rationally dealt with, lead to mental disorder.

The Interpretation of Dreams was far from Freud's final word; in his attempts to chart the mechanism of the unconscious, he constantly revised his theories. Nevertheless, it contained the basis of his subsequent work on the psychology of the individual and his attempts to apply the insights of psychoanalysis to cultural anthropology. Certainly, it expressed that ambiguity which Freud discovered at the heart of human existence, the conflict inherent in what he describes as the pleasure principle, and it explains that spirit of pessimism which was so strong a characteristic of Freud's thought.

Several core themes of Freud's "dream book" became further elaborated in his later writings. The centrality of forbidden wishes modified and deflected by a "censor" remained one such continuing theme. "The censor" was in later work subdivided into the realistic controls of the conscious self, the "ego," and less rational, moralistic restraints and demands of an internalized parental image, the "superego." One core theme, the eroticized love for one's parent of the opposite sex and jealousy of one's same-sex parental rival, recurred in many dreams. This, later labeled the Oedipus complex, was considered by Freud as basic to adult sexual identity and to neurosis.

The mechanism of displaced symbolization that disguises forbidden dream wishes was later elaborated into Freud's many "mechanisms of defense."

Not all of Freud's assumptions in 1900 have withstood the test of time. Freud's theory of motivation rested upon a hydraulic, tension-reducing analogy in which such motives as sex and aggression would build up a sort of pressure that would demand some sort of release. The thrust of more recent psychology gives far more attention than did Freud to the joys of seeking out self-enhancing activities that often involve increased tension and excitement. Major twentieth century psychoanalysts such as Erik H. Erikson give more emphasis than did Freud to the social interactions between parent and child quite apart from the sexual overtones of such relationships.

Freud's writings suffer in several ways from male biases characteristic of views of women prevalent in his time. Freud's account of little girls' family affections and jealousies was heavily flavored by an assumption of the biologically rooted inadequacy of women, an assumption that finds few defenders a century later. It has been charged that Freud too readily dismissed as fantasies reports by female patients of sexual abuse by trusted men. This may or may not be true, but it tends to overlook the fact that Freud, throughout his career, agonized over the relationship between external reality and fantasy in mental life and spent considerable energy attempting to ascertain whether such reports were in fact based in fantasy or in external experience.

SIGNIFICANCE

Many of the ideas found in *The Interpretation of Dreams* retain the vitality of having endured a century of research. Freud's thesis that dreams are meaningful clues to motives important in waking life is still treated with respect by many students of personality and biopsychology. With the discovery by twentieth century neuropsychologists that dreaming episodes in sleep are accompanied by such distinctive neurophysiological signs as rapid eye movements, it became possible to study the nature of dreams with an objectivity greater than was possible for Freud. It appears that dreams are the result of random firing by neurons deep within the brain stem. Such dream episodes occur several times a night, and most are immediately forgotten. However, the few dreams that are remembered may be precisely those that have personal significance.

Fundamentals of Freud's thought survive in psychoanalysis and in scientific psychology. In 1993, some 8,197 members of the International Psychoanalytic Association practiced their healing art. More important, basic Freudian ideas have become a vital, often unrecognized, part of mainstream psychology. Relationships between the quality of childhood-caretaker attachments and adult styles of relating to others is a popular research topic in developmental psychology. The importance of implicit ("unconscious") adaptive styles, to cite another example, has become an important concern of cognitive psychology.

Post-Freudian art, literature, films, and television, no less than psychology, treat human emotions as subtle, complex, and often paradoxical, a view more consistent with Freud's portrayal of human nature than of prior nineteenth century conceptions of human rationality. Most of all, the study of the mind, which was the domain of magic, religion, and speculative philosophy in 1900, has forever become the province of science. Without the stimulus of Freud's ideas, human understanding of life itself would not be at all the same.

—Paul T. Mason, updated by Thomas E. DeWolfe

FURTHER READING

Cohen, Josh. *How to Read Freud*. New York: W. W. Norton, 2005. Useful analysis of key concepts in Freud's writings.

Erikson, Erik. *Childhood and Society*. New York: W. W. Norton, 1950. This work incorporates major post-Freudian developments in psychoanalysis, especially the importance of social factors in childhood.

Gay, Peter. *Freud: A Life for Our Time*. New York: W. W. Norton, 1988. This biography of Freud is comprehensive, thoroughly researched, balanced, and fair, taking into account the criticisms of Freud and also respecting his magnificent achievements.

Jones, Ernest. *The Life and Works of Sigmund Freud*. 3 vols. New York: Basic Books, 1957. An exhaustive work that benefits from the author's long personal association with Freud, but possibly suffers from the positive biases of an admiring disciple.

MacIntyre, Alasdair. *The Unconscious: A Conceptual Analysis*. Rev. ed. New York: Routledge, 2004. A philosophical analysis of Freud's concept of the unconscious, by the foremost moral philosopher of the late twentieth century.

Masson, Jeffrey M. *The Assault on Truth: Freud's Suppression of the Seduction Theory*. New York: Farrar, Straus and Giroux, 1984. This author calls into question Freud's fairness toward women and argues that Freud dismissed as Oedipal fantasies some accounts of real seduction of children.

Neu, Jerome, ed. *The Cambridge Companion to Freud*. New York: Cambridge University Press, 1991. This work contains evaluative essays on such classic Freudian concepts as the interpretation of dreams and on more general topics such as Freud's ideas on women.

Nye, Robert D. *Three Psychologies: Perspectives from Freud, Skinner, and Rogers*. Pacific Grove, Calif.: Brooks-Cole, 1992. This short work contains a clear, succinct, and accurate overview of Freud and psychoanalysis for the introductory student.

Perelberg, Rosine Jozef, ed. *Freud: A Modern Reader*. Philadelphia: Whurr, 2005. Anthology of essays interpreting Freud from the point of view of early twenty-first century scholarship.

Sulloway, Frank J. *Freud: Biologist of the Mind*. New York: Basic Books, 1979. This author seeks to dispel the myth of Freud as a "psychoanalytic hero" alone facing a hostile world.

SEE ALSO: Apr., 1807: Hegel Publishes *The Phenomenology of Spirit*; 1819: Schopenhauer Publishes *The World as Will and Idea*; Feb., 1848: Marx and Engels Publish *The Communist Manifesto*; 1867: Marx Publishes *Das Kapital*; 1897: Ellis Publishes *Sexual Inversion*.

RELATED ARTICLES in *Great Lives from History: The Nineteenth Century, 1801-1900:* Samuel Butler; H. Rider Haggard; Tadano Makuzu.

1900
LEBESGUE DEVELOPS NEW INTEGRATION THEORY

Henri-Léon Lebesgue developed a new theory for integrating discontinuous functions, based on a more general set-theoretic concept of measure, which furthered the development of the calculus.

LOCALE: Rennes, France
CATEGORY: Mathematics

KEY FIGURES
Henri-Léon Lebesgue (1875-1941), French mathematician
Émile Borel (1871-1956), French mathematician and politician
William Henry Young (1863-1943), English mathematician

SUMMARY OF EVENT

Since Euclid's *Stoicheia* (c. 300 B.C.E.; *The Elements of Geometrie of the Most Auncient Philosopher Euclide of Megara*, 1570; commonly known as the *Elements*), the theory of measurements in mathematics generally was thought to encompass little more than systematically comparing the points, lines, or planes to be measured to a standard reference. With Pythagoras's discovery of geometric incommensurables (irrational numbers), it was realized gradually that the question of mathematical measurement, in general, requires more precise and comprehensive consideration of seemingly infinite processes and collections. Development of the differential and integral calculus and limit theory by Sir Isaac Newton and Gottfried Wilhelm Leibniz brought with it the realization that, for most geometric figures, true mathematical measures do not exist a priori, but rather depend on the existence and computability of strictly defined associated limits.

In 1822, French physicist and mathematician Joseph Fourier discovered that computation of sets of harmonic (trigonometric) series used to approximate a given function depended upon appropriate existence and calculations using integrals. Integration, or integral theory, concerns the techniques of finding a function $g(x)$, the first derivatives of which are equal to a given function $f(x)$. These, in turn, depend on how discontinuous the function is. A function is a mathematical expression defining the relation between one (independent) and another (dependent) variable. Although it was known that every continuous function has an integral summation, it was not clear at that time whether or how an integral could be defined

for the many different classes of discontinuous functions; that is, those functions that are not definable at one or more specific points. A function is continuous if it is possible to plot it as a single, unbroken curve.

In 1854, the German mathematician Georg Friedrich Riemann offered the first partial answer to the question of how to integrate discontinuous functions, based on approximating integrands having only a finite number of definitely known discontinuous points by a sum of step functions, instead of the curve-tangent sums of earlier calculus. The sum or measure of the Riemann integral is equal to the area of the region bounded by the curve $f(x)$. Yet, one of the many classic functions of importance to mathematics and physics, for which Riemann integration cannot be defined, is the "salt and pepper" function of Peter Dirichelet, where $f(x) = 1$ if x is rational, and 0 if x is irrational.

Earlier, in 1834, Austrian mathematician-philosopher Bernhard Bolzano gave examples of mathematically continuous functions that are nowhere differentiable and, thus, unintegrable by Riemann's definition. Karl Theodor Weierstrass provided similar examples in 1875. Further motivations for clarifying the notions of continuity and integration arose in 1885, when German mathematician Adolf Harnack paradoxically showed that any countable subset of the real number system could be covered by a collection of intervals of arbitrarily small total length.

As a reaction to these difficulties, between 1880 and 1885, French geometrician Jean Darboux gave a novel definition of continuity, for the first time as a locally definable (versus global) mathematical property for discontinuous functions. Likewise, Camille Jordan, in 1892, first defined analogously the more general notion of "mathematical measure," using finite unions of mathematical intervals to approximate sparse and dense subsets of real numbers. Nevertheless, the opinions of many leading mathematicians such as Henri Poincaré and Charles Hermite differed as to whether discontinuous functions and functions without derivatives were legitimate mathematical objects, as well as how to define the concept of a normal versus a "pathological" function.

The first mathematician to infer from the above results that countable unions of intervals should be used to measure the more general entity of real number subsets was Émile Borel. In 1898, in his *Leçons sur la théorie des fonctions* (lectures on the theory of functions), Borel advocated an abstract axiomatics of constructivistic definitions. Constructivistic, in this case, meant that all proposed definitions should permit explicit construction of actual examples of the mathematical entities referred to. Borel redefined the "measure" of any countable union of real number intervals to be its total length and thereby extended the notion of abstract measurability to progressively more complex sets. Borel sought to generalize Georg Cantor's set theory, as well as to explicitly study "pathological" functions definable in terms of point sets. For Borel, the main problem was how to assign consistently to each pathologic point or singularity an appropriate numerical measure, meaning a nonnegative real number precisely analogous to length, area, and volume. Starting with elementary geometrical figures, Borel sought to define constructively measures to these sets so that formal measures of a line segment, or polygon, is always the same as its Euclidean measure and that the measure of a finite or countably infinite union of nonoverlapping sets is equal to the sum of the measures of all individual sets.

Cantor's set theory had expanded the definition of continuity to include not only geometric smoothness (or nonvariability) of a curve but also its pointwise mapping, or set theoretic correspondence. One of the results of Borel's studies was the well-known Heine-Borel theorem, which states that if a closed set of points on a line can be covered by a set of intervals, such that every point of this set is an interior point of at least one of the intervals, then there exists a finite number of intervals with this "covering" property. For Borel, any such set obtainable by the basic mathematical properties and operations of union and intersection of sets in principle has a measure.

With these ideas as background, in 1900, Henri-Léon Lebesgue sought to enlarge Borel's notion of measurable sets in order to apply it explicitly to the problem of integrating a wider class of pathological functions than those permitted by Riemann's integral. In the preface of his doctoral dissertation, Lebesgue outlined his motivations and methods. In contrast to Borel, Lebesgue employed a nonaxiomatic descriptive approach, one of the key results of which was to solve the problem of defining an integral measure for discontinuous functions in general, insofar as it is necessary here that an infinite but bounded set have finite measure. Lebesgue generalized Riemann's definition of the integral by applying this new definition of measure.

In the second chapter of his dissertation, Lebesgue proposed five criteria necessary for sufficiently widening integration theory, including the need to contain Riemann's definition as a special case to incorporate

only assumptions and results in this extension that are natural, necessary, and computationally useful. Another key insight of Lebesgue's integration theory is that every function with bounded measure is also integrable. Perhaps the most critical property of Borel-Lebesgue measure is its property of summability, or countable additivity. In particular, Lebesgue showed that this property, of term-by-term integrability, gives a definition of the integral much wider and with more stable computational properties in the limit than Riemann's integral. For example, if the approximation to a discontinuous function $f(s)$ approaches $f(x)$, as the number of terms of the approximations approaches infinity, then the integral of this series approximates the integral of the function in the limit; in general, this property of uniform-convergence is not true for Riemann's integration.

As noted in Thomas Hawkins's *Lebesgue's Theory of Integration* (1970), much of the power of Lebesgue's integration results from judicious use of the techniques of monotonic sequences and bracketing. Substituting equivalent monotonic sequences for complicated functions simplifies convergence in the limit. The bracketing technique consists of using the integrals of two well-behaved ("tame") functions to bracket as upper and lower bounds the integral of the pathological function. Instead of subdividing the domain of the independent variable x (abscissa axis), Lebesgue subdivided the range (ordinate axis) of the corresponding function $f(x)$ into subintervals. Therefore, Lebesgue's integration replaces Riemann's integral sums in the limit as sampling intervals approach 0. Lebesgue's theory of the integral also yields other important results, such as extending the fundamental theorem of calculus.

SIGNIFICANCE

Initially, Lebesgue's work met with strong and lasting controversy from Borel. The main point of contention was not so much the mathematical results as the meta-mathematical methods used by each. Lebesgue subsequently developed the ideas of his dissertation further, and soon published these in his two classic texts, *Leçons sur les series trigonométriques* (1906; lessons on the trigonometric series) and *Leçons sur l'integration et la recherche des fonctions primitives* (1904; lessons on integration and analysis of primitive functions). Despite the fact that it was recognized early by some as an important innovation, Lebesgue's integration was comparatively slow to be adopted by the mathematical community at large. In 1906, Lebesgue's contemporary, the English mathematician William Henry Young, independently arrived at a somewhat more general but operationally equivalent definition of Lebesgue-type integration, using the method of monotone sequences. Most textbook discussions of Lebesgue integration have incorporated a combination of Young's notation and formalism with Lebesgue's arguments and examples.

Lebesgue's integral, despite its major advantages, did not generalize completely the concept of integration for all discontinuous functions. For example, Lebesgue integration did not treat the case of unbounded functions and intervals. Subsequently, Arnaud Denjoy in 1912, Thomas Stieltjes in 1913, and Johann Radon and Maurice-René Fréchet in 1915 created other more encompassing definitions of the definite integral over complicated functions. Fréchet, in particular, showed how to generalize Lebesgue's integral to treat functions defined on an arbitrary set without any reference to topological or metric concepts of measure, later leading to Hausdorff dimensional or (Mandelbrot) fractal measures. As further reformulated by Beppo Levi, Lebesgue integrable functions are those that almost always equal the sum of a series of step functions.

Many of the complicated functions of aerodynamics and fluid dynamics, electromagnetic theory, and the theory of probability were for the first time analytically integrable using Lebesgue's method. In his book on the axiomatic foundations of Andrey Markov's probability theory, A. N. Kolmogorov defined a number of operational analogues between the Borel-Lebesgue measure of a set and the probability of an event.

—*Gerardo G. Tango*

FURTHER READING

Bear, H. S. *A Primer of Lebesgue Integration.* 2d ed. San Diego, Calif.: Academic Press, 2002. Explains the principles and importance of Lebesgue's contribution to the calculus.

Craven, B. O. *The Lebesgue Measure and Integral.* Boston: Pitman Press, 1981. An intermediate treatment, but more comprehensive. Includes a modern presentation of Borel's set measure.

Kestelman, Hyman. *Modern Theories of Integration.* Oxford, England: Clarendon Press, 1937. Gives a complete but rather abstract synopsis of contemporary integration theory.

Kline, Morris. *Mathematical Thought from Ancient to Modern Times.* New York: Oxford University Press, 1990. The standard reference for the history of limit and function theory.

Monna, A. F. "The Integral from Riemann to Bourbaki." In *Sets and Integration,* edited by Dirk Van Dalen and A. F. Monna. Groningen, the Netherlands: Wolters-Noordhoff, 1972. Provides a more technical discussion.

Temple, George E J. *The Structure of Lebesgue Integration Theory.* Oxford, England: Clarendon Press, 1971. The most detailed, step-by-step treatment of the modern integration theory.

Young, W. H., and G. C. Young. *The Theory of Sets of Points.* Cambridge, England: Cambridge University Press, 1906. Contains Young's alternative independent development of what is essentially Lebesgue measure-based integration theory.

SEE ALSO: 1819-1833: Babbage Designs a Mechanical Calculator; 1847: Boole Publishes *The Mathematical Analysis of Logic*; 1899: Hilbert Publishes *The Foundations of Geometry.*

RELATED ARTICLE in *Great Lives from History: The Nineteenth Century, 1801-1900:* Joseph Fourier.

1890's

1900
WIECHERT INVENTS THE INVERTED PENDULUM SEISMOGRAPH

Emil Wiechert introduced a damping mechanism that restrained the seismograph pendulum and greatly increased its accuracy. The evolution of the modern seismograph, led by Wiechert's invention, led to an explosion of knowledge about not only earthquakes but also Earth's crust and interior.

LOCALE: Gottingen, Germany
CATEGORIES: Inventions; geology; earth science; science and technology; physics; engineering

KEY FIGURES
Emil Wiechert (1861-1928), German seismologist and geophysicist
John Milne (1850-1913), English seismologist, geologist, and engineer

SUMMARY OF EVENT
Prior to the development of the science of seismology, the study of earthquakes and measurement of the elastic properties of the earth, the natural philosophers of the late nineteenth century held varying views on the composition inside the earth. One view was that if the inside were liquid, then the surface of the earth would rise and fall almost like the tides of the oceans. Another view was that the geological hypothesis of a fluid interior is untenable, and the overall rigidity of the earth's interior is considerable.

The invention of the seismograph, an instrument for recording the phenomena of earthquakes, at the end of the nineteenth century was to open the twentieth century with an explosion of discoveries about the inner earth. The first seismographs were delicate horizontal pendulums that registered singular waves. Such an instrument was used by the German seismologist E. von Rebeur Paschwitz on April 18, 1889, when he correlated horizontal pendulum recordings at Potsdam and Wilhelmshaven with a great earthquake in Tokyo. Four years later, John Milne, an English seismologist, geologist, and mining engineer, invented the first clockwork-powered seismograph. As a result of this invention, when an earthquake occurred, it became possible to record continuously the seismic waves, earth vibrations, produced during an earthquake. Seismic waves carry information to the surface on the structure through which they have passed. The Milne seismograph was the first to record the movements of the earth in all three of their components: up and down, back and forth, and side to side.

An important fact in the study of earthquakes is that there are two types of waves that can be transmitted through a homogeneous, isotropic, elastic solid such as the earth. Isotropic means having the same properties in like degree in all directions. These waves are dilatational (compressional) waves, such as sound waves, which involve particle motions parallel to the direction of the energy; and transverse (shear) waves, which involve motion at right angles to this direction. Emil Wiechert, in 1899, independent of similar work by Richard D. Oldham, an Irish seismologist, determined that the P waves were dilatational and the S waves shear waves.

The Milne seismograph and others developed at the end of the nineteenth century fell short of meeting the demands of a science that was asking ever more complex questions. These early machines measured only a portion of the broad band of wave size and frequencies. Another shortcoming was the tendency of the seismograph's pendulum to keep swinging indefinitely once a strong motion had started it. Without a way to control the pendulum's motion, the seismograph was unable to record accurately the other kinds of waves that arrived later. Wiechert, a German seismologist, started developing a damping mechanism around 1898 that restrained the seismograph pendulum, greatly increasing the seismograph's accuracy. He perfected his early model in 1900. It had one major shortcoming, however, in that it was bulky. It depended upon weights large enough to remain at rest despite the energy transmitted both by the shaking of the instrument's frame and by the mechanical linkage that inscribed the seismic waves on paper.

The Wiechert seismograph, an inverted pendulum, permitted the detection of the vertical component of long earthquake waves. The amplification of the boom movement was achieved by using a system of mechanical levers and recorded by a stylus scratching on smoked paper. It had a mass of seventeen tons supported on a vertical column, which acted as the boom. Its period was about a second, and its magnification was two thousand.

In his experimentation, Wiechert found that the only way to make a seismometer (an instrument for measuring the direction, intensity, and duration of earthquakes) react to the vertical component above was to counteract the force of gravity by a spring. In the inverted pendulum, the mass is held on the right and left by spiral springs. It rests and oscillates upon a sharp horizontal edge turned at right angles to the direction of the movements.

Prior to inventing the inverted pendulum seismograph, Wiechert had suggested the existence of a central core within the earth. He speculated that this central core was appreciably different from the outer shell. In 1901, a year after he invented his seismograph, Wiechert founded the Geophysical Institute in Gottingen, Germany. The institute quickly became a center for the study and compilation of earthquake data from observatories worldwide. One of the important seismologists affiliated with the Geophysical Institute was Beno Gutenberg, a German seismologist who, in 1914, after studying seismic data collected by the institute from worldwide sources, estimated the depth of the boundary between the inner and outer cores at 2,900 kilometers from the earth's surface. Later, Harold Jeffreys, an English seismologist, precisely measured this depth at 2,898 kilometers, plus or minus 4 kilometers.

Wiechert observed that seismograms at many observatories revealed the presence of additional small earth movements, called microseisms. These small movements complicated the problem of the accurate recording of ordinary earthquakes; their form is likely to be related to features that are similar on records traced at observatories distributed over a wide area. One of the features is the approximately simultaneous occurrence of maximum amplitudes at all the observatories involved. These microseisms may persist for many hours at a time and may have more or less regular periods of from 2 to 10 or more seconds. Wiechert suggested that microseisms are generated by the action of rough surf against an extended steep coast; this hypothesis was followed up by Gutenberg. Norwegian and Japanese seismologists have concluded a similar relationship, as suggested by Wiechert.

Shortly after Wiechert's invention, in 1906, Boris Golitsyn, a Russian physicist and seismologist, invented the first electromagnetic seismograph, which did away with the need for mechanical linkage between the pendulum that revealed the earth's movement and the record that transcribed it. With slight modifications, the state of the art in seismographs after Golitsyn was established until 1932, when Hugo Benioff, an American seismologist, perfected a completely different kind of seismograph. It was based on the relative, tiniest movement of two points on the ground, drawing near or separating during the passage of elastic waves of an earthquake, and not the inertia of a pendulum as in earlier seismographs.

SIGNIFICANCE

With the development of the seismograph during the late nineteenth century came an explosion of knowledge about the inner earth. Very early in the twentieth century, Oldham and Wiechert independently postulated the presence in the center of the earth of a large, dense, and at least partially molten core. In 1909, Andrija Mohorovičić, a Yugoslav meteorologist and seismologist, discovered the discontinuity between seismograph recordings of earthquake waves, which led to his discovery of the boundary between the earth's crust and upper mantle. This boundary, called the Mohorovičić Discontinuity, varies from about 10 kilometers beneath the basaltic ocean floor to between 32 and 64 kilometers beneath the granitic continents.

In 1914, Gutenberg, later affiliated with the California Institute of Technology, discovered the boundary between the mantle and the outer core. In 1936, Inge Lehmann, a Danish seismologist, after a number of years of observing waves through the core from Pacific earthquakes and a mathematical model, discovered the boundary between the outer and inner core. These discoveries established the existence of boundaries for the inner and outer core, the mantle and crust.

Around 1924, portable seismographs were being introduced to record seismic waves from quarry blasts and other relatively small explosions. Seismic monitoring of rock blasting in quarries and other methods of mining are now regulated by local laws or are common practice in practically all mining operations in the United States and Europe.

A worldwide network of recording stations in the 1960's, improved seismographs, and computers have all contributed to a greater understanding of the earth in recent times. Some of these discoveries include that the earth's core is not a single molten mass, but consists of an inner and outer core with a transition zone dividing a solid inner core from its surrounding molten rock. The mantle has been found to consist of an upper and lower section. There are concentric envelopes of elusive discontinuities with new ones being detected frequently. It is the region of the upper mantle that commands the special attention of seismologists because it is at the juncture of the mantle and the crust that most earthquakes have their source. Understanding this region is also important for understanding the movement of continental plates.

—*Earl G. Hoover*

FURTHER READING

Bolt, Bruce A. *Inside the Earth: Evidence from Earthquakes*. New York: W. H. Freeman, 1982. An introductory text of a nonmathematical nature for earth science. The principal focus is on earthquake waves,

1890's

main shells of the earth, structural detail, earth vibrations, and physical properties of the earth. Illustrated with simplified diagrams and boxed excerpts of major discoveries in seismicity.

Eiby, G. A. *Earthquakes*. Exeter, N.H.: Heinemann, 1980. This book is intended for general readers who want elemental knowledge about earthquakes; it is a good reference for high school students and college undergraduates. Of particular interest is the chapter on recording an earthquake.

Halacy, D. S., Jr. *Earthquakes: A Natural History*. Indianapolis, Ind.: Bobbs-Merrill, 1974. This is a well-written elementary book designed for high school and lower-level college students as well as general readers. Illustrations and photographs complement the text and are well prepared. A short book covering the basics on earthquakes and is highly recommended.

Stacey, Frank D. *Physics of the Earth*. 3d ed. Brisbane, Australia: Brookfield Press, 1992. The principal audience is the graduate and advanced undergraduate student of physics. Topics covered include the solar system, rotation and figure of the earth, the gravity field, seismology and the internal structure of the earth, and the geomagnetic field.

Tazieff, Haroun. *When the Earth Trembles*. Translated by Patrick O'Brian. New York: Harcourt, Brace & World, 1964. An excellent book for the general reader and high school student. The book has three sections: The first covers the great Chilean earthquake of May, 1960; the second describes the geography of earthquakes in the Mediterranean Belt, Asiatic Belt, Pacific Belt, and Midoceanic Ridge; and the third is on instruments that record earthquakes. The text is well written, illustrated, and contains a brief bibliography.

Walker, Bryce. *Earthquake*. Rev. ed. Alexandria, Va.: Time-Life Books, 1984. This book is structured for the average reader, high school student, and undergraduate college student. It has excellent photographs, many in color and full page, and the text is written in narrative style. Areas covered include the Alaska earthquake of 1964, the history of earthquakes, and seismology from earliest times to 1982.

Wood, Robert Muir. *Earthquakes and Volcanoes*. New York: Weidenfeld & Nicolson, 1987. This is an excellent book for the nontechnical reader and is copiously illustrated with color photographs. It is written in a very understandable format on the causes and prediction of earthquakes. The second part of the book discusses the effects of volcanoes.

SEE ALSO: Apr. 5, 1815: Tambora Volcano Begins Violent Eruption; Nov. 6, 1820: Ampère Reveals Magnetism's Relationship to Electricity; July, 1830: Lyell Publishes *Principles of Geology*; Aug. 27, 1883: Krakatoa Volcano Erupts; July, 1897-July, 1904: Bjerknes Founds Scientific Weather Forecasting; Apr., 1898-1903: Stratosphere and Troposphere Are Discovered.

RELATED ARTICLES in *Great Lives from History: The Nineteenth Century, 1801-1900:* Georges Cuvier; Sir Charles Lyell.

January 14, 1900
PUCCINI'S *TOSCA* PREMIERES IN ROME

The premiere of Giacomo Puccini's Tosca *marked Puccini's departure from the lyric sentimentality then traditional in opera and announced his adoption of the* verismo *style of Italian realism.* Tosca *represented an Italian endorsement of this new style, portraying ordinary people engaged in sordid and violent situations, a style that had first arisen in France.*

LOCALE: Rome, Italy
CATEGORIES: Music; theater

KEY FIGURES
Giacomo Puccini (1858-1924), Italian operatic composer
Victorien Sardou (1831-1908), French playwright
Giuseppe Giacosa (1847-1906), Italian librettist
Luigi Illica (1857-1919), Italian librettist and Giacosa's collaborator
Umberto I (1844-1900), king of Italy, r. 1878-1900

SUMMARY OF EVENT

On January 14, 1900, Giacomo Puccini's opera *Tosca* made its premiere in Rome, the city in which it was set. A glittering crowd of notables took their seats for the sold-out performance. The attendance of members of the royal family and government leaders gave the evening the gloss of an official occasion. The glamour of the evening masked a harsh social reality, however: Italy was a political tinderbox. Strikes and riots paralyzed the nation, and rumors of disturbances and conspiracies at the opera house had people's nerves on edge. A delegation from the Roman police told Leopoldo Mugnone, the conductor, that in case of demonstrations or violence he was to play the royal march to calm the audience.

There had already been attempts on the life of King Umberto I, and there were fears for the safety of Queen Margherita, who was in the audience. Some moments after the opera began, there was a disturbance that brought the performance to a stop, but it turned out to be a quarrel over seating. After the false start, the opera proceeded. The arias were received warmly, and Puccini was called to the stage several times, but the audience's reaction did not approach the unbridled level of enthusiasm that had been anticipated. The reviews the following morning echoed the relatively cool audience reaction. The general theme of the critics was that the opera's plot had overwhelmed the music. Nevertheless, it had been a great moment: Critics, royals, and ordinary patrons alike had witnessed Puccini embracing *verismo*, or realism.

By the time of *Tosca*'s premiere, Puccini was Italy's leading operatic composer. After an unsteady beginning during the 1880's with *Le villi* (1884; the villas) and *Edgar* (1889), he established himself as a composer of the first rank with *Manon Lescaut* (1893) and *La Bohème* (1896; the bohemian woman). When Puccini turned his attention to *Tosca*, he was already regarded as Giuseppe Verdi's musical successor. Puccini had seen the great Sarah Bernhardt perform the title role in Victorien Sardou's play *La Tosca* (pr. 1887, pb. 1909; English translation, 1925) in Florence in 1895, and Giulio Ricordi, Puccini's publisher, was able to secure the rights to the piece. Any doubts about the play's suitability as a subject for opera were swept away when Verdi said that if he were not so old, he would write an opera based on *La Tosca*.

Sardou said that the idea for the play was based on an incident in the French Wars of Religion (1562-1598). A Roman Catholic nobleman promised a Protestant woman that he would save her husband from execution in return for sexual favors. She complied, but she awoke the next morning to see her husband dangling from the gallows. Sardou's play is set against Napoleon I's wars in Italy and includes a much stronger historical element than does Puccini's opera. In the streamlined libretto of the opera, written by Giuseppe Giacosa and Luigi Illica, Floria Tosca is a famous diva, intensely jealous of her lover, Mario Cavaradossi, who is an artist. When Cavaradossi shields Cesare Angelotti, an escaped political prisoner, he is arrested by Rome's chief of police, Baron Scarpia.

Giacomo Puccini. (Library of Congress)

The corrupt and degenerate Scarpia sees in this arrest an opportunity to recover his prisoner, punish Cavaradossi, and seduce Tosca all at once. In the pivotal second act, Scarpia tortures Cavaradossi in Tosca's presence, but the artist steadfastly denies any knowledge of Angelotti's hiding place. When Tosca can take no more, she reveals Angelotti's whereabouts to save Cavaradossi from further torture. Police are sent to arrest Angelotti, who commits suicide, and Cavaradossi is sentenced to death for harboring a fugitive. Scarpia offers Tosca a bargain. If she satisfies his carnal desire, Scarpia will order that a mock execution take place and will provide a safe-conduct pass for Tosca and Cavaradossi to leave Rome. Tosca very reluctantly agrees. Scarpia gives the order for the mock execution, writes out the pass, and gives it to Tosca. Instead of making love to Scarpia, however, Tosca stabs him to death on stage.

In the third act, Tosca rushes to the prison with the

safe-conduct pass. Since Cavaradossi's execution is to take place at dawn, she is certain that the charade will be over long before Scarpia's body is discovered and that they will be able to make their escape. In the brief moments that they have together, Tosca describes what has transpired and happily assures Cavaradossi that the firing squad will fire blanks; she even coaches him in how to make a convincing fall. The guards march Cavaradossi away as Tosca watches. Tosca is lighthearted as the volley is fired, still believing that everything is a sham. As she approaches the body, however, she realizes the truth—Scarpia had lied, and the execution was real. At that moment, Scarpia's lieutenant arrives at the fortress with the news of the baron's murder, and Tosca throws herself from the fortress tower rather than be arrested.

Even in the outlines of the plot, *Tosca*'s realism is apparent. Grand opera of the nineteenth century tended to focus on episodes in the lives of high-born characters caught between love and duty. Furthermore, no conventions at the time prevented a character from singing after being suffocated or stabbed. *Tosca* examined the lives of more ordinary people who were passionate and vengeful. The murders and suicides that Italian *verismo* plots almost invariably included were final. No *verismo* character sings after being killed.

Perhaps one anecdote will suffice to demonstrate Puccini's dedication to realism on the stage. Puccini often traveled around Europe to be present as his works were performed in one opera house after another. In Vienna, Puccini attended a rehearsal that solved a problem that had been nagging him. The opera's most famous aria comes at the moment when Tosca has capitulated to Scarpia's foul demands, and Puccini worried that the aria interrupted the action of the moment. In the Vienna production, Maria Jeritza was singing the title role. During the middle of the second act, an overzealous Baron Scarpia manhandled Jeritza and knocked her to the ground just as the introduction for the aria began. Rather than stop the rehearsal, Jeritza raised herself slightly and sang from the ground. "Exactly right," shouted Puccini. "Never do it any other way." The new staging seemed more realistic to Puccini, and the aria is still usually sung in that manner.

The premiere of *Tosca* signaled an important shift in Italian opera. The most important operatic composer of his generation had produced a full-length work in the new style of *verismo*. Puccini was to go on to hone his realist skills further in such works as *Madama Butterfly* (1904), *La fanciulla del West* (1910; the girl of the West), and *Turandot* (1926).

SIGNIFICANCE

Tosca was the first full-length *verismo* opera to be produced by a composer of the first rank. The roots of *verismo* originated in the novels of Émile Zola, who argued that drama and musical stage works should concern themselves with human issues and should deal with poor, ordinary people in the midst of their miseries and joys. In Italy, Zola's ideas were first taken up by writers. Giovanni Verga, for example, wrote stories about Sicilian peasants. In music, as in literature, nineteenth century realism was at first embraced by the French. A depiction of a promiscuous, lawless factory worker culminating in her onstage murder made Georges Bizet's *Carmen* (1875) a departure point for the *verismo* movement. The Italians quickly followed suit, beginning, however, with lesser composers and one-act operas by more accomplished composers. It was *Tosca*, then, that signaled that this new form of realism had truly arrived in the Italian musical world.

Musical elements closely associated with *verismo* included minor harmonies, wide melodic intervals, orchestral doubling of vocal lines, and the slow pace of dramatic arias. Such characteristics are exemplified by "Vesti la giubba" from Ruggero Leoncavallo's *Pagliacci* (1892) and "E lucevan le stelle" from *Tosca*. Puccini also employed the system of leitmotif (leading motive) in *Tosca*. A leitmotif is a recurrent melodic element that identifies a character. In Scarpia's case, Puccini employed a brief, carefully planned musical statement that included an interval regarded in medieval music as sinister and demoniac. One has only to hear Scarpia's musical motive to be reminded of his ominous presence or influence.

Now that the operas of Richard Strauss, Alban Berg, and Benjamin Britten are standard musical fare, it is difficult to appreciate how new and daring *Tosca* must have seemed in 1900. Contemporary critical responses reflect how novel *Tosca* seemed as it premiered around the world. In London, critics attacked the *verismo* elements of plot.

> Those who were present at the performance of Puccini's opera *Tosca*, were little prepared for the revolting effects produced by musically illustrating the torture and murder scenes of Sardou's play. The alliance of a pure art with scenes so essentially brutal and demoralizing . . . produced a feeling of nausea. . . . What has music to do with a lustful man chasing a defenseless woman or the dying kicks of a murdered scoundrel?

In Boston, critics attacked the score.

At the first hearing much, perhaps most, of Puccini's *Tosca* sounds exceedingly, even ingeniously, ugly. Every now and then one comes across the most ear-flaying succession of chords; then, the instrumentation, although nearly always characteristic, is often distinctly rawboned and hideous. . . .

The plot and music may have come to seem conventional to modern ears, but *Tosca*'s importance remains undiminished. Berg's *Lulu* (1937, 1979) and *Wozzeck* (1925), Dmitri Shostakovich's *Lady Macbeth of Mtsensk* (1932), and Britten's *Peter Grimes* (1945) all owe a debt to the *verismo* ideas of plot, character, and musical style that *Tosca* first fully exemplified.

—Brian R. Dunn

FURTHER READING

Ashbrook, William. *The Operas of Puccini*. Oxford, England: Oxford University Press, 1985. A detailed analysis of Puccini's operas. Although an excellent book, it is technical and will be useful only to someone who reads music and has some understanding of music theory.

Carner, Mosco. *Puccini*. London: Duckworth, 1974. The best and most scholarly English-language biography of Puccini. An enlarged third edition published in 1992 includes an entirely new chapter on *Tosca*.

DiGaetano, John Louis. *Puccini the Thinker*. New York: Peter Lang, 1987. DiGaetano's work assesses the dramatic and intellectual content and development in Puccini's operas. He is particularly interested in the influence of Richard Wagner's operas on Puccini's works. A useful book, although occasionally uncritical in its use of sources.

Greenfeld, Howard. *Puccini*. London: Robert Hale, 1980. A highly readable biography by an ardent fan. The book, though somewhat weak on Puccini's personal life, contains a good discussion of the works and their sources.

Headington, Christopher, Roy Westbrook, and Terry Barfoot. "Verismo." In *Opera: A History*. London: Bodley Head, 1987. An excellent general introduction to opera; particularly good on *verismo*. Although the authors are musical scholars, the language of the book is completely accessible. A fine introduction.

Osborne, Charles. *The Complete Operas of Puccini: A Critical Guide*. London: Victor Gollancz, 1990. Although Osborne is not very fond of *Tosca*, his highly readable book provides an excellent act-by-act description of the action that would be of great help to someone planning to see *Tosca* for the first time. His chapter on *Tosca* also includes a detailed and interesting comparison of Sardou's play and the libretto.

Puccini, Giacomo. *Puccini Among Friends*. Edited by Vincent Seligman. Rev. ed. New York: Benjamin Blom, 1971. A standard English-language edition of Puccini's letters, first published in 1938. *Letters of Giacomo Puccini* (1931; reprinted in 1974) is also a useful source.

SEE ALSO: Feb. 20, 1816: Rossini's *The Barber of Seville* Debuts; Jan. 2, 1843: Wagner's *Flying Dutchman* Debuts; Mar. 3, 1875: Bizet's *Carmen* Premieres in Paris; Aug. 13-17, 1876: First Performance of Wagner's Ring Cycle; Oct. 22, 1883: Metropolitan Opera House Opens in New York.

RELATED ARTICLES in *Great Lives from History: The Nineteenth Century, 1801-1900:* Sarah Bernhardt; Georges Bizet; Émile Zola.

1890's

February, 1900
KODAK INTRODUCES BROWNIE CAMERAS

With the introduction of Brownie cameras, Eastman Kodak became the first company to exploit the mass-market potential of photography by making it accessible to almost everyone.

LOCALE: Rochester, New York
CATEGORIES: Photography; inventions; manufacturing; marketing and advertising

KEY FIGURES
George Eastman (1854-1932), founder of the Eastman Kodak Company
Frank A. Brownell (fl. late nineteenth century), Kodak employee who designed the Brownie
William H. Walker (fl. late nineteenth century), Rochester camera maker who collaborated with Eastman

SUMMARY OF EVENT
In early February of 1900, the first shipments of a new small box camera called the Brownie reached Kodak dealers in the United States and Great Britain. Eager to put photography within the reach of everyone, George Eastman had directed Frank Brownell to design a small camera that could be inexpensively manufactured but still take good photographs. Advertisements for the new Brownie camera proclaimed that everyone—even children—could take good pictures with it. The Brownie was aimed directly at the children's market, a fact indicated by its packaging, which was decorated with drawings of imaginary elves called "Brownies" created by the Canadian illustrator Palmer Cox. Moreover, the camera cost only one dollar.

The Brownie was made of jute board and wood, with a hinged back fastened by a sliding catch. It had an inexpensive two-piece glass lens and a simple rotary shutter that allowed both timed and instantaneous exposures to be made. With a lens aperture of approximately f/14 and a shutter speed of approximately 1/50 of a second, the Brownie was certainly capable of taking acceptable snapshots. It had no viewfinder, but a clip-on reflecting viewfinder was an option. The cameras came loaded with six-exposure rolls of Kodak film that produced square negatives 2.5 inches on a side. This film could be developed, printed, and mounted for forty cents per roll, and new rolls could be purchased for fifteen cents each.

Eastman's first career choice had been banking, but when he failed to receive a promotion that he thought he

deserved, he decided to devote himself to his hobby, photography. Having worked with the complicated wet-plate process of photography, he knew why few amateurs took up photography. The whole process, from plate preparation to printing, was expensive, cumbersome, and time-consuming. Even so, he had already begun to think about the commercial possibilities of photography. After reading about British experiments with dry-plate technology, he set up a small chemical laboratory and came up with a process of his own. The Eastman Dry Plate Company that he then founded became one of the most successful producers of gelatin dry plates.

Dry-plate photography had attracted more amateurs, but it was still a complicated and expensive hobby. Eastman realized that the number of photographers would have to increase considerably if the market for cameras and supplies were to grow significantly. During the early 1880's, he began formulating the policies that would make the Eastman Kodak Company successful in years to come: mass production, low prices, foreign and domestic distribution, and marketing through extensive advertising and by demonstration.

In his efforts to expand the amateur photography market, Eastman first tackled the problem of glass-plate negatives, which were heavy, fragile, and expensive to make. By 1884, his experiments with paper negatives had been successful enough that he changed the name of his company to the Eastman Dry Plate and Film Company. Because flexible roll film needed some devices to hold it flat in camera focal planes, Eastman collaborated with William Walker to develop the Eastman-Walker roll-holder.

Eastman's pioneering manufacture and use of roll films led to the appearance on the market during the 1880's of a wide array of handheld cameras made by several different companies. Such cameras were called detective cameras because they were small and could be used surreptitiously. The most famous of these, introduced by Eastman in 1888, was named the Kodak—a word of no particularly meaning that he invented to be terse, distinctive, and easily pronounced in any language. This camera's simplicity of operation was appealing to the general public and stimulated the growth of amateur photography.

The Kodak camera was a box about seven inches long and four inches wide, with a one-speed shutter and a fixed-focus lens that produced reasonably sharp pictures. It came loaded with enough roll film to make one hundred exposures. The camera's initial price of twenty-five dollars included the cost of processing the first roll of film. The camera also came with a leather case and strap. After exposing a roll of film, a camera owner mailed the entire camera, unopened, to the company plant in Rochester, New York, where the developing and printing were done. For an additional ten dollars, the camera was reloaded and sent back to the customer.

The Kodak was advertised in mass-market publications, rather than in specialized photographic journals, with the slogan, "You press the button, we do the rest." With his introduction of a camera that was easy to use and a service that eliminated the need to know anything about processing negatives, Eastman revolutionized the photographic market. Thousands of people no longer depended upon professional photographers for their portraits but instead learned to make their own. In 1892, the Eastman Dry Plate and Film Company became the Eastman Kodak Company, and by the mid-1890's, 100,000 Kodak cameras had been manufactured and sold, half of them in Europe by Kodak Limited.

After popularizing photography with the first Kodak, in 1900 Eastman turned his attention to the children's market with the introduction of the Brownie. The first five thousand cameras sent to dealers were sold immediately; by the end of the following year, almost one-quarter of a million had been sold. The Kodak Company organized Brownie camera clubs and held competitions specifically for young photographers. The Brownie came with an instruction booklet that gave children simple directions for taking successful pictures, and "The Brownie Boy," an appealing youngster who loved photography, became a standard feature of Kodak's advertisements.

Eastman followed the success of the first Brownie by introducing several additional models between 1901 and 1917. Each elaborated on the original design. These Brownie box cameras were on the market until the early 1930's, and their success inspired other companies to manufacture box cameras of their own. In 1906, for example, the Ansco company produced the Buster Brown camera in three sizes that corresponded to Kodak's Brownie camera range; in 1910 and 1914, Ansco made three additional versions. The Seneca company's Scout box camera, in three sizes, appeared in 1913, and Sears Roebuck's Kewpie cameras, in

five sizes, reached the market in 1916. In Great Britain, Houghtons introduced its first Scout camera in 1901, followed by another series of four box cameras in 1910 sold under the Ensign trademark. Other British manufacturers of box cameras included the James Sinclair company, with its Traveller Una of 1909, and the Thornton-Pickard company, with a Filma camera marketed in four sizes in 1912.

After World War I, several series of box cameras were manufactured in Germany by companies that had formerly concentrated on more advanced and expensive

Early British advertisement for the Brownie camera. The five-shilling price was equivalent to about $1.25 in U.S. currency. (Hulton Archive/Getty Images)

1890's

cameras. The success of box cameras in other countries, led by Kodak's Brownie, undoubtedly prompted this trend in the German photographic industry. The Ernemann Film K series of cameras in three sizes, introduced in 1919, and the all-metal Trapp Little Wonder of 1922 are examples of popular German box cameras.

During the early 1920's, camera manufacturers began making box-camera bodies from metal rather than wood and cardboard. Machine-formed metal was both less expensive and more durable than the traditional hand-worked materials. In 1924, Kodak's two most popular Brownie sizes appeared with aluminum bodies.

In 1928, Kodak Limited of England added two important new features to the Brownie—a built-in portrait lens, which could be brought in front of the taking lens by pressing a lever, and camera bodies in a range of seven different fashion colors. The Beau Brownie cameras, made in 1930, were the most popular of all the colored box cameras. The work of Walter Dorwin Teague, a leading American designer, these cameras had an art deco geometric pattern on the front panel, which was enameled in a color matching the leatherette covering of the camera body. Several other companies, including Ansco, again followed Kodak's lead and introduced their own lines of colored cameras.

During the 1930's, several new box cameras with interesting features appeared, many manufactured by leading film companies. In France, Lumiere advertised a series of box cameras—the Luxbox, Scoutbox, and Lumibox—that ranged from a basic fixed-lens camera to one with an adjustable lens and shutter. In 1933, the German Agfa company restyled its entire range of box cameras, and in 1939, the Italian Ferrania company entered the market with box cameras in two sizes. In 1932, Kodak redesigned its Brownie series to use the new 620 roll film, which it had just introduced. This film and the new Six-20 Brownies inspired other companies to experiment with variations of their own; some box cameras, such as the Certo Double-box, the Coronet Every Distance, and the Ensign E-20 cameras, offered a choice of two picture formats.

Another new trend in cameras was a move toward smaller-format models using standard 127 roll film. In 1934, Kodak marketed the small Baby Brownie. Designed by Teague and made from molded black plastic, this little camera with a folding viewfinder sold for only one dollar—the same price as the original Brownie in 1900. The first Kodak camera made of molded plastic, the Baby Brownie heralded a move toward the use of plastics in camera manufacture. Soon many others, such

as the Altissa series of box cameras and the Voigtlander Brilliant V/6 camera, were being made from this new material.

By the late 1930's, flashbulbs had replaced flash powder for taking pictures in low light. Once again, the Eastman Kodak Company led the way in introducing this new technology as an option on its inexpensive box cameras. The Falcon Press-Flash, marketed in 1939, was the first mass-produced camera to have flash synchronization and was followed the next year by the Six-20 Flash Brownie, which had a detachable flash gun. During the early 1940's, other companies, such as Agfa-Ansco, introduced similar features on their own box cameras.

After World War II, box cameras evolved into eye-level cameras, making them more convenient to carry and use. Many amateur photographers, however, still had trouble handling paper-backed roll film and were taking their cameras back to dealers to be unloaded and reloaded. Kodak therefore developed a new system of film loading, using Kodapak cartridges, which could be mass-produced with a high degree of accuracy by precision plastic-molding techniques. To load cameras, users simply opened the camera backs and inserted film cartridges. This new film was introduced in 1963, along with a series of Instamatic cameras designed for their use. Both the film cartridges and the cameras were immediately successful.

The popularity of film cartridges ended the long history of simple and inexpensive roll film cameras. The last English Brownie was made in 1967, and the last American series of Brownies was discontinued in 1970. Eastman's original marketing strategy of simplifying photography in order to increase the demand for cameras and film continued, however, with the public's acceptance of cartridge-loading cameras such as the Instamatic.

SIGNIFICANCE

From his company's beginning, Eastman recognized that there were two kinds of photographers other than professionals. The first, he declared, were the true amateurs who devoted time enough to acquire skill in the complex film processing systems of the day. The second were those who merely wanted personal pictures or memorabilia of their everyday lives, families, and travels. The second class, he observed, outnumbered the first by almost ten to one. Thus, it was to this second kind of amateur photographer that Eastman appealed, both with his first cameras and with his advertising slogan, "You press the button, we do the rest."

Eastman did much more than simply invent cameras and films; he invented a system and then developed the means for supporting it. This is essentially what the Eastman Kodak Company continued to accomplish with the series of Instamatics and other descendants of the original Brownie. During the decade between 1963 and 1973, for example, approximately sixty million Instamatics were sold throughout the world.

The research, manufacturing, and marketing activities of the Eastman Kodak Company have been so complex and varied that no one would suggest that the company's prosperity rests solely on the success of its line of inexpensive cameras and cartridge films, although these have continued to be important to the company. Like Kodak, however, most large companies in the photographic industry have expanded their research to satisfy ever-growing demands from amateurs. The amateurism that George Eastman recognized and encouraged at the beginning of the twentieth century still flourishes a century later, when the newest trend in amateur photography was digital cameras, which require no film at all.

—*LouAnn Faris Culley*

FURTHER READING

Brayer, Elizabeth. *George Eastman: A Biography*. Baltimore: Johns Hopkins University Press, 1996. First full-length, scholarly biography of the founder of the Eastman Kodak Company.

Coe, Brian. *Kodak Cameras: The First Hundred Years*. Cincinnati, Ohio: Seven Hills Books, 1988. Detailed catalog of Kodak camera models by the former curator of the Kodak Museum in England.

Collins, Douglas. *The Story of Kodak*. New York: Harry N. Abrams, 1990. This first book to present the complete story of the Eastman Kodak Company emphasizes the contributions that Kodak has made to science, art, and popular culture. The author had unlimited access to the company archives as well as the opportunity to interview Kodak's leading researchers.

Cork, Richard. "The End of Art." *New Statesman* 130, no. 4546 (July 16, 2001): 44. Brief survey of the early history of photography.

Eder, Josef Maria. *History of Photography*. Translated by Edward Epstean. New York: Columbia University Press, 1945. This history of the early developments in photography draws on many European sources not available to American writers. Includes a valuable account of Eastman's initial experiments, inventions, and business practices. Technical discussions are easy to understand.

Freund, Gisele. *Photography and Society*. Boston: David R. Godine, 1980. Survey of the history of photography that proceeds to a discussion of the ways in which artistic expression and social forms continually influence and reshape each other. Also discusses photography's essential role in modern life and its indispensable position in both science and industry.

Hirsch, Robert. *Seizing the Light: A History of Photography*. New York: McGraw-Hill, 1999. Detailed, clear, and easily readable history of photography that describes the influence of photography on science, culture, and art.

McKeown, James M., and Joan McKeown. *Collectors Guide to Kodak Cameras*. Grantsburg, Wis.: Centennial Photo Service, 1981. Useful but difficult-to-find guide for collectors of vintage cameras. Like most such guides, it is a trove of historical information.

Taft, Robert. *Photography and the American Scene*. New York: Dover, 1964. Traces the effects of photography on the social history of America and the effect of social life on the progress of photography. Includes a good account of Eastman's early career.

Wade, John. *A Short History of the Camera*. Watford, England: Fountain Press, 1979. Year-by-year history of the development of camera technology and the various companies involved. Well illustrated, with photographs of most of the cameras discussed in the text. Recommended for readers with limited knowledge of how cameras actually work.

West, Nancy Martha. *Kodak and the Lens of Nostalgia*. Charlottesville: University Press of Virginia, 2000. Beautifully illustrated history of early Kodak advertisements that serves as a cultural history of amateur photography.

SEE ALSO: 1839: Daguerre and Niépce Invent Daguerreotype Photography; 1878: Muybridge Photographs a Galloping Horse; May, 1887: Goodwin Develops Celluloid Film; Dec. 15, 1900: General Electric Opens Research Laboratory.

RELATED ARTICLES in *Great Lives from History: The Nineteenth Century, 1801-1900:* Mathew B. Brady; Jacques Daguerre.

1890's

February 27, 1900
BRITISH LABOUR PARTY IS FORMED

Formation of the British Labour Party gave voice to Great Britain's growing industrial working class; the new party ultimately replaced the Liberal Party as one of the country's two major political parties.

ALSO KNOWN AS: Labour Representation Committee
LOCALE: Great Britain
CATEGORIES: Government and politics; social issues and reform; organizations and institutions

KEY FIGURES

Keir Hardie (1856-1915), Scottish miner who became an Independent Labour Party leader
Arthur Henderson (1863-1935), trade union leader who became leader of the Labour Party
George Lansbury (1859-1940), socialist member of the Independent Labour Party who later joined the Labour Party
Ramsay MacDonald (1866-1937), founding member of the Labour Party who would later become prime minister, 1924, 1929-1935

SUMMARY OF EVENT

Although the British Labour Party did not formally exist under that name until after the general election of January, 1906, the party actually become a reality at a London conference in February, 1900, that established the Labour Representation Committee (LRC). The creation of a political organization based upon the working class was the result of a number of intertwined and complex historical developments. The most obvious of these are the political reforms of 1867 and 1884, which gave the vote to male blue-collar workers and increased the electoral power of the working class.

These development alone fail to explain why a working-class political party arose in Great Britain and not in the United States or Germany, both of which also granted the vote to male workers. Excluding the brief significance of the Socialist Party during the early twentieth century, the United States never developed an independent working-class political party, but an explicitly socialist party did have representation in Germany by the 1870's. One must look at the specific historical developments in Great Britain that led to a party that was separate from both mainstream multiclass parties and the Marxist-defined groups predominant on the European continent.

Among the factors that contributed to the birth of Britain's Labour Party was the nearly homogeneous nature of the British working class at the end of the nineteenth century. There was a genuine material basis for class solidarity among laborers as the living standards of unskilled workers rose closer to those of skilled workers, who perceived an erosion in their own social position. The divide-and-conquer approach to governance that was successful in some countries had less chance in Britain. Instead, unskilled workers—preoccupied with achieving some minimum living standards—were able to make common cause with many alienated skilled workers. Furthermore, the decreasing importance of religious and regional differences in Britain made social class a more ready touchstone of identity than in an ethnically and regionally divided nation such as the United States.

None of these considerations assured the formation of a new political party: There remained the possibility of absorption of working-class aspirations by one of the established political parties. The natural candidate for such a development was the Liberal Party, which claimed to share many of the same concerns as those voiced by Labour. The late nineteenth century had seen an alliance between union leaders, working-class voters, and the Liberal Party. However, when faced with ever-increasing demands for a greater role within the party, the Liberal associations proved too intractable to accommodate themselves to the rising labor movement. Thus, in sharp contrast to American urban political machines, which were effective in containing labor discontent, working-class political aspirations in Britain would tend toward the establishment of a new party.

A number of labor leaders initially split from the Liberal Party when they were refused nomination as candidates for Parliament. In 1892, the Scottish miner Keir Hardie was elected to Parliament as an independent labour representative shortly after the Liberal Party denied him its nomination. The following year brought the formation of the Independent Labour Party (ILP), whose express goal was to send to Parliament working-class men who were independent of both the Liberal and Conservative Parties.

This new socialist organization drew support heavily from unions representing unskilled workers, who feared that without parliamentary support they would witness the destruction of their limited gains during the next recession. Although the party was blessed with a number of important leaders who would later make their mark on British politics, including Ramsay MacDonald and George Lansbury, the ILP—even taken together with other left-wing groups—was far too weak to mount a threat to the two established political parties.

It proved essential that a more broad-based labor organization, such as the Trades Union Congress (TUC), join the campaign for a new political party. Although this development had seemed unlikely only a few decades earlier, by February of 1900, the Trades Union Congress voted to become the vehicle that would ultimately form the Labour Party. The relatively rapid conversion of the trade unions to the cause of independent political action was prompted by a series of employer assaults on trade union rights.

Worried about foreign competition, employers had established their own national federations, which conducted lockouts against unionized workers and vigorously opposed union demands. Seventy thousand Scottish miners were defeated in an industrial struggle in 1894, followed by the defeat of the Boot and Shoe Operatives in 1895. Even one of the oldest established trade unions, the Amalgamated Society of Engineers, saw itself defeated by a lockout in 1897-1898.

These industrial assaults on the working class were combined with consistent erosion of the trade unions' legal rights. By the late 1890's, the right to picket—essential if unions were to win strikes—was being threatened in the judicial system. In this context, the Trades Union Congress held in autumn of 1899 considered a resolution from an ILP member from the Amalgamated Society of Railroad Servants to call a special meeting of trade unions, cooperatives, and socialist organizations to design a plan to elect workers to Parliament. After an intense debate that saw leaders of the new unskilled workers pitted against the miners, whose concentration in certain electoral districts forced the Liberal Party to accept their candidates, the motion carried by a vote of 546,000 to 434,000.

The Labour Representation Committee was duly established at a meeting in London on February 27, 1900. Present were 129 delegates, of whom 65 represented unions with 568,000 members—the remainder representing the various socialist societies with fewer than 25,000 members combined. A twelve-member committee was elected with seven trade unionists and five socialists. Although it was in the minority, the ILP was able to elect Ramsay MacDonald secretary of the LRC. During the organization's first year, the trade unions that joined were primarily made up of unskilled workers, although unions representing railroad, boot and shoe, and printing workers joined as well.

A general election took place only six months later, and the results were hardly encouraging. With neither time nor money in great supply, only two of the LRC-endorsed candidates were able to secure victory. There was also tension between the socialists, such as the ILP, and traditional Liberal Party supporters, such as Arthur Henderson. Such problems might have meant the end of the organization had it not been for a further assault on trade union rights that produced a new wave of affiliations. In July of 1901, the House of Lords rendered its famous Taff Vale judgment, which not only reaffirmed limitation on picketing but also proclaimed that unions had to pay for all the costs caused by strike action. Although the legal implications were complicated, trade union leaders soon concluded that they had been forced into an extremely difficult position.

As Labour leaders increasingly questioned the willingness of the existing parties to pass legislation that would reverse Taff Vale, they moved in support of the LRC with the hope of electing their own members to the House of Commons. Unwilling to place their faith in either of the two existing parties, unions began to affiliate with the LRC. Thus, the pre-Taff Vale membership of the LRC, which stood at 376,000, jumped to 469,000 in 1902 and 861,000 by 1903.

SIGNIFICANCE

By the time of the 1906 general election, the Labour Representation Committee was able to run a skillful campaign with fifty serious candidates, resulting in the election of twenty-nine candidates to the House of Commons. When the 1906 Parliament convened, the LRC took the name Labour Party. In 1924, the party won the general elections, and Ramsay MacDonald became the first Labour prime minister. Four other Labour Party leaders served as prime minister during the twentieth century, and during the early twenty-first century, Tony Blair became the first Labour Party leader to hold the office for more than seven consecutive years.

—*William A. Pelz*

FURTHER READING

Cliff, Tony, and Donny Gluckstein. *The Labour Party: A Marxist History.* London: Bookmarks, 1988. Written from a radical left viewpoint, this work provides a thought-provoking, if controversial, treatment of the Labour Party from its beginning.

1890's

Coates, David. *The Labour Party and the Struggle for Socialism*. Cambridge, England: Cambridge University Press, 1975. Although focused on the question of Labour's ability to advance the cause of socialism, this study also addresses broader questions about the party's history.

Davies, Andrew. *To Build a New Jerusalem: The British Labour Party from Keir Hardie to Tony Blair*. London: Abacus, 1996. General history of the Labour Party, from its origins to the eve of Tony Blair's rise to prime minister.

Hobsbawm, Eric. "Workers of the World." In *The Age of Empire, 1875-1914*. New York: Pantheon Books, 1987. Written by a renowned labor historian, this chapter allows readers to situate the birth of the Labour Party within the context of global labor developments.

Jeffreys, Kevin, ed. *Leading Labour: From Keir Hardie to Tony Blair*. London: I. B. Tauris, 1999. Very readable and useful study of all of the major Labour Party leaders during the first century of its existence. Includes a sympathetic account of Keir Hardie's role in establishing the Independent Labour Party.

Morgan, Kenneth O. *Keir Hardie: Radical and Socialist* London: Phoenix Giant, 1997. Biography of the first Labour candidate elected to Parliament that is both readable and reliable. Based on primary and secondary sources.

Pelling, Henry. *Origins of the Labour Party*. Oxford, England: Oxford University Press, 1965. Fine study that examines the many and varied currents that were to come together with the establishment of the Labour Party in 1900.

_____. *A Short History of the Labour Party*. London: Macmillan, 1972. Although somewhat dated and dry in parts, this work remains the best general introduction to the subject.

March 23, 1900
EVANS DISCOVERS CRETE'S MINOAN CIVILIZATION

Evans altered the chronology assigned to the development of Hellenic civilization through his excavations of the Bronze Age site of Knossos, initiating a scholarly controversy on the dominance of Minoan culture on the Greek Peloponnisos.

LOCALE: Kephála (Knossos), Crete
CATEGORY: Archaeology

KEY FIGURES
Arthur Evans (1851-1941), English archaeologist
Duncan Mackenzie (1859-1935), Scottish archaeologist who directed field operations at Knossos
John Pendlebury (1904-1941), English archaeologist who succeeded Mackenzie
Michael Ventris (1922-1956), English classicist and cryptographer who deciphered the "Linear B" script

SUMMARY OF EVENT

Well into his middle age, a period at which most individuals settle into careers and comfortably contemplate retirement, Arthur Evans, the eldest child of Sir John Evans and Harriet Ann Dickinson, discovered a civilization to which he gave the name "Minoan." Although the Minos of legend is familiar to even the most casual reader of myth, no one until Evans's excavations were under way could appreciate its distinctive character.

By Evans's calculations (restated by most contemporary archaeologists to begin only about 2600 B.C.E.), Cretan origins, dated from 3500 B.C.E., reached their zenith around 2200 B.C.E., and ended suddenly about 1100 B.C.E., probably because of a devastating earthquake that necessitated the relocation of government from Crete to the eastern Peloponnisos.

A fortuitous combination of circumstances made Evans's discovery possible. He had intended as early as 1871 to write an archaeological history of the Balkans.

Indeed, he planned permanent residence in the town of Ragusa (now Dubrovnik, Croatia) and emigrated there after his marriage to Margaret Freeman in 1878. The couple shared an enthusiasm for the Balkans, in general, and Ragusa, in particular. They lived in Ragusa for almost four years, through a combination of support from Evans's wealthy father and regular articles Evans wrote for *The Manchester Guardian* on the tense political situation in the Balkans under Austrian occupation. Ultimately, it was these articles and Evans's increasingly outspoken position on Balkan independence that led to his arrest, imprisonment, and expulsion in April, 1882. It was only through the concerted efforts of his wife, brother, and sister that he avoided trial.

Once returned to the family home in Hemel Hempstead, Hertfordshire, England, Evans's family secured for him the post of keeper of the Ashmolean Museum, Oxford, in 1884. The Ashmolean did not resemble the prestigious institution it would become under Evans's leadership. Essentially, it was like a disorganized warehouse, a polyglot collection of archaeological, geological, and historical artifacts. Evans organized and refined the collections, placed the institution on a firm financial basis, and supervised the construction of its handsome building in 1894.

Evans traveled often during his tenure at the Ashmolean and incurred frequent criticism for his long absences. The sudden death of his wife in 1893 was partly responsible for his extensive forays to possible archaeological sites in the Mediterranean, but it is certain that having met Heinrich Schliemann in 1873, only three years after the latter had astounded the archaeological world by unearthing Troy, had excited Evans's imagination to the possibilities of even earlier sites awaiting discovery.

What led Evans to Crete, however, was his having come upon in 1894 several three- and four-sided sealstones of Cretan origin that were offered for sale in an

CRETE IN THE MODERN MEDITERRANEAN REGION

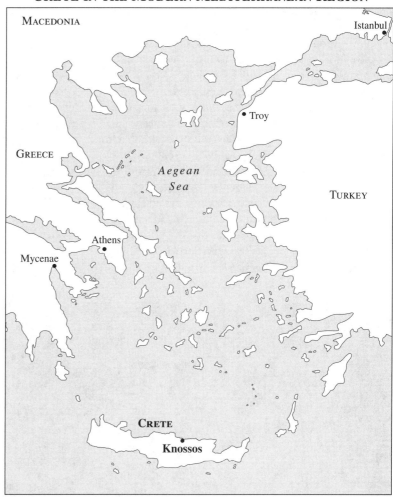

Athens antique shop. They were engraved with the distinctive picture writing Evans would eventually call "Linear A." He recalled similar markings on two vases found by Greek archaeologist Chrestos Tsountas at Mycenae on the Greek Pelponnisos. Evans was convinced that this picture writing indicated a distinct Cretan culture, one that antedated that of the mainland and one that was truly pre-Hellenic. He was determined to prove his hypothesis through excavations on the great mound at Kephála, the modern name for the region that surrounded Knossos, considered the site of the palace of Minos. Evans coined the word "Minoan" to distinguish this culture from that of Mycenae. He used it to identify the culture not only with the king associated with the Daedalean labyrinth and the Minotaur of myth but also to delineate the palace period that preceded the Trojan War.

Evans's friend Federico Halbherr, an Italian archaeologist, convinced him that important discoveries were likely to be found at Knossos. In 1878, Halbherr had unearthed several *pithoi* (large storage jars) on the site, about 6.5 kilometers from the town of Candia. Schliemann, still fresh from his work at Troy and Mycenae, had expressed an interest in excavating there as early as 1878, and he might have done so were it not for his inability to reach financial agreement with the owner of the land. The Turkish authorities then administering Crete repeatedly posed obstacles, but Evans eventually surmounted these by purchasing the land outright. He combined substantial family resources with contributions from the England-based Cretan Exploration Fund he created and, thus, became one of the few archaeologists ever to own the site upon which he excavated.

Evans's unflagging success at Crete lay in his ability to marshal shrewd managerial talent with an uncanny ability to dig in the right place. Immediate and continuing success ensured constant financial support, and though there were interruptions because of the onset of World Wars I and II, the Knossos excavations never lacked the substantial funding they required.

Never had any excavation paid such immediate, continuing, and spectacular dividends. The first day of digging on March 23, 1900, yielded walls and pottery fragments a mere 33 centimeters beneath the topsoil. The second day produced an ancient house and fresco fragments. The third day revealed smoke-blackened walls and broken pottery, including the rims of *pithoi* similar to those discovered by Halbherr. Exactly one week after excavations began, Evans unearthed baked clay bars inscribed with the intriguing linear script, which had first interested Evans in 1894. He would discover two kinds of linear script at Knossos. The first, designated by him as "Linear A," is hieroglyphic in genre and virtually in-

Sir Arthur Evans amid a collection of relics from his Cretan excavations in 1936. His left hand is resting on the throne of Minos. (Hulton Archive/Getty Images)

decipherable, because no inscription bilingual with some known language exists to function as a starting point for translation. "Linear B," however, is different; Evans had hoped until his death that he would be able to decipher it, and he even withheld unpublished several thousand tablets at his home.

Not until 1953 did English classicist Michael Ventris, a cryptographer during World War II, establish that the Linear B script was ideographic (syllabic) pre-Greek. Working from the earlier hypothesis of American Alice Kober that the upright strokes marked word divisions and by noting repetitions, Ventris proved the script's syllabic character and prepared a grid with the ideographs' syllabic equivalents. In effect, Ventris broke the code and revealed, thereby, that the Linear B tablets were largely shorthand inventory lists. The mud-brick upon which they were written was ideal to keep a changing inventory of larder stores and exports. Subsequent discoveries of large tablets at Plyos, Mycenae, and other locations on the Peloponnisos are evidence that Evans's hypothesis regarding the distinctive and independent character of Cretan civilization is questionable.

Evans defended Minoan civilization as dominant and discrete until his death, relegating Mycenaean Greece to the role of its successor, important because successive earthquakes at Knossos necessitated transference of power to the mainland. Archaeologists have subsequently advanced Evans's chronology of Minoan palace settlement and argued that Knossos more likely fell by Mycenaean invasion than by earthquake, probably as early as 1500 B.C.E.

While he was still actively involved in excavating, Evans received severe criticism for the comprehensive restorations of the great palace and its environs. His architect Theodore Fyfe in effect rebuilt large portions of it, often with considerably less evidence than would satisfy contemporary archaeologists. Similarly, the bright colors Émile Gilliéron used in restoring the palace frescos left Evans open to the charge of commercializing the excavation and catering to popular imagination. Still, Evans's daring and flair were responsible for the dramatic unveiling of a brilliant civilization whose discovery might otherwise have been postponed indefinitely.

SIGNIFICANCE

For more than thirty years of his active involvement in the Knossos excavations, Evans repeatedly captured scholarly attention and popular imagination. In part, his colorful personality sustained progress at Knossos, for Evans was the stereotype of an English archaeologist:

immaculately dressed in tropical white linen suit, tie, and always photographed with his walking stick (named Prodger), which he used as a magic wand to uncover astonishing finds. Evans carefully nurtured his public image as a wizard of archaeology. He used it and his facile writing ability to keep the Knossos excavations on a firm financial footing.

Evans's radical restorations also satisfied the general public's notion of what archaeology should be. "Minoan red," the distinctive color used extensively in Gilliéron's restorations, became familiar to the world of art. Wealthy patrons of the Cretan Exploration Fund, as well as others who could afford them, purchased reproductions of Minoan palace art. The homes of European art lovers in the early twentieth century often displayed a bull fresco, a painting of a wasp-waisted serving boy, or the like.

Although such popular attention assured financial stability, the professionals connected with the excavation often found it vaguely embarrassing. Duncan Mackenzie, the rough-edged Scottish archaeologist who supervised daily operations, often disagreed heatedly with Evans's flamboyant methods, and this caused his temporary dismissal on several occasions. Nevertheless, Mackenzie's "day books," painstaking accounts of daily progress, remain the primary source for scholars concerned with the early progress of the excavations. Mackenzie's scientific approach, his careful measuring of soil strata, and his drawings of principal objects found to scale and in context provided a method used by subsequent archaeologists worldwide. After Mackenzie's death, John Pendlebury filled this post and wrote *The Archaeology of Crete: An Introduction* (1939), the comprehensive single-volume account of Minoan archaeology.

The most significant effect of Evans's work was, however, the restructuring of the pre-Greek chronology of settlement on Crete and the eastern Peloponnisos. Evans posited a Neolithic period, which ended about 3500 B.C.E. Likewise, he maintained until his death the preeminence of Minoan over Mycenaean civilization, rejecting the theory of its fall by Mycenaean invasion. Many contemporary archaeologists reject this position and have adjusted Evans's datings, but without Evans's work, the debate would never have begun.

—*Robert J. Forman*

FURTHER READING

Evans, Arthur. *The Palace of Minos*. 1921-1936. Reprint. 4 vols. New York: Biblo & Tannen, 1964. This profusely illustrated account of the excavations gives its entire history with numerous color plates, many

1890's

prepared especially for the set, and numerous painstakingly executed drawings and plans, many of these from Mackenzie's day books. Evans explicates every major object found, discusses the frescos at length, and provides an excellent index.

Hamilakis, Yannis, ed. *Labyrinth Revisited: Rethinking "Minoan" Archaeology*. Oxford, England: Oxbow, 2002. A scholarly collection investigating the cultural history of archaeology as a discipline and how the discipline forms the types of questions asked about, in this case, Minoan civilization.

Horwitz, Sylvia. *The Find of a Lifetime: Sir Arthur Evans and the Discovery of Knossos*. New York: Viking Press, 1981. Popularly written, this volume provides an account of Evans's early life, his experiences in the Balkans, and the circumstances that led him to excavate at Knossos. A good selected bibliography suitable for general readers concludes the volume.

Macgillivray, Joseph Alexander. *Minotaur: Sir Arthur Evans and the Archaeology of the Minoan Myth*. London: Random House, 2001. A biography that suggests that Evans anticipated his discoveries in Crete.

MacKendrick, Paul. *The Greek Stones Speak: The Story of Archaeology in Greek Lands*. New York: St. Martin's Press, 1962. Contains a good account for general readers on the important particulars of the Knossos excavations. Includes photographs of the palace excavations, principal finds, and a reproduction of the syllable grid Ventris published in connection with the deciphering of Linear B.

Palmer, Leonard R. *A New Guide to the Palace of Knossos*. London: Macmillan, 1969. Ideal for general readers and for travelers, this volume provides plates, figures, and plans adapted from Evans's magnum opus on the site, as well as an easy-to-follow text written to incorporate subsequent scholarship on the excavations.

_____. *On the Knossos Tablets: The Find Place of the Knossos Tablets*. Oxford, England: Clarendon Press, 1963. A companion volume to the book cited above, this work discusses the locations and contexts of the tablet hoards. Provides a less technical discussion of linear scripts than the Ventris and Chadwick work, cited below.

Pendlebury, J. D. S. *The Archaeology of Crete: An Introduction*. Reprint. 1939. New York: Biblo & Tannen, 1963. A classic study of Minoan civilization by Evans's site supervisor at Knossos. Discusses the island's geography and principal sites, including those other than Knossos, and provides a concluding discussion of post-Minoan Crete.

Sherratt, Susan. *Arthur Evans, Knossos, and the Priest-King*. Oxford, England: Ashmolean Museum, 2000. A history of the excavation at Knossos and an examination of the famous "priest-king" fresco image. Includes notes and photographs.

Ventris, Michael, and John Chadwick. *Documents in Mycenaean Greek: Three Hundred Selected Tablets from Knossos, Plyos, and Mycenae*. 1956. 2d ed. New York: Cambridge University Press, 1973. This volume offers a complete account of discovery, the linear script writing system, the language, and several hundred of the most representative tablets. The second edition includes commentary on additional tablets.

Willetts, R. F. *The Civilization of Ancient Crete*. Berkeley: University of California Press, 1977. Traces the history of Crete's development and emphasizes the Dorian aristocracy which Evans denied and about which Pendlebury, because of his association with Evans, wrote only obliquely. There is also a good bibliography on the Minoan and Mycenaean world.

SEE ALSO: 1803-1812: Elgin Ships Parthenon Marbles to England; Mar. 22, 1812: Burckhardt Discovers Egypt's Abu Simbel; 1839-1847: Layard Explores and Excavates Assyrian Ruins; Nov., 1839: Stephens Begins Uncovering Mayan Antiquities; Apr., 1870-1873: Schliemann Excavates Ancient Troy.

RELATED ARTICLES in *Great Lives from History: The Nineteenth Century, 1801-1900:* Alexander von Humboldt; Heinrich Schliemann.

May, 1900-September 7, 1901
BOXER REBELLION

The Boxer Rebellion was a peasant revolt, supported by the Chinese government, that attempted to remove all foreigners from Chinese soil. It marked the final, unsuccessful attempt of the Qing Dynasty to throw off the yoke of foreign imperialism.

LOCALE: Northern China, especially Shandong and Chihli Provinces
CATEGORY: Wars, uprisings, and civil unrest

KEY FIGURES
Cixi (Tz'u-hsi; Hsiao-ch'in; Hsien Huang-hau; 1835-1908), China's empress dowager, 1861-1908, who became sole ruler following the coup d'état of 1898
Ronglu (1836-1903), principal adviser to Cixi
Guangxu (1871-1908), Chinese emperor imprisoned by his aunt Cixi in 1898
Alfred von Waldersee (1832-1904), commander of the international relief force sent to Beijing
Zhang Zhidong (Chang Chih-tung; 1837-1909), governor-general of Hunan-Hupei
Li Hongzhang (Li Hung-chang; 1823-1901), influential Chinese official

SUMMARY OF EVENT
After the First Opium War (1839-1842) with Great Britain, China was continually subjected to foreign pressure. The Treaty of Nanjing (1842) following the First Opium War, the Tianjin (Tientsin) Treaty (1858), and the Beijing Convention (1860) following the Second Opium War (1856-1860) allowed a system of foreign enclaves, the Treaty Ports, to be set up in dozens of Chinese cities. Foreign diplomats, not Chinese officials, controlled trade, administration, the collection of customs revenues, and the dispensing of justice in the Treaty Ports. By the late 1890's, this practice of extraterritoriality had been extended to cover all foreigners, and even Chinese subjects who had converted to Christianity were exempt from the power of Chinese courts.

Starting with the cession of Hong Kong to the British in 1842, the Manchu Qing Dynasty had been forced to surrender territory and sovereignty as a result of war or threat. Russia exerted pressure in Manchuria and Central Asia; France took control of Indochina in the second half of the nineteenth century. A newly modernized Japan humiliated China in a war over influence in Korea in 1894-1895 and took Taiwan as a prize. In the wake of the Korean defeat, the older treaty powers redoubled their efforts, and new players, especially Germany, entered the race for Chinese concessions.

Despite persistent attempts at modernization, most notably the "self-strengthening movement" led by the officials Li Hongzhang and Zhang Zhidong, imperial armies and fleets routinely found themselves overmatched. Additionally, the great Taiping Rebellion (1851-1864) and the Nien and Muslim uprisings during the 1860's and 1870's—which by some estimates collectively took upward of thirty million lives—stretched resources to the limit and devastated much of the most productive land in the empire. By the late 1890's, secret societies and antiforeign militia had proliferated, particularly in the northern provinces of Chihli, Shandong, and Shaanxi, where Christian missionary activity and foreign encroachment had most recently become prominent.

In November, 1897, Germany, as part of a comprehensive program of naval expansion, demanded and received a naval base and concession at Jiaozhou Bay in Shandong. The methods by which the Germans consolidated their position, including punitive forays into the surrounding countryside and demands for the safety of their missionaries, increasingly inflamed the sensibilities of local groups and officials. Among the most prominent of these was an association of secret societies called the Yihechuan (Wage-Giles, I-ho ch'üan; the Association of Righteousness and Harmony, most commonly known as the Righteous and Harmonious Fists). As part of its ritual exercises, this group practiced the ancient Chinese martial art of tai chi, which included a form of shadowboxing, prompting the foreign nickname of "Boxers."

The origin of the Boxers is obscure, but it is generally agreed that several of their constituent organizations had taken part in the White Lotus Rebellion of 1796-1804. Their beliefs may be characterized as nativist and fundamentalist, blending Taoist naturalism, Buddhist spirituality, Confucian ethics and politics, and a strong antiforeign bent. Previously, this xenophobia had taken the form of anti-Qing activities, because the Manchus, who had founded the dynasty and still occupied the principal court positions, were ethnically distinct from the Han Chinese majority, having invaded from Manchuria in 1644. Increasingly, however, the emphasis of the group shifted to antimissionary activity, especially after the Germans extended their control over Shandong, the birthplace of Confucius, in 1898.

The Qing government found itself in an increasingly untenable position. On one hand, it faced pressure from the Boxers and other hostile secret societies to protect the empire from foreign encroachment. On the other hand, it had to recognize increasingly strident foreign demands to suppress antiforeign disorder. For a brief period in the summer of 1898, it seemed as if some of these issues would be resolved. Emperor Guangxu, having recently attained his majority, attempted, under the guidance of his adviser Kang Youwei, an ambitious reform of Chinese governmental institutions along the lines of the Meiji Restoration in Japan. However, this Hundred Days of Reform came to an abrupt end in September, 1898, when Guangxu's aunt, the Empress Dowager Cixi, prompted by her chief adviser, Ronglu, and fearful of the consequences of extensive reform, staged a coup d'état. Guangxu was placed under house arrest, Kang Youwei barely escaped with his life, and Cixi ruled outright,

swinging the dynasty toward a much more narrowly antiforeign position.

Encouraged by the tacit support of many local officials in North China, including the governor of Shandong, the Boxers staged increasingly provocative attacks on foreigners. By the summer of 1899, the major Boxer groups in Shandong, led by the Big Sword Society (Dadaohui), had taken as their slogan "fu-Qing, mie-yang" (support the Qing, exterminate the foreigners) and with official support had now become the Yihetuan, or Righteous and Harmonious Militia. The foreign powers, during the winter of 1899-1900, presented the Imperial Court with increasingly heated demands for suppression of the Boxers and threatened to send troops.

Cixi, impressed with the success of the militia in destroying foreign railroads and settlements, and fascinated by their claims of invulnerability to foreign bullets, called upon the army and people to defend the country

Japanese painting of a Russian regiment assaulting the Chinese stronghold at Tianjin. (Library of Congress)

from an anticipated invasion by the foreign powers. Emboldened by this outright imperial support, Boxer groups in Beijing, the metropolitan province of Chihli, and adjacent Shaanxi staged massive antiforeign demonstrations of in May of 1900, beginning the Boxer Rebellion. Hundreds of missionaries and thousands of Chinese converts were wounded and killed, often in deliberately gruesome fashion. A foreign relief force sent from Tianjin was turned back by Boxers and Chinese army units in early June. The German minister to China, Count Clemens von Ketteler, was shot down in the capital's streets. On June 21, 1900, the Qing government declared war on all the treaty powers in China and commanded Boxer militia to besiege Beijing's foreign legation quarter.

An edict of June 21 directed Chinese officials throughout the empire to use their forces in conjunction with the Boxers to attack foreign strong points. With the exception of those in North China with close Boxer affiliations, however, provincial officials in the rest of the empire ignored, defied, or did their best to stall the implementation of the orders. Many of the army commanders, such as future Chinese president Yuan Shikai, maintained a considerable skepticism about the Boxers' combat abilities and did their best to stay aloof from the fighting. Disillusionment with the seemingly futile declaration of war and the leadership that implemented it, sympathy for the captive emperor and the expelled reformers, and the muted influence of more cosmopolitan Chinese officials all served to keep conditions in the capital chaotic and to blunt the force of the Boxers' siege of the legations.

By late July, a powerful international relief force of twenty thousand men, including Germans, Japanese, Americans, British, Russians, French, Austrians, and Italians, had been assembled in Tianjin under the command of Count Alfred von Waldersee. After two weeks of daily skirmishes and several intense fights, the allied forces fought their way to Beijing, entered the city through an unguarded sewer gate, and ended the siege of the legations on August 14. The imperial court fled to Xi'an, most government forces surrendered quickly, and the Boxers, who had proven largely unreliable in battle, melted quickly into the northern Chinese countryside.

Incensed by the brutality meted out to foreigners and

WORDS OF THE BOXERS

In 1900, the rebel Boxers circulated their own placard, excerpted here, condemning in no uncertain terms China's foreign occupiers and the rise of Western "progress" in China.

The Gods assist the Boxers,
The Patriotic Harmonious corps,
It is because the "Foreign Devils" disturb the "Middle
   Kingdom."
Urging the people to join their religion,
To turn their backs on Heaven,
Venerate not the Gods and forget the ancestors.

Men violate the human obligations,
Women commit adultery,
"Foreign Devils" are not produced by mankind,
If you do not believe,
Look at them carefully.

The eyes of all the "Foreign Devils" are bluish,
No rain falls,
The earth is getting dry,
This is because the churches stop Heaven,
The Gods are angry;
The Genii are vexed;
Both come down from the mountain to deliver the
   doctrine. . . .

The great France
Will grow cold and downhearted.
The English and Russians will certainly disperse.
Let the various "Foreign Devils" all be killed.
May the whole Elegant Empire of the Great Ching Dynasty
   be ever prosperous!

Source: Katharine J. Lualdi, ed., *Sources of the Making of the West: Peoples and Cultures* (Boston: Bedford/St. Martin's Press, 2001), vol. 2, pp. 123-124.

Chinese Christians at the hands of the Boxers, the allies launched continuous punitive expeditions into the suburbs of Beijing and Tianjin, burning, looting, and summarily executing suspected Boxers. International forces remained in occupation of the capital until September, 1901, when hostilities formally came to an end. The empress dowager and her court did not return until the beginning of 1902.

The final peace treaty, the Boxer Protocol, accepted by the Chinese on September 7, 1901, was the most severe of the many "unequal treaties" imposed on China during the sixty years following the First Opium War. Among its provisions were allied demands for the exe-

Japanese and British troops storming Tianjin. (Francis R. Niglutsch)

cution, exile, degradation, and dismissal of officials charged with collaborating with the Boxers; the suspension of official examinations (based on classical texts of Confucianism) for five years in cities where Boxer activity had taken place; foreign occupation of the Beijing-Tianjin corridor; the erection of expiatory statues of von Ketteler and other "martyrs"; and a crippling indemnity of $333 million. The indemnity, payable over thirty-nine years at 4 percent interest, required installments nearly matching the annual revenue of the empire.

SIGNIFICANCE

The immediate consequence of the Boxer Rebellion and Protocol was that the Qing Dynasty effectively squandered what was left of its legitimacy in the eyes of both the Chinese and the rest of the world, while the roots of nationalism spread steadily, especially among Chinese communities abroad. While China avoided the fate of partition, the Manchu government appeared to be largely under the control of foreign powers. The weakness and lack of moral prestige of the central government contrib-

uted greatly to the trend toward regionalism that had been growing since midcentury. The most reactionary officials were purged, but people of ability, particularly those with modern or foreign training, tended to avoid taking their place in a government that had proven itself lacking in its hour of crisis. For the city dwellers in the ports and the peasants in the countryside, it appeared that nothing had been accomplished except an increase in foreign arrogance, Manchu ineptitude, and their own misery.

The empire was now in dire financial straits. The customs revenue (already under foreign control), internal transit taxes, and salt tax collectively proved inadequate to service its indemnity. The result was not only a large increase in the tax burden of Chinese subjects but also the wholesale borrowing of money from Western banks to make the scheduled installments.

The Empress Dowager, fearful of reform in 1898, now reluctantly allowed many of the edicts of the Hundred Days of Reform to be implemented. The traditional official examinations were abandoned in favor of more modern curricula. Army training was revamped to provide an emphasis on modern weapons and tactics. A number of sinecure positions in the bureaucracy were eliminated. The most ambitious of these reforms was an alteration of the form of government itself. Chinese officials toured the West, studying various legislative systems. A plan for a constitutional monarchy was prepared, and in 1909 and 1910 elections were held for regional and national parliamentary bodies.

Already, however, the initiative had passed away from the government to a wide spectrum of reformers and revolutionaries for whom the Boxer Rebellion had proven conclusively that the Qing had grown incapable of reform and too weak to rule. These ranged from the exiled Kang Youwei, whose Constitutional Monarchist Party was soon superseded, to radical anarchist cells specializing in bombings and assassinations. Ultimately, the Revolutionary Alliance of Sun Yat-sen, encompassing a variety of republican, nationalist, reform, and secret society organizations, would mount the blow destined to topple this last Chinese dynasty in the Revolution of 1911. On February 12, 1912, the boy emperor Puyi abdicated, ending millennia of imperial rule.

—*Charles A. Desnoyers*

FURTHER READING

Duiker, William J. *Cultures in Collision: The Boxer Rebellion*. San Rafael, Calif.: Presidio Press, 1978. A pioneering attempt to examine the cultural aspects of tradition and modernity as the background for the rise of the Boxers. English language references only.

Esherick, Joseph. *The Origins of the Boxer Uprising*. Berkeley: University of California Press, 1987. A major revisionist study based on extensive Chinese archival material and oral histories. Argues that the Boxers were never antidynastic, but instead that their opposition to Christianity grew out of the "social ecology" of the region. Scholarly yet readable. Numerous appendices and references.

Fleming, Peter. *The Siege at Peking*. London: Hart-Davis, 1959. Competent, solid, in the best tradition of English popular history. Extensive coverage of battle plans, tactics, and fortifications. Dated English language bibliography; no Chinese or Japanese sources.

Laidler, Keith. *The Last Empress*. New York: John Wiley & Sons, 2003. A well-written biography of the dowager empress who ruled China during the Boxer Rebellion; filled with anecdotes.

O'Connor, Richard. *The Spirit Soldiers: A Historical Narrative of the Boxer Rebellion*. New York: Putnam, 1973. Gripping narrative history of the rebellion with an emphasis on explicating Chinese motives and activities. Strong ironic tone in treating the issues of imperialism and international cooperation. Efforts at deeper appreciation of Chinese conditions are undercut by a lack of Chinese sources.

Paludan, Ann. *Chronicles of the Chinese Emperors*. New York: Thames and Hudson, 1998. An excellent account of China's emperors, including an acute portrayal of Cixi.

Price, Eva Jane. *China Journal, 1889-1900: An American Missionary Family During the Boxer Rebellion*. New York: Charles Scribner's Sons, 1989. A fine description of the strengths, shortcomings, and ultimate tragedy of the missionary enterprise in China as seen through the eyes of its practitioners. The letters and journal of the Prices, right up to the hour of their execution at the hands of a fraudulent military escort, reflect their deep love of the people, unflagging fortitude and good humor, and ultimate inability to comprehend fully the reasons for their fate.

Tan, Chester C. *The Boxer Catastrophe*. New York: W. W. Norton, 1971. Classic study, using extensive Chinese source material, of the diplomatic history of the rebellion. Tan's thesis that imperialism and Qing ineptitude were the main causes of the movement has long been the standard interpretation. The volume is scholarly without being overly pedantic, and its great wealth of sources makes it highly useful to the expert as well as to the layperson.

SEE ALSO: Sept., 1839-Aug. 29, 1842: First Opium War; Jan. 11, 1851-late summer, 1864: China's Taiping Rebellion; 1853-1868: Qing Dynasty Confronts the Nian Rebellion; Winter, 1855-Jan. 2, 1878: Muslim Rebellions in China; Oct. 23, 1856-Nov. 6, 1860: Second Opium War; 1860's: China's Self-Strengthening Movement Arises; Nov. 1-2, 1861: Cixi's Coup Preserves Qing Dynasty Power; July 28, 1868: Burlingame Treaty; Aug. 1, 1894-Apr. 17, 1895: Sino-Japanese War; Nov. 14, 1897: Scramble for Chinese Concessions Begins; Sept. 6, 1899-July 3, 1900: Hay Articulates "Open Door" Policy Toward China.

RELATED ARTICLES in *Great Lives from History: The Nineteenth Century, 1801-1900:* Cixi; Li Hongzhang; Zhang Zhidong.

1890's

June, 1900-1904
SUPPRESSION OF YELLOW FEVER

After it was confirmed that yellow fever is transmitted by mosquitoes, the U.S. government undertook a successful campaign to eradicate the disease in the United States and its dependencies by eliminating mosquitoes.

LOCALE: Cuba; Panama
CATEGORY: Health and medicine

KEY FIGURES
Carlos Juan Finlay (1833-1915), physician and
  biologist
William Crawford Gorgas (1854-1920), surgeon in the
  U.S. Army Medical Corps
Walter Reed (1851-1902), head of the Yellow Fever
  Commission

SUMMARY OF EVENT

Throughout the eighteenth and nineteenth centuries, yellow fever, which originated in tropical America, had devastated the Atlantic and Gulf coasts of the United States. During an epidemic in 1878, more than four thousand people died of yellow fever in New Orleans alone. In 1898, after Spain lost the Spanish-American War and withdrew from Cuba, the United States adopted the objective of eradicating yellow fever from that Caribbean island. Because physicians in the United States suspected that the fever was caused by unsanitary conditions in Cuba, initial efforts consisted of large-scale cleanup operations.

The cleanup task was assigned to Major William Crawford Gorgas, a surgeon attached to the U.S. Army of Occupation. Conditions in Cuba, especially in Havana, the country's largest city, had worsened as a result of the insurrection and the war against the Spaniards. Convinced that unsanitary conditions were responsible for the prevalence of yellow fever, Gorgas set about his work with remarkable energy. In 1899, he claimed that Havana was probably the cleanest city in the world. The hypothesis that cleanliness would eliminate yellow fever seemed briefly confirmed: During the first six months of that year, only seven deaths in Havana were attributed to yellow fever.

In August, 1899, new Spanish immigrants began arriving in Cuba in great numbers, and yellow fever again appeared in an epidemic of catastrophic proportions. It became apparent that the low incidence of the disease in the preceding months had not been due to the sanitary conditions introduced by Gorgas but to the scarcity of people who had not developed an immunity to the disease.

In June, 1900, the surgeon general of the United States, George M. Sternberg, appointed a Yellow Fever Commission consisting of four medical doctors: Walter Reed, a major in the U.S. Army Medical Corps and head of the commission; James Carroll and Jesse W. Lazear of the United States; and Aristides Agramonte of Cuba. After the commission arrived in Cuba, its members met with Carlos Juan Finlay, a Cuban physician and biologist serving with Major Gorgas on a special commission to diagnose suspected cases of yellow fever. To Finlay, there was no question about the mechanism of contagion of yellow fever. In 1881, he had announced to a medical congress in Washington, D.C., his conviction that the disease was transmitted by a mosquito then called *Stegomyia calopus*, which was later called *Stegomyia fasciata* and is now known as *Aedes aegypti*.

Walter Reed. (Library of Congress)

Finlay's announcement had been received with skepticism. The concept of insects serving as carriers, or vectors, of human diseases was not widely understood, and Finlay had not shown consistent development of yellow fever in volunteers who had been bitten by mosquitoes that had previously bitten victims of yellow fever. Despite years of experimentation, his strongest arguments remained the correlation of yellow fever cases with the geographical areas in which the mosquito thrived, and certain characteristics of the disease that suggested transmission by injection.

Reed soon became acquainted with Henry Rose Carter, another physician who was studying how yellow fever was spread. In 1898, while he was an inspector for the Public Health Service, Carter had investigated a yellow fever epidemic in Taylor and Orwood, Mississippi. There he observed that people who visited homes of people stricken with yellow fever during the first ten to twelve days of their illnesses seldom contracted the disease, but a large percentage of visitors who visited the homes after that period—even if the patients had died and been removed—were stricken.

Carter presented his findings to Reed, who reasoned that this suggested that an insect carried the disease. Health professionals were just becoming aware of Theobald Smith's discoveries concerning ticks spreading Texas fever and of investigators who had proved that malaria was transmitted by a mosquito species. This gave a new legitimacy to the concept of insect transmission of yellow fever, and the commission decided to undertake a serious investigation of Finlay's theory.

Stegomyia mosquitoes provided by Finlay were used in the experiments. The mosquitoes were first fed on patients infected with yellow fever and then fed on healthy volunteers taken from among U.S. soldiers and Spanish immigrants. Careful records were kept of the progress of the disease in the patients and volunteers. After many failures and Lazear's own death from the disease, the researchers discovered that the disease was infectious only during the first three days of illness. Armed with this information and the knowledge that ten to twelve days must elapse before the disease could be contracted by a second person, the researchers were able to produce yellow fever in nonimmune subjects at will.

After it was established that the disease was transmitted by the *Stegomyia* mosquito, the work of eradicating the plague reverted to Gorgas, who eventually decided to do away with the mosquito itself. Gorgas operated under the authority of the U.S. army and had the cooperation of the mayor of Havana, who declared it a crime for residents to allow mosquitoes to breed on their property. The main effort was a vigorous sanitary campaign engineered and supervised by Gorgas.

With military precision and scientific thoroughness, Gorgas devised a plan of attack based on the habits of the *Stegomyia* mosquito: destruction of its breeding grounds, which usually involved house-to-house searches for stagnant water and the imposition of fines on houses in which mosquito larvae were found; fumigations; division of Havana into districts under Sanitary Department representatives; and quarantines imposed on the houses of people affected by yellow fever. Crews spread oil on standing water and cisterns to kill mosquito larvae, inspected land, ordered standing water drained, stocked ponds with fish that ate mosquito larvae, and educated the public about the health hazards. Other teams followed up on yellow fever victims, sealing their rooms with paper strips, burning pyrethrum powder insecticide to kill mosquitoes, and attracting mosquitoes to lights to be killed directly. Neighbors within range of mosquitoes were watched for symptoms of yellow fever. These techniques were effective, and by the end of 1901, yellow fever ceased to be a serious problem in Cuba.

Gorgas's experience in Havana caused many public health officials in the United States to consider mosquito control not only for the control of yellow fever in the far South, but also for the control of malaria, another mosquito-borne disease. New Orleans, which had almost always faced yellow fever threats, was the first city to seize upon mosquito-control measures to curb the disease.

In 1904, Gorgas was ordered to Panama after the United States had acquired the rights to build a canal through the isthmus, which officials of the French Panama Company had called "the white man's graveyard" when they had tried to build a canal earlier. Yellow fever, as much as corruption among the officials of the French-financed project, thwarted the efforts of the company to build the canal.

In Panama, Gorgas had to battle not only the dreaded mosquito but also the opposition of the authorities in charge of the canal project. It took all Gorgas's persuasive abilities and the specter of an epidemic of catastrophic proportions to convince the canal builders that the eradication of yellow fever depended on the destruction of the *Stegomyia* mosquito. In 1914, the Panama Canal was opened for the first time to commercial transportation. This amazing engineering accomplishment was largely the result of Gorgas's perseverance and insistence on sanitary conditions.

1890's

SIGNIFICANCE

The U.S. policy of establishing public health services and sanitary conditions in occupied countries continued. During the second U.S. occupation of the Dominican Republic, from 1916 to 1922, sanitary regulations were strictly enforced. During the occupation of Haiti in 1915, one of the first measures of the military government was to divide the country into sanitary districts, each in the charge of a public health officer. Such measures instituted in Veracruz in 1914 led to a sharp drop in the mortality rate of the Mexican population, and occupying forces remained free of tropical diseases and pestilences peculiar to the area.

These policies benefited all concerned. Effective pest control and hygienic procedures provided people with far healthier living conditions and enabled other countries to engage in commercial and military relations within the sanitized areas without risking their own citizens' lives.

—Maurice T. Dominguez,
updated by John Richard Schrock

FURTHER READING

Dormandy, Thomas. *Moments of Truth: Four Creators of Modern Medicine*. Hoboken, N.J.: John Wiley & Sons, 2003. Study of four major contributors to modern medical advances, including Walter Reed, who is the subject of six chapters.

Ellis, John H. *Yellow Fever and Public Health in the New South*. Lexington: University Press of Kentucky, 1992. Vividly describes the impact of yellow fever in the epidemic of 1878, including the formation of sanitary associations in New Orleans and other major southern cities.

Finlay, Carlos E. *Carlos Finlay and Yellow Fever*. New York: Oxford University Press, 1940. Interesting account of Finlay's life and the development of his theory on the causes and prevention of yellow fever, from records translated by his son. The son's interpretations and the father's papers are interwoven in a harmonizing but distinguishable fashion.

Gibson, John M. *Physician to the World*. Durham, N.C.: Duke University Press, 1950. Useful biography of Major William Crawford Gorgas.

Greene, Emily, ed. *Occupied Haiti*. New York: Writers Publishing, 1927. Critical report of the U.S. occupation of Haiti, pointing out that the only aspect of the occupation that the Haitians did not resent was the accomplishment of the Service d'Hygiene.

Humphreys, Margaret. *Yellow Fever and the South*. New Brunswick, N.J.: Rutgers University Press, 1992. This careful explanation of the history of yellow fever includes original data on the extent of early epidemics, the succession of discoveries, and the campaign waged following the fuller understanding of insect transmission after 1900.

Pierce, John R., and Jim Writer. *Yellow Jack: How Yellow Fever Ravaged America and Walter Reed Discovered Its Deadly Secrets*. Hoboken, N.J.: John Wiley & Sons, 2005. Lively history of the impact of yellow fever on the United States and Walter Reed's contributions toward its eradication.

Truby, Albert E. *Memoir of Walter Reed: The Yellow Fever Episode*. New York: Paul B. Hoeber, 1943. Study of the methods that Reed and his colleagues used to show how mosquitoes carried yellow fever.

Yellow Fever Studies. Public Health in America. New York: Arno Press, 1977. A collection of critical papers reflecting the major breakthroughs in yellow fever control.

SEE ALSO: May, 1847: Semmelweis Develops Antiseptic Procedures; 1857: Pasteur Begins Developing Germ Theory and Microbiology; 1882-1901: Metchnikoff Advances the Cellular Theory of Immunity; Mar. 24, 1882: Koch Announces His Discovery of the Tuberculosis Bacillus; Dec. 11, 1890: Behring Discovers the Diphtheria Antitoxin; Jan. 23, 1897: "Aspirin" Is Registered as a Trade Name; Aug. 20, 1897: Ross Establishes Malaria's Transmission Vector; 1898: Beijerinck Discovers Viruses; Apr. 24-Dec. 10, 1898: Spanish-American War.

RELATED ARTICLES in *Great Lives from History: The Nineteenth Century, 1801-1900:* Emil von Behring; Robert Koch; Louis Pasteur; Walter Reed.

July 2, 1900
ZEPPELIN COMPLETES THE FIRST FLYING DIRIGIBLE

After a century of experimentation with lighter-than-air craft in different nations, Ferdinand von Zeppelin devised the first prototype of the modern rigid airships, which would play roles in World War I and in international air traffic until 1938.

LOCALE: Manzell, Lake Constance, Germany
CATEGORIES: Space and aviation; transportation; engineering

KEY FIGURES
Ferdinand von Zeppelin (1838-1917), retired German general and advocate of rigid airships
Theodor Kober (1865-1930), Zeppelin's private engineer

SUMMARY OF EVENT
The early history of rigid airships was directed largely by attempts to extend the military potential of lighter-than-air crafts by propulsion and directed flight. After the Montgolfier brothers' balloon launch in France in 1783, engineers—especially in France—began to focus on how the direction of balloon flight could be influenced by machines. Late nineteenth century ideas ranged from rowing through the air with silk-covered oars or movable wings to using rotating fans, airscrews, or propellers powered by steam engines or electric motors. The internal combustion engine, introduced at the end of the nineteenth century and promising higher speeds and more power, was another major step toward the realization of dirigible, or directable, balloons. These craft, however, were not yet rigid.

Rigidity had the advantage of permitting the building of larger airships with wider ranges. Around 1890, the Austro-Hungarian War Ministry turned down a design for a rigid airship devised by the Dalmatian engineer David Schwarz. However, the Russian government accepted the design in 1892. During trials in St. Petersburg in 1893, flaws that became apparent during inflation kept the airship on the ground. Schwarz then took his plans to a third sponsor and succeeded. In 1894, he persuaded a Prussian aeronautical commission to support his research. The second test flight in 1897 in Berlin, however, was troubled by gas leaks in the metal hull and ended in a crash.

Whereas Schwarz's airship consisted of an entirely rigid aluminum cylinder, the German inventor Ferdinand von Zeppelin's design was based on a rigid frame wrapped in a flexible fabric. Zeppelin was familiar with balloons, having been in two wars in which they were used: the U.S. Civil War (1861-1865) and the Franco-Prussian War (1870-1871).

The first thoughts about airships that Zeppelin recorded in his diary were dated March 25, 1874; they were inspired by an article he had read about international post and aviation. Zeppelin soon lost interest in the idea of finding civil uses for airships and came to favor the notion that dirigible balloons might become important in modern warfare. He submitted a request and asked for assistance to build an airship for the German government. In particular, he pointed to the apparent superiority of French military airships. Nationalism was the driving force behind Zeppelin's persistence in his endeavor, and it overshadowed the enormous technical and financial obstacles that he faced.

In order to procure money for his project in 1893, Zeppelin struggled to convince the German military and engineering experts of the utility of his invention. Although a governmental committee judged his work worth minimal funding, the army was skeptical, arguing that the ratio of cost to prospective utility of Zeppelin's machines was unfavorable. The committee finally chose Schwarz's design, but in 1896 the indefatigable Zeppelin won the support of the powerful Union of German Engineers, which helped him to form a stock company, the Association for the Promotion of Airship Flights, two years later. Zeppelin invested almost half of the association's 800,000 marks in capital funds. In 1899, he began construction in Manzell at Lake Constance, and on July 2, 1900, his airship was finished and ready for its first trial.

Together with engineer Theodor Kober, Zeppelin had worked on the design of the ship since May, 1892, shortly after his retirement from the army. By 1894, he and Kober had established the basic design, which, though some of its details were later modified, was to remain the recognized form of the Zeppelin. An improved version was patented in December, 1897.

In the final prototype—the LZ 1—the engineers aimed especially to reduce the weight of the airship as much as possible. They used a light internal combustion motor and devised a latticed container made of aluminum—a lightweight metal that had recently become commercially available because of a new electrolytic process.

Zeppelin's airship was 420 feet (128 meters) long and 38.4 feet (11.7 meters) in maximum diameter. It consisted of a huge zinc-aluminum alloy framework with twenty-four longitudinal girders running from nose to tail and drawn together at each end. Sixteen traverse frame rings held the body together. Over the framework, the engineers had stretched an envelope of smooth cotton cloth to reduce friction as the ship moved through the air and to protect the gas bags inside from direct exposure to the rays of the Sun.

Seventeen separate gas cells made of rubberized cloth were placed inside the framework, all equipped with safety valves. Several were provided with maneuvering valves. Together they contained 4,294,793 cubic feet (121,615 cubic meters) of hydrogen gas, which would lift 24,450 pounds (11,090 kilograms). A bridgelike construction was fixed to the side of the body, attached to which were two motor gondolas, each with a sixteen-horsepower gasoline motor, driving four propellers on the sides.

The dirigible's initial trials were unsuccessful. The two main questions—whether the construction was stable enough and whether its speed was sufficient for practical requirements—could not be answered definitively because small details, such as the breaking of a crankshaft and the jamming of a lateral rudder, prevented normal flying. The first flight lasted no more than eighteen minutes; the ship attained a maximum speed of 8.5 miles per hour (13.7 kilometers per hour). During its three test flights, the airship was in the air for a total of only two hours, and its speed never exceeded 17.5 miles per hour (28.2 kilometers per hour). Lack of money forced Zeppelin to abandon his projects for some years, and his company was liquidated. The LZ 1 was wrecked in the spring of 1901.

Trials with a second airship, which had been financed by industry, the military, and Zeppelin (with the additional help of a lottery), took place in November, 1905, and January, 1906. Both trials were unsuccessful and ended in the destruction of the ship during a storm. By 1906, however, the German government was convinced of the military utility of the airship, although it demanded

Undated photograph of a dirigible landing in the presence of Count Zeppelin and the Crown Prince of Germany. (Library of Congress)

that in order to back the airship financially, future airships would have to be able to fly nonstop for at least twenty-four hours. The third Zeppelin failed to fulfill these conditions in the autumn of 1907.

The breakthrough came with LZ 4. Not only did it prove itself to the military but it also attracted enormous public attention. In the summer of 1908, it flew for more than twenty-four hours and attained the considerable speed of 40 miles per hour (64 kilometers per hour). When, after its forced landing at the end of this flight, the ship was caught in a storm and exploded, spontaneous donations from throughout Germany amounted to more than 6 million marks. The "flying pencil" (a derogatory expression for the rigid airship coined by the German engineer of nonrigid airships, August von Parseval) had become a German national affair. Its advanced technology guaranteed Germany a lasting dominance in the field of airship design.

SIGNIFICANCE

Rigid airship development and operation remained chiefly in German hands, particularly in those of the Zeppelin company and its operating associates. Between 1900 and 1938, 139 of the 161 rigid airships that were made were built in Germany, and 119 of these were of the Zeppelin type. The remaining airships were of an experimental type, the construction of which was abandoned at the end of World War I.

More than 80 percent of airships were built for military purposes. Whereas the British Royal Navy had only four rigid airships at the end of World War I, the German army and navy bought their first airships in 1909 and used more than one hundred improved and enlarged Zeppelins for long-range reconnaissance and bombing during the war. Starting in May, 1915, bombing attacks were flown on the eastern front on Warsaw, Bucharest, and Salonika and on the western front predominantly on England, especially London. The airship attacks had a considerable psychological effect on the British population, although the physical damage they caused did not have a major impact on the war. Furthermore, the British anti-aircraft defense, which used artillery and airplanes, improved rapidly. By 1916, Germany's loss of airships had increased to such an extent that the army abandoned them. The navy, however, continued to employ them until the end of the war, primarily for reconnaissance over water and also for bombing.

Airships were first used for civilian passenger traffic in 1910. By 1914, the Delag (German Aeronautic Stock Company) had acquired seven passenger airships to make recreational circular flights from German cities. Insufficient engine power, ignorance of meteorology, and difficulties in maneuvering the airship on the ground still posed serious problems for regular use. After World War I, the remaining Zeppelins became part of reparation payments, and airship construction for German use was forbidden until 1925.

As airship service over short distances was economically infeasible, partly because of competition from airplanes, long-distance flights became the new specialty for airships during the 1920's and 1930's. Linking the empire by air was the aim of the British airship program between 1924 and 1930. A British airship had succeeded in the first transatlantic flight in 1919. The intended commercial flights, however, especially toward the Far East, never materialized, as a result of the crash of the R-101 in 1930, in which most of the leading British aeronauts were killed.

The American rigid airship program of 1928 to 1935 intended to provide long-range naval reconnaissance and led to the construction of the *Akron* (1931) and the *Macon* (1933). However, the U.S. government stopped the program in 1935 after both airships crashed. Commercial overseas travel by airship was entirely a German concern and as such was exploited for nationalist and, later, fascist propaganda. The world tour of the *Graf Zeppelin* in 1929 was an international success, and exploratory and promotional flights followed. Air connections between Germany and South America started in 1932 on a regular basis, and German airships adorned with Nazi swastikas flew to Lakehurst, New Jersey, in 1936. The explosion of the hydrogen-filled *Hindenburg* in 1937, however, meant the end of the rigid airship. As the U.S. secretary of the interior vetoed the sale of nonflammable helium, fearing its use for military purposes by the Nazi regime, the German government had to stop transatlantic flights for safety reasons. In 1940, the last two remaining rigid airships were wrecked.

—Matthias Dörries

FURTHER READING

Beaubois, Henry. *Airships*. Translated and adapted by Michael Kelly and Angela Kelly. New York: Two Continents Publishing Group, 1976. Comprehensive collection of pictures and drawings of all the airships built through the mid-1970's, starting with the first balloons and ending with the radar-equipped Goodyear ZPG-3W of the U.S. Navy and blimps used for publicity.

Brooks, Peter W. *Historic Airships*. London: H. Evelyn,

1973. Dense but clear account of the history of rigid airships. Brooks also provides useful tables and reliable statistics concerning the technical aspects and operation of airships.

Kirschner, Edwin J. *The Zeppelin in the Atomic Age*. Urbana: University of Illinois Press, 1957. This book appeared shortly before the end of the U.S. military airship program. It discusses the possibility of commercial transport using atomic-powered airships, with a strong emphasis on economic considerations.

Meyer, Henry Cord. "France Perceives the Zeppelins, 1924-1937." *South Atlantic Quarterly* 78 (1979): 107-121. Description of the French perception of Zeppelins as a symbol of new German political and technological strength after World War I. Recapitulating the struggles concerning permission for German airships to fly over France, it reflects on the political implications of modern technology.

Payne, Lee. *Lighter than Air: An Illustrated History of the Airship*. Rev. ed. New York: Orion Books, 1991. Broad history of all varieties of lighter-than-air craft.

Robinson, Douglas H. *Giants in the Sky*. Seattle: University of Washington Press, 1973. Accurate and insightful survey of the history of airships by the leading authority on rigid airships.

Robinson, Douglas H., and Charles L. Keller. *"Up Ship!" A History of the U.S. Navy's Rigid Airships, 1919-1935*. Annapolis: Naval Institute Press, 1982. Based on documents of the National Archives. Presents a detailed and precise history of the U.S. Navy's rigid airships but does not avoid romanticism in describing military weaponry.

Syon, Guillaume de. *Zeppelin! Germany and the Airship, 1900-1939*. Baltimore: Johns Hopkins University Press, 2002. Solid and well-written study of Zeppelin's dirigibles, with special attention to their place in German culture and history.

Toland, John. *The Great Dirigibles: Their Triumphs and Disasters*. New York: Dover, 1972. Popular history of the early dirigibles.

SEE ALSO: Aug. 17, 1807: Maiden Voyage of the *Clermont*; May 22-June 20, 1819: *Savannah* Is the First Steamship to Cross the Atlantic; c. 1845: Clipper Ship Era Begins; 1847: Hamburg-Amerika Shipping Line Begins; Jan. 31, 1858: Brunel Launches the SS *Great Eastern*.

RELATED ARTICLES in *Great Lives from History: The Nineteenth Century, 1801-1900:* George Cayley; Gottlieb Daimler.

September 8, 1900
GALVESTON HURRICANE

The category 4 hurricane that struck Galveston, Texas, was the deadliest natural disaster in U.S. history. The low-lying barrier island was battered by 120-mile-per-hour winds that killed several thousand people and destroyed two-thirds of Galveston's buildings, including more than thirty-six hundred homes.

LOCALE: Galveston, Texas
CATEGORIES: Disasters; natural disasters; environment and ecology

KEY FIGURES
Isaac M. Cline (1861-1955), U.S. Weather Bureau climatologist and physician
Clara Barton (1821-1912), president of the American Red Cross

SUMMARY OF EVENT
In 1900, Galveston was a vibrant city of thirty-seven thousand people. Located at the eastern end of a thirty-mile-long barrier island, the area's cotton production made Galveston the third-busiest commercial port in the United States and one of the wealthiest cities in the state of Texas. With an opera house and medical college, Galveston also could boast of being the first in Texas to have telephone and electrical service. The city's prestige was evident in ornately designed office buildings and residential areas echoing Greek Revival and Romanesque architectural styles. Galveston's streets, however, built over sand, were only four to seven feet above sea level. The city was also relatively isolated from the mainland. One wagon bridge and three wooden railroad trestles provided links to the mainland two miles away.

Most adult Galvestonians had lived through hurricanes and viewed them as inconveniences rather than serious threats. Hurricanes had never severely damaged the island, so many believed that natural defenses protected the city from storms. However, after a powerful hurricane in 1886 destroyed the nearby port town of Indian-

Typical wreckage from the Galveston Hurricane. The large building at the left is the high school for black students. (Library of Congress)

ola, some residents called for construction of a seawall to provide a storm barrier. Despite frequent discussion the wall was not constructed. Ironically, developers increased the city's vulnerability to waves and storm surge by removing coastal vegetation and moving sand from beach dunes to fill low-lying areas.

On August 27, 1900, an unnamed tropical depression began forming in the equatorial mid-Atlantic. Gaining energy, the storm moved westward through the Greater Antilles causing damage on the island of Jamaica. First word of the storm came on Tuesday, September 4, when the U.S. Weather Bureau received cables from ships encountering rough seas and high winds off the coast of Cuba. Passing Key West, Florida, on September 6, the storm intensified, drawing energy from unusually high water temperatures in the Gulf of Mexico. Isaac M.

Cline, head of the U.S. Weather Bureau's Galveston Station, had been monitoring the situation. On September 7, he placed Galveston under a storm warning. A brief story appeared that day in the *Galveston News*, noting a disturbance in the Gulf of Mexico but offering few details. As the afternoon wore on, ocean swells began to intensify. A few sightseers from Houston came to watch large waves pounding the shoreline.

The morning of September 8 began with a pleasant autumn breeze. Few seemed alarmed that seawater had begun inundating homes near the waterfront. Such flooding, known as overflow, was relatively common in Galveston. For most residents nothing about the morning's weather suggested an approaching storm. Seeing that few people had taken the storm warning seriously, Cline drove a horse-drawn buggy along the waterfront urging residents within three blocks of the ocean to seek higher ground. By noon, wind speeds had increased and rain began to fall.

Despite signs of the approaching storm, few people evacuated to the mainland. As water levels rose residents moved to the upper stories of buildings or to higher ground near the city's center. At 3:30 that afternoon, Cline drafted a message to the Weather Bureau office in Washington, D.C., advising that a great loss of life was imminent and requesting immediate assistance. Wading through waist-deep water, he arrived at the Western Union office only to find that telegraph lines had been knocked out by the storm.

By 4 P.M., winds increased to hurricane force. Breaking free from its moorings, a steamship slammed into all four bridges to the mainland, preventing an evacuation of the island. Buildings near the shoreline were the first to be wiped away by the wind and the rising storm surge. People attempting to move away from beach areas to higher ground were struck by flying wood and masonry.

At 6:30, a large wave moved ashore in advance of the hurricane's eye, causing a sudden four-foot surge. Survivors clung to rooftops, the tops of trees, or floating debris. Huddled together, some found shelter on the upper floors of large mansions and other buildings, such as the Tremont Hotel, in the center of the city. More than four hundred people crowded into City Hall. About a half-hour later, wind speeds reached 120 miles per hour. Water that now covered the entire island reached its peak depth within a few hours. By 11 P.M., the worst of the storm had passed and the water level started to subside within most parts of the city.

During the early hours of Sunday morning, the winds began to subside. As the sun came up the storm's catastrophic devastation was evident. The tremendous force of the wind, coupled with the storm surge, had pushed buildings off their foundations. Two-thirds of the city's structures had been razed, including thirty-six hundred homes. Among buildings destroyed was St. Mary's Orphanage, where ten Catholic nuns and

---

MEMORIALIZING THE GALVESTON HURRICANE

A Galveston-area school teacher remembers her students in an undated poem written after the hurricane. One stanza is excerpted here.

> And then—oh, the next night's horror!
> I cannot, I will not tell
> Of the souls that to death were hurried,
> Or the waters that rang their knell.
> And I heard—oh, my God, that hearing!
> That only a few were left;
> That the waters had taken my pupils,
> And me of their love bereft. . . .

Another woman living in the Galveston area wrote a series of letters, originally in German, to her daughters living outside the devastated Gulf region. Excerpted here are two letters, the first dated just three days after the hurricane struck.

[letter of Sept. 11, 1900]

My dear Daughters:

You will have read in the papers about the terrible disaster that has happened to our island. The storm struck as far as Austin and all along the Coast; in New Orleans it is said that 4,700 people lost their lives. . . .

There is no electricity as the chimney of the power house is down; and we have only cistern water. The city water tower still stands and they hope to have it back in order soon. During the storm night we sat in the dark. A Mallory ship has come into port and reports that the Gulf is filled with bodies. . . .

[letter of Sept. 14, 1900]

The havoc here is indescribable. The remaining houses are so damaged they cannot be used as they are and will take months to repair. Workmen are so absurd in their charges that only a few people can afford to have repairs done. . . .

It will never be known how many were killed or drowned in the storm. Whole parts of the town have vanished completely. A great many people are being evacuated, especially women and children, in order to relieve the housing and feeding problems. Already food and clothing is being sent in from outside.

Sources: Bertie Dinkelaker, "In Loving Memory of My Little Scholars Lost at Poolville, Galveston County, Texas" (undated); Georges Anna Dorothea Marckmann Focke, "September Eighth 1900: An Account of That Day by a Mother to Her Daughters Far Away" (1956 edition; original in German). Galveston and Texas History Center, Rosenberg Library, Galveston, Texas.

ninety children perished; a few scattered bricks were all that remained of the building. Within a few hours, Galveston had been transformed from a wealthy vacation destination to a ruined landscape of uprooted trees, broken timbers, and buckled sidewalks.

Because bridges and telegraph lines were damaged, word of the devastation had not reached the mainland. Departing on Sunday, volunteers carrying messages to the governor of Texas and the president of the United States navigated a twenty-foot steam launch ten miles across Galveston Bay to Texas City on the mainland. The messages were not received until Monday, September 10.

Rescue workers arriving from Houston by train and ship were stunned by the carnage. The dead were scattered everywhere among the rubble of homes and businesses. An initial estimate of five hundred killed was soon determined to be too low, as the search revealed more victims, many battered beyond recognition. On Sunday morning, Galveston's mayor held an emergency town meeting. Because there was no functional city government, an ad hoc central relief committee was appointed and martial law implemented to stop looting.

Every able-bodied man was required to participate in the cleanup, which was made even more miserable by heat, humidity, and the unbearable stench. Citizen squads worked to dispose of bodies by loading them onto barges to be dumped into the gulf. This process had to be stopped when it was discovered that corpses were floating back to shore. Unable to bury the large number of victims, workers had to burn the bodies in funeral pyres. Survivors received emergency shelter in army tents and makeshift buildings constructed from salvageable timber. Seventy-eight-year-old Clara Barton, founder of the American Red Cross, was among those who traveled to Galveston to help survivors. Within a week after the storm, telegraph and water services had been restored to portions of the city.

SIGNIFICANCE

Calls to rebuild the city began soon after the storm. In an effort to avoid a repeat of the disaster, city leaders developed plans to build a seawall and raise the island's elevation by seventeen feet. The first section of the wall was completed in 1904, and subsequent sections were constructed during the next fifty-five years, eventually extending the wall's length to ten miles. Sixteen million cubic yards of sand were dredged from Galveston's ship channel to provide fill for raising the city's elevation. Gas, water, and sewer pipes along with streetcar lines, houses, and other buildings were lifted up. An all-weather bridge to the mainland was constructed to replace the wagon bridge destroyed by the storm.

Although several hurricanes have struck the United States with greater intensity or have been more costly, such as Hurricanes Katrina and Rita in 2005, no hurricane has been more deadly than the 1900 storm in Galveston. The number of persons killed by the Galveston hurricane was greater than the combined death tolls of the 1871 Great Chicago Fire, the 1889 Johnstown flood, and the 1906 San Francisco earthquake. Galveston's low-lying topography and lack of barriers to wind and rising water contributed to the magnitude of devastation. However, the complacency of island residents toward the impending danger was also a major factor in the high death toll.

A series of measures, including the construction of a seawall, were implemented after the storm to prevent similar disasters. Galveston saw another hurricane in 1915, which had been comparable in strength to the 1900 hurricane. Although 275 persons were killed, the seawall and other measures were credited with preventing the death toll from being substantially higher. In the years after the 1900 storm, scientific weather forecasting and radio communications with ships have contributed to more accurate predictions of hurricane magnitudes and movements.

—*Thomas A. Wikle*

FURTHER READING

Cartwright, Gary. *Galveston: A History of the Island*. Fort Worth: Texas Christian University Press, 1998. Relates the story of Galveston's rise as a commercial center, the impact of the 1900 hurricane, and its aftermath.

Galveston and Texas History Center, Rosenberg Library. 1900 storm exhibit. Available at http://www.gthcenter.org/. A collection of eyewitness accounts of the 1900 Galveston hurricane in letters, documents, and photographs. Accessed February 11, 2006.

Green, Nathan, ed. *Story of the 1900 Galveston Hurricane*. Gretna, La.: Pelican, 2000. A series of firsthand accounts of the Galveston hurricane.

Larson, Erik. *Isaac's Storm: A Man, a Time, and the Deadliest Hurricane in History*. New York: Crown, 1999. The personal story of the Galveston hurricane as told by Isaac M. Cline, Galveston's chief meteorologist.

SEE ALSO: Oct. 8-10, 1871: Great Chicago Fire; May 31, 1889: Johnstown Flood.

RELATED ARTICLE in *Great Lives from History: The Nineteenth Century, 1801-1900:* Clara Barton.

1890's

November 8, 1900
DREISER PUBLISHES *SISTER CARRIE*

Theodore Dreiser's novel Sister Carrie, *published despite misgivings concerning its frank treatment of sexuality, became a beacon to later American writers intent on breaking literary taboos. It is considered by many one of the best modern novels.*

LOCALE: New York, New York
CATEGORY: Literature

KEY FIGURES
Theodore Dreiser (1871-1945), American novelist who was a leading figure in American literary naturalism
Frank Norris (1870-1902), American naturalistic novelist
Walter Hines Page (1855-1918) and
Frank Nelson Doubleday (1862-1934), American publishers

SUMMARY OF EVENT
By 1899, Theodore Dreiser was a young veteran of print journalism, with experience on daily newspapers in Chicago, Pittsburgh, New York, and St. Louis, Missouri. In September of that year in New York (or possibly a few months earlier at a friend's house in Maumee, Ohio), Dreiser began writing the story of a girl from a small Wisconsin town who becomes a kept woman in Chicago and, eventually, a Broadway starlet. The novel, which Dreiser finished in March of 1900, would entangle him in one of the most famous disputes in American publishing history.

Dreiser sent the completed manuscript to a publishing house in May, but it was rejected, although an editor suggested that Doubleday, Page & Company might be interested in the work. In doubt was the suitability of the novel's frank portrayal of sexuality in an era of Victorian literary proscriptions. The heroine, Carrie Meeber, a character based in part on one of Dreiser's own sisters, lives with two men without benefit of matrimony. Perhaps most dubious of all, according to the standards of the day, Carrie's transgressions are not punished beyond her consignment to a vague nonfulfillment at novel's end.

Despite this cause for caution, Doubleday, Page accepted the manuscript for publication, reasoning that the work received unbridled enthusiasm by the publisher's first reader, the California naturalistic novelist Frank Norris. In 1899, the firm (then called Doubleday, McClure) had brought out Norris's violent tale of a brutish San Francisco dentist, *McTeague*. Norris, whose popu-

larity with his publishers gained him substantial influence, pronounced *Sister Carrie* "a wonder" and one of the most pleasing novels he had read "in *any* form, published or otherwise."

Impressed by Norris's response, Walter Hines Page wrote to Dreiser and accepted the novel in the absence of his partner, Frank N. Doubleday, who was traveling in Europe. When the signed agreement arrived from Page, Dreiser had every reason to believe that his career as a fiction writer had been launched. Soon, however, Doubleday and his wife Neltje returned from Europe, where they had been trying to acquire the publishing rights to French writer Émile Zola's novels. Doubleday, a somewhat moralistic Episcopalian in spite of his relatively liberal attitude toward *McTeague* and Zola's novels, read Dreiser's manuscript and objected to the publishing agreement on the grounds that the work was immoral and because, in any event, it was unlikely to sell. Neltje Doubleday also read the book and concurred in her husband's judgment.

On July 19, at Frank Doubleday's insistence, Page wrote to Dreiser explaining the growing misgivings at the publishing house about the manuscript and asking for release from the agreement. Dreiser decided to fight for his legal rights. A series of conflicts ensued, and Dreiser, who first tried courteous insistence, finally threatened legal action. Doubleday, Page representatives responded with offers to find him a different publisher and other attempts to mollify. Eventually, Doubleday agreed in exasperation to honor the agreement but to commit to only one edition. In a concession bespeaking surprising goodwill under the circumstances, Doubleday put Norris in charge of publicity, and the latter sent out 127 review copies appended with promotional material and his own personal letters.

By the actual day of publication, November 8, 1900, Norris and Dreiser were certain the novel would be a huge, immediate success. They were mistaken. Few reviewers were favorable, and those that were favorable found much to criticize. The overwhelming majority of reviewers found the novel's subject matter unacceptably crude according to prevailing tastes and judged the style totally graceless. The response of the public was equally disheartening. Only 456 copies had sold by February of 1902, netting Dreiser royalties of $68.40.

Dreiser's disappointment was profound and sustained. In the short run, his perceived failure in this first attempt at long fiction, added to his family and marital troubles, sent his already brooding psyche into a deep depression, and he was on the verge of suicide for several months. He was helped by his brother, the celebrated songwriter Paul Dresser (Johann Paul Dreiser, Jr.), who arranged for his treatment in a sanitarium. After recovering his equilibrium, Dreiser achieved notable financial success while pursuing a career as an editor of women's magazines. He might have stayed with this work permanently had he not been made to resign because of an affair of the heart involving an assistant's daughter. Forced to try writing literature again as a way of making a living, he went on to become one of the nation's leading novelists and the author of one of its most important twentieth century works of fiction, *An American Tragedy* (1925).

Dreiser, though, was never able to forgot his troubles with Doubleday, Page over the manuscript of *Sister Carrie*, even though the novel's subsequent publication in England spurred the slow but steady growth of its reputation in America. Throughout his later life, he returned again and again to the story of the conflict with his first publisher, often embellishing it with half-truths and outright falsehoods. Almost always, these elaborated stories made Neltje Doubleday the blue-nosed villain of the piece, a bit of misinformation he apparently picked up from Norris. For many years, the legends Dreiser circulated about the circumstances surrounding the Doubleday affair were taken at face value, but later scholarship served to set the record straight.

SIGNIFICANCE

Because *Sister Carrie* was effectively neutralized at the time of its appearance by the combination of its less-than-enthusiastic publisher, mostly negative reviews, and negligible sales, it had no appreciable immediate impact. Not until the modest success of his second novel, *Jennie Gerhardt* (1911), did Dreiser attract the concentrated attention of important critics and writers, who then discovered and reconsidered the ultimately more respected earlier novel.

Undoubtedly, the most important of the first literary critics impressed by Dreiser was the

SISTER CARRIE AND HURSTWOOD

Theodore Dreiser became somewhat of a literary icon for his forthright treatment, in his 1900 novel Sister Carrie, *of a woman's sexuality outside marriage. The following excerpt from the novel shows Carrie responding to the gazes of her married lover Hurstwood.*

Hurstwood's glance was as effective as the spoken words of a lover, and more. They called for no immediate decision, and could not be answered.

People in general attach too much importance to words. They are under the illusion that talking effects great results. As a matter of fact, words are, as a rule, the shallowest portion of all the argument. They but dimly represent the great surging feelings and desires which lie behind. When the distraction of the tongue is removed, the heart listens.

In this conversation she [Carrie] heard, instead of his words, the voices of the things which he represented. How suave was the counsel of his appearance! How feelingly did his superior state speak for itself! The growing desire he felt for her lay upon her spirit as a gentle hand. She did not need to tremble at all, because it was invisible; she did not need to worry over what other people would say—what she herself would say—because it had no tangibility. She was being pleaded with, persuaded, led into denying old rights and assuming new ones, and yet there were no words to prove it. Such conversation as was indulged in held the same relationship to the actual mental enactments of the twain that the low music of the orchestra does to the dramatic incident which it is used to cover.

"Have you ever seen the houses along the Lake Shore on the North Side?" asked Hurstwood.

"Why, I was just over there this afternoon—Mrs. Hale and I. Aren't they beautiful?"

"They're very fine," he answered.

"Oh, me," said Carrie, pensively. "I wish I could live in such a place."

"You're not happy," said Hurstwood, slowly, after a slight pause.

He had raised his eyes solemnly and was looking into her own. He assumed that he had struck a deep chord. Now was a slight chance to say a word in his own behalf. He leaned over quietly and continued his steady gaze. He felt the critical character of the period. She endeavored to stir, but it was useless. The whole strength of a man's nature was working. He had good cause to urge him on. He looked and looked, and the longer the situation lasted the more difficult it became. The little shop-girl was getting into deep water. She was letting her few supports float away from her.

"Oh," she said at last, "you mustn't look at me like that."

"I can't help it," he answered.

Source: Sister Carrie, *edited by Claude Simpson (Cambridge, Mass.: Riverside Press, 1959), pp. 103-104.*

1890's

acerbic Henry Louis Mencken. Dreiser had published some of Mencken's early essays while working as a magazine editor. The two became fast friends, a circumstance that positioned Mencken to mount his famous defense of Dreiser when Dreiser's 1915 novel *The "Genius"* was attacked for its "lewd" and "obscene" material by the New York Society for the Suppression of Vice.

The notoriety of the temporary suppression of *The "Genius,"* coupled with the growing legend of his earlier troubles with Doubleday over *Sister Carrie*, helped establish Dreiser as an antiestablishment icon for the next generation of writers, which included F. Scott Fitzgerald, James T. Farrell, Richard Wright, and many others. By the time *An American Tragedy*, Dreiser's epic novel fictionalizing a famous murder case, became a best seller following its publication in 1925, *Sister Carrie* had come to be regarded as a national classic.

What subsequent writers discovered in *Sister Carrie*, however, was not simply a novel of historic importance in the battle against Victorian literary squeamishness. Equally important were other trendsetting aspects of the work as well as its attempt to come to intellectual grips with the modern world, in which the failure of faith necessitated a search for a substitute, secular salvation. First, the novel's heroine, Carrie Meeber, is a lower-middle-class midwesterner who speaks ungrammatically. These qualities sharply differentiate her not only from the protagonists of romantic novels but also even from the protagonists of earlier American realists such as Henry James and William Dean Howells, whose "slice of life" fiction carefully avoided such less-than-genteel types. Moreover, Chicago and New York, the settings for *Sister Carrie*, are rendered so palpably that the novel is justly regarded as a pioneering picture of the newly urbanized America teeming with seeking immigrants. As such, it provided a precedent for later city novelists such as John Dos Passos, Nelson Algren, and Hubert Selby, Jr.

Perhaps the most widespread and long-lasting influence *Sister Carrie* has had on later writers, however, stems from the book's attempt to construe the meaning of modern American life. In the novel, Dreiser weds the growing spiritual skepticism of the age to a national context. He was prepared for this mission by his reading and experiences in the years preceding the novel's publication. His reading had made him, at least nominally, a philosophic naturalist who believed that God was dead, that life was meaningless, that humans are helpless victims of their heredity and environment, and that blind chance shapes events.

Dreiser's experiences led him to brood about the disillusionment that almost inevitably resulted from the attainment of his desires and about his continued longing for fulfillment in spite of the evidence of his emotions. Dreiser incorporated his reading of naturalistic philosophy into *Sister Carrie* through the voice of an omniscient narrator who comments on and assesses the heroine's development. He made use of his experience by giving Carrie the same wants and urges that had prodded his own progress through life. In the novel, Carrie achieves material, sexual, artistic, and social success as well as fame, but her ultimate dissatisfaction leads her to contemplate an alternative agenda, the subsuming of the self in devotion to the less fortunate.

The American writers who came after Dreiser were forced to face a world that *Sister Carrie* had helped to define. Whether they accepted or rejected the bleak twentieth century determinism of the novel, they had to acknowledge that the philosophy contributed mightily to the skeptical attitude dominant among American intellectuals. Succeeding writers who sought thereafter to signal the significance of contemporary American life often walked the same road taken by Dreiser.

A notable example of the influence of *Sister Carrie* on a later work is Fitzgerald's *The Great Gatsby* (1925), often singled out as the finest novel about the American Dream. Its mythic hero, Jay Gatsby, tragically pursues most of the same ends that had mesmerized Carrie; moreover, Fitzgerald ends his novel with a poetic evocation of the very desire and disillusionment over which Dreiser had brooded at the close of his story. *Sister Carrie* can be seen as well as the ancestor of the many other novels that excoriate American materialism, works as diverse yet typical as Sinclair Lewis's *Babbitt* (1922) and Joan Didion's *Play It as It Lays* (1970).

In 1981, *Sister Carrie* enjoyed a second debut somewhat more auspicious than its first. The University of Pennsylvania's Dreiser Project, a scholarly endeavor aimed at providing definitive editions of the novelist's works, published a version based on the *Sister Carrie* holograph. This version restores some thirty-six thousand words deleted in the process that led to the Doubleday, Page edition in 1900. Even this later version, though, met with the seemingly inevitable controversy that plagued most of Dreiser's book launchings. The Pennsylvania edition eliminates the final scene, in which Carrie muses on her experience while rocking in her chair—a deletion justified on the grounds that Dreiser had added it a few weeks after he had ostensibly finished the manuscript.

—*The Editors*

FURTHER READING

Dreiser, Theodore. *Letters of Theodore Dreiser*. Edited by Robert H. Elias. 3 vols. Philadelphia: University of Pennsylvania Press, 1959. Contains scattered references to *Sister Carrie* written to correspondents over Dreiser's entire life. Many references add to the legend surrounding the suppression of the novel by Doubleday, Page in 1900.

_____. *Sister Carrie*. Philadelphia: University of Pennsylvania Press, 1981. Part of a scholarly project aimed at re-creating the definitive texts of Dreiser's novels as he would have authorized them. Restores passages eliminated in the process of creating and publishing the novel in 1899 and 1900. Amplifies especially the characters of Carrie and Hurstwood.

_____. *Theodore Dreiser's Uncollected Magazine Articles, 1897-1902*, edited by Yoshinobu Hakutani. Newark: University of Delaware Press, 2003. Brings into one volume Dreiser's journalistic works. Includes a bibliography and an index.

Dudley, Dorothy. *Forgotten Frontiers: Dreiser and the Land of the Free*. New York: Harrison Smith and Robert Haas, 1932. Biography that attempts to place Dreiser in a national context. Written in a somewhat florid style uncharacteristic of biographies. Dudley's advantage over more recent biographers was her interviews with Dreiser. Contains no scholarly apparatus or photographs.

Elias, Robert H. *Theodore Dreiser: Apostle of Nature*. New York: Alfred A. Knopf, 1948. An early critical biography completed as a doctoral dissertation. Elias's advantage over other biographers was his training in literary criticism and the availability of resource persons just a few years after Dreiser's death in 1945. Contains an index and a few photographs.

Lingeman, Richard. *Theodore Dreiser: At the Gates of the City, 1871-1907*. New York: G. P. Putnam's Sons, 1986. The first volume of the definitive biography. A much more sympathetic approach to Dreiser's life than the work of W. A. Swanberg and more sensitive in its approach to the novels. Contains photographs, index, and bibliography. The second volume, published in 1990, is entitled *Theodore Dreiser: An American Journey, 1908-1945*.

Newlin, Keith, ed. *A Theodore Dreiser Encyclopedia*. Westport, Conn.: Greenwood Press, 2003. A comprehensive collection of all things Dreiser, in a format that makes it easy to locate select information on the writer. Includes a bibliography and an index.

Pizer, Donald. *The Novels of Theodore Dreiser: A Critical Study*. Minneapolis: University of Minnesota Press, 1976. Sets out to establish sources and elucidate the composition process for each of the novels. Separate chapter on each novel. Discussion of *Sister Carrie* composition especially helpful. Contains index and endnotes.

Rush, Frederic E., and Donald Pizer, eds. *Theodore Dreiser: Interviews*. Urbana: University of Illinois Press, 2004. A collection of interviews with the novelist Dreiser, edited by scholars of his work. Includes a bibliography and index.

Salzman, Jack, ed. *Theodore Dreiser: The Critical Reception*. New York: David Lewis, 1972. A collection of contemporary reviews of Dreiser's books. Includes several of the original responses to the 1900 Doubleday, Page edition of *Sister Carrie* and an introductory essay by Salzman that puts Dreiser's literary reception and subsequent reputation in historical context.

Swanberg, W. A. *Dreiser*. New York: Charles Scribner's Sons, 1965. The first serious and comprehensive biography. Swanberg's jaundiced view of Dreiser's private life did not sit well with the surviving members of the novelist's family. Reliable on factual details but deficient in literary judgment. Contains photographs and index. Superseded by Lingeman's two-volume biography cited above.

SEE ALSO: 1807: Bowdler Publishes *The Family Shakespeare*; c. 1830's-1860's: American Renaissance in Literature; Fall, 1848: Pre-Raphaelite Brotherhood Begins; Oct. 1-Dec. 15, 1856: Flaubert Publishes *Madame Bovary*; c. 1865: Naturalist Movement Begins; 1870's: Aesthetic Movement Arises; 1879: *A Doll's House* Introduces Modern Realistic Drama; c. 1884-1924: Decadent Movement Flourishes.

RELATED ARTICLES in *Great Lives from History: The Nineteenth Century, 1801-1900:* Honoré de Balzac; Charles Baudelaire; Gustave Flaubert; Oscar Wilde; Émile Zola.

1890's

December 14, 1900
ARTICULATION OF QUANTUM THEORY

In attempting to resolve anomalies in the traditional explanation of radiation emitted from certain heated objects, Max Planck restricted the object's "resonators" to discrete (or quantized) energies, an ad hoc solution that proved to have revolutionary implications.

LOCALE: Berlin, Germany

CATEGORIES: Physics; science and technology

KEY FIGURES

Max Planck (1858-1947), German physicist

Albert Einstein (1879-1955), German-born Swiss American physicist

Rudolf Clausius (1822-1888), German physicist

Ludwig Eduard Boltzmann (1844-1906), Austrian physicist

Wilhelm Wien (1864-1928), German physicist

SUMMARY OF EVENT

Although Max Planck has traditionally been closely associated with the origin of quantum theory, some scholars have come to question whether he actually proposed the theory's basic idea: that radiant energy is transmitted in discrete packets. Planck was reluctant to accept the idea of quantized energy. In his autobiography, he credits Albert Einstein with the idea. The question of Planck's precise contribution to quantum theory therefore naturally arises.

During the first fifteen years of his scientific career, Planck devoted his efforts to clarifying, developing, and applying the laws of thermodynamics to a variety of problems. The first law of thermodynamics (the law of conservation of energy) states that, although energy can be changed into different forms, the total energy of an isolated system remains the same. The second law of thermodynamics, which involves the direction of energy flow, states that heat energy moves spontaneously from hot to cold regions or, more generally, that the amount of useless energy in an isolated system (called entropy) increases when an irreversible process occurs in that system.

This phenomenon of irreversibility fascinated Planck, who became an avid student of the writings of Rudolf Clausius, who, in 1865, had introduced the term "entropy" as a measure of the amount of thermal energy incapable of doing work (later seen as a measure of a system's disorder). Planck came to believe that the second law of thermodynamics had absolute validity. During the 1880's and 1890's, he tried to convince his fellow physicists that entropy constitutes a principle of irreversibility, and—largely through Ludwig Eduard Boltzmann's statistical arguments about the equipartition of energy in describing the behavior of a gas—Planck's views on entropy prevailed.

During the 1890's, Planck became interested in measurements of the radiation from very hot objects being made at a technical institute in Berlin. The theoretical construct used to understand this radiation was the "blackbody," an idealized object that totally absorbs all radiation falling on it. By the laws of thermodynamics, this perfect absorber must also be a perfect emitter of radiation. Experimenters found that they could approximate a blackbody with a hollow metal box containing a pinhole. After heating the box to a uniform temperature, researchers studied the radiation emitted through the pinhole. They were surprised to discover that this radiation did not depend either on the type of metal or the size and shape of the box.

The "blackbody radiation" depended only on the temperature, and when the brightness (or intensity) of this radiation was plotted as a function of its color (or wavelength) for various temperatures, a set of humplike curves was generated. With higher temperatures, the curves kept their basic shape but their maxima shifted toward the shorter wavelengths (the ultraviolet portion of the spectrum). A family of these curves, the "normal spectral energy distribution," represented for Planck "something absolute." He very much wanted to find a satisfactory theoretical explanation of these experimental curves.

Wilhelm Wien, who studied blackbody radiation both experimentally and theoretically, devised an equation that accounted for the experimental results at high frequencies but not at low frequencies. The English physicist Lord Rayleigh, on the other hand, formulated an equation that fit the low frequencies but not the high. Wien had also found an empirical relationship between the temperature and the wavelength at the peak of the curve, and Boltzmann had discovered a relationship between the temperature and total radiated energy. However, no scientist had been able to provide a theoretical explanation of the entire family of curves.

For several years, Planck toiled at solving the mystery of the energy distribution of radiated heat by relying solely on the principles of thermodynamics. He chose this path, because these principles had, for him, absolute validity. He did not need to know about the ultimate nature of the atoms making up the metal box. However, he did posit that the box's walls contained what he called "simple linear oscillators or resonators." (He did not describe exactly what these oscillators were, but some scholars have interpreted them as idealized atoms.) Heating the walls set the oscillators into vibrations, causing radiant energy to stream into the cavity and then to emanate from the pinhole. Planck found that he could derive Wien's formula, explaining some aspects of this radiant energy, when he assumed a simple relationship between the energy and entropy of these oscillators as they absorbed and emitted radiation.

Bolzmann's criticism of this analysis forced Planck to study the interrelationship between entropy and probability, which in turn led him to develop a statistical analysis of the number of ways of distributing a certain amount of energy among many oscillators of a certain frequency. To get a match with experimental results, he needed to construct this distribution in multiples of an energy element. It is unclear whether he intended these energy elements to correspond with actual physical entities, such as quantized energy packets, or whether he used them simply as convenient calculational devices in his combinatorial analysis.

Until 1978, when science historian Thomas Kuhn argued that Planck did not discover the quantization of radiant energy, Planck's work was commonly interpreted to indicate that he had understood oscillators as actually emitting radiation in multiples of a definite energy that was proportional to its frequency. The proportionality constant, h, which came to be called "Planck's constant," is an extremely small number that has the units of mechanical action. Planck saw this constant as a "mysterious messenger" from the microworld. He insisted that the "introduction of the quantum of action h" into physicists' theories about the atom "should be done as conservatively as possible." He knew that the classical wave theory of light had been shown to be true with many experimental observations, and he therefore wanted to preserve a model in which radiation was continuous rather than discrete.

Nevertheless, Planck must have realized that he had accomplished something very important, because on December 14, 1900, when he first made his ideas on quantum theory public, he told his son Erwin that he had just made a discovery "as important as Newton's." On the other hand, he saw his greatest claim to fame in his radiation-law formula, because it agreed perfectly with energy distributions of radiations determined in laboratories for all wavelengths and temperatures. The task of interpreting this equation and Planck's formula relating energy and frequency fell, for the most part, to others.

SIGNIFICANCE

The person who most profoundly understood the significance of Planck's work on quantum theory was Albert Einstein. He wholeheartedly embraced the idea of quantized energy and used it extensively in his work. For example, he used light quanta to explain the previously inexplicable photoelectric effect, an achievement for which he received the 1921 Nobel Prize in Physics. Planck had won the 1918 Nobel Prize for "his discovery

Max Planck. (Library of Congress)

1890's

of energy quanta." By extending the discontinuity of energy to light, as well as to the entire electromagnetic spectrum, and by his quantum studies of the interactions between light and matter, Einstein revealed the great power of the quantum idea.

In 1913, Niels Bohr developed his quantum theory of the hydrogen atom, using quantized electron energy states to account for the hydrogen spectrum. The full-fledged importance of the quantum idea became clear in quantum mechanics, developed in the 1920's by such eminent physicists as Louis de Broglie, Werner Heisenberg, and Erwin Schrödinger. So momentous was this new quantum theory that it has become the dominant theoretical tool for helping physicists and chemists understand the microrealm of atoms and molecules.

—*Robert J. Paradowski*

FURTHER READING

Brush, Stephen G. *Cautious Revolutionaries: Maxwell, Planck, Hubble*. College Park, Md.: American Association of Physics Teachers, 2002. Brush, a historian of physics, argues that Planck intended his quantum hypothesis as a mathematical device, not a physical discontinuity. Includes bibliographical references.

Cline, Barbara Lovett. *Men Who Made a New Physics*. Chicago: University of Chicago Press, 1987. Originally published as *The Questioners* in 1965, this reprint provides general readers with an accessible account of the evolution of quantum theory. The two chapters on the early work of Planck are particularly well done. Index.

Duck, Ian. *One Hundred Years of Planck's Quantum*. River Edge, N.J.: World Scientific, 2000. Surveys the history of quantum theory from Planck's discovery of the quantum to the end of the twentieth century. Includes bibliographical references and indexes.

Heilbron, J. L. *The Dilemmas of an Upright Man: Max Planck as a Spokesman for German Science*. Berkeley: University of California Press, 1986. This brief biography by a respected historian of science surveys Planck's life and achievements against the background of political turmoil in Germany. Extensive bibliography, index.

Kuhn, Thomas S. *Black-Body Theory and the Quantum Discontinuity, 1894-1912*. New York: Oxford University Press, 1978. This narrative analysis of Planck's great "discovery" is a controversial reinterpretation of Planck's ideas and writings. Kuhn maintains that the revolutionary idea of quantized energy did not originate in Planck's work but in the work of Albert Einstein, Paul Ehrenfest, and Hendrik Lorentz. Extensive notes with references to primary and secondary sources, bibliography, and index.

SEE ALSO: 1803-1808: Dalton Formulates the Atomic Theory of Matter; Nov. 6, 1820: Ampère Reveals Magnetism's Relationship to Electricity; Oct., 1831: Faraday Converts Magnetic Force into Electricity; 1850-1865: Clausius Formulates the Second Law of Thermodynamics; 1869-1871: Mendeleyev Develops the Periodic Table of Elements; Nov. 9, 1895: Röntgen Discovers X Rays.

RELATED ARTICLES in *Great Lives from History: The Nineteenth Century, 1801-1900:* The Becquerel Family; Josiah Willard Gibbs; Sir William Rowan Hamilton; Hermann von Helmholtz; Baron Kelvin; Albert A. Michelson; Henri Poincaré.

December 15, 1900
GENERAL ELECTRIC OPENS RESEARCH LABORATORY

The opening of General Electric's research laboratory marked the integration of science as a fundamental force in American industry and manufacturing.

LOCALE: Schenectady, New York
CATEGORIES: Manufacturing; trade and commerce; science and technology

KEY FIGURES

Charles Proteus Steinmetz (1865-1923), German émigré and electrical engineer
Edwin W. Rice, Jr. (1862-1935), vice president of General Electric responsible for manufacturing and engineering
Willis R. Whitney (1868-1958), chemist who became the first director of General Electric's research laboratory
Irving Langmuir (1881-1957), General Electric lab scientist
William David Coolidge (1873-1975), physicist for General Electric
Charles A. Coffin (1844-1926), first president of General Electric Company

SUMMARY OF EVENT

The opening of the General Electric (GE) research laboratory in Schenectady, New York, on December 15, 1900, marked the first effort by an American corporation to make science part of its competitive strategy. Faced with innovations in lamp design and materials developed by the competition, GE decided that its survival depended on using scientific talent dedicated to basic research. Adopted as a defensive measure to preserve GE's dominance in the market, the research lab soon developed a number of new products that would significantly broaden GE's market. Once seen as a risky and possibly unnecessary venture, the research lab captured a central role in giving GE a major place in the electrical industry.

Formed by the merger of Thomson-Houston and Edison General Electric in 1892, GE immediately dominated the lamp market and looked forward to a profitable future. The company soon confronted hard times, as the 1893 depression crippled the electrical market. Charles A. Coffin, GE's president, sold millions of dollars of holdings of securities issued by local power companies and significantly trimmed the company's workforce during the mid- and late 1890's. Eventually these policies restored GE's financial stability.

The company faced threats from other quarters. Engaged in one of the first industries based on the combination of science and technology, electrical manufacturers always faced the possibility of innovations undermining their stability. As insurance, GE and the other major electrical manufacturer, Westinghouse, had exchanged patents on key technology in 1897. This arrangement enabled GE to hold a strong position in the lamp market.

Reluctant to spend money on basic research, GE depended on buying research undertaken by independent inventors. During the 1890's, for example, GE bought the services and patents of inventors Charles Bradley and Ernst Danielson to regain a competitive edge against Westinghouse, which had made advances in a number of key areas. These relationships were always short term, limited in cost, and outside the company's daily activities. As important, Coffin and others at GE subscribed to the notion that people who engaged in such innovation demonstrated work habits and personality traits ill-suited for the highly structured corporate workplace.

Charles Proteus Steinmetz. (Library of Congress)

Despite GE's cautious attitude toward innovation and its practitioners, the company maintained a number of laboratories. These usually focused on testing materials used in manufacturing and in standardizing measurements. Basic long-term research was not part of their mission.

The director of GE's calculating department, Charles Proteus Steinmetz, realized as early as 1897 that his company's future rested with a research lab. Rebuffed in his early efforts, Steinmetz finally succeeded in winning approval for a research laboratory in 1900. He also grasped the threat posed to GE by work done in Germany on lamp design and materials.

Germany had pioneered research labs during the late nineteenth century. By 1900, the country's scientists had developed innovations that made gas lamps competitive and had enhanced filaments for incandescent lamps. Both of these innovations challenged GE's position. In the United States, research on the mercury vapor lamp by Westinghouse-employed Peter Cooper-Hewett also created a potential threat to GE. Supported by Edwin W. Rice, Jr., the GE vice president responsible for manufacturing and engineering, Steinmetz successfully urged that a new GE research lab focus on these threats to GE's dominance in the market.

Rice contacted Professor Charles R. Cross at the Massachusetts Institute of Technology (MIT). Cross, a longtime advocate of applied research, had established close ties with industry. He suggested colleague Willis R. Whitney, who had earned his Ph.D. in physical chemistry at the University of Leipzig. Wedded to the academic environment, Whitney reluctantly agreed to part-time work in the lab. Eventually the demands of his new position forced Whitney to petition for a one-year leave from MIT in August, 1901, a leave that soon became permanent.

Whitney expressed uneasiness over the long-term nature of the lab's basic research in the light of the company's cost-conscious administration. He sought ways to justify the lab's continued existence by using the lab's resources to assist company engineers in solving production problems. These applied research projects demonstrated the lab's usefulness and brought visible returns to the company. Whitney broadened this policy to include manufacturing of specialized items including X-ray and radio tubes. This activity reached such proportions that GE created the commercial department in 1916 to sell these products.

Whitney maintained a balance between the demands of the corporation and the morale of his staff. He pro-

vided a large and growing library of scientific journals and books that served as guides for literature searches by the professional staff members when they began new projects. He urged his scientists, however, to rely on experimentation rather than on scholarly theories that were untested in the marketplace. Whitney also scoured the professional staff reports for results that could pass the scrutiny of patent officials and guarantee GE a lock on new commercial technology. Demanding in many ways, Whitney still made every effort to develop a keen understanding of his staff's abilities. Above all, he emphasized the cooperative approach, an important notion in a team-based effort. He reinforced this policy by refusing to reward any single person in the case of a successful patent that seemed to promise great profits for GE.

Aware of the academic backgrounds of his scientists, Whitney deliberately retained some elements of a university setting. He actively encouraged independent research and urged publication of his staff's work once GE attorneys had secured patents or when the research promised no immediate commercial application. Whitney's own academic commitment was manifest in his associations with professional societies such as the American Chemical Society and the American Electrochemical Society.

Whitney's university ties proved useful in recruiting talented scientists for GE's lab. In 1904, he lured the brilliant William D. Coolidge from MIT to work on GE's most pressing problem, that of the tungsten filament. His work produced the ductile tungsten filament, far superior to the more delicate tungsten filament developed in Germany. Patented in 1913, Coolidge's discovery secured for GE the long-sought dominance in the lamp market and generated a fortune in profits for the company. Coolidge's work demonstrated conclusively the necessity of basic research in technology-based industries.

Whitney also recruited physical chemist Irving Langmuir from the Stevens Institute of Technology. More than other members of the professional staff, Langmuir showed incredible talents in theoretical work that frequently translated into commercial products. His gas-filled bulb solved the problem of GE's lightbulbs blackening after extended use. He also developed a vacuum tube in 1912 that brought GE into the radio market. Langmuir's achievements earned him the Nobel Prize in 1932, the first industrial scientist to merit this prestigious award.

The work of Coolidge, Langmuir, and others facilitated the lab's move from the defensive posture that dominated its early years to a more aggressive product development strategy. The lab's ongoing research opened up markets in radio, medicine, the military, and consumer appliances. The efforts of GE's researchers guaranteed the company's dominance in the electrical industry and made possible the transition from the trial-and-error methods of nineteenth century inventors to the team approach based on high-level skills in chemistry, physics, and engineering.

SIGNIFICANCE

The confluence of large companies at the end of the nineteenth century and the emergence of a well-educated scientific community created conditions that encouraged the spread of research labs once General Electric had demonstrated its worth in the market. By the early twentieth century, numerous and highly specialized professional societies had appeared in all the areas essential to technology-based companies.

Universities had also developed curricula appropriate to preparing students in these fields. As early as 1882, MIT offered a bachelor's degree in electrical engineering, while institutions such as Carnegie Tech devoted their energies to the scientific and technical disciplines. During the late nineteenth century, chemistry and physics training grew faster in the United States than in any industrializing country except Germany. These changes occurred at the same time that America's new corporations demanded scientific training and specialized knowledge acquired only in universities.

Industrial research moved beyond large-scale enterprise by the 1920's. Individually lacking sufficient capital, smaller companies collectively set up their own labs, usually through the medium of a trade association. Private research facilities also appeared before the end of the decade. These trends made basic research a pervasive part of the American economy. By the 1990's, thousands of research labs operated throughout American industry, with combined annual budgets in excess of $40 billion.

—*Edward J. Davies II*

FURTHER READING

Birr, Kendall. *Pioneering in Industrial Research: The Story of the General Electric Research Laboratory.* Washington, D.C.: Public Affairs Press, 1957. The first scholarly work on the topic. Provides a good overview of the development of the GE lab and the roles of its participants. The first two chapters outline the background to industrial research and the GE lab.

_____. "Science in American Industry." In *Science and Society in the United States*, edited by David Van Tassel and Michael G. Hall. Homewood, Ill.: Dorsey Press, 1966. Provides a brief background on the evolution of science and its increasing interaction with industry. Discusses the rise of organized research in the twentieth century.

Galambos, Louis. "The American Economy and the Reorganization of the Sources of Knowledge." In *The Organization of Knowledge in Modern America*, edited by Alexandra Oleson and John Voss. Baltimore: Johns Hopkins University Press, 1979. Includes an effective description of the relationship between science and the rise of large-scale companies.

Gorowitz, Bernard, et al., eds. *The General Electric Story: A Heritage of Innovation, 1876-1999.* 3d ed. Schenectady, N.Y.: Hall of Electrical History, 2000. The third edition of a series of photo histories of General Electric, combined in one volume.

Hughes, Thomas P. *American Genesis: A Century of Invention and Technological Enthusiasm, 1870-1970.* New York: Viking, 1989. A must read for an understanding of technology's role in American society. Chapter 4 analyzes the appearance of industrial labs in key industries. Good coverage of the GE, AT&T, and Du Pont labs.

Kline, Ronald R. *Steinmetz: Engineer and Socialist.* Baltimore: Johns Hopkins University Press, 1992. Provides a detailed account of Steinmetz's role in the formation of the GE lab and his disagreements with Whitney that led to Steinmetz's departure. Essential reading to understand much of the immediate background to the creation of the GE lab.

Mees, C. E. Kenneth, and John A. Leermakers. *The Organization of Industrial Scientific Research.* 2d ed. New York: McGraw-Hill, 1950. Provides invaluable information on the ways research labs were organized and functioned, from finance and building design to patents and associations for industrial research. Includes numerous examples of industrial research labs from many industries.

Noble, David F. *America by Design: Science, Technology, and the Rise of Corporate Capitalism.* New York: Alfred A. Knopf, 1977. A work very critical of the impact of science and technology on American society. Valuable insights into the changes in American industry during the late nineteenth and early twentieth centuries. An effective analysis of the role of patents in scientific research and the importance of universities to industry.

Rae, John. "The Application of Science to Industry." In *The Organization of Knowledge in Modern America,*

1860-1920, edited by Alexandra Oleson and John Voss. Baltimore: Johns Hopkins University Press, 1979. Covers the roles of government and private industry in research.

Reich, Leonard S. *The Making of American Industrial Research: Science and Business at GE and Bell, 1876-1926*. New York: Cambridge University Press, 1985. Provides a systematic comparison of the industrial research at GE and Bell. It should be a starting point for anyone interested in understanding the origins and evolution of this process in American industry. An essential work in the field.

Wise, George. *Willis R. Whitney, General Electric, and the Origins of Industrial Research*. New York: Columbia University Press, 1985. Provides an effective analysis of Whitney's role in the creation of the GE lab. Explains the reasons for Whitney's decreasing role as an active researcher and highlights his role in the larger scientific community.

SEE ALSO: c. 1801-1810: Davy Develops the Arc Lamp; Oct., 1831: Faraday Converts Magnetic Force into Electricity; Apr., 1869: Westinghouse Patents His Air Brake; Oct. 21, 1879: Edison Demonstrates the Incandescent Lamp; Mar. 11, 1891: Strowger Patents Automatic Dial Telephone System; Nov. 16, 1896: First U.S. Hydroelectric Plant Opens at Niagara Falls; Feb., 1900: Kodak Introduces Brownie Cameras.

RELATED ARTICLES in *Great Lives from History: The Nineteenth Century, 1801-1900:* Eleuthère Irénée Du Pont; Thomas Alva Edison; Michael Faraday; Sir William Robert Grove; Aleksandr Stepanovich Popov; Charles Proteus Steinmetz; Nikola Tesla; George Westinghouse.

Appendixes

TIME LINE

This time line includes the events and developments covered in the essays in this publication. Those topics which are printed in small capital letters are treated in depth in this chronologically arranged publication under the dates shown. More than 750 other important events and developments are also included here. Each event is tagged by a general region or regions; by this means, the time line can be used to consider general trends in the same region over time. However, because many events, although occurring in one or two regions nevertheless had a global or cross-regional impact, they have been left in chronological order to facilitate a better understanding of simultaneous events and their occasional interaction. The abbreviation "c." is used below to stand for "circa."

–John Powell

DATE	REGION	EVENT
Oct. 25, 1760-Jan. 29, 1820	Europe	Reign of King George III of Great Britain
Feb. 9, 1796-Sept. 2, 1820	East Asia	Reign of the Jiaqing Emperor of China
1799-1804	South America	Alexander von Humboldt and Aimé Bonpland Explore South America, Mexico, and Cuba
1800	Europe	Madame de Staël Publishes *De la littérature considérée dans ses rapports avec les institutions sociales* (*A Treatise on Ancient and Modern Literature*, 1803; also known as *The Influence of Literature upon Society*, 1813)
1800-1864	North America	Inuit Settlers Emigrate from Canada to Northern Greenland
Mar. 14, 1800-Aug. 20, 1823	Europe	Pontificate of Pius VII
19th cent.	Middle East	ARABIC LITERARY RENAISSANCE
19th cent.	Europe	DEVELOPMENT OF WORKING-CLASS LIBRARIES
19th cent.	Europe	SPREAD OF THE WALTZ
1801	Europe	EMERGENCE OF THE PRIMITIVES
1801	Europe	Franz K. Achard Builds the First Sugar-Beet Factory
c. 1801-1810	Europe	DAVY DEVELOPS THE ARC LAMP
c. 1801-1850	North America	PROFESSIONAL THEATERS SPREAD THROUGHOUT AMERICA
Jan. 1, 1801	Europe	FIRST ASTEROID IS DISCOVERED
Jan. 20, 1801	North America	John Marshall Is Appointed Chief Justice of the U.S. Supreme Court
Feb. 17, 1801	North America	HOUSE OF REPRESENTATIVES ELECTS JEFFERSON PRESIDENT
Mar. 3, 1801	North America	U.S. President John Adams Leaves Office
Mar. 4, 1801-Mar. 3, 1809	North America	U.S. Presidency of Thomas Jefferson
Mar. 21, 1801	Africa	Britain Defeats France at the Second Battle of Aboukir (Wars of Napoleon)
Mar. 23, 1801-Dec. 1, 1825	Europe	Reign of Czar Alexander I of Russia
June 19, 1801-July, 1803	Australia	Thomas-Nicholas Baudin Explores the East, South, and West Coasts of Australia
Summer, 1801-Summer, 1805	Africa	TRIPOLITAN WAR
June 27, 1801	Africa	Cairo Falls to British Troops (Wars of Napoleon)
July 18, 1801	Europe	Napoleon Signs a Concordat with the Pope
Nov. 16, 1801	North America	First Edition of the *New York Evening Post*
Dec. 6, 1801-Aug., 1803	Australia	FLINDERS EXPLORES AUSTRALIA
1802	Europe	BRITAIN ADOPTS GAS LIGHTING

DATE	REGION	EVENT
1802	Europe	William Paley Publishes *Natural Theology: Or, Evidences of the Existence and Attributes of the Deity*
Jan., 1802	Europe	COBBETT FOUNDS THE *POLITICAL REGISTER*
Mar. 16, 1802	North America	U.S. MILITARY ACADEMY IS ESTABLISHED
Mar. 24, 1802	Europe	TREVITHICK PATENTS THE HIGH-PRESSURE STEAM ENGINE
Mar. 27, 1802	Europe	Treaty of Amiens Between Britain and France
Apr. 10, 1802	South Asia	LAMBTON BEGINS TRIGONOMETRICAL SURVEY OF INDIA
May 19, 1802	Europe	French Legion of Honor Is Established
June, 1802-1820	Southeast Asia	Emperor Gia Long Unites Vietnam
1803-1805	South Asia	Britain Defeats Maratha Confederacy in Second Maratha War
1803-1808	Europe	DALTON FORMULATES THE ATOMIC THEORY OF MATTER
1803-1812	Europe	ELGIN SHIPS PARTHENON MARBLES TO ENGLAND
Feb. 24, 1803	North America	*MARBURY V. MADISON*
May 9, 1803	North America	LOUISIANA PURCHASE
Sept. 7, 1803	Australia	GREAT BRITAIN BEGINS COLONIZING TASMANIA
Sept. 20, 1803	Europe	Irish Rebel Robert Emmett Is Executed
Sept. 23, 1803	South Asia	Britain Defeats the Maratha Confederacy at the Battle of Assaye (Second Maratha War)
1804	Europe	BRITISH AND FOREIGN BIBLE SOCIETY IS FOUNDED
1804	Europe	George Cayley Builds and Flies the First Fixed-Wing Glider
1804	Africa	Onset of the Fulani Jihad in Northern Nigeria
1804	East Asia	Russian Envoy Unsuccessfully Attempts to Negotiate a Commercial Treaty with Japan
1804	Europe	SAUSSURE PUBLISHES HIS RESEARCH ON PLANT METABOLISM
Jan., 1804	North America	OHIO ENACTS THE FIRST BLACK CODES
Feb. 14, 1804-1816	Europe	Serbian Uprisings Against the Ottoman Empire
Mar. 21, 1804	Europe	The Napoleonic Code Becomes the Civil Law of France
May 14, 1804-Sept. 23, 1806	North America	LEWIS AND CLARK EXPEDITION
May 18-July 9, 1804	North America	Alexander von Humboldt visits the United States and President Thomas Jefferson
July 11, 1804	North America	Aaron Burr Kills Alexander Hamilton in a Duel
Aug. 11, 1804-Mar. 2, 1835	Europe	Reign of Emperor Francis I of Austria
Sept. 25, 1804	North America	TWELFTH AMENDMENT IS RATIFIED
Dec. 2, 1804	Europe	BONAPARTE IS CROWNED NAPOLEON I
1805	Europe	Rockets Are First Used by the British Army
1805-1806	Africa	Mungo Park Explores the Niger River
1805-1848	Africa/Middle East	Muḥammad ʿAlī Pasha Establishes Egypt's Independence from the Ottoman Empire
Mar., 1805-Sept. 1, 1807	North America	BURR'S CONSPIRACY
Mar. 1, 1805	North America	Supreme Court Justice Samuel Chase Is Acquitted of Impeachment Charges
Apr. 7, 1805	Europe	BEETHOVEN'S *EROICA* SYMPHONY INTRODUCES THE ROMANTIC AGE
May 4, 1805-1830	Africa	EXPLORATION OF WEST AFRICA
Oct. 21, 1805	Europe	BATTLE OF TRAFALGAR

DATE	REGION	EVENT
Dec. 2, 1805	Europe	BATTLE OF AUSTERLITZ
Dec. 26, 1805	Europe	Truce Between Austria and France Will Lead to the Treaty of Pressburg
1806	Europe	Napoleon I Dissolves the Holy Roman Empire and Forms the Confederation of the Rhine
1806-1820	Caribbean/West Indies	Civil War in Haiti
Mar. 29, 1806	North America	Authorization of the Cumberland Road, the First U.S. Federal Highway
June 5, 1806	Europe	Napoleon Appoints Louis Bonaparte King of Holland
July 15, 1806-July 1, 1807	North America	PIKE EXPLORES THE AMERICAN SOUTHWEST
Oct. 12-14, 1806	Europe	French Victories in the Simultaneous Battles of Jena and Auerstadt (Napoleonic Wars)
Nov. 21, 1806	Europe	Napoleon Proclaims the Berlin Decrees, Banning Trade with Britain
1807	Africa	Ashanti Empire Invades Fante Territory in the Gold Coast
1807	Europe	BOWDLER PUBLISHES *THE FAMILY SHAKESPEARE*
1807	Europe	First Ascot Gold Cup in Horse Racing
1807	Europe	Jacques-Louis David completes *The Coronation of Napoleon*
1807	Europe	Ottoman Sultan Selim III Is Deposed
1807	Europe	William Wordsworth Publishes "Ode: Intimations of Immortality"
1807-1834	Europe	MOORE PUBLISHES *IRISH MELODIES*
1807-1834	Europe	Publication of the Multivolume *Voyage aux régions équixoiales du Nouveau Continent*, Describing the Explorations of Humboldt and Bonpland
1807-1850	North America	RISE OF THE KNICKERBOCKER SCHOOL
Mar. 2, 1807	North America	CONGRESS BANS IMPORTATION OF AFRICAN SLAVES
Mar. 25, 1807	Europe	British Slave Trade Is Ended by Parliament
Mar. 25, 1807	Europe	England's Oystermouth Railway Becomes the World's First Railway to Carry Passengers
Apr., 1807	Europe	HEGEL PUBLISHES *THE PHENOMENOLOGY OF SPIRIT*
June 13-14, 1807	Europe	France Triumphs over Russia in the Battle of Friedland (Wars of Napoleon)
June 22, 1807	North America	Chesapeake-Leopard Affair Leads to Public Outrage in the United States
July 7-9, 1807	Europe	France, Prussia, and Russia Conclude the Peace of Tilsit, Creating the Grand Duchy of Warsaw
Aug. 17, 1807	North America	MAIDEN VOYAGE OF THE *CLERMONT*
Oct. 9, 1807	Europe	Serfdom Is Abolished in Prussia
Dec. 27, 1807-Mar. 1, 1809	North America	Jefferson's Embargo Act Cripples American Trade
1808	Europe	Academy of Fine Arts Founded in Munich
1808	Africa	Fulani Invade Bornu
1808	Europe	Johann Wolfgang von Goethe Publishes *Faust*, Part 1
1808-Dec. 3, 1810	South Asia	British Siege of Mauritius Leads to Its Occupation
1808-1821	South America/Europe	Rio de Janeiro Serves as Capital of the Portuguese Empire
1808-1826	Middle East	OTTOMANS SUPPRESS THE JANISSARY REVOLT
1808-1826	South America	South American Wars of Independence

DATE	REGION	EVENT
Jan. 26, 1808	Australia	Rum Rebellion in New South Wales
Feb. 2, 1808	Europe	French Troops Occupy the Papal States
Feb. 21, 1808-Sept., 1809	Europe	Russo-Finnish War
Mar. 26, 1808	Europe	Charles IV of Spain Abdicates in Favor of Ferdinand VII
Apr., 1808	North America	TENSKWATAWA FOUNDS PROPHETSTOWN
Apr. 6, 1808	North America	AMERICAN FUR COMPANY IS CHARTERED
May 2, 1808	Europe	DOS DE MAYO INSURRECTION IN SPAIN
May 2, 1808-Nov., 1813	Europe	PENINSULAR WAR IN SPAIN
June 15, 1808-Aug. 17, 1808, Dec. 20, 1808-Feb. 20, 1809	Europe	France Seizes Spanish Fortress in the Siege of Saragossa (Wars of Napoleon)
July 5, 1808	South America	Spain Forces Britain to Evacuate the Rio de la Plata Region in the Battle of Buenos Aires (Wars of Napoleon)
Oct. 2, 1808	Europe	Johann Wolfgang von Goethe and Napoleon Bonaparte Meet at the Congress of Erfurt
Nov. 15, 1808-July 1, 1839	Europe	Reign of Sultan Mahmud II of the Ottoman Empire
Dec. 22, 1808	Europe	Ludwig van Beethoven Conducts His Fifth and Sixth Symphonies and Piano Concerto No. 5 in Vienna
1809	Europe	LAMARCK PUBLISHES *ZOOLOGICAL PHILOSOPHY*
1809	Europe	Marie Madeline Sophie Blanchard Becomes the First Woman to Die in Flight
1809-1811	Arctic	Matvey Gedenshrom and P. Pshenitsin Map the New Siberian Islands
Jan. 16, 1809	Europe	British Gain Foothold in Spain at the Battle of Corunna (Wars of Napoleon)
Feb. 3, 1809	North America	Illinois Territory Is Created
Mar. 4, 1809-Mar. 3, 1817	North America	U.S. Presidency of James Madison
May 12, 1809	Europe	British Troops Drive the French from Oporto (Wars of Napoleon)
May 21, 1809	Europe	Dartmoor Prison Opens in England
July 5-6, 1809	Europe	French Victory in the Battle of Wagram Effectively Ends the Fifth Coalition
July 6, 1809	Europe	French Troops Arrest Pope Pius VII
July 16, 1809	South America	Pedro Domingo Murillo Leads the Revolt of Upper Peru
July 28, 1809	Europe	Tactical but Indecisive Victory for the British at the Battle of Talavera (Wars of Napoleon)
Aug. 10, 1809	South America	Ecuador Declares Independence from Spain
Aug. 11, 1809	Europe	Earthquake Sinks the Azores Village of São Miguel
Sept. 18, 1809	Europe	Royal Opera House Opens in London
1810	Pacific Islands	Kamehameha I Unifies the Hawaiian Islands, Becoming Hawaii's First King
Jan. 10, 1810	Europe	Napoleon Marries Marie-Louise of Austria
Mar. 16, 1810	North America	*FLETCHER V. PECK*
Apr. 19, 1810	South America	Spanish Governor Is Expelled from Venezuela
Apr. 27, 1810	Europe	Beethoven Composes *Für Elise*
May 25, 1810	South America	Spanish Viceroy Is Expelled from Buenos Aires
July 20, 1810	South America	First Representative Council in Colombia Resists Spanish Authority

DATE	REGION	EVENT
Sept. 8, 1810-May, 1812	North America	ASTORIAN EXPEDITIONS EXPLORE THE PACIFIC NORTHWEST COAST
Sept. 16, 1810	North America	HIDALGO ISSUES EL GRITO DE DOLORES
Sept. 16, 1810-Sept. 28, 1821	North America	MEXICAN WAR OF INDEPENDENCE
Sept. 18, 1810	South America	Chilean National Junta Forms
Oct. 27, 1810	North America	United States Annexes West Florida from Spain
1811	South America	José Gervasio Artigas Launches Uruguayan Revolt Against Spain
1811-1818	Middle East	EGYPT FIGHTS THE WAHHĀBĪS
1811-1840	North America	CONSTRUCTION OF THE NATIONAL ROAD
Jan. 8, 1811	North America	Charles Deslandes (or Deslonde) Leads an Unsuccessful Slave Revolt in Louisiana
Mar. 1, 1811	Africa	MUḤAMMAD ʿALĪ HAS THE MAMLŪKS MASSACRED
Mar. 11, 1811-1816	Europe	LUDDITES DESTROY INDUSTRIAL MACHINES
Mar. 25, 1811	Europe	First Sighting of the Great Comet of 1811
May 14, 1811	South America	Paraguay Overthrows Local Spanish Leaders and Declares Independence
Sept., 1811	Europe	First Rosh Hoshanna Kibbutz to the Grave of Rabbi Nachman of Breslov
Sept. 20, 1811	Europe	KRUPP WORKS OPEN AT ESSEN
Nov. 7, 1811	North America	BATTLE OF TIPPECANOE
Nov. 16, 1811	North America	New Madrid Earthquake Reverses the Course of the Mississippi River
1812	North America	Disguised Lucy Brewer Enlists as a Marine
1812-1815	Europe	BROTHERS GRIMM PUBLISH FAIRY TALES
Feb. 2, 1812	North America	Russia Establishes a Fur Trading Post at Fort Ross, California
Mar. 22, 1812	Africa	BURCKHARDT DISCOVERS EGYPT'S ABU SIMBEL
Mar. 26, 1812	South America	Earthquake Destroys Caracas, Venezuela
May 28, 1812	Europe	Treaty of Bucharest Grants Bessarabia to Russia
June 18, 1812-Dec. 24, 1814	North America	WAR OF 1812
June 23-Dec. 14, 1812	Europe	NAPOLEON INVADES RUSSIA
July 12, 1812	North America	U.S. Invasion of Canada
July 22, 1812	Europe	BATTLE OF SALAMANCA
Aug. 19, 1812	North America	USS *Constitution* Defeats British Frigate *Guerriere* off Nova Scotia
Sept. 7, 1812	Europe	BATTLE OF BORODINO
Sept. 14, 1812	Europe	Russians Burn Moscow as Napoleon Approaches the City
Oct. 19, 1812	Europe	Napoleon Begins His Retreat from Moscow
1813	Europe	Founder of Toxicology Mathieu Orfila Publishes *A General System of Toxicology: Or, A Treatise on Poisons*
1813	North America	FOUNDING OF McGILL UNIVERSITY
1813	Europe	Founding of the London Philharmonic Society
Mar., 1813-Dec. 9, 1824	South America	BOLÍVAR'S MILITARY CAMPAIGNS
May, 1813	Australia	Gregory Blaxland, William Lawson, and William Wentworth Cross the Blue Mountains of Australia
May 2, 1813	Europe	Napoleon Forces Allies to Withdraw at the Battle of Lutzen (Wars of Napoleon)

DATE	REGION	EVENT
June 21, 1813	Europe	French Are Routed and Driven Back Across the Pyrenees at the Battle of Vitoria (Wars of Napoleon)
July 12, 1813	Europe	Sectarian Riots in Belfast
July 27, 1813-Aug. 9, 1814	North America	CREEK WAR
Aug. 26-27, 1813	Europe	Brilliant Tactical Victory for Napoleon at the Battle of Dresden (Wars of Napoleon)
Sept. 10, 1813	North America	American Fleet Destroys an English Flotilla at the Battle of Lake Erie (War of 1812)
Oct. 5, 1813	North America	BATTLE OF THE THAMES
Oct. 16-19, 1813	Europe	BATTLE OF LEIPZIG
Nov. 5, 1813	Middle East	Treaty of Gulestan Ends a Russo-Persian War and Consolidates Russia's Position in the Caucasus
1814	South America	Berbice, Demerara, and Essequibo Are Transferred from Holland to Britain, Becoming British Guiana
1814	Europe	FRAUNHOFER INVENTS THE SPECTROSCOPE
1814	Europe	SCOTT PUBLISHES *WAVERLEY*
1814-Sept. 20, 1840	South America	Personal Rule of José Gaspar Rodríguez Francia in Paraguay
1814-1879	Middle East	EXPLORATION OF ARABIA
Jan. 14, 1814	Europe	Denmark Cedes Norway to Sweden in Return for Pomerania
Feb. 21, 1814	Europe	Great Stock Exchange Hoax
Mar., 1814	Europe	GOYA PAINTS *THIRD OF MAY 1808: EXECUTION OF THE CITIZENS OF MADRID*
Spring, 1814-1830	North America	COMMUNITARIAN EXPERIMENTS AT NEW HARMONY
Mar. 27, 1814	North America	Andrew Jackson Defeats Creek and Cherokee Indians at the Battle of Horseshoe Bend (War of 1812)
Apr. 11, 1814-July 29, 1830	Europe	FRANCE'S BOURBON DYNASTY IS RESTORED
May 2, 1814-Sept. 16, 1824	Europe	Reign of King Louis XVIII of France
Aug. 13, 1814	Africa	BRITAIN ACQUIRES THE CAPE COLONY
Sept. 6-11, 1814	North America	Americans Force British to Withdraw in the Battle of Lake Champlain, or Plattsburgh (War of 1812)
Sept. 14, 1814	North America	Francis Scott Key Writes "The Star-Spangled Banner"
Sept. 15, 1814-June 11, 1815	Europe	CONGRESS OF VIENNA
Dec. 15, 1814-Jan. 5, 1815	North America	HARTFORD CONVENTION
1815	Southeast Asia	Britain Restores Java to the Netherlands
1815	Europe	Netherlands Is Granted Sovereignty over Belgium and Luxembourg
1815	South Asia	Second Kandyan War Ends Sri Lankan Independence
c. 1815-1830	North America	WESTWARD AMERICAN MIGRATION BEGINS
c. 1815-1848	Europe	BIEDERMEIER FURNITURE STYLE BECOMES POPULAR
c. 1815-1930	North America	Almost 5 Million European Immigrants Arrive in Canada
c. 1815-1930	South America	More than 6 Million European Immigrants Arrive in Argentina
c. 1815-1930	North America	More than 32 Million European Immigrants Arrive in the United States
Jan. 8, 1815	North America	BATTLE OF NEW ORLEANS
Feb. 17, 1815	North America	TREATY OF GHENT TAKES EFFECT
Feb. 17, 1815-May 6, 1816	South America	Spanish Reconquest of New Granada

DATE	REGION	EVENT
Mar. 20, 1815	Europe	Napoleon Reenters Paris After His Escape from Elba
Apr. 5, 1815	Southeast Asia	TAMBORA VOLCANO BEGINS VIOLENT ERUPTION
June 1, 1815-Aug., 1817	North America	RED RIVER RAIDS
June 8-9, 1815	Europe	ORGANIZATION OF THE GERMAN CONFEDERATION
June 18, 1815	Europe	BATTLE OF WATERLOO
Sept. 26, 1815	Europe	Russia, Austria, and Prussia Conclude the Holy Alliance as a Defense Against European Revolution
Oct. 15, 1815	Europe	Napoleon Begins Exile on St. Helena
Nov. 20, 1815	Europe	SECOND PEACE OF PARIS
Dec. 16, 1815	South America/Europe	Brazil Is Integrated into the United Kingdom of Portugal, Brazil, and the Algarve
1816	Europe	*Blackwood's Magazine* Is Founded
1816	Africa	Britain Establishes Banjul as an Anti-Slaving Port in the Gambia
1816	Europe	LAËNNEC INVENTS THE STETHOSCOPE
1816-1825	Europe	Reign of Ferdinand I as King of the Two Sicilies
1816-1837	East Asia	Reign of Tsultrim Gyatso as Tenth Dalai Lama in Tibet
Feb. 20, 1816	Europe	ROSSINI'S *THE BARBER OF SEVILLE* DEBUTS
Apr., 1816	North America	SECOND BANK OF THE UNITED STATES IS CHARTERED
Apr. 9, 1816	North America	AFRICAN METHODIST EPISCOPAL CHURCH IS FOUNDED
May 8, 1816	North America	AMERICAN BIBLE SOCIETY IS FOUNDED
June 19, 1816	North America	Metis Uprising Against the North West Company Leaves Twenty-One Dead at Seven Oaks (Manitoba, Canada)
July 9, 1816	South America	Argentina Gains Independence from Spain
Dec., 1816	Europe	RISE OF THE COCKNEY SCHOOL
1817	Europe	RICARDO IDENTIFIES SEVEN KEY ECONOMIC PRINCIPLES
1817	North America	Rush-Bagot Agreement Limits the Number of Battleships on the Great Lakes
c. 1817-1828	Africa	ZULU EXPANSION
1817-1861	Africa	Missionary Robert Moffat Explores Southern Africa as Far North as Zimbabwe
Jan. 18, 1817-July 28, 1821	South America	SAN MARTÍN'S MILITARY CAMPAIGNS
Feb. 12, 1817	South America	Chilean Victory over Spanish Royalists at the Battle of Chacabuco (Latin American Wars of Independence)
Mar. 4, 1817-Mar. 3, 1825	North America	U.S. Presidency of James Monroe
Nov. 5, 1817-June 3, 1818	South Asia	THIRD MARATHA WAR
Nov. 21, 1817-Mar. 27, 1858	North America	SEMINOLE WARS
1818	Europe/North America	Black Ball Line of Sailing Packets Begins Regular Liverpool-New York Service
1818	Europe	Prado Museum Is Founded in Madrid
1818	Africa	Seku Amadu Launches Jihad Against the Bambara Empire
1818-1829	Australia	Allan Cunningham Explores East Central Australia
1818-1854	Arctic	SEARCH FOR THE NORTHWEST PASSAGE
Feb. 12, 1818	South America	Chile Proclaims Its Independence from Spain
Mar. 11, 1818	Europe	Mary Shelley Publishes *Frankenstein: Or, The Modern Prometheus*

DATE	REGION	EVENT
Apr. 5, 1818	South America	Battle of Maipo Secures Chilean Independence
Oct. 20, 1818	North America	U.S.-British Convention Establishes U.S. Boundary with Canada
Dec. 24, 1818	Europe	Franz Gruber and Joseph Mohn Compose "Stille Nacht, heilige Nacht," Which Becomes the Christmas Carol "Silent Night"
1819	Europe	John Kidd Extracts Naphthalene from Coal Tar
1819	Europe	SCHOPENHAUER PUBLISHES *THE WORLD AS WILL AND IDEA*
1819-1820	North America	IRVING'S *SKETCH BOOK* TRANSFORMS AMERICAN LITERATURE
1819-1820	North America	Washington Irving's "Rip Van Winkle" Is Published
1819-1833	Europe	BABBAGE DESIGNS A MECHANICAL CALCULATOR
Jan. 29-Feb. 7, 1819	Europe	Sir Thomas Stamford Raffles Lays the Foundation for a British Colony at Singapore
Feb. 22, 1819	North America	ADAMS-ONÍS TREATY GIVES THE UNITED STATES FLORIDA
Mar. 6, 1819	North America	*McCULLOCH V. MARYLAND*
May, 1819	North America	UNITARIAN CHURCH IS FOUNDED
May 22-June 20, 1819	North America/Europe	*SAVANNAH* IS THE FIRST STEAMSHIP TO CROSS THE ATLANTIC
Aug. 7, 1819	South America	Simón Bolívar Leads Colombian Patriots to Victory in the Battle of Boyacá (Latin American Wars of Independence)
Aug. 16, 1819	Europe	Peterloo Massacre in England
Dec. 11-30, 1819	Europe	BRITISH PARLIAMENT PASSES THE SIX ACTS
Dec. 17, 1819	South America	Congress of Angostura Establishes Independence of Gran Colombia from Spain
1820's	East Asia	CHINA'S STELE SCHOOL OF CALLIGRAPHY EMERGES
1820's-1830's	North America	FREE PUBLIC SCHOOL MOVEMENT
1820's-1850's	North America	SOCIAL REFORM MOVEMENT
1820	South America	Argentina Establishes a Penal Colony on the Falkland Islands
1820	Pacific Islands	Development of Whaling Industry in the North Pacific
1820	Europe	JESUITS ARE EXPELLED FROM RUSSIA, NAPLES, AND SPAIN
1820	Europe	Karl Ritter Assumes the first Europe University Professorship in Geography in Berlin and Begins to Establish the Connection Between Geography and Human History
1820	Middle East	Peace Treaty Ends Piracy in the Persian Gulf
1820-early 1840's	Antarctica	EUROPEANS EXPLORE THE ANTARCTIC
1820-1841	Southeast Asia	Reign of Emperor Minh Mang in Vietnam
c. 1820-1860	South America	*COSTUMBRISMO* MOVEMENT
1820-1864	Africa	Fulani Expand the Islamic Empire
Jan., 1820	Antarctica	Fabian Bellingshausen Sights the Landmass of Antarctica
Jan., 1820-Aug. 31, 1823	Europe	Spanish Civil War
Jan. 29, 1820-June 26, 1830	Europe	Reign of King George IV of Great Britain
Feb. 6, 1820	North America/Africa	African American Settlers Sail from New York to Freetown, Sierra Leone
Feb. 23, 1820	Europe	LONDON'S CATO STREET CONSPIRATORS PLOT ASSASSINATIONS
Mar. 3, 1820	North America	MISSOURI COMPROMISE
Apr., 1820	Europe	Hans Christian Ørsted Discovers the Relationship Between Magnetism and Electricity
Apr., 1820	Europe	Scottish Insurrection

DATE	REGION	EVENT
Apr. 24, 1820	North America	CONGRESS PASSES LAND ACT OF 1820
July 2, 1820-Mar., 1821	Europe	NEAPOLITAN REVOLUTION
Aug. 24-Sept. 15, 1820	Europe	Constitutionalist Revolts in Portugal
Oct. 3, 1820-Feb. 25, 1850	East Asia	Reign of the Daoguang Emperor of China
Oct. 20-Nov. 19, 1820	Europe	At Congress of Troppau, Russia, Prussia, and Austria Agree on Armed Intervention Against Republican Movements
Nov. 6, 1820	Europe	AMPÈRE REVEALS MAGNETISM'S RELATIONSHIP TO ELECTRICITY
1821	Europe	*Manchester Guardian* Is Founded in England
1821-1824	North America	Lachine Canal Is Built in Canada
Mar. 7, 1821-Sept. 29, 1829	Europe	GREEKS FIGHT FOR INDEPENDENCE FROM THE OTTOMAN EMPIRE
June 24, 1821	South America	Battle of Carabobo Establishes the Independence of Colombia
July 28, 1821	South America	Peru Declares Independence from Spain
Sept., 1821	North America	SANTA FE TRAIL OPENS
1822	Europe	Britain's Royal Academy of Music Is Founded
1822	Central America	El Salvador Petitions the United States for Statehood
1822	Africa	Liberia Is Founded as a Home for Freed Slaves
1822-1824	Europe	Jean-François Champollion Translates the First Egyptian Hieroglyphs from the Rosetta Stone
1822-1827	Africa	Hugh Clapperton Explores the Sahara, Reaching Sokoto
1822-1831	North America	JEDEDIAH SMITH EXPLORES THE FAR WEST
1822-1874	Africa	EXPLORATION OF NORTH AFRICA
Feb. 9, 1822	Caribbean/West Indies	Haiti Invades Santo Domingo
May 24, 1822	South America	Victory by Revolutionaries in the Battle of Pichincha Establishes Ecuadoran Independence (Latin American Wars of Independence)
May 30, 1822	North America	Denmark's Vesey Slave Uprising Is Thwarted
July 27, 1822	South America	Simón Bolívar and José de San Martín Meet in Guayaquil
Sept. 7, 1822	South America	BRAZIL BECOMES INDEPENDENT
Oct. 20-30, 1822	Europe	GREAT BRITAIN WITHDRAWS FROM THE CONCERT OF EUROPE
Oct. 22, 1822-Apr. 7, 1831	South America	Reign of Emperor Dom Pedro I of Brazil
1823-1826	Australia	John Oxley Surveys Much of What Becomes New South Wales
1823-1831	East Asia	HOKUSAI PRODUCES *THIRTY-SIX VIEWS OF MOUNT FUJI*
May, 1823	North America	HARTFORD FEMALE SEMINARY IS FOUNDED
July, 1823-1840	Central America	United Provinces of Central America Experiment with Republican Democracy
July 24, 1823	South America	Patriot Forces Establish Venezuelan Independence at the Battle of Lake Maracaibo (Latin American Wars of Independence)
Oct. 5, 1823	Europe	WAKLEY INTRODUCES *THE LANCET*
Dec. 2, 1823	North America	PRESIDENT MONROE ARTICULATES THE MONROE DOCTRINE
1824	Europe	BRITISH PARLIAMENT REPEALS THE COMBINATION ACTS
1824	East Asia	Ferdinand von Wrangel Maps the Northeastern Coast of Siberia
1824	Europe	Lord Byron Is Killed During the Greek War for Independence from Turkey
1824	Europe	PARIS SALON OF 1824
1824	Europe	RANKE DEVELOPS SYSTEMATIC HISTORY

DATE	REGION	EVENT
1824-1826	Southeast Asia	First Anglo-Burmese War
1824-1829	North America	First Welland Canal Built in Canada
Feb. 20, 1824	Europe	BUCKLAND PRESENTS THE FIRST PUBLIC DINOSAUR DESCRIPTION
Mar. 2, 1824	North America	*GIBBONS V. OGDEN*
Mar. 11, 1824	North America	U.S. Bureau of Indian Affairs Is Created as Part of the War Department
Mar. 17, 1824	Europe	Anglo-Dutch Treaty Resolves Lingering Colonial Differences
May 7, 1824	Europe	FIRST PERFORMANCE OF BEETHOVEN'S NINTH SYMPHONY
Sept. 16, 1824-Aug. 2, 1830	Europe	Reign of King Charles X of France
Oct. 21, 1824	Europe	Joseph Aspdin Patents Portland Cement
Nov. 5, 1824	North America	Rensselaer School Becomes the First Technological University in the English-Speaking World
Dec. 1, 1824-Feb. 9, 1825	North America	U.S. ELECTION OF 1824
Dec. 9, 1824	South America	Patriot Victory at the Battle of Ayachuco Assures Peruvian Independence (Latin American Wars of Independence)
1825	North America	*Commonwealth v. Blanding*
1825	Africa	Egypt Founds Khartoum at the Confluence of the Blue and White Nile Rivers
1825	Europe	Great Britain Repeals Laws Prohibiting Emigration, Leading to a Major Movement of Immigrants from England and Ireland
1825-1830	Southeast Asia	GREAT JAVA WAR
Mar. 4, 1825-Mar. 3, 1829	North America	U.S. Presidency of John Quincy Adams
Aug. 25, 1825-Aug. 27, 1828	South America	Uruguay Gains Independence from Brazil
Sept. 27, 1825	Europe	STOCKTON AND DARLINGTON RAILWAY OPENS
Oct. 26, 1825	North America	ERIE CANAL OPENS
Dec. 1, 1825-Mar. 2, 1855	Europe	Reign of Czar Nicholas I of Russia
Dec. 26, 1825	Europe	DECEMBRIST REVOLT
1826	Europe	Construction of the Menai Strait Bridge off the Northwest Coast of Wales
c. 1826-1827	Europe	FIRST MEETINGS OF THE PLYMOUTH BRETHREN
1826-1840	Central America	Civil Wars of the Central American Federation
1826-1842	Europe	YOUNG GERMANY MOVEMENT
Feb. 11, 1826	Europe	University of London Is Founded
Feb. 13, 1826	North America	American Temperance Society Is Established
Apr. 1, 1826	Europe	Samuel Morey Patents One of the First Internal Combustion Engines
July 16, 1826-Feb. 2, 1828	Middle East	Russo-Persian War Extends Russian Influence in the Caucusus
Aug. 18, 1826	Africa	Alexander Gordon Laing Is the First European to Reach Timbuktu
1827	North America	First African American Newspaper, *Freedom's Journal*, Is Published in New York
Mar. 7, 1827	Europe	Edward Gibbon Wakefield Abducts Wealth Heiress Ellen Turner
1828	Africa	Basel Mission to the Gold Coast
1828	South Asia	Ram Mohan Roy founds Brahmo Sámaj, the Western-Influence Society of God
1828-1834	Europe	PORTUGAL'S MIGUELITE WARS
1828-1842	Europe	ARNOLD REFORMS RUGBY SCHOOL

DATE	REGION	EVENT
Jan. 22, 1828	Europe	Duke of Wellington Becomes Britain's Prime Minister
Feb. 21, 1828	North America	CHEROKEE PHOENIX BEGINS PUBLICATION
Feb. 21, 1828	Middle East	Turkmanchai Treaty with Persia Grants Russian Control Over Armenia and Azerbaijan
Apr. 26, 1828-Aug. 28, 1829	Europe	SECOND RUSSO-TURKISH WAR
May 9, 1828-Apr. 13, 1829	Europe	ROMAN CATHOLIC EMANCIPATION
May 26, 1828	Europe	Discovery of the Feral Child, Kaspar Hausser, in Nuremberg, Germany
Sept. 22, 1828	Africa	Shaka Zulu Is Assassinated
Sept. 29, 1828	Europe	Russia Captures the Ottoman City of Varna
Nov., 1828	North America	WEBSTER PUBLISHES THE FIRST AMERICAN DICTIONARY OF ENGLISH
Dec. 3, 1828	North America	U.S. ELECTION OF 1828
1829	Europe	First Oxford-Cambridge Boat Race
1829	Europe	George Stephenson Builds the Steam Locomotive *Rocket*
1829	Europe	Louis Braille Invents Printing for the Blind
1829	North America	Mexico Abolishes Slavery
1829	Europe	Charles Wheatstone Patents the Concertina
1829-1836	Europe/North America	IRISH IMMIGRATION TO CANADA
1829-1848	Europe	Honoré de Balzac Publishes *La Comédie humaine* (*The Human Comedy*)
1829-1852	South America	Leadership of Juan Manuel de Rosas in Argentina
Mar. 4, 1829-Mar. 3, 1837	North America	U.S. Presidency of Andrew Jackson
June 5, 1829	Caribbean/West Indies	HMS *Pickle* Captures the Slaver *Voladora* off the Coast of Cuba
July 23, 1829	North America	William Burt Obtains a Patent for the Typographer, an Early Typewriter
Sept. 24, 1829	Europe	TREATY OF ADRIANOPLE
Oct. 1, 1829	Africa	University of Cape Town Is Founded
Dec. 4, 1829	South Asia	BRITISH ABOLISH SUTTEE IN INDIA
1830's-1840's	Pacific Islands	SCIENTISTS STUDY REMAINS OF GIANT MOAS
c. 1830's-1860's	North America	AMERICAN RENAISSANCE IN LITERATURE
1830	Australia	Charles Sturt Explores the Murray River System
1830	Europe	Gibraltar Becomes a Colony of Britain
1830	Europe	Joseph Whitworth Develops the Standard Screw Gauge
1830-1831	Europe/North America	Joseph Henry and Michael Faraday Independently Discover Electromagnetic Induction
1830-1842	North America	TRAIL OF TEARS
c. 1830-1865	North America	SOUTHERNERS ADVANCE PROSLAVERY ARGUMENTS
c. 1830-1870	Europe	BARBIZON SCHOOL OF LANDSCAPE PAINTING FLOURISHES
Jan. 7, 1830	North America	BALTIMORE AND OHIO RAILROAD OPENS
Jan. 19-27, 1830	North America	WEBSTER AND HAYNE DEBATE SLAVERY AND WESTWARD EXPANSION
Mar. 3, 1830	Europe	HUGO'S *HERNANI* INCITES RIOTING
Apr. 6, 1830	North America	SMITH FOUNDS THE MORMON CHURCH
May 13, 1830	South America	Ecuador Separates from Gran Colombia

Date	Region	Event
May 28, 1830	North America	Congress Passes Indian Removal Act
June 14-July 5, 1830	Africa	France Conquers Algeria
June 26, 1830-June 20, 1837	Europe	Reign of King William IV of Great Britain
July, 1830	Europe	Charles-Maurice de Talleyrand-Périgord Is Appointed French Ambassador to England
July, 1830	Europe	Lyell Publishes *Principles of Geology*
July 17, 1830	Europe	In France, Barthélemy Thimonnier Is Granted a Patent for His Sewing Machine
July 29, 1830	Europe	July Revolution Deposes Charles X
Aug. 9, 1830-Feb. 24, 1848	Europe	Reign of Louis-Phillipe, the Citizen King of France
Aug. 25, 1830-May 21, 1833	Europe	Belgian Revolution
Sept. 15, 1830	Europe	Liverpool and Manchester Railway Opens
Oct.-Dec., 1830	Europe	Delacroix Paints *Liberty Leading the People*
Nov., 1830-Oct., 1865	Europe	Prominence of Lord Palmerston as British Foreign Secretary and Prime Minister
Nov. 8, 1830-May 22, 1859	Europe	Ferdinand II Reigns over the Kingdom of the Two Sicilies
Nov. 29, 1830-Aug. 15, 1831	Europe	First Polish Rebellion
Dec. 5, 1830	Europe	Hector Berlioz Premiers *Symphonie phantastique* in Paris
Dec. 20, 1830	Europe	Recognition of Belgian Independence by the European Powers
1831	Africa	Brothers Richard and John Lander Explore the Course of the Lower Niger River
1831	North America	Female Literary Association Formed in Philadelphia
1831	Europe	Mazzini Founds Young Italy
1831	Middle East	Muḥammad ʿAlī Pasha Conquers Syria
1831-1834	East Asia	Hiroshige Completes *The Tokaido Fifty-Three Stations*
1831-1846	Australia	Thomas Mitchell's Explorations Lead to the Rapid Expansion of Pastoralism in the Australian Interior
Jan. 1, 1831	North America	Garrison Begins Publishing *The Liberator*
Feb.-Mar., 1831	Europe	Liberal Revolts Against Austria Throughout Central and Northern Italy
Feb. 2, 1831-June 1, 1846	Europe	Pontificate of Pope Gregory XVI
Feb. 14, 1831	Africa	Ethiopian Crown Beats Back a Rebellion in the Battle of Debre Abbay (Ethiopian Civil War)
Mar. 10, 1831	Europe	Founding of the French Foreign Legion
Mar. 18, 1831, and Mar. 3, 1832	North America	Cherokee Cases
Apr. 7, 1831-Dec. 5, 1891	South America	Reign of Emperor Dom Pedro II of Brazil
Apr. 11, 1831	South America	Mass Killing of Charrua Indians at Salsipuedes
May, 1831-Feb., 1832	North America	Tocqueville Visits America
Summer, 1831	North America	McCormick Invents the Reaper
Aug. 21, 1831	North America	Turner Launches Slave Insurrection
Oct., 1831	Europe	Faraday Converts Magnetic Force into Electricity
Dec. 27, 1831-Oct. 2, 1836	South America	Charles Darwin Voyages Around the World on HMS *Beagle*
1832	Central America	Anastasio Aquino Leads an Indigenous Revolt Against Creoles and Mestizos in El Salvador
1832-1841	Middle East	Turko-Egyptian Wars

DATE	REGION	EVENT
1832-1847	Africa	ABDELKADER LEADS ALGERIA AGAINST FRANCE
Feb. 12, 1832	Europe	Cholera Epidemic Claims Three Thousand Lives in London
Feb. 12, 1832	South America	Ecuador Annexes the Galápagos Islands
Mar. 12, 1832	Europe	LA SYLPHIDE INAUGURATES ROMANTIC BALLET'S GOLDEN AGE
May 7, 1832	Europe	Prince of Bavaria Is Chosen as King of the Newly Established Kingdom of Greece
June 4, 1832	Europe	BRITISH PARLIAMENT PASSES THE REFORM ACT OF 1832
June 15, 1832	Middle East	Egyptian Forces Seize Damascus
July 10, 1832	North America	JACKSON VETOES RECHARTERING OF THE BANK OF THE UNITED STATES
Nov. 24, 1832-Jan. 21, 1833	North America	NULLIFICATION CONTROVERSY
Dec. 4-23, 1832	Europe	The Netherlands Loses Antwerp to French Attack (War of Belgian Independence)
1833	Europe	BRITISH PARLIAMENT PASSES THE FACTORY ACT
1833	North America	Lucretia Mott Founds the Philadelphia Female Anti-Slavery Society
Jan., 1833	South America	GREAT BRITAIN OCCUPIES THE FALKLAND ISLANDS
May 16, 1833-Aug. 9, 1855	North America	Political Influence of Antonio López de Santa Anna in Mexico
July 14, 1833	Europe	OXFORD MOVEMENT BEGINS
Aug. 28, 1833	World	SLAVERY IS ABOLISHED THROUGHOUT THE BRITISH EMPIRE
Sept. 3, 1833	North America	BIRTH OF THE PENNY PRESS
Sept. 29, 1833-1849	Europe	CARLIST WARS UNSETTLE SPAIN
Dec., 1833	North America	AMERICAN ANTI-SLAVERY SOCIETY IS FOUNDED
Dec. 3, 1833	North America	OBERLIN COLLEGE OPENS
1834	Europe	Composer Hector Berlioz Completes His Symphony *Harold en Italie* (*Harold in Italy*)
Jan. 1, 1834	Europe	GERMAN STATES JOIN TO FORM CUSTOMS UNION
Apr. 14, 1834	North America	CLAY BEGINS AMERICAN WHIG PARTY
Aug. 14, 1834	Europe	BRITISH PARLIAMENT PASSES NEW POOR LAW
Oct. 14, 1834	North America	BLAIR PATENTS HIS FIRST SEED PLANTER
1835	North America	FINNEY LECTURES ON "REVIVALS OF RELIGION"
1835	Europe	Gaetano Donizetti's Opera *Lucia di Lammermoor* Premiers in Naples
1835	Africa	SOUTH AFRICA'S GREAT TREK BEGINS
1835-1836	Europe	STRAUSS PUBLISHES *THE LIFE OF JESUS CRITICALLY EXAMINED*
1835-1845	South America	Brazilian Antiregency Uprisings
1835-1848	North America	Newspaper Owner Joseph Howe Advocates Responsible Government for Canada
1835-1863	South Asia	Reign of Dost Mohammed as Emir in Afghanistan
Jan., 1835-July, 1836	North America	Construction of Canada's First Railway
Jan. 30, 1835	North America	Unsuccessful Assassination Attempt Against U.S. President Andrew Jackson
Mar. 2, 1835	Europe	Reign of Emperor Ferdinand I of Austria
May 5, 1835	Europe	First Railway in Continental Europe Opens in Belgium
May 8, 1835	Europe	ANDERSEN PUBLISHES HIS FIRST FAIRY TALES

DATE	REGION	EVENT
Aug. 16, 1835	Australia	MELBOURNE, AUSTRALIA, IS FOUNDED
Sept. 7, 1835	South America	Charles Darwin Arrives in the Galápagos Islands Aboard HMS *Beagle*
Sept. 9, 1835	Europe	BRITISH PARLIAMENT PASSES MUNICIPAL CORPORATIONS ACT
Oct. 2, 1835-Apr. 21, 1836	North America	TEXAS REVOLUTION
Dec. 7, 1835	Europe	First German Railway Opens
1836	North America	Angelina Grimké's *Appeal to the Christian Women of the South* Urges Women to Protest Slavery
1836	Europe	Architect Augustus Welby Northmore Pugin Publishes *Contrasts: Or, A Parallel Between the Noble Edifices of the Fourteenth and Fifteenth Centuries and Similar Buildings of the Present*
1836	North America	First Chartered Women's College, Wesleyan College, Opens in Macon, Georgia
1836	North America	TRANSCENDENTAL MOVEMENT ARISES IN NEW ENGLAND
Feb. 23-Mar. 6, 1836	North America	Texans Slow Mexican Troops but Are Defeated at the Siege of the Alamo (Texas War of Independence)
Feb. 25, 1836	North America	COLT PATENTS THE REVOLVER
Mar. 2, 1836	North America	Texas Declares Its Independence from Mexico
Apr. 21, 1836	North America	Texans Rout Mexican Troops at the Battle of San Jacinto (Texas War of Independence)
July 21, 1836	North America	CHAMPLAIN AND ST. LAWRENCE RAILROAD OPENS
Oct. 28, 1836-Feb. 20, 1839	South America	Peru-Bolivian Confederation
Dec. 28, 1836	Australia	Colony of South Australia Is Proclaimed
1837	North America	John Deere Develops a Steel Plow
1837-1853	East Asia	Shogunate of Tokugawa Ieyoshi in Japan
Jan. 4, 1837	Europe	Charles Darwin Presents Bird and Mammal Specimens from the *Beagle* Voyage to the Zoological Society in London
Jan. 12, 1837	Europe	MAZZINI BEGINS LONDON EXILE
Mar. 4, 1837-Mar. 3, 1841	North America	U.S. Presidency of Martin Van Buren
Mar. 17, 1837	North America	PANIC OF 1837 BEGINS
June 11, 1837	North America	Broad Street Riot in Boston
June 20, 1837-Jan. 22, 1901	Europe	Reign of Queen Victoria of Great Britain
Oct. 23-Dec. 16, 1837	North America	REBELLIONS ROCK BRITISH CANADA
Nov. 8, 1837	North America	MOUNT HOLYOKE FEMALE SEMINARY OPENS
Nov. 25, 1837	North America	Patriot Louis-Joseph Papineau Flees to the United States to Avoid Arrest
1838	North America	France Blockades Mexico During the Pastry War
1838	Africa	James Wellsted Charts the Omani Coast
1838	East Asia	Nakayama Miki Founds the Tenri Sect in Japan
1838	Europe	National Gallery Opens in London
1838-1839	North America	AROOSTOOK WAR
1838-1839	Europe	SCHWANN AND VIRCHOW DEVELOP CELL THEORY
Apr. 4-23, 1838	Europe	*Sirius* and *Great Western* Make the First All-Steam Transatlantic Voyages
May 8, 1838-Apr. 10, 1848	Europe	CHARTIST MOVEMENT
June 28, 1838	Europe	QUEEN VICTORIA'S CORONATION

DATE	REGION	EVENT
Sept. 28, 1838-1858	South Asia	Reign of Mughal Emperor Bahadur Shah II of India
Nov. 3, 1838	South Asia	*Bombay Times* and the *Journal of Commerce* Are Founded
Dec. 16, 1838	Africa	Trekking Boers Beat Back the Zulu at the Battle of Blood River (South African Frontier Wars)
1839	Europe	BLANC PUBLISHES *THE ORGANIZATION OF LABOUR*
1839	Europe	DAGUERRE AND NIÉPCE INVENT DAGUERREOTYPE PHOTOGRAPHY
1839	North America	Lord Durham Recommends the Assimilation of French-Speaking Canadians
1839	North America	Mississippi Passes First Married Women's Property Act
1839-1842	South Asia	FIRST AFGHAN WAR
1839-1847	Middle East	LAYARD EXPLORES AND EXCAVATES ASSYRIAN RUINS
Jan. 19, 1839	Middle East	Britain Annexes Aden
Jan. 20, 1839	South America	Chilean Army Defeats Peruvian-Bolivian Coalition in the Battle of Yungay (Chilean Recovery Expedition)
Mar. 26, 1839	Europe	First Staging of the Henley Royal Regatta
Apr. 9, 1839	Europe	First Commercial Electric Telegraph Line Opens in England
Apr. 19, 1839	Europe	Treaty of London Establishes the Independence of Belgium
June 22, 1839	Europe	Louis Daguerre Receives Patent for His Camera
July 1, 1839-June 25, 1861	Europe	Reign of Sultan Abd-ul-Mejid of the Ottoman Empire, Who Begins the Tanzimat Program of Modernization
July 2, 1839	North America	*AMISTAD* SLAVE REVOLT
Sept., 1839-Aug. 29, 1842	East Asia	FIRST OPIUM WAR
Oct. 3, 1839	Europe	First Railway Opens on the Italian Peninsula
Nov., 1839	Central America	STEPHENS BEGINS UNCOVERING MAYAN ANTIQUITIES
Nov. 25, 1839	South Asia	Giant Cyclone Kills 300,000 in India
1840's-1850's	North America	AMERICAN ERA OF "OLD" IMMIGRATION
1840's-1880's	Europe	RUSSIAN REALIST MOVEMENT
1840	North America	Catherine Brewer Becomes the First Woman to Graduate from College in the United States
1840	Europe	Cunard Line Is Founded, Becoming One of the Largest Carriers of Transatlantic Immigrants
1840	North America	First Issue of the *Lowell Offering* Is Published
1840	Europe	First Photograph of the Moon Is Taken
1840	Antarctica	French Expedition Nears the South Magnetic Pole
1840	Europe	LIEBIG ADVOCATES ARTIFICIAL FERTILIZERS
1840	Europe	Max Schneckenburger writes *Die Wacht am Rhine* (*The Watch on the Rhine*)
1840	Middle East/Africa	Omani Ruler Imam Sayyid Said Transfers Capital to Zanzibar
1840-Sept. 10, 1862	South America	Political Influence of Carlos Antonio López in Paraguay
Jan. 10, 1840	Europe	GREAT BRITAIN ESTABLISHES PENNY POSTAGE
Jan. 19, 1840	Antarctica	American Captain Charles Wilkes Claims Wilkes Land for the United States
Jan. 22, 1840	Pacific Islands	British Colonists Reach New Zealand, Establishing Wellington
Feb. 6, 1840	Pacific Islands	Treaty of Waitaingi Grants British Sovereignty in New Zealand
Apr. 27, 1840-Feb., 1852	Europe	BRITISH HOUSES OF PARLIAMENT ARE REBUILT

DATE	REGION	EVENT
May 7, 1840	North America	Great Natchez Tornado Kills 317 in Mississippi
Sept. 10, 1840	Middle East	Anglo-Ottoman Force Bombards Egyptians in Beirut
Dec. 2, 1840	North America	U.S. ELECTION OF 1840
1841	Australia	Edward John Eyre Completes the First Transcontinental Journey Across Australia
Jan., 1841	Antarctica	James Ross Forces a Passage Through Antarctic Pack Ice
Jan. 26, 1841	East Asia	British Troops Occupy Hong Kong (First Opium War)
Feb. 10, 1841	North America	UPPER AND LOWER CANADA UNITE
Mar. 4, 1841-Apr. 4, 1841	North America	U.S. Presidency of William Henry Harrison
Apr. 4, 1841-Mar. 3, 1845	North America	U.S. Presidency of John Tyler
Sept. 4, 1841	North America	CONGRESS PASSES PREEMPTION ACT OF 1841
Sept. 24, 1841	Southeast Asia	Britain Annexes Sarawak
1842	Europe	Charles James Apperley (Nimrod) Publishes *The Life of a Sportsman*
1842	Europe	Giuseppe Verdi's Nationalistic Opera *Nabucco* Debuts
1842	Europe	TENNYSON PUBLISHES "MORTE D'ARTHUR"
1842	East Asia	Treaty of Nanking Opens British Trade to Chinese Ports
Mar., 1842	North America	*COMMONWEALTH V. HUNT*
Mar. 5, 1842	North America	Mexican Troops Briefly Invade the Republic of Texas
May, 1842-1854	North America	FRÉMONT EXPLORES THE AMERICAN WEST
May 14, 1842	Europe	First Edition of the *Illustrated London News*
May 18, 1842	North America	RHODE ISLAND'S DORR REBELLION
Aug. 9, 1842	North America	WEBSTER-ASHBURTON TREATY SETTLES MAINE'S CANADIAN BORDER
1843	Central Asia	Alexander von Humboldt Publishes *Central Asia*
1843	Africa	Britain Occupies Natal in Southern Africa
1843	Europe	CARLYLE PUBLISHES *PAST AND PRESENT*
Jan. 2, 1843	Europe	WAGNER'S *FLYING DUTCHMAN* DEBUTS
Feb. 6, 1843	North America	FIRST MINSTREL SHOWS
Feb. 17, 1843	South Asia	British Victory at the Battle of Miani Leads to Annexation of the Sind
Sept. 2, 1843	Europe	WILSON LAUNCHES *THE ECONOMIST*
Oct. 13, 1843	North America	B'nai Brith Founded in New York City
Dec. 17, 1843	Europe	Charles Dickens Publishes "A Christmas Carol"
1844	Southeast Asia	Thailand Establishes a Protectorate in Cambodia
Jan. 15, 1844	North America	University of Notre Dame Chartered
Feb. 27, 1844	Caribbean/West Indies	Dominican Republic Gains Independence from Haiti
May 6-July 5, 1844	North America	ANTI-IRISH RIOTS ERUPT IN PHILADELPHIA
May 23, 1844	Middle East	Babism Established in Persia
May 24, 1844	North America	MORSE SENDS FIRST TELEGRAPH MESSAGE
June 15, 1844	North America	GOODYEAR PATENTS VULCANIZED RUBBER
July 3, 1844	Europe	Extinction of the Great Auk
Aug., 1844-Jan., 1846	Australia	The Ill-Fated Expedition of Charles Sturt Dispels Notions of an Inland Sea
Oct. 22, 1844	North America	Millerites Expect the Return of Jesus

DATE	REGION	EVENT
Dec. 4, 1844-Apr. 14, 1865	Central America	Political Influence of Jose Rafael Carrera in Guatemala
1845	Europe	Alexander von Humboldt Publishes the First Volume of *Kosmos*
c. 1845	North America	CLIPPER SHIP ERA BEGINS
1845	Australia	Edward John Eyre Publishes *Discoveries in Central Australia*
1845	Europe	First Photograph Taken of the Sun
c. 1845	North America	MODERN BASEBALL BEGINS
1845	North America	*White v. Nicholls*
1845-1847	Arctic	Franklin Expedition Perishes Seeking the Northwest Passage
1845-1849	South Asia	Sikh Wars
1845-1854	Europe	GREAT IRISH FAMINE
1845-1860	Europe/North America	More than 1.7 Million Irish Immigrate to the United States
Jan. 29, 1845	North America	Edgar Allan Poe Publishes "The Raven"
Mar. 4, 1845-Mar. 3, 1849	North America	U.S. Presidency of James K. Polk
Mar. 11, 1845	Pacific Islands	Maoris Burn Kororarake (Flagstaff War)
July 4, 1845-Sept. 6, 1847	North America	Henry David Thoreau Lives at Walden Pond
Oct. 9, 1845	Europe	NEWMAN BECOMES A ROMAN CATHOLIC
Dec. 21-22, 1845	South Asia	British Force Sikhs to Withdraw Beyond the Sutlej River in the Battle of Ferozeshah (First Sikh War)
Dec. 29, 1845	North America	Republic of Texas Is Admitted as the Twenty-Eighth State of the United States
1846	Europe	Paris Opera House Installs Electric-Arc Lighting
Jan. 28, 1846	South Asia	British Destroy Ranjur Singh's Army at the Battle of Aliwal (First Sikh War)
Feb. 4, 1846	North America	MORMONS BEGIN MIGRATION TO UTAH
May 8, 1846	North America	BATTLE OF PALO ALTO
May 13, 1846-Feb. 2, 1848	North America	MEXICAN WAR
May 17, 1846	Europe	Adolphe Sax Patents the Saxophone
June 14-July 7, 1846	North America	Bear Flag Republic Revolts Against Mexico
June 15, 1846	Europe	BRITISH PARLIAMENT REPEALS THE CORN LAWS
June 15, 1846	North America	UNITED STATES ACQUIRES OREGON TERRITORY
June 16, 1846-Feb. 7, 1878	Europe	Pontificate of Pope Pius IX
June 30, 1846-Jan. 13, 1847	North America	UNITED STATES OCCUPIES CALIFORNIA AND THE SOUTHWEST
Aug. 1, 1846	North America	ESTABLISHMENT OF INDEPENDENT U.S. TREASURY
Aug. 10, 1846	North America	SMITHSONIAN INSTITUTION IS FOUNDED
Sept. 10, 1846	North America	HOWE PATENTS HIS SEWING MACHINE
Sept. 21-24, 1846	North America	U.S. Forces Continue Southern Advance with Victory at the Battle of Monterrey (Mexican War)
Sept. 23, 1846	Europe	Discovery of Planet Neptune by Johann Gottfried Galle and Heinrich Louis d'Arrest
Oct. 16, 1846	North America	SAFE SURGICAL ANESTHESIA IS DEMONSTRATED
Dec. 2, 1846	Central America	Bidlack-Mallarino Treaty Grants U.S. Transit Rights Across the Isthmus of Panama
1847	Europe	BOOLE PUBLISHES *THE MATHEMATICAL ANALYSIS OF LOGIC*
1847	Europe	HAMBURG-AMERIKA SHIPPING LINE BEGINS
Jan. 19-Feb. 3, 1847	North America	TAOS REBELLION

DATE	REGION	EVENT
Feb. 22-23, 1847	North America	American Victory at Battle of Buena Vista Ends the Northern Campaign (Mexican War)
Apr. 17-18, 1847	North America	American Victory at the Battle of Cerro Gordo Enables Continued March on Mexico City (Mexican War)
May, 1847	Europe	SEMMELWEIS DEVELOPS ANTISEPTIC PROCEDURES
June 1, 1847	Europe	First Communist Congress Meets in London
July 26, 1847	Africa	LIBERIA PROCLAIMS ITS INDEPENDENCE
Sept. 12-13, 1847	North America	BATTLE OF CHAPULTEPEC
Oct. 28, 1847-Feb. 19, 1848	North America	Donner Party Settlers Traveling from Illinois to California Are Trapped by Heavy Snows
Dec. 3, 1847	North America	DOUGLASS LAUNCHES *THE NORTH STAR*
1848	North America	Shaker Joseph Brackett Writes the Song "Simple Gifts"
1848-1852	South America	Alfred Russel Wallace Undertakes Botanical Study of the Amazon River Basin
1848-1889	Africa	EXPLORATION OF EAST AFRICA
Jan. 12, 1848	Europe	Liberal Rising in Palermo Against Bourbon Rule
Jan. 12, 1848-Aug. 28, 1849	Europe	ITALIAN REVOLUTION OF 1848
Jan. 24, 1848	North America	CALIFORNIA GOLD RUSH BEGINS
Jan. 26, 1848	North America	Henry David Thoreau Presents His Ideas on Civil Disobedience to the Concord Lyceum
Feb., 1848	Europe	MARX AND ENGELS PUBLISH *THE COMMUNIST MANIFESTO*
Feb. 2, 1848	North America	TREATY OF GUADALUPE HIDALGO ENDS MEXICAN WAR
Feb. 22-June, 1848	Europe	PARIS REVOLUTION OF 1848
Mar. 3-Nov. 3, 1848	Europe	PRUSSIAN REVOLUTION OF 1848
Mar. 7, 1848	Pacific Islands	Great Mahele Land Division Permits Foreign Ownership of Land in Hawaii
Mar. 13, 1848-Mar. 4, 1849	Europe	Austrian Revolutions of 1848
Apr., 1848-Mar., 1849	South Asia	SECOND ANGLO-SIKH WAR
Apr. 10, 1848	Europe	Monster Chartist Rally in London
Apr. 27, 1848	World	France Abolishes Slavery
May 11, 1848	Africa	Johann Rebmann Sights Snow-Covered Mount Kilimanjaro
July 4, 1848	North America	GROUND IS BROKEN FOR THE WASHINGTON MONUMENT
July 19-20, 1848	North America	SENECA FALLS CONVENTION
July 26, 1848	South Asia	Matale Rebellion Against British Rule in Ceylon
July 29, 1848	Europe	Tipperary Revolt in Ireland Put Down by British Police
Aug. 28, 1848	Caribbean/West Indies	Mathieu Luis Represents Guadaloupe in the French Parliament, Becoming France's First Black Representative
Sept. 12, 1848	Europe	SWISS CONFEDERATION IS FORMED
Sept. 17, 1848-May 1, 1896	Middle East	Reign of Shah Nāsir al-Din of Persia
Fall, 1848	Europe	PRE-RAPHAELITE BROTHERHOOD BEGINS
Dec. 2, 1848-Nov. 21, 1916	Europe	Reign of Emperor Francis (Franz) Joseph I
Dec. 10, 1848	Europe	Prince Louis Napoleon Elected First President of the Second French Republic
1849	North America/East Asia	CHINESE BEGIN IMMIGRATING TO CALIFORNIA
Jan. 13, 1849	South Asia	Sher Singh Fights the British to a Draw in the Battle of Chilianwala (Second Sikh War)

DATE	REGION	EVENT
Jan. 23, 1849	North America	Elizabeth Blackwell Becomes the First Woman in the United States to Be Awarded a Medical Degree
Feb. 21, 1849	South Asia	Decisive Defeat of the Sikhs in the Battle of Gujarat, Leading to British Annexation of the Punjab (Second Sikh War)
Mar. 4, 1849-July 9, 1850	North America	U.S. Presidency of Zachary Taylor
Apr. 25, 1849	North America	FIRST TEST OF CANADA'S RESPONSIBLE GOVERNMENT
May 17, 1849	North America	Great St. Louis Fire
July, 1849	North America	Harriet Tubman Escapes from Slavery
Dec., 1849	Europe	DOSTOEVSKI IS EXILED TO SIBERIA
1850's-1880's	North America	RISE OF BURLESQUE AND VAUDEVILLE
1850	Australia	Britain Grants Responsible Government to the Australian Colonies
1850	Europe	First Photograph of a Star Is Taken
1850	North America	FIRST U.S. PETROLEUM REFINERY IS BUILT
1850-1851	Europe	Joseph Paxton Designs and Builds the Crystal Palace in London
1850-1852	Africa	Arab Merchants Traverse Africa from Dar es Salaam to Benguela
1850-1855	Africa	Heinrich Barth Explores North and Central Africa
c. 1850-1860	North America	UNDERGROUND RAILROAD FLOURISHES
1850-1865	Europe	CLAUSIUS FORMULATES THE SECOND LAW OF THERMODYNAMICS
Jan. 29-Sept. 20, 1850	North America	COMPROMISE OF 1850
Mar. 9, 1850-Aug. 22, 1861	East Asia	Reign of the Xianfeng Emperor of China
Apr. 4, 1850	North America	Los Angeles, California, Is Incorporated
May, 1850-Jan. 27, 1855	Central America	Completion of the Panama Railway
May 6, 1850	North America	CALIFORNIA'S BLOODY ISLAND MASSACRE
July 9, 1850-Mar. 3, 1853	North America	U.S. Presidency of Millard Fillmore
Aug. 28, 1850	Europe	Richard Wagner's Opera *Lohengrin* Premiers
Sept. 9, 1850	North America	California Is Admitted as the Thirty-First U.S. State
Sept. 18, 1850	North America	SECOND FUGITIVE SLAVE LAW
Nov. 5, 1850	Europe	TENNYSON BECOMES ENGLAND'S POET LAUREATE
Dec. 16, 1850	Pacific Islands	Canterbury Pilgrims Arrive in Lyttleton, New Zealand
1851	Middle East	Dar ol-Foonon Is Established as First Modern University in Persia
1851	Australia	GOLD IS DISCOVERED IN NEW SOUTH WALES
1851	North America	MELVILLE PUBLISHES *MOBY DICK*
1851-1854	Europe	COMTE ADVANCES HIS THEORY OF POSITIVISM
1851-1868	Southeast Asia	Reign of King Rama IV in Thailand
1851-1900	Europe/North America	More than 4.4 Million Germans Immigrate to the United States
Jan. 11, 1851-late summer, 1864	East Asia	CHINA'S TAIPING REBELLION
Mar. 30, 1851	Europe	First Census Is Taken in the United Kingdom
May 1-Oct. 15, 1851	Europe	LONDON HOSTS THE FIRST WORLD'S FAIR
May 28-29, 1851	North America	AKRON WOMAN'S RIGHTS CONVENTION
July, 1851	Europe	Adolf Anderssen Wins "The Immortal Game" of Chess over Lionel Kieseritzky
Aug. 22, 1851	North America	*AMERICA* WINS THE FIRST AMERICA'S CUP RACE
Sept. 18, 1851	North America	MODERN *NEW YORK TIMES* IS FOUNDED

DATE	REGION	EVENT
Nov. 13, 1851	Europe	First Permanent Underwater Telegraph Cable Links France and England
1852	Africa	Al-Hajj Umar Proclaims Jihad in West Africa
1852	Southeast Asia	Second Anglo-Burmese War Leads to British Annexation of Southern Burma
1852	North America	STOWE PUBLISHES *UNCLE TOM'S CABIN*
1852	North America	Université Laval, North America's First French-Language University, Is Founded
1852	Europe	William Henry Fox Talbot Patents Photoengraving
1852-1878	Europe	Montenegrin Wars of Independence
Jan. 17, 1852	Africa	Britain Recognizes Independence of the Transvaal
Mar., 1852-Sept., 1853	Europe	DICKENS PUBLISHES *BLEAK HOUSE*
Sept. 24, 1852	Europe	Henri Giffard Creates the First Steam-Powered Airship
Nov. 10, 1852	North America	CANADA'S GRAND TRUNK RAILWAY IS INCORPORATED
Dec. 2, 1852	Europe	LOUIS NAPOLEON BONAPARTE BECOMES EMPEROR OF FRANCE
1853	South America	Argentine Constitution Encourages European Immigration
1853	Europe	Georges Eugène Haussmann Modernizes Paris with Improved Public Works, Boulevards, and Parks
1853	Europe	Robert Smith Surtees Publishes *Mr. Sponge's Sporting Tour*
1853	North America	Stephen Foster Writes "My Old Kentucky Home"
1853	North America	Yellow Fever Epidemic Kills Almost Eight Thousand in New Orleans
1853-1868	East Asia	QING DYNASTY CONFRONTS THE NIAN REBELLION
1853-1878	Southeast Asia	Reign of King Mindon Min in Burma
Jan. 19, 1853	Europe	Giuseppe Verdi's Opera *Il Trovatore* Premiers in Rome
Mar. 2, 1853-1857	North America	PACIFIC RAILROAD SURVEYS
Mar. 4, 1853-Mar. 3, 1857	North America	U.S. Presidency of Franklin Pierce
July 6, 1853	North America	NATIONAL COUNCIL OF COLORED PEOPLE IS FOUNDED
July 8, 1853	East Asia	U.S. Commodore Matthew C. Perry Arrives in Edo (Tokyo) Bay
Aug. 12, 1853	Pacific Islands	Britain Grants Responsible Government to New Zealand
Sept. 12, 1853	Middle East	BURTON ENTERS MECCA IN DISGUISE
Oct. 4, 1853-Mar. 30, 1856	Europe	CRIMEAN WAR
Nov. 17, 1853	Africa	LIVINGSTONE SEES THE VICTORIA FALLS
Nov. 30, 1853	Europe	Russia Destroys the Turkish Fleet at the Battle of Sinope (Crimean War)
Dec. 31, 1853	North America	GADSDEN PURCHASE COMPLETES THE U.S.-MEXICAN BORDER
1854-1862	Southeast Asia	WALLACE'S EXPEDITIONS GIVE RISE TO BIOGEOGRAPHY
1854-1868	Europe	Eugène-Emmanuel Viollet-le-Duc Publishes *Dictionnaire raisonné de l'architecture française du XIe au XVIe siècle* (dictionary of French architecture from the eleventh to the sixteenth century)
1854-1885	Central Asia	Russia Occupies Central Asia
Jan. 1, 1854	North America	Lincoln University (originally the Ashmun Institute) Is Chartered as the First Black College in the United States
Jan. 13, 1854	North America	Anthony Faas Receives a U.S. Patent for a Modern Accordian

DATE	REGION	EVENT
Feb. 17, 1854	Africa	Britain Recognizes the Independence of the Orange Free State in Southern Africa
Mar. 31, 1854	East Asia	PERRY OPENS JAPAN TO WESTERN TRADE
May 30, 1854	North America	CONGRESS PASSES THE KANSAS-NEBRASKA ACT
June 6, 1854	North America	U.S.-Canadian Reciprocity Treaty Reduces Customs Duties
July 6, 1854	North America	BIRTH OF THE REPUBLICAN PARTY
Sept. 20, 1854	Europe	Anglo-French-Turkish Armies Advance with a Victory over Russia at the Battle of Alma (Crimean War)
Oct. 17, 1854-Sept. 11, 1855	Europe	SIEGE OF SEVASTOPOL
Oct. 25, 1854	Europe	BATTLE OF BALAKLAVA
Nov. 4, 1854	Europe	NIGHTINGALE TAKES CHARGE OF NURSING IN THE CRIMEA
Nov. 5, 1854	Europe	Russian Troops Fail to Lift the Siege of Sevastopol in the Battle of Inkerman (Crimean War)
Dec. 8, 1854	Europe	PIUS IX DECREES THE IMMACULATE CONCEPTION DOGMA
1855	Europe	BESSEMER PATENTS IMPROVED STEEL-PROCESSING METHOD
1855	Europe	COURBET ESTABLISHES REALIST ART MOVEMENT
1855	Central America	First Highway for Wheeled Traffic Begins in El Salvador
1855-1868	Africa	Reign of Emperor Teodoros in Ethiopia
Jan. 23, 1855	North America	First Bridge over the Mississippi River Opens
Mar. 2, 1855-Mar. 13, 1881	Europe	Reign of Czar Alexander II
June 16, 1855-May 1, 1857	Central America	WALKER INVADES NICARAGUA
June 29, 1855	Europe	*Daily Telegraph* Begins Publication in Britain
Winter, 1855-Jan. 2, 1878	East Asia	MUSLIM REBELLIONS IN CHINA
Mar. 5, 1856	Europe	Fire Destroys Covent Garden Theatre in London
Mar. 30, 1856	Europe	Treaty of Paris Ends the Crimean War
Apr. 15, 1856	Central America	"Watermelon War" Race Riot in Panama City
Apr. 16, 1856	South Asia	Declaration of Paris Makes Herāt Part of Afghanistan
May, 1856-Aug., 1858	North America	BLEEDING KANSAS
May 22, 1856	North America	Congressman Preston Brooks Assaults Senator Charles Sumner in the Hall of the U.S. Senate Following Sumner's Verbal Attack on Brooks's Uncle, Senator Andrew Pickens Butler
Aug., 1856	Europe	NEANDERTHAL SKULL IS FOUND IN GERMANY
Oct., 1856	North America	Toronto-Montreal Line of the Grand Trunk Railway Opens
Oct. 1-Dec. 15, 1856	Europe	FLAUBERT PUBLISHES *MADAME BOVARY*
Oct. 23, 1856-Nov. 6, 1860	East Asia	SECOND OPIUM WAR
1857	Europe	PASTEUR BEGINS DEVELOPING GERM THEORY AND MICROBIOLOGY
Jan. 1, 1857	North America	FIRST AFRICAN AMERICAN UNIVERSITY OPENS
Feb. 16, 1857	North America	Gallaudet, the First University for the Deaf, Is Founded
Mar. 4, 1857-Mar. 3, 1861	North America	U.S. Presidency of James Buchanan
Mar. 6, 1857	North America	*DRED SCOTT V. SANDFORD*
Mar. 21, 1857	East Asia	Earthquake Near Tokyo Kills 100,000
Mar. 23, 1857	North America	OTIS INSTALLS THE FIRST PASSENGER ELEVATOR
May 10, 1857-July 8, 1858	South Asia	SEPOY MUTINY AGAINST BRITISH RULE
May 11, 1857	South Asia	Indian Troops Take Delhi from the British (Sepoy Mutiny)

DATE	REGION	EVENT
May 12, 1857	North America	NEW YORK INFIRMARY FOR INDIGENT WOMEN AND CHILDREN OPENS
June, 1857-Feb. 13, 1858	Africa	Richard Francis Burton and John Hanning Speke Explore the Region Between Mombasa and Lake Tanganyika
June 4-Dec. 6, 1857	South Asia	Battle, Siege, and Massacre at Cawnpore (Sepoy Mutiny)
Aug.-Dec., 1857	North America	TEXAS'S CART WAR
Aug. 28, 1857	Europe	BRITISH PARLIAMENT PASSES THE MATRIMONIAL CAUSES ACT
Dec., 1857-Jan., 1861	North America	War of Reform in Mexico
Dec. 16, 1857	Europe	Earthquake Kills Eleven Thousand in Naples, Italy
1858	North America	Fenian Brotherhood Is Founded
1858	Europe	Rebuilding of Ringstrasse in Vienna
Jan. 14, 1858	Europe	Orsini Plot to Assassinate French President Napoleon III Fails
Jan. 31, 1858	Europe	BRUNEL LAUNCHES THE SS *GREAT EASTERN*
Feb. 11-July 16, 1858	Europe	VIRGIN MARY APPEARS TO BERNADETTE SOUBIROUS
Mar. 23, 1858	North America	FRASER RIVER GOLD RUSH BEGINS
June 16-Oct. 15, 1858	North America	LINCOLN-DOUGLAS DEBATES
June 23, 1858	Europe	Edgar Mortara Is Kidnapped from His Jewish Family by Papal Guards
July 26, 1858	Europe	ROTHSCHILD IS FIRST JEWISH MEMBER OF BRITISH PARLIAMENT
Aug., 1858	Southeast Asia	FRANCE AND SPAIN INVADE VIETNAM
Aug. 2, 1858	Africa	John Hanning Speke Reaches and Names Lake Victoria
Aug. 7, 1858	Australia	First Australian-Rules Football Match Is Played in Melbourne
1859	Middle East	*Codex Sinaiticus* Is Discovered by Constantine von Tischendorf
1859	Europe	MILL PUBLISHES *ON LIBERTY*
1859	Europe	SMILES PUBLISHES *SELF-HELP*
1859	Southeast Asia	Treaty of Lisbon Divides the Island of Timor Between Portugal and the Netherlands
1859-1861	Africa	Henri Duveyrier Studies the Taureg Tribes of Northern Africa
1859-1875	South America	Political Influence of Gabriel García Moreno in Ecuador
1859-1878	Europe	Russia Gains Control of the Caucasus Region
Jan. 24, 1859	Europe	Moldavia and Walachia Unite Under the Name Romania
Apr. 29-Nov., 1859	Europe	Austro-Sardinian War
June 4, 1859	Europe	Franco-Sardinian Forces Defeat Austria at the Battle of Magenta (Austro-Sardinian War)
June 24, 1859	Europe	BATTLE OF SOLFERINO
July, 1859	North America	LAST SLAVE SHIP DOCKS AT MOBILE
July 6, 1859	Australia	Colony of Queensland Separates from New South Wales
July 11, 1859	Europe	NAPOLEON III AND FRANCIS JOSEPH I MEET AT VILLAFRANCA
Aug. 27, 1859	North America	COMMERCIAL OIL DRILLING BEGINS
Sept. 7, 1859	Europe	London's Big Ben Clock and Thirteen-Ton Bell Become Fully Functional
Sept. 16, 1859	Africa	David Livingstone Reaches Lake Nyasa
Oct. 16-18, 1859	North America	BROWN'S RAID ON HARPERS FERRY
Nov. 24, 1859	Europe	DARWIN PUBLISHES *ON THE ORIGIN OF SPECIES*
Dec. 2, 1859	North America	John Brown Is Hanged for His Raid on Harpers Ferry

DATE	REGION	EVENT
1860's	East Asia	CHINA'S SELF-STRENGTHENING MOVEMENT ARISES
1860	North America	Gail Borden Opens a Factory to Produce Evaporated Milk
1860	Europe	LENOIR PATENTS THE INTERNAL COMBUSTION ENGINE
1860-1900	North America	Foreign-Born Population of the United States Averages Almost 14 Percent of the Total Population
Mar., 1860-Feb., 1861	Southeast Asia	Vietnamese Lay Siege to French-Held Saigon
Mar. 5, 1860-May 15, 1872	Pacific Islands	Second Maori War Leads to the Disruption of Maori Society
Spring, 1860	Middle East	Ottoman Massacre of Christians in Damascus, Syria
Mar. 24, 1860	Europe	France Annexes Savoy and Nice
Apr. 3, 1860-Oct. 26, 1861	North America	PONY EXPRESS EXPEDITES TRANSCONTINENTAL MAIL
Apr. 30, 1860-1865	North America	APACHE AND NAVAJO WAR
May-July, 1860	Europe	GARIBALDI'S REDSHIRTS LAND IN SICILY
Aug. 22, 1860	Europe	Giuseppe Garibaldi's Red Shirts Cross from Sicily to the Italian Mainland (Wars of Italian Independence)
Oct. 16, 1860	East Asia	British and French Troops Burn the Imperial Summer Palace in China
Nov. 6, 1860	North America	LINCOLN IS ELECTED U.S. PRESIDENT
1861	Europe	*ARCHAEOPTERYX LITHOGRAPHICA* IS DISCOVERED
1861	Europe	MORRIS FOUNDS DESIGN FIRM
1861	Europe	Pasteurization of Beer, Wine, and Milk Is Introduced
1861-1863, 1867-1872	North America	Benito Juárez Serves as President of Mexico
1861-1864	North America	Balloons Are Used for Reconnaissance During the American Civil War
Jan. 2, 1861-Mar. 9, 1888	Europe	Reign of Kaiser William (Wilhelm) I of Germany
Feb. 6, 1861-Sept. 4, 1886	North America	APACHE WARS
Feb. 8, 1861	North America	ESTABLISHMENT OF THE CONFEDERATE STATES OF AMERICA
Mar. 3, 1861	Europe	EMANCIPATION OF RUSSIAN SERFS
Mar. 4, 1861	North America	LINCOLN IS INAUGURATED PRESIDENT
Mar. 17, 1861	Europe	ITALY IS PROCLAIMED A KINGDOM
Apr. 12, 1861-Apr. 9, 1865	North America	U.S. CIVIL WAR
June 25, 1861-May 30, 1876	Europe	Reign of Sultan Abd-ul-Aziz of the Ottoman Empire
July 21, 1861	North America	FIRST BATTLE OF BULL RUN
Oct. 24, 1861	North America	TRANSCONTINENTAL TELEGRAPH IS COMPLETED
Oct. 31, 1861-June 19, 1867	North America	FRANCE OCCUPIES MEXICO
Nov. 1-2, 1861	East Asia	CIXI'S COUP PRESERVES QING DYNASTY POWER
1862	Europe	SPENCER INTRODUCES PRINCIPLES OF SOCIAL DARWINISM
1862-1863	Middle East	William Palgrave Becomes the First European to Cross the Arabian Desert from West to East
Jan., 1862	North America	Spanish, French, and British Troops Land in Mexico
Jan. 1, 1862	Africa	Britain Annexes Lagos Island, Nigeria
Mar. 9, 1862	North America	BATTLE OF THE *MONITOR* AND THE *VIRGINIA*
May 5, 1862	North America	Mexico Wins a Moral Victory over France at the Battle of Puebla (Cinco de Mayo)
May 20, 1862	North America	LINCOLN SIGNS THE HOMESTEAD ACT
July 1, 1862	Europe	Russian State Library Is Founded

DATE	REGION	EVENT
July 2, 1862	North America	LINCOLN SIGNS THE MORRILL LAND GRANT ACT
July 17, 1862	North America	U.S. Congress Enables African Americans to Serve Legally in the Union Army
Aug. 17, 1862-Dec. 28, 1863	North America	GREAT SIOUX WAR
Aug. 17, 1862-Dec. 28, 1863	Africa	John Hanning Speke Reaches and Names Ripon Falls, the Source of the Nile River
Sept. 24, 1862	Europe	BISMARCK BECOMES PRUSSIA'S MINISTER-PRESIDENT
Nov., 1862	Pacific Islands	SLAVE TRADERS BEGIN RAVAGING EASTER ISLAND
1863	Middle East	BAHĀʾĪSM TAKES FORM
1863	Southeast Asia	Cambodia Becomes an Autonomous French Protectorate
1863	Europe	Henry Clifton Sorby Discovers the Microstructure of Steel
1863	World	The Netherlands Becomes the Last European Nation to Abolish Slavery
1863-1913	Europe	GREECE UNIFIES UNDER THE GLÜCKSBURG DYNASTY
Jan. 1, 1863	North America	LINCOLN ISSUES THE EMANCIPATION PROCLAMATION
Jan. 10, 1863	Europe	FIRST UNDERGROUND RAILROAD OPENS IN LONDON
Jan. 22-Sept., 1863	Europe	RUSSIA CRUSHES POLISH REBELLION
Feb. 25, 1863-June 3, 1864	North America	CONGRESS PASSES THE NATIONAL BANK ACTS
Mar. 3, 1863	North America	UNION ENACTS THE FIRST NATIONAL DRAFT LAW
May 15, 1863	Europe	PARIS'S SALON DES REFUSÉS OPENS
May 23, 1863	Europe	Ferdinand Lassalle Organizes Europe's First Socialist Workers' Party, the Social Democratic Labor Party, in Germany
May 31, 1863	Europe	First Running of the Prix de l'Arc de Triomphe Horse Race
July 1-Nov. 25, 1863	North America	BATTLES OF GETTYSBURG, VICKSBURG, AND CHATTANOOGA
Aug., 1863-Sept., 1866	North America	LONG WALK OF THE NAVAJOS
Dec. 8, 1863-Apr. 24, 1877	North America	RECONSTRUCTION OF THE SOUTH
1864	North America	Archduke Maximilian of France Becomes Emperor of Mexico
1864	Europe	HILL LAUNCHES HOUSING REFORM IN LONDON
1864	Europe	James Clerk Maxwell Discovers Microwaves
1864	Europe	John Wisden Publishes the First *Wisden Cricketers' Almanack*
1864	Europe	Russia Annexes Abkhazia and Circassia
1864	North America	U.S. Congress Passes an Immigration Act Legalizing Contract Labor and Encouraging Immigration as a Means of Developing the Economy
1864-1876	Europe	International Workingman's Association Promotes Marxism
Jan. 21-June 21, 1864	Pacific Islands	British Troops Regain Control of Tauranga Harbor (Second Maori War)
Feb. 1-Oct. 30, 1864	Europe	DANISH-PRUSSIAN WAR
Mar. 14, 1864	Africa	Samuel Baker Reaches and Names Lake Albert
Apr., 1864-Feb., 1866	South America	Chincha Islands War
Apr. 22, 1864	North America	"IN GOD WE TRUST" APPEARS ON U.S. COINS
June 15, 1864	North America	Arlington National Cemetery Is Established
Aug. 22, 1864	Europe	INTERNATIONAL RED CROSS IS LAUNCHED
Sept. 1-Oct. 27, 1864	North America	Charlottetown and Quebec Conferences Lay a Foundation for Canadian Confederation

Date	Region	Event
Sept. 28, 1864	Europe	FIRST INTERNATIONAL IS FOUNDED
Oct. 12, 1864-Mar. 1, 1870	South America	War of the Triple Alliance
Nov. 15, 1864-Apr. 18, 1865	North America	SHERMAN MARCHES THROUGH GEORGIA AND THE CAROLINAS
Nov. 29, 1864	North America	SAND CREEK MASSACRE
Dec. 8, 1864	Europe	PIUS IX ISSUES THE SYLLABUS OF ERRORS
1865	Africa	Friedrich Gerhard Rohlfs Becomes First European to Cross Africa from the Mediterranean to the Gulf of Guinea
1865	World	International Telegraphic Union Is Founded to Supervise International Communications
1865	Europe	MENDEL PROPOSES LAWS OF HEREDITY
c. 1865	Europe	NATURALIST MOVEMENT BEGINS
1865-1868	Africa	BASUTO WAR
1865-1869	Europe	Leo Tolstoy Publishes *War and Peace*
1865-1870	East Asia	Persecution of Christians in Korea
Jan., 1865-Apr., 1866	Central Asia	Nain Singh Travels Across Tibet and Surveys Monasteries
Mar. 3, 1865	North America	CONGRESS CREATES THE FREEDMEN'S BUREAU
Apr. 9 and 14, 1865	North America	SURRENDER AT APPOMATTOX AND ASSASSINATION OF LINCOLN
Apr. 15, 1865-Mar. 3, 1869	North America	U.S. Presidency of Andrew Johnson
Apr. 27, 1865	North America	Explosion of the Steamboat *Sultana* Kills Seventeen Hundred
May 1, 1865-June 20, 1870	South America	PARAGUAYAN WAR
June 23, 1865	North America	WATIE IS LAST CONFEDERATE GENERAL TO SURRENDER
July, 1865	Europe	BOOTH ESTABLISHES THE SALVATION ARMY
July 14, 1865	Europe	Edward Whymper Becomes the First Climber to Scale the Matterhorn
July 27, 1865	South America	Welsh Settlers Arrive in the Chubut Valley, Argentina
Sept. 26, 1865	North America	VASSAR COLLEGE OPENS
Oct. 7-12, 1865	Caribbean/West Indies	MORANT BAY REBELLION
Nov. 24, 1865	North America	MISSISSIPPI ENACTS FIRST POST-CIVIL WAR BLACK CODE
Dec. 6, 1865	North America	THIRTEENTH AMENDMENT IS RATIFIED
1866	North America	BIRTH OF THE KU KLUX KLAN
1866	North America	Young Women's Christian Association Forms in Boston
1866-1867	Europe	NORTH GERMAN CONFEDERATION IS FORMED
Feb. 25, 1866-1901	North America	Calaveras Skull Hoax
Apr. 9, 1866	North America	CIVIL RIGHTS ACT OF 1866
Apr. 10, 1866	North America	American Society for the Prevention of Cruelty to Animals Is Founded
May and July, 1866	North America	MEMPHIS AND NEW ORLEANS RACE RIOTS
May 2, 1866	South America	Peru Holds Off the Spanish Fleet at the Battle of Callao (Chincha Islands War)
May 10, 1866	North America	SUFFRAGISTS PROTEST THE FOURTEENTH AMENDMENT
June, 1866-1871	Europe	FENIAN RISINGS FOR IRISH INDEPENDENCE
June 1, 1866	North America	American Fenians Capture Fort Erie
June 13, 1866-Nov. 6, 1868	North America	RED CLOUD'S WAR
June 15-Aug. 23, 1866	Europe	AUSTRIA AND PRUSSIA'S SEVEN WEEKS' WAR
June 15, 1866-June 29, 1868	Southeast Asia	Mekong River Expedition

DATE	REGION	EVENT
July 3, 1866	Europe	BATTLE OF KÖNNIGGRÄTZ
July 27, 1866	North America	FIRST TRANSATLANTIC CABLE IS COMPLETED
Dec. 21, 1866	North America	FETTERMAN MASSACRE
1867	North America	CHISHOLM TRAIL OPENS
1867	Africa	Diamonds Are Discovered at Kimberley
1867	North America	Dorothea Dix Investigates Jails, Poorhouses, and Mental Hospitals
1867	Europe	Football Association Is Founded in England
1867	Europe	LISTER PUBLISHES HIS THEORY ON ANTISEPTIC SURGERY
1867	Europe	Marketing of Paperback Series Begins with Johann Wolfgang von Goethe's *Faust*
1867	Europe	MARX PUBLISHES *DAS KAPITAL*
1867	Europe	World's Fair in Paris Introduces Japanese Art to the West
Jan. 1, 1867	North America	John Augustus Roebling Engineers the Longest Suspension Bridge in the World, Linking Covington, Kentucky, with Cincinnati, Ohio
Jan. 30, 1867-July 30, 1912	East Asia	Reign of Emperor Meiji (Mutsuhito) of Japan
Mar. 2, 1867	North America	U.S. DEPARTMENT OF EDUCATION IS CREATED
Mar. 30, 1867	North America	RUSSIA SELLS ALASKA TO THE UNITED STATES
Apr. 1, 1867	Southeast Asia	Strait Settlement of Singapore Is Made a British Crown Colony
May 29, 1867	Europe	AUSTRIAN AUSGLEICH
July 1, 1867	North America	BRITISH NORTH AMERICA ACT
Aug., 1867	Europe	BRITISH PARLIAMENT PASSES THE REFORM ACT OF 1867
Sept., 1867	Europe	Fenian Rising Is Thwarted by British
Oct., 1867	Europe	NOBEL PATENTS DYNAMITE
Oct. 21, 1867	North America	MEDICINE LODGE CREEK TREATY
Dec. 4, 1867	North America	NATIONAL GRANGE IS FORMED
1868	Europe	BAKUNIN FOUNDS THE SOCIAL DEMOCRATIC ALLIANCE
1868	North America	British Case of *Regina v. Hicklin* Establishes the "Hicklin Rule" for Identifying Obscenity
1868	Australia	LAST CONVICTS LAND IN WESTERN AUSTRALIA
1868-1910	Southeast Asia	Reign of King Rama V in Thailand
Jan. 3, 1868	East Asia	JAPAN'S MEIJI RESTORATION
Feb. 24-May 26, 1868	North America	IMPEACHMENT OF ANDREW JOHNSON
Feb. 27, 1868-Apr. 19, 1881	Europe	Disraeli Leads the British Conservative Party
Mar., 1868	Europe	LARTET DISCOVERS THE FIRST CRO-MAGNON REMAINS
Apr., 1868	Africa	BRITISH EXPEDITION TO ETHIOPIA
Apr. 6, 1868	East Asia	PROMULGATION OF JAPAN'S CHARTER OATH
June 2, 1868	Europe	GREAT BRITAIN'S FIRST TRADES UNION CONGRESS FORMS
June 23, 1868	North America	SHOLES PATENTS A PRACTICAL TYPEWRITER
July 9, 1868	North America	FOURTEENTH AMENDMENT IS RATIFIED
July 28, 1868	North America	BURLINGAME TREATY
Aug. 16, 1868	South America	Tsunami in Chile Kills Seventy Thousand
Sept. 23, 1868	Caribbean/West Indies	Puerto Rican Rebels Declare Independence from Spain
Sept. 30, 1868	Europe	SPANISH REVOLUTION OF 1868

DATE	REGION	EVENT
Oct. 10, 1868-Feb. 10, 1878	Caribbean/West Indies	CUBA'S TEN YEARS' WAR
Nov. 27, 1868	North America	WASHITA RIVER MASSACRE
Dec. 3, 1868-Feb. 20, 1874	Europe	GLADSTONE BECOMES PRIME MINISTER OF BRITAIN
1869	North America	BASEBALL'S FIRST PROFESSIONAL CLUB FORMS
1869	Africa	Basutoland Is Made a British Protectorate
1869	Europe	FIRST MODERN DEPARTMENT STORE OPENS IN PARIS
c. 1869	Europe	GOLDEN AGE OF FLAMENCO BEGINS
1869-1871	Europe	MENDELEYEV DEVELOPS THE PERIODIC TABLE OF ELEMENTS
1869-1874	Africa	Gustav Nachtigal Explores the Central Saharan Region and Darfur
Mar. 4, 1869-Mar. 3, 1877	North America	U.S. Presidency of Ulysses S. Grant
Apr., 1869	North America	WESTINGHOUSE PATENTS HIS AIR BRAKE
Apr. 8, 1869	North America	American Museum of Natural History Opens in New York City
May, 1869	North America	WOMAN SUFFRAGE ASSOCIATIONS BEGIN FORMING
May 10, 1869	North America	FIRST TRANSCONTINENTAL RAILROAD IS COMPLETED
May 29, 1869	Europe	British Parliament Ends Public Hanging
July 4, 1869	Europe	University of Bucharest Founded in Romania
Aug. 9, 1869	Europe	Social Democratic Workers' Party Is Founded in Germany
Sept. 24, 1869-1877	North America	SCANDALS ROCK THE GRANT ADMINISTRATION
Oct. 11, 1869-July 15, 1870	North America	FIRST RIEL REBELLION
Nov. 3, 1869-Feb. 13, 1861	Europe	Combined Forces of Giuseppe Garibaldi and the Piedmont Capture the Final Neapolitan Stronghold in the Siege of Gaeta
Nov. 4, 1869	Europe	Scientific Journal *Nature* Begins Publication
Nov. 17, 1869	Africa	SUEZ CANAL OPENS
Dec., 1869	North America	WYOMING GIVES WOMEN THE VOTE
Dec. 8, 1869-Oct. 20, 1870	Europe	VATICAN I DECREES PAPAL INFALLIBILITY DOGMA
1870's	Europe	AESTHETIC MOVEMENT ARISES
1870's	East Asia	JAPAN EXPANDS INTO KOREA
1870-1871	Europe	French Use Observation Balloons During the Franco-Prussian War
1870-1871	North America	WATCH TOWER BIBLE AND TRACT SOCIETY IS FOUNDED
1870-1888	South America	Period of Influence of Antonio Guzmán Blanco in Venezuela
Jan. 10, 1870	North America	STANDARD OIL COMPANY IS INCORPORATED
Apr., 1870-1873	Europe	SCHLIEMANN EXCAVATES ANCIENT TROY
May 12, 1870	North America	Province of Manitoba Is Created
July 19, 1870-Jan. 28, 1871	Europe	FRANCO-PRUSSIAN WAR
Sept. 1, 1870	Europe	BATTLE OF SEDAN
Sept. 20, 1870	Europe	Italian Troops End the Temporal Power of the Pope
Sept. 20, 1870-Jan. 28, 1871	Europe	PRUSSIAN ARMY BESIEGES PARIS
Oct. 8, 1870	Europe	French Minister Léon Gambetta Escapes Paris in a Balloon Craft
1871	Europe	DARWIN PUBLISHES *THE DESCENT OF MAN*
1871	Europe	Eugène Pottier Writes the Socialist Anthem "The International"
1871	Europe	London Conference Redefines Russian Rights in the Black Sea
1871	Europe	Rome Becomes the Capital of Italy
1871	Europe	Rugby Football Union Is Founded in England
1871-1876	North America	DÍAZ DRIVES MEXICO INTO CIVIL WAR

DATE	REGION	EVENT
1871-1877	Europe	KULTURKAMPF AGAINST THE CATHOLIC CHURCH IN GERMANY
c. 1871-1883	North America	GREAT AMERICAN BUFFALO SLAUGHTER
1871-1885	Central Asia	PRZHEVALSKY EXPLORES CENTRAL ASIA
1871-1890	Central America	Henry Meiggs and Minor Keith Build a Railroad in Costa Rica
Jan. 18, 1871	Europe	GERMAN STATES UNITE WITHIN GERMAN EMPIRE
Feb. 13, 1871-1875	Europe	THIRD FRENCH REPUBLIC IS ESTABLISHED
Mar. 3, 1871	North America	GRANT SIGNS INDIAN APPROPRIATION ACT
Mar. 18-May 28, 1871	Europe	PARIS COMMUNE
Mar. 29, 1871	Europe	Royal Albert Hall Opens in London
Apr. 10, 1871	North America	BARNUM CREATES THE FIRST MODERN AMERICAN CIRCUS
May 8, 1871	North America	TREATY OF WASHINGTON SETTLES U.S. CLAIMS VS. BRITAIN
July 20, 1871	North America	British Columbia Joins the Canadian Confederation
Oct., 1871	Africa	Henry Morton Stanley Finds David Livingstone at Ujiji
Oct. 8-10, 1871	North America	GREAT CHICAGO FIRE
1872	Africa	Britain Grants Self-Government to Cape Colony
1872	North America	DOMINION LANDS ACT FOSTERS CANADIAN SETTLEMENT
1872	East Asia	Opening of the First Japanese Railway
1872	North America	Victoria Woodhull Runs for President of the United States on the Equal Rights Party Ticket
1872-Feb. 27, 1876	Europe	Third Carlist War
Jan. 9, 1872	South America	Paraguay Grants Brazil Free Navigation of the Rio Paraguay
Feb. 20, 1872	North America	METROPOLITAN MUSEUM OF ART OPENS
Mar. 1, 1872	North America	YELLOWSTONE BECOMES THE FIRST U.S. NATIONAL PARK
Aug., 1872	North America	WARD LAUNCHES A MAIL-ORDER BUSINESS
Sept. 1, 1872	North America	Mayan Attack on Orange Walk, British Honduras
Nov. 7-Dec. 4, 1872	Europe	Mystery of the Abandoned Ship *Mary Celeste*
1873	North America	Canada's Conservative Government Is Rocked by the Pacific Scandal
1873	Australia	Ernest Giles Traverses Australia's Gibson Desert
1873	Europe	Founding of the International Meteorological Organization
1873	Australia	Peter Warburton Crosses the Great Sandy Desert of Australia
1873	North America	UKRAINIAN MENNONITES BEGIN SETTLING IN CANADA
1873-1875	Africa	Verney Lovett Cameron Becomes the First European to Complete an East-West Crossing of Equatorial Africa
1873-1880	Africa	EXPLORATION OF AFRICA'S CONGO BASIN
1873-1897	Africa	ZANZIBAR OUTLAWS SLAVERY
1873-1916	South America	Dutch Begin to Import Hindu Laborers to Suriname from India
Jan. 22, 1873-Feb. 13, 1874	Africa	SECOND BRITISH-ASHANTI WAR
Feb. 12, 1873	North America	"CRIME OF 1873"
Mar. 3, 1873	North America	CONGRESS PASSES THE COMSTOCK ANTIOBSCENITY LAW
May, 1873	Africa	Death of David Livingstone at Lake Bangweulu
May, 1873-Apr. 2, 1885	Central America	Justo Rufino Barrios Attempts Liberal Reforms in Guatemala
May 6-Oct. 22, 1873	Europe	THREE EMPERORS' LEAGUE IS FORMED
May 23, 1873	North America	CANADA FORMS THE NORTH-WEST MOUNTED POLICE
June 17-18, 1873	North America	ANTHONY IS TRIED FOR VOTING

DATE	REGION	EVENT
Nov. 5, 1873-Oct. 9, 1878	North America	CANADA'S MACKENZIE ERA
1874	Europe	Denmark Grants Home Rule to Iceland
1874	World	Founding of the Universal Postal Union
1874	Europe	Lawn Tennis Is Invented in England
1874	Africa	Mande State Is Established Under Samory Touré
1874-Aug., 1877	Africa	Henry Morton Stanley Traverses Africa, Completing the First Descent of the Congo River
1874-1879	Europe	Bedřich Smetana, Father of Czech National Music, Composes the Cycle of Symphonic Poems *Má vlast* (*My Fatherland*)
1874-1897	Arctic	Multinational Expeditions Explore Franz Josef Land
Apr. 15, 1874	Europe	FIRST IMPRESSIONIST EXHIBITION
May 20, 1874	North America	Levi Strauss and Jacob Davis Patent Blue Denim Pants with Copper Rivets
June 27, 1874-June 2, 1875	North America	RED RIVER WAR
Oct. 19, 1874	Europe	University of Zagreb Is Founded
Nov. 24, 1874	North America	GLIDDEN PATENTS BARBED WIRE
1875	Africa	Britain Acquires a Ruling Interest in the Suez Canal
1875	North America	SUPREME COURT OF CANADA IS ESTABLISHED
1875-1877	Europe	Leo Tolstoy Publishes *Anna Karenina*
Mar. 1, 1875	North America	U.S. Congress Enacts a Civil Rights Act Banning Discrimination in Public Facilities
Mar. 3, 1875	Europe	BIZET'S *CARMEN* PREMIERES IN PARIS
Mar. 3, 1875	North America	CONGRESS ENACTS THE PAGE LAW
Mar. 9, 1875	North America	*MINOR V. HAPPERSETT*
May 17, 1875	North America	Running of the First Kentucky Derby
Sept., 1875	North America	THEOSOPHICAL SOCIETY IS FOUNDED
Oct. 30, 1875	North America	EDDY ESTABLISHES THE CHRISTIAN SCIENCE MOVEMENT
Late 1870's	Europe	POST-IMPRESSIONIST MOVEMENT BEGINS
1876	Europe	Britain's Royal Titles Act Makes Queen Victoria Empress of India
1876	North America	CANADA'S INDIAN ACT
1876	East Asia	Japan Pressures Korea to Open Ports to Trade
1876	Europe	SPANISH CONSTITUTION OF 1876
1876-1877	North America	SIOUX WAR
1876-1878	Africa	Charles Doughty Lives Two Years Among the Arabian Bedouin
1876-1878	South Asia	Famine Leaves More than 5 Million Dead in India
Feb. 2, 1876	North America	National Baseball League Is Formed
Feb. 3, 1876	South America	Agreement to Settle the Border Between Argentina and Paraguay
May, 1876	Europe	BULGARIAN REVOLT AGAINST THE OTTOMAN EMPIRE
May, 1876	Europe	Meeting of Verney Lovett Cameron and King Leopold II of Belgium
May, 1876	Europe	OTTO INVENTS A PRACTICAL INTERNAL COMBUSTION ENGINE
May 10-Nov. 10, 1876	North America	PHILADELPHIA HOSTS THE CENTENNIAL EXPOSITION
June 25, 1876	North America	BATTLE OF THE LITTLE BIGHORN
June 25, 1876	North America	BELL DEMONSTRATES THE TELEPHONE
July 1, 1876	North America	Intercolonial Railway Links Central Canada with the Maritimes

DATE	REGION	EVENT
July 4, 1876	North America	DECLARATION OF THE RIGHTS OF WOMEN
July 8, 1876	Europe	Agreement Between Austria-Hungary and Russia on the Partition of the Balkan Peninsula
Aug. 13-17, 1876	Europe	FIRST PERFORMANCE OF WAGNER'S RING CYCLE
Aug. 31, 1876-Apr. 27, 1909	Europe	Reign of Sultan Abd-ul-Hamid II of the Ottoman Empire
Sept. 7, 1876	North America	James-Younger Gang Is Decimated in a Bank Robbery Attempt
Oct. 4-6, 1876	North America	AMERICAN LIBRARY ASSOCIATION IS FOUNDED
Oct. 31, 1876	South Asia	A Cyclone Strikes India, Killing 200,000
Nov. 29, 1876-Nov. 30, 1880, Dec. 1, 1884-1910	North America	Porfirio Díaz Serves as President of Mexico
1877	North America	*Ex Parte Jackson* Enables Congress to Prohibit Information About Lotteries from the U.S. Mail
1877	Europe	*The Fishing Gazette* Is First Published in England
Jan.-Sept. 24, 1877	East Asia	FORMER SAMURAI RISE IN SATSUMA REBELLION
Mar. 5, 1877	North America	HAYES BECOMES PRESIDENT
Apr. 24, 1877-Jan. 31, 1878	Europe	THIRD RUSSO-TURKISH WAR
June 15-Oct. 5, 1877	North America	NEZ PERCE WAR
July 9, 1877	Europe	First Wimbledon Tennis Tournament Is Held
July 20, 1877	North America	Baltimore and Ohio Railway Riots Leave Nine Dead
Sept. 10-Dec. 17, 1877	North America	TEXAS'S SALINERO REVOLT
Dec. 24, 1877	North America	EDISON PATENTS THE CYLINDER PHONOGRAPH
1878	Europe	Austria Gains Control of Bosnia
1878	Europe	James Whistler Sues John Ruskin for Libel
1878	North America	MUYBRIDGE PHOTOGRAPHS A GALLOPING HORSE
1878-1899	Europe	IRVING MANAGES LONDON'S LYCEUM THEATRE
Feb. 18, 1878	North America	Ranchers and Entrepreneurs in New Mexico Clash in the Lincoln County War
Feb. 20, 1878-July 20, 1903	Europe	Pontificate of Pope Leo XIII
Mar. 3, 1878	Europe	Treaty of San Stefano Recognizes the Independence of Serbia, Montenegro, and Romania from the Ottoman Empire
May 28, 1878	Europe	W. S. Gilbert and Arthur Sullivan's Comic Opera *H.M.S. Pinafore: Or, The Lass That Loved a Sailor* Premiers in London
June 13-July 13, 1878	Europe	CONGRESS OF BERLIN
Sept., 1878	North America	MACDONALD RETURNS AS CANADA'S PRIME MINISTER
Oct. 19, 1878	Europe	GERMANY PASSES ANTI-SOCIALIST LAW
Nov. 21, 1878-1880	South Asia	Second Afghan War
1879	Europe	*A DOLL'S HOUSE* INTRODUCES MODERN REALISTIC DRAMA
1879	Arctic	Nils Adolf Erik Nordenskjöld Locates the Northeast Passage
1879	North America	POWELL PUBLISHES HIS REPORT ON THE AMERICAN WEST
Jan. 22-23, 1879	Africa	BATTLES OF ISANDLWANA AND RORKE'S DRIFT
Jan. 22-Aug., 1879	Africa	ZULU WAR
Mar. 3, 1879	North America	U.S. Geological Survey Is Instituted
Mar. 12, 1879	North America	John A. Macdonald Introduces His National Policy for Canada

DATE	REGION	EVENT
Apr. 5, 1879-Oct. 20, 1883	South America	WAR OF THE PACIFIC
Oct. 7, 1879	Europe	Dual Alliance Signed Between Germany and Austria-Hungary
Oct. 8, 1879	South America	Chilean Victory at the Battle of Angamos Enables Ground Forces to Invade Peru and Bolivia (War of the Pacific)
Oct. 21, 1879	North America	EDISON DEMONSTRATES THE INCANDESCENT LAMP
Dec. 30, 1879	Europe	W. S. Gilbert and Arthur Sullivan's Comic Opera *The Pirates of Penzance: Or, The Slave of Duty* Premiers
1880's	North America	BRAHMIN SCHOOL OF AMERICAN LITERATURE FLOURISHES
1880's	Central America	Compagnie Universelle du Canal Interocéanique Attempts to Build a Canal Across the Isthmus of Panama
1880's	Europe	ROUX DEVELOPS THE THEORY OF MITOSIS
1880's-1890's	North America	RISE OF YELLOW JOURNALISM
1880	North America	Mary H. Myers Becomes First American Woman to Pilot Her Own Balloon
1880	Europe	Statutes (Definition of Time) Act Establishes Greenwich Mean Time as the British Standard
June 29, 1880	Pacific Islands	France Annexes Tahiti
July, 1880-Jan., 1881	South America	Submarine *Toro* Is Used in War of the Pacific
July 7, 1880	South America	Heroic Charge Leads to Chilean Victory in the Battle of Arica (War of the Pacific)
Sept.-Nov., 1880	Europe	IRISH TENANT FARMERS STAGE FIRST "BOYCOTT"
Sept. 5, 1880	Europe	Electric Tram Is Successfully Tested in St. Petersburg, Russia
Oct., 1880	South America	United States Fails to Negotiate a Diplomatic End to the War of the Pacific
Oct. 15, 1880	North America	Apache Leader Victorio Is Killed by the Mexican Army
Dec. 16, 1880-Mar. 6, 1881	Africa	FIRST BOER WAR
Dec. 30, 1880	Africa	Transvaal Becomes the South African Republic
1881	South America	Argentina and Chile Agree on Chilean Sovereignty over the Straits of Magellan
1881-1884	North America	Nineteenth Century Immigration to the United States Peaks, Averaging 620,000 Per Year
1881-1889	Europe	BISMARCK INTRODUCES SOCIAL SECURITY PROGRAMS IN GERMANY
Jan. 16-24, 1881	Central Asia	Russians Conquer the Turcoman Stronghold at Geok-Tepe
Mar. 4, 1881-Sept. 19, 1881	North America	U.S. Presidency of James Garfield
Mar. 13, 1881-Nov. 1, 1894	Europe	Reign of Czar Alexander III of Russia
May 12, 1881	Africa	France Makes Tunisia a Protectorate
May 21, 1881	North America	Clara Barton Founds the American Red Cross
July, 1881-1883	Europe	STEVENSON PUBLISHES *TREASURE ISLAND*
Sept. 19, 1881-Mar. 3, 1885	North America	U.S. Presidency of Chester A. Arthur
Oct. 10, 1881	Europe	LONDON'S SAVOY THEATRE OPENS
Oct. 26, 1881	North America	Earp Brothers and Doc Holliday Confront and Kill Three Outlaws in a Gunfight at the O.K. Corral
1882	Europe	FIRST BIRTH CONTROL CLINIC OPENS IN AMSTERDAM
1882	Europe	Founding of the Berlin Philharmonic Orchestra

DATE	REGION	EVENT
1882-1884	North America	Nineteenth Century Immigration Peaks in Canada, Averaging More than 116,000 Per Year
1882-1900	Europe	Nikola Tesla Develops the Rotating Magnetic Field Principle, Helping Improve Alternating Current Motors
1882-1901	Europe	METCHNIKOFF ADVANCES THE CELLULAR THEORY OF IMMUNITY
Jan. 2, 1882	North America	STANDARD OIL TRUST IS ORGANIZED
Mar. 22, 1882	North America	Polygamy Is Outlawed in the United States
Mar. 24, 1882	Europe	KOCH ANNOUNCES HIS DISCOVERY OF THE TUBERCULOSIS BACILLUS
Apr., 1882-1885	Southeast Asia	FRENCH INDOCHINA WAR
Apr. 3, 1882	North America	Outlaw Jesse James Is Shot to Death
May 2, 1882	Europe	KILMAINHAM TREATY MAKES CONCESSIONS TO IRISH NATIONALISTS
May 9, 1882	North America	ARTHUR SIGNS THE CHINESE EXCLUSION ACT
May 20, 1882	Europe	TRIPLE ALLIANCE IS FORMED
June 6, 1882	South Asia	Cyclone in the Arabian Sea Leaves 100,000 Dead in India
July 11, 1882	Africa	Bombardment of Alexandria by the British Fleet
July 23, 1882-Jan. 9, 1885	East Asia	KOREAN MILITARY MUTINIES AGAINST JAPANESE RULE
Aug. 20, 1882	Europe	Peter Ilich Tchaikovsky's *1812 Overture* Debuts in Moscow
Sept. 13, 1882	Africa	BATTLE OF TEL EL KEBIR
Nov. 12, 1882	North America	SAN FRANCISCO'S CHINESE SIX COMPANIES ASSOCIATION FORMS
1883	Europe	GALTON DEFINES "EUGENICS"
1883-1885	North America	WORLD'S FIRST SKYSCRAPER IS BUILT
Jan. 16, 1883	North America	PENDLETON ACT REFORMS THE FEDERAL CIVIL SERVICE
Feb.-Apr., 1883	Africa	Germany Establishes Itself in Southwest Africa at Angra Pequena (Lüderitz)
May 24, 1883	North America	BROOKLYN BRIDGE OPENS
Aug. 12, 1883	Europe	Death of the Last Quagga
Aug. 27, 1883	Southeast Asia	KRAKATOA VOLCANO ERUPTS
Oct. 4, 1883	Europe	*Orient Express* Train Departs Paris on Its Inaugural Run
Oct. 15, 1883	North America	CIVIL RIGHTS CASES
Oct. 22, 1883	North America	METROPOLITAN OPERA HOUSE OPENS IN NEW YORK
Nov. 3, 1883	Europe	GAUDÍ BEGINS BARCELONA'S TEMPLO EXPIATORIO DE LA SAGRADA FAMÍLIA
1884	Europe	Horatio Phillips Invents the Airfoil
1884	Europe	MAXIM PATENTS HIS MACHINE GUN
1884	Europe	NEW GUILDS PROMOTE THE ARTS AND CRAFTS MOVEMENT
c. 1884-1924	Europe	DECADENT MOVEMENT FLOURISHES
Jan., 1884	Europe	FABIAN SOCIETY IS FOUNDED
Jan. 25, 1884	South Asia	INDIAN LEGISLATIVE COUNCIL ENACTS THE ILBERT BILL
Mar. 13, 1884-Jan. 26, 1885	Africa	SIEGE OF KHARTOUM
June 21, 1884	Africa	GOLD IS DISCOVERED IN THE TRANSVAAL
July 5, 1884	Africa	Germany Annexes Cameroon in West Africa
Oct., 1884	World	International Meridian Conference Creates Twenty-Four Time Zones Worldwide

DATE	REGION	EVENT
Nov. 4, 1884	North America	U.S. ELECTION OF 1884
Nov. 15, 1884-Feb. 26, 1885	Europe	BERLIN CONFERENCE LAYS GROUNDWORK FOR THE PARTITION OF AFRICA
Dec., 1884-Feb., 1885	North America	TWAIN PUBLISHES *ADVENTURES OF HUCKLEBERRY FINN*
Dec. 6, 1884	Europe	BRITISH PARLIAMENT PASSES THE FRANCHISE ACT OF 1884
1885	South Asia	INDIAN NATIONAL CONGRESS IS FOUNDED
1885-1886	Southeast Asia	Third Burmese War
Jan. 20, 1885	North America	L. A. Thompson Patents the Roller Coaster
Feb. 9, 1885	Pacific Islands	Japanese Workers Begin Arriving in the Hawaiian Islands
Mar., 1885	Central Asia	Panjdeh Crisis in Afghanistan Nearly Leads to War Between Britain and Russia
Mar. 4, 1885-Mar. 3, 1889; Mar. 4, 1893-Mar. 3, 1897	North America	U.S. Presidency of Grover Cleveland
Mar. 19, 1885	North America	SECOND RIEL REBELLION BEGINS
Mar. 31, 1885	Africa	British Establish a Protectorate over Bechuanaland (Botswana)
Sept. 2, 1885	North America	Rock Springs Massacre Leaves Twenty-Eight Chinese Dead
Sept. 6, 1885	Europe	Unification of Bulgaria
1886	Southeast Asia	Britain Annexes Burma
1886	Europe	RISE OF THE SYMBOLIST MOVEMENT
Jan., 1886-1889	Europe	FRENCH RIGHT WING REVIVES DURING BOULANGER CRISIS
Jan. 29, 1886	Europe	BENZ PATENTS THE FIRST PRACTICAL AUTOMOBILE
May 4, 1886	North America	Haymarket Riot Leaves Eleven Dead in Chicago, Illinois
May 8, 1886	North America	PEMBERTON INTRODUCES COCA-COLA
June, 1886-Sept. 9, 1893	Europe	IRISH HOME RULE DEBATE DOMINATES BRITISH POLITICS
Oct. 7, 1886	Caribbean/West Indies	Spain Abolishes Slavery in Cuba
Oct. 28, 1886	North America	STATUE OF LIBERTY IS DEDICATED
Dec. 8, 1886	North America	AMERICAN FEDERATION OF LABOR IS FOUNDED
1887	Europe	Halford Mackinder, Future Author of the *Theory of Eurasia as the Center of Geopolitical Power*, Is Appointed a Reader in Geography at Oxford University
1887	East Asia	Japan Annexes Iwo Jima
1887	Europe	Ottomar Anschütz Demonstrates His Electrotachyscope
1887	North America	Samuel Pierpont Langley Constructs a Manned Flying Apparatus
1887	East Asia	Yellow River Floods in China Leave More than 900,000 Dead
Feb. 2, 1887	North America	First Groundhog Day Is Observed in Punxsutawney, Pennsylvania
Feb. 4, 1887	North America	INTERSTATE COMMERCE ACT
Feb. 5, 1887	Europe	Giuseppe Verdi's Opera *Otello* Premiers at La Scala in Milan
Feb. 8, 1887	North America	GENERAL ALLOTMENT ACT ERODES INDIAN TRIBAL UNITY
Mar., 1887-Dec., 1889	Africa	Emin Pasha Relief Expedition, to Assist British Equatoria Against a Mahdist Threat, Is the Century's Last Major European Expedition into the African Interior
Mar. 3, 1887	North America	Anne Sullivan Begins to Teach Helen Keller
Mar. 13, 1887	North America	AMERICAN PROTECTIVE ASSOCIATION IS FORMED
May, 1887	North America	GOODWIN DEVELOPS CELLULOID FILM
May 9, 1887	Europe	Buffalo Bill's Wild West Show Plays in London

DATE	REGION	EVENT
Oct. 1, 1887	South Asia	Britain Annexes Baluchistan
Dec., 1887	Europe	CONAN DOYLE INTRODUCES SHERLOCK HOLMES
1888	Southeast Asia	Brunei Becomes a Protectorate of Great Britain
1888	North America	George Eastman Markets the First Kodak Camera
1888	Europe	RODIN EXHIBITS *THE THINKER*
1888-1906	Europe	RAMÓN Y CAJAL SHOWS HOW NEURONS WORK IN THE NERVOUS SYSTEM
Mar., 1888	Africa	Samuel Teleki Reaches and Names Lake Rudolf (now Lake Turkana)
Mar. 13, 1888	Africa	RHODES AMALGAMATES KIMBERLEY DIAMONDFIELDS
Apr. 11, 1888	Europe	Concertgebouw Opens in Amersterdam
June 15, 1888-Nov. 9, 1918	Europe	Reign of Kaiser William II of Germany
Aug.-Nov., 1888	Europe	Jack the Ripper Commits Serial Killings in London
Oct., 1888	Europe	Louis Aimé Augustin Le Prince Shoots His *Roundhay Garden Scene*, Believed to Be the First Motion Picture
Dec. 7, 1888	Europe	DUNLOP PATENTS THE PNEUMATIC TIRE
1889	Pacific Islands	Britain, the United States, and Germany Agree to Joint Supervision of the Samoan Islands
1889	North America	Eastman Kodak Begins to Manufacture Roll Film on Celluloid
1889	Europe	GREAT BRITAIN STRENGTHENS ITS ROYAL NAVY
1889-1916	Europe	Second International Coordinates the Work of Socialist Parties and Organizations
Feb. 11, 1889	East Asia	JAPAN ADOPTS A NEW CONSTITUTION
Mar. 4, 1889-Mar. 3, 1893	North America	U.S. Presidency of Benjamin Harrison
Mar. 31, 1889	Europe	EIFFEL TOWER IS DEDICATED
Apr. 22, 1889	North America	Fifty Thousand Settlers Join the Oklahoma Land Run
May 31, 1889	North America	JOHNSTOWN FLOOD
Aug. 14, 1889	Europe	Great London Dock Strike Strengthens the Dockers' Union
Sept. 18, 1889	North America	ADDAMS OPENS CHICAGO'S HULL-HOUSE
Oct., 1889-Apr., 1890	Western Hemisphere	FIRST PAN-AMERICAN CONGRESS
Nov., 1889-Jan., 1894	Africa	DAHOMEY-FRENCH WARS
Nov. 14, 1889-Jan. 25, 1890	World	Muckraking Journalist Elizabeth Seaman (known as Nellie Bly) Travels Around the World in a Record Seventy-Two Days
1890's	North America	RISE OF TIN PAN ALLEY MUSIC
1890	Europe	Germany Regains Helgoland from Britain
1890	Europe	Luxembourg Breaks with the Netherlands
1890	North America	MISSISSIPPI CONSTITUTION DISFRANCHISES BLACK VOTERS
1890	North America	U.S. CENSUS BUREAU ANNOUNCES CLOSING OF THE FRONTIER
Jan. 5, 1890	North America	United Mine Workers of America Is Founded
Feb. 17-18, 1890	North America	WOMEN'S RIGHTS ASSOCIATIONS UNITE
Mar. 4, 1890	Europe	Cantilevered Railway Bridge Is Completed Across Scotland's Firth of Forth
July 10, 1890	North America	Wyoming Enters the Union as the First State with Full Female Suffrage
July 20, 1890	North America	HARRISON SIGNS THE SHERMAN ANTITRUST ACT

DATE	REGION	EVENT
Dec. 11, 1890	Europe	BEHRING DISCOVERS THE DIPHTHERIA ANTITOXIN
Dec. 29, 1890	North America	WOUNDED KNEE MASSACRE
1891	Pacific Islands	French Painter Paul Gauguin Settles in Tahiti
1891	North America	NAISMITH INVENTS BASKETBALL
1891	Europe	Otto Lilienthal Develops and Popularizes the Hang Glider
1891	Africa	Portugal Agrees to British Control of Rhodesia
1891	North America	Thomas Edison Applies for a Patent on the Kinetoscope
1891-1904	Europe/East Asia	Building of the Trans-Siberian Railway
Jan. 6-Aug. 28, 1891	South America	Chilean Civil War
Mar. 11, 1891	North America	STROWGER PATENTS AUTOMATIC DIAL TELEPHONE SYSTEM
May 5, 1891	North America	Peter Ilich Tchaikovsky Conducts the Opening Performance at the Music Hall (Later Carnegie Hall) in New York City
May 15, 1891	Europe	PAPAL ENCYCLICAL ON LABOR
Aug. 28, 1891	South America	Battle of La Placilla Is a Turning Point in the Chilean Civil War
1892	North America	AMERICA'S "NEW" IMMIGRATION ERA BEGINS
1892	North America	Gasoline Tractor Is First Used for Farming
1892	North America	Stanley Cup Is Donated as a Hockey Trophy
1892-1895	Europe	TOULOUSE-LAUTREC PAINTS *AT THE MOULIN ROUGE*
Jan. 1, 1892	North America	ELLIS ISLAND IMMIGRATION DEPOT OPENS
Feb., 1892	Europe	DIESEL PATENTS THE DIESEL ENGINE
May 4, 1892	North America	ANTI-JAPANESE YELLOW PERIL CAMPAIGN BEGINS
May 28, 1892	North America	John Muir Establishes the Sierra Club
July 4-5, 1892	North America	BIRTH OF THE PEOPLE'S PARTY
July 6, 1892	North America	Pinkerton Detectives Put Down the Homestead Strike, Leaving Ten Dead
Aug. 3, 1892	Europe	HARDIE BECOMES PARLIAMENT'S FIRST LABOUR MEMBER
1893	South Asia	Indian Football Association Is Founded
1893	Europe	MUNCH PAINTS *THE SCREAM*
1893-1896	Arctic	NANSEN ATTEMPTS TO REACH THE NORTH POLE
Jan. 17, 1893	Pacific Islands	U.S. Marines Assist in Overthrow of Queen Liliuokalani
May 1-Oct. 30, 1893	North America	CHICAGO WORLD'S FAIR
Sept. 19, 1893	Pacific Islands	NEW ZEALAND WOMEN WIN VOTING RIGHTS
Oct., 1893-Oct., 1897	Africa	BRITISH SUBDUE AFRICAN RESISTANCE IN RHODESIA
Oct. 27, 1893	North America	NATIONAL COUNCIL OF WOMEN OF CANADA IS FOUNDED
1894	Africa	France Establishes a Protectorate in Dahomey
1894	Europe	Paul Vidal de La Blache Publishes *Atlas général Vidal-Lablache: Histoire et géographie*
1894-1895	North America	KELLOGG'S CORN FLAKES LAUNCH THE DRY CEREAL INDUSTRY
1894-1896	Europe	OTTOMANS ATTEMPT TO EXTERMINATE ARMENIANS
Jan. 4, 1894	Europe	FRANCO-RUSSIAN ALLIANCE
May 11-July 11, 1894	North America	PULLMAN STRIKE
July 8, 1894-Jan. 1, 1896	East Asia	KABO REFORMS BEGIN MODERNIZATION OF KOREAN GOVERNMENT
Aug., 1894-June, 1897	Europe	Ottomans Massacre Armenians
Aug. 1, 1894-Apr. 17, 1895	East Asia	SINO-JAPANESE WAR

DATE	REGION	EVENT
Oct., 1894-July, 1906	Europe	DREYFUS AFFAIR
Nov. 1, 1894-Mar. 2, 1917	Europe	Reign of Czar Nicholas II of Russia
Dec. 22, 1894	Europe	DEBUSSY'S *PRELUDE TO THE AFTERNOON OF A FAUN* PREMIERES
1895	South America	Liberal Revolution in Ecuador
1895	South America	Non-Native Population of Argentina Exceeds Twenty-Five Percent
1895	World	Sixth International Geophysical Conference Encourages Antarctic Exploration
1895-1898	North America	HEARST-PULITZER CIRCULATION WAR
Jan. 24, 1895	Pacific Islands	HAWAII'S LAST MONARCH ABDICATES
Jan. 27, 1895	Europe	TCHAIKOVSKY'S *SWAN LAKE* IS STAGED IN ST. PETERSBURG
Feb. 24, 1895-1898	Caribbean/West Indies	CUBAN WAR OF INDEPENDENCE
Apr. 6, 1895-May 25, 1895	Europe	Oscar Wilde Is Arrested and Convicted of Gross Indecency
Apr. 17, 1895	East Asia	Treaty of Shimonoseki Ends the Sino-Japanese War
May 10, 1895	North America	CHINESE CALIFORNIANS FORM NATIVE SONS OF THE GOLDEN STATE
June 20, 1895	Europe	GERMANY'S KIEL CANAL OPENS
Sept. 18, 1895	North America	WASHINGTON'S ATLANTA COMPROMISE SPEECH
Oct. 2, 1895	North America	Canada's Yukon Territory Separates from the Northwest Territories
Nov. 9, 1895	Europe	RÖNTGEN DISCOVERS X RAYS
Nov. 27, 1895	Europe	NOBEL BEQUEATHS FUNDS FOR THE NOBEL PRIZES
Dec. 28, 1895	North America	FIRST COMMERCIAL PROJECTION OF MOTION PICTURES
Dec. 28, 1895	Europe	Lumière Brothers Open Le Cinématographe in Paris
Dec. 29, 1895-Jan. 2, 1896	Africa	JAMESON RAID
1896	North America	BROOKS BROTHERS INTRODUCES BUTTON-DOWN SHIRTS
1896	Europe	Charles and Émile Pathé Found the Pathé Frères, Producing and Distributing Motion Pictures Worldwide
1896	Africa	France Conquers Madagascar
1896	South Asia	Great Stone Pillar of Aśoka Discovered at Lubini
1896	North America	IMMIGRANT FARMERS BEGIN SETTLING WESTERN CANADA
1896	Southeast Asia	Malay States Form a Federation Under British Influence
Feb., 1896-Aug., 1897	Europe	HERZL FOUNDS THE ZIONIST MOVEMENT
Feb. 11, 1896	Europe	Oscar Wilde's Play *Salomé* Debuts in Paris
Mar., 1896-Nov., 1899	Africa	SUDANESE WAR
Mar. 1, 1896	Africa	ETHIOPIA REPELS ITALIAN INVASION
Apr., 1896	Europe	*The Soldier's Courtship*, Britain's First Story Film, Is Released
Apr. 6, 1896	Europe	MODERN OLYMPIC GAMES ARE INAUGURATED
May 1, 1896	Middle East	Assassination of Shah Nāsir al-Din of Persia
May 6, 1896	North America	Samuel Pierpont Langley Makes the First Successful Unmanned Heavier-than-Air Flight
May 18, 1896	North America	*PLESSY V. FERGUSON*
June, 1896	Europe	MARCONI PATENTS THE WIRELESS TELEGRAPH
June 9, 1896	East Asia	Lobanov-Yamagata Agreement on Russo-Japanese Cooperation in Korea

DATE	REGION	EVENT
July 11, 1896	North America	LAURIER BECOMES THE FIRST FRENCH CANADIAN PRIME MINISTER
Aug. 17, 1896	North America	KLONDIKE GOLD RUSH BEGINS
Nov. 3, 1896	North America	MCKINLEY IS ELECTED PRESIDENT
Nov. 16, 1896	North America	FIRST U.S. HYDROELECTRIC PLANT OPENS AT NIAGARA FALLS
Dec. 30, 1896	Southeast Asia	Poet José Rizal Is Executed in the Philippines for Rebellion
1897	Europe	ELLIS PUBLISHES *SEXUAL INVERSION*
1897	Europe	Friedrich Ratzel Publishes *Politische Geographie*
1897	Africa	Slavery Is Banned in Zanzibar
1897-1901	North America	ABEL AND TAKAMINE ISOLATE ADRENALINE
Jan. 21-May 20, 1897	Europe	GRECO-TURKISH WAR
Jan. 23, 1897	Europe	"ASPIRIN" IS REGISTERED AS A TRADE NAME
Mar. 4, 1897-Sept. 14, 1901	North America	U.S. Presidency of William McKinley
July, 1897-July, 1904	Europe	BJERKNES FOUNDS SCIENTIFIC WEATHER FORECASTING
July 24, 1897	North America	CONGRESS PASSES DINGLEY TARIFF ACT
Aug. 20, 1897	Europe	ROSS ESTABLISHES MALARIA'S TRANSMISSION VECTOR
Nov. 1, 1897	North America	NEW LIBRARY OF CONGRESS BUILDING OPENS
Nov. 14, 1897	East Asia	SCRAMBLE FOR CHINESE CONCESSIONS BEGINS
1898	Europe	BEIJERINCK DISCOVERS VIRUSES
1898	Caribbean/West Indies	Cameramen Film War in Cuba
1898	North America	Doukhobors Begin to Settle in Saskatchewan
1898	Europe	George Albert Smith Uses Double Exposure for Special Effects in the Film *Cinderella and the Fairy Godmother*
Jan. 13, 1898	Europe	Émile Zola Publishes "J'accuse," His Protest of the Anti-Semitic Conviction of Captain Alfred Dreyfus for Treason, in the Parisian Newspaper *L'Aurore*
Mar., 1898	Europe	RUSSIAN SOCIAL-DEMOCRATIC LABOR PARTY IS FORMED
Mar. 28, 1898	North America	*UNITED STATES V. WONG KIM ARK*
Apr., 1898-1903	Europe	STRATOSPHERE AND TROPOSPHERE ARE DISCOVERED
Apr. 24-Dec. 10, 1898	Caribbean/West Indies/ Southeast Asia	SPANISH-AMERICAN WAR
June 11-Sept. 21, 1898	East Asia	Hundred Days Reform Movement
July 10-Nov. 3, 1898	Africa	FASHODA INCIDENT PITS FRANCE VS. BRITAIN
Oct. 14, 1898	Europe	MOSCOW ART THEATER IS FOUNDED
1899	Europe	Auguste Blaise Baron Perfects His System of Sound Cinema
1899	Africa	Britain and France Exchange African Territories
1899	Southeast Asia	France Establishes a Protectorate in Laos
1899	Europe	HILBERT PUBLISHES *THE FOUNDATIONS OF GEOMETRY*
1899	North America	JOPLIN POPULARIZES RAGTIME MUSIC AND DANCE
1899	Central America/ Caribbean	United Fruit Company Forms, Consolidating Holdings in Central America and the Caribbean
1899	Central America	Vaccaro Brothers Begin Importing Bananas from Honduras to New Orleans
1899-1900	Europe	REDISCOVERY OF MENDEL'S HEREDITARY THEORY

DATE	REGION	EVENT
1899-1902	Europe	Britain Uses Balloons and Kites for Observation During the Boer War
Feb. 4, 1899-July 4, 1902	Southeast Asia	PHILIPPINE INSURRECTION
May 18-July, 1899	Europe	FIRST HAGUE PEACE CONFERENCE
Sept. 6, 1899-July 3, 1900	East Asia	HAY ARTICULATES "OPEN DOOR" POLICY TOWARD CHINA
Oct. 11, 1899-May 31, 1902	Africa	SOUTH AFRICAN WAR
Oct. 13, 1899-May 17, 1900	Africa	SIEGE OF MAFEKING
Nov. 25, 1899	Middle East	Baghdad Railway Concession Is Granted to Germany
Winter, 1899-1900	Antarctica	Expedition Led by Carsten Borchgrevink Is First to Winter in the Antarctic
1900	Europe	FREUD PUBLISHES *THE INTERPRETATION OF DREAMS*
1900	Europe	LEBESGUE DEVELOPS NEW INTEGRATION THEORY
1900	Europe	Léon Gaumont Demonstrates Synchronized Sound and Pictures
1900	North America	Railroad Engineer Octave Chanute Advises Orville and Wilbur Wright, Alexander Graham Bell, and Samuel Langley on Aviation Projects
1900	Europe	WIECHERT INVENTS THE INVERTED PENDULUM SEISMOGRAPH
Jan. 14, 1900	Europe	PUCCINI'S *TOSCA* PREMIERES IN ROME
Feb., 1900	North America	KODAK INTRODUCES BROWNIE CAMERAS
Feb. 27, 1900	Europe	BRITISH LABOUR PARTY IS FORMED
Mar. 23, 1900	Europe	EVANS DISCOVERS CRETE'S MINOAN CIVILIZATION
May, 1900-Sept. 7, 1901	East Asia	BOXER REBELLION
June, 1900-1904	Central America	SUPPRESSION OF YELLOW FEVER
July 2, 1900	Europe	ZEPPELIN COMPLETES THE FIRST FLYING DIRIGIBLE
Sept. 8, 1900	North America	GALVESTON HURRICANE
Nov. 8, 1900	North America	DREISER PUBLISHES *SISTER CARRIE*
Dec. 14, 1900	Europe	ARTICULATION OF QUANTUM THEORY
Dec. 14, 1900	Africa	Franco-Italian Agreement Establishes Division of Power in North Africa
Dec. 15, 1900	North America	GENERAL ELECTRIC OPENS RESEARCH LABORATORY
Dec. 23, 1900	North America	First Wireless Radio Broadcast

GLOSSARY

Abolitionists: Men and women who campaigned for a complete end to slavery, led most notably in England by William Wilberforce in the 1770's and in the United States by William Lloyd Garrison in the 1830's.

Aborigines: People native to a region; in the nineteenth century, most often used to designate the native inhabitants of Australia.

Aesthetic movement: A literary and artistic movement of nineteenth century England based upon the principle of "art for art's sake," suggesting that the arts or a work of art need not support a larger social or moral purpose. *See also* Decadent movement.

Afrikaners: A distinct ethnic group inhabiting modern South Africa and Namibia, descended mainly from seventeenth century Dutch Calvinists but augmented by French Huguenots and German, Scandinavian, and English Protestants. *See also* Boers.

Agnosticism: The philosophical view that it is impossible to know whether or not God exists.

Agricultural Revolution: The application of new farming and animal husbandry techniques that allowed greater agricultural productivity in the eighteenth century, thus enabling more workers to move into industrial jobs. As the nineteenth century progressed, agricultural development continued, aided by the development of chemical fertilizers and the invention of mechanized farm implements.

Amir: *See* Emir.

Anarchism: An antiauthoritarian political ideology that argues against coercive social institutions, favoring voluntary association of citizens.

Anglican: Of or belonging to the Protestant Church of England.

Annexation: The legal incorporation of a smaller, weaker territory into a larger state or empire; in the case of imperial annexations of the nineteenth century, it implies coercion or cooperation with one indigenous group against another. *See also* Imperialism, Protectorate.

Anti-Semitism: Hostility toward Jews on the basis of their religion and/or ethnicity; anti-Jewish legal disabilities and prejudice were widespread throughout Europe during the nineteenth century and led to overt persecution in Russia.

Antiseptic: A substance that prevents the reproduction of bacteria, fungi, viruses, and other microorganisms, and thus aids in avoiding infection; became widely used in surgery from the 1860's.

Antitrust laws: Laws designed to prohibit anticompetitive behavior in the economy; the term was used most frequently in the United States.

Archaeology: The study of the material artifacts left by a culture, including tools, buildings, daily objects, and written inscriptions.

Aristocracy: A class of hereditary nobility in Europe, established by royal grants of titles and lands. In the Middle Ages grants were made for military service; by the nineteenth century they were made for a wide range of services to a monarch. *See also* Gentry.

Arts and Crafts movement: An English aesthetic movement emphasizing the simplicity and virtue of crafts produced by hand, as opposed those produced by machines; spawned around 1880, it gained adherents in most European countries throughout the final two decades of the nineteenth century.

Atheism: The belief that there is no God or supernatural being.

Bābism: A religious reform movement that originated in Persia (Iran) in the mid-nineteenth century and eventually led to the development of the Baha'i religion.

Balkans: The large triangular peninsula of southeastern Europe bordered on the west by the Adriatic Sea, on the east by the Black Sea, and on the south by the Mediterranean Sea; controlled by the Ottoman Empire at the beginning of the nineteenth century, most of the nationalities of the peninsula became independent between 1820 and 1900.

Baptists: One of the most rapidly growing Christian denominations of nineteenth century England and the United States, emphasizing congregational autonomy, separation of church and state, and the responsibility of each individual directly to God.

Bimetallism: An economic system in which the standard of currency can be fixed in either gold or silver; became the focus of controversies during the 1890's, particularly in the United States and India.

Black codes: State and local laws passed mainly in the southern United States to restrict the freedom of former slaves. *See also* Jim Crow laws.

Boers: The descendants of seventeenth and eighteenth century Dutch settlers in southern Africa; in the nineteenth century the term was specifically used to designate citizens of the Boer republics of the Transvaal and the Orange Free State. *See also* Afrikaners.

Bonapartists: In France, supporters of the family line of

Napoleon Bonaparte as legitimate rulers of the country; they clashed with others who believed that the Bourbon family represented the legitimate royal line and with those who favored a republican form of government; Napoleon III (r. 1852-1870) was the only member of the Bonaparte family to succeed his uncle on the throne.

Bosporus: The narrow waterway connecting the Black Sea with the Sea of Marmara. *See also* Dardanelles, Straits.

Bourbon Dynasty: The hereditary ruling family of all or parts of France from 1555 to 1792, when Louis XVI was executed during the French Revolution; throughout the nineteenth century, Monarchists supported the restoration of the Bourbon Dynasty in opposition to Bonapartists and Republicans, though only Louis XVIII (r. 1814-1824) and Charles X (r. 1824-1830) were ever raised to the throne.

Bowdlerize: To remove morally objectionable content in literature in order to make suitable for family reading; named after Thomas Bowdler, who in 1818 published *The Family Shakespeare*.

Boxers: Chinese members of the Righteous Harmony Society who led an unsuccessful rebellion against Western influence and extraterritoriality in China (1900).

Boyar: A Russian noble—that is, a member of the landed military aristocracy—ranking just below a ruling prince.

Boycott: A collective agreement to refrain from doing business with a person or firm in order to bring about social or political change; named after Captain Charles Boycott, who evicted Irish tenants and as a result was socially ostracized in 1880.

Broad constructionist: A person who accepts the doctrine of implied powers in the Constitution.

Bull: A formal papal letter or document issuing an authoritative statement or policy. Named after the pope's lead seal, or *bulla*.

Bushido: The code of conduct of the samurai (Japanese warrior class), stressing martial prowess, discipline, bravery, and unwavering loyalty to one's lord. *See also* Samurai, Shogun.

Cabinet: The body of secretaries or ministers appointed by a president or prime minister to head executive departments and formulate government policy.

Caliph: An Islamic ruler claiming both spiritual and secular authority as the successor of the Prophet Muḥammad. *See also* Imam, Islam, Sharif.

Calvinism: The theology based on the teachings of John Calvin in the sixteenth century, which places supreme faith in God and asserts human fallibility and predestination. *See also* Catholicism, Presbyterian, Protestantism.

Canon law: The system of governing the Roman Catholic Church, its bishops, clerics, and laypersons. *See also* Catholicism, Clerics or clergy.

Capitalism: An economic system in which the means of production are privately owned and in which the production, value, and distribution of goods and services are regulated by supply and demand.

Carbonari: Secret revolutionary societies that promoted Italian independence during the first half of the nineteenth century.

Cardinal: A high official in the Roman Catholic Church, second only to the pope in authority. Cardinals are appointed by the pope, and the College of Cardinals is the body that elects a new pope.

Carpetbaggers: Northerners who traveled to the South after the U.S. Civil War to take advantage of business and political opportunities afforded during the period of Reconstruction. *See also* Reconstruction.

Caste system: In India, a system of rigid social hierarchy, rooted in Hindu teachings, in which each person is born into a specific social rank.

Categorical imperative: The internal sense of moral duty that all people possess, according to the philosophical doctrines of German philosopher Immanuel Kant.

Cathedral or cathedral church: The central church in a diocese, the seat of a bishop's cathedra, or throne.

Catholicism: From the Greek *catholicos*, meaning "universal," Catholicism is a branch of Christianity organized in a strict hierarchy and subscribing to a complex body of religious dogma, including belief in transubstantiation, in papal infallibility, and in justification by faith in combination with good works. The two Catholic Churches are the Roman Catholic Church and the Eastern Orthodox Church. *See also* Calvinism, Eastern Orthodox Church, Islam, Judaism, Presbyterian, Protestantism.

Caudillo: An authoritarian politico-military leader who gains the support of the common people through populist programs of reform, relying on an attending cult of personality; most commonly applied in Latin American countries.

Cell theory: Developed in the 1830's by German physiologist Theodor Schwann, who argued that cells are the basic unit of structure in all living things.

Centennial: A one-hundred-year anniversary.

Chartists: In Great Britain, supporters during the 1830's and 1840's of the People's Charter, which called for greater public access to the political structure, including universal male suffrage, the secret ballot, and pay for members of Parliament.

Cholera: A bacterial, water-borne disease that killed millions of people in all parts of the world during the nineteenth century.

Christianity: The religion derived from the teachings of Jesus Christ and from the words of the Bible, including the New Testament, which is considered sacred scripture. Christianity is practiced by Roman Catholic, Protestant, and Eastern Orthodox bodies. *See also* Anglican, Baptists, Catholicism, Congregational, Congregationalists, Eastern Orthodox Church, Evangelicalism, Islam, Judaism, Protestantism, Presbyterian, Second Great Awakening, Unitarianism.

Civil rights: Protections and privileges granted to citizens by law.

Civil war: War between two factions within the same country; in the United States, used to designate the rebellion of the slaveholding Southern states (Confederacy) against the federal government between 1861 and 1865. *See also* Confederacy.

Classical economics: The theory that economies operate according to natural, self-regulating laws such as supply and demand, and that government intervention should be strictly minimized.

Clerics or clergy: A general term for all members of the Church, including abbots, monks, priests, friars, bishops, archbishops, cardinals, and others.

Colonialism: The control and subjugation by one power, such as a country or empire, over an area made up of those who become dependent upon that power. *See also* Annexation, Colony, Governor, Imperialism.

Colony: A territory taken, usually by force, and occupied by peoples of a different, usually distant nation—in the nineteenth century, mostly countries of Western Europe. *See also* Colonialism, Governor.

Commerce: The exchange and buying and selling of commodities, usually on a large scale and between multiple locations. The eighteenth and nineteenth centuries witnessed a rapid increase in commerce because of rising trade between countries and regions of the world, mostly by sea. *See also* Colonialism, Commodity, Consumption.

Commodity: Any good that circulates as an article of exchange in a money economy. *See also* Commerce, Consumption.

Commoner: One who is not a member of the clergy or of a noble or a royal family. *See also* Peasant, Serf.

Confederacy: A confederation or alliance of groups or countries; when capitalized, this term generally refers to the Confederate States of America, which sought independence from the United States of America between 1860 and 1865. *See also* Civil war.

Congregational: Of or relating to the Protestant churches that developed in seventeenth century England, which affirmed the critical importance and autonomy of local congregations. Final authority in church matters rested with each congregation. "Congregationalism" is the practice of those who believe in Congregational administration and worship. *See also* Episcopacy, Presbyterian, Protestantism.

Congregationalists: Christian denomination descended from the Puritans, emphasizing the governing authority of each congregation; during the nineteenth century, various congregations evolved in a variety of generally liberal ways.

Congress system: Diplomatic system established by Great Britain, Prussia, Austria, and Russia in Vienna following the defeat of France in 1814-1815, relying upon consultation among the great powers regarding any territorial changes and emphasizing balance of power and the rule of legitimate dynastic families; France was readmitted to the status of power in 1818.

Conservatism: The nineteenth century political ideology based upon the ideas of English philosopher Edmund Burke, who argued that all historical situations are unique and should be evaluated accordingly and that change should be incremental and rooted in accepted norms and practices.

Consort: A spouse; when used in conjunction with a royal title, "consort" becomes the title of a royal spouse: queen consort, prince consort, and so forth.

Constitution: Generally, a written exposition of governing structures, principles, and protections, and one of the chief hallmarks of nineteenth century political liberalism; the British constitution, however, was not written, being the collective laws, practices, and customs related to governance.

Constitutional monarchy: *See* Limited (constitutional) monarchy.

Consulate: In France, a form of government replacing the Directory, which lasted until 1804. Napoleon was invited to join the Third Consul but soon became First Consul.

Consumption: The process of satisfying wants and desires through purchasing and using goods and services. The use of these goods results in their transformation, deterioration, or destruction, which ensures that individuals will continue to purchase new goods, thereby maintaining an economy. *See also* Commerce, Commodity.

Continental Divide: The geologically elevated line dividing the primary watersheds of North America; although there are several continental divides, this Great Divide runs from Alaska in the north to Central America, roughly along the Rocky Mountains and the Sierra Madre Oriental, separating the waters that eventually drain into either the Pacific or the Atlantic Ocean.

Corn Laws: Import tariffs imposed in 1815 in order to maintain the high wheat prices that had evolved out of the period of Napoleonic Wars (1799-1815); while the tariffs protected British farmers, they also raised the price of bread and eventually led to a split in the Tory Party during the 1840's.

Cossack: The term "cossack" comes from the Turkic for "free warriors." The Cossacks, frontier warriors in southern Russia, lived as free persons. Slaves and peasants fleeing serfdom often would join them. *See also* Hetman, Peasant, Serf.

Costumbrismo **movement:** A literary and artistic movement emphasizing daily life, manners, and customs; originating in Spain, it spread throughout the Latin American world during the nineteenth century.

Cotton gin (engine): A mechanical device built to separate cotton fibers from the hull, thus speeding the processing of raw cotton; developed in 1792 by Eli Whitney, it was continually improved throughout the nineteenth century.

Count: From the Latin *comes* (companion) and the Middle French *comte*, the French or continental equivalent of an earl. The office became a noble title, ranked below duke.

Coup d'état: The armed overthrow of a government by its own army.

Creed: A formal statement of belief, often religious or theological.

Creole: A person of Spanish descent born in the New World. *See also* Indigenous, Mestizo.

Crimea: The large peninsula extending into the northern Black Sea; during the nineteenth century, part of Russia and site of the majority of fighting during the Crimean War (1853-1856); now part of the modern state of Ukraine.

Crown: Referring to the sovereign authority of a king, queen, czar, emperor, or empress. *See also* Czar.

Czar: A Russian or other Slavic emperor. The word "czar" is derived from the Roman title "caesar" and suggests a ruler of equal stature to the emperors of imperial Rome.

Daguerreotype: An early type of photograph developed by Frenchman J. M. Daguerre during the 1830's.

Daimyo: Great territorial lords in Japan. *See also* Samurai, Shogun.

Dardanelles: The narrow waterway connecting the Aegean Sea and the Sea of Marmara. *See also* Bosporus, Straits.

Darwinism: *See* Evolution, Social Darwinism.

Decadent movement: A literary and artistic movement of Central and Western Europe, emphasizing artistic artifice and the inherently diseased or decaying condition of life; during the late nineteenth century, the Decadents provided stinging critiques of hierarchical and bourgeois society, especially in England, France, and Germany. *See also* Aesthetic movement.

Deccan: The region of India between the Narmada and Krishna Rivers.

Devshirme: A levy of Christian boys, enslaved for training and recruitment to serve in various parts of the administration of the Ottoman Empire. The recruits formed the Janissary corps and also served in the sultan's household. *See also* Janissaries, Sultan.

Diaspora: The collective worldwide population of a particular ethnic or cultural group after their displacement from their homeland after war or other means of oppression. *See also* Immigration.

Diesel engines: A type of internal combustion engine developed during the 1890's by German engineer Rudolf Diesel. *See also* Internal combustion engine.

Diocese: The basic administrative and territorial unit of the Catholic Church. Each diocese is governed by a bishop. *See also* Cathedral, Catholicism.

Diphtheria: A highly contagious bacterial respiratory disease prevalent during the nineteenth century.

Direct representation: The selection of representatives to an assembly by citizens who vote directly for the delegates who will represent them.

Dissenters: Members of non-Anglican Protestant denominations in England, formally prohibited from serving in Parliament or taking degrees at Oxford and Cambridge, though compromises were reached throughout the century.

Divine right: The concept that God bestowed upon kings the right to rule.

Dogma: The body of beliefs and doctrines formally held and sanctioned by a church.

Domestic system of textile production: An economic system in which agents distribute wool, yarn, or other products used to manufacture textiles to laborers working in their homes; the laborers then spin yarn or weave cloth in anticipation of the return of the agent who will transport the finished product. *See also* Putting-out system.

Dominion: A self-governing, white settlement colony within the British empire that recognizes the authority of the British monarch.

Duke, duchess: From Roman *dux*, a governor, especially of a military jurisdiction; later, a member of the nobility who was lord over several counties (headed by "counts"), who could pass the title duke or duchess to offspring. *See also* Count.

Dynamite: An explosive utilizing nitroglycerin, developed by Swedish chemist Alfred Nobel in the 1860's.

Dynastic state: A state organized under the rule of a royal family perceived to have legitimate rule over a particular territory—at odds with the organizing principle of nationalism that gained strength throughout the nineteenth century.

Dynasty: A line of rulers who succeed one another based on their familial relationships. *See also* Colonialism, Colony, Dynastic state, Empire.

Eastern Orthodox Church: A group of self-governing national churches in Eastern Europe and the Balkan Peninsula that split from the Roman Catholic Church in 1054. While the patriarch, or leader, of each branch of Orthodoxy is ranked hierarchically in relation to the others, each branch is essentially self-governing, and the relationship among the various branches is that of a loose federation. *See also* Catholicism, Christianity.

Ecclesiastical: Of or relating to a church.

Edict: An order, command, or proclamation with legal authority.

Emancipation: The process of freeing or of becoming free or equal; for the nineteenth century it most often refers to the freeing of slaves in the West, the ending of serfdom in Russia, and gaining of legal equality by Catholics in Great Britain.

Emigration: The leaving or moving out of people from a region or country to settle permanently elsewhere. *See also* Immigration.

Emir: A general title given to Islamic military commanders, rulers, and governors.

Empire: A large realm, ruled by an emperor or empress, which consists of previously distinct political units joined together under a ruler's central authority. *See also* Colonialism, Colony, Dynasty.

Empresario: An agent who received a land grant from the Spanish or Mexican government in return for settling subjects there.

Enclosure: The consolidation of common lands by British landlords to make agriculture work more efficiently; it usually required an act of Parliament.

Enlightened despotism: Rule by absolute monarchs who embraced reason and progressive reforms as means of improving their societies but who refused to accept the enlightened doctrine that sovereignty resides in the people; during the nineteenth century, this concept increasingly came under attack from proponents of liberalism. *See also* Divine right, Enlightenment.

Enlightenment: A European worldview progressively developed during the eighteenth and early nineteenth centuries that rejected divine revelation and a fixed religious and social order in favor of reason, the social contract theory of government, and the desirability and potential of human progress.

Entrepreneur: One who takes risks in business with the hope of making a profit. *See also* Laissez-faire.

Episcopacy: A system of church governance in which the bishops hold all authority. *See also* Congregational, Presbyterian, Protestantism.

Era of Good Feelings: In the United States, the period between 1815 and 1824, marked by the absence of serious political party divisions and a focus on nationalism and economic development.

Established church: Any church given special legal protections by a government and supported in part by public taxes.

Eugenics: A social philosophy advocating various forms of intervention (selective breeding, sterilization, gene therapy) to produce healthier human traits; during the nineteenth century this philosophy formed a pseudo-scientific basis for racism and other types of discrimination.

Evangelicalism: A conservative movement within Christianity that emphasizes personal salvation through belief in the atoning work of Jesus Christ and a commitment to sharing that message with others who are unredeemed.

Evolution: The scientific theory that all life rose from a single source, developing separate species across long periods of time according to Charles Darwin's theory of natural selection: the tendency for organisms with the most adaptable traits to survive, reproduce, and pass those traits to offspring. *See also* Social Darwinism.

Exclusion: The process or state of omitting or not allowing entrance. Prior to 1882, the United States had an open immigration policy, but in that year passed the first measure—the Chinese Exclusion Act—to prohibit a specific ethnic group from entering the country.

Exposition: *See* World's fair.

Fabians: British socialists who pursued education of the electorate to effect socialist changes, rejecting violence and revolution.

Famine: The absence of adequate food resources, leading to widespread starvation, disease, and death; famines killed tens of millions of people in China and India during the nineteenth century, while the Great Potato Famine of 1845-1849 led to a million deaths in Ireland and mass migration to England, Canada, and the United States. *See also* Potato blight.

Fatwa: A legal opinion or ruling issued by an Islamic legal scholar, or mufti. *See also* Imam, Mufti.

Free-Soil Party: Comprising largely antislavery U.S. Democrats after failure of the Wilmot Proviso in 1846, this group merged with the Republican Party during the mid-1850's.

Free trade: The unrestricted exchange of goods with few or no tariffs. *See also* Commerce, Commodity.

Freedmen: Former slaves freed during the U.S. Civil War and protected by Reconstruction-era civil rights legislation. *See also* Civil rights, Civil war, Reconstruction.

Fugitive slave laws: Laws passed by the U.S. Congress before the Civil War to provide for the return of escaped slaves; a particularly stringent fugitive slave law was passed as part of the Compromise of 1850, establishing commissioners with special jurisdiction and imposing fines on those who refused to comply with the law.

Gatling gun: The first machine gun significantly used in war, introduced in the U.S. Civil War; it required hand cranking but loaded automatically and could fire at a rate of more than one thousand rounds per minute. *See also* Machine gun, Maxim gun.

Genetics: The study of genes and their role in hereditary variation; in 1865, the monk Gregor Mendel published the results of his study of flower color in pea plants, which led in 1900 to the beginnings of modern

genetics when researchers rediscovered and followed up on his work.

Genocide: The attempt to destroy an entire ethnic or racial group.

Gentry: Landholding families ranked just below the aristocracy in terms of social status. *See also* Aristocracy, Noble.

Germ theory: The once controversial theory that microorganisms cause disease, supported in the nineteenth century by the work of Louis Pasteur, John Snow, and others.

German Confederation: A decentralized collection of thirty-nine German states established in 1806 from the remnants of the Holy Roman Empire. Until 1866 Austria and Prussia vied for control of the German Confederation, with Prussia gaining supremacy by its victory that year in the Austro-Prussian War.

Gold Coast: Coastal area of West Africa, corresponding roughly with the coast of modern-day Ghana. *See also* Ivory Coast, Transatlantic slave trade.

Gold rushes: Sudden influxes of miners and service providers to areas where large deposits of gold were discovered; significant gold rushes occurred in California (1848-1849), Australia (1851), South Africa (1886), and the Canadian Klondike (1897-1899).

Gothic: A style of European architecture between the twelfth and sixteenth centuries, especially, characterized by ornateness, strong vertical lines, and pointed arches. The Gothic style strongly influenced artists and architects in the nineteenth century.

Governor: The proxy representative of an emperor or central government who rules over a colony or an imperial territory. *See also* Colonialism, Colony, Empire.

Grand duke: The ruler of a sovereign territory called a grand duchy.

Grand prince: The ruler of a Russian city-state. *See also* Czar.

Gujarat: A region of western India.

Habsburg Dynasty: The hereditary ruling family of the Austrian Empire between 1278 and 1918, and usually also of the Holy Roman Empire until its dissolution in 1806; their rule was lost as a result of defeat in World War I.

Hadith: A tradition or commentary related to the life or teachings of Muḥammad, used with varying degrees of authority as guides to the application of teachings found in the Qu'rān. *See also* Islam.

Hanoverian Dynasty: The hereditary ruling family of

the British Empire between 1714 and 1901; Queen Victoria (r. 1837-1901) was the last of the British Hanoverian monarchs.

Hegelianism: The philosophical system of Georg Wilhelm Friedrich Hegel, supporting the concept that all aspects of reality can be expressed in rational terms; important in the development of Marxist philosophy. *See also* Marxism.

Hetman: A Cossack leader. *See also* Cossack.

Hinduism: The collective term used by Europeans to denote the variety of Indian beliefs and ritual practices.

Hohenzollerns: The hereditary ruling family of Brandenburg-Prussia (1415-1918) and the German Empire (1871-1918); their rule was lost as a result of defeat in World War I.

Holy Roman Empire: A loosely organized state established during the ninth century, incorporating most of the German and northern Italian states and dominated by Austria (Habsburg Dynasty). During the Napoleonic Wars, the Holy Roman Empire was abolished (1806), and its more than three hundred principalities were consolidated into thirty-nine larger states, banded together in the decentralized German Confederation.

Home rule: Control of most or all domestic political matters by a dependency; in the nineteenth century, the British government granted home rule—or responsible self-government, as it was sometimes called—to most white settlement colonies, but failed to pass a similar measure for Ireland. *See also* Imperialism, Responsible government.

Homesteading: Settlement of an undeveloped piece of land, usually with the expectation of gaining free or inexpensive land; in the nineteenth century many nations used homestead laws to encourage agriculturalists to settle in remote or undeveloped regions.

House: A royal or noble family. *See also* Aristocracy, Dynasty, Empire.

House of Commons: The lower house of the British parliament, comprising representatives elected by the most wealthy citizens in the country. *See also* Aristocracy, House of Lords, Parliament.

House of Lords: The upper house of the British parliament, comprising "peers" representing the aristocratic families of the land. *See also* Aristocracy, House of Commons, Parliament.

Idealism: A philosophical approach that suggests that reality is primarily found in the mind, rather than in physical circumstances.

Imam: An Islamic religious and political leader. Also, an Islamic ruler in East Africa. In the Shīʿite tradition, the imam is a perfect guide for the people and can be appointed only by Allah. *See also* Caliph, Fatwa, Sultan, Ulama.

Immigration: The voluntary influx of people into a country not of their birth or citizenship, usually for the purpose of gaining economic opportunities or personal freedoms. *See also* Diaspora, Emigration.

Imperialism: Imposed rule over a people or country not in the ruling nation's jurisdiction. European nations, the United States, and Japan became increasingly imperialistic after 1880. *See also* Annexation, Colonialism.

Impressionism: A late nineteenth century style of painting characterized by extensive use of light, treatment of ordinary themes, and use of visible brushstrokes. *See also* Post-Impressionism.

Indigenous: A person or thing native to a particular region. "Indigenous" has replaced the terms "Indian" or "American Indian" in many contexts that refer to the early peoples of the Americas. *See also* Creole, Mestizo.

Industrial Revolution: The mechanization of Western economies that began with textile production in Britain during the second half of the eighteenth century and continued throughout the nineteenth century. *See also* Agricultural Revolution.

Influenza: One of a group of infectious viral diseases that spread rapidly, causing regional and global epidemics that during the nineteenth century killed millions of people.

Internal combustion engine: An engine that burns (usually fossil) fuel in a confined space to produce energy. *See also* Diesel engine, Steam engine.

Invisible hand: A term used by Adam Smith to illustrate the natural law of supply and demand, which works to allocate resources in a given market; understood in the nineteenth century as the basis for free trade policies.

Irredenta: An area outside a state's borders, claimed on the basis of common ethnicity with the population; irredentist areas become points of international contention in periods of heightened nationalism.

Islam: The religion founded by the Prophet Muḥammad, which, after his death in 632, began to spread throughout the world and contribute to intellectual advancement and the blending of the arts. A person who practices Islam is a Muslim. *See also* Catholicism, Christianity, Jihad, Judaism, Muslim, Protestantism.

Ivory Coast: The coastal area of West Africa corresponding roughly with the coast of the modern-day republic of Côte d'Ivoire. *See also* Gold Coast, Transatlantic slave trade.

Janissaries: From the Turkish for "new corps" or "new soldier," an elite corps of non-Muslim children, usually Christians from the Balkans, recruited as slaves of the sultan in the eighteenth and nineteenth centuries. The Janissaries played a key role in the rise of the Ottoman Empire, with some holding high governmental positions. The corps eventually declined in significance beginning in the early eighteenth century. *See also* Devshirme.

Jihad: A holy "war" waged by Muslims against those who do not follow Islam, considered by many Muslims a duty imposed by holy law. *See also* Fatwa, Islam.

Jim Crow laws: State and local laws enacted in the American South after Reconstruction to limit the civil rights of freed slaves. *See also* Civil rights, Reconstruction.

Judaism: The religion characterized by belief in one transcendent God who has revealed himself to Abraham, Moses, and the Hebrew prophets. Judaism is practiced in accordance with Scriptures and rabbinic traditions. *See also* Catholicism, Christianity, Eastern Orthodox Church, Islam, Protestantism.

Judicial review: An implied constitutional power by which federal (U.S.) courts review and determine the constitutionality of acts passed by Congress and state legislatures. *See also* Separation of powers.

Kabuki: A popular Japanese drama developed in the seventeenth century by Izumo no Okuni, which combines song, dance, and other varieties of performance. Elaborate, detailed, and ornately costumed and designed, Kabuki plays are based not only on legends and myths but also on historical subjects.

Kinetoscope: An early version of the motion-picture projector. *See also* Vitascope.

King: A male monarch who ruled a large region and under whom ruled subordinate lords. A king's title was usually hereditary and most often for life. *See also* Czar, Dynasty, Empire, Queen, Sultan.

Knights of Labor: One of the earliest successful labor unions in the United States, founded in 1869 and characterized by open membership not restricted by skill level, trade, gender, or race. *See also* Labor union, Trade(s) union.

Know-Nothings: A secretive U.S. political movement of the 1850's, organized in response to massive immigration, and particularly to the role of Irish immigrants in the Democratic Party; its antislavery elements generally merged with the Republican Party from 1856.

Ku Klux Klan: White supremacist organization founded by former Confederates in 1866 to oppose the civil rights measures afforded to freed slaves during Reconstruction. *See also* Civil rights, Confederacy, Reconstruction.

Kulturkampf: The "culture struggle" waged by Otto von Bismarck to strengthen the power of the new unified German state at the expense of the Roman Catholic Church; most prominent between 1871 and 1878.

Labor union: A voluntary association of laborers, organized for the purpose of enhancing work conditions or benefits by collective action. *See also* Knights of Labor, Strike, Trade(s) union.

Laissez-faire: French phrase meaning "allow to do." In economics the doctrine of minimal government interference in the working of an economy. *See also* Commerce, Entrepreneur.

Lamarckianism: A theory based on the work of Jean-Baptiste Lamarck (1744-1829) suggesting that individual organisms (plants and animals, including humans) could pass acquired traits to offspring through inheritance; the theory was debunked and superseded by the work of Charles Darwin, Gregor Mendel, and later geneticists. *See also* Evolution, Genetics.

Land-grant colleges: Colleges and universities in the United States funded by grants of federal lands to the states, initially by the provisions of the Morrill Act of 1862; designed to provide education in agriculture, mechanics, military, and other "practical" arts.

Liberalism: A dominant political ideology of the nineteenth century, founded upon individualism and free trade, favoring representative government, rule of law, and written constitutions.

Limited (constitutional) monarchy: A system of government in which the powers of the monarch are subject to legislation passed by representative assemblies. *See also* House of Commons, House of Lords, Parliament, Separation of powers.

Low Countries: Informally used in the nineteenth century to refer to the Netherlands, Belgium, and Luxembourg, though historically covering the broad, low-lying regions near the coastal areas of the Rhine, Scheldt, and Meuse Rivers.

Luddites: English opponents of the free market economy and the growing influence of machinery, known for destroying textile machinery between 1811 and 1813.

Machine gun: A firearm with fully or partially automatic features; the manually cranked Gatling gun was introduced as an important weapon during the U.S. Civil War. *See also* Civil war, Gatling gun, Maxim gun.

Mahdi: The prophesied redeemer of Islam; more specifically, the title taken by Muhammad Ahmad in the Sudan during the 1880's and 1890's.

Mail-order trade: The buying and selling of goods by mail; although practiced to a small degree in the eighteenth century, the mail-order trade did not become widespread until after the mid-nineteenth century, when communication and transportation technologies enhanced profitability.

Malaria: A debilitating, infectious disease occurring mainly in tropical regions; it proved to be a temporary barrier to European imperial expansion during the nineteenth century.

Mamlūks: Originally non-Muslim slaves who were converted and specially trained to serve the Ottoman sultan; they formed an elite military caste that challenged Ottoman and Egyptian rule in the nineteenth century.

Manifest destiny: The belief, commonly held in the United States during the expansionistic 1830's and 1840's, that God or fate had predetermined America's greatness and thus established a basis for expansion into Mexican, Native American, and other territories.

Maoris: The indigenous peoples of New Zealand, descended from Polynesian settlers.

Maroon: A runaway or rebellious slave. More specifically, a member of a community of runaway slaves in the West Indies and South America.

Marxism: A political ideology founded by Karl Marx and Friedrich Engels in the 1840's, based upon concepts of class struggle, material reality, and ultimate worldwide revolution of the proletariat (workers) against the owners and managers of capital; the foundation of modern socialist and communist political movements. *See also* Socialism, Utopian socialism.

Maxim gun: The first fully automatic machine gun, introduced by Britain during the 1880's. *See also* Gatling gun, Machine gun.

Mecca: An Arabian city and spiritual capital of the Islamic world; the Qu'rān requires that all Muslims who have sufficient wealth make at least one pilgrimage to Mecca.

Meiji Restoration: The 1868 restoration of the authority of the emperor in Japan after 265 years of rule by the Tokugawa shoguns; more generally indicates the beginning of economic and social modernization in Japan. *See also* Tokugawas.

Mennonites: A communitarian Protestant sect committed to nonviolence and pacifism; thousands of Mennonites immigrated to the United States and Canada from various parts of Europe during the nineteenth century, primarily in search of religious tolerance.

Mestizo: In Spanish America, a person of mixed Spanish and indigenous ancestry. *See also* Creole, Indigenous.

Methodism: A pietistic movement within the Church of England led by the brothers John and Charles Wesley, which developed into a separate denomination late in the eighteenth century. *See also* Anglican, Pietism, Protestantism.

Metis: The descendants of seventeenth and eighteenth century relationships between mainly indigenous women and French Canadian and Scottish men; by the nineteenth century a distinct Metis ethnicity had emerged in Western Canada, challenging efforts to unify Canada.

Mfecane: An African term roughly meaning "the crushing," used to designate the tumultuous period of rapid Zulu expansion throughout parts of southern Africa between about 1815 and 1835.

Militia: Nonmilitary citizens organized to provide paramilitary services.

Minstrelsy: A form of entertainment popular in the United States during the nineteenth century, including songs, skits, dances, and comedy, often performed in blackface. *See also* Vaudeville.

Mission: A colonial ministry whose task is to convert indigenous peoples to Christianity. *See also* Catholicism, Christianity, Colonialism, Indigenous, Mission system, Missionary.

Mission system: A chain of missions (usually centered on compounds that included a church, housing, and gardens) established by Spain in the American Southwest to convert indigenous peoples to Catholicism. *See also* Catholicism, Christianity, Colonialism, Indigenous.

Missionary: An agent of the Catholic or other Christian church commissioned to travel to a colony or other "distant" location to gain converts from among indigenous populations. *See also* Catholicism, Christianity, Colonialism, Indigenous, Mission.

Missouri Compromise (1820): A complicated agreement between proslavery and antislavery forces in the

United States, admitting Maine to the Union as a free state and Missouri as a slave state and dividing the remainder of the Louisiana Purchase territory between areas that would remain free and areas that were or could become slaveholding.

Modernism: A late nineteenth century artistic and aesthetic style characterized by fragmentation, abstraction, dissonance, decadence, and experimentation; elements were adopted throughout the arts, including painting, sculpting, music, poetry, and literature.

Monastery: A place where monks or nuns lived a religious life, frequently including a chapter house for meetings as well as sleeping quarters and various other facilities depending on the work of the monastery.

Monroe Doctrine: The 1823 declaration by President James Monroe that the Western Hemisphere was no longer open to European colonization, aimed at curbing the possible restoration of Spanish and Portuguese influence in Central and South America and tacitly supported by Great Britain.

Monsoon: Strong and predictable seasonal winds in the Indian Ocean that enabled merchants to engage in regular trade between South Asia and the east coast of Africa.

Mormons: The common name for members of the Church of Jesus Christ of Latter-day Saints, a Christian religious sect established by Joseph Smith in upstate New York in 1830; considered heretical by most orthodox Christian denominations because of the sect's belief in a new revelation in the Book of Mormon and the early church's practice of polygamy. Mormons were attacked, and they eventually trekked to Utah under the leadership of Brigham Young in the 1840's.

Morse code: A method developed by Samuel F. B. Morse in the 1830's for transmitting written messages electrically across wires; the code employed a standard set of short and long pulses (dots and dashes), tapped out on a device at the sender's end, to indicate specific letters and numbers. *See also* Telegraph.

Mufti: A specialist in Islamic law who is not a public official but a private scholar who functions as a consultant. *See also* Fatwa, Imam.

Mulatto: In Spanish America, a person of mixed African and European descent. *See also* Creole, Indigenous, Mestizo.

Muslim: One who practices the religion of Islam. *See also* Islam.

Mysticism: The practice within many religious faiths, including Christianity and Islam, which emphasizes the nonrational, spiritual, and felt rather than intellectual aspects of religious truth as an emotional or transcendent experience. *See also* Quietism, Sufism.

Nationalism: One of the dominant ideologies of the nineteenth century, based on the doctrine that ethnic or historical unity is the soundest basis for state organization; the rise of nationalism worked against the dynastic state structure that was common throughout central and eastern Europe at the beginning of the nineteenth century and, along with colonialism, transformed the world geopolitically by the beginning of the twentieth century. *See also* Colonialism.

Nativism: A strong mistrust of ethnic, religious, or political minorities within one's own culture; massive immigration into the United States, Canada, Argentina, and other Western Hemispheric countries led to a variety of nativist movements in these countries during the nineteenth century. *See also* Immigration, Know-Nothings.

Natural rights: As part of enlightened thought, an understanding that all human beings possessed rights such as life, liberty, property, freedom of speech and religion, and equality before the law, simply by virtue of their humanity; a foundation of nineteenth century liberalism. *See also* Enlightenment.

Naturalism: An artistic style emphasizing an extremely precise realistic portrayal of an object as it appears in nature, emphasizing the importance of environment in shaping one's reality. *See also* Realism.

Nawab: A semiautonomous Muslim prince who cooperated with British colonialists in British India.

Neoclassicism: An aesthetic approach based upon Greek and Roman models, emphasizing balance and order. Neoclassicism developed during the eighteenth century in response to the ornamentation of the Baroque period.

Nobel Prizes: Annual awards established in 1895 through the bequest of Alfred B. Nobel, Swedish inventor of dynamite, to promote discoveries from all nations in physics, chemistry, medicine, literature, and peace; the first awards were made in 1901.

Noble: A member of the landed aristocracy. *See also* Aristocracy, Gentry.

Nullification: The legal concept that a state within the United States of America has the authority to declare a federal measure unconstitutional; the issue was settled substantially but not finally in favor of federal authority during the nullification crisis of 1832-1833.

Old Believers: Conservative members of the Russian Orthodox Church who were labeled dissidents for opposing church reforms; by the late nineteenth century they comprised about one quarter of Russian Christians. *See also* Eastern Orthodox Church, Patriarch.

Open door policy: An international policy recognizing equal access to free commercial transactions in a region, usually as a pretext for the extension of imperial influence; though suggested as applying generally throughout the colonial world during the nineteenth century, the term most often refers to the accepted international policy toward China proposed by U.S. secretary of state John Hay in 1899-1900. *See also* Imperialism.

Orthodox Church: A type of Eastern Catholicism that formally broke with the Roman Catholic Church in the eleventh century, organizing itself along national rather than international lines; prominent Eastern Orthodox churches developed in Russia, Greece, and Serbia.

Ottomans: Turkish rulers of large parts of the Islamic world from the thirteenth century until 1922. Their conquest in 1453 of the seat of the Byzantine Empire and Eastern Christian Orthodoxy, Constantinople, marked their ascendant power. The Ottoman Empire was a significant geopolitical entity during the eighteenth and nineteenth centuries, waning in the latter part of the nineteenth century. *See also* Islam, Safavids, Sultan.

Palatinate: A county or principality ruled by a lord whose rights included those of a king, such as the right to coin money or appoint judges. Also, in Germany, the proper name of a principality. *See also* Palatine.

Palatine: The lord of a palatinate or a resident of the (German) Palatinate. *See also* Palatinate.

Pan-American congresses: Meetings of many states of the Western Hemisphere to address common problems; one met in Panama in 1826, but was not attended by the United States because of divisions over slavery; eighteen American states, including the United States, attended the first International Conference of American States which met in Washington, D.C.

Panic: A fear of economic instability similar to a depression; panics became more common in the nineteenth century as industrialization and accumulation of capital spread.

Papal infallibility: The doctrine that Papal statements on faith and morals are without error and binding on all Roman Catholics; formally proclaimed at the Vatican Council in 1870.

Papal States: Until 1870, a sovereign Italian city-state, which was based in Rome and ruled by the pope and served as the spiritual seat of his papacy; after 1870 the papal territory was reduced to the tiny Vatican City, also sovereign. *See also* Catholicism, Pope.

Paris Commune: The socialist government that briefly ruled in Paris between March and May, 1871, in the aftermath of France's defeat at the hands of Germany.

Parliament: An assembly of representatives, usually a mix of nobles, clergy, and commoners, which functions as a legislative body serving under the sovereignty of a monarch. *See also* House of Commons, House of Lords.

Paşa: The highest title of rank or honor in the Ottoman Empire. The title evolved to include governors of foreign territories and viziers of a domestic government. *See also* Ottomans, Sultan, Vizier.

Pasteurization: A process for heating food in order to destroy harmful bacteria and other organisms; named for French chemist Louis Pasteur, who perfected the process in the 1860's.

Patriarch: The head of one of the self-governing branches of the Eastern Orthodox Church. *See also* Catholicism, Eastern Orthodox Church, Pope.

Patron: One who financially or materially supports an artist, composer, poet, or other creative individual.

Patronage: The practice of awarding titles and making appointments to government and other positions to gain political support.

Peasant: The lowest rank of commoner, who works the land in order to subsist. *See also* Aristocracy, Commoner, Noble, Serf.

Peninsulares: Persons born in Spain who settled in the New World.

Penny press: Inexpensive tabloid newspapers that became possible in the mid-nineteenth century because of improvements in mechanized printing and papermaking.

Periodic table of elements: A systematic, tabular method of displaying the chemical elements according to several of their properties, such as atomic weight; first proposed by Russian chemist Dmitry Mendeleyev in the 1860's.

Persia: A term used by Westerners until the early twentieth century to describe the region always known to Iranians as Iran.

Pietism: A way of Christian worship and belief that promoted religion of the heart rather than of the mind.

Pietism is closely associated with the rise of Methodism. *See also* Methodism.

Pilgrimage: A journey to a sacred shrine by Christians seeking to show their piety, fulfill vows, or gain absolution for sins. Other religions also have pilgrimage traditions, such as the pilgrimage to Mecca by Muslims, the pilgrimages made by early Chinese Buddhists to India, and the pilgrimages made by Jews to the Holy Land. *See also* Christianity, Islam.

Plantation economy: An economic system organized for producing cash crops such as sugar, cotton, tobacco, rice, coffee, and tea, and most commonly utilizing slave labor. *See also* Commerce, Transatlantic slave trade.

Political economy: The branch of knowledge related to the relationship between economies and knowledge.

Pony Express: A system of horse riders and stations that enabled mail to be carried rapidly from the Missouri River to the Pacific Ocean in 1860 and 1861; it declined with the advent of the telegraph, the rapid development of transcontinental railways, and competition from coach-borne services.

Pope: The spiritual leader of the Roman Catholic Church and temporal ruler of the Papal States. *See also* Catholicism, Christianity, Papal States, Patriarch.

Populism: A political ideology based upon the premise that the interests of the masses are best served when common men (and sometimes women) are given access to the political process; populism spawned the People's Party in the United States in the 1890's.

Positivism: A philosophy recognizing scientific knowledge as the only acceptable basis for understanding; Auguste Comte, who developed positivism, suggested that scientific explanations for phenomena superseded the supernatural and metaphysical explanations that had been common in earlier ages.

Post-Impressionism: An artistic style named for its reaction to preceding and contemporary Impressionist artists. Post-Impressionists highlighted use of vivid colors, pronounced brushstrokes and heavy layers of paint, and distortion of forms for effect; most often associated with artists including Vincent van Gogh, Paul Cézanne, and Paul Gaugin. *See also* Impressionism.

Potato blight: A water mold known as *Phytophthora infestans* that frequently caused failure in potato crops across Europe during the eighteenth and nineteenth centuries; it was the cause of the Great Potato Famine of 1845-1849 in Ireland.

Pre-Raphaelite Brotherhood: An artistic reform movement founded in England in 1848 that rejected mechanistic approaches to painting.

Presbyterian: A Protestant Christian church that is mostly Calvinistic in doctrine. "Presbyterianism" is a system of church governance favored as more democratic than Episcopalianism because it is characterized by a graded system of representative ecclesiastical bodies. *See also* Calvinism, Catholicism, Christianity, Congregational, Ecclesiastical, Episcopacy, Presbytery, Protestantism.

Presbytery: The ruling body in Presbyterian churches. Also, the part of a church reserved for clergy who officiate. *See also* Clerics or clergy, Presbyterian, Protestantism.

Presidio: In Spanish America, a military post.

Protectorate: A form of imperial control in which native rulers govern their lands with support from a technologically superior country. *See also* Colony, Imperialism, Sphere of influence.

Protestantism: A branch of Christianity, incorporating many different churches, which "protests" and rejects Catholic tradition, especially its doctrine of papal infallibility, and believes instead in a religion of all believers who read the Bible for themselves rather than having it interpreted to them by clergy. *See also* Calvinism, Catholicism, Christianity, Clerics or clergy, Ecclesiastical, Episcopacy, Presbyterian, Quakerism.

Prussia: One of two large and powerful German states (the other being Austria) that vied for influence with the thirty-nine German principalities that existed in 1815 after the Napoleonic Wars; under Otto von Bismarck in the 1860's, Prussia unified all German states except Austria and remained the dominant force in the new German Empire.

Putting-out system: An early system of manufacturing in which merchants furnished households with raw materials that would be processed by workers in their own homes; the system declined throughout Europe as the Industrial Revolution spread during the early decades of the nineteenth century. *See also* Domestic system of textile production, Industrial Revolution.

Qing Dynasty: The last ruling dynasty in China, ruling from 1644 until 1911; China reached its peak under the Qing Dynasty in the late eighteenth century but gradually fell under European and Japanese influence as the nineteenth century progressed. Also known as the Manchu Dynasty.

Quakerism: A Protestant group that began in seventeenth century England and rejected ritualized forms of worship. Traditional Quaker worship services are not led by ordained ministers and do not involve the recitation of a religious creed. Women play a major role in Quakerism, since Quakers believe that men and women are equally suited to preach the word of God. Quaker religious beliefs are egalitarian and humanitarian. *See also* Protestantism.

Queen: A female monarch who rules a large region. A queen's title, unlike that of the king—which was usually hereditary—was often gained upon marriage to a king. Some wives of kings were called "consorts," or "queen consorts," instead of "queens." Also, queens would become "regents" if they lived after the death of their husband-kings and were pronounced virtual rulers during the minority of a monarch to be, usually the queen's son. *See also* Consort, King, Queen-mother, Regent.

Queen-mother: A former queen who is the mother of a current ruler. *See also* Queen, Regent.

Quietism: In religion, quietism refers to a mysticism that teaches, among other things, suppression of the will to obtain spiritual peace and perfection. Politically, quietism is the withdrawn or passive attitude or policy toward world affairs. *See also* Mysticism.

Raison d'état: The concept that the interests of the state ("reasons of state"), rather than moral or philosophical concerns, may justify a course of action.

Rajputs: Members of a Hindu warrior caste from northwest India.

Realism: In art, the attempt to depict objects, human figures, or scenes as they appear in real life, that is, without distortion or stylization; in literature it was characterized by a depiction of ordinary people or events without authorial commentary. *See also* Naturalism.

Realpolitik: A commitment to pursuing realistic or practical political solutions, rather than idealistic or ideological ones.

Reconstruction: The period of political, economic, and social reconstruction of the union following the U.S. Civil War, generally 1865-1877; characterized by military occupation of the South by the North and passage of a number of civil rights measures and programs to assist freed slaves and bring them into political equality, but ineffective in the face of Southern opposition and given up by the federal government by 1877.

Recusant: An English Roman Catholic, especially from the sixteenth century until Catholic emancipation (1828), who refused to obey the teachings of and participate in the services of the Church of England, thereby committing a statutory offense. *See also* Catholicism, Protestantism.

Redshirts: Informal name given to the soldiers of Giuseppe Garibaldi in the 1850's and early 1860's as they fought for Italian unification and independence; the red shirt was easily distinguished in the absence of a more expensive, formal uniform.

Regent: One who temporarily governs in place of a monarch or other ruler when the latter is too young or infirm to govern for himself or herself. Often, a regent is the monarch's mother. *See also* Queen, Queen-mother.

Republic: A political unit not ruled by a monarch, especially one governed by a group of representatives chosen by and responsible to its citizens. *See also* Parliament.

Republican Party: Founded in the United States in 1854 as a coalition between antislavery Whigs, Northern Democrats, and Free-Soilers who sought to limit the extension of slavery; Abraham Lincoln was the first president to be elected as a Republican.

Responsible government: Home rule, or self-government, granted by the British government to various of its colonies. *See also* Home rule.

Revolutions of 1848: A series of liberal revolutions against autocratic rule that broke out across Europe in the wake of revolt in Paris in February, 1848; although many of these uprisings were briefly successful, only the revolution in the Piedmont against Austrian control led to the establishment of a permanent liberal government.

Romanov Dynasty: The hereditary ruling family of Russia from 1613 to 1917 (Oldenburg-Romanov from 1762); the last Romanov czar, Nicholas II, abdicated in 1917 and was executed by the newly installed communist government.

Romanticism: A broad artistic and cultural movement that influenced most Western countries, reaching its peak between 1800 and 1850; decrying the Enlightenment (late eighteenth and early nineteenth century) emphasis on reason, the movement instead valued intuition and emotion, nature, the supernatural, and the unique qualities of the individual.

Royalist: One who favors monarchical government and the power of a ruler. *See also* Divine right, Tory, Whig.

Ṣafavids: An Islamic empire in Iran (Persia), founded in 1501 and ended in 1722. Shī'ite Islam, developed by the early Ṣafavids, continues to be the dominant religion of Iran into the twenty-first century. *See also* Islam.

Samurai: A member of the Japanese warrior caste, especially a warrior who served a daimyo and who subscribed to a strict code of conduct called Bushido. *See also* Bushido, Daimyo, Shogun.

Satire: A literary style that uses wit, sarcasm, humor, irony, parody, and other literary devices to point out human vices, follies, and immorality.

Scientific socialism: *See* Marxism.

Scramble for Africa: The period between 1880 and 1914, when European countries gained control of virtually the entire continent, excepting only Liberia and Abyssinia (Ethiopia); marked by increasingly direct forms of control, rather than simply by economic influence.

Second Empire: The antiparliamentary, imperial regime of French emperor Napoleon III (r. 1852-1870), who was driven from power when Prussia invaded France in 1870.

Second Great Awakening: A great spiritual revival that swept through the United States during the first quarter of the nineteenth century, leading to greater piety, involvement in reform movements, the strengthening of evangelical denominations including Baptists and Methodists, and the creation of new denominations including the Disciples of Christ and the Mormons.

Second Republic: The constitutional republican government in France (1848-1852), formed in the wake of revolution in 1848 and ended by Napoleon III's coup d'état. *See also* Bonapartists.

Secular: Nonreligious, either in content or in context. Thus, "secular" can be a simple antonym of "religious," but it can also refer to members of the clergy who live and act in the public sphere rather than spending their lives in religious seclusion in a monastery or abbey.

Segregation: Social separation of races or ethnic groups, particularly in housing, education, and public facilities; most widely applied to freed slaves in the American South and Jews in Russia during the nineteenth century. *See also* Jim Crow laws, Anti-Semitism.

Separation of powers: Any system of divided governmental powers, advocated by Montesquieu in his *De l'esprit des loix* (1748; *The Spirit of the Laws*, 1750). Influential in the development of the U.S. Constitution. *See also* Direct representation, Judicial review, Limited (constitutional) monarchy, Parliament.

Serf: A peasant bound to the land through contract. Serfs were given a parcel of land on which to live and work, but any surplus they produced was owed to their landlord as rent, tax, or tribute; serfdom was gradually abolished in Europe throughout the nineteenth century. *See also* Commoner, Gentry, Peasant.

Settlement houses: Housing settlements established in poor, urban neighborhoods to enable social workers to assist the poor; these developed generally after 1884, sparked by growing urban populations and rapid increases in immigration.

Settler colony: A colonial territory of a European state, suited by climate and local conditions, for large-scale immigration and settlement according to European patterns; Canada, Australia, and New Zealand were settler colonies in the British Empire. *See also* Dominion.

Sharia: Islamic holy law. *See also* Caliph, Fatwa, Islam, Ulama.

Sharif: A Muslim who claims descent from the Prophet Muḥammad. *See also* Caliph, Imam, Islam.

Shia: The Muslims of the Shīʿite branch of Islam. *See also* Imam, Shīʿite, Sunni.

Shīʿite: The branch of Islam that holds that ʿAlī ibn Abī Ṭālib and the imams are the only rightful successors of the Prophet Muḥammad and that the last imam will someday return. *See also* Imam, Shia, Sunni.

Shintoism: The traditional animistic religion of Japan.

Shogun: A Japanese military ruler. *See also* Bushido, Daimyo, Samurai.

Shogunate system: The system of government in Japan in which the emperor exercised only titular authority while the shoguns (regional military dictators) exercised actual political power.

Sino-: A prefix used in the West and Japan to designate association with China; taken from an early transliteration of China into English.

Sioux: A group of plains Indian tribes of the northern United States and Southern Canada.

Smallpox: A contagious viral disease responsible for killing millions of people around the world; the main disease responsible for the destruction of Native American cultures following the arrival of Europeans in the late fifteenth century; vaccines to protect against smallpox became increasingly common in the West during the nineteenth century.

Social Darwinism: The social theory that Charles Darwin's evolutionary biological ideas, founded upon the doctrine of "survival of the fittest," could also be applied to competing social and national groups. The main promulgator of this notion was social philosopher Herbert Spencer (1820-1903); Darwin himself would recognize that the application of his theory of natural selection to sociological situations made no sense from an evolutionary perspective. *See also* Evolution.

Social reform movements: A variety of Western liberal efforts to provide more just and humane treatment to the poor, handicapped, prisoners, and others without access to sources of wealth and power; the Progressive movement in the United States and temperance movements in many Western countries also emphasized moral purification. *See also* Temperance movements.

Socialism: An economic system in which the major means of economic production are controlled by the people or the state that represents them, rather than by individuals.

Sociology: The academic discipline devoted to the study of human society and social institutions; the term was coined by Frenchman Auguste Comte in the 1830's.

Sphere of influence: A form of imperial control in which the economic interests of a technologically dominant state indirectly influence the governance of a region by an indigenous ruler.

State: An autonomous, self-governing, sovereign political unit. *See also* Parliament.

States' rights: The belief that ultimate political sovereignty rests with state, rather than central, governments; frequently applied in the United States to the Southern belief that federal coercion in a variety of matters was unconstitutional.

Steam engine: An external combustion engine that uses the thermal power of steam to drive machinery; one of the most important industrial developments of the nineteenth century. *See also* Thermodynamics.

Steamships: Ships powered by steam engines, and thus not dependent upon variable wind power.

Straits: The two narrow waterways (Bosporus and Dardanelles) connecting the Black Sea and the Mediterranean Sea; "the Straits question" was of supreme importance throughout the nineteenth century as Russia sought to gain control of these strategic waterways from a weakening Ottoman Empire. *See also* Bosporus, Dardanelles.

Strike: A collective decision by laborers to withhold work from employers in order to gain better work conditions, higher wages, or other concessions; an important tactic of socialist movements. *See also* Socialism.

Succession: The passing of sovereign authority from one person or group to another person or group, or the rules governing that process.

Suffrage: The political right to vote; during the nineteenth century, Western liberal socialist movements generally promoted a broad extension of suffrage to free males, and in some cases to women.

Sufism: Islamic mysticism. A Sufi is one who practices Sufism. *See also* Islam, Mysticism, Quietism.

Sultan: Beginning in the eleventh century, any political and military ruler of an Islamic state or emirate (as opposed to the caliph, the religious authority of the Islamic state). Applied mostly to Ottoman rulers. *See also* Caliph, Ottomans.

Sunni: Muslims who adhere to the orthodox tradition of Islam, which acknowledges the first four caliphs, the religious authorities of Islam, as rightful successors of the Prophet Muḥammad. *See also* Imam, Islam, Shia, Shīʿite.

Suttee: The Indian custom of a wife being burned on the funeral pyre of her deceased husband; never common, the practice was banned by the British in 1829.

Swahili: A Bantu language spoken in coastal East Africa that incorporates many Arabic words.

Symbolism: A late nineteenth century artistic style characterized by subjectivity and symbolic representation of an artist's insight and inner vision.

Tammany Hall: A New York political society originating in the 1790's and dominating city politics from the 1850's through the early twentieth century; closely affiliated with the rising tide of immigration from mid-century.

Tariff: A tax levied on imported goods.

Telegraph: The long-distance, electrical transmission of written messages by wire, most often using a code of dots and dashes. *See also* Morse code.

Temperance movements: Movements organized to limit or prohibit the sale or consumption of alcoholic beverages; although common in many Western countries in the latter part of the nineteenth century, extreme limitations were never the majority view. *See also* Social reform movements.

Textile: Material made from fibers such as wool, cotton, or linen; the spinning and weaving of such fibers became the first widely mechanized industry during the late eighteenth and early nineteenth centuries.

Thermodynamics: The physical laws governing the movement and effect of dynamic energy, and the study of these as a subdiscipline of physics; the discovery and investigation of these principles is associated in the nineteenth century especially with the development of the steam engine. *See also* Steam engine.

Third Republic: The ruling government of France between invasions by Germany in 1870 and 1940; the first sustained and stable republic in France. *See also* Second Empire, Second Republic.

Tokugawas: The family name of the shoguns who ruled Japan between 1603 and 1868. *See also* Meiji Restoration.

Tory: In England, the party that supported royal power in the face of challenges by Parliament. Opposed by the Whigs, and one of the two dominant political parties until the present; during the nineteenth century they were more commonly called the Conservative Party. *See also* Parliament, Royalist, Whig.

Trade(s) union: A voluntary association of laborers, organized by skill or trade, for the purpose of enhancing work conditions or benefits by collective action; in Europe, often they were heavily involved in the political process. *See also* Knights of Labor, Labor union, Strike.

Trail of Tears: Refers to the forced relocation of Native Americans from the southeastern states to Indian Territory (later primarily Oklahoma Territory) between 1830 and 1838 as a result of the Indian Removal Act (1830); the removal led to some four thousand deaths as Native Americans were forced to trek on foot toward their new, unfamiliar home.

Transatlantic slave trade: The trade in slaves, mostly from Africa, that crossed the Atlantic Ocean from and between East Africa, Europe, North America, and South America.

Transcendentalism: A philosophical and cultural movement that originated in New England during the 1830's, suggesting that true spiritualism transcends rational and physical proofs; Ralph Waldo Emerson and Henry David Thoreau were noted Transcendentalists.

Transportation: The British policy from the late eighteenth century to the mid-nineteenth century of shipping persons convicted of the most serious offenses to Australia as an alternative to capital punishment.

Transvaal: The region of southern Africa "beyond the Vaal" River, occupied by Boer settlers in the 1830's and 1840's as British administrators and settlers began to occupy the region around Cape Town. *See also* Boers.

Treaty: An agreement or arrangement, made by negotiation, between nations, especially two nations.

Tributary system: A system in which countries in East and Southeast Asia not under the direct control of empires based in China nevertheless enrolled as tributary states, acknowledging the superiority of the emperors in China in exchange for trading rights or strategic alliances.

Tsar: *See* Czar.

Tuberculosis: An infectious bacterial disease that most commonly affects the lungs and progresses toward death when untreated; the disease afflicted many during the nineteenth century, when it was also called "consumption."

Tweed Ring: William Marcy Tweed and his political associates, who dominated New York politics and systematically looted the New York City treasury between 1860 and Tweed's conviction in 1873. *See also* Tammany Hall.

Typhoid fever: A bacterial disease common in most parts of the world, transmitted through food or water contaminated with human feces.

Uitlanders: The Afrikaans word for "foreigner," used to denote the wave of immigrants who swamped the Transvaal in the wake of the discovery of gold in the Witwatersrand in 1885.

Ulama: Muslim religious scholars who serve as interpreters of Islamic law. *See also* Caliph, Imam, Islam, Sharia.

Umma: The community of all Muslims, as distinguished from kinship affiliations common in early Middle Eastern lands. *See also* Islam.

Underground Railroad: The network of secret routes and safe houses for transporting slaves from the slave-holding states of the U.S. South to freedom in Canada; the most prominent routes crossed Ohio and Indiana, and it is estimated that between thirty thousand and eighty thousand slaves reached freedom by this means.

Unitarian Church: A variety of religious movements that accept the unity of God, as opposed to Christian Trinitarianism; Unitarians in the nineteenth century tended to be rationalists.

Unitarianism: A religious system that teaches the unity of God, as opposed to a Trinitarian godhead; recognizes Jesus as a moral teacher and is generally committed to understanding a kind of humanistic wisdom common to all cultures; prominent in the mid-nineteenth century, but declined rapidly in the twentieth.

Urdu: A Persian-influenced literary form of the Hindi language, written in Arabic characters and widely spoken along the trade routes of southern Asia.

Utilitarianism: A philosophy of ethics that calculates

action based upon the greatest happiness for the greatest number; it was first given coherence by Jeremy Bentham at the end of the eighteenth century and was developed in the nineteenth century by John Stuart Mill.

Utopian socialism: The early and unsuccessful forms of egalitarian and collective social organization designed to produce ideal societies; Karl Marx introduced the term as opposed to his version of "scientific" socialism.

Vatican: The seat of papal authority, Vatican City is a tiny independent state of about 108 acres completely surrounded by Rome, Italy; the term also refers to an important council of 1869-1870, in which the doctrine of papal infallibility was proclaimed.

Vaudeville: A form of American entertainment that included a wide range of acts, including song, dance, acrobatics, animal acts, magic, and lectures; unlike minstrelsy, vaudeville was directed toward mixed audiences among the middle classes and was performed in nondrinking halls designed specially for the entertainments. *See also* Minstrelsy.

Vitascope: The prototype of the modern film projector; developed by Charles Francis Jenkins and Thomas Armat in the 1890's. *See also* Kinetoscope.

Vizier: A title given to high officials of Islamic nations. In the Ottoman Empire beginning around 1453, the viziers were specifically ministers to the sultan. The chief minister was known as the grand vizier, and members of the council who assisted and filled in for the grand vizier were called dome viziers. Use of the title was later expanded to include other important domestic officials, as well as provincial governors. *See also* Caliph, Imam, Islam, Sultan.

Wahhābiism: A fundamentalist branch of Sunni Islam—named for the Wahhābī movement in the Arabia peninsula, beginning in the eighteenth century—that sought to restore the pure form of the religion; adherents were often at odds with the Ottoman government.

Wall Street: The heart of the financial district in lower Manhattan, and home to the first permanent New York Stock Exchange in 1817; more generally refers to American financial markets as a whole.

Whig: In seventeenth century England, a political party opposed to absolute royal authority and favoring increased parliamentary power; one of two dominant political parties through the 1850's, when it combined with philosophic radicals and Conservative free traders to form the modern Liberal Party. *See also* Parliament, Royalist, Tory.

World's fair: The display of a range of internationally manufactured goods, handicrafts, artwork, and inventions in order to promote a nation's commerce, usually lasting several months or years. Also referred to as expositions. There were thirteen officially sanctioned events between 1851 and 1900, including fairs in London (1851), Paris (1867), Philadelphia (1876), Melbourne (1880), and Chicago (1893).

X rays: A form of electromagnetic radiation that could be used in conjunction with photographic techniques to make it possible to see through soft objects such as skin in order to observe underlying hard objects such as bones; first described by German scientist Wilhelm Röntgen in 1895, the use of X rays became the basis of modern medical imaging.

Yellow fever: An acute viral disease of mainly tropical regions, often leading to widespread epidemics.

Yellow journalism: A term frequently used to designate the use of sensationalism by many U.S. newspapers in the 1880's and 1890's, with little professional regard for truth or verification; taken from the cartoon "The Yellow Kid," which appeared in a number of prominent newspapers, including Joseph Pulitzer's *New York World* and William Randolph Hearst's *New York Journal.*

Young Turk movement: A revolutionary movement against the autocratic rule of Abdül Hamid II, who had suspended the Ottoman constitution in 1878; the successful revolt of 1908 did not lead to political consensus among the revolutionaries.

Zen: A Japanese form of Buddhism based on disciplined meditation and closely associated with the samurai code of Bushido. *See also* Bushido, Samurai.

Zionism: A political ideology developed during the 1880's and characterized by a commitment to the creation of a Jewish national state; orthodox Zionists would accept only Palestine as a location, while some romantic Zionists considered locations in Argentina and Uganda. *See also* Anti-Semitism.

Zulu: A Bantu ethnic group of Southern Africa that became the dominant native military state of the region under the leadership of Shaka between 1816 and 1828.

—John Powell

Bibliography

CONTENTS

INTRODUCTION

The past third of a century has seen a remarkable revival in the study of almost every aspect of the nineteenth century, particularly in the West. The bibliography below will provide a good starting point for general areas of research, though it is by no means exhaustive. Emphasis here has been placed on broad studies, rather than narrowly focused monographs or journal articles. More recent works have been preferred to older ones, though many of the best older works are also included.

Of the many general historical resources that are useful in researching nineteenth century themes, two are especially helpful: *The Encyclopedia of World History*, edited by Peter N. Stearns (Boston: Houghton Mifflin, 2001), is a detailed and comprehensive compendium of world events, arranged chronologically and extensively annotated to provide an invaluable reference narrative; it is supported by an exhaustive index and an excellent,

searchable CD-ROM. *The American Historical Association's Guide to Historical Literature*, edited by Mary Beth Norton et al. (3d ed., 2 vols., New York: Oxford University Press, 1995), is the best comprehensive, annotated bibliography available, covering the most important works in all areas of worldwide research—a tall task but one that specialist section editors achieve remarkably well. Though the work is somewhat dated, it is still an essential point of departure for research into unfamiliar areas.

A Note on Databases and Web Sites: Of many organizations promoting the study of nineteenth century culture, see especially the Centre for Nineteenth Century Studies at the University of Sheffield (http://www.c19 .group.Shef.ac.uk); the North American Victorian Studies Association (http://www.cla.purdue .edu/academic/engl/ navsa/index.cfm); the Centre for Nineteenth-Century Studies at Birkbeck College, University of London (http:// www .bbk.ac.uk/eh/research/centreforc19thstudies); the

Nineteenth Century Studies Association (http://www
.msu.edu/~floyd/ncsa/); and the Interdisciplinary Nineteenth Century Studies (http://www.nd.edu/~incshp/).
The most comprehensive set of links to Web sites related
to world history and related public domain documents
for all geographical areas in the nineteenth century is the
Internet Modern History Sourcebook Project: The Long
Nineteenth Century http://www.fordham.edu/halsall/
mod/modsbook3.html. The most extensive searchable
database for English-language materials is ProQuest's
C19: The Nineteenth Century Index, which is linked to
the full-text references it cites. *C19* provides records for
more than 11 million documents, including books and
periodicals found in a variety of printed and microform
editions, including the *Nineteenth Century Short Title
Catalogue* (a union catalog of materials published in all
languages in the English-speaking world, 1801-1900);
The Nineteenth Century from Chadwyck-Healey's ongoing microform project (more than 30,000 titles); *Periodicals Index Online* and *Periodicals Archive Online*
(covering more than 3.5 million articles from more than
nine hundred scholarly journals); the *Wellesley Index to
Victorian Periodicals* (the standard guide to British periodicals of the period, including more than ninety thousand article records); the *British House of Commons Parliamentary Papers*; and *Palmer's Index to the Times*
(1790-1905).

More than one hundred academic discussion networks,
most of which cover nineteenth century topics, can be
found at H-Net (http://www.h-net.org/lists/). Access to
virtually all important Web sites associated with Victorian
organizations, discussion groups, bibliographies, and related materials can be found at one or more of the following sites: Research Resources for Nineteenth Century
Studies (http://www.sciper.leeds.ac.uk/resources/index
.htm) provides an extensive guide to research in nineteenth-century topics, including finding aids; the Victorian Web covers literature, history, and culture and includes links to an extensive array of primary texts (http://
www.victorianweb.org/); the Victorian Research Web includes links to academic journals devoted to nineteenth-
century topics, bibliographies, links to discussion groups,
and an extensive collection of links to related topics (http:/
/victorianresearch.org/); and Research Resources for the
Study of Nineteenth-Century Ireland contains extensive
and wide-ranging resources on both Irish history and culture and the Irish diaspora (http://www.qub.ac.uk/en/socs/
research.htm). For more on Web sites and databases, see
"Electronic Resources" in this volume.

—John Powell

GENERAL STUDIES, SURVEYS, AND REFERENCE WORKS

Abernethy, David B. *The Dynamics of Global Dominance: European Overseas Empires, 1415-1980*.
New Haven, Conn.: Yale University Press, 2000.

Bayly, C. A. *The Birth of the Modern World, 1780-1914*.
Malden, Mass.: Blackwell, 2004.

Belchem, John, and Richard Price, eds. *A Dictionary of
Nineteenth-Century World History*. Malden, Mass.:
Blackwell, 1994.

Cohen, Robin, ed. *The Cambridge Survey of World Migration*. Cambridge, England: Cambridge University
Press, 1995.

Cook, Chris, and John Paxton. *European Political Facts,
1789-1848*. New York: Facts On File, 1981.

De Vries, Leonard. *History as Hot News, 1865-1897:
The Late Nineteenth-Century World as Seen Through
the Eyes of the "Illustrated London News" and the
"Graphic."* New York: St. Martin's Press, 1974.

Farr, James R., ed. *Industrial Revolution in Europe,
1789-1914*. Vol. 9 in *World Eras*. Farmington Hills,
Mich.: Thomson Gale, 2002.

Fiero, Gloria K. *Romanticism, Realism, and the Nineteenth-Century World*. Vol. 5 in *The Humanistic Tradition*. New York: McGraw-Hill Humanities, 2005.

Haywood, John. *Historical Atlas of the Nineteenth-
Century World*. New York: Barnes and Noble, 2002.

Manning, Patrick. *Migration in World History*. New
York: Routledge, 2005.

Norton, Mary Beth, et al., eds. *The American Historical
Association's Guide to Historical Literature*. 3d ed. 2
vols. New York: Oxford University Press, 1995.

Nugent, Walter. *Crossings: The Great Transatlantic Migrations, 1870-1914*. Bloomington: Indiana University Press, 1992.

Parker, Geoffrey, ed. *Hammond Atlas of World History*.
5th ed. Maplewood, N.J.: Hammond, 1999.

Pearson, Raymond. *Longman Companion to European
Nationalism, 1789-1920*. New York: Longman,
1994.

Stearns, Peter N., ed. *The Encyclopedia of World History*. Boston: Houghton Mifflin, 2001.

Thackeray, Frank W., and John E. Findling. *Events That
Changed the World in the Nineteenth Century*. Westport, Conn.: Greenwood Press, 1996.

Thernstrom, Stephan, ed. *Harvard Encyclopedia of
American Ethnic Groups*. Cambridge, Mass.: Belknap Press of Harvard University, 1980.

Walford's Guide to Reference Material: Vol. 1, *Science
and Technology*; Vol. 2, *Social and Historical Sci-*

ences, Philosophy and Religion; Vol. 3, *Generalia, Language and Literature, the Arts.* 7th ed. 3 vols. London: Library Association, 1996-1998.

Wiener, Pete, ed. *Dictionary of the History of Ideas: Studies of Selected Pivotal Ideas.* 5 vols. New York: Charles Scribner's Sons, 1973-1974.

Winks, Robin W., and Joan Neuberger. *Europe and the Making of Modernity, 1815-1914.* New York: Oxford University Press, 2005.

Wintle, Justin, ed. *Makers of Nineteenth Century Culture, 1800-1914.* London: Routledge & Kegan Paul, 1982.

AFRICA

Adamson, Kay. *Political and Economic Thought and Practice in Nineteenth-Century France and the Colonization of Algeria.* Lewiston, N.Y.: E. Mellen Press, 2002.

Alpern, S. B. *Amazons of Black Sparta: The Women Warriors of Dahomey.* New York: New York University Press, 1998.

Barry, Boubacar. *Senegambia and the Atlantic Slave Trade.* Translated by Ayi Kwei Armah. New York: Cambridge University Press, 1998.

Bates, Darrell. *The Fashoda Incident of 1898: Encounter on the Nile.* New York: Oxford University Press, 1984.

Bay, Edna. *Wives of the Leopard: Gender, Politics, and Culture in the Kingdom of Dahomey.* Charlottesville: University Press of Virginia, 1998.

Clancy-Smith, Julia A. *Rebel and Saint: Muslim Notables, Populist Protest, Colonial Encounters (Algeria and Tunisia, 1800-1904).* Berkeley: University of California Press, 1994.

Cooper, Frederick. *From Slaves to Squatters: Plantation Labor and Agriculture in Zanzibar and Coastal Kenya, 1890-1925.* New Haven, Conn.: Yale University Press, 1981.

Cope, Richard. *Ploughshare of War: The Origins of the Anglo-Zulu War of 1879.* Pietermaritzburg: University of Natal Press, 1999.

Dodds, Glen Lyndon. *The Zulus and Matabele: Warrior Nations.* Harrisburg, Pa.: Arms and Armour Press, 1998.

Dugard, Martin. *Into Africa: The Epic Adventures of Stanley and Livingstone.* New York: Broadway Books, 2004.

Edgerton, Robert B. *The Fall of the Asante Empire: The Hundred-Year War for Africa's Gold Coast.* New York: Free Press, 1995.

Fage, J. D. *A History of Africa.* 4th ed. New York: Routledge, 2001.

_____, ed. *The Cambridge History of Africa.* Vols. 5-6. Cambridge, England: Cambridge University Press, 1977, 1985.

Giliomee, Hermann B. *The Afrikaners: Biography of a People.* Charlottesville: University of Virginia Press, 2003.

Hamilton, Carolyn, ed. *The Mfecane Aftermath: Reconstructive Debates in Southern African History.* Bloomington: Indiana University Press, 1996.

Knight, Ian. *The Zulu War: 1879.* Oxford, England: Osprey, 2003.

Lāpiso Dé Delébo. *The Italo-Ethiopian War of 1887-1896: From Dogali to Adwa.* Addis Ababa: Artistic Print Enterprise, 1996.

Le May, G. H. L. *The Afrikaners: A Historical Interpretation.* Oxford, England: Blackwell, 1995.

Manning, Patrick. *Francophone Sub-Saharan Africa, 1880-1985.* New York: Cambridge University Press, 1985.

Nicoll, Fergus. *Sword of the Prophet: The Mahdi of Sudan and the Death of General Gordon.* Stroud, England: Sutton, 2004.

Northrup, David. *Africa's Discovery of Europe, 1450-1850.* New York: Oxford University Press, 2002.

Pakenham, Thomas. *The Scramble for Africa.* New York: Random House, 1991.

Paulin, Christopher M. *White Men's Dreams, Black Men's Blood: African Labor and British Expansionism in Southern Africa, 1877-1895.* Trenton, N.J.: Africa World Press, 2001.

Porch, Douglas. *The Conquest of the Sahara.* New York: Knopf, 1984.

Reader, John. *Africa: A Biography of the Continent.* New York: Vintage, 1999.

Sattin, Anthony. *The Gates of Africa: Death, Discovery, and the Search for Timbuktu.* New York: St. Martin's Press, 2005.

Sheriff, Abdul. *Slaves, Spices, and Ivory in Zanzibar.* Athens: Ohio University Press, 1987.

Thomas, Anthony. *Rhodes: Race for Africa.* New York: Thomas Dunne Books, 1997.

Thompson, Leonard. *The History of South Africa.* 3d ed. New Haven, Conn.: Yale University Press, 2001.

Vandervort, Bruce. *Wars of Imperial Conquest in Africa, 1830-1914.* Bloomington: Indiana University Press, 1998.

Worger, William H. *South Africa's City of Diamonds: Mine Workers and Monopoly Capitalism in Kimber-*

ley, 1867-1895. New Haven, Conn.: Yale University Press, 1987.

Worger, William H., Nancy L. Clark, and Edward A. Alpers, eds. *Africa and the West: A Documentary History from the Slave Trade to Independence*. Phoenix, Ariz.: Oryx Press, 2001.

AGRICULTURE, MINING, AND THE WEST IN NORTH AMERICA

Alonzo, Armando C. *Tejano Legacy: Rancheros and Settlers in South Texas, 1734-1900*. Albuquerque: University of New Mexico Press, 1998.

Billington, Ray A. *Westward Expansion: A History of the American Frontier*. New York: Macmillan, 1967.

Brands, H. W. *The Age of Gold: The California Gold Rush and the New American Dream*. New York: Doubleday, 2002.

Buck, Solon J. *The Granger Movement: A Study of Agricultural Organization and Its Political, Economic, and Social Manifestations, 1870-1880*. Lincoln: University of Nebraska Press, 1963.

Carstensen, Vernon, ed. *The Public Lands: Studies in the History of the Public Domain*. Madison: University of Wisconsin Press, 1963.

Chambers, J. D., and G. E. Mingay. *The Agricultural Revolution, 1750-1880*. London: B. T. Batsford, 1966.

Clark, Thomas D., and John D. W. Guice. *Frontiers in Conflict: The Old Southwest, 1795-1830*. Albuquerque: University of New Mexico Press, 1989.

Corbett, Christopher. *Orphans Preferred: The Twisted Truth and Lasting Legend of the Pony Express*. New York: Broadway Books, 2003.

Dary, David. *The Santa Fe Trail: Its History, Legends, and Lore*. Reprint. New York: Penguin, 2002.

De León, Arnoldo. *The Tejano Community, 1836-1900*. Albuquerque: University of New Mexico Press, 1982.

Diamond, Henry L., and Patrick F. Noonan, eds. *Land Use in America*. Washington, D.C.: Island Press, 1996.

Dirlik, Arif, and Malcolm Yeung, eds. *Chinese on the American Frontier*. Lanham, Md.: Rowman & Littlefield, 2001.

Feller, Daniel. *The Public Lands in Jacksonian Politics*. Madison: University of Wisconsin Press, 1984.

Fite, Gilbert C. *The Farmers' Frontier, 1865-1900*. New York: Holt, Rinehart and Winston, 1966.

Gordon, Mary M., ed. *Overland to California with the Pioneer Line*. Urbana: University of Illinois Press, 1984.

Hall, Thomas D. *Social Change in the Southwest, 1850-1880*. Lawrence: University Press of Kansas, 1989.

Hobhouse, Henry. *Seeds of Change: Five Plants That Transformed Mankind*. New York: Harper & Row, 1986.

Holliday, J. S. *The World Rushed In: The California Gold Rush Experience*. Norman: University of Oklahoma Press, 2002.

Hoseason, David. *Harvesters and Harvesting, 1840-1900*. London: Croom Helm, 1982.

Isenberg, Andrew C. *The Destruction of the Bison: An Environmental History, 1750-1920*. New York: Cambridge University Press, 2000.

Isern, Thomas D. *Bull Threshers and Bindlestiffs: Harvesting and Threshing on the North American Plains*. Lawrence: University Press of Kansas, 1990.

Johnson, Susan Lee. *Roaring Camp: The Social World of the California Gold Rush*. New York: W. W. Norton, 2000.

Krell, Alan. *The Devil's Rope: A Cultural History of Barbed Wire*. London: Reaktion Books, 2002.

Lanza, Michael L. *Agrarianism and Reconstruction Politics: The Southern Homestead Act*. Baton Rouge: Louisiana State University Press, 1990.

Lavender, David. *The Great West*. Boston: Houghton Mifflin, 1985.

Limerick, Patricia N. *The Legacy of Conquest: The Unbroken Past of the American West*. New York: W. W. Norton, 1987.

Moeller, Bill, and Jan Moeller. *The Pony Express: A Photographic History*. Missoula, Mont.: Mountain Press, 2002.

Montgomery, M. R. *Jefferson and the Gun-Men: How the West Was Almost Lost*. New York: Crown, 2000.

Musgrave, Toby, and Will Musgrave. *An Empire of Plants: People and Plants That Changed the World*. London: Cassell, 2000.

O'Neal, Bill. *Cattlemen vs. Sheepherders: Five Decades of Violence in the West, 1880-1920*. Austin, Tex.: Eakin Press, 1989.

Paul, Rodman W. *The Far West and the Great Plains in Transition, 1859-1900*. New York: Harper & Row, 1988.

Rohrbough, Malcolm J. *The Land Office Business: The Settlement and Administration of American Public Lands, 1789-1837*. New York: Oxford University Press, 1968.

Ronda, James P. *Astoria and Empire*. Lincoln: University of Nebraska Press, 1990.

Strom, Claire. *Profiting from the Plains: The Great*

Northern Railway and Corporate Development of the American West. Seattle: University of Washington Press, 2003.

Tilghman, Wendy B. *The Great Plains Experience*. Lincoln, Nebr.: University of Mid-America, 1981.

Turner, Frederick Jackson. *The Frontier in American History*. 1920. Reprint. New York: Dover Publications, 1996.

Vestal, Stanley. *The Old Santa Fe Trail*. Boston: Houghton Mifflin, 1939.

Wade, Richard C. *The Urban Frontier: The Rise of Western Cities, 1790-1830*. Cambridge, Mass.: Harvard University Press, 1959.

Weber, David J. *The Mexican Frontier, 1821-1846: The American Southwest Under Mexico*. Albuquerque: University of New Mexico Press, 1982.

White, Richard. *"It's Your Misfortune and None of My Own": A History of the American West*. Norman: University of Oklahoma Press, 1991.

Wishart, David J. *The Fur Trade of the American West, 1807-1840*. Lincoln: University of Nebraska Press, 1992.

Woods, Thomas A. *Knights of the Plow: Oliver H. Kelley and the Origins of the Grange in Republican Ideology*. Ames: Iowa State University Press, 1991.

ARCHAEOLOGY

Adkins, Lesley, and Roy Adkins. *The Keys of Egypt: The Obsession to Decipher Egyptian Hieroglyphs*. New York: HarperCollins, 2000.

Allen, Susan Heuck. *Finding the Walls of Troy: Frank Calvert and Heinrich Schliemann at Hisarlik*. Berkeley: University of California Press, 1999.

Bourbon, Fabio. *The Lost Cities of the Mayas: The Life, Art, and Discoveries of Frederick Catherwood*. Shrewsbury, England: Swan Hill Press, 1999.

Evans, R. Tripp. *Romancing the Maya: Mexican Antiquity in the American Imagination, 1820-1915*. Austin: University of Texas Press, 2004.

Flenley, John, and Paul Bahn. *The Enigmas of Easter Island: Island on the Edge*. 2d ed. New York: Oxford University Press, 2003.

Glassman, Steve. *On the Trail of the Maya Explorer: Tracing the Epic Journey of John Lloyd Stephens*. Tuscaloosa: University of Alabama Press, 2003.

Greene, Jerome A., and Douglas D. Scott. *Finding Sand Creek: History, Archeology, and the 1864 Massacre Site*. Norman: University of Oklahoma Press, 2004.

Hamilakis, Yannis, ed. *Labyrinth Revisited: Rethinking*

"Minoan" Archaeology. Oxford, England: Oxbow, 2002.

Horwitz, Sylvia. *The Find of a Lifetime: Sir Arthur Evans and the Discovery of Knossos*. New York: Viking Press, 1981.

Larsen, Mogens Trolle. *The Conquest of Assyria: Excavations in an Antique Land, 1840-1860*. New York: Routledge, 1996.

Layard, Austen Henry. *Nineveh and Its Remains*. 1849. Reprint. Piscataway, N.J.: Georgias Press, 2004.

Macgillivray, Joseph Alexander. *Minotaur: Sir Arthur Evans and the Archaeology of the Minoan Myth*. London: Random House, 2001.

Meyerson, Daniel. *The Linguist and the Emperor: Napoleon and Champollion's Quest to Decipher the Rosetta Stone*. New York: Ballantine Books, 2004.

Romer, John, and Elizabeth Romer. *The History of Archaeology*. New York: Checkmark Books, 2001.

Runnels, Curtis. *The Archaeology of Heinrich Schliemann: An Annotated Bibliographic Handlist*. Boston: Archaeological Institute of America, 2002.

Russell, John Malcolm. *From Nineveh to New York: The Strange Story of the Assyrian Reliefs in the Metropolitan Museum and the Hidden Masterpiece at Canford School*. New Haven, Conn.: Yale University Press, 1997.

Schnapp, Alain. *The Discovery of the Past and the Origins of Archeology*. London: British Museum Press, 1996.

Sherratt, Susan. *Arthur Evans, Knossos, and the Priest-King*. Oxford, England: Ashmolean Museum, 2000.

Stephens, John Lloyd. *Incidents of Travel in Central America, Chiapas, and Yucatan*. Edited by Karl Ackerman. Washington, D.C.: Smithsonian Institution Press, 1993.

Traill, David A. *Schliemann of Troy: Treasure and Deceit*. New York: St. Martin's Press, 1995.

Von Hagen, Victor Wolfgang. *Maya Explorer: John Lloyd Stephens and the Lost Cities of Central America and Yucatán*. 1947. Reprint. San Francisco, Calif.: Chronicle Books, 1990.

ART AND ARCHITECTURE

Barnhart, Richard, et al. Three *Thousand Years of Chinese Painting*. New Haven, Conn.: Yale University Press, 2002.

Bergdoll, Barry. *European Architecture, 1750-1890*. New York: Oxford University Press, 2000.

Berger, Patricia. *Empire of Emptiness: Buddhist Art and*

Political Authority in Qing China. Honolulu: University of Hawaii Press, 2003.

Bernheimer, Charles. *Decadent Subjects: The Idea of Decadence in Art, Literature, Philosophy, and Culture of the Fin de Siècle in Europe*. Edited by T. Jefferson Kline and Naomi Schor. Baltimore: Johns Hopkins University Press, 2002.

Brettell, Richard R. *Impression: Painting Quickly in France, 1860-1890*. New Haven, Conn.: Yale University Press, 2000.

Bryson, Norman. *Tradition and Desire: From David to Delacroix*. Cambridge, England: Cambridge University Press, 1984.

Calinescu, Matei. *Five Faces of Modernity: Modernism, Avant-Garde, Decadence, Kitsch, Postmodernism*. Rev. ed. Bloomington: Indiana University Press, 1987.

Clark, Kenneth. *The Gothic Revival: An Essay in the History of Taste*. Harmondsworth, England: Penguin Books, 1964.

Craske, Matthew. *Art in Europe, 1700-1830: A History of the Visual Arts in an Era of Unprecedented Urban Economic Growth*. Oxford, England: Oxford University Press, 1997.

Denvir, Bernard. *The Chronicle of Impressionism: An Intimate Diary of the Lives and World of the Great Artists*. London: Thames and Hudson, 2000.

_____. *The Thames and Hudson Encyclopedia of Impressionism*. London: Thames and Hudson, 1990.

Fahr-Becker, Gabriele. *Japanese Prints*. Cologne, Germany: Taschen, 1999.

Fu, Shen C. Y. *Traces of the Brush: Studies in Chinese Calligraphy*. New Haven, Conn.: Yale University Art Gallery, 1977.

Guth, Christine. *Art of Edo Japan: The Artist and the City, 1615-1868*. New York: Harry N. Abrams, 1996.

Halliwell, Sarah, ed. *Who and When? Impressionism and Postimpressionism: Artists, Writers, and Composers*. London: Marshall Cavendish, 1998.

Hawksley, Lucinda. *Essential Pre-Raphaelites*. Bath, England: Parragon, 1999.

Hodin, Paul. *Edvard Munch*. London: Thames and Hudson, 1985.

Kolinsky, Dorothy. *The Artist and the Camera: Degas to Picasso*. New Haven, Conn.: Yale University Press, 1999.

Lambert, Ray. *John Constable and the Theory of Landscape Painting*. Cambridge, England: Cambridge University Press, 2005.

Lerman, Leo. *The Museum: One Hundred Years and the Metropolitan Museum of Art*. New York: Viking Press, 1969.

Marrinan, Michael. *Painting Politics for Louis Philippe: Art and Ideology in Orleanist France, 1830-1848*. New Haven, Conn.: Yale University Press, 1988.

Meyer, Barbara. *In the Arts and Crafts Style*. New York: Chronicle Books, 1992.

Moudry, Roberta. *The American Skyscraper: Cultural Histories*. New York: Cambridge University Press, 2005.

Nagata, Seiji. *Hokusai: Genius of the Japanese Ukiyo-e*. New York: Kodansha International, 1995.

Newland, Amy, ed. *The Commercial and Cultural Climate of Japanese Printmaking*. Hotei Academic European Studies on Japan 2. Amsterdam: Hotei, 2004.

Salter, Rebecca. *Japanese Woodblock Printing*. Honolulu: University of Hawaii Press, 2001.

Stevenson, Michael. *Both Curious and Valuable: African Art from Late Nineteenth-Century South-East Africa*. London: Michael Graham-Stewart, 2005.

Todd, Pamela. *The Arts and Crafts Companion*. New York: Bulfinch Press, 2004.

Visona, Monica Blackmun, et al. *History of Art in Africa*. New York: Prentice Hall, 2003.

Weir, David. *Decadence and the Makings of Modernism*. Amherst: University of Massachusetts Press, 1995.

Wells, Matthew. *Skyscrapers: Structure and Design*. New Haven, Conn.: Yale University Press, 2005.

AUSTRALIA

Bosworth, Michal. *Convict Fremantle: A Place of Promise and Punishment*. Perth: University of Western Australia Press, 2004.

Burgmann, Verity, and Jenny Lee, eds. *Constructing a Culture: A People's History of Australia Since 1788*. Ringwood, Vic.: Penguin, 1988.

Clark, Charles Manning. *A History of Australia*. 6 vols. 1962. Reprint. Carleton: Melbourne University Press, 1999.

Coupe, Robert. *Australia's Gold Rushes*. Frenchs Forest, N.S.W.: New Holland Books, 2004.

Day, David. *Claiming a Continent: A New History of Australia*. New York: HarperCollins, 2001.

Healy, Chris. *In the Ruins of Colonialism: History as Social Memory*. Melbourne, Vic.: Cambridge University Press, 1997.

Hughes, Robert. *The Fatal Shore*. 1987. Reprint. New York: Vintage, 1996.

Macintyre, Stuart. *A Concise History of Australia*. New York: Cambridge University Press, 2000.

Rude, George. *Protest and Punishment: The Story of the Social and Political Protestors Transported to Australia, 1788-1868*. Oxford, England: Clarendon Press, 1978.

West, John. *The History of Tasmania*. Sydney: Angus & Robertson, 1971.

Windschuttle, Keith. *The Fabrication of Aboriginal History*. Paddington, Tas.: Macleay Press, 2002.

THE BALKANS

Castellan, Georges. *History of the Balkans: From Mohammed the Conqueror to Stalin*. Translated by Nicholas Bradley. Boulder, Colo.: East European Monographs, 1992.

Clark, James Franklin. *The Pen and the Sword: Studies in Bulgarian History*. New York: Columbia University Press, 1988.

Clogg, Richard, ed. *The Struggle for Greek Independence: Essays to Mark the 150th Anniversary of the Greek War of Independence*. Hamden, Conn.: Archon Books, 1973.

Crampton, R. J. *A Concise History of Bulgaria*. New York: Cambridge University Press, 1997.

Dakin, Douglas. *The Greek Struggle for Independence, 1821-1833*. Berkeley: University of California Press, 1973.

Djordjevic, Dimitrije, and Stephen Fischer-Galati. *The Balkan Revolutionary Tradition*. New York: Columbia University Press, 1981.

Fleming, K. E. *The Muslim Bonaparte*. Princeton, N.J.: Princeton University Press, 2000.

Glenny, Misha. *The Balkans: Nationalism, War, and the Great Powers, 1804-1999*. New York: Penguin Books, 1999.

Jelavich, Barbara. *History of the Balkans*. 2 vols. New York: Cambridge University Press, 1983.

_____. *Russia's Balkan Entanglements, 1806-1914*. Cambridge, England: Cambridge University Press, 2004.

Jelavich, Charles, and Barbara Jelavich. *The Establishment of the Balkan National States, 1804-1920*. Vol. 8 in *A History of East Central Europe*. Seattle: University of Washington Press, 1977.

Palairet, Michael R., et al. *The Balkan Economies c. 1800-1914: Evolution Without Development*. Cambridge, England: Cambridge University Press, 2003.

Roudometof, Victor. *Nationalism, Globalization, and Orthodoxy: The Social Origins of Ethnic Conflict in the Balkans*. Westport, Conn.: Greenwood Press, 2001.

Stavrianos, L. S. *The Balkans, 1815-1914*. New York: Holt, Rinehart and Winston, 1965.

_____. *The Balkans Since 1453*. New York: New York University Press, 2000.

Stojanovic, Mihailo D. *The Great Powers and the Balkans, 1875-1878*. New York: Cambridge University Press, 1968.

Tzvetkov, Plamen. *A History of the Balkans: A Regional Overview from a Bulgarian Perspective*. San Francisco, Calif.: Edwin Mellen Press, 1993.

BUSINESS, ECONOMICS, AND FINANCE

Allen, Frederick L. *Secret Formula: How Brilliant Marketing and Relentless Salesmanship Made Coca-Cola the Best Known Product in the World*. New York: HarperCollins, 1995.

Ash, Juliet, and Lee Wright, eds. *Components of Dress: Design, Manufacturing, and Image-Making in the Fashion Industry*. New York: Routledge, 1988.

Batty, Peter. *The House of Krupp*. Rev. ed. Lanham, Md.: Cooper Square Press, 2002.

Becker, William H. *The Dynamics of Business-Government Relations: Industry and Exports, 1893-1921*. Chicago: University of Chicago Press, 1982.

Bigelow, Gordon. *Fiction, Famine, and the Rise of Economics in Victorian Britain and Ireland*. New York: Cambridge University Press, 2003.

Bissell, D. C. *The First Conglomerate: 145 Years of the Singer Sewing Machine Company*. Brunswick, Maine: Audenreed Press, 1999.

Blanke, David. *Sowing the American Dream: How Consumer Culture Took Root in the Rural Midwest*. Athens: Ohio University Press, 2000.

Bodenhorn, Howard. *A History of Banking in Antebellum America: Financial Markets and Economic Development in an Era of Nation-Building*. New York: Cambridge University Press, 2000.

Brands, H. W. *Masters of Enterprise: Giants of American Business from John Jacob Astor and J. P. Morgan to Bill Gates and Oprah Winfrey*. New York: Free Press, 1999.

Brown, Marion A. *The Second Bank of the United States and Ohio, 1803-1860: A Collision of Interests*. Lewiston, N.Y.: Edwin Mellen Press, 1998.

Bruce, Scott, and Bill Crawford. *Cerealizing America: The Unsweetened Story of American Breakfast Cereal*. Boston: Faber and Faber, 1995.

Cameron, Rondo. *A Concise Economic History of the World*. New York: Oxford University Press, 1993.

Churchman, Nancy. *David Ricardo on Public Debt*. New York: Palgrave, 2001.

Clapham, J. H. *The Economic Development of France and Germany, 1815-1914*. Cambridge, England: Cambridge University Press, 1936.

_____. *An Economic History of Modern Britain: The Early Railway Age*. Cambridge, England: Cambridge University Press, 1939.

Crossick, Geoffrey, and Serge Jaumain, eds. *Cathedrals of Consumption: The European Department Store, 1850-1939*. Burlington, Vt.: Ashgate, 1999.

Doti, Lynne Pierson, and Larry Schweikart. *Banking in the American West: From the Gold Rush to Deregulation*. Norman: University of Oklahoma Press, 1991.

Edwards, Ruth Dudley. *The Pursuit of Reason: The Economist, 1843-1943*. London: Hamish Hamilton, 1993.

Eichengreen, Barry J. *Capital Flows and Crises*. Cambridge, Mass.: MIT Press, 2003.

Ferguson, Niall. *The House of Rothschild: Money's Prophets, 1798-1848*. New York: Penguin Books, 1999.

Foley, Duncan. *Understanding Capital: Marx's Economic Theory*. Cambridge, Mass.: Harvard University Press, 1986.

Friedman, Milton, and Anna J. Schwartz. *A Monetary History of the United States, 1867-1960*. Princeton, N.J.: Princeton University Press, 1963.

Haeger, John D. *John Jacob Astor: Business and Finance in the Early Republic*. Detroit: Wayne State University Press, 1991.

Hays, Constance L. *The Real Thing: Truth and Power of the Coca-Cola Company*. New York: Random House, 2004.

Hixson, William F. *Triumph of the Bankers: Money and Banking in the Eighteenth and Nineteenth Centuries*. Westport, Conn.: Praeger, 1993.

Hoge, Cecil C. *The First Hundred Years Are the Toughest: What Can We Learn from the Century of Competition Between Sears and Wards*. Berkeley, Calif.: Ten Speed Press, 1988.

Hylton, Keith N. *Antitrust Law: Economic Theory and Common Law Evolution*. New York: Cambridge University Press, 2003.

Kahan, Arcadius. *Russian Economic History: The Nineteenth Century*. Chicago: University of Chicago Press, 1989.

Kaplan, Edward S. *The Bank of the United States and the American Economy*. Westport, Conn.: Greenwood Press, 1999.

Kolchin, Peter. *Unfree Labor: American Slavery and Russian Serfdom*. Cambridge, Mass.: Belknap Press of Harvard University Press, 1987.

Kovaleff, Theodore P., ed. *The Antitrust Impulse: An Economic, Historical, and Legal Analysis*. 2 vols. Armonk, N.Y.: M. E. Sharpe, 1994.

Lancaster, William. *The Department Store: A Social History*. London: Leicester Press, 1995.

Laughlin, J. Laurence. *The History of Bimetallism in the United States*. 4th ed. New York: Greenwood Press, 1968.

Leach, William R. *Land of Desire: Merchants, Power, and the Rise of a New American Culture*. New York: Vintage Books, 1994.

Livesay, Harold C. *American Made: Men Who Shaped the American Economy*. Boston: Little, Brown, 1979.

Livingston, James. *Origins of the Federal Reserve System: Money, Class, and Corporate Capitalism, 1890-1913*. Ithaca, N.Y.: Cornell University Press, 1986.

Madsen, Axel. *The Marshall Fields: The Evolution of an American Business Dynasty*. Hoboken, N.J.: John Wiley & Sons, 2002.

Miller, Michael Barry. *The Bon Marché: Bourgeois Culture and the Department Store, 1869-1920*. Princeton, N.J.: Princeton University Press, 1981.

Mullineux, A. W. *Business Cycles and Financial Crises*. Ann Arbor: University of Michigan Press, 1990.

Northrup, Cynthia Clark, and Elaine C. Prange Turney, eds. *Encyclopedia of Tariffs and Trade in U.S. History*. Westport, Conn.: Greenwood Press, 2003.

O'Rourke, Kevin H., and Jeffrey G. Williamson, eds. *Globalization and History: A History of a Nineteenth-Century Atlantic Economy*. Cambridge, Mass.: MIT Press, 2001.

Pendergrast, Mark. *For God, Country, and Coca-Cola: The Definition of the Great American Soft Drink and the Company That Makes It*. 2d ed. New York: Basic Books, 2000.

Ricardo, David. *The Principles of Political Economy and Taxation*. Introduction by Michael P. Fogarty. London: J. M. Dent & Sons, 1969.

Rothbard, Murray N. *A History of Money and Banking in the United States: The Colonial Era to World War II*. Auburn, Ala.: Ludwig Von Mises Institute, 2002.

Schwartz, Vanessa R. *Spectacular Realities: Early Mass Culture in Fin-de-Siècle Paris*. Berkeley: University of California Press, 1999.

Schwarz, Richard W. *John Harvey Kellogg, M.D.* Nashville, Tenn.: Southern, 1970.

Schweikart, Larry. *Banking in the American South from*

the Age of Jackson to Reconstruction. Baton Rouge: Louisiana State University Press, 1987.

Sheridan, Richard. *Sugar and Slavery: An Economic History of the British West Indies.* Kingston, Jamaica: University of West Indies Press, 2000.

Timberlake, Richard H. *Monetary Policy in the United States: An Intellectual and Institutional History.* Chicago: University of Chicago Press, 1993.

_____. *The Origins of Central Banking in the United States.* Cambridge, Mass.: Harvard University Press, 1978.

Wendel, Charles H. *One Hundred Fifty Years of International Harvester.* Osceola, Wis.: Motorbooks International, 1993.

Whitten, David O., and Bessie E. Whitten. *The Birth of Big Business in the United States, 1860-1914: Commercial, Extractive, and Industrial Enterprise.* Westport, Conn.: Praeger, 2006.

Witzel, Gyuel Young, and Michael Karl Witzel. *The Sparkling Story of Coca-Cola.* Stillwater, Minn.: Voyager Press, 2002.

CANADA

Beahan, William, and Stanley Horrall. *Red Coats on the Prairies: The North-West Mounted Police, 1886-1900.* Regina, Sask.: Centax Books, 1998.

Beal, Bob, and Rod Macleod. *Prairie Fire: The 1885 North-West Rebellion.* Edmonton: Hurtig, 1984.

Berton, Pierre. *The Promised Land: Settling the West, 1896-1914.* Toronto, Ont.: McClelland & Stewart, 1984.

Brown, Jennifer S. H., Jacqueline Peterson, Robert K. Thomas, and Marcel Giraud, eds. *New Peoples: Being and Becoming Métis in North America.* St. Paul: Minnesota Historical Society, 2001.

Brown, R. Craig, ed. *The Illustrated History of Canada.* 4th ed. Toronto: Key Porter Books, 2003.

Buckner, Phillip A. *The Transition to Responsible Government: British Policy in British North America, 1815-1850.* Westport, Conn.: Greenwood, 1985.

Bumsted, J. M. *The Peoples of Canada: A Post-Confederation History.* New York: Oxford University Press, 2004.

Cruise, David, and Alison Griffiths. *The Great Adventure: How the Mounties Conquered the West.* Toronto, Ont.: Viking Press, 1996.

Dickason, Olive Patricia. *Canada's First Nations: A History of Founding Peoples from Earliest Times.* Norman: University of Oklahoma Press, 1992.

Draper, Paula, Franca Iacovetta, and Robert Ventresca,

eds. *A Nation of Immigrants: Women, Workers, and Communities in Canadian History, 1840's-1960's.* Toronto, Ont.: University of Toronto Press, 1998.

Flanagan, Thomas. *Riel and the Rebellion.* Toronto: University of Toronto Press, 2000.

Galbraith, John S. *The Hudson's Bay Company as an Imperial Factor, 1821-1869.* Berkeley: University of California Press, 1957.

Giraud, Marcel. *The Metis in the Canadian West.* Translated by George Woodcock. 2 vols. Lincoln: University of Nebraska Press, 1986.

Gough, Barry M. *Gunboat Frontier: British Maritime Authority and Northwest Coast Indians, 1846-1890.* Vancouver: University of British Columbia Press, 1984.

Hall, David J. *Clifford Sifton.* 2 vols. Vancouver: University of British Columbia Press, 1981, 1985.

Harris, R. Cole, and John Warkentin. *Canada Before Confederation: A Study in Historical Geography.* Carleton, Ont.: Carleton University Press, 1991.

Holt, Thomas C. *The Problem of Freedom: Race, Labor, and Politics in Jamaica and Britain, 1832-1938.* Baltimore: Johns Hopkins University Press, 1992.

Houston, Cecil J., and William J. Smyth. *Irish Emigration and Canadian Settlement: Patterns, Links, and Letters.* Toronto: University of Toronto Press, 1990.

McMillan, Alan D. *Native Peoples and Cultures of Canada: An Anthropological Overview.* Vancouver: Douglas & McIntyre, 1988.

McNairn, Jeffrey L. *The Capacity to Judge: Public Opinion and Deliberative Democracy in Upper Canada, 1791-1854.* Toronto: University of Toronto Press, 2000.

Mann, Susan. *The Dream of a Nation: A Social and Intellectual History of Quebec.* 2d ed. Montreal: McGill-Queen's University Press, 2002.

Mansergh, Nicholas. *The Durham Report to the Anglo-Irish Treaty.* Vol. 1 in *The Commonwealth Experience.* Toronto: University of Toronto Press, 1982.

Martin, Ged. *Britain and the Origins of Canadian Confederation, 1837-1867.* London: Macmillan, 1995.

Miller, J. R. *Skyscrapers Hide the Heavens: A History of Indian-White Relations in Canada.* Rev. ed. Toronto: University of Toronto Press, 1991.

Morse, Kathryn Taylor. *The Nature of Gold: An Environmental History of the Klondike Gold Rush.* Seattle: University of Washington Press, 2003.

Owram, Doug. *Promise of Eden: The Canadian Expansionist Movement and the Idea of the West, 1856-1900.* Toronto: University of Toronto Press, 1980.

Satzewich, Vic, and Terry Wotherspoon. *First Nations: Race, Class, and Gender Relations.* Scarborough, Ont.: Nelson Canada, 1993.

Saywell, John T. *The Lawmakers: Judicial Power and the Shaping of Canadian Federalism.* Toronto: University of Toronto Press, 2002.

See, Scott W. *The History of Canada.* Westport, Conn.: Greenwood Press, 2001.

Sewell, John. *Mackenzie: A Political Biography of William Lyon Mackenzie.* Toronto: J. Lorimer, 2002.

Siggins, Maggie. *Riel: A Life of Revolution.* Toronto: HarperCollins, 1994.

Silver, A. I. *The French-Canadian Idea of Confederation, 1864-1900.* 2d ed. Toronto, Ont.: University of Toronto Press, 1997.

Spigelman, Martin. *Wilfrid Laurier.* Rev. ed. Markham, Ont.: Fitzhenry & Whiteside, 2000.

Tennant, Paul. *Aboriginal Peoples and Politics: The Indian Land Question in British Columbia, 1849-1989.* Vancouver: University of British Columbia Press, 1990.

Troper, Harold M. *Only Farmers Need Apply: Official Canadian Government Encouragement of Immigration from the United States, 1896-1911.* Toronto, Ont.: Griffin House, 1972.

Tulchinsky, Gerald J. J. *The River Barons: Montreal Businessmen and the Growth of Industry and Transportation, 1837-1853.* Toronto, Ont.: Toronto University Press, 1977.

Waite, P. B. *The Life and Times of Confederation, 1864-1867: Politics, Newspapers, and the Union of British North America.* 3d ed. Toronto, Ont.: Robin Brass Studio, 2001.

Wallace, Jim. *A Trying Time.* Winnipeg, Man.: Bunker to Bunker Books, 1998.

Ward, John Manning. *Colonial Self-Government: The British Experience, 1759-1856.* London: Macmillan, 1976.

Wilson, J. Donald., et al., eds. *Canadian Education: A History.* Scarborough, Ont.: Prentice-Hall/Canada, 1970.

Woods, Shirley E., Jr. *The Molson Saga, 1763-1983.* Toronto, Ont.: Doubleday Canada, 1983.

CARIBBEAN

Bakan, Abigail B. *Ideology and Class Conflict in Jamaica: The Politics of Rebellion.* Quebec: McGill-Queen's University Press, 1990.

Fraginals, Manuel Moreno. *The Long Nineteenth Century: Nineteenth Century Transformations.* Vol. 4 in *General History of the Caribbean.* New York: Palgrave Macmillan, 2006.

Gott, Richard. *Cuba: A New History.* New Haven, Conn.: Yale University Press, 2004.

Schmidt-Nowara, Christopher. *Empire and Antislavery: Spain, Cuba, and Puerto Rico, 1833-1874.* Pittsburgh, Pa.: University of Pittsburgh Press, 1999.

Sheridan, Richard. *Sugar and Slavery: An Economic History of the British West Indies.* Kingston, Jamaica: University of West Indies Press, 2000.

Thomas, Hugh. *Cuba: The Pursuit of Freedom.* New York: Harper & Row, 1971.

Turton, Peter. *Jose Marti: Architect of Cuba's Freedom.* London: Zed Books, 1986.

DANCE

Cohen, Selma Jeanne, ed. *International Encyclopedia of Dance.* 6 vols. New York: Oxford University Press, 1998.

Foster, Susan Leigh. *Choreography and Narrative: Ballet's Staging of Story and Desire.* Bloomington: Indiana University Press, 1996.

Garafola, Lynn, ed. *Rethinking the Sylph: New Perspectives on the Romantic Ballet.* Hanover, N.H.: Wesleyan University Press, 1997.

Leblon, Bernard. *Gypsies and Flamenco: The Emergence of the Art of Flamenco in Andalusia.* Hertfordshire, England: University of Hertfordshire Press, 2003.

Lee, Carol. *Ballet in Western Culture: A History of Its Origins and Evolution.* New York: Routledge, 2002.

Reeser, Educard. *The History of the Waltz.* Translated by W. A. G. Doyle-Davidson. Stockholm: Continental, 1949.

Scholl, Tim. *From Petipa to Balanchine: Classical Revival and the Modernization of Ballet.* Reprint. New York: Routledge, 2001.

Souritz, Elisabeth. *The Great History of the Russian Ballet: Its Art and Choreography.* Richford, Vt.: Parkstone Press, 1999.

Yaraman, Sevin H. *Revolving Embrace: The Waltz as Sex, Steps, and Sound.* Hillsdale, N.Y.: Pendragon Press, 2002.

DIPLOMACY

Alsop, Susan Mary. *The Congress Dances: Vienna, 1814-1815.* New York: Harper & Row, 1984.

Alvarez, Alejandro. *The Monroe Doctrine: Its Importance in the International Life of the States of the New World.* Buffalo, N.Y.: William S. Hein, 2003.

Bourne, Kenneth. *Britain and the Balance of Power in North America, 1815-1908*. Berkeley: University of California Press, 1967.

Bridge, F. R., and Roger Bullen. *The Great Powers and the European States System, 1815-1914*. 2d ed. New York: Longman, 2005.

Calleo, David. *The German Problem Reconsidered: Germany and the World Order, 1870 to the Present*. London: Cambridge University Press, 1978.

Chapman, Tim. *The Congress of Vienna: Origins, Processes, and Results*. New York: Routledge, 1998.

Clarke, John. *British Diplomacy and Foreign Policy, 1782-1865: The National Interest*. London: Unwin Hyman, 1989.

Cooper, Sandi E. *Patriotic Pacifism: Waging War on War in Europe, 1815-1914*. New York: Oxford University Press, 1991.

Cushing, Caleb. *The Treaty of Washington: Its Negotiation, Execution, and the Discussions Relating Thereto*. Freeport, N.Y.: Books for Libraries Press, 1970.

Davis, John R. *Britain and the German Zollverein, 1848-66*. New York: St. Martin's Press, 1997.

Edwards, E. W. *British Diplomacy and Finance in China, 1895-1914*. Oxford, England: Oxford University Press, 1987.

Graham, Gerald S. *The China Station: War and Diplomacy, 1830-1860*. Oxford, England: Clarendon Press, 1978.

Healy, David. *James G. Blaine and Latin America*. Columbia: University of Missouri Press, 2001.

Jones, Howard. *To the Webster-Ashburton Treaty: A Study in Anglo-American Relations, 1783-1843*. Chapel Hill: University of North Carolina Press, 1977.

Kennan, George F. *American Diplomacy*. Expanded ed. Chicago: University of Chicago Press, 1984.

_____. *The Fateful Alliance: France, Russia, and the Coming of the First World War*. New York: Pantheon Books, 1984.

Kissinger, Henry. *Diplomacy*. New York: Simon & Schuster, 1994.

_____. *A World Restored: Metternich, Castlereagh, and the Problems of Peace, 1815-1822*. Reprint. Boston: Houghton Mifflin, 1973.

Langer, William L. *The Diplomacy of Imperialism*. New York: Alfred A. Knopf, 1950.

_____. *European Alliances and Alignments, 1871-1890*. 2d ed. New York: Alfred A. Knopf, 1950.

Medlicott, W. N. *The Congress of Berlin and After: A Diplomatic History of the Near East Settlement, 1878-1880*. 2d ed. Hamden, Conn.: Archon Books, 1962.

Merk, Frederick. *The Oregon Question: Essays in Anglo-American Diplomacy and Politics*. Cambridge, Mass.: Harvard University Press, 1967.

Offner, John L. *An Unwanted War: The Diplomacy of the United States and Spain over Cuba, 1895-1898*. Chapel Hill: University of North Carolina Press, 1992.

Pletcher, David M. *The Diplomacy of Annexation: Texas, Oregon, and the Mexican War*. Columbia: University of Missouri Press, 1973.

Saab, Ann Pottinger. *The Origins of the Crimean Alliance*. Charlottesville: University Press of Virginia, 1977.

Schmitt, Bernadotte E. *Triple Alliance and Triple Entente*. New York: Howard Fertig, 1971.

Seton-Watson, R. W. *Disraeli, Gladstone, and the Eastern Question: A Study in Diplomacy and Party Politics*. 1935. Reprint. New York: W. W. Norton, 1972.

Stagg, J. C. A. *Mr. Madison's War: Politics, Diplomacy, and Warfare in the Early American Republic, 1783-1830*. Princeton, N.J.: Princeton University Press, 1983.

Thomas, Daniel. *The Guarantee of Belgian Independence and Neutrality in European Diplomacy, 1830's-1930's*. Kingston, R.I.: D. H. Thomas, 1983.

Troubetzkoy, Alexis S. *The Road to Balaklava: Stumbling into War with Russia*. Toronto, Ont.: Trafalgar Press, 1986.

Wetzel, David. *The Crimean War: A Diplomatic History*. Boulder, Colo.: East European Monographs, 1985.

Yasamee, F. A. K. *Ottoman Diplomacy: Abdülhamid II and the Great Powers*. Istanbul: Isis Press, 1996.

EAST ASIA

Allinson, Gary D. *The Columbia Guide to Modern Japanese History*. New York: Columbia University Press, 1999.

Beasley, W. G. *Japanese Imperialism, 1894-1945*. Oxford, England: Clarendon Press, 1987.

Beer, Lawrence, and John Maki. *From Imperial Myth to Democracy: Japan's Two Constitutions, 1889-2002*. Boulder: University Press of Colorado, 2002.

Buruma, Ian. *Inventing Japan*. New York: Modern Library, 2003.

Dudden, Alexis. *Japan's Colonization of Korea: Discourse and Power*. Honolulu: University of Hawaii Press, 2005.

Duiker, William J. *Cultures in Collision: The Boxer Rebellion*. San Rafael, Calif.: Presidio Press, 1978.

Duus, Peter. *Modern Japan*. 2d ed. Boston: Houghton Mifflin, 1998.

Ebrey, Patricia Buckley. *The Cambridge Illustrated History of China*. New York: Cambridge University Press, 1999.

Edgerton, Robert B. *Warriors of the Rising Sun: A History of the Japanese Military*. Boulder: Westview Press, 1997.

Edwards, E. W. *British Diplomacy and Finance in China, 1895-1914*. Oxford, England: Oxford University Press, 1987.

Fairbank, John K. *China Perceived: Images and Policies in Chinese-American Relations*. New York: Alfred A. Knopf, 1974.

Fairbank, John K., and Merle Goldman. *China: A New History*. Cambridge, Mass.: Harvard University Press, 1998.

Fairbank, John K., Edwin O. Reischauer, and Albert M. Craig. *East Asia: Tradition and Transformation*. Rev. ed. Boston: Houghton Mifflin, 1989.

Graham, Gerald S. *The China Station: War and Diplomacy, 1830-1860*. Oxford, England: Clarendon Press, 1978.

Hsu, Immanuel C. Y. *The Rise of Modern China*. 6th ed. New York: Oxford University Press, 2000.

Hu, Sheng. *From the Opium Wars to the May Fourth Movement*. Beijing: The People's Press, 1981.

Ikegami, Eiko. *The Taming of the Samurai: Honorific Individualism and the Making of Modern Japan*. Cambridge, Mass.: Harvard University Press, 1995.

Jansen, Marius B. *The Making of Modern Japan*. Cambridge, Mass.: Harvard University Press, 2000.

_____, ed. *The Emergence of Meiji Japan*. New York: Cambridge University Press, 1995.

_____, ed. *The Nineteenth Century*. Vol. 5 in *The Cambridge History of Japan*. Cambridge, England: Cambridge University Press, 1989.

Joe, Wanne. *A Cultural History of Modern Korea*. Elizabeth, N.J.: Hollym Press, 2000.

Kim, Hodong. *Holy War in China: The Muslim Rebellion and State in Chinese Central Asia, 1864-1877*. Stanford, Calif.: Stanford University Press, 2004.

Laidler, Keith. *The Last Empress*. New York: John Wiley & Sons, 2003.

Lee, Robert. *France and the Exploitation of China, 1895-1901*. Oxford, England: Oxford University Press, 1989.

Melancon, Glenn. *Britain's China Policy and the Opium Crisis*. Burlington, Vt.: Ashgate, 2003.

Michael, Franz. *The Taiping Rebellion: History and Documents*. 3 vols. Seattle: University of Washington Press, 1966-1971.

Oliver, Robert. *A History of the Korean People in Modern Times*. Newark: University of Delaware Press, 1993.

Ravina, Mark. *The Last Samurai: The Life and Battles of Saigō Takamori*. Hoboken, N.J.: John Wiley & Sons, 2004.

Shin, Yong-ha. *Modern Korean History and Nationalism*. Translated by N. N. Pankaj. Seoul, Republic of Korea: Jimoondang, 2000.

Smith, Richard J. *China's Cultural Heritage: The Qing Dynasty, 1644-1912*. 2d ed. Boulder, Colo.: Westview Press, 1994.

Spencer, Jonathan. *The Search for Modern China*. 2d ed. New York: Norton, 1999.

Tennant, Roger. *A History of Korea*. London: Kegan Paul International, 1996.

Tsai, Shih-shan Henry. *China and the Overseas Chinese in the United States, 1868-1911*. Fayetteville: University of Arkansas Press, 1983.

Twitchett, Denis, and Frederick W. Mote, eds. *The Cambridge History of China*. Vol. 10. Cambridge, England: Cambridge University Press, 1998.

Wilson, George. *Patriots and Redeemers in Japan: Motives in the Meiji Restoration*. Chicago: University of Chicago Press, 1992.

Wright, Mary Clabaugh. *The Last Stand of Chinese Conservatism: The T'ung Chich Restoration, 1862-1874*. Stanford, Calif.: Stanford University Press, 1957.

EDUCATION

Battles, Matthew. *Library: An Unquiet History*. New York: Norton, 2003.

Bowen, James. *A History of Western Education: The Modern West—Europe and the New World*. New York: Routledge, 2003.

Burleigh, Nina. *The Stranger and the Statesman: James Smithson, John Quincy Adams, and the Making of America's Greatest Museum, the Smithsonian*. New York: Morrow, 2003.

Chandos, John. *Boys Together*. New Haven, Conn.: Yale University Press, 1984.

Fletcher, Robert S. *A History of Oberlin College from Its Foundation Through the Civil War*. 2 vols. Oberlin, Ohio: Oberlin College Press, 1943.

Graves, Frank Pierrepont. *A History of Education in Modern Times*. Honolulu: University Press of the Pacific, 2004.

Hafertepe, Kenneth. *America's Castle: The Evolution of*

the Smithsonian Building and Its Institution, 1840-1878. Washington, D.C.: Smithsonian Institution Press, 1984.

Harris, Michael H. *History of Libraries in the Western World*. Metuchen, N.J.: Scarecrow Press, 1995.

Horowitz, Helen Lefkowitz. *Campus Life: Undergraduate Cultures from the End of the Eighteenth Century to the Present*. New York: Alfred A. Knopf, 1987.

Lasser, Carol. *Educating Men and Women Together: Co-education in a Changing World*. Urbana: University of Illinois Press, in conjunction with Oberlin College, 1987.

Lerner, Fred. *The Story of Libraries: From the Invention of Writing to the Computer Age*. New York: Continuum, 1998.

McClellan, B. Edward, and William J. Reese, eds. *The Social History of American Education*. Urbana: University of Illinois Press, 1988.

Pulliam, John D., and James J. Van Patten. *History of Education in America*. 8th ed. Upper Saddle River, N.J.: Merrill, 2003.

Rasmussen, Wayne D. *Taking the University to the People: Seventy-Five Years of Cooperative Extension*. Ames: Iowa State University Press, 1989.

Spring, Joel. *The American School, 1642-1990*. 2d ed. New York: Longman, 1990.

Story, Ronald. *The Forging of an Aristocracy: Harvard and the Boston Upper Class, 1800-1870*. Middletown, Conn.: Wesleyan University Press, 1980.

Taylor, James Monroe. *Before Vassar Opened: A Contribution to the History of the Higher Education of Women in America*. Boston: Houghton Mifflin, 1914.

Thelin, John R. *A History of American Higher Education*. Baltimore: Johns Hopkins University Press, 2004.

Vincent, David. *The Rise of Mass Literacy*. Cambridge, England: Polity, 2000.

Warren, Donald R. *To Enforce Education: A History of the Founding Years of the United States Office of Education*. Detroit: Wayne State University Press, 1974.

Wilson, J. Donald., et al., eds. *Canadian Education: A History*. Scarborough, Ont.: Prentice-Hall/Canada, 1970.

Woodson, Carter G. *The Education of the Negro Prior to 1861*. New York: Arno Press, 1968.

ENGLAND, SCOTLAND, AND IRELAND

Bailey, Brian. *The Luddite Rebellion*. New York: New York University Press, 1998.

Bartlett, Thomas. *The Fall and Rise of the Irish Nation: The Catholic Question, 1690-1830*. Savage, Md.: Barnes & Noble Books, 1992.

Bew, Paul. *Land and the National Question in Ireland, 1858-1882*. Dublin: Gill and Macmillan, 1978.

Boyce, D. George, and Alan O'Day, eds. *Ireland in Transition, 1867-1921*. New York: Routledge, 2004.

Briggs, Asa. *The Age of Improvement, 1783-1867*. 2d ed. New York: Longman, 2000.

_____. *Victorian Cities*. New York: Harper & Row, 1963.

_____. *Victorian People: A Reassessment of Persons and Themes, 1851-1867*. Chicago: University of Chicago Press, 1955.

Chambers, J. D., and G. E. Mingay. *The Agricultural Revolution, 1750-1880*. London: B. T. Batsford, 1966.

Charlton, John. *The Chartists: The First National Workers' Movement*. London: Pluto Press, 1997.

Clark, Samuel. *Social Origins of the Irish Land War*. Princeton, N.J.: Princeton University Press, 1979.

Cole, G. D. H., and Raymond Postgate. *The British Common People, 1746-1946*. London: Methuen, 1961.

Davies, Andrew. *To Build a New Jerusalem: The British Labour Party from Keir Hardie to Tony Blair*. London: Abacus, 1996.

Drescher, Seymour. *The Mighty Experiment: Free Labor Versus Slavery in British Emancipation*. New York: Oxford University Press, 2002.

Driver, Felix. *Power and Pauperism: The Workhouse System, 1834-1884*. New York: Cambridge University Press, 1993.

Finlayson, Geoffrey. *Citizen, State, and Social Welfare in Britain, 1780-1930*. Oxford, England: Clarendon Press, 1994.

Halévy, Élie. *A History of the English People in the Nineteenth Century*. 6 vols. Translated by E. I. Watkin. 2d rev. ed. New York: Peter Smith, 1949.

Hamlin, Christopher. *Public Health and Social Justice in the Age of Chadwick: Britain, 1800-1854*. Cambridge, England: Cambridge University Press, 1998.

Hilton, Boyd. *A Mad, Bad, and Dangerous People? England, 1783-1846*. New York: Oxford University Press, 2006.

Hinde, Wendy. *Catholic Emancipation: A Shake to Men's Minds*. Oxford, England: Blackwell, 1992.

Hobhouse, Hermione. *The Crystal Palace and the Great Exhibition*. New York: Athlone Press, 2002.

Hoppen, K. Theodore. *The Mid-Victorian Generation, 1846-1886*. New York: Oxford University Press, 2000.

Jenkins, T. A. *Gladstone, Whiggery, and the Liberal*

Party, 1874-1886. Oxford, England: Clarendon Press, 1988.

Jordan, Donald E., Jr. *Land and Popular Politics in Ireland: County Mayo from the Plantation to the Land War*. Cambridge, England: Cambridge University Press, 1994.

King, Carla, ed. *Famine, Land, and Culture in Ireland*. Dublin: University College Dublin Press, 2000.

Loughlin, James. *Gladstone, Home Rule, and the Ulster Question, 1882-1893*. Dublin: Gill & MacMillan, 1986.

Mansergh, Nicholas. *The Irish Question, 1840-1921*. Buffalo, N.Y.: University of Toronto Press, 1975.

Melancon, Glenn. *Britain's China Policy and the Opium Crisis*. Burlington, Vt.: Ashgate, 2003.

Mitchell, Sally, ed. *Victorian Britain: An Encyclopaedia*. New York: Garland, 1988.

Mokyr, Joel. *Why Ireland Starved: A Quantitative and Analytical History of the Irish Economy, 1800-1850*. London: Allen & Unwin, 1985.

Moody, T. W. *The Fenian Movement*. Cork, Ireland: Mercer Press, 1968.

Moran, Gerard. *Sending Out Ireland's Poor: Assisted Emigration to North America in the Nineteenth Century*. Portland, Oreg.: Four Courts Press, 2004.

O'Day, Alan. *Irish Home Rule, 1867-1921*. Manchester: Manchester University Press, 1998.

O'Ferrall, Fergus. *Catholic Emancipation: Daniel O'Connell and the Birth of Irish Democracy, 1820-1830*. Dublin: Gill & Macmillan, 1985.

Ó'Gráda, Cormac. *Ireland Before and After the Famine: Explorations in Economic History, 1800-1925*. New York: Manchester University Press, 1988.

Parry, Jonathan P. *The Rise and Fall of Liberal Government in Victorian Britain*. New Haven, Conn.: Yale University Press, 1993.

Pickering, Paul A. *Chartism and the Chartists in Manchester and Salford*. New York: St. Martin's Press, 1995.

Pickering, Paul A., and Alex Tyrell. *The People's Bread: A History of the Anti-Corn Law League*. New York: Leicester University Press, 2000.

Roberts, Stephen, ed. *The People's Charter: Democratic Agitation in Early Victorian Britain*. London: Merlin Press, 2004.

Rose, Michael E., ed. *The Poor and the City: The English Poor Law in Its Urban Context, 1834-1914*. New York: St. Martin's Press, 1985.

Sack, James L. *From Jacobite to Conservative: Reaction and Orthodoxy in Britain, c. 1760-1832*. Cambridge, England: Cambridge University Press, 1993.

Scally, Robert J. *The End of Hidden Ireland: Rebellion, Famine and Emigration*. New York: Oxford University Press, 1995.

Smith, Robert A. *Late Georgian and Regency England*. Cambridge, England: Cambridge University Press, 2004.

Stevenson, John. *Popular Disturbances in England, 1700-1832*. 2d ed. London: Longman, 1992.

Stone, Lawrence. *Broken Lives: Separation and Divorce in England, 1660-1857*. Oxford, England: Oxford University Press, 1993.

Woodham-Smith, Cecil B. *The Great Hunger: Ireland, 1845-1849*. New York: Harper & Row, 1962.

EXPLORATION AND THE SEA

Ambrose, Stephen E. *Undaunted Courage: Meriwether Lewis, Thomas Jefferson, and the Opening of the American West*. New York: Simon & Schuster, 1996.

Berton, Pierre. *The Arctic Grail: The Quest for the North West Passage and the North Pole, 1818-1909*. Toronto, Ont.: McClelland and Stewart, 1988.

Chaffin, Tom. *Pathfinder: John Charles Frémont and the Course of American Empire*. New York: Hill & Wang, 2002.

Dale, Harrison C., ed. *The Ashley-Smith Explorations and the Discovery of a Central Route to the Pacific, 1822-1829*. Rev. ed. Glendale, Calif.: Arthur H. Clark, 1941.

Dugard, Martin. *Into Africa: The Epic Adventures of Stanley and Livingstone*. New York: Broadway Books, 2004.

Eyraud, Eugène, et al. *Early Visitors to Easter Island 1864-1877: The Reports of Eugene Eyraud, Hippolyte Roussel, Pierre Loti, and Alphonse Pinart*. Translated by Ann M. Altman. Los Osos, Calif.: Easter Island Foundation, 2004.

Fernandez-Armesto, Felipe, ed. *The Times Atlas of World Exploration*. New York: HarperCollins, 1991.

Goetzmann, William H. *Exploration and Empire: The Explorer and the Scientist in the Winning of the American West*. New York: Alfred A. Knopf, 1966.

Gurney, Alan. *The Race to the White Continent: Voyages to the Antarctic*. W. W. Norton, 2000.

Hearn, Chester G. *Tracks in the Sea: Matthew Fontaine Maury and the Mapping of the Oceans*. Camden, Maine: International Maritime/McGraw-Hill, 2002.

Hemming, John. *Atlas of Exploration*. New York: Oxford University Press, 1997.

Herman, Arthur. *To Rule the Waves: How the British Navy Shaped the Modern World*. New York: Harper-Collins 2004.

Jones, Charles H. *Africa: The History of Exploration and Adventure as Given in the Leading Authorities from Herodotus to Livingstone*. Reprint. Westport, Conn.: Negro University Press, 1970.

Jones, Landon Y. *William Clark and the Shaping of the West*. New York: Hill & Wang, 2004.

Keay, John. *The Great Arc: The Dramatic Tale of How India Was Mapped and Everest Was Named*. New York: HarperCollins, 2000.

Kukla, Jon. *A Wilderness So Immense: The Louisiana Purchase and the Destiny of America*. New York: Alfred A. Knopf, 2003.

La Gueriviere, Jean de. *The Exploration of Africa*. Woodstock, N.Y.: Overlook Duckworth, 2003.

McGrath, Patrick. *The Lewis and Clark Expedition*. Morristown, N.J.: Silver Burdett, 1985.

Markham, Clements R. *The Lands of Silence: A History of Arctic and Antarctic Exploration*. Mansfield Centre, Conn.: Martino, 2005.

Mills, William J., ed. *Exploring Polar Frontiers: A Historical Encyclopedia*. Santa Barbara, Calif.: ABC-Clio, 2003.

Nansen, Fridtjof. *The Farthest North*. Northampton, Mass.: Interlink Books, 2003.

Newman, James L. *Imperial Footprints*. Washington, D.C.: Brassey's, 2004.

Rayfield, Donald. *The Dream of Lhasa: The Life of Nikolay Przhevalsky, 1839-1888, Explorer of Central Asia*. Athens: Ohio University Press, 1976.

Rice, Tony. *Three Centuries of Natural History Exploration*. New York: Clarkson Potter, 1999.

Ronda, James P. *Lewis and Clark Among the Indians*. Lincoln: University of Nebraska Press, 1984.

Sanford, William R., and Carl R. Green. *Zebulon Pike: Explorer of the Southwest*. Springfield, N.J.: Enslow, 1996.

Savours, Ann. *The Search for the North West Passage*. New York: St. Martin's Press, 1999.

Stockwell, Foster. *Westerners in China: A History of Exploration and Trade, Ancient Times Through the Present*. Jefferson, N.C.: McFarland, 2003.

Trench, Richard. *Arabian Travellers*. Topsfield, Mass.: Salem House, 1986.

Wilford, John Noble. *The Mapmakers*. Rev. ed. New York: Alfred A. Knopf, 2000.

FRANCE

Aminzade, Ronald. *Ballots and Barricades: Class Formation and Republican Politics in France, 1830-1871*. Princeton, N.J.: Princeton University Press, 1993.

Bertier de Sauvigny, Guillaume de. *The Bourbon Restoration*. Philadelphia: University of Pennsylvania Press, 1966.

Burns, Michael. *Rural Society and French Politics: Boulangism and the Dreyfus Affair*. Princeton, N.J.: Princeton University Press, 1984.

Charlton, D. G. *Positivist Thought in France During the Second Empire, 1852-1870*. Oxford, England: Clarendon Press, 1959.

Christiansen, Rupert. *Paris Babylon: A Social History of the Paris Commune*. New York: Viking, 1995.

Crook, Malcolm. *Revolutionary France: 1788-1880*. New York: Oxford University Press, 2002.

Dwyer, Philip G. *Talleyrand*. London: Longman, 2002.

Echard, William E. *Napoleon III and the Concert of Europe*. Baton Rouge: Louisiana State University Press, 1983.

Fortescue, William. *The Third Republic in France, 1870-1940: Conflicts and Continuities*. London: Routledge, 2000.

Forth, Christopher E. *The Dreyfus Affair and the Crisis of French Manhood*. Baltimore: Johns Hopkins University Press, 2004.

Furet, François. *Revolutionary France, 1770-1880*. Translated by Antonia Nevill. Oxford, England: Blackwell, 1992.

Horne, Alistair. *The Fall of Paris: The Siege and the Commune, 1870-71*. New York: Pan Macmillan, 2002.

Irvine, William. *The Boulanger Affair Reconsidered: Royalism, Boulangism, and the Origins of the Radical Right in France*. New York: Oxford University Press, 1989.

Lehning, James R. *Peasant and French: Cultural Context in Rural France During the Nineteenth Century*. New York: Cambridge University Press, 1995.

_____. *To Be a Citizen: The Political Culture of the Early French Third Republic*. Ithaca, N.Y.: Cornell University Press, 2001.

McMillan, James, and William Doyle. *Modern France: 1880-2002*. New York: Oxford University Press, 2003.

Magraw, Roger. *France, 1815-1914: The Bourgeois Century*. New York: Oxford University Press, 1986.

Mayeur, Jean-Marie, and Madeleine Rebérioux. *The*

Third Republic from Its Origins to the Great War, 1871-1914. Translated by J. R. Foster. New York: Cambridge University Press, 1987.

Taithe, Bertrand. *Citizenship and Wars: France in Turmoil, 1870-1871.* London: Routledge, 2001.

Wright, Gordon. *France in Modern Times: From the Enlightenment to the Present.* 5th ed. New York: W. W. Norton, 1995.

HABSBURG EMPIRE

Beller, Steven. *Francis Joseph.* London: Longman, 1996.

Bridge, F. R. *The Habsburg Monarchy Among the Great Powers, 1815-1918.* New York: Berg, 1990.

Crankshaw, Edward. *The Fall of the House of Habsburg.* New York: Penguin, 1983.

Kann, Robert A., and Zdenek V. David. *The Peoples of the Eastern Habsburg Lands, 1526-1918.* Seattle: University of Washington Press, 1984.

Lendvai, Paul. *The Hungarians: A Thousand Years of Victory in Defeat.* Translated by Jefferson Decker. Princeton, N.J.: Princeton University Press, 2004.

Pamlenyi, Ervin, ed. *A History of Hungary.* London: Collet's, 1975.

Pavlovic, Darko. *The Austrian Army, 1836-1866.* London: Osprey, 1999.

Sked, Alan. *The Decline and Fall of the Habsburg Empire, 1815-1918.* London: Longman, 1989.

Wawro, Geoffrey. *The Austro Prussian War: Austria's War with Prussia and Italy in 1866.* New York: Cambridge University Press, 1996.

Wheatcroft, Andrew. *The Habsburgs.* Reprint. New York: Penguin, 1997.

IMPERIALISM, EMPIRE, AND COLONIAL AFFAIRS

Abernethy, David B. *The Dynamics of Global Dominance: European Overseas Empires, 1415-1980.* New Haven, Conn.: Yale University Press, 2000.

Adamson, Kay. *Political and Economic Thought and Practice in Nineteenth-Century France and the Colonization of Algeria.* Lewiston, N.Y.: E. Mellen Press, 2002.

Bates, Darrell. *The Fashoda Incident of 1898: Encounter on the Nile.* New York: Oxford University Press, 1984.

Danziger, Raphael. *Abd al-Qadir and the Algerians: Resistance to the French and Internal Consolidation.* New York: Holmes & Meier, 1977.

Duiker, William J. *Cultures in Collision: The Boxer Rebellion.* San Rafael, Calif.: Presidio Press, 1978.

Edgerton, Robert B. *The Fall of the Asante Empire: The Hundred-Year War for Africa's Gold Coast.* New York: Free Press, 1995.

Eng, Pierre van der. *The "Colonial Drain" from Indonesia, 1823-1890.* Canberra: Economics Division, Research School of Pacific Studies, Australian National University, 1993.

Etherington, Norman. *The Great Treks: The Transformation of Southern Africa, 1815-1854.* Harlow, England: Pearson Education, 2001.

Farwell, Byron. *The Great Anglo-Boer War.* New York: W. W. Norton, 1990.

Grant, Kevin. *A Civilized Savagery: Britain and the New Slaveries in Africa, 1884-1926.* Philadelphia: Taylor & Francis, 2004.

Grigsby, Darcy Grimaldo. *Extremities: Painting Empire in Post-revolutionary France.* New Haven, Conn.: Yale University Press, 2002.

Hevia, James L. *English Lessons: The Pedagogy of Imperialism in Nineteenth-Century China.* Durham, N.C.: Duke University Press, 2003.

Hibbert, Christopher. *Great Mutiny: India, 1857.* New York: Penguin Books, 1980.

Hochschild, Adam. *King Leopold's Ghost.* Boston: Houghton Mifflin, 1998.

Holt, Thomas C. *The Problem of Freedom: Race, Labor, and Politics in Jamaica and Britain, 1832-1938.* Baltimore: Johns Hopkins University Press, 1992.

Hopkirk, Peter. *The Great Game: The Struggle for Empire in Central Asia.* New York: Kodansha International, 1994.

James, Lawrence. *Raj: The Making and Unmaking of British India.* New York: St. Martin's Press, 1998.

Karnow, Stanley. *In Our Image: America's Empire in the Philippines.* New York: Random House, 1989.

Karsh, Efraim. *Islamic Imperialism.* New Haven, Conn.: Yale University Press, 2006.

Knight, Ian. *The Zulu War: 1879.* Oxford, England: Osprey, 2003.

Lāpiso Dé Delébo. *The Italo-Ethiopian War of 1887-1896: From Dogali to Adwa.* Addis Ababa: Artistic Print Enterprise, 1996.

McLynn, Frank. *Hearts of Darkness: The European Exploration of Africa.* New York: Carroll & Graf, 1992.

Manning, Patrick. *Francophone Sub-Saharan Africa: 1880-1985.* New York: Cambridge University Press, 1985.

Maxwell, Leigh. *The Ashanti Ring: Sir Garnet Wolseley's Campaigns, 1870-1882.* London: Secker & Warburg, 1985.

Metcalfe, Thomas R. *Ideologies of the Raj.* Cambridge, England: Cambridge University Press, 1994.

Meyer, Karl E., and Shareen Blair Brysac. *Tournament of Shadows: The Great Game and the Race for Empire in Central Asia.* Washington, D.C.: Counterpoint, 1999.

Neillands, Robin. *The Dervish Wars: Gordon and Kitchener in the Sudan, 1880-1898.* London: John Murray, 1996.

O'Ballance, Edgar. *Afghan Wars, 1839-1992: What Britain Gave Up and the Soviet Union Lost.* New York: Brassey's, 1993.

Pakenham, Thomas. *The Scramble for Africa.* New York: Random House, 1991.

Porch, Douglas. *The Conquest of the Sahara.* New York: Knopf, 1984.

Porter, Andrew, ed. *The Nineteenth Century.* Vol. 3 in *Oxford History of the British Empire.* New York: Oxford University Press, 2001.

Schmidt-Nowara, Christopher. *Empire and Antislavery: Spain, Cuba, and Puerto Rico, 1833-1874.* Pittsburgh, Pa.: University of Pittsburgh Press, 1999.

Singer, Barnett, and John Langdon. *Cultured Force: Makers and Defenders of the French Colonial Empire.* Madison: University of Wisconsin Press, 2004.

Tate, D. J. M. *The Making of Modern South-East Asia: The European Conquest.* Kuala Lumpur, Malaysia: Oxford University Press, 1977.

Vandervort, Bruce. *Wars of Imperial Conquest in Africa, 1830-1914.* Bloomington: Indiana University Press, 1998.

Waller, John H. *Gordon of Khartoum: The Saga of a Victorian Hero.* New York: Atheneum, 1988.

INDIA AND SOUTH ASIA

Alavi, Seema. *The Sepoys and the Company: Tradition and Transition, 1770-1830.* New York: Oxford University Press, 1995.

Andrews, Charles F., and Girija K. Mookerjee. *The Rise and Growth of Congress in India, 1832-1920.* 2d ed. Meerut: Meenakshi Prakashan, 1967.

Basham, A. L., ed. *A Cultural History of India.* Oxford, England: Clarendon Press, 1975.

Edney, Mathew H. *Mapping an Empire: The Geographical Construction of British India, 1765-1843.* New Delhi: Oxford University Press, 1999.

Gordon, Stewart. *The Marathas, 1600-1818.* Cambridge, England: Cambridge University Press, 1993.

James, Lawrence. *Raj: The Making and Unmaking of British India.* New York: St. Martin's Press, 1998.

Metcalfe, Thomas R. *Ideologies of the Raj.* Cambridge, England: Cambridge University Press, 1994.

O'Ballance, Edgar. *Afghan Wars, 1839-1992: What Britain Gave Up and the Soviet Union Lost.* New York: Brassey's, 1993.

Sen, Mala. *Death by Fire: Sati, Dowry, Death, and Female Infanticide in Modern India.* New Brunswick, N.J.: Rutgers University Press, 2002.

Singh, Khushwant. *How the Sikhs Lost Their Kingdom.* New Delhi, India: UBS, 1996.

Yasin, Madhavi. *Emergence of Nationalism, Congress, and Separatism.* Delhi, India: Raj, 1996.

ITALY

Beales, Derek, and Eugenio Biagini. *The Risorgimento and the Unification of Italy.* Rev. 2d ed. Harlow, England: Longman, 2002.

Crippa, Maria Antonietta. *Antoni Gaudí, 1852-1926: From Nature to Architecture.* Cologne: Taschen, 2004.

Davis, John A., ed. *Italy in the Nineteenth Century, 1796-1900.* New York: Oxford University Press, 2000.

Di Scala, Spencer. *Italy from Revolution to Republic, 1700 to the Present.* 3d ed. Boulder, Colo.: Westview Press, 2004.

Mack Smith, Denis, ed. *Mazzini.* New Haven, Conn.: Yale University Press, 1994.

_____, ed. *The Making of Italy, 1796-1870.* New York: Walker, 1968.

Riall, Lucy. *The Italian Risorgimento: State, Society, and National Unification.* London: Routledge, 1994.

Romani, George T. *The Neapolitan Revolution of 1820-1821.* Evanston, Ill.: Northwestern University Press, 1950.

Sarti, Roland. *Mazzini: A Life for the Religion of Politics.* Westport, Conn.: Praeger, 1997.

Trevelyan, George Macaulay. *Garibaldi and the Thousand.* Reprint. New York: AMS Press, 1979.

Turnbull, Patrick. *Solferino: The Birth of a Nation.* New York: St. Martin's Press, 1985.

Wawro, Geoffrey. *The Austro-Prussian War: Austria's War with Prussia and Italy in 1866.* Rev. ed. New York: Cambridge University Press, 1997.

JEWISH HISTORY

Avineri, Shlomo. *The Making of Modern Zionism: Intellectual Origins of the Jewish State.* 1970. Reprint. New York: Basic Books, 1990.

Gorny, Yosef. *Zionism and the Arabs, 1882-1948: A*

Study of Ideology. Oxford, England: Clarendon Press, 1987.

Herzl, Theodor. *The Jews' State.* Translated by Henk Overberg. Northvale, N.J.: Jason Aronson, 1997.

Laqueur, Walter. *A History of Zionism.* Reprint. New York: Schocken, 2003.

Lindemann, Albert S. *The Jew Accused: Three Anti-Semitic Affairs (Dreyfus, Beilis, Frank), 1894-1915.* New York: Cambridge University Press, 1991.

Pawel, Ernest. *The Labyrinth of Exile: A Life of Theodor Herzl.* New York: Farrar Straus Giroux, 1992.

Sachar, Howard M. *A History of Israel: From the Rise of Zionism to Our Time.* 2d rev. ed. New York: Knopf, 1996.

Tobias, Henry J. *The Jewish Bund in Russia: From Its Origins to 1905.* Stanford, Calif.: Stanford University Press, 1972.

Weintraub, Stanley. *Charlotte and Lionel: A Rothschild Love Story.* New York: Free Press, 2003.

Wilson, Stephen. *Ideology and Experience: Antisemitism in France at the Time of the Dreyfus Affair.* Rutherford, N.J.: Fairleigh Dickinson University Press, 1982.

LABOR AND WORKERS

Daunton, Martin, ed. *Housing the Workers: A Comparative History, 1850-1914.* London: Leicester University Press, 1990.

Drescher, Seymour. *The Mighty Experiment: Free Labor Versus Slavery in British Emancipation.* New York: Oxford University Press, 2002.

Dubofsky, Melvin, and Foster Rhea Dulles. *Labor in America: A History.* 7th ed. Wheeling, Ill.: Harlan Davidson, 2004.

Greene, Julie. *Pure and Simple Politics: The American Federation of Labor and Political Activism, 1881-1917.* New York: Cambridge University Press, 1998.

Howell, David. *British Workers and the Independent Labour Party, 1888-1906.* London: Palgrave Macmillan, 1983.

Jeffreys, Kevin, ed. *Leading Labour: From Keir Hardie to Tony Blair.* London: I. B. Tauris, 1999.

Kessler-Harris, Alice, ed. *Protecting Women: Labor Legislation in Europe, the United States, and Australia, 1880-1920.* Urbana: University of Illinois Press, 1995.

Laurie, Bruce. *Artisans into Workers: Labor in Nineteenth Century America.* New York: Hill and Wang, 1989.

Reid, Alistair J. *United We Stand: A History of Britain's Trade Unions.* London: Allen Lane, 2004.

Rule, John, ed. *British Trade Unionism, 1750-1850.* New York: Longman, 1988.

Sale, Kirkpatrick. *Rebels Against the Future: The Luddites and Their War on the Industrial Revolution—Lessons for the Computer Age.* Reading, Mass.: Addison-Wesley, 1995.

Sheehan, James J. *Industrialization and Industrial Labor in Nineteenth Century Europe.* New York: John Wiley & Sons, 1973.

Thompson, Dorothy. *The Chartists: Popular Politics in the Industrial Revolution.* New York: Pantheon Books, 1984.

Thompson, E. P. *The Making of the English Working Class.* New York: Vintage, 1963.

Tomlins, Christopher L. *The State and the Unions: Labor Relations, Law, and the Organized Labor Movement in America, 1880-1960.* New York: Cambridge University Press, 1985.

Voss, Kim. *The Making of American Exceptionalism: The Knights of Labor and Class Formation in the Nineteenth Century.* Ithaca, N.Y.: Cornell University Press, 1993.

LITERATURE, THE PRESS, AND PUBLISHING

Badawi, M. M. *A Short History of Modern Arabic Literature.* Oxford, England: Clarendon Press, 1993.

Bercovich, Sacvan. *Cambridge History of American Literature.* 8 vols. Cambridge, England: Cambridge University Press, 1994-2006.

Boullata, Issa J., and Terri DeYoung, eds. *Tradition and Modernity in Arabic Literature.* Fayetteville: University of Arkansas Press, 1997.

Campbell, W. Joseph. *Yellow Journalism: Puncturing the Myths, Defining the Legacies.* Westport, Conn.: Praeger, 2001.

Chai, Leon. *Aestheticism: The Religion of Art in Post-Romantic Literature.* New York: Columbia University Press, 1990.

Constable, Liz, et al., eds. *Perennial Decay: On the Aesthetics and Politics of Decadence.* Philadelphia: University of Pennsylvania Press, 1999.

Davis, Paul, et al., eds. *The Nineteenth Century, 1800-1900.* Book 5 in *The Bedford Anthology of World Literature.* Boston: Bedford/St. Martin's, 2003.

Echevarria, Roberto Gonzalez, ed. *The Cambridge History of Latin American Literature.* Cambridge, England: Cambridge University Press, 1996.

Franco, Jean. *An Introduction to Spanish American Lit-*

erature. 1969. Reprint. New York: Cambridge University Press, 1994.

Gies, David T. *The Cambridge History of Spanish Literature*. Cambridge, England: Cambridge University Press, 2005.

Grossman, Jay. *Reconstituting the American Renaissance: Emerson, Whitman, and the Politics of Representation*. Durham, N.C.: Duke University Press, 2003.

Hohendahl, Peter Uwe. *Building a National Literature: The Case of Germany, 1830-1870*. Ithaca, N.Y.: Cornell University Press, 1989.

Lehan, Richard. *Realism and Naturalism: The Novel in an Age of Transition*. Madison: University of Wisconsin Press, 2005.

Loving, Jerome. *Lost in the Customhouse: Authorship in the American Renaissance*. Iowa City: University of Iowa Press, 1993.

Matthiessen, F. O. *American Renaissance: Art and Expression in the Age of Emerson and Whitman*. 1941. Reprint. New York: Oxford University Press, 1968.

Mostow, Joshua S., et al. *The Columbia Companion to Modern East Asian Literature*. New York: Columbia University Press, 2000.

Reid, Margaret. *Cultural Secrets as Narrative Form: Story Telling in Nineteenth-Century America*. Columbus: Ohio State University Press, 2004.

Romaine, Suzanne, ed. *1776-1997*. Vol. 4 in *The Cambridge History of the English Language*. Cambridge, England: Cambridge University Press, 1998.

Sagarra, Eda. *Germany in the Nineteenth Century: History and Literature*. New York: Peter Lang, 2001.

Smythe, Ted Curtis. *The Gilded Age Press, 1850-1900*. Westport, Conn.: Praeger, 2003.

Travers, Martin, ed. *An Introduction to Modern European Literature: From Romanticism to Postmodernism*. London: Palgrave Macmillan, 1997.

Turnell, Martin. *The Rise of the French Novel*. New York: New Directions, 1978.

Turner, Hy B. *When Giants Ruled: The Story of Park Row, New York's Great Newspaper Street*. New York: Fordham University Press, 1999.

Weinberg, Arthur, and Lila Weinberg, eds. *The Muckrakers*. Urbana: University of Illinois Press, 2001.

MATHEMATICS

Bear, H. S. *A Primer of Lebesgue Integration*. 2d ed. San Diego, Calif.: Academic Press, 2002.

Boyer, Carl B. *A History of Mathematics*. Rev. ed. New York: John Wiley & Sons, 1991.

Cole, K. C. *The Universe and the Teacup: The Mathematics of Truth and Beauty*. Fort Washington, Pa.: Harvest Books, 1999.

Davis, Martin. *Engines of Logic: Mathematicians and the Origin of the Computer*. New York: W. W. Norton, 2000.

Gasser, James, ed. *A Boole Anthology: Recent and Classical Studies in the Logic of George Boole*. Dordrecht, the Netherlands: Kluwer, 2000.

Grattan-Guinness, Ivor. *The Norton History of the Mathematical Sciences*. New York: W. W. Norton, 1999.

Jacquette, Dale. *On Boole*. Belmont, Calif.: Wadsworth, 2002.

Kline, Morris. *Mathematical Thought from Ancient to Modern Times*. New York: Oxford University Press, 1990.

Mlodinow, Leonard. *Euclid's Window: The Story of Geometry from Parallel Lines to Hyperspace*. New York: Free Press, 2001.

Smith, G. C. *The Boole-De Morgan Correspondence, 1842-1864*. New York: Oxford University Press, 1982.

Swade, Doron. *The Difference Engine: Charles Babbage and the Quest to Build the First Computer*. New York: Viking Press, 2001.

Van Heijenoort, Jean. *From Frege to Gödel: A Source Book in Mathematical Logic, 1879-1931*. Cambridge, Mass.: Harvard University Press, 2002.

Young, W. H., and G. C. Young. *The Theory of Sets of Points*. Cambridge, England: Cambridge University Press, 1906.

MEDICINE AND HEALTH

Bynum, W. E. *Science and Practice of Medicine in the Nineteenth Century*. Cambridge, England: Cambridge University Press, 1994.

Chase, Allan. *Magic Shots*. New York: William Morrow, 1982.

Curtin, Philip D. *Death by Migration: Europe's Encounter with the Tropical World in the Nineteenth Century*. Cambridge, England: Cambridge University Press, 1989.

Dormandy, Thomas. *Moments of Truth: Four Creators of Modern Medicine*. Hoboken, N.J.: Wiley, 2003.

Duncum, Barbara M. *The Development of Inhalation Anaesthesia with Special Reference to the Years, 1846-1900*. London: Oxford University Press, 1947.

Fenster, Julie M. *Ether Day: The Strange Tale of America's Greatest Medical Discovery and the Haunted Men Who Made It*. New York: HarperCollins, 2001.

Forsyth, David P. *The Humanitarians: The International Committee of the Red Cross*. New York: Cambridge University Press, 2005.

Gaw, Jerry L. *"A Time to Heal": The Diffusion of Listerism in Victorian Britain*. Philadelphia: American Philosophical Society, 1999.

Kamminga, Harmke, and Andrew Cunningham, eds. *The Science and Culture of Nutrition, 1840-1940*. The Wellcome Institute Series in the History of Medicine/ Clio Medica 32. Atlanta: Rodopi, 1995.

Money, John. *The Destroying Angel: Sex, Fitness, and Food in the Legacy of Degeneracy Theory, Graham Crackers, Corn Flakes, and American Health History*. Amherst, N.Y.: Prometheus Books, 1985.

Parish, A. J. *A History of Immunization*. Edinburgh: E. & S. Livingstone, 1965.

Porter, Roy. *The Greatest Benefit to Mankind: A Medical History of Humanity*. New York: W. W. Norton, 1999.

Robinson, Daniel N. *An Intellectual History of Psychology*. 3d ed. Madison: University of Wisconsin Press, 1995.

Shryock, Richard Harrison. *Medicine and Society in America, 1660-1860*. New York: New York University Press, 1960.

Singer, Charles. *A Short History of Anatomy and Physiology from the Greeks to Harvey*. New York: Dover, 1957.

Small, Hugh. *Florence Nightingale, Avenging Angel*. London: Constable, 1998.

Viney, Wayne. *A History of Psychology: Ideas and Context*. Boston: Allyn & Bacon, 1993.

Waller, John. *The Discovery of the Germ: Twenty Years That Transformed the Way We Think About Disease*. New York: Columbia University Press, 2002.

Wolfe, Richard J. *Tarnish Idol: William T. G. Morton and the Introduction of Surgical Anesthesia*. San Anselmo, Calif.: Norman, 2001.

MILITARY

Adkin, Mark. *The Charge: Why the Light Brigade Was Lost*. London: Leo Cooper, 1996.

Ambrose, Stephen. *Duty, Honor, Country: A History of West Point*. Baltimore: Johns Hopkins University Press, 1966.

Badsey, Stephen. *Essential Histories: The Franco-Prussian War, 1870-1871*. London: Osprey, 2003.

Bauer, K. Jack. *The Mexican War, 1846-1848*. Lincoln: University of Nebraska Press, 1992.

Baumgart, Winfried. *The Crimean War, 1853-1856*. New York: Oxford University Press, 1999.

Blumberg, Arnold. *A Carefully Planned Accident: The Italian War of 1859*. Cranbury, N.J.: Associated University Press, 1990.

Borneman, Walter R. *1812: The War That Forged a Nation*. New York: HarperCollins, 2004.

Brewer, David. *The Greek War of Independence*. New York: Overlook, 2001.

Brighton, Terry. *Hell Riders: The True Story of the Charge of the Light Brigade*. New York: Henry Holt, 2004.

Britt, Albert Sidney. *The Wars of Napoleon*. Wayne, N.J.: Avery Publishing Group, 1985.

Bucholz, Arden. *Moltke and the German Wars, 1864-1871*. New York: Palgrave, 2001.

Clowes, William Laird. *The Royal Navy: A History from the Earliest Times to 1900*. 7 vols. London: Chatham, 1997.

Coleman, Terry. *The Nelson Touch: The Life and Legend of Horatio Nelson*. New York: Oxford University Press, 2002.

Corrigan, Gordon. *Wellington: A Military Life*. London: Hambledon and London, 2001.

Crackel, Theodore J. *Mr. Jefferson's Army: Political and Social Reform of the Military Establishment, 1801-1809*. New York: New York University Press, 1987.

_____. *West Point: A Bicentennial History*. Lawrence: University Press of Kansas, 2002.

Elting, John R. *Amateurs to Arms! A Military History of the War of 1812*. Chapel Hill, N.C.: Algonquin Books, 1991.

Esdaile, Charles J. *Fighting Napoleon: Guerrillas, Bandits, and Adventurers in Spain, 1808-1814*. New Haven, Conn.: Yale University Press, 2004.

Esherick, Joseph W. *The Origins of the Boxer Uprising*. Berkeley: University of California Press, 1987.

Farwell, Byron. *The Encyclopedia of Nineteenth-Century Land Warfare: An Illustrated World View*. New York: W. W. Norton, 2001.

Gat, Azar. *The Development of Military Thought: The Nineteenth Century*. New York: Oxford University Press, 1992.

Gates, David. *Warfare in the Nineteenth Century*. London: Palgrave Macmillan, 2001.

Hickey, Donald R. *The War of 1812: A Forgotten Conflict*. Urbana: University of Illinois Press, 1989.

Howard, Michael E. *The Franco-Prussian War: The German Invasion of France*. New York: Dorset Press, 1990.

Jones, Howard. *Great Britain and the Confederate Navy, 1861-1865.* Bloomington: University of Indiana Press, 2004.

Keegan, John. *The Price of Admiralty: The Evolution of Naval Warfare.* New York: Viking, 1988.

Kennedy, Paul M. *The Rise and Fall of British Naval Mastery.* New York: Charles Scribner's Sons, 1976.

_____. *The Rise and Fall of the Great Powers: Economic Change and Military Conflict from 1500 to 2000.* New York: Random House, 1987.

Massie, Robert. *Dreadnought.* New York: Random House, 1991.

May, Robert E. *Manifest Destiny's Underworld: Filibustering in Antebellum America.* Chapel Hill: University of North Carolina Press, 2002.

Pakenham, Thomas. *The Boer War.* New York: Random House, 1979.

Rothenberg, Gunther E. *The Napoleonic Wars.* London: Cassell, 1999.

Schom, Alan. *One Hundred Days: Napoleon's Road to Waterloo.* New York: Atheneum, 1992.

Sutherland, Jonathan, and Diane Canwell. *The Zulu Kings and Their Armies.* Barnsley, England: Pen and Sword Military, 2005.

Utley, Robert M. *Frontier Regulars: The United States Army and the Indian, 1866-1891.* Lincoln: University of Nebraska Press, 1984.

Wawro, Geoffrey. *The Franco-Prussian War.* New York: Cambridge University Press, 2003.

Winders, Richard Bruce. *Mr. Polk's Army: The American Military Experience in the Mexican War.* College Station: Texas A&M University Press, 1997.

MUSIC

Abraham, Gerald, ed. *Romanticism, 1830-1890.* Vol. 9 in *The New Oxford History of Music.* New York: Oxford University Press, 1990.

Allison, John. *Great Opera Houses of the World.* London: Rolls House, 2004.

Bent, Ian, ed. *Music Theory in the Age of Romanticism.* Cambridge, England: Cambridge University Press, 1996.

Berlin, Edward A. *Ragtime: A Musical and Cultural History.* 1980. Reprint. Berkeley: University of California Press, 2002.

Carner, Mosco. *The Waltz.* London: M. Parrish, 1948.

Cooper, Barry. *The Beethoven Compendium: A Guide to Beethoven's Life and Music.* New York: Thames and Hudson, 1996.

Dahlhaus, Carl. *Nineteenth-Century Music.* Berkeley: University of California Press, 1991.

Davis, Leith. *Music, Postcolonialism, and Gender: The Construction of Irish National Identity, 1724-1874.* Notre Dame, Ind.: University of Notre Dame Press, 2006.

Dean, Winton. *Georges Bizet: His Life and Work.* 3d ed. London: J. M. Dent & Sons, 1975.

Fiedler, Johanna. *The Mayhem Behind the Music at the Metropolitan Opera.* New York: Nan A. Talese, 2001.

Furia, Philip. *The Poets of Tin Pan Alley: A History of America's Great Lyricists.* New York: Oxford University Press, 1990.

Griffiths, Paul. *A Concise History of Avant-Garde Music from Debussy to Boulez.* New York: Oxford University Press, 1978.

Hyman, Alan. *Sullivan and His Satellites: A Survey of English Operettas, 1860-1914.* London: Chappell, 1978.

Jasen, David A., and Gene Jones. *That American Rag: The Story of Ragtime in the United States.* New York: Schirmer Books, 2000.

Kamen, Henry A. *Music in New Orleans: The Formative Years, 1791-1841.* Baton Rouge: Louisiana State University Press, 1984.

Kolodin, Irving. *The Metropolitan Opera, 1883-1966.* New York: A. A. Knopf, 1966.

Levy, David. *Beethoven: The Ninth Symphony.* Rev. ed. New Haven, Conn.: Yale University Press, 2003.

May, Thomas. *Decoding Wagner: An Invitation to His World of Music Drama.* Pompton Plains, N.J.: Amadeus Press, 2004.

Rosselli, John. *The Opera Industry in Italy from Cimarosa to Verdi: The Role of the Impresario.* New York: Cambridge University Press, 1984.

Scherer, F. M. *Quarter Notes and Bank Notes: The Economics of Music Composition in the Eighteenth and Nineteenth Centuries.* Princeton, N.J.: Princeton University Press, 2003.

Schonberg, Harold C. *The Lives of the Great Composers.* 3d ed. New York: Norton, 1997.

Tawa, Nicholas E. *The Way to Tin Pan Alley: American Popular Song, 1866-1910.* New York: Schirmer Books/Macmillan, 1990.

NATIVE AMERICANS AND FIRST NATIONS

Axelrod, Alan. *Chronicle of the Indian Wars.* New York: Prentice Hall, 1993.

Barrett, Carole, and Harvey Markowitz, eds. *American*

Indian Biographies. Rev. ed. Pasadena, Calif.: Salem Press, 2005.

Braund, Kathryn E. Holland. *Deerskins and Duffels: The Creek Indian Trade with Anglo-America, 1685-1815*. Lincoln: University of Nebraska Press, 1993.

Brown, Dee. *Bury My Heart at Wounded Knee: An Indian History of the American West*. New York: Holt, Rinehart & Winston, 1970.

Brown, Jennifer S. H., Jacqueline Peterson, Robert K. Thomas, and Marcel Giraud, eds. *New Peoples: Being and Becoming Métis in North America*. St. Paul: Minnesota Historical Society, 2001.

Dickason, Olive Patricia. *Canada's First Nations: A History of Founding Peoples from Earliest Times*. Norman: University of Oklahoma Press, 1992.

Dowd, Gregory Evans. *A Spirited Resistance: The North American Indian Struggle for Unity, 1745-1815*. Baltimore: Johns Hopkins University Press, 1992.

Giraud, Marcel. *The Metis in the Canadian West*. Translated by George Woodcock. 2 vols. Lincoln: University of Nebraska Press, 1986.

Gough, Barry M. *Gunboat Frontier: British Maritime Authority and Northwest Coast Indians, 1846-1890*. Vancouver: University of British Columbia Press, 1984.

Haley, James L. *The Buffalo War: The History of the Red River Indian Uprising of 1874*. Austin, Tex.: State House Press, 1998.

Handbook of Middle American Indians. 16 vols. Austin: University of Texas Press, 1964-1976.

Jahoda, Gloria. *The Trail of Tears*. New York: Wings Books, 1995.

Josephy, Alvin M., Jr. *Civil War in the American West*. New York: Alfred A. Knopf, 1991.

Lazarus, Edward. *Black Hills, White Justice: The Sioux Nation Versus the United States, 1775 to the Present*. New York: HarperCollins, 1991.

McLoughlin, William G. *Cherokees and Missionaries, 1789-1839*. New Haven, Conn.: Yale University Press, 1984.

McMillan, Alan D. *Native Peoples and Cultures of Canada: An Anthropological Overview*. Vancouver: Douglas & McIntyre, 1988.

McPherson, Robert S. *The Northern Navajo Frontier, 1860-1900: Expansion Through Adversity*. Albuquerque: University of New Mexico Press, 1988.

Markowitz, Harvey, ed. *American Indians*. 3 vols. Pasadena, Calif.: Salem Press, 1995.

Miller, J. R. *Skyscrapers Hide the Heavens: A History of*

Indian-White Relations in Canada. Rev. ed. Toronto: University of Toronto Press, 1991.

Missall, John, and Mary Lou Missall. *The Seminole Wars: America's Longest Indian Conflict*. Gainesville: University Press of Florida, 2004.

O'Brien, Sean Michael. *In Bitterness and in Tears: Andrew Jackson's Destruction of the Creeks and Seminoles*. Guilford, Conn.: Lyons Press, 2005.

Ogle, Ralph Hedrick. *Federal Control of the Western Apaches, 1848-1886*. Albuquerque: University of New Mexico Press, 1970.

Prucha, Francis Paul. *American Indian Treaties*. Berkeley: University of California Press, 1994.

Robinson, Charles M., III. *The Plains Wars, 1757-1900*. New York: Routledge, 2003.

Rollings, Willard H. *The Comanche*. New York: Chelsea House, 1989.

Satzewich, Vic, and Terry Wotherspoon. *First Nations: Race, Class, and Gender Relations*. Scarborough, Ont.: Nelson Canada, 1993.

Sturtevant, William C. *Handbook of North American Indians*. 20 vols. Washington, D.C.: Smithsonian Institution Press, 2004.

Sugden, John. *Tecumseh: A Life*. New York: Henry Holt, 1998.

Tanner, Helen Hornbeck, ed. *The Settling of North America: The Atlas of the Great Migration into North America from the Ice Age to the Present*. New York: Macmillan, 1995.

Tennant, Paul. *Aboriginal Peoples and Politics: The Indian Land Question in British Columbia, 1849-1989*. Vancouver: University of British Columbia Press, 1990.

Utley, Robert M. *The Indian Frontier of the American West, 1846-1890*. Albuquerque: University of New Mexico Press, 1984.

Utley, Robert M., and Wilcomb B. Washburn. *The Indian Wars*. Boston: Houghton Mifflin, 1985.

Waldman, Carl, ed. *Atlas of the North American Indian*. New York: Facts On File, 1985.

Williams, Robert A. *The American Indian in Western Legal Thought*. New York: Oxford University Press, 1990.

OTTOMAN EMPIRE, PERSIA, AND THE MIDDLE EAST

Cleveland, William L. *A History of the Modern Middle East*. Boulder, Colo.: Westview Press, 1994.

Dadrian, Vahakn N. *The History of the Armenian Genocide: Ethnic Conflict from the Balkans to Anatolia to the Caucasus*. New York: Berghahn Books, 2003.

_____. *Warrant for Genocide: Key Elements of the Turko-Armenian Conflict*. New Brunswick, N.J.: Transaction, 1999.

Daly, M. W., ed. *Modern Egypt from 1517 to the End of the Twentieth Century*. Vol. 2 in *The Cambridge History of Egypt*. New York: Cambridge University Press, 1998.

Esposito, John. *The Oxford History of Islam*. New York: Oxford University Press, 2000.

Fahmy, Khaled. *All the Pasha's Men: Mehmed Ali, His Army, and the Making of Modern Egypt*. New York: Cambridge University Press, 1997.

Goodwin, Godfrey. *The Janissaries*. London: Saqi, 1997.

Hunter, F. Robert. *Egypt Under the Khedives, 1805-1879: From Household Government to Modern Bureaucracy*. Pittsburgh: University of Pittsburgh Press, 1988.

Karpat, Kemal H. *The Politicization of Islam: Reconstructing Identity, State, Faith, and Community in the Late Ottoman State*. New York: Oxford University Press, 2001.

Lewis, Bernard. *The Emergence of Modern Turkey*. New York: Oxford University Press, 2002.

Medlicott, W. N. *The Congress of Berlin and After: A Diplomatic History of the Near East Settlement, 1878-1880*. 2d ed. Hamden, Conn.: Archon Books, 1962.

Mishaqa, Mikhayil. *Murder, Mayhem, Pillage, and Plunder: The History of Lebanon in the Eighteenth and Nineteenth Centuries*. Translated by W. M. Thackston, Jr. Albany: State University of New York Press, 1988.

Nicolle, David. *Armies of the Ottoman Empire, 1775-1820*. London: Osprey, 1998.

Philipp, Thomas, and Ulrich Haarmann, eds. *The Mamluks in Egyptian Politics and Society*. Cambridge, England: Cambridge University Press, 1998.

Robinson, Francis. *Atlas of the Islamic World Since 1500*. New York: Facts On File, 1982.

Willis, Michael. *The Islamist Challenge in Algeria: A Political History*. New York: New York University Press, 1996.

Yapp, M. E. *A History of the Near East: The Making of the Modern Near East, 1792-1923*. New York: Longman, 1987.

Yasamee, F. A. K. *Ottoman Diplomacy: Abdülhamid II and the Great Powers*. Istanbul: Isis Press, 1996.

PHILOSOPHY

Berger, Fred R. *Happiness, Justice, and Freedom: The Moral and Political Philosophy of John Stuart Mill*. Berkeley: University of California Press, 1984.

Comte, Auguste. *System of Positive Polity*. New York: B. Franklin, 1968.

Craig, Edward, ed. *Routledge Encyclopedia of Philosophy*. 10 vols. New York: Routledge, 1998.

Edwards, Paul, ed. *The Encyclopedia of Philosophy*. 8 vols. New York: Macmillan, 1967.

Harris, Henry Silton. *Hegel's Development: Night Thoughts, Jena, 1801-1806*. Oxford, England: Clarendon Press, 1983.

Himmelfarb, Gertrude. *On Liberty and Liberalism: The Case of John Stuart Mill*. New York: Alfred A. Knopf, 1974.

Houlgate, Stephen. *An Introduction to Hegel: Freedom, Truth, and History*. 2d ed. Malden, Mass.: Blackwell, 2005.

Levin, Michael. *J. S. Mill on Civilization and Barbarism*. London: Routledge, 2004.

Magee, Bryan. *The Philosophy of Schopenhauer*. Oxford, England: Oxford University Press, 1997.

Manuel, Frank. *The New World of Henri Saint-Simon*. Cambridge, Mass.: Harvard University Press, 1956.

Mill, John Stuart. *John Stuart Mill: A Selection of His Works*. Edited by John M. Robson. New York: Odyssey Press, 1966.

Parkinson, G. H. R., and S. G. Shanker, ed. *Routledge History of Philosophy*. 10 vols. New York: Routledge, 2003.

Popkin, Richard, ed. *The Columbia History of Western Philosophy*. New York: Columbia University Press, 1999.

Roth, John K., ed. *World Philosophers and Their Works*. 3 vols. Pasadena, Calif.: Salem Press, 2000.

Scharff, Robert C. *Comte After Positivism*. New York: Cambridge University Press, 1995.

Weinstein, D. *Equal Freedom and Utility: Herbert Spencer's Liberal Utilitarianism*. New York: Cambridge University Press, 1998.

West, Henry R. *An Introduction to Mill's Utilitarian Ethics*. New York: Cambridge University Press, 2004.

PHOTOGRAPHY AND FILM

Abel, Richard. *The Ciné Goes to Town: French Cinema, 1896-1914*. Berkeley: University of California Press, 1994.

Elsaesser, Thomas, with Adam Barker, eds. *Early Cinema: Space, Frame, Narrative*. London: BFI, 1990.

Freund, Gisele. *Photography and Society*. Boston: David R. Godine, 1980.

Hirsch, Robert. *Seizing the Light: A History of Photography*. New York: McGraw-Hill, 1999.

Marien, Mary Warner. *Photography: A Cultural History*. New York: Harry N. Abrams, 2002.

Newhall, Beaumont. *History of Photography: From 1839 to the Present*. New York: Museum of Modern Art, 1982.

Rosenblum, Naomi. *A World History of Photography*. 3d ed. New York: Abbeville Press, 1997.

Sullivan, George. *In the Wake of Battle: The Civil War Images of Mathew Brady*. New York: Prestel, 2004.

West, Nancy Martha. *Kodak and the Lens of Nostalgia*. Charlottesville: University Press of Virginia, 2000.

POLITICAL THOUGHT AND THE HISTORY OF IDEAS

Baron, Samuel H. *Plekhanov: The Father of Russian Marxism*. Stanford, Calif.: Stanford University Press, 1963.

Beecher, Jonathan. *Victor Considerant and the Rise and Fall of French Romantic Socialism*. Berkeley: University of California Press, 2001.

Benson, Thomas W. *Rhetoric and Political Culture in Nineteenth-Century America*. Ann Arbor: University of Michigan Press, 1997.

Brewer, Anthony. *A Guide to Marx's "Capital."* Cambridge, England: Cambridge University Press, 1984.

Ehrenberg, John. *Proudhon and His Age*. Atlantic Highlands, N.J.: Humanities Press, 1996.

Francis, Mark, and John Morrow. *A History of English Political Thought in the Nineteenth Century*. London: Duckworth, 1994.

Gilbert, Felix. *History: Politics or Culture? Reflections on Ranke and Burckhardt*. Princeton, N.J.: Princeton University Press, 1990.

Gray, John. *Liberalisms: Essays in Political Philosophy*. New York: Routledge, 1991.

Gray, T. S. *The Political Philosophy of Herbert Spencer*. Aldershot, Hampshire, England: Avebury Press, 1996.

Hartz, Louis, and Paul Roazen, eds. *The Necessity of Choice: Nineteenth Century Political Thought*. New Brunswick, N.J.: Transaction, 1990.

Hereth, Michael. *Alexis de Tocqueville: Threats to Freedom in Democracy*. Translated by George Bogardus. Durham, N.C.: Duke University Press, 1986.

Iggers, Georg G., and James Powell, eds. *Leopold von Ranke and the Shaping of the Historical Discipline*. Syracuse, N.Y.: Syracuse University Press, 1990.

Kahan, Alan S. *Liberalism in Nineteenth Century Europe*. Houndmills, Basingstoke, England: Palgrave Macmillan, 2003.

McCann, Charles R. *Individualism and the Social Order: The Social Element in Liberal Thought*. London: Routledge, 2004.

McLaughlin, Paul. *Mikhail Bakunin: The Philosophical Basis of His Theory of Anarchism*. New York: Algora, 2002.

Marsden, Richard. *The Nature of Capital: Marx After Foucault*. London: Routledge, 1999.

Marx, Karl, and Frederick Engels. *On the Paris Commune*. Moscow: Progress Publishers, 1971.

Mayer, David N. *The Constitutional Thought of Thomas Jefferson*. Charlottesville: University Press of Virginia, 1994.

Mecklenberg, Frank, and Manfred Stassen, eds. *German Essays on Socialism in the Nineteenth Century: Theory, History, and Political Organization, 1844-1914*. New York: Continuum International, 1990.

Morgan, Edmund Sears. *The Meaning of Independence: John Adams, George Washington, Thomas Jefferson*. Rev. ed. Charlottesville: University of Virginia Press, 2004.

Morland, David. *Demanding the Impossible? Human Nature and Politics in Nineteenth-Century Anarchism*. London: Cassell, 1997.

Shankman, Kimberly Christner. *Compromise and the Constitution: The Political Thought of Henry Clay*. Lanham, Md.: Lexington Books, 1999.

Steger, Manfred B., and Terrell Carver, eds. *Engels After Marx*. University Park: Pennsylvania State University Press, 1999.

Struik, Dirk J., ed. *Birth of the Communist Manifesto*. New York: International Publishers, 1971.

Wolin, Sheldon S. *Tocqueville Between Worlds: The Making of a Political and Theoretical Life*. Princeton, N.J.: Princeton University Press, 2001.

POPULAR CULTURE AND DAILY LIFE

Adams, Bluford. *E. Pluribus Barnum: The Great Showman and the Making of Popular Culture*. Minneapolis: University of Minnesota Press, 1997.

Allen, Robert C. *Horrible Prettiness: Burlesque and American Culture*. Chapel Hill, N.C.: University of North Carolina Press, 1991.

Ash, Juliet, and Lee Wright, eds. *Components of Dress: Design, Manufacturing, and Image-Making in the Fashion Industry*. New York: Routledge, 1988.

Block, David. *Baseball Before We Knew It: A Search for*

the Roots of the Game. Lincoln: University of Nebraska Press, 2005.

Boucher, François. *Twenty Thousand Years of Fashion: The History of Costume and Personal Adornment*. Rev. ed. New York: Harry N. Abrams, 1987.

Burnett, J. *A Social History of Housing, 1815-1985*. 2d ed. London: Methuen, 1986.

Cockrell, Dale. *Demons of Disorder: Early Blackface Minstrels and Their World*. New York: Cambridge University Press, 1997.

Cook, James W. *The Arts of Deception: Playing with Fraud in the Age of Barnum*. Cambridge, Mass.: Harvard University Press, 2001.

Coubertin, Pierre de. *Olympic Memoirs*. Lausanne, Switzerland: International Olympic Committee, 1979.

Culhane, John. *The American Circus: An Illustrated History*. New York: Henry Holt, 1990.

Davis, Susan G. *Parades and Power: Street Theatre in Nineteenth-Century Philadelphia*. Philadelphia: Temple University Press, 1986.

Dennett, Andrea Stulman. *Weird and Wonderful: The Dime Museum in America*. New York: New York University Press, 1997.

Erdman, Andrew L. *Blue Vaudeville: Sex, Morals, and the Mass Marketing of Amusement, 1895-1915*. Jefferson, N.C.: McFarland, 2004.

Ewen, David. *The Life and Death of Tin Pan Alley: The Golden Age of American Popular Music*. New York: Funk & Wagnalls, 1964.

Harter, Jim. *Food and Drink: A Pictorial Archive from Nineteenth-Century Sources*. New York: Dover, 1980.

Johnston, Lucy. *Nineteenth-Century Fashion in Detail*. London: Victoria and Albert Museum, 2005.

Kirsch, George B. *The Creation of American Team Sports: Baseball and Cricket, 1838-1872*. Urbana: University of Illinois Press, 1989.

Larson, Erik. *The Devil in the White City: Murder, Magic, and Madness at the Fair That Changed America*. New York: Crown, 2003.

Lipscomb, F. W. *A Hundred Years of the America's Cup*. Greenwich, Conn.: New York Graphic Society, 1971.

Llewellyn Smith, M. *Olympics in Athens, 1896: The Invention of the Modern Olympic Games*. London: Profile Books, 2004.

McCutcheon, Mark. *Everyday Life in the 1800's: A Guide for Writers, Students, and Historians*. New York: Writer's Digest Books, 2001.

Mahar, William J. *Behind the Burnt Cork Mask: Early Blackface Minstrelsy and Antebellum American Pop-*

ular Culture. Urbana: University of Illinois Press, 1999.

Peterson, Robert W. *Cages to Jump Shots: Pro Basketball's Early Years*. Lincoln: University of Nebraska Press, 2002.

Purbrick, Louise, ed. *The Great Exhibition of 1851: New Interdisciplinary Essays*. New York: Manchester University Press, 2001.

Snyder, Robert W. *The Voice of the City: Vaudeville and Popular Culture in New York*. Reprint. Chicago: Ivan R. Dee, 2000.

Toll, Robert C. *Blacking Up: The Minstrel Show in Nineteenth-Century America*. London: Oxford University Press, 1974.

Webb, Bernice Larson. *The Basketball Man: James Naismith*. Lawrence: University Press of Kansas, 1973.

Wittke, Carl. *Tambo and Bones: A History of the American Minstrel Stage*. Reprint. New York: Greenwood, 1968.

Young, David C. *The Modern Olympics: A Struggle for Revival*. Baltimore: Johns Hopkins University Press, 1996.

PRUSSIA AND GERMANY

Alter, Peter. *The German Question and Europe: A History*. London: Arnold, 2000.

Berghann, V. R. *Imperial Germany, 1871-1918: Economy, Society, Culture, and Politics*. Rev. and expanded ed. New York: Berghann Books, 2005.

Blackbourn, David. *History of Germany, 1780-1918: The Long Nineteenth Century*. London: Blackwell, 2002.

Craig, Gordon A. *Germany, 1866-1945*. New York: Oxford University Press, 1978.

Feuchtwanger, Edgar. *Imperial Germany, 1850-1918*. London: Routledge, 2001.

Hargreaves, David. *Bismarck and German Unification*. Houndmills, England: Macmillan, 1991.

Henderson, W. O. *The Rise of German Industrial Power, 1834-1914*. Berkeley: University of California Press, 1975.

Holborn, Hajo. *A History of Modern Germany*. 3 vols. New York: Alfred A. Knopf, 1964.

Lee, Stephen J. *Imperial Germany, 1871-1918*. London: Routledge, 1999.

Manchester, William. *The Arms of Krupp, 1587-1968*. Boston: Little Brown, 1968.

Nipperdey, Thomas. *Germany from Napoleon to Bismarck*. Princeton, N.J.: Princeton University Press, 1996.

Ross, Ronald J. *The Failure of Bismarck's Kulturkampf: Catholicism and State Power in Wilhelmine, Germany*. Washington, D.C.: Catholic University Press, 1998.

Sheehan, James J. *German History, 1770-1886*. Oxford, England: Clarendon Press, 1989.

Showalter, Dennis E. *The Wars of German Unification*. London: Arnold, 2004.

Siemann, Wolfram. *The German Revolution of 1848-49*. New York: Palgrave Macmillan, 1998.

Simpson, William. *The Second Reich: Germany, 1871-1918*. New York: Cambridge University Press, 1995.

Smith, Helmut W. *German Nationalism and Political Conflict, 1870-1912*. Princeton, N.J.: Princeton University Press, 1995.

Williamson, D. G. *Bismarck and Germany, 1862-1890*. 2d ed. London: Longman, 1998.

RELIGION

Abzug, Robert H. *Cosmos Crumbling: American Reform and the Religious Imagination*. New York: Oxford University Press, 1994.

Asad, Talal. *Formations of the Secular: Christianity, Islam, Modernity*. Stanford, Calif.: Stanford University Press, 2003.

Barth, Karl. *Protestant Theology in the Nineteenth Century: Its Background and History*. Grand Rapids, Mich.: Eerdman's, 2002.

Buescher, John B. *The Other Side of Salvation: Spiritualism and the Nineteenth-Century Religious Experience*. Boston: Skinner House, 2004.

Chadwick, Owen. *A History of the Popes, 1830-1914*. New York: Oxford University Press, 1998.

_____. *The Secularization of the European Mind in the Nineteenth Century*. Reprint. Cambridge, England: Cambridge University Press, 1990.

Coppa, Frank J. *The Modern Papacy Since 1789*. London: Longman, 1998.

George, Carol V. R. *Segregated Sabbaths: Richard Allen and the Rise of Independent Black Churches, 1760-1840*. New York: Oxford University Press, 1973.

Grant, Robert M., and David Tracy. *A Short History of the Interpretation of the Bible*. Rev. ed. London: SCM, 1996.

McDannell, Colleen. *Material Christianity: Religion and Popular Culture in America*. New Haven, Conn.: Yale University Press, 1996.

McKivigan, John R. *The War Against Proslavery Religion: Abolitionism and the Northern Churches, 1830-1865*. Ithaca, N.Y.: Cornell University Press, 1984.

Mandelker, Ira L. *Religion, Society, and Utopia in Nineteenth-Century America*. Amherst: University of Massachusetts Press, 1984.

Matovina, Timothy M. *Tejano Religion and Ethnicity: San Antonio, 1821-1860*. Austin: University of Texas Press, 1995.

Nasr, Seyed Hossein. *Islam: Religion, History and Civilization*. San Francisco: HarperSanFrancisco, 2002.

Nockles, Peter B. *The Oxford Movement in Context: Anglican High Churchmanship, 1760-1857*. Cambridge, England: Cambridge University Press, 1996.

Noll, Mark A. *The Old Religion in the New World: The History of North American Christianity*. Grand Rapids, Mich.: Wm. B. Eerdmans, 2001.

Nord, David Paul. *Faith in Reading: Religious Publishing and the Birth of Mass Media in America*. New York: Oxford University Press, 2004.

Noss, David S. *A History of the World's Religions*. 11th ed. Englewood Cliffs, N.J.: Prentice Hall, 2002.

Wacker, Grant. *Religion in Nineteenth Century America*. New York: Oxford University Press, 2000.

Walker, Pamela J. *Pulling the Devil's Kingdom Down: The Salvation Army in Victorian Britain*. Berkeley: University of California Press, 2001.

RUSSIA AND POLAND

Davies, Norman. *God's Playground: A History of Poland*. New York: Columbia University Press, 1984.

Field, Daniel. *The End of Serfdom: Nobility and Bureaucracy in Russia, 1855-1861*. Cambridge, Mass.: Harvard University Press, 1976.

Jelavich, Barbara. *Russia's Balkan Entanglements, 1806-1914*. New York: Cambridge University Press, 1991.

Lincoln, W. Bruce. *The Great Reforms: Autocracy, Bureaucracy, and the Politics of Change in Imperial Russia*. DeKalb: Northern Illinois University Press, 1990.

MacKenzie, David. *Imperial Dreams, Harsh Realities: Tsarist Russian Foreign Policy, 1815-1917*. Fort Worth, Tex.: Harcourt Brace College, 1994.

Marks, Steven. *How Russia Shaped the Modern World: From Art to Anti-Semitism, Ballet to Bolshevism*. Princeton, N.J.: Princeton University Press, 2003.

Menning, Bruce W. *Bayonets Before Bullets: The Imperial Russian Army, 1861-1914*. Bloomington: Indiana University Press, 1992.

Moss, Walter G. *Russia in the Age of Alexander II, Tolstoy, and Dostoevsky*. London: Anthem Press, 2002.

Polunov, Alexander. *Russia in the Nineteenth Century:*

Autocracy, Reform, and Social Change, 1814-1914. Translated by Marshall S. Shatz, edited by Thomas C. Owen and Larissa G. Zakharova. Armonk, N.Y.: M. E. Sharpe, 2005.

Saunders, David. *Russia in the Age of Reaction and Reform, 1801-1881.* New York: Longman, 1992.

Walicki, Andrzej. *A History of Russian Thought: From the Enlightenment to Marxism.* Stanford, Calif.: Stanford University Press, 1993.

Wandyc, Piotr S. *The Lands of Partitioned Poland, 1795-1918.* Seattle: University of Washington Press, 1996.

SCIENCE

Alioto, Anthony M. *A History of Western Science.* 2d ed. Upper Saddle River, N.J.: Prentice Hall, 1993.

Baker, John. *The Cell Theory: A Restatement, History, and Critique.* New York: Garland, 1988.

Bland, Lucy, and Laura Doan. *Sexology in Culture: Labeling Bodies and Desires.* Chicago: University of Chicago Press, 1998.

Bowler, Peter J. *Charles Darwin: The Man and His Influence.* Cambridge, England: Cambridge University Press, 1996.

_____. *Evolution: The History of an Idea.* Rev. ed. Berkeley: University of California Press, 1989.

Brock, William H. *The Chemical Tree: A History of Chemistry.* New York: W. W. Norton, 2000.

_____. *Justus von Liebig: The Chemical Gatekeeper.* Cambridge, England: Cambridge University Press, 1997.

Brookes, Martin. *Extreme Measures: The Dark Visions and Bright Ideas of Francis Galton.* New York: Bloomsbury, 2004.

Brush, Stephen G. *Cautious Revolutionaries: Maxwell, Planck, Hubble.* College Park, Md.: American Association of Physics Teachers, 2002.

Bynum, W. F., E. J. Browne, and R. Porter, eds. *Dictionary of the History of Science.* London: Macmillan, 1981.

Cantor, Geoffrey. *Michael Faraday, Sandemanian and Scientist: A Study of Science and Religion in the Nineteenth Century.* New York: St. Martin's Press, 1991.

Carlson, Elof Axel. *Mendel's Legacy: The Origin of Classical Genetics.* Woodbury, N.Y.: Cold Spring Harbor Laboratory Press, 2004.

Corsi, Pietro. *The Age of Lamarck: Evolutionary Theories in France, 1790-1830.* Berkeley: University of California Press, 1988.

Darrigol, Oliver. *Electrodynamics from Ampere to Einstein.* New York: Oxford University Press, 2000.

Duck, Ian. *One Hundred Years of Planck's Quantum.* River Edge, N.J.: World Scientific, 2000.

Edelson, Edward. *Gregor Mendel and the Roots of Genetics.* Oxford, England: Oxford University Press, 2001.

Finger, Stanley. *Minds Behind the Brain: A History of the Pioneers and Their Discoveries.* New York: Oxford University Press, 2000.

Gay, Peter. *Freud: A Life for Our Time.* New York: W. W. Norton, 1988.

Geison, Gerald. *The Private Science of Louis Pasteur.* Princeton, N.J.: Princeton University Press, 1995.

Golinski, Jan. *Science as Public Culture: Chemistry and Enlightenment in Britain, 1760-1820.* Cambridge, England: Cambridge University Press, 1992.

Gordin, Michael D. *A Well-Ordered Thing: Dmitrii Mendeleev and the Shadow of the Periodic Table.* New York: Basic Books, 2004.

Greene, Mott T. *Geology in the Nineteenth Century: Changing Views of a Changing World.* Ithaca, N.Y.: Cornell University Press, 1982.

Heilbron, J. L. *The Dilemmas of an Upright Man: Max Planck as a Spokesman for German Science.* Berkeley: University of California Press, 1986.

Kevles, Daniel J. *In the Name of Eugenics: Genetics and the Uses of Human Heredity.* Cambridge, Mass.: Harvard University Press, 1995.

Keynes, Milo, ed. *Sir Francis Galton, FRS: The Legacy of His Ideas.* London: Macmillan, 1993.

Klaver, J. M. I. *Geology and Religious Sentiment: The Effect of Geological Discoveries on English Society and Literature Between 1829 and 1859.* New York: Brill, 1997.

Knight, David. *The Age of Science: The Scientific Worldview in the Nineteenth Century.* Reprint. London: Blackwell, 1988.

Kuhn, Thomas S. *Black-Body Theory and the Quantum Discontinuity, 1894-1912.* New York: Oxford University Press, 1978.

Kutzbach, Gisela. *The Thermal Theory of Cyclones: A History of Meteorological Thought in the Nineteenth Century.* Boston: American Meteorological Society, 1979.

Lamarck, Jean-Baptiste. *Zoological Philosophy: An Exposition with Regard to the Natural History of Animals.* Translated by Hugh Elliot. Chicago: University of Chicago Press, 1984.

Lyell, Charles. *Elements of Geology*. London: John Murray, 1838.

MacIntyre, Alasdair. *The Unconscious: A Conceptual Analysis*. Rev. ed. New York: Routledge, 2004.

Miller, David Philip. *Discovering Water: James Watt, Henry Cavendish, and the Nineteenth Century "Water Controversy."* Burlington, Vt.: Ashgate, 2004.

Morris, Richard. *The Last Sorcerers: The Path from Alchemy to the Periodic Table*. Washington, D.C.: Joseph Henry Press, 2003.

Morton, A. G. *History of Botanical Science: An Account of Botany from Ancient Times to the Present Day*. London: Academic Press, 1981.

North, John. *The Norton History of Astronomy and Cosmology*. New York: W. W. Norton, 1995.

Purrington, Robert D. *Physics in the Nineteenth Century*. New Brunswick, N.J.: Rutgers University Press, 1997.

Ruse, Michael. *The Darwinian Revolution: Science Red in Tooth and Claw*. 2d ed. Chicago: University of Chicago Press, 1999.

Smyth, Albert Leslie. *John Dalton, 1766-1844*. Aldershot, England: Ashgate, 1998.

Strathern, Paul. *Mendeleyev's Dream: The Quest for the Elements*. New York: Berkeley Books, 2000.

Sturge, M. D. *Statistical and Thermal Physics: Fundamentals and Applications*. Natick, Mass.: A K Peters, 2003.

Sturtevant, A. H. *A History of Genetics*. 1965. Reprint. Cold Spring Harbor, N.Y.: Cold Spring Harbor Press, 2001.

Wallace, Alfred Russel. *The Malay Archipelago: A Narrative of Travel with Studies of Man and Nature*. 1869. Reprint. Hong Kong: Periplus, 2000.

Waller, John. *Einstein's Luck: The Truth Behind Some of the Greatest Scientific Discoveries*. New York: Oxford University Press, 2002.

Weber, Alan S. *Nineteenth-Century Science: An Anthology*. Peterborough, Ont.: Broadview Press, 2000.

Wilson, Leonard G. *Charles Lyell*. 2 vols. New Haven, Conn.: Yale University Press, 1972.

SLAVERY AND THE AFRICAN AMERICAN EXPERIENCE

Anderson, Eric, and Alfred A. Moss, Jr., eds. *The Facts of Reconstruction: Essays in Honor of John Hope Franklin*. Baton Rouge: Louisiana State University Press, 1991.

Baker, Houston A., Jr. *Turning South Again: Re-thinking Modernism/Re-reading Booker T. Washington*. Durham, N.C.: Duke University Press, 2001.

Bell, Derrick. *Race, Racism, and American Law*. 2d ed. Boston: Little, Brown, 1980.

Brundage, Fitzhugh, ed. *Booker T. Washington and Black Progress: "Up from Slavery" One Hundred Years Later*. Gainesville: University Press of Florida, 2003.

Chesebrough, David B. *Frederick Douglass: Oratory from Slavery*. Westport, Conn.: Greenwood Press, 1998.

Clinton, Catherine. *Harriet Tubman: The Road to Freedom*. New York: Little, Brown, 2004.

Drescher, Seymour. *The Mighty Experiment: Free Labor Versus Slavery in British Emancipation*. New York: Oxford University Press, 2002.

Dvorak, Katharine L. *An African American Exodus*. Brooklyn, N.Y.: Carlson, 1991.

Franklin, John Hope, and Alfred A. Moss, Jr. *From Slavery to Freedom: A History of African Americans*. 8th ed. Boston: McGraw-Hill, 2000.

French, Scot. *The Rebellious Slave: Nat Turner in American Memory*. Boston: Houghton Mifflin, 2004.

Greenberg, Kenneth S., ed. *Nat Turner: A Slave Rebellion in History and Memory*. New York: Oxford University Press, 2003.

Humez, Jean M. *Harriet Tubman: The Life and the Life Stories*. Madison: University of Wisconsin Press, 2003.

Jones, Howard. *Mutiny on the "Amistad": The Saga of a Slave Revolt and Its Impact on American Abolition, Law, and Diplomacy*. New York: Oxford University Press, 1987.

Larson, Kate Clifford. *Bound for the Promised Land: Harriet Tubman, Portrait of an American Hero*. New York: Ballantine, 2004.

Levine, Robert S. *Martin Delany, Frederick Douglass, and the Politics of Representative Identity*. Chapel Hill: University of North Carolina Press, 1997.

Litwack, Leon F. *Been in the Storm So Long: The Aftermath of Slavery*. New York: Alfred A. Knopf, 1979.

Mabee, Carleton. *Sojourner Truth: Slave, Prophet, Legend*. New York: New York University Press, 1993.

Martin, Waldo E. *The Mind of Frederick Douglass*. Chapel Hill: University of North Carolina Press, 1984.

Nieman, Donald G. *Promises to Keep: African-Americans and the Constitutional Order, 1776 to the Present*. New York: Oxford University Press, 1991.

Rasmussen, R. Kent. *Farewell to Jim Crow: The Rise*

and Fall of Segregation in America. New York: Facts On File, 1997.

Sluby, Patricia Carter. *The Inventive Spirit of African Americans: Patented Ingenuity.* Westport, Conn.: Praeger, 2004.

Thomas, Hugh. *The Slave Trade: The Story of the Atlantic Slave Trade, 1440-1870.* New York: Simon & Schuster, 1999.

Tise, Larry E. *Proslavery: A History of the Defense of Slavery in America, 1701-1840.* Athens: University of Georgia Press, 1987.

Verney, Kevern. *The Art of the Possible: Booker T. Washington and Black Leadership in the United States, 1881-1925.* New York: Routledge, 2001.

SOUTHEAST ASIA, AUSTRALASIA, AND THE PACIFIC

Brands, H. W. *Bound to Empire: The United States and the Philippines.* New York: Oxford University Press, 1992.

Chapuis, Oscar. *A History of Vietnam.* Westport, Conn.: Greenwood Press, 1995.

_____. *The Last Emperors of Vietnam: From Tu Duc to Bao Dai.* Westport, Conn.: Greenwood Press, 2000.

Daws, Gavan, and Marty Fujita. *Archipelago: The Islands of Indonesia, from the Nineteenth-Century Discoveries of Alfred Russel Wallace to the Fate of Forests and Reefs in the Twenty-First Century.* Berkeley: University of California Press, 1999.

Eng, Pierre van der. *The "Colonial Drain" from Indonesia, 1823-1890.* Canberra: Economics Division, Research School of Pacific Studies, Australian National University, 1993.

Guzzetti, Paula. *Last Hawaiian Queen, Liliuokalani.* London: Marshall Cavendish, 1997.

Hall, D. G. E. *A History of South-East Asia.* 4th ed. New York: St. Martin's Press, 1981.

Karnov, Stanley. *In Our Image: America's Empire in the Philippines.* New York: Random House, 1989.

McCall, Grant. *Rapanui: Tradition and Survival on Easter Island.* Honolulu: University of Hawaii Press, 1994.

Maude, H. E. *Slavers in Paradise: The Peruvian Slave Trade in Polynesia, 1862-1864.* Stanford, Calif.: Stanford University Press, 1981.

Osborne, Thomas J. *Empire Can Wait: American Opposition to Hawaiian Annexation, 1893-1898.* Kent, Ohio: Kent State University Press, 1981.

Pluvier, Jan M. *Historical Atlas of South-East Asia.*
Leiden, the Netherlands: Brill Academic Publishers, 1995.

Ricklefs, M. C. *A History of Modern Indonesia Since c. 1200.* 3d ed. Stanford, Calif.: Stanford University Press, 2001.

Tarling, Nicholas, ed. *From c. 1800 to the 1930's.* Vol. 2, part 1 in *The Cambridge History of Southeast Asia.* New York: Cambridge University Press, 2000.

Tate, D. J. M. *The Making of Modern South-East Asia: The European Conquest.* Kuala Lumpur, Malaysia: Oxford University Press, 1977.

SPAIN, PORTUGAL, AND LATIN AMERICA

Anderson, James Maxwell. *The History of Portugal.* Westport, Conn.: Greenwood Press, 2000.

Anna, Timothy E. *The Mexican Empire of Iturbide.* Lincoln: University of Nebraska Press, 1990.

Archer, Chirston I., ed. *The Birth of Modern Mexico, 1780-1824.* Wilmington, Del.: Scholarly Resources, 2003.

Barahona, Renato. *Vizcaya on the Eve of Carlism: Politics and Society, 1800-1833.* Reno: University of Nevada Press, 1989.

Barman, Roderick J. *Brazil: The Forging of a Nation, 1798-1852.* Stanford, Calif.: Stanford University Press, 1988.

_____. *Citizen Emperor: Pedro II and the Making of Brazil, 1825-1891.* Stanford, Calif.: Stanford University Press, 1999.

Barton, Simon. *A History of Spain.* London: Palgrave McMillan, 2004.

Bazant, Jan. *A Concise History of Mexico from Hidalgo to Cárdenas, 1805-1940.* Cambridge, England: Cambridge University Press, 1977.

Belnap, Jeffrey, and Raul Fernandez. *Jose Marti's "Our America": From National to Hemispheric Cultural Studies.* Durham, N.C.: Duke University Press, 1998.

Birmingham, David. *A Concise History of Portugal.* 2d ed. Cambridge, England: Cambridge University Press, 2003.

Burr, Robert N. *By Reason or Force: Chile and the Balancing of Power in South America, 1830-1905.* Berkeley: University of California Press, 1967.

Carr, Raymond, ed. *Spain: A History.* New York: Oxford University Press, 2000.

Crow, John A. *Spain, the Root and the Flower: An Interpretation of Spain and the Spanish People.* 3d ed. Berkeley: University of California Press, 1985.

Farcau, Bruce W. *The Ten Cents War: Chile, Peru, and*

Bolivia in the War of the Pacific, 1879-1884. Westport, Conn.: Praeger, 2000.

Ferrer, Ada. *Insurgent Cuba: Race, Nation, and Revolution, 1868-1898.* Chapel Hill: University of North Carolina Press, 1999.

Graham, Richard. *Independence in Latin America: A Comparative Approach.* New York: McGraw-Hill, 1994.

Harvey, Robert. *Liberators: Latin America's Struggle for Independence, 1810-1830.* Woodstock, N.Y.: Overlook Press, 2000.

Healy, David. *James G. Blaine and Latin America.* Columbia: University of Missouri Press, 2001.

Jaksić, Iván, ed. *The Political Power of the Word: Press and Oratory in Nineteenth-Century Latin America.* London: Institute of Latin American Studies, 2002.

Keen, Benjamin. *A History of Latin America.* Boston: Houghton Mifflin, 1996.

Kraay, Hendrick. *Race, State, and Armed Forces in Independence-Era Brazil: Bahia, 1790's-1840's.* Stanford, Calif.: Stanford University Press, 2002.

Kraay, Hendrick, and Thomas L. Whigham, eds. *I Die with My Country: Perspectives on the Paraguayan War, 1864-1870.* Lincoln: University of Nebraska Press, 2004.

Krauze, Enrique. *Mexico: Biography of Power.* New York: HarperCollins, 1997.

Leone, Bruno. *The Mexican War of Independence.* San Diego, Calif.: Lucent Books, 1996.

Leuchars, Chris. *To the Bitter End: Paraguay and the War of the Triple Alliance.* Westport, Conn.: Greenwood Press, 2002.

Loveman, Brian. *Chile: The Legacy of Hispanic Capitalism.* 3d ed. New York: Oxford University Press, 2001.

Lynch, John. *Bourbon Spain, 1700-1808.* Oxford, England: Basil Blackwell, 1989.

_____. *The Spanish American Revolutions, 1808-1826.* New York: W. W. Norton, 1973.

Maude, H. E. *Slavers in Paradise: The Peruvian Slave Trade in Polynesia, 1862-1864.* Stanford, Calif.: Stanford University Press, 1981.

Meyer, Michael C., and William H. Beezley, eds. *The Oxford History of Mexico.* New York: Oxford University Press, 2000.

Meyer, Michael C., William L. Sherman, and Susan M. Deeds. *The Course of Mexican History.* 7th ed. New York: Oxford University Press, 2003.

Rodriguez O., Jaime E. *The Independence of Spanish America.* New York: Cambridge University Press, 1998.

Ruiz, Ramón Eduardo. *Triumphs and Tragedy: A History of the Mexican People.* New York: W. W. Norton, 1992.

Safford, Frank, and Marco Palacios. *Colombia: Fragmented Land, Divided Society.* New York: Oxford University Press, 2002.

Sater, William F. *Chile and the War of the Pacific.* Lincoln: University of Nebraska Press, 1986.

Scheina, Robert L. *Santa Anna: A Curse upon Mexico.* Washington, D.C.: Brassey's, 2002.

Schmidt-Nowara, Christopher. *Empire and Antislavery: Spain, Cuba, and Puerto Rico, 1833-1874.* Pittsburgh, Pa.: University of Pittsburgh Press, 1999.

Schultz, Kirsten. *Tropical Versailles: Empire, Monarchy, and the Portuguese Royal Court in Rio de Janeiro, 1808-1821.* New York: Routledge, 2001.

Thomas, Hugh. *Cuba: The Pursuit of Freedom.* New York: Harper & Row, 1971.

Wasserman, Mark. *Everyday Life and Politics in Nineteenth Century Mexico: Men, Women, and War.* Albuquerque: University of New Mexico Press, 2000.

Whigham, Thomas L. *The Paraguayan War: Causes and Early Conduct.* Lincoln: University of Nebraska Press, 2002.

TECHNOLOGY, INVENTION, AND INDUSTRY

Adas, Michael. *Machines as the Measure of Men: Science, Technology, and Ideologies of Western Dominance.* Ithaca, N.Y.: Cornell University Press, 1989.

Ambrose, Stephen E. *Nothing Like It in the World: The Men Who Built the Transcontinental Railroad, 1863-1869.* New York: Simon & Schuster, 2000.

Andreae, Christopher. *Lines of Country: An Atlas of Railway and Waterway History in Canada.* Cartography by Geoffrey Matthews. Erin, Ont.: Boston Mills Press, 1997.

Bankstron, John. *Karl Benz and the Single Cylinder Engine.* Hockessin: Mitchell Land, 2004.

Barger, M. Susan, and William B. White. *The Daguerreotype: Nineteenth Century Technology and Modern Science.* Baltimore: Johns Hopkins University Press, 2000.

Beauchamp, Ken. *History of Telegraphy.* London: Institution of Electrical Engineers, 2001.

Black, Brian. *Petrolia: The Landscape of America's First Oil Boom.* Baltimore: Johns Hopkins University Press, 2000.

Bodsworth, C., ed. *Sir Henry Bessemer: Father of the Steel Industry.* London: IOM Communications, 1998.

Bowers, B. *Lengthening the Day: A History of Lighting*

Technology. New York: Oxford University Press, 1998.

Cadbury, Deborah. *Dreams of Iron and Steel: Seven Wonders of the Nineteenth Century, from the Building of the London Sewers to the Panama Canal.* New York: Fourth Estate, 2004.

Cardwell, D. S. L. *Turning Points in Western Technology: A Study of Technology, Science, and History.* New York: Science History, 1972.

Coe, Lewis. *The Telegraph: A History of Morse's Invention and Its Predecessors in the United States.* Jefferson, N.C.: McFarland, 1993.

Collins, Douglas. *The Story of Kodak.* New York: Harry N. Abrams, 1990.

Cooper, Paul W., and Stanley R. Kurowski. *Introduction to the Technology of Explosives.* New York: Wiley-VCH, 1997.

Crothers, William L. *The American-Built Clipper Ship, 1850-1856: Characteristics, Construction, and Details.* Camden, Maine: International Marine/Ragged Mountain Press, 2000.

Daniels, Jeff. *Driving Force: The Evolution of the Car Engine.* Newbury Park, Calif.: Haynes, 2002.

De Syon, Guillaume. *Zeppelin! Germany and the Airship, 1900-1939.* Baltimore: Johns Hopkins University Press, 2002.

Dillon, Maureen. *Artificial Sunshine: A Social History of Domestic Lighting.* London: National Trust, 2002.

Douglas, George H. *All Aboard! The Railroad in American Life.* New York: Paragon House, 1992.

_____. *Skyscrapers: A Social History of the Very Tall Building in America.* Jefferson, N.C.: McFarland, 2004.

Dubois, Muriel L., and Miriam Butts. *Industrial Revolution Comes to America.* Amawalk, N.Y.: Jackdaw, 2001.

Eckermann, Eric. *World History of the Automobile.* New York: Society of Automotive Engineers, 2001.

Economides, Michael, and Ronald Oligney. *The Color of Oil: The History, the Money, and the Politics of the World's Biggest Business.* Katey, Tex.: Round Oak, 2000.

Emmerson, Andrew. *The Underground Pioneers: Victorian London and Its First Underground Railways.* Harrow Weald, Middlesex, England: Capital Transport, 2000.

Evans, Eric J. *The Forging of the Modern State: Early Industrial Britain, 1783-1870.* 2d ed. New York: Longman, 1996.

Faith, Nicholas. *The World the Railways Made.* New York: Carroll & Graf, 1991.

Fischer, Claude S. *America Calling: A Social History of the Telephone to 1940.* Berkeley: University of California Press, 1992.

Fishlow, Albert. *American Railroads and the Transformation of the Antebellum Economy.* Cambridge, Mass.: Harvard University Press, 1965.

Fox, Stephen. *The Ocean Railway: Isambard Kingdom Brunel, Samuel Cunard, and the Great Atlantic Steamships.* London: HarperCollins, 2003.

French, Michael J. *The U.S. Tire Industry: A History.* Boston: Twayne, 1992.

Friedel, Robert D. *Edison's Electric Light: Biography of an Invention.* New Brunswick, N.J.: Rutgers University Press, 1986.

Gabler, Edwin. *The American Telegrapher: A Social History, 1860-1900.* New Brunswick, N.J.: Rutgers University Press, 1988.

Glancey, Jonathan. *The Car: The Illustrated History of the Automobile.* London: Carlton Books, 2003.

Gleasner, Diana C. *Dynamite: Inventions That Changed Our Lives.* New York: Walker, 1982.

Goetz, Alisa, ed. *Up Down Across: Elevators, Escalators, and Moving Sidewalks.* London: Merrell, 2003.

Goldberg, Vicki. *Photography in Print: Writings from 1816 to the Present.* Albuquerque: University of New Mexico Press, 1988.

Goodwin, Jason. *Otis: Giving Rise to the Modern City.* Chicago: Ivan R. Dee, 2001.

Gorowitz, Bernard, et al., eds. *The General Electric Story: A Heritage of Innovation, 1876-1999.* 3d ed. Schenectady, N.Y.: Hall of Electrical History, 2000.

Grant, Ellsworth S. *The Colt Armory: A History of Colt's Manufacturing Company.* Lincoln, R.I.: Mowbray, 1995.

Grant, H. Roger. *The Railroad: The Life Story of a Technology.* Westport, Conn.: Greenwood Press, 2005.

Gray, Lee Edward. *From Ascending Rooms to Express Elevators: A History of the Passenger Elevator in the Nineteenth Century.* Mobile, Ala.: Elevator World, 2002.

Harter, Jim. *World Railways of the Nineteenth Century.* Baltimore: Johns Hopkins University Press, 2005.

Hearn, Chester G. *Circuits in the Sea: The Men, the Ships, and the Atlantic Cable.* Westport, Conn.: Praeger, 2004.

Hendricks, Gordon. *Edward Muybridge.* Mineola, N.Y.: Dover Books, 2001.

Hughes, Thomas P. *Networks of Power: Electrification in*

Western Society, 1880-1930. Baltimore: Johns Hopkins University Press, 1983.

Hungerford, Edward. *The Story of the Baltimore and Ohio Railroad.* 2 vols. New York: G. P. Putnam's Sons, 1928.

Jonnes, Jill. *Empires of Light: Edison, Tesla, Westinghouse, and the Race to Electrify the World.* New York: Random House, 2003.

Kanfer, Stefan. *The Last Empire: De Beers, Diamonds, and the World.* New York: Noonday Press, 1993.

Karabell, Zachary. *Parting the Desert: The Creation of the Suez Canal.* New York: Alfred A. Knopf, 2003.

Kelly, Jack. *Gunpowder: Alchemy, Bombards, and Pyrotechnics: The History of the Explosive That Changed the World.* New York: Basic Books, 2004.

Korman, Richard. *The Goodyear Story: An Inventor's Obsession and Struggle for a Rubber Monopoly.* San Francisco, Calif.: Encounter Books, 2002.

Landau, Sarah Bradford, and Carl W. Condit. *Rise of the New York Skyscraper, 1865-1913.* New Haven, Conn.: Yale University Press, 1996.

Lottman, Herbert R. *The Michelin Men: Driving an Empire.* London: I. B. Tauris, 2003.

Lumley, John L. *Engines: An Introduction.* Cambridge, England: Cambridge University Press, 1999.

McMillan, James. *The Dunlop Story: The Life, Death, and Re-birth of a Multi-national.* London: Weidenfeld and Nicolson, 1989.

Martin, Albro. *Railroads Triumphant: The Growth, Rejection, and Rebirth of a Vital American Force.* New York: Oxford University Press, 1992.

Mayer, Lynn Rhodes, and Ken Vose. *Makin' Tracks: The Saga of the Transcontinental Railroad.* New York: Barnes & Noble Books, 1995.

Misa, Thomas J. *A Nation of Steel: The Making of Modern America, 1865-1925.* Baltimore: Johns Hopkins University Press, 1995.

Mokyr, Joel. *The Lever of Riches: Technological Creativity and Economic Progress.* New York: Oxford University Press, 1990.

Morgan, Kenneth. *The Birth of Industrial Britain: Social Change, 1750-1850.* Harlow, Essex, England: Pearson/Longman, 2004.

Musser, Charles. *Before the Nickelodeon: Edwin S. Porter and the Edison Manufacturing Company.* Berkeley: University of California Press, 1991.

Noonan, Jon. *Nineteenth-Century Inventors.* New York: Facts On File, 1992.

Payne, Lee. *Lighter than Air: An Illustrated History of the Airship.* Rev. ed. New York: Orion Books, 1991.

Prodger, Philip, and Tom Gunning. *Time Stands Still: Muybridge and the Instantaneous Photography Movement.* Oxford, England: Oxford University Press, 2003.

Pulkrabek, Willard W. *Engineering Fundamentals of the Internal Combustion Engine.* Upper Saddle River, N.J.: Pearson/Prentice Hall, 2004.

Reich, Leonard S. *The Making of American Industrial Research: Science and Business at GE and Bell, 1876-1926.* New York: Cambridge University Press, 1985.

Ross, David. *The Willing Servant: A History of the Steam Engine.* Stroud, Gloucestershire, England: Tempus, 2004.

Shagena, Jack L. *Who Really Invented the Steamboat? Fulton's Clermont Coup: A History of the Steamboat Contributions of William Henry, James Rumsey, John Fitch, Oliver Evans, Nathan Read, Samuel Morey, Robert Fulton, John Stevens, and Others.* Amherst, N.Y.: Humanity Books, 2004.

Shaw, Ronald E. *Erie Water West: A History of the Erie Canal, 1792-1854.* Lexington: University Press of Kentucky, 1966.

Singer, Charles, et al., eds. *The Late Nineteenth Century, 1850 to 1900.* Vol. 5 in *A History of Technology.* Oxford, England: Clarendon Press, 1954-1958.

Speight, James G., and Baki Ozum. *Petroleum Refining Processes.* New York: Marcel Dekker, 2001.

Standage, Tom. *The Victorian Internet: The Remarkable Story of the Telegraph and the Nineteenth Century On-line Pioneers.* New York: Walker, 1998.

Stone, Richard D. *The Interstate Commerce Commission and the Railroad Industry: A History of Regulatory Policy.* New York: Praeger, 1991.

Van Dulken, Stephen. *Inventing the Nineteenth Century: One Hundred Inventions That Shaped the Victorian Age.* New York: New York University Press, 2001.

Weigold, Marilyn E. *Silent Builder: Emily Warren Roebling and the Brooklyn Bridge.* Port Washington, N.Y.: Associated Faculty Press, 1984.

Wengenroth, Ulrich. *Enterprise and Technology: The German and British Steel Industries, 1865-1895.* New York: Cambridge University Press, 1993.

Williams, Trevor I. *A History of the British Gas Industry.* New York: Oxford University Press, 1981.

Wormser, Richard. *The Iron Horse: How Railroads Changed America.* New York: Walker, 1993.

THEATER

Bank, Rosemarie, K. *Theatre Culture in America, 1825-1860*. Cambridge, England: Cambridge University Press, 1997.

Kroen, Sheryl. *Politics and Theater: The Crisis of Legitimacy in Restoration France, 1815-1830*. Berkeley: University of California Press, 2000.

Naylor, David, and Joan Dillon. *American Theatres: Performance Halls of the Nineteenth Century*. New York: John Wiley & Sons, 1997.

Richardson, Gary A. *American Drama from the Colonial Period Through World War I*. New York: Twayne, 1993.

Swift, E. Anthony. *Popular Theater and Society in Tsarist Russia*. Berkeley: University of California Press, 2002.

Trussler, Simon. *The Cambridge Illustrated History of the British Theatre*. Cambridge, England: Cambridge University Press, 2000.

UNITED STATES
General

Abernathy, M. Glenn. *Civil Liberties Under the Constitution*. 5th ed. Columbia: University of South Carolina Press, 1989.

Bodnar, John. *The Transplanted: A History of Immigrants in Urban America*. Bloomington: Indiana University Press, 1985.

Daniels, Roger. *Asian America: Chinese and Japanese in the United States Since 1850*. Seattle: University of Washington Press, 1988.

_____. *Coming to America: A History of Immigration and Ethnicity in American Life*. 2d ed. New York: HarperCollins, 2002.

_____. *The Golden Door: American Immigration Policy and Immigrants Since 1882*. New York: Hill and Wang, 2004.

Ely, John Hart. *Democracy and Distrust: A Theory of Judicial Review*. Cambridge, Mass.: Harvard University Press, 1980.

Foner, Nancy. *From Ellis Island to JFK: New York's Two Great Waves of Immigration*. New Haven, Conn.: Yale University Press, 2000.

Friedman, Lawrence J. *Gregarious Saints: Self and Community in American Abolitionism, 1830-1870*. New York: Cambridge University Press, 1982.

Gabaccia, Donna R. *Immigration and American Diversity: A Social and Cultural History*. Malden, Mass.: Blackwell, 2002.

Gould, Lewis L. *Grand Old Party: A History of the Republicans*. New York: Random House, 2003.

Greene, Victor R. *A Singing Ambivalence: American Immigrants Between Old World and New, 1830-1930*. Kent, Ohio: Kent State University Press, 2004.

Handlin, Oscar. *The Uprooted*. 2d ed. Boston: Little, Brown, 1973.

Hansen, Marcus Lee. *The Atlantic Migration, 1607-1860: A History of the Continuing Settlement of the United States*. New York: Harper & Brothers, 1961.

Hensley, Thomas R., Christopher E. Smith, and Joyce A. Baugh. *The Changing Supreme Court: Constitutional Rights and Liberties*. St. Paul, Minn.: West Publishing, 1997.

Holder, Angela Roddey. *The Meaning of the Constitution*. New York: Barron's, 1987.

Huebner, Timothy S. *The Taney Court: Justices, Rulings, and Legacy*. Santa Barbara, Calif.: ABC-Clio, 2003.

Hyman, Harold M., and William M. Wiecek. *Equal Justice Under Law: Constitutional Development, 1835-1875*. New York: Harper & Row, 1982.

Johannsen, Robert W. *The Frontier, the Union, and Stephen A. Douglas*. Urbana: University of Illinois Press, 1989.

Knobel, Dale T. *America for the Americans: The Nativist Movement in the United States*. New York: Twayne, 1996.

Langley, Lester D. *America and the Americas: The United States in the Western Hemisphere*. Athens: University of Georgia Press, 1989.

LeMay, Michael C. *From Open Door to Dutch Door: An Analysis of U.S. Immigration Policy Since 1820*. New York: Praeger, 1987.

Lipset, Seymour Martin, and Earl Raab. *The Politics of Unreason: Right-Wing Extremism in America, 1790-1970*. New York: Harper & Row, 1970.

McFeely, William S. *Grant*. New York: W. W. Norton, 1981.

McPherson, James M. *The Struggle for Equality: Abolitionists and the Negro in the Civil War and Reconstruction*. Princeton, N.J.: Princeton University Press, 1964.

Meier, Matt S., and Feliciano Ribera. *Mexican Americans, American Mexicans: From Conquistadors to Chicanos*. Rev. ed. New York: Hill & Wang, 1993.

Miller, Kerby A. *Emigrants and Exiles: Ireland and the Irish Exodus to North America*. New York: Oxford University Press, 1985.

Nasaw, David. *The Chief: The Life of William Randolph Hearst*. Boston: Houghton Mifflin, 2000.

Neely, Mark E., Jr. *The Last Best Hope of Earth: Abraham Lincoln and the Promise of America*. Cambridge, Mass.: Harvard University Press, 1993.

Pascoe, Elaine. *Neighbors at Odds: U.S. Policy in Latin America*. New York: Franklin Watts, 1990.

Peskin, Allan. *Winfield Scott and the Profession of Arms*. Kent, Ohio: Kent State University Press, 2003.

Pierson, Michael D. *Free Hearts and Free Home: Gender and American Antislavery Politics*. Chapel Hill: University of North Carolina Press, 2003.

Robinson, Judith. *The Hearsts: An American Dynasty*. Newark: University of Delaware Press, 1991.

Rugoff, Milton. *The Beechers: An American Family in the Nineteenth Century*. New York: Harper & Row, 1981.

Schwartz, Bernard. *A History of the Supreme Court*. New York: Oxford University Press, 1993.

Silverman, Kenneth. *Lightning Man: The Accursed Life of Samuel F. B. Morse*. New York: Alfred A. Knopf, 2003.

Taylor, John M. *William Henry Seward: Lincoln's Right Hand*. New York: HarperCollins, 1991.

Thomas, Emory M. *Robert E. Lee: A Biography*. New York: W. W. Norton, 1995.

Thompson, Brian. *Devastating Eden: The Search for Utopia in America*. London: HarperCollins, 2004.

Versluis, Arthur. *The Esoteric Origins of the American Renaissance*. New York: Oxford University Press, 2001.

Wright, Russell O. *Presidential Elections in the United States: A Statistical History, 1860-1992*. Jefferson, N.C.: McFarland Press, 1995.

Zinn, Howard. *A People's History of the United States*. New York: Harper & Row, 1980.

Antebellum Period

Abbott, Richard H. *Cotton and Capital: Boston Businessmen and Antislavery Reform, 1854-1868*. Amherst: University of Massachusetts Press, 1991.

Aitken, Thomas. *Albert Gallatin: Early America's Swiss-Born Statesman*. New York: Vantage Press, 1985.

Bartlett, Irving H. *John C. Calhoun: A Biography*. New York: W. W. Norton, 1993.

Baxter, Maurice G. *Henry Clay and the American System*. Lexington: University Press of Kentucky, 1995.

_____. *One and Inseparable: Daniel Webster and the Union*. Cambridge, Mass.: Harvard University Press, 1984.

Bergeron, Paul H. *The Presidency of James K. Polk*. Lawrence: University Press of Kansas, 1987.

Blackburn, Robin. *The Overthrow of Colonial Slavery, 1776-1848*. New York: Verso, 1988.

Buel, Richard, Jr. *America on the Brink: How the Political Struggle over the War of 1812 Almost Destroyed the Young Republic*. London: Palgrave Macmillan, 2005.

Cain, William E., ed. *William Lloyd Garrison and the Fight Against Slavery: Selections from "The Liberator."* Boston: Bedford Books of St. Martin's Press, 1995.

Cantrell, Gregg. *Stephen F. Austin: Empresario of Texas*. New Haven, Conn.: Yale University Press, 1999.

Clinton, Robert Lowry. *"Marbury v. Madison" and Judicial Review*. Lawrence: University Press of Kansas, 1989.

Cornog, Evan. *The Birth of Empire: DeWitt Clinton and the American Experience, 1769-1828*. New York: Oxford University Press, 1998.

Cunningham, Noble E., Jr. *In Pursuit of Reason: The Life of Thomas Jefferson*. Baton Rouge: Louisiana State University Press, 1987.

_____. *The Presidency of James Monroe*. Lawrence: University Press of Kansas, 1996.

Davis, William C. *Three Roads to the Alamo: The Lives and Fortunes of David Crockett, James Bowie, and William Barret Travis*. New York: HarperCollins, 1998.

Elkins, Stanley, and Eric McKitrick. *The Age of Federalism*. New York: Oxford University Press, 1993.

Ellis, Richard E. *Andrew Jackson*. Washington, D.C.: CQ Press, 2003.

Faust, Drew Gilpin. *The Ideology of Slavery: Proslavery Thought in the Antebellum South, 1830-1860*. Baton Rouge: Louisiana State University Press, 1981.

Flemingo, Thomas. *Louisiana Purchase*. New York: John Wiley & Sons, 2003.

Foner, Eric. *Free Soil, Free Labor, Free Men: The Ideology of the Republican Party Before the Civil War*. New York: Oxford University Press, 1970.

Freehling, William W. *The Road to Disunion: Secessionists at Bay, 1776-1854*. New York: Oxford University Press, 1990.

Garrison, William Lloyd. *William Lloyd Garrison and the Fight Against Slavery: Selections from "The Liberator."* Edited with an introduction by William E. Cain. Boston: Bedford Books of St. Martin's Press, 1995.

Gienapp, William E. *The Origins of the Republican Party, 1852-1856*. New York: Oxford University Press, 1987.

Gossett, Thomas F. *"Uncle Tom's Cabin" and American Culture*. Dallas, Tex.: Southern Methodist University Press, 1985.

Griffin, Clifford S. *Their Brothers' Keepers: Moral Stewardship in the United States, 1800-1865*. New Brunswick, N.J.: Rutgers University Press, 1960.

Guarneri, Carl J. *The Utopian Alternative: Fourierism in Nineteenth-Century America*. Ithaca, N.Y.: Cornell University Press, 1991.

Holzer, Harold, ed. *The Lincoln-Douglas Debates*. New York: HarperCollins, 1993.

Johnson, Herbert A. *The Chief Justiceship of John Marshall, 1801-1835*. Columbia: University of South Carolina Press, 1997.

Kuroda, Tadahisa. *The Origins of the Twelfth Amendment: The Electoral College in the Early Republic, 1787-1804*. Westport, Conn.: Greenwood Press, 1994.

Lack, Paul D. *The Texas Revolutionary Experience: A Political and Social History, 1835-1836*. College Station: Texas A&M Press, 1992.

Lomask, Milton. *Aaron Burr: The Conspiracy and Years of Exile, 1805-1806*. New York: Farrar, Straus, Giroux, 1982.

McCullough, David. *John Adams*. New York: Simon and Schuster, 2002.

Mayer, Henry. *All on Fire: William Lloyd Garrison and the Abolition of Slavery*. New York: St. Martin's Press, 1998.

Melton, Buckner F., Jr. *Aaron Burr: Conspiracy to Treason*. New York: Wiley, 2002.

Meyer, Daniel. *Stephen Douglas and the American Union*. Chicago: University of Chicago Press, 1994.

Monroe, Dan. *The Republican Vision of John Tyler*. College Station: Texas A&M University Press, 2003.

Montejano, David. *Anglos and Mexicans in the Making of Texas, 1836-1986*. Austin: University of Texas Press, 1987.

Nagel, Paul C. *John Quincy Adams: A Public Life, a Private Life*. New York: Random House, 1997.

Newman, Richard S. *The Transformation of American Abolitionism: Fighting Slavery in the Early Republic*. Chapel Hill: University of North Carolina Press, 2002.

Newmyer, R. Kent. *John Marshall and the Heroic Age of the Supreme Court*. Baton Rouge: Louisiana State University Press, 2001.

Niven, John. *Martin Van Buren: The Romantic Age of American Politics*. New York: Oxford University Press, 1983.

Petersen, Merrill D. *The Great Triumvirate: Webster, Clay, and Calhoun*. New York: Oxford University Press, 1987.

Peterson, Norma Lois. *The Presidencies of William Henry Harrison and John Tyler*. Lawrence: University Press of Kansas, 1989.

Randall, Willard S. *Thomas Jefferson: A Life*. New York: Henry Holt, 1993.

Reeves, Richard. *American Journey: Traveling with Tocqueville in Search of "Democracy in America."* New York: Simon & Schuster, 1982.

Remini, Robert V. *Andrew Jackson and the Course of American Empire*. 3 vols. New York: Harper & Row, 1977-1984.

_____. *Daniel Webster: The Man and His Time*. New York: W. W. Norton, 1997.

_____. *John Quincy Adams*. New York: Times Books, 2002.

Reynolds, David S. *John Brown, Abolitionist: The Man Who Killed Slavery, Sparked the Civil War, and Seeded Civil Rights*. New York: Alfred A. Knopf, 2005.

Risjord, Norman K. *Thomas Jefferson*. Madison, Wis.: Madison House, 1994.

Seigenthaler, John. *James K. Polk*. New York: Times Books, 2003.

Sibley, Joel H. *Martin Van Buren and the Emergence of American Popular Politics*. Lanham, Md.: Rowman & Littlefield, 2002.

Smith, Craig R. *Daniel Webster and the Oratory of Civil Religion*. Columbia: University of Missouri Press, 2005.

Smith, Elbert B. *The Presidencies of Zachary Taylor and Millard Fillmore*. Lawrence: University Press of Kansas, 1988.

Smith, Jean E. *John Marshall: Definer of a Nation*. New York: Henry Holt, 1996.

Stewart, James Brewer. *William Lloyd Garrison and the Challenge of Emancipation*. Arlington Heights, Ill.: Harlan Davidson, 1992.

Unger, Harlow Giles. *Noah Webster: The Life and Times of an American Patriot*. New York: John Wiley & Sons, 1998.

Watson, Harry L. *Andrew Jackson vs. Henry Clay: Democracy and Development in Antebellum America*. Boston: Bedford Books of St. Martin's Press, 1998.

Watts, Steven. *The Republic Reborn: War and the*

Making of Liberal America, 1790-1820. Baltimore: Johns Hopkins University Press, 1987.

Weeks, William E. *John Quincy Adams and American Global Empire*. Lexington: University Press of Kentucky, 1992.

Weisberger, Bernard A. *America Afire: Jefferson, Adams, and the Revolutionary Election of 1800*. New York: William Morrow, 2000.

Widmer, Ted. *Martin Van Buren*. New York: Times Books, 2005.

Civil War Period

Benét, Stephen Vincent. *John Brown's Body*. Chicago: Elephant Paperbacks, 1990.

Bonekemper, Edward H. III. *A Victor, Not a Butcher: Ulysses S. Grant's Overlooked Military Genius*. Washington, D.C.: Regnery, 2004.

Boyer, Richard O. *The Legend of John Brown: A Biography and a History*. New York: Alfred A. Knopf, 1972.

Brandt, Nat. *The Town That Started the Civil War*. Syracuse, N.Y.: Syracuse University Press, 1990.

Bunting, Josiah, III. *Ulysses S. Grant*. New York: Times Books, 2004.

Catton, Bruce. *Mister Lincoln's Army*. Garden City, N.Y.: Doubleday, 1951.

Cleaves, Freeman. *Meade of Gettysburg*. New York: Morningside Press, 1980.

Collins, Bruce. *The Origins of America's Civil War*. New York: Holmes & Meier, 1981.

Cooper, William J., Jr. *Jefferson Davis: American*. New York: Alfred A. Knopf, 2000.

Cozzens, Peter. *The Shipwreck of Their Hopes: The Battles for Chattanooga*. Urbana: University of Illinois Press, 1994.

Davis, William C. *First Blood: Fort Sumter to Bull Run*. Alexandria: Time-Life Books, 1983.

_____. *A Government of Our Own: The Making of the Confederacy*. New York: Free Press, 1994.

_____. *Jefferson Davis: The Man and His Hour*. New York: HarperPerennial, 1991.

Davis, William C., and Bell L. Wiley, eds. *Civil War Album: A Complete Photographic History of the Civil War—Fort Sumter to Appomattox*. New York: Tess Press, 2000.

Detzer, David. *Donnybrook: The Battle of Bull Run, 1861*. Orlando, Fla.: Harcourt, 2004.

Donald, David Herbert. *Lincoln*. New York: Simon & Schuster, 1995.

Foner, Eric, ed. *Politics and Ideology in the Age of the Civil War*. New York: Oxford University Press, 1980.

Foote, Shelby. *The Civil War: A Narrative*. 9 vols. New York: Random House, 1958.

Fowler, William M., Jr. *Under Two Flags: The American Navy in the Civil War*. New York: W. W. Norton, 1990.

Gaines, W. Craig. *The Confederate Cherokees: John Drew's Regiment of Mounted Rifles*. Baton Rouge: Louisiana State University Press, 1989.

Gienapp, William E. *Abraham Lincoln and Civil War America: A Biography*. New York: Oxford University Press, 2002.

Glatthaar, Joseph T. *The March to the Sea and Beyond: Sherman's Troops in the Savannah and Carolinas Campaigns*. New York: New York University Press, 1985.

Groom, Winston. *Shrouds of Glory: From Atlanta to Nashville, the Last Great Campaign of the Civil War*. New York: Grove Press, 1995.

Guelzo, Allen C. *Lincoln's Emancipation Proclamation: The End of Slavery in America*. New York: Simon & Schuster, 2004.

Hathaway, Herman, and Richard E. Beringer. *Jefferson Davis: Confederate President*. Lawrence: University Press of Kansas, 2002.

Hendrickson, Robert. *Sumter: The First Day of the Civil War*. New York: Dell, 1991.

Horn, John. *The Petersburg Campaign, June, 1864-April, 1865*. Conshohocken, Pa.: Combined Books, 1993.

Hutton, Paul Andrew. *Phil Sheridan and His Army*. Lincoln: University of Nebraska Press, 1985.

Ingram, E. Renée. *In View of the Great Want of Labor: A Legislative History of African American Conscription in the Confederacy*. Westminster, Md.: Willowbend Books, 2002.

Jones, Archer. *Civil War Command and Strategy*. New York: Free Press, 1992.

Josephy, Alvin M., Jr. *Civil War in the American West*. New York: Alfred A. Knopf, 1991.

Kennett, Lee. *Sherman: A Soldier's Life*. New York: HarperCollins, 2001.

Luraghi, Raimondo. *A History of the Confederate Navy*. Translated by Paolo E. Coletta. Annapolis, Md.: Naval Institute Press, 1996.

McDonald, JoAnna H. *We Shall Meet Again: The First Battle of Manassas (Bull Run), July 18-21, 1861*. New York: Oxford University Press, 2000.

McPherson, James M. *Abraham Lincoln and the Second American Revolution*. New York: Oxford University Press, 1990.

_____. *Battle Cry of Freedom.* New York: Oxford University Press, 1988.

_____. *Ordeal by Fire: The Civil War and Reconstruction.* New York: Alfred A. Knopf, 1982.

Marszalek, John F. *Sherman's Other War: The General and the Civil War Press.* Memphis, Tenn.: Memphis State University Press, 1981.

Marvel, William. *Lee's Last Retreat: The Flight to Appomattox.* Chapel Hill: University of North Carolina Press, 2002.

Neillands, Robin. *Grant: The Man Who Won the Civil War.* Cold Spring Harbor, N.Y.: Cold Spring Press, 2004.

Nelson, James L. *Reign of Iron: The Story of the First Battling Ironclads, the "Monitor" and the "Merrimack."* New York: William Morrow, 2004.

Oates, Stephen B. *Our Fiery Trial: Abraham Lincoln, John Brown, and the Civil War Era.* Amherst: University of Massachusetts Press, 1979.

_____. *To Purge This Land with Blood: A Biography of John Brown.* 2d ed. Amherst: University of Massachusetts Press, 1984.

_____. *With Malice Toward None.* New York: HarperPerennial, 1994.

Osborn, Thomas W. *The Fiery Trail.* Knoxville: University of Tennessee Press, 1986.

Reck, W. Emerson. *A. Lincoln: His Last Twenty-Four Hours.* Columbia: University of South Carolina Press, 1994.

Reid, Brian Holden. *The Civil War and the Wars of the Nineteenth Century.* London: Collins, 2006.

Richardson, Heather Cox. *The Greatest Nation on Earth: Republican Economic Policies During the Civil War.* Cambridge, Mass.: Harvard University Press, 1997.

Schecter, Barnet. *The Devil's Own Work: The Civil War Draft Riots and the Fight to Reconstruct America.* New York: Walker, 2005.

Sinisi, Kyle S. *Sacred Debts: State Civil War Claims and American Federalism, 1861-1880.* New York: Fordham University Press, 2003.

Stampp, Kenneth, ed. *The Causes of the Civil War.* Rev. ed. Englewood Cliffs, N.J.: Prentice-Hall, 1974.

Still, William N., Jr., ed. *The Confederate Navy: The Ships, Men, and Organization, 1861-65.* Annapolis, Md.: Naval Institute Press, 1996.

Sullivan, George. *In the Wake of Battle: The Civil War Images of Mathew Brady.* New York: Prestel, 2004.

Thomas, Emory M. *The Confederacy as a Revolutionary Experience.* Columbia: University of South Carolina Press, 1991.

Weighley, Russell F. *A Great Civil War: A Military and Political History, 1861-1865.* Bloomington: Indiana University Press, 2000.

Winks, Robin W. *Canada and the United States: The Civil War Years.* Baltimore: Johns Hopkins University Press, 1960.

Woodworth, S. E. *Jefferson Davis and His Generals: The Failure of Confederate Command in the West.* Lawrence: University Press of Kansas, 1990.

Post-Civil War Period

Ackerman, Kenneth D. *Dark Horse: The Surprise Election and Political Murder of President James A. Garfield.* New York: Carroll & Graf, 2003.

Argersinger, Peter H. *The Limits of Agrarian Radicalism: Western Populism and American Politics.* Lawrence: University Press of Kansas, 1995.

Bogue, Allan G. *Frederick Jackson Turner: Strange Roads Going Down.* Norman: University of Oklahoma Press, 1998.

Brownstone, David M., Irene M. Franck, and Douglas L. Brownstone, eds. *Island of Hope, Island of Tears.* New York: Penguin Books, 1986.

Carson, Mina. *Settlement Folk: Social Thought and the American Settlement Movement, 1885-1930.* Chicago: University of Chicago Press, 1990.

Carter, Dan T. *When the War Was Over: The Failure of Self-Reconstruction in the South, 1865-1867.* Baton Rouge: Louisiana State University Press, 1985.

Cashman, Sean Dennis. *America in the Gilded Age: From the Death of Lincoln to the Rise of Theodore Roosevelt.* 3d ed. New York: New York University Press, 1993.

Chernow, Ron D. *Titan: The Life of John D. Rockefeller, Sr.* New York: Random House, 1998.

Dobson, John. *Reticent Expansionism: The Foreign Policy of William McKinley.* Pittsburgh: Duquesne University Press, 1988.

Fireside, Harvey. *Separate and Unequal: Homer Plessy and the Supreme Court Decision That Legalized Racism.* New York: Carroll & Graf, 2004.

Foner, Eric. *Reconstruction: America's Unfinished Revolution, 1863-1877.* New York: Harper & Row, 1988.

Gould, Lewis L. *The Presidency of William McKinley.* Lawrence: University Press of Kansas, 1980.

Graff, Henry F. *Grover Cleveland.* New York: Times Books, 2002.

Griffiths, David B. *Populism in the Western United States*. Lewiston, Idaho: Edwin Mellen Press, 1992.

Hoogenboom, Ari. *Rutherford B. Hayes: Warrior and President*. Lawrence: University Press of Kansas, 1995.

Jeffers, H. Paul. *An Honest President: The Life and Presidencies of Grover Cleveland*. New York: William Morrow, 2000.

Jones, Stanley L. *The Presidential Election of 1896*. Madison: University of Wisconsin Press, 1964.

McGerr, Michael. *The Decline of Popular Politics: The American North, 1865-1928*. New York: Oxford University Press, 1986.

McMath, Robert C. *American Populism: A Social History, 1877-1898*. New York: Hill and Wang, 1993.

Mandelbaum, Seymour J. *Boss Tweed's New York*. Chicago: I. R. Dee, 1990.

Morris, Roy, Jr. *Fraud of the Century: Rutherford B. Hayes, Samuel Tilden, and the Stolen Election of 1876*. New York: Simon & Schuster, 2003.

Ostler, Jeffrey. *Prairie Populism: The Fate of Agrarian Radicalism in Kansas, Nebraska, and Iowa, 1880-1892*. Lawrence: University Press of Kansas, 1993.

Phillips, Kevin. *William McKinley*. New York: Times Books/Henry Holt, 2003.

Rehnquist, William H. *Centennial Crisis: The Disputed Election of 1876*. New York: Random House, 2004.

Simpson, Brooks D. *The Reconstruction Presidents*. Lawrence: University Press of Kansas, 1998.

Stauffer, John. *The Black Hearts of Men: Radical Abolitionists and the Transformation of Race*. Cambridge, Mass.: Harvard University Press, 2002.

Summers, Mark Wahlgren. *The Era of Good Stealings*. New York: Oxford University Press, 1993.

Sutherland, Daniel E. *The Confederate Carpetbaggers*. Baton Rouge: Louisiana State University Press, 1988.

Traxel, David. *1898: The Birth of the American Century*. New York: A. A. Knopf, 1998.

Trefousse, Hans L. *Carl Schurz: A Biography*. Knoxville: University of Tennessee Press, 1982.

_____. *Impeachment of a President: Andrew Johnson, the Blacks, and Reconstruction*. New York: Fordham University Press, 1999.

_____. *Rutherford B. Hayes*. New York: Times Books, 2002.

_____. *Thaddeus Stevens: Nineteenth-Century Egalitarian*. Chapel Hill: University of North Carolina Press, 1997.

Trelease, Allen W. *White Terror: The Ku Klux Klan Conspiracy and the Southern Reconstruction*. Baton Rouge: Louisiana State University Press, 1995.

Tutorow, Norman E. *The Governor: The Life and Legacy of Leland Stanford, a California Colossus*. 2 vols. Spokane, Wash.: Arthur H. Clark, 2004.

Welch, Richard E. *The Presidencies of Grover Cleveland*. Lawrence: University Press of Kansas, 1988.

Williams, R. Hal. *Years of Decision: American Politics in the 1890's*. Prospect Heights, Ill.: Waveland Books, 1993.

WOMEN AND WOMEN'S ISSUES

Arneil, Barbara. *Politics and Feminism*. Malden, Mass.: Blackwell, 1999.

Back, Kurt W. *Family Planning and Population Control: The Challenges of a Successful Movement*. Boston: Twayne, 1989.

Baker, Jean H, ed. *Votes for Women: The Struggle for Suffrage Revisited*. Oxford, England: Oxford University Press, 2002.

Baly, Monica E. *Florence Nightingale and the Nursing Legacy*. 2d ed. London: Whurr, 1997.

Banner, Lois W. *Elizabeth Cady Stanton: A Radical for Woman's Rights*. Boston: Little, Brown, 1980.

Barry, Kathleen. *Susan B. Anthony: A Biography of a Singular Feminist*. New York: Ballantine Books, 1988.

Bartlett, Ken. *Lessons to Be Learned: Thought-Provoking Octavia Hill Commemoration Day Sermons*. Wisbech, England: O. Hill Birthplace Museum Trust, 1996.

Beeton, Beverly. *Women Vote in the West: The Woman Suffrage Movement, 1869-1896*. New York: Garland, 1986.

Beisel, Nicola Kay. *Imperiled Innocents: Anthony Comstock and Family Reproduction in Victorian America*. Princeton, N.J.: Princeton University Press, 1997.

Besant, Annie, and Charles Knowlton. *"A Dirty, Filthy Book": The Writings of Charles Knowlton and Annie Besant on Reproductive Physiology and Birth Control and an Account of the Bradlaugh-Besant Trial*. Edited by Sripati Chandrasekhar. Berkeley: University of California Press, 1981.

Blackwell, Alice Stone. *Lucy Stone: Pioneer of Woman's Rights*. 2d ed. 1930. Reprint. Charlottesville: University Press of Virginia, 2001.

Blackwell, Elizabeth. *Pioneer Work in Opening the Medical Profession to Women*. Reprint. Amherst, N.Y.: Humanity Books, 2004.

Boyd, Nancy. *Josephine Butler, Octavia Hill, Florence*

Nightingale: Three Victorian Women Who Changed Their World. London: Palgrave Macmillan, 1982.

Boydston, Jeanne, Mary Kelley, and Anne Margolis. *The Limits of Sisterhood: The Beecher Sisters on Women's Rights and Woman's Sphere*. Chapel Hill: University of North Carolina Press, 1988.

Brodie, Janet Farrell. *Contraception and Abortion in Nineteenth-Century America*. Ithaca, N.Y.: Cornell University Press, 1994.

Buhle, Mari Jo, and Paul Buhle, eds. *The Concise History of Woman Suffrage: Selections from the Classic Work of Stanton, Anthony, Gage, and Harper*. Urbana: University of Illinois Press, 1978.

Burton, David H. *Clara Barton: In the Service of Humanity*. Westport, Conn.: Greenwood Press, 1995.

Bushnell, Horace. *Women's Suffrage: The Reform Against Nature*. New York: C. Scribner, 1869.

Bystydzienski, Jill M., and Joti Sekhon, eds. *Democratization and Women's Grassroots Movements*. Bloomington: Indiana University Press, 1999.

Carr-Gomm, Richard. *Octavia Hill and the Individual*. London: O. Hill Society, 1996.

Catt, Carrie Chapman, and Nettie Rogers Shuler. *Woman Suffrage and Politics*. New York: Charles Scribner's Sons, 1926.

Clayton, Peter John. *Octavia Hill, 1838-1912: Born in Wisbech*. Wisbech, England: Wisbech Society and Preservation Trust, 1993.

Clinton, Catherine. *The Other Civil War: American Women in the Nineteenth Century*. New York: Hill & Wang, 1984.

Cromwell, Otelia. *Lucretia Mott*. Cambridge, Mass.: Harvard University Press, 1958.

Donovan, Josephine. *Feminist Theory: The Intellectual Traditions of American Feminism*. New York: Frederick Ungar, 1985.

DuBois, Ellen Carol. *Feminism and Suffrage: The Emergence of an Independent Women's Movement in America, 1848-1869*. Ithaca, N.Y.: Cornell University Press, 1978.

_____, ed. *Elizabeth Cady Stanton, Susan B. Anthony: Correspondence, Writings, Speeches*. New York: Schocken Books, 1981.

_____, ed. *Women Suffrage and Women's Rights*. New York: New York University Press, 1998.

Flexner, Eleanor. *Century of Struggle: The Woman's Rights Movement in the United States*. New York: Atheneum, 1973.

Foner, Philip S. *Women and the American Labor Movement: From the First Trade Unions to the Present*. New York: Free Press, 1979.

Glenn, Susan A. *Female Spectacle: The Theatrical Roots of Modern Feminism*. Cambridge, Mass.: Harvard University Press, 2000.

Glowacki, Peggy, and Julia Hendry. *Hull-House*. Charleston, S.C.: Arcadia, 2004.

Goldstein, Leslie Friedman. *The Constitutional Rights of Women: Cases in Law and Social Change*. Rev. ed. Madison: University of Wisconsin Press, 1988.

Gordon, Linda. *The Moral Property of Women: A History of Birth Control Politics in America*. Urbana: University of Illinois Press, 2002.

Griffin, Elizabeth. *In Her Own Right: The Life of Elizabeth Cady Stanton*. New York: Oxford University Press, 1984.

Grimshaw, Patricia. *Women's Suffrage in New Zealand*. 2d ed. Auckland, New Zealand: Auckland University Press, 1987.

Gurko, Miriam. *The Ladies of Seneca Falls: The Birth of the Women's Rights Movement*. New York: Macmillan, 1974.

Hedrick, Joan D. *Harriet Beecher Stowe: A Life*. New York: Oxford University Press, 1994.

Hill, Octavia. *Octavia Hill and the Social Housing Debate: Essays and Letters by Octavia Hill*. Edited by Robert Whalan. Reprint. London: Civitas Institute for the Study of Civil Society, 2000.

Hirsch, Pam. *Barbara Leigh Smith Bodichon, 1827-1891: Feminist, Artist and Rebel*. London: Chatto & Windus, 1998.

Holcombe, Lee. *Wives and Property: Reform of the Married Women's Property Law in Nineteenth-Century England*. Toronto: University of Toronto Press, 1983.

Kern, Kathi. *Mrs. Stanton's Bible*. Ithaca, N.Y.: Cornell University Press, 2001.

Kessler-Harris, Alice, ed. *Protecting Women: Labor Legislation in Europe, the United States, and Australia, 1880-1920*. Urbana: University of Illinois Press, 1995.

Kousser, J. Morgan. *The Shaping of Southern Politics: Suffrage Restriction and the Establishment of the One-Party South, 1880-1910*. New Haven, Conn.: Yale University Press, 1974.

Lasser, Carol, and Marlene Merrill, eds. *Soul Mates: The Oberlin Correspondence of Lucy Stone and Antoinette Brown, 1846-1850*. Oberlin, Ohio: Oberlin College, 1983.

Levin, Miriam R. *Defining Women's Scientific Enter-*

prise: Mount Holyoke Faculty and the Rise of American Science. Hanover, N.H.: University Press of New England, 2005.

Marshall, Susan E. *Splintered Sisterhood: Gender and Class in the Campaign Against Women Suffrage.* Madison: University of Wisconsin Press, 1997.

Martin, Jane Roland. *Reclaiming a Conversation: The Ideal of the Educated Woman.* New Haven, Conn.: Yale University Press, 1985.

Mazour, Anatole G. *Women in Exile: Wives of the Decembrists.* Tallahassee, Fla.: Diplomatic Press, 1975.

Morantz-Sanchez, Regina. *Sympathy and Science: Women Physicians in American Medicine.* Rev. ed. Chapel Hill: University of North Carolina Press, 2000.

More, Ellen S. *Restoring the Balance: Women Physicians and the Profession of Medicine, 1850-1995.* Cambridge, Mass.: Harvard University Press, 1999.

Mott, Lucretia. *Selected Letters of Lucretia Coffin Mott.* Edited by Beverly Wilson Palmer, Holly Byers Ochoa, and Carol Faulkner. Urbana: University of Illinois Press, 2002.

Orr, Clarissa Campbell. *Women in the Victorian World.* Manchester, England: Manchester University Press, 1995.

Riley, Glenda. *The Female Frontier: A Comparative View of Women on the Prairie and the Plains.* Lawrence: University Press of Kansas, 1988.

Schwarkopf, Jutta. *Women in the Chartist Movement.* New York: St. Martin's Press, 1991.

Shapiro, Thomas M. *Population Control Politics: Women, Sterilization, and Reproductive Choice.* Philadelphia: Temple University Press, 1985.

Stanton, Elizabeth Cady. *Eighty Years and More: Reminiscences, 1815-1897.* 1898. Reprint. Introduction by Ellen Carol DuBois. Afterword by Ann D. Gordon. Boston: Northeastern University Press, 1993.

Stanton, Elizabeth Cady, Susan B. Anthony, and Matilda Joslyn Gage, eds. *History of Woman Suffrage.* Rochester, N.Y.: Mann, 1886.

Stetson, Dorothy M. *Woman's Issue: The Politics of Family Law Reform in England.* Westport, Conn.: Greenwood Press, 1982.

Stratton, Joanna. *Pioneer Women: Voices from the Kansas Frontier.* New York: Simon & Schuster, 1981.

Strong-Boag, Veronica, and Anita Clair Fellman, eds. *Rethinking Canada: The Promise of Women's History.* New York: Oxford University Press, 1997.

Tone, Andrea. *Controlling Reproduction: An American History.* Wilmington, Del.: SR Books, 1997.

_____. *Devices and Desires: A History of Contraceptives in America.* New York: Hill & Wang, 2001.

Underhill, Lois Beachy. *The Woman Who Ran for President: The Many Lives of Victoria Woodhull.* Bridgehampton, N.Y.: Bridge Works, 1995.

Vernon, Betty D. *Margaret Cole, 1893-1980: A Political Biography.* Dover, N.H.: Croom Helm, 1986.

Wagner, Sally. *A Time of Protest: Suffragists Challenge the Republic, 1870-1887.* 2d ed. Carmichael, Calif.: Sky Carrier Press, 1988.

Walter, Lynn, ed. *Women's Rights: A Global View.* Westport, Conn.: Greenwood Press, 2001.

Weimann, Jeanne Madeline. *The Fair Women.* Chicago: Academy Chicago, 1981.

Wellman, Judith. *The Road to Seneca Falls: Elizabeth Cady Stanton and the First Women's Rights Convention.* Urbana: University of Illinois Press, 2004.

White, Barbara A. *The Beecher Sisters.* New Haven, Conn.: Yale University Press, 2003.

ELECTRONIC RESOURCES

WEB SITES

The sites listed below were visited by the editors of Salem Press in March, 2006. Because URLs frequently change or are moved, the accuracy of these sites cannot be guaranteed; however, long-standing sites, such as those of university departments, national organizations, and government agencies, generally maintain links when sites move or upgrade their offerings.

GENERAL

Centre for Nineteenth-Century Studies at Birkbeck College, University of London
http://www.bbk.ac.uk/eh/research/
centreforc19thstudies
The CNCS, founded in 1996, is an interdisciplinary project focusing on the period 1790-1914, as "a time when important cultural formations and literary and historical relationships emerge over a number of decades." The center studies the Romantic, Victorian and Edwardian periods in order to address cross-disciplinary trends such as the idea of democracy, gender debates, the popular culture "industry," and new accounts of subjectivity and scientific culture.

Centre for Nineteenth Century Studies at the University of Sheffield
http://www.c19.group.shef.ac.uk/
The center has an interdisciplinary focus that targets "the whole breadth of the 'long Nineteenth Century,' from c. 1789-c. 1914, covering British, American, and European history, literature, and culture." Holds seminars and conferences, and works with archives, museums, and galleries to support research and academic programs. Has access to important collections in the history of labor, social, political, and medical history, as well as those of the University of Sheffield library, with more than a million volumes of both primary and secondary works.

H-Net
http://www.h-net.org/lists/
More than one hundred academic discussion networks, most of which cover nineteenth century topics, can be found at H-Net.

Interdisciplinary Nineteenth Century Studies
http://www.nd.edu/~incshp/
INCS is an international group of scholars dedicated to interdisciplinary discussion and research. The organization sponsors annual meetings and enjoys a collaborative relationship with Nineteenth-Century Contexts: An Interdisciplinary Journal. INCS encourages scholarly work that transcends disciplinary boundaries in its approach to cultural studies.

Internet Modern History Sourcebook: The Long Nineteenth Century
http://www.fordham.edu/halsall/mod/modsbook3.html
This highly regarded Web site contain an extensive collection of primary source materials about every conceivable aspect of nineteenth century history, politics, and culture, compiled by Paul Halsall of Fordham University. The site includes a wide range of information about Europe, with specific sections on the Council of Vienna, nationalism, conservatism, liberalism, the revolts of 1848, and significant events in Britain, Austro-Hungary, Italy, and other European countries. There are also numerous pages about the United States (see United States, below). Other sections of the site contain documents about nineteenth century Canada, Australia, New Zealand, the Middle East, and Japanese expansion. Halsall has also collected primary source documents describing the second Industrial Revolution and how socialism, Marxism, and imperialism in Africa, China, and India were responses to economic growth. Additional sections contain information about Charles Darwin's theories, social Darwinism, and nineteenth century science and religion. This site is a "must use" for anyone doing research about the nineteenth century.

Nineteenth Century Studies Association
http://www.msu.edu/~floyd/ncsa/
Sponsors conferences on topics in the nineteenth century, such as "Race and Ethnicity in the 19th Century" (Susquehanna University, Selinsgrove, Pennsylvania, 2007).

North American Victorian Studies Association

http://www.cla.purdue.edu/academic/engl/navsa/
index.cfm

Established in 2002, the NAVSA provides "a continental forum for the discussion of the Victorian period, to encourage a wide variety of theoretical and disciplinary approaches to the field, and to further the interests of scholars of the period." Projects include initiating Web-based archival projects that make Victorian texts more easily accessible to members.

Research Resources for Nineteenth Century Studies

http://www.sciper.leeds.ac.uk/resources/index.htm

Provides an extensive guide to research in nineteenth century topics, including finding aids.

Victorian Web Sites

http://www.lang.nagoya-u.ac.jp/~matsuoka/
Victorian.html

This page at The Victorian Web provides links to more than 150 Web sites about various aspects of Victorian era history, culture, art, and literature, as well as links to journals and organizations dedicated to the study of the nineteenth century.

WebChron: Web Chronology Project Then Again

http://www.thenagain.info/WebChron/index.html

The Web Chronology Project originally was created by the History Department at North Park University in Chicago. It is now administered by David Koeller, the project's originator, as part of his "Then Again" Web site. The site contains a series of hyperlinked time lines tracing developments in the United States, Africa south of the Sahara, the Middle East and West Asia, India and South Asia, China and East Asia, Russia and Eastern Europe, and western and central Europe. Other chronologies provide information about Islam, Christianity, and Judaism, as well as art, music, literature, and speculative thought in the Western tradition.

World History International

http://history-world.org

A wealth of information about history from the Neolithic period to the present. Users can access the "Contents A-Z" page for a list of pages with essays about the Americas; Africa, Australia, and the Sea Islands; art and architecture; Asia and the Middle East; Europe; science; world religions; and other general topics. The Americas section includes essays about the American Civil War, Ku Klux Klan, Lewis and Clark, Manifest Destiny, the Mormon migrations, Monroe Doctrine, Reconstruction, and the Spanish American War. There are also three essays about the establishment of Latin American states, the Latin American plantation colony, and Latin American revolts. The Africa section includes essays about the Boer War and David Livingstone's discoveries in Africa.

AFRICA

Humanities 211: Culture and Literature of Africa

http://web.cocc.edu/cagatucci/classes/hum211/

This site was created for a course taught by Cora Agatucci, a professor of English at Central Oregon Community College. The site includes a five-part time line of African history. Part 3, "African Slave Trade and European Imperialism," offers an overview of African history between the fifteenth and early nineteenth centuries, including information on the abolitionist movement in England and the United States and the European exploration of Africa. Part 4, "Anti-colonialism and Reconstruction," provides information and Web links to events occurring in the nineteenth to the mid-twentieth centuries, including the height of global imperialism, the Zulu Wars, and the Boer War.

Internet African History Sourcebook

http://www.fordham.edu/halsall/africa/
africasbook.html

Contains information about African history, including documents regarding African societies, the abolition of slavery, exploration and missionary activity, South Africa, and British, Belgian, and French Africa.

ART AND ARCHITECTURE

Art History Resources on the Web: Part 12, Nineteenth Century Art

http://witcombe.sbc.edu/ARTHLinks5.html

Chris Witcombe, a professor of art history at Sweet Briar College in Virginia, compiled this extensive list of Web sites about art history. This page of the site specifically deals with nineteenth century painting, sculpture, and architecture, featuring hundreds of links to information about Neoclassicism, Romanticism, Realism, and other art styles and about individual artists, sculptors, and architects of the period.

A Digital Archive of American Architecture: Nineteenth Century

http://www.bc.edu/bc_org/avp/cas/fnart/fa267/
　　fa267_19.html

Professor Jeffrey Howe of Boston College created this slide collection of nineteenth century American architecture, which includes examples of buildings created in the Neoclassic, Greek, Gothic, Egyptian Revival, Richardson Romanesque, and other styles. Slides also depict period houses, churches, and public and commercial structures.

A Digital Archive of Architecture: Nineteenth Century Architecture

http://www.bc.edu/bc_org/avp/cas/fnart/arch/
　　19arch_europe.html

Professor Jeffrey Howe of Boston College created this Web site of European architecture. This page features examples of nineteenth century architecture, including buildings designed in the Greek Revival, High Victorian Gothic, and Second Empire Baroque styles. There also is information about the Eiffel Tower, the Vienna Secessionists, and Charles Rennie Mackintosh and the Glasgow School of Art.

Metropolitan Museum of Art: Timeline of Art History

http://www.metmuseum.org/toah/splash.htm

The museum's Web site describes itself as a "chronological, geographical, and thematic exploration of the history of art from around the world, as illustrated especially by the Metropolitan Museum of Art's collection." The time line for the period from 1800 to 1900 contains artworks, maps, and chronologies organized by regions of the world, including North America, South America, Europe, Central America and Mexico, Africa, Oceania, and several areas of Asia. The site also features numerous pages devoted to specific topics, including European art in the nineteenth century, arts of the United States in the nineteenth century, and African, Asian, and Islamic art.

WebMuseum, Paris: Famous Art Works Exhibition

http://www.ibiblio.org/wm/paint/

This Web collection of European and American paintings from 1250 through the twentieth century includes two pages specifically about nineteenth century art: "Revolution and Restoration" and "Impressionism." Each page contains links to information describing painting styles and providing biographical

information about specific artists, including Eugène Delacroix, John Constable, Vincent van Gogh, Édouard Manet, and Mary Cassatt. Additional information about artists is accessible through the artist index, an alphabetical listing of artists whose work is featured on the site.

ASIA

Internet East Asian History Sourcebook

http://www.fordham.edu/halsall/eastasia/
　　eastasiasbook.html

This site provides primary source materials tracing historical and cultural developments in China, Japan, Korea, and other East Asian nations. It includes separate sections focusing on religious traditions; the Western intrusion, including European and American imperialism, British East Asia, and the work of missionaries; Japan as a world power; and Chinese history from 1840 through 1949.

CANADA

The Canadian Encyclopedia

http://thecanadianencyclopedia.com/

The Canadian Encyclopedia provides authoritative information on what the site describes as "all things Canadian." The Feature Articles section contains numerous articles about a broad range of nineteenth century people and events, including George Brown and rebellion in Upper Canada, as well as articles about culture, sports, exploration, the military, and society. An extensive time line chronicles significant events throughout Canadian history.

Dictionary of Canadian Biography Online

http://www.biographi.ca/EN/index.html

The online version of the *Dictionary of Canadian Biography* contains thousands of biographies about significant Canadians. The biographies can be accessed via alphabetical listings or through the site's search engine.

oCanada.ca: Canadian History, Nineteenth Century

http://www.ocanada.ca/history/history_19.php

The oCanada.ca Web site contains a time line listing significant events in Canadian history, including this page featuring a chronology of events occurring in the nineteenth century.

ECONOMICS

The History of Economic Thought

http://cepa.newschool.edu/het/

Created by the Department of Economics at the New School for Social Research, this site features biographical information and excerpts of texts from more than five hundred economists who can be accessed via an alphabetical index. Friedrich Engels, Thomas Robert Malthus, Karl Marx, John Stuart Mill, David Ricardo, and Robert Owen are among the nineteenth century giants featured here. Another section of the site describes various schools of economic thought; the section about classical economics features information about Utilitarianism, Karl Marx and Marxism, and David Ricardo and the classical Ricardian school, while the section about alternative economic schools features information about Utopians, socialists, and Fabian socialists.

McMaster University Archive for the History of Economic Thought

http://socserv2.socsci.mcmaster.ca/~econ/ugcm/3113/

An extensive collection of texts about economics, organized by author. The site includes the writings of Thomas Carlyle, Horace Greeley, Karl Marx, John Stuart Mill, Simon Newcomb, Henry Sidgwick, Pierre-Joseph Proudhon, and Herbert Spencer, among other nineteenth century thinkers.

EXPLORATION

Lewis and Clark—PBS

http://www.pbs.org/lewisandclark/index.html

This Web site was designed to accompany Ken Burns's documentary film *The Journey of the Corps of Discovery*, aired by the Public Broadcasting System (PBS). One section of the site, "Inside the Corps," contains information about the members of the corps and an essay placing the expedition within the context of early nineteenth century American politics and history. "Native Americans" describes how the Indians were long familiar with the lands that Lewis and Clark "discovered." The archive contains searchable excerpts from expedition journals, a time line, maps, and a list of related Web links. The site also includes an interactive trail map and "Into the Unknown," an interactive feature that allows users to pretend they are leading the famed expedition.

Nineteenth Century Exploration of Australia

http://www.wku.edu/~smithch/australia/

This look at the exploration of the interior of Australia features maps and pages detailing the expeditions of individual explorers who trekked throughout the continent in the nineteenth century.

Pathfinders and Passageways: The Exploration of Canada

http://www.collectionscanada.ca/explorers/index-e.html

Created by the Library and Archives of Canada, the site chronicles the many people who discovered and explored the country. It includes several pages devoted to nineteenth century exploration, including information on discoveries in the Arctic and attempts to discover a Northwest Passage.

FRANCE

Gallica: XIX Seicle

http://gallica.bnf.fr/

This French-language site, created by the Bibliothèque Nationale de France, features the library's collections and other materials about French history and culture. The page about the nineteenth century links to images and information about French history, law, science, and philosophy. The literature section provides overviews of various movements in nineteenth century French literature and information about the French theater and the French novel of that period, including separate pages devoted to authors Stendhal, Émile Zola, Victor Hugo, and Honoré de Balzac.

Napoleon Bonaparte Internet Guide

http://www.napoleonbonaparte.nl/

A guide to help users readily access what its creator describes as "the best Napoleonic sites in the world." There are hundreds of links to sites about Napoleon, the Napoleonic era, and other topics, as well as articles about Napoleon.

Nineteenth Century France

http://www.fordham.edu/halsall/mod/
modsbook3.html#France

This page of Web links about nineteenth century France is part of "Internet Modern History Sourcebook: The Long Nineteenth Century," created by Paul Halsall of Fordham University. The page provides primary source documents about the revolts of 1848, the Franco Prussian War, the Paris Commune, and the Third Republic.

Nineteenth Century Paris Project

http://gallery.sjsu.edu/paris/

Designed by Kathleen Cohen, a professor of art history at San Jose State University, and her students, this site is a beautifully illustrated, user-friendly compendium of information about life in nineteenth century Paris. It is divided into general categories: architecture; French politics and government; social classes; technology, describing various industries and technological developments; women's fashion; furniture; music, including audio clips of music by Hector Berlioz, Georges Bizet, and other composers; the Academy, an overview of "official" French painting and sculpture before Impressionism; breaking away, an overview of the work of the Impressionists and subsequent artists; mass-produced art; and the Symbolist movement in painting and poetry. The section on social classes is especially interesting, featuring a chronology of major events in nineteenth century Parisian history and descriptions of life for men, women, and children of the upper, middle, and lower classes.

GERMANY

Germany Under Bismarck

http://www.historyhome.co.uk/europe/bismarck2.htm

This series of pages about Otto von Bismarck constitutes part of "A Web of English History," a collection of links about late eighteenth and nineteenth century British history. The pages devoted to the Iron Chancellor include a biography, collection of quotations, a time line outlining significant nineteenth century developments leading to the eventual unification of Germany, information about Bismarck's foreign policy and the Franco-Prussian War of 1870-1871, and an overview of Bismarck's domestic German policies.

Nineteenth Century Germany

http://www.fordham.edu/halsall/mod/
modsbook3.html#Germany

This page of Web links about nineteenth century Germany is part of "Internet Modern History Sourcebook: The Long Nineteenth Century," created by Paul Halsall of Fordham University. The page provides primary source documents about German unification, Otto von Bismarck, and Kaiser Wilhelm II.

GREAT BRITAIN

Chartism

http://www.spartacus.schoolnet.co.uk/chartism.htm

One of the many excellent Web sites created by Spartacus Educational, a British organization that creates Web sites designed for history instruction. This site provides information about the people and events associated with the Chartist movement in the 1830's and 1840's. The movement aimed to restore perceived inequities in the Reform Act of 1832 by demanding suffrage for all British men (including the working class), and designated electoral districts, annual general elections, secret ballots, and other electoral reforms. The site contains individual pages about movement leaders, movement tactics, British newspapers' opinions of Chartism, and the nineteenth century parliamentary reform acts relevant to the movement.

The Monarchy, 1042-1952

http://www.spartacus.schoolnet.co.uk/monarchy.htm

Contains individual pages about each of the British monarchs who reigned from 1042 to 1952, with portraits, biographical details, significant historical facts about their reigns, and links to sites with additional information. This site is particularly valuable for its page about Queen Victoria, which details the many events of her life and her unusually long nineteenth century reign.

Prime Ministers, 1760-1960

http://www.spartacus.schoolnet.co.uk/pm.htm

A site designed by Spartacus Educational, a British organization that creates Web sites designed for history instruction. Provides portraits, biographies, and information about significant events that occurred during the terms of Britain's prime ministers, with links to sites with additional information. Benjamin Disraeli, William Gladstone, Sir Robert Peel, Lord Liverpool, and the other nineteenth century prime ministers are included on the site. The individual pages about each prime minister are easily accessed via a central list of the prime ministers, in chronological order of their terms in office.

Research Resources for the Study of Nineteenth-Century Ireland

http://www.qub.ac.uk/en/socs/research.htm

Contains extensive and wide-ranging resources on both Irish history and culture and the Irish diaspora.

Victoria Research Web

http://victorianresearch.org/

Includes links to academic journals devoted to nineteenth century topics, bibliographies, links to discussion groups, and an extensive collection of links to related topics.

The Victorian Dictionary: Exploring Victorian London

http://www.victorianlondon.org/

This quirky but entertaining and informative site provides a range of information about life in nineteenth century London. Articles, many of which are illustrated, can be accessed through an alphabetical list of topics, including advertising, death and dying, childhood, education, the legal system, women, shops and shopping, clothing and fashions, and food and drink. The section about people profiles a broad spectrum of nineteenth century Londoners, ranging from Queen Victoria to Joseph Merrick (better known as the Elephant Man).

The Victorian Web

http://victorian.lang.nagoya-u.ac.jp/victorianweb/

One of the finest Web sites about the nineteenth century, maintained by the National University of Singapore, is an online version of information originally designed for a course at Brown University. The site provides a wealth of information about Great Britain during the reign of Queen Victoria, including political and social history, gender matters, science, technology, economics, and culture. It also provides lists of Web books, a bibliography, and links to related Web sites.

A Web of English History

http://www.historyhome.co.uk/

This site is an exceptionally good source of information about British politics and history between 1760 and 1830. It includes Peel Web, named for Sir Robert Peel, the dominant figure in Parliament from 1830 through 1850 and a two-time prime minister in the nineteenth century. In addition to its biographical information about Peel, the site provides primary and secondary source materials about other prime ministers of the eighteenth and nineteenth centuries, British political and economic affairs, political parties and reform movements, British foreign policy, and contemporary political literature. There is also a section devoted to nineteenth century Irish history, including

information on the Irish Famine and the campaign to repeal the Corn Laws.

ITALY

The Italian Unification

http://www.arcaini.com/ITALY/ItalyHistory/
ItalianUnification.htm

This page from "The History of Italy" Web site provides an overview of Italian unification. It features a time line detailing historical developments from 1672 through 1871 and an essay about the country's unification in the nineteenth century, focusing on Giuseppe Mazzini, Giuseppe Garibaldi, and Count Cavour.

LATIN AMERICA

Casahistoria: Latin American Home Page

http://www.casahistoria.net/latam.html

Casahistoria was created by a teacher in Buenos Aires, Argentina, who wanted to provide a list of Web resources for his undergraduate history students. The site contains information in English and Spanish, including a page of links about Latin American history and culture, with two sections pertaining to the nineteenth century. Independence from Spain links to pages about Simón Bolívar, José de San Martín, Mexican independence, and the Spanish-American War. The "Nineteenth Century" section includes a time line of Latin American history from 1800 through 1998 and information about the Triple Alliance War and British and American involvement in Latin America.

Internet Modern History Sourcebook: The Long Nineteenth Century

http://www.fordham.edu/halsall/mod/modsbook3.html

In this collection of primary source documents, Paul Halsall of Fordham University includes a section about Latin America. The section features information about the region's independence from Spain and about several Latin American nations, including Argentina, Brazil, and Cuba.

LITERATURE

Authors Discussed in the Victorian Web

http://victorian.lang.nagoya-u.ac.jp/victorianweb/

The Victorian Web's home page links to a section called "Authors," providing an alphabetical listing of more than seventy British authors from the Victorian era. The list links to additional pages of information about the individual authors, including biographies, bibliographies, analyses of their work, and, in some cases, excerpts of their writing. Oscar Wilde, Charles Dickens, Alfred, Lord Tennyson, Charlotte Brontë, and George Eliot are among the authors included in this excellent compilation. The page also includes links to information about some pre-Victorians, such as Lord Byron, Jane Austen, Alexander Pope, and other eighteenth and early nineteenth century authors.

The Cambridge History of English and American Literature: An Encyclopedia in Eighteen Volumes

http://www.bartleby.com/cambridge/

An exhaustively comprehensive examination of all forms of writing in Great Britain and the United States, including literature; legal, political, and church writing; history; journalism; children's literature; and philosophy. Volumes 12 through 14 contain essays and literary texts composed during the Romantic revival and the Victorian era in England. Volumes 15 through 17 focus on early and later national literature from the United States, including information on Walt Whitman, O. Henry, Mark Twain, Henry James, and Abraham Lincoln.

Literary Resources on the Net: Victorian British

http://andromeda.rutgers.edu/~jlynch/Lit/

Jack Lynch, associate professor of English at Rutgers University, has compiled a thorough collection of Web resources about literature. The home page provides a link to a separate page containing information about Victorian era British literature. That page includes links to e-texts and Web sites, discussions of Victorian theater and literary movements, and information about individual authors, including Robert and Elizabeth Barrett Browning, Sir Arthur Conan Doyle, Thomas Hardy, and Lewis Carroll.

Nineteenth Century British and Irish Authors

http://www.lang.nagoya-u.ac.jp/~matsuoka/19th-authors.html

This site, maintained by Nagoya University in Japan, links to information about 411 nineteenth century British and Irish poets, novelists, playwrights, and other writers. The authors are listed chronologically by birth date, from 1751 until 1865. The page also provides a link for information about additional authors not included in the list.

Romantic Links, Electronic Texts, and Home Pages

http://www.english.upenn.edu/~mgamer/Romantic/index.html

This page is part of "The Penn English Web Site," created by Michael Gamer, associate professor of English at the University of Pennsylvania. It includes a wide range of materials about eighteenth and nineteenth century Romantic literature. The site is divided into several sections, including information about associations and journals devoted to the study of Romantic literature; general links; electronic texts from the eighteenth and nineteenth centuries; university professors' personal home pages about these centuries; and Web sites about individual authors, including Lord Byron, William Wordsworth, the Brontë sisters, Percy Bysshe Shelley, and John Keats.

Voice of the Shuttle: Romantics

http://vos.ucsb.edu/browse.asp?id=2750

An excellent collection of Web resources about the humanities compiled by professors at the University of California, Santa Barbara. This page contains links to essays, literary criticism, and examples of prose, poetry, and drama from a long list of British authors from the late eighteenth and early nineteenth centuries.

Voice of the Shuttle: Victorians

http://vos.ucsb.edu/browse.asp?id=2751

Another page from Voice of the Shuttle, this one focusing on British writers from the Victorian era. The page contains links to numerous Web sites, essays, selected writings, and other resources.

WWW.Twainquotes.com

http://www.twainquotes.com/

A good place to begin a Web-based study of Mark Twain, this illustrated site, designed by independent scholar Barbara Schmidt, features texts of some of Twain's newspaper articles, selected interviews, and a lengthy collection of the author's quotes, organized alphabetically by subject. The site also provides links to other Twain Web sites.

MATHEMATICS

The MacTutor History of Mathematics Archive

http://www-groups.dcs.st-and.ac.uk/~history/index.html

A very comprehensive Web site, created and maintained by the School of Mathematics and Statistics at the University of St. Andrews, Scotland. The site features biographies of prominent mathematicians which can be accessed by either an alphabetical or chronological index. It also contains information about math history, with separate pages explaining important mathematical discoveries and concepts. Niels Henrik Abel, Gottlob Frege, Sofia Kovalevskaia, Nikolay Ivanovich Lobachevsky, and Charlotte Angus Scott are among the mathematicians included.

MUSIC

American Singing: Nineteenth Century Song Sheets
http://memory.loc.gov/ammem/amsshtml/
  amsshome.html

This collection of several hundred song sheets is part of the American Memory Project, the Library of Congress's collection of sound recordings, images, maps, sheet music, and other materials aimed at documenting the American experience. Song sheets, or single printed sheets containing lyrics but no music, were a popular form of entertainment during the nineteenth century. The collection focuses on song sheets published from the beginning of the nineteenth century until the 1880's, with the majority dating from the 1850's through the 1870's, the zenith of the song sheet craze. The song sheets can be accessed by title, author's name, or publisher and are presented in both thumbnail and enlarged formats.

Carolina Classical Connection: Classical Period Music
Links
http://www.carolinaclassical.com/links.html

The Classical MIDI Connection: The Classical Period
http://www.classicalmidiconnection.com/cmc/
  classical.html

The Classical MIDI Connection: The Romantic Period
http://www.classicalmidiconnection.com/cmc/
  romantic.html

A collection of music midi files. Midi, or musical instrument digital interface, is a digital technology that allows electronic musical instruments and computers to communicate with one another and enables people to listen to music on their computers. The site has an alphabetized list of composers with links to midi files of their music. Separate pages are devoted to music of specific eras. The Classical Period page contains an extensive collection of links and midi files for Ludwig van Beethoven and Franz Schubert. The Romantic period page features a wide range of nineteenth century composers, including Frédéric Chopin, Johannes Brahms, Antonín Dvořák, Edvard Grieg, Félix Mendelssohn, Camille Saint-Saëns, John Philip Sousa, and Sir Arthur Sullivan.

Public Domain Music
http://www.pdmusic.org

This collection of midi and text files of lyrics for American music in the public domain contains many examples of nineteenth century music. The files can be accessed through a list of composers, with an especially good selection of work by Stephen Collins Foster. Files are also organized by style of music, with the Minstrel Songs, Old and New section featuring nineteenth century compositions. Four additional pages are specifically devoted to nineteenth century music: Music from 1800 through 1860; two pages of Civil War-era music; and Music from 1866 through 1899.

Romantic Era Music Links
http://www.carolinaclassical.com/romantic.html

A collection of links to a wide variety of music-related Web sites, with biographical information on composers, descriptions of musical genres and types of compositions, and encoded music files. The page with links to the Classical period includes information on Ludwig van Beethoven. The Romantic era page contains links to information about Scott Joplin, John Philip Sousa, Franz Schubert, Richard Wagner, Peter Ilich Tchaikovsky, Hector Berlioz, Franz Lizst, and many other nineteenth century composers.

PHILOSOPHY

Philosophy Pages
http://www.philosophypages.com/

An easily accessible site aimed at students of the Western philosophical tradition. Users can access information via a dictionary of philosophical terms and names, a survey of the history of Western philosophy, and a time line. "Philosophy Pages" also provides links to other philosophy Web sites, recommended books for further study, and essays examining the ideas of several major nineteenth century philosophers, including William James, Karl Marx, Friedrich Nietzsche, and Søren Kierkegaard.

Stanford Encyclopedia of Philosophy

http://plato.stanford.edu/contents.html

A collection of articles about various aspects of philosophy which can be accessed through an alphabetical table of contents. Includes articles about Darwinism, F. H. Bradley, Ralph Waldo Emerson, Karl Marx, and Arthur Schopenhauer.

The Victorian Web: Philosophy Overview

http://victorian.lang.nagoya-u.ac.jp/victorianweb/

The Victorian Web home page includes a philosophy section that provides an overview of nineteenth century British moral, religious, political, economic, and aesthetic philosophy, including information about John Stuart Mill, Herbert Spencer and Social Darwinism, David Ricardo, and John Ruskin.

The Web of American Transcendentalism

http://www.vcu.edu/engweb/transcendentalism/
    index.html

Virginia Commonwealth University graduate students created this comprehensive Web site to supplement their study of American Transcendentalism. One section of the site contains biographical information and texts of works by American Transcendentalist authors such as Ralph Waldo Emerson, Henry David Thoreau, and Bronson Alcott. "Ideas and Thought" provides an overview of Transcendentalists' views on nature, aesthetics, religion, education, and other topics, while "Roots and Influences" explores the origins of Transcendentalism and its legacy in American literature, religion, philosophy, and political and social reform. A bibliography and selected Web list recommend resources for further research.

RELIGION

Religion and the New Republic

http://www.loc.gov/exhibits/religion/re107.html

This page is part of "Religion and the Founding of the American Republic," a Web site accompanying an exhibit at the Library of Congress. The page describes various aspects of religion in the United States from 1800 until the Civil War, focusing on evangelism, which the site describes as the "grand absorbing theme" of American life. The page includes information about evangelical camp meetings, pictures of re-

ligious revivals, and pages from revival hymnals. There is additional information about the emergence of the African American church, the Shakers, the Mormons, nineteenth century American religious leaders, and the role of church-related benevolent societies.

Religion in Victorian Britain

http://victorian.lang.nagoya-u.ac.jp/victorianweb/

Includes a section titled "Religion," a page of links to information about numerous aspects of Victorian era religion in Great Britain, including a time line of religion and philosophy and an examination of the relationship of science and religion. There is also information about specific church denominations and sects, including the Evangelical and Oxford movements.

What Is the Oxford Movement?

http://parishes.oxford.anglican.org/puseyhouse/
    oxfdmove.htm

This is part of the Web site for the Pusey House and Library in Oxford, England, a site dedicated to the nineteenth century theologian E. B. Pusey. The page describes the involvement of Pusey, John Henry Newman, John Keble, and others in the Oxford Movement, an attempt to bring about a Catholic revival within the Church of England.

William Ellery Channing and American Unitarianism

http://xroads.virginia.edu/%7EHYPER/DETOC/
    religion/channing.html

An overview of the life of William Ellery Channing and his role in establishing the Unitarian religion in the United States, part of a Web site created by the University of Virginia. The site includes a brief look at Channing's life and career; the text of his speech "Unitarian Christianity," delivered on May 5, 1819; and Alexis de Tocqueville's account of his 1831 interview with Channing, excerpted from the book *Tocqueville and Beaumont in America* (1938), by George Wilson Pierson.

RUSSIA

Russia, 1860-1945

http://www.spartacus.schoolnet.co.uk/
    RussiaIssues.htm

An examination of Russian history from 1860 until

the end World War II, including information about the events and issues in the mid- and late nineteenth century that led to the Russian Revolution. The nature of the Romanov Dynasty, the role of the Russian Orthodox Church, Jewish pogroms, and Czar Alexander II's Emancipation Manifesto are among the topics explored here.

SCIENCE AND MEDICINE

Eric Weisstein's World of Science

http://scienceworld.wolfram.com/

This online reference has been compiled by a research scientist and former professor of astronomy. It contains several encyclopedias of information about astronomy, chemistry, mathematics, and physics. There also are brief biographies and portraits of noteworthy scientists, including Louis Pasteur, Humphrey Davy, Charles Babbage, Niels Henrik Abel, Georges Cuvier, and other nineteenth century figures.

From Quackery to Bacteriology: The Emergence of Modern Medicine in Nineteenth Century America

http://www.cl.utoledo.edu/canaday/quackery/quack-index.html

The Web site was created to accompany an exhibit tracing the development of medicine through printed works that was mounted in 1994 at the University of Toledo Libraries. The site features illustrations, which can be viewed in both thumbnail and enlarged sizes, and text describing nineteenth century medicine, including scientific treatments for disease, alternative health treatments, quackery, patent medicine, women's health care, mental health, physical fitness and nutrition, nursing, medical education, and medicine during the Civil War.

History of Western Biomedicine

http://www.mic.ki.se/West.html#West3

Compiled by the Karolinska Institutet in Sweden, this site contains links to Web sites discussing various aspects of medical and scientific history from ancient times into the twenty-first century. The section "Modern Period, 1601-" includes a list of sites about nineteenth century scientific and medical developments, including the history of the stethoscope, hearing aids, anesthesia, medicine in the American Civil War, and biographical information about John Dalton, Michael Faraday, Elizabeth Blackwell, Louis Braille, Ernst

Haeckel, Florence Nightingale, Louis Pasteur, Joseph Lister, and Ferdinand Julius Cohn.

THEATER

Nineteenth Century Actors Photographs

http://content.lib.washington.edu/
19thcenturyactorsweb/

One of the digital collections of the University of Washington Libraries, this site features 610 studio portraits of entertainers, actors, and actresses who performed on the American stage in the mid- to late nineteenth century. The photographs are organized and accessed by categories of entertainers and theater professionals, including comedians, theater dramatists, theater managers, musicians and singers, blackface entertainers, and women. There also is an essay about nineteenth century American theater.

Theatre Database: Nineteenth Century Theatre

http://www.theatredatabase.com/19th_century/

The pages on this site link to biographical information and other Web sites about nineteenth century playwrights and actors, including Henrik Ibsen, W. S. Gilbert, William Charles Macready, and Edmund Kean. There are also Web links to articles about drama in the nineteenth century and the rise of Romanticism in French drama.

TRADE, COMMERCE, AND TECHNOLOGY

Cotton Times: Understanding the Industrial Revolution

http://www.cottontimes.co.uk/index.html

A comprehensive examination of the Industrial Revolution in Great Britain. The site begins its exploration with information about the innovations in the cotton industry in eighteenth century Lancashire, which spurred what the site describes as "history's greatest upheaval." Among the site's features are a time line of events from 1700 to 1900, an alphabetical listing of key figures associated with the Industrial Revolution; separate sections providing biographical information about significant inventors, inventions, engineers, and reformers; overviews of workers' riots, rallies, and confrontations; and descriptions of the lives of adult and child factory workers. In addition, the site provides a bibliography for further research, a glossary, and links to related Web sites.

Internet History Sourcebook: The Long Nineteenth Century: The Second Industrial Revolution and Advanced Capitalism

http://www.fordham.edu/halsall/mod/modsbook3.html

Paul Halsall's collection of nineteenth century primary source documents contains a section that links to materials about the lives of workers; new technologies, including electricity and technological advances in the steel and chemical industries; efficiency, automation, and the assembly line; and the modern corporation.

Nineteenth Century Inventions: 1800-1850

http://inventors.about.com/library/weekly/aa111100a.htm

Nineteenth Century Inventions: 1851-1899

http://inventors.about.com/library/weekly/aa111100b.htm

These two pages from About.com's time line of inventions are devoted to the nineteenth century. The time line links to additional pages describing inventors and inventions of the period, including information about Rudolf Diesel, Alexander Graham Bell, Thomas Alva Edison, Alfred Nobel, Sir Humphry Davy, Richard Trevithick, and the invention of the battery, tin can, microphone, gas lighting, matches, photography, and motion pictures.

UNITED STATES

Abraham Lincoln Papers at the Library of Congress

http://memory.loc.gov/ammem/alhtml/malhome.html

The site provides digitized access to twenty thousand of Abraham Lincoln's documents, the majority dating from his presidency. The site is divided into three series of general correspondence: Series 1, from 1833 to 1916; Series 2, 1858 to 1865; and Series 3, 1837 to 1897. The general correspondence includes letters, drafts of speeches, pamphlets, newspaper clippings, and notes. Lincoln's draft of the Emancipation Proclamation is one of the site's particularly valuable documents. The site features additional information about the Emancipation Proclamation and Lincoln's assassination.

The American Civil War Homepage

http://sunsite.utk.edu/civil-war/cwarhp.html

In the site's own words, this is a collection of "hyper-

text links to the most useful identified electronic files about the American Civil War." The site, maintained by George H. Hoemann, an assistant dean at the University of Tennessee, is unusually extensive, with a wealth of information arranged categorically. The compendium of links features information about the antebellum period and the secession crisis; photos and other images of the war; biographical information about important historical figures, such as Abraham Lincoln, Robert E. Lee, Ulysses S. Grant, and Stonewall Jackson; descriptions of battles and campaigns; and Web sites about individual regiments and battalions.

American Cultural History: The Nineteenth Century

http://kclibrary.nhmccd.edu/19thcentury.html

This accessible and well-illustrated site was created at Kingwood College in Kingwood, Texas. It provides a time line with individual pages for each decade of the nineteenth century, from 1800 to 1890. Each page provides information about American art, architecture, business, economy, books, literature, migration and immigration, education, music, theater, pastimes, science, technology, and social movements during the decade examined. The pages also contain links to other Web sites and recommended books and videotapes for further research.

AmericanPresident.org

http://www.americanpresident.org/

This accessible and inclusive site was created by the Miller Center of Public Affairs at the University of Virginia, a research institution that studies the American presidency. The "Presidency in History" section contains several pages of information about each of the presidents, illustrated with period drawings, photographs, and other images; there are brief biographies of each president, followed by more extensive pages of information about each president's life before and after his term in office, his campaigns and elections, and significant domestic and foreign affairs during his administration. In addition, there are biographies of each First Lady, brief biographies of key cabinet members, lists of presidential staff members and advisers, and links to additional resources.

American West

http://www.spartacus.schoolnet.co.uk/USAamericanwest.htm

Spartacus Educational has compiled this collection of biographies and other information about the exploration, expansion, and settlement of the western United States during the late eighteenth and nineteenth centuries. Many of the pages are enhanced with excerpts from diaries, newspapers, and other primary source materials. The site provides access to pages with information about a broad range of topics, including explorers; frontiersmen, mountain men, and fur trappers, such as Kit Carson and Davy Crockett; Jesse James, Billy the Kid, and other criminals and outlaws; soldiers; migrants and settlers; missionaries and religious leaders; judges and lawmen, including Wild Bill Hickok and Wyatt Earp; politicians; Calamity Jane, Belle Starr, and other women of the West; inventors and businessmen; artists and writers; Native American leaders and tribes; and significant events and issues related to the western expansion.

America's Reconstruction: People and Politics After the Civil War

http://www.digitalhistory.uh.edu/reconstruction/index.html

This excellent overview of the Reconstruction era was created by Eric Foner, the De Witt Clinton Professor of History at Columbia University, and Olivia Mahoney, director of historical documentation at the Chicago Historical Society. It contains text, photographs, cartoons, and other images about the abolition of slavery and the reconstruction of the South after the Civil War. The site is divided by subjects, providing information about the Emancipation Proclamation and the condition of newly freed slaves during the Civil War; responses to slavery by both black and white Americans; an explanation of how many former slaves became a source of free labor after the Civil War; and the politics of Reconstruction, including details of the administration of President Andrew Johnson. The site also provides a Reconstruction time line and links to other resources.

Avalon Project at Yale Law School: Nineteenth Century Documents

http://www.yale.edu/lawweb/avalon/19th.htm

A collection of digitized primary source materials relevant to the fields of law, history, economics, politics, diplomacy, and government. A separate page, "Nineteenth Century Documents," features numerous legal and political documents, listed in alphabetical order, including the presidents' inaugural addresses and an-

nual messages; papers from the Confederate States of America; Abraham Lincoln's Gettysburg Address; treaties between the United States and other nations, including Native American nations; documents pertaining to the Louisiana Purchase; and laws relating to slavery and Native Americans.

First Person Narratives of the American South, 1860-1920

http://memory.loc.gov/ammem/award97/ncuhtml/fpnashome.html

A compilation of printed texts from the libraries of the University of North Carolina, Chapel Hill, featuring what the site describes as a look at the "nineteenth century American South from the viewpoints of Southerners." While some of the narrators are prominent historical figures, many others are unknown women, African Americans, military men who enlisted during the Civil War, laborers, and Native Americans. The site's texts were found in diaries, the narratives of former slaves, autobiographies, memoirs, and travel accounts. These narratives can be accessed through indexes of authors, titles, and subjects.

The Frederick Douglass Papers at the Library of Congress

http://memory.loc.gov/ammem/doughtml/doughome.html

The Library of Congress created this digitized collection about Frederick Douglass, a former slave who became a major leader of the abolitionist movement. The site features 7,400 items, with 38,000 images, about Douglass's life as an escaped slave, abolitionist, orator, editor, and public servant covering the years 1841 through 1864, with the majority of the papers dating from 1862 through 1895. The papers include Douglass's correspondence, speeches, articles written by him and his contemporaries, a draft of his autobiography, his financial and legal papers, and scrapbooks. In addition to the papers, the site features a time line of Douglass's life, links to complete online texts of all three of his autobiographies, and a Douglass family tree.

Internet Modern History Sourcebook: The Long Nineteenth Century

http://www.fordham.edu/halsall/mod/modsbook3.html

Among the site's collection of primary source materials is an extensive section devoted to the United States. The section features documents regarding

American expansion and the Manifest Destiny; the antebellum conflict between North and South; the Civil War, Reconstruction, and Jim Crow; immigration and its effects; American culture; the legal framework of American life; and the Gilded Age.

Selected Civil War Photographs

http://memory.loc.gov/ammem/cwphtml/
    cwphome.html

Another site created by the Library of Congress as part of the library's American Memory project. "Selected Civil War Photographs" contains digitized versions of 1,318 photographs, the majority of them taken under the direction of famed photographer Mathew B. Brady, depicting scenes of military personnel, battle preparations, and the aftermath of Civil War battles. While some of the subjects of the photographs are Confederate and Union army and navy officers, there also are images of enlisted men and infantry units. The images are featured in both thumbnail and enlarged versions.

Slavery

http://www.spartacus.schoolnet.co.uk/USAslavery.htm

An excellent overview of American slavery, this site provides numerous pages containing accounts from Harriet Tubman, Frederick Douglass, Henry Box Brown, Sojourner Truth, and other slaves; descriptions of the slave trade, plantation system, the Underground Railroad, and slaves' lives; discussions of the significant events and issues in the abolition movement; and biographical information about major abolitionists in the United States and Britain. The historical information on many of the pages is enhanced with excerpts from diaries, journals, newspaper reports, and other primary source documents.

Slaves and the Courts, 1740-1860

http://memory.loc.gov/ammem/sthtml/sthome.html

The Library of Congress has organized this digitized collection of about one hundred pamphlets and books published between 1772 and 1889 which pertain to the experiences of African American slaves in the American colonies and the United States. The materials include information about trials and cases relating to slavery, legal arguments for and against slavery, examinations of cases and legal decisions, journals, and other works about the legal system and slavery. The documents on the site can be accessed through indexes of subjects, authors, and titles.

Thomas Jefferson Digital Archive

http://etext.lib.virginia.edu/jefferson/

A compendium of electronic information about Jefferson, one of the most significant presidents of the nineteenth century, compiled by the University of Virginia. The site includes more than seventeen hundred digitized texts to or by Jefferson, including letters and manuscripts; an online version of *The Jefferson Cyclopedia: A Comprehensive Collection of the Views of Thomas Jefferson*, containing Jefferson's views on government, politics, law, religion, and other subjects; and a collection of Jefferson's quotes. There also is an electronic text of B. L. Rayner's *Life of Thomas Jefferson*, a biography originally published in 1834.

WAR, RIOTS, AND REVOLUTION (*See also* UNITED STATES, *above, for sites about the U.S. Civil War*)

Anglo Boer War Museum

http://www.anglo-boer.co.za/index.html

The museum, located in Bloemfontein, South Africa, has designed this Web site describing the conflict fought from 1899 to 1902 between the British and soldiers from the Boer republics of the Transvaal and the Orange Free State. It includes an overview outlining the causes of the war, information about important people involved in the conflict, and an explanation of the role of black people in the war.

Chicago Anarchists on Trial: Evidence from the Haymarket Affair, 1886-1887

http://memory.loc.gov/ammem/award98/ichihtml/
    hayhome.html

A collection, compiled and digitized by the Library of Congress, of manuscripts, broadsides, photographs, and prints about the Haymarket affair, a violent confrontation between labor protesters and Chicago police that took place on May 4, 1886. The site includes materials pertaining to the anarchists' meeting and bombing on May 4; a thirty-two-hundred-page transcript of proceedings from the subsequent trial of the men who allegedly incited the bombing; and information about the defendants' convictions, appeals, and execution. Among the materials are two dozen two-dimensional artifacts, including labor banners, an unexploded bomb, and articles from the Chicago police department. A Haymarket chronology and excerpts from the autobiographies of defendants August Spies and Albert Parsons are also available on the site.

Cinco de Mayo, 1862, La Batalla de Puebla

http://www.nacnet.org/assunta/spa5may.htm

Part of a Web site describing Mexican and Chicano holiday traditions, this page provides a brief overview, in both English and Spanish, of the battle on May 5, 1862, in which the Mexican imperial monarchy was overthrown. It also contains a bibliography of English- and Spanish-language books and encyclopedias containing additional information about the battle.

Encyclopedia of 1848 Revolutions

http://www.cats.ohiou.edu/~Chastain/index.htm

An online version of the encyclopedia that describes itself as "the only complete history of all the 1848 revolutions." The site features numerous essays by historians and professors describing the movements toward liberty, economic equality, and nationalism that developed throughout the world during the nineteenth century. The essay topics include information about German and Italian unification, communism, life in nineteenth century France and the 1848 revolution in that country, Jewish emancipation, political developments in Poland and Hungary, women's rights, and the United States' reaction to the revolutions of 1848.

Napoleon, His Army and Enemies: Armies, Campaigns, Battles, Tactics, Commanders

http://web2.airmail.net/napoleon/index.html

According to its home page, this site contains more than "1,800 illustrations, maps, charts, articles about Napoleon's strategy and tactics, about the French, Polish, Prussian, Austrian, Russian, and British armies, their organization, commanders, uniforms, books, clubs, re-enactment groups" and other information about the Napoleonic Wars in Europe. It outlines individual battles fought between 1796 and 1815 and describes military tactics of the period.

The U.S.-Mexican War

http://www.dmwv.org/mexwar/mexwar1.htm

Created by the Descendants of Mexican War veterans, the site provides an overview of the conflict. It includes a concise history of the war; images; maps; descriptions of historic battle sites in the United States and Mexico; and speeches, legislation, battle reports, and other primary source documents. There also is a list of frequently asked questions about the war, a chronology of the conflict, and statistics.

War of 1812-1814

http://members.tripod.com/~war1812/

This examination of the war between the United States and Britain includes an explanation of the events in Europe and the United States leading to the conflict; numerous pages describing individual battles; descriptions and illustrations of the weapons used during the war; and information about the role of American and British soldiers, women, and Native Americans in the war. The site also provides links to several other Web sites about the War of 1812.

The World of 1898: The Spanish-American War

http://www.loc.gov/rr/hispanic/1898/

The Hispanic Division of the Library of Congress has compiled this compendium of resources about the Spanish-American War, the period before the war, and the people who either fought in or commented about the conflict. There are separate sections about Cuba, the Philippines, Puerto Rico, and Spain featuring overview essays, maps, chronologies, and indexes of cities that were significant to the conflict. Another section focuses on the literary response to the war, with comments from Mark Twain, Stephen Crane, Walt Whitman, and Puerto Rican and Cuban writers. There also is a selected bibliography of Spanish-language books about the conflict.

WOMEN

Civil War Women: Primary Sources on the Internet

http://odyssey.lib.duke.edu/women/cwdocs.html

Compiled by Duke University, this is a collection of links to individual diaries, letters, and other primary source materials, available on the Internet, about women in the Civil War.

Emancipation of Women, 1750-1920

http://www.spartacus.schoolnet.co.uk/women.htm

Another of the many accessible and comprehensive Web sites designed by Spartacus Educational, a British organization that creates Web sites designed for history instruction. *Emancipation of Women* focuses on the women's suffrage movement in Great Britain. It provides individual pages about key figures in the movement, such as Millicent Garrett Fawcett, Elizabeth Fry, and Harriet Martineau, and the organizations with which they were affiliated, including the Society of Friends, the Unitarian Society, and the

Women's Social and Political Union. In addition, there are descriptions of schooling, marriage, careers, birth control, and other aspects of women's life in nineteenth century Britain; explanations of the strategy and tactics that women used to attain the vote; and examinations of Parliamentary reform laws enacted between 1832 and 1928. Each page contains numerous links to additional pages of information.

Internet Modern History Sourcebook: The Long Nineteenth Century

http://www.fordham.edu/halsall/mod/modsbook3.html

A section of this site contains primary source materials about nineteenth century feminism in the United States and Great Britain. It includes excerpts from Mary Wollstonecraft's *A Vindication of the Rights of Woman*, the text of the 1848 Seneca Falls Declaration, and additional information about the women's suffrage movement and the temperance movement.

Not for Ourselves Alone: The Story of Elizabeth Cady Stanton and Susan B. Anthony

http://www.pbs.org/stantonanthony/

This site was created in connection with a documentary aired by the Public Broadcasting System (PBS) focusing on the two leaders of the nineteenth century American women's right movement. It features streaming video, illustrations, and texts providing biographical and historical information about Anthony and Stanton and the fight for equal rights and suffrage from 1830 through 1920. Each page of biographical and historical data is accompanied by a chronology of cultural and political events and essays and primary source documents that place the women's lives in a broader historical context.

Transcendentalist Women Part 1

http://womenshistory.about.com/library/weekly/
aa031599.htm

Transcendentalist Women Part 2

http://womenshistory.about.com/library/weekly/
aa032299.htm

Contains two articles written by June Johnson Lewis, a teacher and Unitarian minister, about the role of women in the American Transcendentalist movement. Part 1 focuses on Margaret Fuller and Mary Moody Emerson; part 2 discusses Harriet Martineau, Julia Ward Howe, and Elizabeth Palmer Peabody and her sisters, Mary Tyler Peabody Mann and Sophia Amelia Peabody Hawthorne. The site provides links to other Web sites with additional information about these women.

Victorian Women Writers Project

http://www.indiana.edu/~letrs/vwwp/

Created and maintained by Indiana University, the project aims, in its own words, "to produce accurate transcriptions of works by British women writers of the nineteenth century." Dollie Radford, Ouida, Ella Hepworth Dixon, and Catherine Mumford Booth are among the writers whose works are included in the collection.

Women's Suffrage

http://www.spartacus.schoolnet.co.uk/USAwomen.htm

Designed by Spartacus Educational, this site focuses on the women's suffrage movement in the United States. It provides biographical information on a wide range of women's rights campaigners, including Susan B. Anthony, Lucy Stone, and Margaret Fuller, and about campaign organizations, including the American Women's Suffrage Association and the National Association of Colored Women. There are also biographies of the women artists involved in the suffrage movement and of the men who supported women's efforts to attain the vote.

SUBSCRIPTION WEB SITES

The following sites are posted on the World Wide Web but are available only to paying subscribers. Many public, college, and university libraries subscribe to these sources; readers can ask reference librarians if they are available at their local libraries.

GENERAL

Oxford Reference Online

http://www.oxfordreference.com

The Core Collection of Oxford Reference Online is a virtual reference library of more than one hundred dictionaries, language reference, and subject reference books published by the Oxford University Press. The electronic versions of the books are fully indexed and cross-searchable and provide information on a wide range of subjects, including art, architecture, biological sciences, economics and business, history, law, literature, mathematics, medicine, military history, performing arts, political science, social science, religion, and philosophy. The Premium Collection contains all of the features of the Core Collection plus electronic versions of the Oxford Companions Series.

Oxford Scholarship Online

http:www.oxfordscholarship.com

Oxford Scholarship Online contains the electronic versions of more than one thousand books about economics, finance, philosophy, political science, and religion that are published by the Oxford University Press. The site contains the full texts of these books plus advanced searching capabilities.

ART

Grove Art Online

http://www.groveart.com

This authoritative and comprehensive site provides information about the visual arts from prehistory to the present. In addition to its more than 130,000 art images, the site contains articles on a range of subjects, including fine arts, architecture, China, South America, Africa, and other world cultures, as well as biographies and links to museum and gallery Web sites.

BRITISH ISLES

Oxford Dictionary of National Biography Online

http://www.oxforddnb.com/

The online version of the revised *Dictionary of Na-*

tional Biography is a highly authoritative reference source of biographical information. According to the site's description, the dictionary contains more than "50,000 biographies of people who shaped the history of the British Isles and beyond, from the earliest times to the year 2002."

HISTORY

Daily Life Through History Online

http://dailylife.greenwood.com/login.asp

The site, created by Greenwood Electronic Media, contains articles and entries describing the religious, domestic, economic, material, political, recreational, and intellectual life of people throughout history. It contains information from *The Greenwood Encyclopedia of Daily Life* as well as other books, reference works, and primary source documents. Users can also access chronologies, time lines, and hundreds of Web links.

MUSIC

Grove Music Online

http://www.grovemusic.com

The online version of the highly regarded *The New Grove Dictionary of Music and Musicians* features more than forty-five hundred articles on musicians, instruments, and musical techniques, genres, and styles. In addition to its articles and biographies, the site provides more than five hundred audio clips of music, and links to images, sound, and related Web sites.

SCIENCE

Access Science: McGraw-Hill Encyclopedia of Science and Technology Online

http://www.accessscience.com

An online version of the *McGraw Hill Encyclopedia of Science and Technology* and *McGraw Hill Dictionary of Scientific and Technical Terms* containing the information found in the latest editions of these books. Users can access biographies, more than three thousand articles, and science news.

ELECTRONIC DATABASES

Electronic databases usually do not have their own URLs. Instead, public, college, and university libraries subscribe to these databases and install them on their Web sites, where they are available only to library card holders or specified patrons. Readers can check library Web sites to see if these databases are installed, or can ask reference librarians if these databases are available.

BIOGRAPHY

Biography Resource Center

Produced by Thomson Gale, Biography Resource Center includes biographies of more than 335,000 prominent people throughout history that were previously published in Thompson Gale reference sources. It also features full-text biographical articles from almost three hundred magazines.

Biography Resource Center: African Americans

An electronic collection of almost 30,000 biographies of African Americans who have attained prominence in a number of areas, including the arts, business, government, history, literature, politics, and science. Produced by Thomson Gale, the database's biographies were culled from the company's Biography Resource Center database. In addition to the biographies, the database provides links to related Web sites, about two thousand portraits, and more than forty-two thousand full-text articles from almost three hundred magazines.

Wilson Biographies Plus Illustrated

Produced by H. W. Wilson Co., this database contains more than 140,000 narrative profiles, more than thirty-six thousand images, bibliographies, and links to related material. The database's content derives from some of Wilson's reference books, including *Current Biography* and the World Authors series, as well as from information licensed from other reference publishers.

HISTORY

American Broadsides and Ephemera

Readex, a division of NewsBank, Inc., has created this digital collection of broadsides and other materials that is based on the American Antiquarian Society's extensive collection of broadsides and ephemera. The database contains about fifteen thousand broadsides printed between 1820 and 1876 and about fifteen thousand pieces of ephemera printed between 1760 and 1900. The single-sheet printed broadsides present information on a diverse range of subjects, including contemporary accounts of the Civil War, descriptions of natural disasters, and official proclamations. There are also several digitized ephemera collections, including colored cards advertising the routes and departures of clipper ships, trade cards describing goods and services available to the public, letterhead stationery, menus, and theater and music programs.

American History Online

This database, produced by Facts On File, contains information about more than five hundred years of political, military, social, and cultural history. Its content derives from the company's publications, including the *Encyclopedia of American History*, as well as the *Landmark Documents in American History* database. Users can access information about historical events and topics, biographies of significant people, more than thirteen hundred primary source documents, time lines, essays providing an overview of significant time periods, maps, charts, and more than thirteen hundred images. In addition, the database includes almost five hundred entries from the *Encyclopedia of the Lewis and Clark Expedition*.

American Slavery: A Composite Autobiography

American Slavery: A Composite Autobiography, created by Greenwood Electronic Media, is an electronic collection of the almost four thousand narratives of former slaves that was compiled by the Works Progress Administration between 1936 and 1938. The narratives describe the experiences of slavery in the United States and what life was like after the slaves were freed. The narratives can be searched by surname, location, age, and subject index headings. The online collection provides links to related Web sites and enables users to listen to the archives of Folk Culture Sound recordings.

American Women's History Online

An electronic database focusing on five hundred years of American women's history. Produced by Facts On File, the database contains more than twenty-three hundred biographies; entries about issues pertaining to women, such as court cases and legislation, events, and social issues; primary source documents; time lines containing hyperlinked entries, including a time line of women's suffrage; more than six hundred images; maps; and charts.

C19: The Nineteenth Century Index

The most extensive searchable database for English-language materials is ProQuest's C19, which is linked to the full-text references it cites. C19 provides records for more than 11 million documents, including books and periodicals found in a variety of printed and microform editions, such as the *Nineteenth Century Short Title Catalogue* (a union catalog of materials published in all languages in the English-speaking world, 1801-1900); *The Nineteenth Century* from Chadwyck-Healey's ongoing microform project (more than thirty thousand titles); *Periodicals Index Online* and *Periodicals Archive Online* (covering more than 3.5 million articles from more than nine hundred scholarly journals); an American Periodicals series; the *Wellesley Index to Victorian Periodicals* (the standard guide to British periodicals of the period, including more than ninety thousand article records); the *British House of Commons Parliamentary Papers*; and *Palmer's Index to the Times* (1790-1905).

History Center: World

History Center: World is an electronic collection compiled by Thomson Gale featuring information from the company's publications as well as primary source documents and full-text articles from academic journals and periodicals.

History Reference Center

A product of Ebsco Information Services, the History Reference Center is a comprehensive world history database. It contains the contents of more than one thousand encyclopedias, reference works, and nonfiction books, the full text of articles published in about sixty history periodicals, thousands of historical documents, biographies, photographs, maps, and historical film and video.

History Resource Center: U.S.

History Resource Center: U.S., produced by Thomson Gale, provides primary source documents from digital archives, the full texts of current periodical articles, and multimedia reference articles about United States history. Database users also can access audio and video clips of historic speeches and events and link to digitized special collections.

MagillOnHistory

Available on the EbscoHost platform, Salem Press's MagillOnHistory database offers the full contents of the company's Great Lives from History and Great Events from History series as well as entries from its many history and social science encyclopedias, such as the award-winning Ready Reference: American Indians, and its decades series, *The Fifties*, *The Sixties*, and The Seventies. Several thousand full-length essays cross-link to coverage of historical events with biographies about prominent persons from ancient times to the twenty-first century. Updated quarterly.

World History Online

Created by Facts On File, World History Online covers the wide range of historical events from ancient times to the present. Its content includes more than ten thousand biographies; subject entries describing more than fourteen thousand events, places, and cultural events; hundreds of primary source documents; time lines, and more than 650 maps and charts.

LITERATURE

Literary Reference Online

An electronic examination of the lives and works of writers throughout history produced by Facts On File. Among its features are author biographies searchable by type of writing or time period and information about the plots, themes, social context, and importance of literary works. Literary Reference Online also contains a guide to more than thirty-five thousand literary characters, a glossary of literary terms, and articles on literary movements, literary groups, magazines, and newspapers.

Literature Resource Center

Literature Resource Center, produced by Thomson Gale, includes biographies, bibliographies, and critical analyses of authors from a wide range of literary disciplines, countries, and eras. The database also features plot summaries, the full text of articles from literary journals, and critical essays.

MagillOnLiteraturePlus

Available on the EbscoHost platform, MagillOnLiteraturePlus is a comprehensive, integrated literature database produced by Salem Press. The database incorporates the full contents of Salem's many reference works and, as of 2006, featured information from *Masterplots* (series I and II), *Cyclopedia of World Authors*, *Cyclopedia of Literary Characters*, *Cyclopedia of Literary Places*, *Critical Surveys of Literature*, *Magill's Literary Annual*, *World Philosophers and Their Works*, and *Magill Book Reviews*. The database examines more than thirty-five thousand works and more than ten thousand writers, poets, dramatists, essayists, and philosophers. Essays feature critical analysis as well as plot summaries, biographical information, character profiles, and authoritative listings of authors' works and the dates of publication. The majority of the essays also include annotated bibliographies to help users conduct additional research. Updated quarterly.

—Rebecca Kuzins

CHRONOLOGICAL LIST OF ENTRIES

June 18, 1812-Dec. 24, 1814: War of 1812
June 23-Dec. 14, 1812: Napoleon Invades Russia
July 22, 1812: Battle of Salamanca
Sept. 7, 1812: Battle of Borodino
1813: Founding of McGill University
Mar., 1813-Dec. 9, 1824: Bolívar's Military Campaigns
July 27, 1813-Aug. 9, 1814: Creek War
Oct. 5, 1813: Battle of the Thames
Oct. 16-19, 1813: Battle of Leipzig
1814: Fraunhofer Invents the Spectroscope
1814: Scott Publishes *Waverley*
1814-1879: Exploration of Arabia
Mar., 1814: Goya Paints *Third of May 1808: Execution of the Citizens of Madrid*
Spring, 1814-1830: Communitarian Experiments at New Harmony
Apr. 11, 1814-July 29, 1830: France's Bourbon Dynasty Is Restored
Aug. 13, 1814: Britain Acquires the Cape Colony
Sept. 15, 1814-June 11, 1815: Congress of Vienna
Dec. 15, 1814-Jan. 5, 1815: Hartford Convention
c. 1815-1830: Westward American Migration Begins
c. 1815-1848: Biedermeier Furniture Style Becomes Popular
Jan. 8, 1815: Battle of New Orleans
Feb. 17, 1815: Treaty of Ghent Takes Effect
Apr. 5, 1815: Tambora Volcano Begins Violent Eruption
June 1, 1815-Aug., 1817: Red River Raids
June 8-9, 1815: Organization of the German Confederation

June 18, 1815: Battle of Waterloo
Nov. 20, 1815: Second Peace of Paris
1816: Laënnec Invents the Stethoscope
Feb. 20, 1816: Rossini's *The Barber of Seville* Debuts
Apr., 1816: Second Bank of the United States Is Chartered
Apr. 9, 1816: African Methodist Episcopal Church Is Founded
May 8, 1816: American Bible Society Is Founded
Dec., 1816: Rise of the Cockney School
1817: Ricardo Identifies Seven Key Economic Principles
c. 1817-1828: Zulu Expansion
Jan. 18, 1817-July 28, 1821: San Martín's Military Campaigns
Nov. 5, 1817-June 3, 1818: Third Maratha War
Nov. 21, 1817-Mar. 27, 1858: Seminole Wars
1818-1854: Search for the Northwest Passage
1819: Schopenhauer Publishes *The World as Will and Idea*
1819-1820: Irving's *Sketch Book* Transforms American Literature
1819-1833: Babbage Designs a Mechanical Calculator
Feb. 22, 1819: Adams-Onís Treaty Gives the United States Florida
Mar. 6, 1819: *McCulloch v. Maryland*
May, 1819: Unitarian Church Is Founded
May 22-June 20, 1819: *Savannah* Is the First Steamship to Cross the Atlantic
Dec. 11-30, 1819: British Parliament Passes the Six Acts

1820's

1820's: China's Stele School of Calligraphy Emerges
1820's-1830's: Free Public School Movement
1820's-1850's: Social Reform Movement
1820: Jesuits Are Expelled from Russia, Naples, and Spain
1820-early 1840's: Europeans Explore the Antarctic
c. 1820-1860: *Costumbrismo* Movement
Feb. 23, 1820: London's Cato Street Conspirators Plot Assassinations
Mar. 3, 1820: Missouri Compromise
Apr. 24, 1820: Congress Passes Land Act of 1820
July 2, 1820-Mar., 1821: Neapolitan Revolution

Nov. 6, 1820: Ampère Reveals Magnetism's Relationship to Electricity
Mar. 7, 1821-Sept. 29, 1829: Greeks Fight for Independence from the Ottoman Empire
Sept., 1821: Santa Fe Trail Opens
1822-1831: Jedediah Smith Explores the Far West
1822-1874: Exploration of North Africa
Sept. 7, 1822: Brazil Becomes Independent
Oct. 20-30, 1822: Great Britain Withdraws from the Concert of Europe
1823-1831: Hokusai Produces *Thirty-Six Views of Mount Fuji*

May, 1823: Hartford Female Seminary Is Founded

Oct. 5, 1823: Wakley Introduces *The Lancet*

Dec. 2, 1823: President Monroe Articulates the Monroe Doctrine

1824: British Parliament Repeals the Combination Acts

1824: Paris Salon of 1824

1824: Ranke Develops Systematic History

Feb. 20, 1824: Buckland Presents the First Public Dinosaur Description

Mar. 2, 1824: *Gibbons v. Ogden*

May 7, 1824: First Performance of Beethoven's Ninth Symphony

Dec. 1, 1824-Feb. 9, 1825: U.S. Election of 1824

1825-1830: Great Java War

July 29, 1825: Stockton and Darlington Railway Opens

Oct. 26, 1825: Erie Canal Opens

Dec. 26, 1825: Decembrist Revolt

c. 1826-1827: First Meetings of the Plymouth Brethren

1826-1842: Young Germany Movement

1828-1834: Portugal's Miguelite Wars

1828-1842: Arnold Reforms Rugby School

Feb. 21, 1828: *Cherokee Phoenix* Begins Publication

Apr. 26, 1828-Aug. 28, 1829: Second Russo-Turkish War

May 9, 1828-Apr. 13, 1829: Roman Catholic Emancipation

Nov., 1828: Webster Publishes the First American Dictionary of English

Dec. 3, 1828: U.S. Election of 1828

1829-1836: Irish Immigration to Canada

Sept. 24, 1829: Treaty of Adrianople

Dec. 4, 1829: British Abolish Suttee in India

1830's

1830's-1840's: Scientists Study Remains of Giant Moas

c. 1830's-1860's: American Renaissance in Literature

1830-1842: Trail of Tears

c. 1830-1865: Southerners Advance Proslavery Arguments

c. 1830-1870: Barbizon School of Landscape Painting Flourishes

Jan. 7, 1830: Baltimore and Ohio Railroad Opens

Jan. 19-27, 1830: Webster and Hayne Debate Slavery and Westward Expansion

Mar. 3, 1830: Hugo's *Hernani* Incites Rioting

Apr. 6, 1830: Smith Founds the Mormon Church

May 28, 1830: Congress Passes Indian Removal Act

June 14-July 5, 1830: France Conquers Algeria

July, 1830: Lyell Publishes *Principles of Geology*

July 29, 1830: July Revolution Deposes Charles X

Aug. 25, 1830-May 21, 1833: Belgian Revolution

Oct.-Dec., 1830: Delacroix Paints *Liberty Leading the People*

Nov. 29, 1830-Aug. 15, 1831: First Polish Rebellion

1831: Mazzini Founds Young Italy

1831-1834: Hiroshige Completes *The Tokaido Fifty-Three Stations*

Jan. 1, 1831: Garrison Begins Publishing *The Liberator*

Mar. 18, 1831, and Mar. 3, 1832: Cherokee Cases

May, 1831-Feb., 1832: Tocqueville Visits America

Summer, 1831: McCormick Invents the Reaper

Aug. 21, 1831: Turner Launches Slave Insurrection

Oct., 1831: Faraday Converts Magnetic Force into Electricity

1832-1841: Turko-Egyptian Wars

1832-1847: Abdelkader Leads Algeria Against France

Mar. 12, 1832: *La Sylphide* Inaugurates Romantic Ballet's Golden Age

June 4, 1832: British Parliament Passes the Reform Act of 1832

July 10, 1832: Jackson Vetoes Rechartering of the Bank of the United States

Nov. 24, 1832-Jan. 21, 1833: Nullification Controversy

1833: British Parliament Passes the Factory Act

Jan., 1833: Great Britain Occupies the Falkland Islands

July 14, 1833: Oxford Movement Begins

Aug. 28, 1833: Slavery Is Abolished Throughout the British Empire

Sept. 3, 1833: Birth of the Penny Press

Sept. 29, 1833-1849: Carlist Wars Unsettle Spain

Dec., 1833: American Anti-Slavery Society Is Founded

Dec. 3, 1833: Oberlin College Opens

Jan. 1, 1834: German States Join to Form Customs
    Union
Apr. 14, 1834: Clay Begins American Whig Party
Aug. 14, 1834: British Parliament Passes New Poor
    Law
Oct. 14, 1834: Blair Patents His First Seed Planter
1835: Finney Lectures on "Revivals of Religion"
1835: South Africa's Great Trek Begins
1835-1836: Strauss Publishes *The Life of Jesus
    Critically Examined*
May 8, 1835: Andersen Publishes His First Fairy Tales
Aug. 16, 1835: Melbourne, Australia, Is Founded
Sept. 9, 1835: British Parliament Passes Municipal
    Corporations Act
Oct. 2, 1835-Apr. 21, 1836: Texas Revolution
1836: Transcendental Movement Arises in New
    England
Feb. 25, 1836: Colt Patents the Revolver
July 21, 1836: Champlain and St. Lawrence Railroad
    Opens

Jan. 12, 1837: Mazzini Begins London Exile
Mar. 17, 1837: Panic of 1837 Begins
Oct. 23-Dec. 16, 1837: Rebellions Rock British
    Canada
Nov. 8, 1837: Mount Holyoke Female Seminary Opens
1838-1839: Aroostook War
1838-1839: Schwann and Virchow Develop Cell
    Theory
May 8, 1838-Apr. 10, 1848: Chartist Movement
June 28, 1838: Queen Victoria's Coronation
1839: Blanc Publishes *The Organization of Labour*
1839: Daguerre and Niépce Invent Daguerreotype
    Photography
1839-1842: First Afghan War
1839-1847: Layard Explores and Excavates Assyrian
    Ruins
July 2, 1839: *Amistad* Slave Revolt
Sept., 1839-Aug. 29, 1842: First Opium War
Nov., 1839: Stephens Begins Uncovering Mayan
    Antiquities

1840's

1840's-1850's: American Era of "Old" Immigration
1840's-1880's: Russian Realist Movement
1840: Liebig Advocates Artificial Fertilizers
Jan. 10, 1840: Great Britain Establishes Penny
    Postage
Apr. 27, 1840-Feb., 1852: British Houses of
    Parliament Are Rebuilt
Dec. 2, 1840: U.S. Election of 1840
Feb. 10, 1841: Upper and Lower Canada Unite
Sept. 4, 1841: Congress Passes Preemption Act of
    1841
1842: Tennyson Publishes "Morte d'Arthur"
Mar., 1842: *Commonwealth v. Hunt*
May, 1842-1854: Frémont Explores the American
    West
May 18, 1842: Rhode Island's Dorr Rebellion
Aug. 9, 1842: Webster-Ashburton Treaty Settles
    Maine's Canadian Border
1843: Carlyle Publishes *Past and Present*
Jan. 2, 1843: Wagner's *Flying Dutchman* Debuts
Feb., 1843: First Minstrel Shows
Sept. 2, 1843: Wilson Launches *The Economist*
May 6-July 5, 1844: Anti-Irish Riots Erupt in
    Philadelphia

May 24, 1844: Morse Sends First Telegraph Message
June 11, 1844: Goodyear Patents Vulcanized Rubber
c. 1845: Clipper Ship Era Begins
c. 1845: Modern Baseball Begins
1845-1854: Great Irish Famine
Oct. 9, 1845: Newman Becomes a Roman Catholic
Feb. 4, 1846: Mormons Begin Migration to Utah
May 8, 1846: Battle of Palo Alto
May 13, 1846-Feb. 2, 1848: Mexican War
June 15, 1846: British Parliament Repeals the Corn
    Laws
June 15, 1846: United States Acquires Oregon
    Territory
June 30, 1846-Jan. 13, 1847: United States Occupies
    California and the Southwest
Aug. 1, 1846: Establishment of Independent U.S.
    Treasury
Aug. 10, 1846: Smithsonian Institution Is Founded
Sept. 10, 1846: Howe Patents His Sewing Machine
Oct. 16, 1846: Safe Surgical Anesthesia Is
    Demonstrated
1847: Boole Publishes *The Mathematical Analysis of
    Logic*
1847: Hamburg-Amerika Shipping Line Begins

1850's

1860's

1870's

1870's: Aesthetic Movement Arises

1870's: Japan Expands into Korea

1870-1871: Watch Tower Bible and Tract Society Is Founded

Jan. 10, 1870: Standard Oil Company Is Incorporated

Apr., 1870-1873: Schliemann Excavates Ancient Troy

July 19, 1870-Jan. 28, 1871: Franco-Prussian War

Sept. 1, 1870: Battle of Sedan

Sept. 20, 1870-Jan. 28, 1871: Prussian Army Besieges Paris

1871: Darwin Publishes *The Descent of Man*

1871-1876: Díaz Drives Mexico into Civil War

1871-1877: Kulturkampf Against the Catholic Church in Germany

c. 1871-1883: Great American Buffalo Slaughter

1871-1885: Przhevalsky Explores Central Asia

Jan. 18, 1871: German States Unite Within German Empire

Feb. 13, 1871-1875: Third French Republic Is Established

Mar. 3, 1871: Grant Signs Indian Appropriation Act

Mar. 18-May 28, 1871: Paris Commune

Apr. 10, 1871: Barnum Creates the First Modern American Circus

May 8, 1871: Treaty of Washington Settles U.S. Claims vs. Britain

Oct. 8-10, 1871: Great Chicago Fire

1872: Dominion Lands Act Fosters Canadian Settlement

Feb. 20, 1872: Metropolitan Museum of Art Opens

Mar. 1, 1872: Yellowstone Becomes the First U.S. National Park

Aug., 1872: Ward Launches a Mail-Order Business

1873: Ukrainian Mennonites Begin Settling in Canada

1873-1880: Exploration of Africa's Congo Basin

1873-1897: Zanzibar Outlaws Slavery

Jan. 22, 1873-Feb. 13, 1874: Second British-Ashanti War

Feb. 12, 1873: "Crime of 1873"

Mar. 3, 1873: Congress Passes the Comstock Antiobscenity Law

May 6-Oct. 22, 1873: Three Emperors' League Is Formed

May 23, 1873: Canada Forms the North-West Mounted Police

June 17-18, 1873: Anthony Is Tried for Voting

Nov. 5, 1873-Oct. 9, 1878: Canada's Mackenzie Era

Apr. 15, 1874: First Impressionist Exhibition

June 27, 1874-June 2, 1875: Red River War

Nov. 24, 1874: Glidden Patents Barbed Wire

1875: Supreme Court of Canada Is Established

Mar. 3, 1875: Bizet's *Carmen* Premieres in Paris

Mar. 3, 1875: Congress Enacts the Page Law

Mar. 9, 1875: *Minor v. Happersett*

Sept., 1875: Theosophical Society Is Founded

Oct. 30, 1875: Eddy Establishes the Christian Science Movement

Late 1870's: Post-Impressionist Movement Begins

1876: Canada's Indian Act

1876: Spanish Constitution of 1876

1876-1877: Sioux War

May, 1876: Bulgarian Revolt Against the Ottoman Empire

May, 1876: Otto Invents a Practical Internal Combustion Engine

May 10-Nov. 10, 1876: Philadelphia Hosts the Centennial Exposition

June 25, 1876: Battle of the Little Bighorn

June 25, 1876: Bell Demonstrates the Telephone

July 4, 1876: Declaration of the Rights of Women

Aug. 13-17, 1876: First Performance of Wagner's Ring Cycle

Oct. 4-6, 1876: American Library Association Is Founded

Jan.-Sept. 24, 1877: Former Samurai Rise in Satsuma Rebellion

Mar. 5, 1877: Hayes Becomes President

Apr. 24, 1877-Jan. 31, 1878: Third Russo-Turkish War

June 15-Oct. 5, 1877: Nez Perce War

Sept. 10-Dec. 17, 1877: Texas's Salinero Revolt

Dec. 24, 1877: Edison Patents the Cylinder Phonograph

1878: Muybridge Photographs a Galloping Horse

1878-1899: Irving Manages London's Lyceum Theatre

June 13-July 13, 1878: Congress of Berlin

Sept., 1878: Macdonald Returns as Canada's Prime Minister

Oct. 19, 1878: Germany Passes Anti-Socialist Law

1879: *A Doll's House* Introduces Modern Realistic Drama

1879: Powell Publishes His Report on the American West

Jan. 22-23, 1879: Battles of Isandlwana and Rorke's Drift

Jan. 22-Aug., 1879: Zulu War

Apr. 5, 1879-Oct. 20, 1883: War of the Pacific

Oct. 21, 1879: Edison Demonstrates the Incandescent Lamp

1880's

1880's: Brahmin School of American Literature Flourishes

1880's: Roux Develops the Theory of Mitosis

1880's-1890's: Rise of Yellow Journalism

Sept.-Nov., 1880: Irish Tenant Farmers Stage First "Boycott"

Dec. 16, 1880-Mar. 6, 1881: First Boer War

1881-1889: Bismarck Introduces Social Security Programs in Germany

July, 1881-1883: Stevenson Publishes *Treasure Island*

Oct. 10, 1881: London's Savoy Theatre Opens

1882: First Birth Control Clinic Opens in Amsterdam

1882-1901: Metchnikoff Advances the Cellular Theory of Immunity

Jan. 2, 1882: Standard Oil Trust Is Organized

Mar. 24, 1882: Koch Announces His Discovery of the Tuberculosis Bacillus

Apr., 1882-1885: French Indochina War

May 2, 1882: Kilmainham Treaty Makes Concessions to Irish Nationalists

May 9, 1882: Arthur Signs the Chinese Exclusion Act

May 20, 1882: Triple Alliance Is Formed

July 23, 1882-Jan. 9, 1885: Korean Military Mutinies Against Japanese Rule

Sept. 13, 1882: Battle of Tel el Kebir

Nov. 12, 1882: San Francisco's Chinese Six Companies Association Forms

1883: Galton Defines "Eugenics"

1883-1885: World's First Skyscraper Is Built

Jan. 16, 1883: Pendleton Act Reforms the Federal Civil Service

May 24, 1883: Brooklyn Bridge Opens

Aug. 27, 1883: Krakatoa Volcano Erupts

Oct. 15, 1883: Civil Rights Cases

Oct. 22, 1883: Metropolitan Opera House Opens in New York

Nov. 3, 1883: Gaudí Begins Barcelona's Templo Expiatorio de la Sagrada Família

1884: Maxim Patents His Machine Gun

1884: New Guilds Promote the Arts and Crafts Movement

c. 1884-1924: Decadent Movement Flourishes

Jan., 1884: Fabian Society Is Founded

Jan. 25, 1884: Indian Legislative Council Enacts the Ilbert Bill

Mar. 13, 1884-Jan. 26, 1885: Siege of Khartoum

June 21, 1884: Gold Is Discovered in the Transvaal

Nov. 4, 1884: U.S. Election of 1884

Nov. 15, 1884-Feb. 26, 1885: Berlin Conference Lays Groundwork for the Partition of Africa

Dec., 1884-Feb., 1885: Twain Publishes *Adventures of Huckleberry Finn*

Dec. 6, 1884: British Parliament Passes the Franchise Act of 1884

1885: Indian National Congress Is Founded

Mar. 19, 1885: Second Riel Rebellion Begins

1886: Rise of the Symbolist Movement

Jan., 1886-1889: French Right Wing Revives During Boulanger Crisis

Jan. 29, 1886: Benz Patents the First Practical Automobile

May 8, 1886: Pemberton Introduces Coca-Cola

June, 1886-Sept. 9, 1893: Irish Home Rule Debate Dominates British Politics

Oct. 28, 1886: Statue of Liberty Is Dedicated

Dec. 8, 1886: American Federation of Labor Is Founded

Feb. 4, 1887: Interstate Commerce Act

Feb. 8, 1887: General Allotment Act Erodes Indian Tribal Unity

Mar. 13, 1887: American Protective Association Is Formed

May, 1887: Goodwin Develops Celluloid Film

Dec., 1887: Conan Doyle Introduces Sherlock Holmes

1888: Rodin Exhibits *The Thinker*

1888-1906: Ramón y Cajal Shows How Neurons Work in the Nervous System

Mar. 13, 1888: Rhodes Amalgamates Kimberley Diamondfields

Dec. 7, 1888: Dunlop Patents the Pneumatic Tire
1889: Great Britain Strengthens Its Royal Navy
Feb. 11, 1889: Japan Adopts a New Constitution
Mar. 31, 1889: Eiffel Tower Is Dedicated

May 31, 1889: Johnstown Flood
Sept. 18, 1889: Addams Opens Chicago's Hull-House
Oct., 1889-Apr., 1890: First Pan-American Congress
Nov., 1889-Jan., 1894: Dahomey-French Wars

1890's

1890's: Rise of Tin Pan Alley Music
1890: Mississippi Constitution Disfranchises Black
    Voters
1890: U.S. Census Bureau Announces Closing of the
    Frontier
Feb. 17-18, 1890: Women's Rights Associations Unite
July 20, 1890: Harrison Signs the Sherman Antitrust
    Act
Dec. 11, 1890: Behring Discovers the Diphtheria
    Antitoxin
Dec. 29, 1890: Wounded Knee Massacre
1891: Naismith Invents Basketball
Mar. 11, 1891: Strowger Patents Automatic Dial
    Telephone System
May 15, 1891: Papal Encyclical on Labor
1892: America's "New" Immigration Era Begins
1892-1895: Toulouse-Lautrec Paints *At the Moulin
    Rouge*
Jan. 1, 1892: Ellis Island Immigration Depot Opens
Feb., 1892: Diesel Patents the Diesel Engine
May 4, 1892: Anti-Japanese Yellow Peril Campaign
    Begins
July 4-5, 1892: Birth of the People's Party
Aug. 3, 1892: Hardie Becomes Parliament's First
    Labour Member
1893: Munch Paints *The Scream*
1893-1896: Nansen Attempts to Reach the North
    Pole
May 1-Oct. 30, 1893: Chicago World's Fair
Sept. 19, 1893: New Zealand Women Win Voting
    Rights
Oct., 1893-Oct., 1897: British Subdue African
    Resistance in Rhodesia
Oct. 27, 1893: National Council of Women of Canada
    Is Founded
1894-1895: Kellogg's Corn Flakes Launch the Dry
    Cereal Industry
1894-1896: Ottomans Attempt to Exterminate
    Armenians
Jan. 4, 1894: Franco-Russian Alliance

May 11-July 11, 1894: Pullman Strike
July 8, 1894-Jan. 1, 1896: Kabo Reforms Begin
    Modernization of Korean Government
Aug. 1, 1894-Apr. 17, 1895: Sino-Japanese War
Oct., 1894-July, 1906: Dreyfus Affair
Dec. 22, 1894: Debussy's *Prelude to the Afternoon of
    a Faun* Premieres
1895-1898: Hearst-Pulitzer Circulation War
Jan. 24, 1895: Hawaii's Last Monarch Abdicates
Jan. 27, 1895: Tchaikovsky's *Swan Lake* Is Staged in
    St. Petersburg
Feb. 24, 1895-1898: Cuban War of Independence
May 10, 1895: Chinese Californians Form Native Sons
    of the Golden State
June 20, 1895: Germany's Kiel Canal Opens
Sept. 18, 1895: Washington's Atlanta Compromise
    Speech
Nov. 9, 1895: Röntgen Discovers X Rays
Nov. 27, 1895: Nobel Bequeaths Funds for the Nobel
    Prizes
Dec. 28, 1895: First Commercial Projection of Motion
    Pictures
Dec. 29, 1895-Jan. 2, 1896: Jameson Raid
1896: Brooks Brothers Introduces Button-Down Shirts
1896: Immigrant Farmers Begin Settling Western
    Canada
Feb., 1896-Aug., 1897: Herzl Founds the Zionist
    Movement
Mar., 1896-Nov., 1899: Sudanese War
Mar. 1, 1896: Ethiopia Repels Italian Invasion
Apr. 6, 1896: Modern Olympic Games Are
    Inaugurated
May 18, 1896: *Plessy v. Ferguson*
June, 1896: Marconi Patents the Wireless Telegraph
July 11, 1896: Laurier Becomes the First French
    Canadian Prime Minister
Aug. 17, 1896: Klondike Gold Rush Begins
Nov. 3, 1896: McKinley Is Elected President
Nov. 16, 1896: First U.S. Hydroelectric Plant Opens at
    Niagara Falls

GEOGRAPHICAL INDEX

List of Geographical Regions

CATEGORY INDEX

List of Categories

AGRICULTURE

Summer, 1831: McCormick Invents the Reaper, 496
Oct. 14, 1834: Blair Patents His First Seed Planter, 557
1840: Liebig Advocates Artificial Fertilizers, 638
1845-1854: Great Irish Famine, 696

June 15, 1846: British Parliament Repeals the Corn Laws, 715
Dec. 4, 1867: National Grange Is Formed, 1231
1872: Dominion Lands Act Fosters Canadian Settlement, 1369

COLONIZATION

COMMUNICATIONS

CRIME AND SCANDALS

EDUCATION

ENGINEERING

ENVIRONMENT AND ECOLOGY

EXPLORATION AND DISCOVERY

FASHION AND DESIGN

GENETICS

HEALTH AND MEDICINE

JOURNALISM

LAWS, ACTS, AND LEGAL HISTORY

Literature

Great Events from History

Indexes

PERSONAGES INDEX

Subject Index

RGS. *See* Royal Geographical Society

Rhett, Robert Barnwell, 1022-1023

Rhine, Confederation of the, 239, 1349

Rhineland, 217, 244, 549

Rhode Island; constitution, 664-666; Dorr rebellion, 664-666; education, 311; Royal Charter, 664; School of Design, 446; slavery in, 1167; suffrage, 664-666; and War of 1812, 219; woman suffrage, 1426

Rhodes, Cecil, 214; and diamondfields, 1674-1676; and goldfields, 1612, 1614; and Jameson Raid, 1824; and Rhodesia, 1763-1768; and South African War, 1932

Rhodes, James Ford, 854

Rhodesia, 1763-1768, 1932, 1935

Ricardo, David, 267-269, 525, 715

Rice, Edwin W., Jr, 1983-1984

Rice, Thomas Dartmouth, 675-676

Richardson, James, 345-346

Richardson, William, 1298

Richelieu, duc de. *See* Plessis, Armand-Emmanuel du

Richmond, Virginia, 1012; and Confederacy, 1024-1025, 1045, 1102, 1128, 1146-1147; port of, 1063; siege of, 1127

Richter, Hans, 1464-1465

Rickets, 924

Ricketts, John Bill, 1360

Ridge, John, 460, 462-463

Ridge, Major, 440, 460, 462

Ridgeway, Battle of, 1185

Riel, Louis, 1299-1301, 1401, 1854; execution of, 1854; second rebellion, 1633-1635, 1854

Riel Rebellion, First (1869-1870), 1299-1301, 1401

Riel Rebellion, Second (1885), 1401, 1633-1635

Riemann, Georg Friedrich, 1941

Rifāʾah Rāfiʿ aṭ-Ṭahtawi, 1-2

Rigdon, Sidney, 457

Rights of Man, The (Paine), 62

Rimbaud, Arthur, 1636

Rimsky-Korsakov, Nikolay, 1791-1792

Rinderpest, 1766

Ring Cycle (Wagner), 672, 1464-1466, 1590

Ring des Nibelungen, Der. See Ring Cycle

Ring of the Nibelung, The. See Ring Cycle

Ring Thunder, 1188

Ringgold, Samuel, 707-709

Rio de Janeiro, 348-349, 1151

Rio Grande, 92, 771-772, 882, 1228; and Mexican War, 707

"Rip Van Winkle" (Irving), 100, 289

Ripley, George, 581-582

Ripon, first marquis of, 1606-1608, 1630

Risorgimento. *See* Italian unification movement; Italy, unification of

Rivas, Patricio, 915

Rivaz, François Isaac de, 998

Rivière, Henri, 1553

Roberts, Edmund, 888

Roberts, Frederick Sleigh, 1932-1933, 1935-1936

Roberts, Issachar J., 836, 838

Roberts, Joseph Jenkins, 748-749

Roberts, William R., 1184

Roberts v. Boston (1849), 1849

Robertson, Colin, 238

Robinson, Charles, 919-920

Robinson, Emily, 844

Robinson, Frank M., 1643

Robinson, George Augustus, 56

Robinson, Sir Hercules, 1824

Robinson, John Hamilton, 90, 92

Robinson, Peter, 423-424

Robinson and Wife v. Memphis & Charleston Railroad Company (1883), 1586

Rochefort, Victor-Henri, 1638

Rockefeller, John D., 1318-1321, 1547-1550, 1712

Rockefeller, William, 1318-1321, 1547-1548

Rockhill, William Woodville, 1928-1931

Rocky Mountain Fur Company, 120, 342-344

Rocky Mountains, 1228, 1375; exploration of, 65, 68, 661-663, 1504; and fur trade, 120; and Zebulon Pike, 91; and railroads, 867

Rodin, Auguste, 1669-1671

Rodríguez, José María, 1592

Roebling, Emily, 1580, 1582

Roebling, John Augustus, 1580-1583

Roebling, Washington Augustus, 1580-1583

Roebuck, Alvah C., 1378-1379

Roebuck, John Arthur, 797-798

Roesler, Hermann, 1683-1684

Rogers, Harrison G., 342-343

Rogers, Moses, 303-305

Rogers, Stevens, 303-305

Rogier, Charles, 474-475

Rohlfs, Friedrich Gerhard, 345-346

Rolfe, Robert Monsey, 952-953

Rolph, John, 595-596

Roman Catholic Church; and French Revolution (1789), 906; in Germany, 1340-1342, 1534; and Holy Land, 877; Immaculate Conception dogma, 906-908, 959, 1308; Index of Forbidden Books, 906; Inquisition, 139, 141, 906; and Italian unification movement, 906; Jesuits, 315-317; and Kulturkampf, 1340-1342, 1534; and Lourdes apparitions, 959; in Mexico, 1338; and Napoleon I, 72; papacy, 906; papal encyclical on labor, 1727-1729; and papal infallibility dogma, 1307-1309; in Spain, 1440; Syllabus of Errors, 1133-1135, 1308, 1534; and United States, 782; Vatican I, 908

Roman Catholic emancipation, 33-34, 414-418, 515

C